USING THE NEW
DB2

IBM's
Object-Relational
Database
System

The Morgan Kaufmann Series in Data Management Systems

Series Editor, Jim Gray

USING THE NEW

DB2

IBM's
Object-Relational
Database
System

Don Chamberlin

IBM ALMADEN RESEARCH CENTER

Morgan Kaufmann Publishers, Inc.

SAN FRANCISCO, CALIFORNIA

Senior Editor Diane D. Cerra
Production Manager Yonie Overton
Production Editor Cheri Palmer
Editorial Assistant Jane Elliott
Cover Design Ross Carron Design
Editorial Illustration (cover, half-title,
* chapter openers, selected section*
* heads)* Duane Bibby

Technical Illustration Cherie Plumlee
Text Design Donna Davis
Composition Fog Press
Copyeditor Sharilyn Hovind
Proofreader Jennifer McClain
Indexer Ty Koontz
Printer Courier Corporation

Morgan Kaufmann Publishers, Inc.
Editorial and Sales Office
340 Pine Street, Sixth Floor
San Francisco, CA 94104-3205
USA
Telephone 415 / 392-2665
Facsimile 415 / 982-2665
Internet mkp@mkp.com
Web site http://www.mkp.com

Library of Congress Cataloging-in-Publication Data

Chamberlin, D. D. (Donald Dean)
      Using the new DB2 : IBM's object-relational database system / Don
Chamberlin.
          p. cm. -- (Morgan Kaufmann series in data management systems)
      Includes bibliographical references and index.
      ISBN 1-55860-373-5 (pbk.)
      1. IBM Database 2. 2. Object-oriented databases. I. Title.
II. Series.
QA76.9.D3C4225   1996
005.75'65--dc20   95-50341
                                                                        CIP

This book is dedicated to the
members of the System R team
and to the memory of Raymond F. Boyce

Foreword

by Donald J. Haderle
*IBM Fellow and Director of Data Management Architecture and Technology,
IBM Software Solutions Division*

Very simply, the purpose of a database management system is to store and retrieve data with surety. Twenty-five years ago, Dr. E. F. Codd proposed the relational data model to accomplish this purpose, combining strong mathematical foundations with an intuitive, commonsense user interface. One of the most important advantages of the relational model is its data independence, which promises to make relational systems adaptable to changing sets of requirements.

The first great challenge faced by relational systems was to meet the needs of a broad range of applications, from online transaction processing to decision support, with adequate performance and reasonable cost. For the first time, the SQL-based database systems of the 1980s provided a single language to span the whole range of applications, with support for multiple views of data and independence from physical data structures. Because of the success of these systems, relational databases have become ubiquitous and SQL has become a world standard database language.

Today, the world of database management is rapidly changing, driven by advances in processing power, storage capacity, and communications bandwidth. A new set of challenges faces today's database systems. Some of these challenges derive from the need to store and retrieve new types of very large objects with complex state and behavior, including multimedia objects and engineering designs. Today's systems also need to increase the value of stored data by capturing more of its semantic content. They need to capture business rules and enable these rules to be shared across all the applications that access common data. A new type of database system is emerging to meet these challenges and is described by the term *object-relational system*.

With DB2 Version 2 for common servers, IBM introduces a set of extensions to SQL to meet the demands of a new generation of database applications. DB2 Version 2 provides new functions and datatypes, including datatypes for storing large objects. More important, it provides a means for users to define additional functions and datatypes of their own to meet the specialized needs of their applications. Using these features, users can store and manipulate objects such as graphic images, audio and video streams, fingerprints, and spatial and temporal data, retrieving and processing each object according to its specialized characteristics.

DB2 Version 2 also provides a rich variety of active data features, including constraints and triggers that can be used to capture data semantics and encapsulate business rules. By representing this information in the database rather than in application code, redundancy can be eliminated and the global integrity of the database can be protected.

Using the New DB2 provides a good general overview of DB2 Version 2 and an in-depth study of the new features that make it an object-relational system. As a designer of the original SQL and a member of the DB2 development team, Don Chamberlin brings perspective to his readers on how the various features of the system fit together into a synergistic whole. Don's book provides many examples that motivate the advanced features of DB2 and illustrate how they can be used to solve real problems. After reading this book, you will be well equipped to use DB2 Version 2 to develop advanced database applications, and you will be confident that relational database management systems are evolving to meet the challenges of a new decade.

Foreword

by Jim Gray
Microsoft Research

Twenty years ago, Don Chamberlin designed the SEQUEL language and led its first implementation, in an experimental database system called System R. That effort spawned the SQL relational database standard, IBM's DB2 product family, and many successful software companies. Computer scientists at IBM's Almaden Research Center have been experimenting with relational database systems since the relational model was first introduced. They prototyped a distributed relational system called R* (pronounced "R-star") and an extensible relational system called Starburst. They made major contributions to data modelling, transaction management, and workflow. They have also worked closely with IBM's product divisions to help bring you IBM's DB2 product family.

Now, 20 years later, many of these ideas have come together in a new relational product, DB2 Version 2 for common servers, developed by IBM in Toronto, Canada and San Jose, California. DB2 Version 2 shares the DB2 name, but it is a brand-new code base with a radical new architecture. This new system is portable to many hardware and software platforms including Intel/NT, SPARC/Solaris, HPPA/HPUX, PowerPC/AIX, and Intel/OS/2.

DB2 Version 2 is a substantial advance over traditional relational systems. It integrates object-oriented ideas with the SQL language to produce an object-relational database management system. It includes major innovations in query optimization, recursive union, active databases (triggers), and stored procedures.

In short, DB2 Version 2 is a revolutionary product from IBM. Since it is a third-generation SQL system, I think of it as Don's grandchild. Many bright people contributed to the early relational systems, but the basic design of SQL was created by Don and his colleague, Ray Boyce.

Don is a great visionary and designer, but his greatest talent is as an expositor. He writes and speaks in crystal-clear prose. He makes complex ideas simple—seemingly trivial. Unfortunately for him, when you make something simple, most people are not impressed with how complex it could have been.

Since you are reading this, you are probably wondering about object-relational systems or about DB2 Version 2. You probably wish for a guru to guide you through the hype and smoke and mirrors. Well, this is where you should start. I have read this book twice, and it is GREAT!

No other book will explain the concepts so clearly. No other book will take you from concept to running code in as few words. No other book will skip the irrelevant details. Don is a scientist, a teacher, and a programmer. This book combines these three perspectives into a unified and very readable presentation. It teaches both the ideas and the techniques needed to build object-relational database applications.

If you want to use DB2 Version 2, this is a good book to teach you the basics. It also teaches style and the more advanced topics. If you want to learn about object-relational database systems, this book gives you a detailed tour of a real one, warts and all. Either way, it is well worth the time you invest in it.

Contents

Preface

In 1995, IBM announced an important new addition to its DB2 family of database products. The announcement included new high-function relational database products for OS/2, Windows NT, AIX, and several other UNIX-based platforms, sharing a common code base. Because the new products share a code base and run on similar platforms, they are collectively known as the "common server" version of DB2. Each of the common server products has a platform-specific name and version number, as in "DB2 for AIX, Version 2." This book is a user's guide for all the common server DB2 products.

The common server products introduce an important new generation of IBM database systems, incorporating new technology developed at IBM's Research Division, where the relational data model originated. Your investment in learning about these products will be rewarded by a large payoff in functionality, performance, and productivity.

When you are trying to learn how to use a new system, the best kind of help is a friendly guide who can answer your questions and lead you over the rough spots. The second best kind of help is a set of working examples that you can refer to when writing programs of your own. The objective of this book is to provide both of these kinds of help to users of the common server DB2 products.

This book provides a general overview of DB2 in all its aspects and focuses in depth on the interfaces that support application developers and end users. It also includes a less detailed overview of facilities for database administrators. It is intended to be complementary to the IBM product documentation, providing a more narrative style and more explanatory material about the reasoning behind various product features and how these features are intended to be used. Occasionally, references are made to product manuals, such as *DB2 SQL Reference* and *DB2 Administration Guide*, where additional details can be found. The book contains many examples of code written in SQL, C, and C++, including several complete application programs that can be used as templates for developing your own applications. It also contains dozens of practical tips that are distilled from many hours of experience in developing DB2 applications.

You'll find that *Using the New DB2* is self-contained and accessible, whether or not you are familiar with previous versions of DB2. It does not assume that you have any prior knowledge of the SQL language or of relational database terminology. The book covers elementary database management, but its main emphasis is on the advanced features that are being introduced for the first time in the common server DB2 products. These products include the largest set of new database functionality to be released by IBM since the original IBM relational products of the early 1980s. Some of the new features that the book examines in detail include support for constraints and triggers, user-defined types and functions, large objects, and recursive queries.

These are interesting times in the field of database management. Two quite different paradigms are currently vying for the hearts and minds of database users. The *relational approach* offers data independence, multiple views of data, and a high-level set-oriented query language. The *object-oriented approach* offers abstract data types, orthogonal persistence, and seamless integration with a host programming language. It is not hard to see that the strengths of these two approaches are complementary and that some form of convergence between the two is a reasonable prediction for the future.

The task of combining the advantages of relational and object-oriented database systems has been a focus of research and development for the past several years and will not be completed quickly. It involves the efforts of database vendors, users, and standards committees. DB2 for common servers represents IBM's first step toward this goal, starting from a relational system and moving in an object-oriented direction. The goal of the new products is to incorporate object-oriented functionality without sacrificing the advantages of commercially proven relational systems. The new DB2 products include facilities for storing large objects with complex state and behavior and for invoking the behavior of these objects in SQL queries. Certain features that are often associated with object-oriented database systems—such as inheritance, inter-object references, and method-based indexes—are not yet included in the DB2 products, but they represent directions in which the products may evolve. The subtitle of this book, *IBM's Object-Relational Database System*, is meant to suggest that IBM, like other vendors, is seeking a synthesis of the relational and object-oriented approaches and that DB2 Version 2 for common servers does not represent the end of that process, but only the beginning.

My hope is that at least two different classes of readers will find value in this book. Users of the DB2 family of products will benefit from having a complete single-volume tutorial and reference on all aspects of the common server DB2 products. At the same time, readers who have a general interest in database systems and in the convergence of the relational and object-oriented paradigms will find in this book a discussion of IBM's approach to this important problem, illustrated by many practical examples.

Acknowledgments

I am very grateful for the encouragement and support I have received from IBM in the preparation of this book, and especially for the help and cooperation provided by the DB2 development teams at IBM's Almaden, Santa Teresa, and Toronto laboratories. Special thanks are due to all those who reviewed the manuscript and made many helpful suggestions, including (but not limited to) Michael Au, Paul Bird, Mike Carey, Jyh-Herng Chow, Bobbie Cochrane, Mark Hecht, Richard Hedges, Peter Kutschera, Toby Lehman, Margaret Li, Bruce Lindsay, Guy Lohman, Nelson Mattos, Kathy McKnight, John McPherson, Rodolphe Michel, Pat O'Neil, Frank Pellow, Hamid Pirahesh, Berthold Reinwald, Berni Schiefer, Pat Selinger, Eugene Shekita, Peter Shum, Richard Sidle, Lorie Strain, Rick Swagerman, Marty Wildberger, Bob Wilson, George Wilson, and Calisto Zuzarte. Thanks also to Jim Gray and Bruce Spatz for their guidance in the writing of this book, to Cheri Palmer and the staff at Morgan Kaufmann for their expert help in its production, to Duane Bibby for his wonderful illustrations, and to Carlene Nakagawa for her patience and skill in testing the examples.

1 Introduction

I n 1981, IBM introduced its first relational database system, SQL/DS, which ran under an operating system called DOS/VSE and supported the database language SQL, or Structured Query Language. SQL/DS was followed in 1983 by the DB2 product, which provided support for SQL under the MVS operating system. Over time, DB2 grew into a family of database products that now encompasses all IBM platforms from personal computer to mainframe and several non-IBM platforms as well.

In 1993, IBM announced DB2 for OS/2 and DB2 for AIX, two relational database systems with a common code base. In 1995, the company released major functional enhancements to these products, including support not just for OS/2 and AIX but for a variety of personal computer and workstation platforms. This new generation of database products is collectively referred to as the "common server" version of DB2, and this book is a comprehensive user's guide to these products.

Each of the products in the DB2 family is identified by a platform-specific name and a version number. This practice can be somewhat confusing, because the version numbers are not synchronized across the various platforms. For example, in 1996 the most current products available are DB2 for MVS Version 4, DB2 for OS/400 Version 3, and DB2 for AIX Version 2. A decimal digit after the version number identifies a specific release—for example, DB2 for AIX Version 2.1.

This book describes the DB2 Version 2.1 products for all personal computer and workstation platforms, including OS/2, Windows NT, AIX, HP-UX, Solaris, and SINIX. Throughout the book, the symbol V2 denotes this family of products and the symbol V1 denotes the predecessor products, DB2 Version 1 for AIX and OS/2.

The V2 family of products introduces the largest set of new database features to be released by IBM since the original SQL/DS announcement in 1981. These new features are clustered in four main categories: First, the power and orthogonality of the SQL language are greatly expanded by the inclusion of several new query features, including recursive queries. Second, a collection of object-oriented features enables V2 to store complex objects and to invoke the behavior of these objects in SQL statements. Third, a set of "active data" features including constraints and triggers is provided to protect data integrity and to enforce business rules. Fourth, V2 includes a number of performance enhancements, including powerful new techniques for query optimization and improved control over physical storage media.

The goal of this book is to provide an easy-to-read tutorial and reference for the common server DB2 products, with emphasis on the features that are new in V2 and with many examples to explain and motivate the features as they are introduced. You may wish to use it in conjunction with the IBM product manuals, which provide additional details that are beyond this book's scope, such as lists of error codes. The book includes occasional references to IBM manuals where further details can be found on a particular subject. The IBM publication numbers by which all these manuals can be ordered are listed in Appendix F.

1.1 ABOUT THIS BOOK

This book is organized as follows:

Chapter 1 provides a general overview of V2 and a summary of the different ways in which the product can be used. The chapter also includes a brief historical perspective on the SQL language and a discussion of how early decisions in its development have influenced V2 and other current relational systems.

Chapter 2 describes the basics of how to define, access, and manipulate data using SQL, both as a stand-alone query language and as a database language embedded in the C and C++ programming languages. For experienced users of relational database systems, much of this material will be a review. At the end of Chapter 2, there is a list of the features described in this chapter that are being introduced for the first time in V2. If you are an experienced user of V1 and are in the process of upgrading to V2, you may want to go directly to this list and then read selectively about the features that are of interest to you.

Chapter 3 describes some new V2 features that make SQL a much more powerful query language. This chapter will show you how to write recursive queries and how you can use a subquery anywhere that a scalar value or a table is expected. The features described in this chapter implement many aspects of the ANSI/ISO SQL92 Standard and remove many long-standing limitations of SQL in the areas of orthogonality and closure.

Chapter 4 introduces the new object-oriented features of V2, including support for large objects, user-defined datatypes, and user-defined functions. The chapter includes an example to show how you can use these features to define your own classes of objects with complex state and behavior, store these objects in your database, and invoke their behavior in SQL queries.

Chapter 5 describes another important area of new V2 functionality called *active data*. The term *active data* refers to rules and actions that are automatically invoked when the database is updated. The main active data features supported by V2 are constraints and triggers, which can be used together to protect the integrity of your data and to enforce the policies of your business. This chapter includes a comprehensive example that illustrates the use of constraints and triggers as well as user-defined datatypes and functions.

Chapter 6 describes the two different interfaces provided by V2 to support dynamic applications. Dynamic applications are applications that need to execute SQL statements generated "on the fly"—that is, SQL statements that are not known at the time the application is compiled. An example of a dynamic application is an interactive query interface, which must be able to execute user-generated SQL statements and display their results. V2 provides two ways to develop dynamic applications, called the *Call Level Interface* (CLI) and *Embedded Dynamic SQL*.

Chapter 7 describes how to write stored procedures. A stored procedure is a program that is installed and executed on a server machine but can be invoked from a separate client machine. By using stored procedures containing SQL statements, you can localize much of your application logic on the database server and minimize the network traffic between client and server.

Chapter 8 provides an overview of database administration tasks and of the tools provided by V2 for accomplishing these tasks. The tasks discussed in this chapter include creating and configuring databases, managing physical space, managing database backup and recovery, bulk loading data, monitoring and tuning the performance of the database, and examining the access plans of individual SQL statements.

The book concludes with six appendices:

- Appendix A lists the special registers such as CURRENT TIME and CURRENT DATE that can be used in SQL statements.

- Appendix B lists all the built-in functions supported by V2, a much more comprehensive set of functions than in previous IBM products.

- Appendix C lists the typecodes that are used to identify datatypes of values that are exchanged between the database and an application program.

- Appendix D describes the system catalog tables that V2 uses to maintain a description of the content of the database.

- Appendix E describes the syntax used to declare variables used for exchange of values between the database and a C or C++ program.

- Appendix F lists the IBM publications that pertain to V2 and gives the publication numbers by which they can be ordered.

1.1.1 **Notational Conventions**

The SQL language is insensitive to upper- and lowercase letters in keywords and in the names of tables and columns. Thus the following SQL queries are equivalent:

```
SELECT AVG(SALARY) FROM EMPLOYEES;
select avg(salary) from employees;
Select Avg(Salary) From Employees;
```

The only place in SQL where upper- and lowercasing is significant is inside a quoted string. But there are two kinds of quoted strings: strings enclosed in single quotes denote data values, and strings enclosed in double quotes denote identifiers (names). The following example illustrates both kinds of quoted strings:

```
SELECT avg(salary) FROM "Employees" WHERE job = 'Typist';
```

In the above example, we are searching for data in a table named "Employees" (not "EMPLOYEES" or "employees") and we are searching for the data value 'Typist' (not 'TYPIST' or 'typist').

Since SQL is insensitive to upper- and lowercasing except inside quoted strings, the SQL examples in this book have been written using a convention that is intended to make them consistent and easy to read. This convention is as follows:

1. SQL keywords are written in uppercase. Examples: SELECT, FROM, WHERE.

2. The names of tables and columns, when used in queries, are written in lowercase. Examples: employees, salary, job. However, when used in text outside of SQL queries, names of tables and columns are capitalized.

3. The names of functions are written in lowercase. This applies both to built-in functions and to new functions defined by users. Examples: avg, sum, length, substr.

4. The names of datatypes are written in lowercase with an initial capital. This applies both to built-in datatypes and to new datatypes defined by users. Examples: Integer, Varchar, Blob, Complex.

The following example illustrates this convention applied to some simple SQL statements:

```
SELECT name, salary, bonus
FROM employees
WHERE bonus > salary AND location = 'Armonk';

CREATE TABLE games
    (hometeam     Varchar(20),
     visitors     Varchar(20),
     gamedate     Date,
     homescore    Integer,
     visitorscore Integer);
```

1.1.2 Syntax Diagrams

This book makes extensive use of syntax diagrams to describe how to write SQL statements and clauses. A syntax diagram represents all the ways of constructing a valid statement or clause as a set of paths through the diagram from the starting symbol ├─ to the ending symbol ─▶│. The symbol ─▶ means "continued on the next line." Along a path, words appearing in uppercase (such as ORDER BY) represent words that must appear in the statement or clause, and words appearing in lowercase (such as column-name and integer) can be replaced by symbols of the user's choice (for example, specific column names or integers). "Loops" inside a syntax diagram represent parts of the path that can be used more than once. The name of the element (statement or clause) that is defined by a syntax diagram is shown on the border around the diagram. For example, the following syntax diagram defines an element named "order-by-clause," which consists of the words ORDER BY followed by a list of column names or integers separated by commas, with an optional word ASC or DESC after each column name or integer.

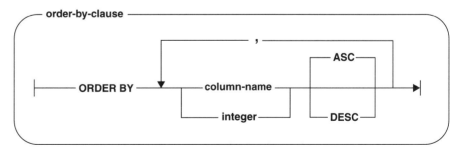

When a path fragment is printed above an empty path fragment, such as ASC in the above example, that fragment represents a default option that is effective if no other option is specified. Thus, in the above example, the ASC option is effective whenever the DESC option is not specified.

Occasionally an SQL statement may contain a series of options that can be specified in any order. This is denoted by a sequence of bullets in the syntax diagram. The fragments between the bullets can be written in any order. For example, the following diagram represents a syntax in which a size option, a color option, and a speed option can be specified in any order.

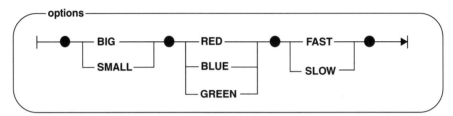

In some cases, a syntax diagram will contain some elements that are defined by lower-level syntax diagrams of their own. For example, the following diagram shows how a "search condition" can be built up from combinations of predicates and other search conditions, connected by the words AND, OR, and NOT. The elements *predicate* and *search-condition* are enclosed in small ovals to indicate that they are defined by syntax diagrams of their own. This syntax diagram is recursive, because the element named *search-condition* is used inside its own definition. (Any syntax diagram in the book can easily be found by looking for its element name in the index.)

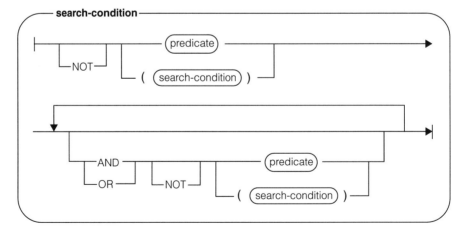

1.1.3 Examples

This book contains many examples, some written in pure SQL and some written using SQL embedded in a host programming language. Although the V2 product supports several different host programming languages, all the embedded-SQL examples in this book will use the C and C++ languages. These host languages were chosen because of their widespread use on the platforms supported by V2. Details of how SQL can be embedded in other host programming languages such as FORTRAN, COBOL, and REXX can be found in the *DB2 Application Programming Guide.*

Since V2 supports several different operating system platforms, the examples in this book are designed to be platform-independent except as noted. The only general exception to this rule involves filenames. OS/2 and Windows NT generally use the "\" character as a delimiter in filenames, whereas UNIX-based platforms such as AIX generally use the "/" character for the same purpose. Filenames in this book will be written using the UNIX convention, but can easily be converted to OS/2-style filenames by replacing "/" with "\". For example, the UNIX filename "/u/images/boat.gif" is equivalent to the OS/2 filename "\u\images\boat.gif".

1.1.4 Tips

During the course of creating and testing the examples in this book, I often encountered small tidbits of information that I felt would be helpful to users in developing applications of their own. A lot of this information was collected the hard way: by making mistakes and figuring out why things didn't work as I expected. Whenever I felt that users would benefit from some such piece of information or advice, I included it in the form of a "Tip." To help you identify them and find them quickly, tips are printed in a special format as shown in the example below. I have tried to include in these tips the kind of information that distinguishes a veteran user from a beginner and that is usually accumulated by painful experience. I hope that reading these tips will save you the many hours it would take to find this information out for yourself.

 TIP: If you are planning to put on both socks and shoes, you should put the socks on first.

1.2 PRODUCT OVERVIEW

The V2 family of products can be configured and used in a variety of ways. This section discusses some of the ways in which V2 products can be installed in a client-server environment, as well as some of the ways in which users can interact with V2. It also briefly discusses some other products that are closely related to V2 or that provide functionality complementary to that of V2.

1.2.1 The Client-Server Connection

A client-server computing environment consists of a set of computers connected together by some kind of network, often a local area network (LAN). A given machine, or *node,* in the network can act as a *server* (provider of services to other nodes), or as a *client* (requester of services from other nodes), or as both a client and a server. In a client-server database environment, server nodes generally manage databases and client nodes generally run database applications and support interactive users. When an application program or end user at a client node needs to access data in a database, software on the client node sends a request to the server node on which the data resides. Various protocols have been developed for handling the interactions between client and server nodes. Generally, these protocols are transparent to the database application or end user, who may not know or care on which server node the data actually resides. The V2 products can be used to configure individual machines as client nodes, server nodes, or both.

The V2 database engine is available in two versions: a single-user version and a server version. Figure 1-1 illustrates an installation of the single-user version, which supports only applications that run on the same machine where the database is installed. (Multiple applications can access the database at the same time, as long as they are all running on the local machine.) The single-user version of V2 includes toolkits for database administration and for developing new database applications. All the facilities described in this book are available in the single-user version of V2, subject to the limitation that only local applications are supported.

Figure 1-2 illustrates an installation of the server version of V2, which supports both local and remote applications. Each remote application runs on a client node that communicates with the server by means of a piece of software called a *Client Application Enabler* (CAE). Provided with the server version of V2 are CAEs for all the supported client platforms, including AIX, OS/2, Windows, and DOS. Client nodes of several different types can connect to the same V2 server node. Several network communication protocols are supported for the client-server connections, including APPC, TCP/IP, NetBios, and IPX/SPX. (For definitions of these protocols and information about which protocols are supported by a particular platform, see the *DB2 Planning Guide* for that platform.)

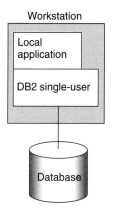

Figure 1-1: Single-User Installation of V2

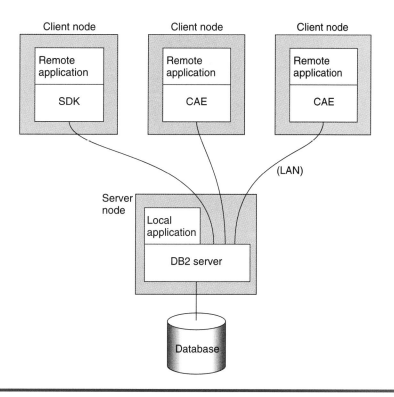

Figure 1-2: Client-Server Installation of V2

The CAEs for the various client platforms contain all the software necessary to run remote applications and to perform database administration tasks. However, to develop new database applications in a client-server environment, an additional product is needed called a *Software Developer's Kit* (SDK). An SDK for a given platform includes all the features of the CAE for that platform, and, in addition, includes host language precompilers, header files, code samples, and all the other tools necessary to develop new V2 applications. Figure 1-2 illustrates a configuration in which a V2 server is connected to three client nodes, two of which are running CAE and one of which is running SDK.

Figure 1-2 illustrates V2 client and server nodes connected to each other by a local area network. However, V2 nodes can also participate in networks of heterogeneous machines that are distributed throughout the world, using a protocol called *Distributed Relational Database Architecture* (DRDA). The DRDA protocol consists of two parts: the *Application Requestor* (AR) protocol and the *Application Server* (AS) protocol. Any system that implements the AR protocol can connect as a client to any server system that implements the AS protocol. All the database products in the DB2 family—and many competitive products as well—implement the DRDA protocols and can interconnect with each other with full generality. Thus, for example, a machine in San Francisco running DB2 for OS/2 might issue database requests to a machine in London running DB2 for MVS (or vice versa).

The AS side of the DRDA protocol is automatically included in every V2 server. Thus, your V2 server node can accept requests from any DRDA client node without requiring any additional software.

The AR side of the DRDA protocol is supported for V2 platforms by a separate product called *Distributed Database Connection Services* (DDCS). In its simplest configuration, DDCS can be installed by itself on a client node, enabling applications running on that client to connect to any DRDA-compliant server machine and to access databases on that server machine as though they were local databases. This configuration is illustrated by Figure 1-3, in which a client machine uses DDCS to connect to a database on a host system running DB2 for MVS.

Figure 1-4 illustrates the use of DDCS in a more complex configuration. Here, DDCS has been installed on the same machine as a V2 server. The DDCS installation includes a router that examines incoming requests from clients and routes them to the proper destination. Requests directed to databases that are managed by the V2 server system are handled locally, and requests directed to other databases are handled by DDCS, which forwards them to the proper server machine using the DRDA protocol. In this configuration, DDCS serves as a *gateway* that concentrates requests from a local cluster of V2 clients, making it unnecessary for each client machine to have its own DDCS installation.

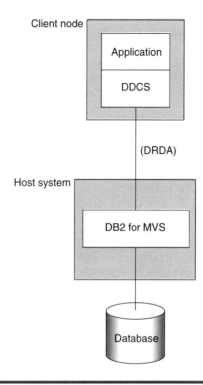

Figure 1-3: Installation of DDCS on a Client Machine

1.2.2 Nodes, Instances, and Databases

As shown in Figures 1-2, 1-3, and 1-4, a client-server database environment can include many machines, or nodes. On any given node, a product from the V2 family may be installed one or more times. For example, a server node might have two separate installations of the V2 database engine, one for testing and one for production. Each separate installation of V2 is called an *instance* and has an *instance name,* which is chosen when the product is installed.

It is sometimes necessary (for example, when creating a new database) to specify which instance of V2 is to be used. This can be done by setting an environment variable called DB2INSTANCE to the desired instance name or by using an ATTACH command as in the following example:

```
ATTACH TO db2test;
```

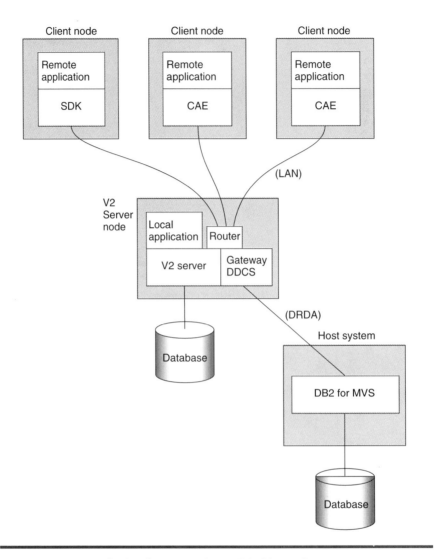

Figure 1-4: Example Configuration Using DDCS as a Gateway

Each instance of the V2 database engine can create and manage one or more *databases*. A database is a collection of data, organized in the form of *tables*. Each database belongs to a particular V2 instance and resides on the node where that instance is installed. Each database has a name, which is chosen at the time the database is created. Each database has a set of *system catalog*

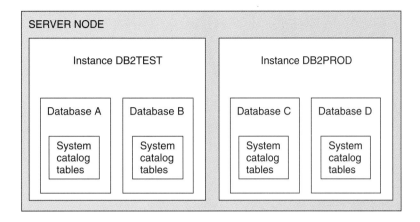

Figure 1-5: V2 Instances and Databases

tables, which are automatically maintained by the system, containing information about the tables and other objects that are stored in the database and about users of the database and their access privileges. Information about the database can be retrieved from the system catalog tables using SQL queries. (System catalog tables are discussed in detail in Appendix D.)

Figure 1-5 shows an example of the relationships among V2 instances and databases. In the example, two V2 instances are installed on the same server node, and each instance manages two databases.

In a client-server environment, client applications must be able to connect to databases on various servers. Therefore, one of the important tasks of the CAE is to keep a list of all the server nodes and databases that are accessible from a given client node. This list is kept in the form of *directories,* which are maintained at each client node. There are two kinds of directories:

1. A *node directory* is maintained by each client instance to record information about other nodes in the network and how to communicate with them. The information in the node directory is maintained by commands such as CATA-LOG NODE, UNCATALOG NODE, and LIST NODE DIRECTORY.

2. *Database directories* are also maintained by each client instance, to record information about databases that are available in the network and where they reside. For each database in its directory, a client can assign a name, called an *alias,* that serves as the name of the database as viewed from that particular client. The information in the database directories is maintained by commands such as CATALOG DATABASE, UNCATALOG DATABASE, and LIST DATABASE DIRECTORY.

It is important not to confuse the node directories and database directories, which exist at the DB2-instance level and are not accessible via SQL, with the system catalog tables, which exist at the database level and are accessible via SQL. It is perhaps unfortunate that some of the commands to maintain the node and database directories have names such as CATALOG NODE and CATALOG DATABASE, since these commands have nothing to do with system catalog tables. (Management of node and database directories is discussed in more depth in Section 8.3.)

1.2.3 The Command Line Processor

There are several different ways in which users can interact with the V2 system. One of these ways that is very simple and direct is by means of a user interface called the *Command Line Processor* (CLP). The CLP is provided with both the single-user and server versions of V2 and is also a part of the SDK, which can be installed on a client machine. The V2 CAEs also include a restricted version of the CLP that is able to execute only a limited set of commands.

The CLP accepts and processes commands and SQL statements, either from the keyboard or from a file, and displays the results. The CLP can be invoked from your operating system command prompt by means of the db2 command, which is described in Section 2.6.

The commands and statements that can be processed by the CLP fall into the following general categories:

1. *Commands that affect the behavior of the CLP itself.* These commands control options such as where input comes from, where output is saved, and how errors are handled. The commands for controlling CLP options are described in more detail in Section 2.6.

2. *SQL statements, to access and manipulate data in the database.* We will refer to SQL statements that are executed via the CLP as *interactive SQL statements*. The CAE version of the CLP does not support interactive SQL statements. Examples of interactive SQL statements include

   SELECT: Retrieves data from the database.

   INSERT, DELETE, UPDATE: Used to modify data in the database.

   CREATE, ALTER, DROP: Used to create, modify, and delete objects in the database such as tables, views, indexes, constraints, triggers, datatypes, and functions.

   COMMIT, ROLLBACK: Used to group database changes into units of work called *transactions*. COMMIT causes a series of changes to become permanent, and ROLLBACK cancels all the changes since the last COMMIT.

   GRANT, REVOKE: Used to control access to data by granting or revoking access privileges to various users.

Interactive SQL statements will be examined in more detail in Chapter 2 and Chapter 3.

3. *Commands that invoke system utilities.* Examples of these commands include

CREATE DATABASE, DROP DATABASE: Invoke utilities to create new databases and specify their configurations and to delete databases.

PREP, BIND, REBIND: Invoke utilities for preparing (compiling) new database applications written in host programming languages.

BACKUP, RESTORE, RESTART, ROLLFORWARD: Invoke utilities for protecting the database against processor or media failure and for recovering from failures.

LOAD, UNLOAD, EXPORT, IMPORT: Invoke utilities for exchanging bulk data between the database and external files.

GET, LIST: Invoke utilities that display information about the database. These commands have many options. For example, LIST TABLES displays a list of the tables in the database, and GET AUTHORIZATIONS displays a list of your access privileges for the database.

REORG, RUNSTATS: Invoke utilities to reorganize the physical storage of tables to improve their performance and to collect statistical data used by the system optimizer.

CATALOG, UNCATALOG: Invoke utilities to manage the database and node directories at your local node.

Most of the system utilities can be invoked in three different ways: by means of commands issued from the CLP, as described above; by means of a graphic user interface called the *Database Director;* and by means of function calls from application programs. Commands are described in more detail in Chapter 8, and the Database Director is discussed in Section 8.8. Interfaces for calling system utilities from application programs are documented in the *DB2 API Reference.*

1.2.4 Application Programs

As we have seen, the CLP allows you to submit SQL statements to V2 for processing, either interactively or through a file. But many database applications require programming-language features, such as looping and branching, that are not currently supported by SQL. For this reason, V2 allows SQL statements to be embedded in certain host programming languages, including C, C++, FORTRAN, COBOL, and REXX. This book discusses how database applications can be developed using SQL statements embedded in C and C++ programs. A discussion of embedding SQL in the other host languages can be found in the *DB2 Application Programming Guide.*

There are two main ways of embedding SQL statements in a host language program: *static SQL* and *dynamic SQL*. A static SQL statement is a statement that is known at the time the application is written. The form of the statement, as well as the names of the tables and columns accessed by the statement, must be known and fixed in order for the statement to be static. The only part of a static statement that can remain unknown at compile time is the specific data value to be searched for or updated, which can be represented by a variable in the host program. For example, the following static SQL statement searches for an employee whose employee number matches the C variable x, and updates that employee's salary to the value in the C variable y. The names of the table (EMPLOYEES) and columns (EMPNO and SALARY) accessed by this statement are fixed at compile time.

```
UPDATE employees SET salary = :y WHERE empno = :x
```

Static SQL statements have an important advantage: since the structure of the statement is known at compile time, the work of analyzing the statement and choosing an efficient access plan for implementing the statement can be done at compile time.[1] When the application program runs, then, its static SQL statements can be executed using the preselected access plan without further attention by the V2 optimizer. This minimizes the execution time of your application program, particularly if it invokes a given SQL statement multiple times. For this reason, static SQL statements are often used in high-performance applications that perform the same operation repeatedly, such as a banking application that updates customer accounts.

Static SQL statements exchange data with the application program by means of *host program variables*, which are C-language variables that are prefixed by a colon when used inside an SQL statement. Host program variables can be used to exchange both input and output values. For example, in the following SQL statement, variable :x provides an input value (a search argument) and variable :y retrieves an output value:

```
SELECT jobcode INTO :y FROM employees WHERE empno = :x
```

An SQL statement often returns multiple results, such as the names and addresses of all suppliers of a given part. Multiple results are delivered to a host program by means of a language feature called a *cursor*. A cursor is associated with a specific SQL statement and represents the *result set* returned by

---

1. At this point, I am using the term *compile time* somewhat loosely. As you will see shortly, the database system adds a new step, called *precompilation,* to the process of preparing an application program for execution.

that statement, which consists of zero or more rows. Each time a FETCH statement is applied to a given cursor, it returns one row from the result set (for example, the name and address of a supplier) into the host program variables named in the FETCH statement.

When an SQL statement is embedded in an application program, it is prefixed by the words EXEC SQL. All host language variables that are used inside SQL statements must be declared in a special *SQL Declare Section*, which is also prefixed by the words EXEC SQL. This prefix identifies the SQL statements inside the host program and distinguishes them from host language statements.

The process of preparing a database application in the C language to run under V2 is illustrated in Figure 1-6. The process consists of the following steps:

1. Prepare your application program, with embedded SQL statements, in a file with extension `sqc` (represented by `myprog.sqc` in Figure 1-6). Your file should include the header file `<sqlenv.h>`. Each of your SQL statements should be preceded by EXEC SQL.

2. Using the CLP, connect to the database that you wish to use, then use the PREP command to invoke the V2 precompiler. The precompiler removes the SQL statements from your source program and replaces them with calls to the run-time library of the database manager. It also generates and stores in the database a *package* containing a *section* for each of the static SQL statements in your program. The sections contain the encoded access plans that were selected by the V2 optimizer to execute your SQL statements. At run time, your program calls the database system and causes it to retrieve and execute these access plans.

   If you choose the BINDFILE option of the PREP command, the precompiler will generate a file, called a *bind file*, containing all the SQL statements and other information needed to generate a package for your program. The package can then be generated from the bind file and stored in the database by using the BIND command of the CLP. The advantage of creating a bind file is that you can use it repeatedly to *rebind* your program without invoking the precompiler. Each time you bind or rebind your program, the V2 optimizer chooses an optimal access plan for your SQL statements, based on the indexes and other database conditions at bind-time.

3. Use your favorite C compiler and linker to compile and link the pure C program generated by the V2 precompiler. You may link the program to functions in an object library if necessary. But remember that you must never modify the C program that was generated by the precompiler. If you need to modify your application, modify the `.sqc` file and repeat the PREP command.

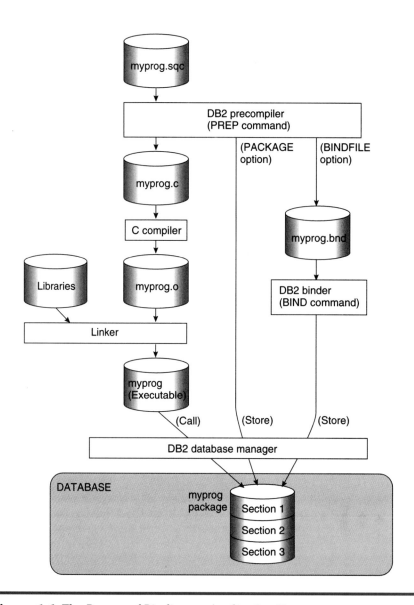

Figure 1-6: The Process of Binding an Application Program

When the above steps are complete, your application program is ready to run. You can invoke it by typing its name at the operating system prompt, like any compiled C program. When your program runs, it calls the V2 run-time library to execute the plans corresponding to your original SQL statements. V2 finds these plans inside the package that was stored in the database for your program either at PREP-time or at BIND-time.

1.2.5 Dynamic Applications

The previous section discusses static SQL statements, which are known at the time the application is written (except possibly for data values that can be obtained from host variables). Some applications, however, have a need to construct and execute new SQL statements at run time. Since these SQL statements are not written into the application, they cannot be optimized and converted to a package by the precompiler as can static SQL statements. Instead, they must be submitted to the optimizer while the application program is running, using special facilities designed for this purpose. SQL statements that are generated by a running program are called *dynamic SQL statements*, and the applications that generate them are called *dynamic applications*.

An excellent example of a dynamic application is the CLP. The function of the CLP is to prompt a user to enter SQL statements, which are then submitted to the system for processing. Although the CLP is shipped with the V2 system, it is written using exactly the same dynamic SQL facilities that are available to application developers. Using these facilities, you can write a CLP of your own, perhaps supporting a graphic interface or some other technique to help users construct interactive SQL statements.

Another example of a dynamic application is a general-purpose bulk loader. The purpose of this program is to create tables and load them with data, under the direction of some control file. Since the bulk loader does not know in advance the name of the table to be loaded or the number and datatypes of its columns, the bulk loader cannot be written using static SQL statements. The bulk loader will need to generate and execute a CREATE TABLE statement and a suitable INSERT statement for loading the data. By making careful use of dynamic SQL facilities, the bulk loader will cause the INSERT statement to be parsed and optimized only once, even though it is executed repeatedly as rows are inserted into the new table.

In general, dynamic SQL statements incur a performance penalty compared to static SQL statements, because they must be parsed and optimized at run time. For this reason, dynamic SQL statements are not generally used in high-performance applications involving short, predefined transactions. For example, a reservation system for car rentals would be likely to use static SQL statements, whereas a decision-support system for long-range planning would be more likely to use dynamic SQL statements.

V2 provides two separate facilities for processing dynamic SQL statements: *Call Level Interface* (CLI) and *Embedded Dynamic SQL*. These two facilities represent different approaches to accomplishing the same task. Each is described briefly here and revisited in more detail in Chapter 6.

Call Level Interface (CLI)

The V2 Call Level Interface (CLI) is based on Microsoft's *Open Database Connectivity* (ODBC) interface, supporting all the Level 1 features of ODBC and most of the Level 2 features. The Call Level Interface, as its name suggests, is a set of function calls that can be embedded in programs to access a database. At present, CLI is supported only for the C and C++ languages.

An important advantage of CLI is that application programs that use it do not need to be precompiled. This means that these programs can be distributed in the form of object code, since there is no need to submit source code to a precompiler. An application written using CLI can also be more portable than applications written using other V2 interfaces, since it can be ported to other database systems that support ODBC. In order to preserve this portability, however, a CLI-based application must confine itself to SQL features that are implemented on all the database systems of interest. V2 supports many advanced SQL features, such as user-defined datatypes and functions, that are available through the V2 CLI interface but are not supported on other systems.

If portability or object-code distribution is of great importance to an application, that application can be written using CLI rather than static SQL, even though all its SQL statements are known in advance. However, a static program written using CLI gives up the advantage of having its SQL statements optimized in advance and must pay the performance cost of invoking the SQL optimizer each time it is run. Also, CLI does not provide the same guarantee of *conservative binding semantics* that is provided by static SQL. Conservative binding semantics ensures that, once a program is bound, its behavior will not change until it is explicitly rebound. Since a CLI program goes through the function-selection process each time it runs, it is possible (but not very likely) that two runs of the program could end up invoking different functions. (For example, this might happen if a new function was created between the two runs of the program.)

The following are brief descriptions of some of the call interfaces supported by CLI:

SQLPrepare: This call prepares an SQL statement for execution by submitting it to the V2 optimizer.

SQLExecute: This call executes an SQL statement that was previously prepared by SQLPrepare. A statement can be prepared once and executed repeatedly.

SQLNumResultCols and SQLDescribeCol: These calls are used after preparing an SQL statement that queries the database, in order to get a description of the result set. The calls return the number of columns in the result set, and their datatypes, so that the application program can fetch the actual data and place it in the appropriate host variables.

SQLFetch: This call is used to fetch data from a result set and place it in one or more host variables.

CLI also supports many other calls for connecting to and interacting with databases—these will be discussed in greater detail in Chapter 6.

Embedded Dynamic SQL

Like CLI, Embedded Dynamic SQL permits an application program to generate SQL statements at run time and submit them to the database system to be optimized and executed. Unlike CLI, however, Embedded Dynamic SQL can be used with any of the host programming languages supported by V2.

Like static SQL, Embedded Dynamic SQL relies on the use of a precompiler—in fact, the same precompiler that is used for static SQL. For this reason, users who wish to mix together dynamic and static SQL statements in the same application, or who are familiar with the use of an SQL precompiler, may find Embedded Dynamic SQL more convenient than CLI.

Like static SQL statements, Embedded Dynamic SQL statements must be prefixed by EXEC SQL, which enables the precompiler to distinguish them from host language statements. The precompiler replaces each Embedded Dynamic SQL statement with a call to the V2 run-time library, as it does for static SQL. In the dynamic case, however, the call does not invoke an access plan that was prepared in advance and stored in the database for later execution. Instead, the call invokes database facilities to optimize and execute an SQL statement at run time.

The following is a brief description of some Embedded Dynamic SQL statements. The similarity between these statements and the CLI functions summarized above should be clear.

PREPARE: This statement submits a dynamic SQL statement, contained in a host variable, to V2 to be optimized and prepared for execution.

EXECUTE: This statement executes an SQL statement that was previously prepared by a PREPARE statement.

DESCRIBE: This statement is used after preparing an SQL statement that queries the database in order to get a description of the number of columns in the result set and their datatypes. This information is needed by the application program in order to fetch the actual data and place it into the appropriate host variables.

FETCH: The result of a dynamic query is delivered to the host program in the same way as the result of a static query: by applying FETCH statements to a cursor that represents the result set. In order to fetch data whose datatype is not known at compile time, the FETCH statement has a special dynamic option called FETCH USING DESCRIPTOR.

The details of these and other Embedded Dynamic SQL statements are discussed in Chapter 6.

1.2.6 Stored Procedures

In a client-server environment, applications are often invoked from a client machine to run against a database on a server machine. If such an application contains many SQL statements, each SQL statement is sent across the network from the client to the server in a separate message. Under certain circumstances, the number of messages between client and server can be reduced and the performance of the application improved, by using a technique called a *stored procedure*. You may wish to consider using a stored procedure if your application has the following characteristics:

1. It is invoked repeatedly from a client machine but uses a database on a server machine.

2. It contains several SQL statements but does a limited amount of end-user interaction. Specifically, the application needs to gather all its input data into a set of host variables, then execute a series of SQL statements without user interaction, then deliver all its output using a set of host variables.

A stored procedure is an application program that is written according to certain conventions, then precompiled and bound to a particular database on the server machine. A separate program, called the *client application,* is installed on the client machine. The client application must connect to the database in which the stored procedure is bound, using an SQL CONNECT statement. The client application can then invoke the stored procedure by means of an SQL statement, CALL, which names the stored procedure and provides a list of host variables that are used to exchange data with the stored procedure, in both directions. All the variables named in the CALL statement are passed to the stored procedure as inputs and can be reused by the stored procedure to return output to the client application.

A client application can use the SQL CALL statement to invoke stored procedures on any database system that supports the *Database Application Remote Interface* (DARI) or *Distributed Relational Database Architecture* (DRDA) protocol. This includes not only all the products in the V2 family but also DB2 products on other platforms such as MVS and OS/400.

The SQL CALL statement is a new feature of V2. An older application programming interface for stored procedures, called sqleproc, is still supported but can only be used to invoke stored procedures on servers that support the DARI protocol.

In addition to the native facilities of V2 for creating and invoking stored procedures, a separate product called *DataBasic* is available that provides a specialized environment for developing stored procedures. DataBasic allows you to create and test stored procedures using the BASIC programming language with embedded SQL. DataBasic is used on a client machine, and it provides tools for developing stored procedures, testing them on the client machine, then installing them on a server machine for production use. (Stored procedures are discussed in more detail in Chapter 7.)

1.2.7 User Roles

As we have seen, there are many ways of interacting with a system as complex as V2. Since the purpose of a database system is to manage shared data, it is reasonable to expect that a system like V2 will have many users and that these users will fall into several different categories. Users may vary widely in their degree of expertise and their need for access to the facilities of the system and to the data that it stores. Therefore, V2 recognizes several categories of users and has a system of authorities and privileges to control their activities. The roles in which users can interact with V2 are summarized below. The system of authorities and privileges that supports and enforces these roles is discussed further in Section 2.10.

1. *System administrator.* The role of system administrator is the most powerful user role recognized by V2. System adminstrators are considered to own all the resources of the database system and are authorized to execute any system command. The *System Administration* authority applies to a V2 instance (installation of the database system), which may include several databases. The user group that holds this authority is specified at the time the system is installed.

   V2 also recognizes two subsets of System Administration authority: *System Control* and *System Maintenance.* Holders of System Control authority can control the physical resources of the database system, while holders of System Maintenance authority can perform maintenance operations such as starting and stopping the server and backing up and restoring databases. However, unlike System Administration, the System Control and System Maintenance authorities do not convey the right to access or modify user data.

2. *Database administrator.* The role of database administrator applies to a specific database and carries with it the authority to create, destroy, access, and modify all objects in that database. Database administrators can also grant to other users the right to create objects and to access and modify individual objects such as tables, views, and indexes.

3. *Application developer.* One of the important user roles in V2 is that of a developer of new database applications. An application developer need not be a database administrator, but, in order to be effective, must hold both some general *authorities* and some specific *privileges*.

   The *authorities* needed by application developers apply to the database as a whole and include CONNECT (the right to connect to the database), CREATETAB (the right to create tables in the database), and BINDADD (the right to create new application programs, or packages, in the database). An application developer will probably need all three of these authorities.

   The *privileges* needed by application developers apply to specific objects in the database such as tables, views, and packages. In general, the creator of a new object receives a full set of privileges on the object, which the creator can then grant selectively to other users as desired. Each type of object has a certain set of privileges that are applicable to it. For example, the privileges that apply to tables include SELECT, INSERT, DELETE, UPDATE, and some other specialized privileges as described in Section 2.10.

   When a new application program is bound to a database (by a PREP or BIND command), the SQL statements in the program are checked against the authorities and privileges of the user who is binding the program. For example, to bind a program that updates the CUSTOMERS table, a user must hold the UPDATE privilege on that table. However, once the program has been bound, users need only the EXECUTE privilege on the package in order to run it. This enables the holder of a privilege (such as UPDATE on CUSTOMERS) to *encapsulate* this privilege in a program that exercises it in a specific way (perhaps updating customer addresses but not their credit ratings). The ability to run the program can then be granted to users who do not hold a generalized UPDATE privilege on CUSTOMERS.

4. *End user.* The user role in V2 that requires the least level of authorization is that of the end user. In order to run an existing application, a user needs only CONNECT authority on the database and EXECUTE privilege on the application's package. In fact, if CONNECT on the database and EXECUTE on the package have been granted to PUBLIC, a user can run the application without any authorization at all.

   If a user wishes to use the CLP to run interactive SQL statements against the database, performing various actions such as retrieving and updating data and creating new tables, the user must hold the specific privileges that are required to perform these actions.

1.2.8 Related Products

V2 is a member of a large family of related IBM software products. Some of these products are database managers that provide functionality similar to that of V2 on various other platforms; others are auxiliary products that interact with database managers to provide additional functionality. In the case of some auxiliary products based on V1, a V2-based version of the product has not been announced at the time of publication. This section provides only a brief overview of each product—interested users should consult IBM literature for details on functionality and availability.

DB2 Family of Database Managers

As we have noted, V2 is called the "common server" version of DB2 because it supports many personal computer and workstation platforms. In addition to the common server DB2 products, the DB2 family of database managers includes DB2 for MVS, DB2 for OS/400, and DB2 for VM and VSE.

Distributed Database Connection Services (DDCS)

As discussed in previous sections, DDCS is the product that enables V2 clients to connect to any database server in the DB2 family or to any other server that implements the Distributed Relational Database Architecture (DRDA) Application Server protocol.

DB2 Parallel Edition

DB2 Parallel Edition is based on DB2 for AIX, Version 1, the predecessor product to V2, which we refer to as V1. DB2 Parallel Edition provides V1 functionality on the IBM SP2 hardware platform, which is a shared-nothing multiprocessor system that connects multiple Risc System/6000 processors using a high-speed switch and a special version of AIX. A parallel optimizer enables DB2 Parallel Edition to support high-performance applications by executing queries in parallel using multiple processors, with near-linear scalability. Although DB2 Parallel Edition does not yet support the advanced functions of V2 such as user-defined datatypes, functions, and triggers, it is reasonable to expect these features to be incorporated into future versions of the Parallel Edition.

Relational Extenders

The V2 system provides the infrastructure needed to create user-defined datatypes and functions, enabling users to define and store objects with complex state and behavior. IBM also provides a set of Relational Extenders that exploit this infrastructure by providing definitions for specific datatypes and functions. For example, the Text Extender allows you to store large text documents in V2 and to search for documents that contain specific text, synonyms of a word or phrase, or multiple words or phrases in proximity. IBM offers relational extenders for Text, Image, Audio, Video, and Fingerprints, all developed specifically for use with the V2 system. Over time, additional extenders are likely to become available from IBM and other sources.

Visualizer

Visualizer is a series of products that run on the OS/2, AIX, and Windows platforms, connecting to database managers in the DB2 family and providing interactive query functions with a graphic user interface. The Visualizer products enable users to interact with DB2 databases without requiring knowledge of SQL syntax. The individual products in the Visualizer series provide features for querying and updating DB2 databases and for generating reports, charts, and maps based on data retrieved from DB2. One of the Visualizer products, Ultimedia Query for OS/2, supports browsing through multimedia data such as audio, video, and images, including searching for images by content based on color, texture, and shape.

DataJoiner

DataJoiner is a "middleware" product that enables users to interact with data from multiple heterogeneous sources, providing an image of a single relational database. DataJoiner supports client applications on AIX, OS/2, DOS, Windows, Solaris, and HP-UX operating system platforms, allowing them to connect to databases managed by the DB2 family of products as well as competitive systems such as Oracle and Sybase and nonrelational systems such as IMS and VSAM. DataJoiner masks the differences among these various systems, presenting to the client an image of a single database system that supports the external interfaces of DB2 for AIX, Version 1 (V1). All the data in the heterogeneous network appears to the client in the form of tables in a single relational database. DataJoiner includes an optimizer for cross-platform queries that enables an SQL query, for example, to join a table stored in a DB2 database in San Francisco with a table stored in an Oracle database in Chicago. Data manipulation statements (SELECT, INSERT, DELETE, and UPDATE) are independent of the location of the stored data, but data definition statements (such as CREATE TABLE) are less well standardized and must be written in the native language of the system on which the data is stored.

Data Replicator Products

IBM provides three products for keeping databases consistent by propagating updates from one database to another. *DataPropagator Relational* propagates updates between members of the DB2 relational database family of products, at user-specified intervals or triggered by specific events. For example, Data-Propagator Relational might be used to download daily changes from an operational database using DB2 for MVS to a decision-support database using DB2 for AIX, automatically performing user-specified computations on each download. *DataPropagator NonRelational* performs a similar function in propagating changes between DB2 databases and IMS databases, in both directions. *DataRefresher* is a related product that provides refresh copying of data from sources in MVS to targets on various platforms.

DataHub

DataHub has two versions: DataHub for OS/2 and DataHub for UNIX. Both products provide graphic user interfaces for administering networks of database systems from a single control point. DataHub for OS/2 can perform administrative functions for any database system in the DB2 family, and DataHub for UNIX can perform similar functions for DB2, Oracle, Sybase, and Ingres systems running on various UNIX platforms. Using DataHub, an administrator can create and modify database objects such as tables and views, perform backup and recovery, grant and revoke user privileges, and monitor database activity and resource utilization. DataHub for UNIX also has a rule-based "watchdog" feature that can invoke automatic actions when specified events or conditions are detected in the database network.

DataGuide

DataGuide is an OS/2-based database dictionary product that can be used for storing "meta-data" about the information available in DB2 and other databases. DataGuide provides tools for extracting this information from database systems and for displaying it in a convenient format. DataGuide might be thought of as a "card catalog" for searching among the information assets of a corporation.

DataBasic

DataBasic is a development environment based on the BASIC programming language that can be used to create and debug stored procedures and user-defined functions for use with V2. Using DataBasic, a developer can quickly create, test, and install a stored procedure or user-defined function on a V2 database server. DataBasic provides a safe environment for developing stored procedures, because BASIC is an interpreted language that does not allow programs to access memory via pointers. DataBasic also provides a closer coupling between BASIC and SQL than is available in other host programming languages.

VisualAge and VisualGen

VisualAge and VisualGen are development environments for database applications based on the visual programming paradigm. These environments allow you to create an end-user interface by assembling predefined components such as buttons and dialog boxes, and to bind these user-interface components to functions that access DB2 databases. VisualAge and VisualGen each has a scripting language that is used for writing those parts of the application logic that are not predefined. In the case of VisualAge, the scripting language is Smalltalk, and the resulting application program can be generated in either Smalltalk or C++. VisualGen, on the other hand, has a unique scripting language of its own, and can generate application programs in either C++ or COBOL.

ADSTAR Distributed Storage Manager

The ADSTAR Distributed Storage Manager (ADSM) is a network-based facility for creating and managing backup copies of stored data. V2 databases can be backed up via network connections to ADSM servers running on a variety of platforms. The backups can be invoked either explicitly or according to an automatic schedule. ADSM also provides facilities for automating policies about how long backups should be kept and for examining the list of available backups.

1.3 A BRIEF HISTORY OF SQL

Since SQL is so central to the user interface of V2, a brief discussion of the early history of the language may be helpful in understanding how some V2 features came to be the way they are. In the discussion that follows, references to source materials are provided in square brackets. A list of these references can be found in Section 1.3.4.

Before 1970, databases were usually viewed as territories through which computer programs might "navigate," following pointers from one record to another along fixed pathways, perhaps leaving breadcrumbs (sometimes called "currency status indicators") behind in case they lost their way. In 1970, Dr. E. F. Codd proposed a completely new paradigm for thinking about data, in which all meaningful relationships among data records are represented by data values rather than by hidden pointers or connections.

Codd's insight made it possible to express database queries in a nonprocedural language, thus making queries independent of the structures and algorithms used in the database implementation—a concept that Codd called *data independence*. Codd's 1970 paper, "A Relational Model of Data for Large Shared Data Banks" [Codd 70], is one of the most influential and widely cited papers in all of computer science and was the basis for Codd's receiving the ACM Turing Award in 1981.

Codd's original paper noted that queries against data stored in the form of relations could be expressed either using the first-order predicate calculus or using a collection of relational operators such as join and projection. In subsequent papers, he developed these two approaches into two database access languages, which came to be known as the *relational calculus* [Codd 71a] and the *relational algebra* [Codd 71b]. Much of the early work on implementation of the relational model was focused on the operators of the relational algebra, and an algebra-based prototype was constructed at IBM's Peterlee laboratory in England [Todd 75].

1.3.1 System R

In the early 1970s, the benefits of the relational model for user productivity and data independence were reasonably well known, but important questions remained about whether a relational database system could be built to store large amounts of data in a multiuser environment with adequate performance for production use. In 1973, a project was begun at the IBM Research Laboratory in San Jose, California, to study these questions by building an industrial-strength relational prototype, which came to be known as System R [Astrahan 76]. At about the same time, a similar relational database project, known as Ingres, was formed at the University of California at Berkeley [Stonebraker 76]. The System R and Ingres projects both built successful prototypes, demonstrating that the relational model could be implemented efficiently and could support both ad hoc queries and transaction processing on production data. Both prototypes were extensively tested by experimental users, and both ultimately led to commercial products. For their work in developing the infrastructure to support the relational data model, the designers of System R and Ingres jointly received the ACM Software Systems Award in 1988.

Rather than implementing the relational algebra or calculus, the designers of System R developed a new database language, which was originally known as *Structured English Query Language*, or SEQUEL [Chamberlin 74]. The designers of SEQUEL attempted to develop a language that was easy to learn and use, basing the language on familiar English keywords and avoiding potentially difficult concepts such as the division operator of the relational algebra. The SEQUEL designers also included a number of features that were not present in either of Codd's original languages, such as update operators and a grouping operator. (C. J. Date has subsequently shown how these features could be added to the relational algebra and calculus [Date 95].) Finally, the SEQUEL designers attempted to provide a syntax that would unify several operations that had traditionally been considered separate and unrelated, including query, data manipulation, data definition (for example, definition of views), and data control (for example, constraints on data values).

The early history of the SEQUEL language is inextricable from the history of System R. The project conducted a series of human-factor tests on the language using college students as subjects [Reisner 75] and published a series of papers on various features of the language [Boyce 73, Chamberlin 76] and its implementation [Selinger 79, Chamberlin 81]. In the late 1970s, it was discovered that the name SEQUEL conflicted with an existing trademark, so the name was shortened to SQL, or Structured Query Language. The System R prototype was used over a period of three years by experimental users in a number of locations. Summaries of the lessons learned during this period can be found in [Chamberlin 80] and [Astrahan 80].

1.3.2 Products and Standards

Although SQL was developed and prototyped at IBM, the first commercial product based on SQL was released by a small company called Relational Software, Inc., in 1979. This product was called Oracle, a name that was later adopted by the company, which is no longer small. Oracle was first implemented under the UNIX operating system on Digital PDP-11 machines and later ported to other platforms. In the same year, a relational database product based on the Ingres prototype was released, also in the UNIX environment, by a new company called Relational Technology, Inc. The Ingres product initially implemented a query language called *QUEL* and later added support for SQL.

The first commercial implementation of SQL from IBM, called *SQL/Data System*, was released in February 1981 under a System/370 operating system called DOS/VSE. This release was followed by a series of IBM products that extended support for SQL to all of IBM's operating system environments: SQL/Data System for VM/370 in 1983, DB2 for MVS in 1983, SQL/400 in 1988, and OS/2 Database Manager in 1987. The "common server" DB2 products described in this book are the latest addition to the DB2 family.

During the 1980s, SQL was implemented by all major relational database suppliers and is now the world's most widely used database language. In order to promote portability among the many SQL implementations, the American National Standards Institute (ANSI) undertook a project to develop a standard specification for SQL. The result, called *Database Language SQL,* was approved as an ANSI Standard (number X3.135-1986) in October 1986. The same language was adopted by the International Organization for Standardization (ISO) as an International Standard (number 9075-1987) in June 1987 and has subsequently been accepted by the national standards organizations of Canada, the United Kingdom, France, Germany, Japan, and other countries.

SQL continues to be a focus for standardization activities. The ANSI/ISO Standard for SQL was updated in 1989 by the addition of an Integrity Enhancement feature that supports specification of constraints on data values and on relationships between tables. A much larger version of the Standard, containing many new features, was adopted by ANSI and ISO in 1992 and is often referred to as *SQL92* [ANSI 92]. An even more comprehensive version of SQL, informally known as *SQL3*, is currently under development in ANSI and ISO committees. Meanwhile, the formidable size of the ANSI/ISO Standard has prompted a number of users and suppliers of database systems to form an independent consortium, now called the *X/Open SQL Access Group*, which has published a standard specification of its own that is a subset of SQL92 [X/Open 92].

1.3.3 Some Controversial Decisions

During the early development of SQL and System R, some decisions were made that were ultimately to generate a great deal more controversy than anyone anticipated. Chief among these were the decisions to support null values and to permit duplicate rows to occur in tables and in query results. I will devote a small amount of space here to examining the reasons for these decisions and the context in which they were made. My purpose here is historical rather than persuasive—I recognize that nulls and duplicates are religious topics, and I do not expect anyone to have a conversion experience after reading this chapter.

For the most part, the designers of System R were practical people rather than theoreticians, and this orientation was reflected in many of their decisions. To a large extent, the philosophy of the System R user interface can be expressed by three principles: (1) Use common sense; (2) Model the real world; and (3) Trust the user. Some examples will help us to see how these principles were applied to the issues of nulls and duplicates.

Consider a database containing student records for a large university. Suppose that each student is uniquely identified by some primary key such as a social security number. One application program written for this database might print a set of mailing labels, perhaps to send a registration bulletin to all the students. The query to retrieve the students' names and addresses is a very simple one and might be written as follows:

```
SELECT name, address FROM students;
```

This query returns a large amount of data—perhaps 35,000 rows. Since neither name nor address (nor their combination) is declared to be a key, the system does not know whether the collection of names and addresses retrieved by this query contains any duplicates. If the semantics of the query language are defined in such a way that duplicates are guaranteed to be eliminated from every query result, the system will be forced to search for duplicate pairs of names and addresses, probably by making a temporary copy of all the data and sorting it. Now, sorting 35,000 records is not entirely free, even today, and in the mid-1970s it was even more expensive. A good commonsense question to ask here is: What value is added to this query result by eliminating duplicates? The user who wrote the query probably knows that it is unlikely that two or more students with the same name will be found at the same address. And in the case that two students with identical names and addresses do exist, the writer of the program may very well choose to print a mailing label for each of them (and let them figure out who gets which label). Because of examples such as this, it was decided that SQL would make elimination of duplicate rows from query results optional, trusting the user to decide when the cost of this operation is justified. The minor issue of default behavior was decided on the basis of maximizing performance and minimizing cost—that is, the system would undertake the costly and time-consuming operation of eliminating duplicates only when asked to do so.

Of course, permitting duplicate rows in query results is not the same thing as permitting duplicate rows in tables. The System R designers were aware that a relation, as defined in Codd's groundbreaking paper, is a subset of the Cartesian product of a set of domains, and that this definition permits no duplicate rows. Certainly this formal definition of a relation is a useful one and should be supported by every database system. But the System R designers also considered it possible that some users (perhaps untutored in set theory) would appreciate a more flexible concept of a table as a container for storing information, in which duplicate rows and null values could be either permitted or not permitted according to the user's choice. As an example of an application in which duplicate rows might be meaningful, consider a table of real estate transactions that records the zip code, date, and selling price of each transaction. The designer of the table might be interested only in statistical queries, such as finding the average selling price of parcels in zip code 90210 in a given year or finding zip codes in which properties have sold for more than $1 million. Now, it might be rare, but it is certainly not impossible for two parcels in the same zip code to be sold on the same day for the same price. A reasonable commonsense question might be: Should users be *required* to take precautions against storing this kind of "duplicate" data? In order to guarantee uniqueness of rows, another column would need to be added to the table, perhaps containing a parcel number. Indeed, since the very same parcel might change hands twice on the same day, it might be necessary for the application to generate a synthetic key for each transaction, and for the system to maintain some kind of index on the key to guarantee uniqueness. SQL trusts the database designer to decide whether the costs of generating and maintaining such a unique key are justified. To impose these costs on all applications regardless of their semantics seems a little heavy-handed, and seemed even more so in 1975 given the costs of storage and processing at that time.

Turning to the issue of nulls forces us to confront, head-on, the fact that databases are sometimes used to model the real world. Consider a table that records the temperature, barometric pressure, wind direction and velocity, and other weather-related data for various dates and locations. Suppose that at the weather station in Fairbanks, Alaska, on January 17, 1989, someone dropped the only barometer on the floor and broke it, and as a result the barometric pressure at that particular place and time is forever unknown. This is the kind of nasty problem that tends to happen in the real world, and it presents database designers with some unpalatable options.

One such option, proposed by C. J. Date [Date 92], is to choose one of the possible values of the barometric pressure column and to dedicate it forever to representing missing information. This approach leads to at least two serious problems. The least serious of these problems is that some columns may not be able to spare a value to represent missing data, since all possible values are meaningful. This situation, though certainly possible, is probably rare (if the barometric pressure in Fairbanks reaches zero, for example, representation of missing values will be the least of our problems). A much more serious problem is the fact that using a valid data value to represent missing information requires explicit defensive code to be written into *every* application that interacts with the database. For example, if zero is chosen as the representation of a missing barometric pressure, the following query will return wrong answers quietly and without any warning.

```
SELECT avg(pressure)
FROM weather
WHERE location = 'Fairbanks';
```

In order to obtain the correct answer, the query above (and every similar query in every application) would need to be rewritten as follows (assuming that zero is chosen as the representation for an unknown pressure):

```
SELECT avg(pressure)
FROM weather
WHERE location = 'Fairbanks'
AND pressure <> 0;
```

A second unpalatable option for representing missing information is to "double up" each column with an auxiliary column containing a flag that indicates whether the value in the original column is valid or missing.

Needless to say, this approach significantly increases the storage required by the database and still requires defensive coding in every application program as illustrated in the example above.

A third unpalatable option is for the database system to explicitly represent missing information by a null, or "out of band," value that is qualitatively different from, and not comparable to, a normal value. This approach leads to the three-valued logic that is part of the ANSI/ISO SQL Standard and has been implemented by V2 and by many other relational systems. It also leads to some (by now) well-documented anomalies. For example, in SQL the expression avg(salary) is not necessarily equal to the expression sum(salary) / count(*). Furthermore, the following query, which might reasonably be supposed to return all the rows of the EMPLOYEES table, will fail to return any employees with null salaries:

```
SELECT *
FROM employees
WHERE salary > 10000
OR salary < 10000
OR salary = 10000;
```

The presence of nulls also places some limitations on query optimizers. For example, certain techniques for transforming queries into other equivalent queries are valid under two-valued logic but not under three-valued logic, so optimizers that use these techniques must observe certain limitations in the presence of nulls.[2]

Faced with these unpalatable options, the designers of SQL fell back to the principle "Trust the user." Providing support for explicit nulls and three-valued logic in the database system gives users the tools to represent missing data with minimal cost and without requiring defensive coding in every application. At the same time, supporting the NOT NULL constraint at the column level allows users to avoid the anomalies associated with null values where this is considered important. Since none of the options for representing missing information is flawless, and since users are paying the bills, it seems appropriate that users should be able to choose the approach they find least troublesome.

Before leaving the null subject, I would like to observe that nulls can sometimes give database users the flexibility they need to deal with unanticipated situations. As an example, consider a database maintained by a government agency to record information about vehicles sold in the United States. Such a

2. The V2 optimizer does in fact use query-transformation techniques and does limit their use in order to avoid null-related anomalies.

database might contain a VEHICLES table with a column named MPG containing a measure of fuel efficiency in miles per gallon. Various applications might make use of this information; for example, the following query might be used to enforce standards for fleet average fuel efficiency:

```
SELECT manufacturer, avg(mpg)
FROM vehicles
GROUP BY manufacturer;
```

Imagine the problems that might be caused at this agency by the introduction of the first electric car. The MPG column is obviously inapplicable to such a vehicle, but dedicating some numeric value in this column to represent "inapplicable" would invalidate existing applications such as the average fuel efficiency query shown above. This problem may be caused by a lack of omniscience on the part of the original database designers, but this failing is unfortunately fairly common. The theoretically correct approach might be to redesign the database, perhaps adding a POWERSOURCE column and rewriting all existing applications. But programmers and database designers are not always plentiful, and problems like this are sometimes discovered on Wednesday afternoon when a final report is due on Friday. Partly because of gritty examples like this one, the designers of SQL and System R decided that nulls should be part of the bag of tools available to users to get their work done.

When the original SQL designers decided to allow users the options of handling nulls and duplicates, they viewed these features as minor conveniences, not as major departures from orthodoxy, taken at the risk of excommunication. Twenty years later, a great deal has been said, much of it rather loudly, on the issues of nulls and duplicates. E. F. Codd, originator of the relational data model, has stated that he does not consider a database system to be "fully relational" unless it supports not just one but two kinds of missing data [Codd 90]. Other well-known writers on things relational insist that the concept of nulls should be abolished altogether. In the end, I believe that the true arbiters of the null and duplicate-row issues will be users of database systems. If users find that these concepts are helpful in solving real problems, they will continue to use them. If, on the other hand, users are convinced that nulls and duplicates are harmful, they will avoid these features and scrupulously use options such as NOT NULL, PRIMARY KEY, and SELECT DISTINCT. By supporting these options, V2 makes it easy for users to "vote with their data."

1.3.4 References

[ANSI 92] *Database Language SQL*. Standard No. X3.135-1992. New York: American National Standards Institute, 1992.

[Astrahan 76] Astrahan, M. M., M. W. Blasgen, D. D. Chamberlin, K. P. Eswaran, J. N. Gray, P. P. Griffiths, W. F. King, R. A. Lorie, P. R. McJones, J. W. Mehl, G. R. Putzolu, I. L. Traiger, B. Wade, and V. Watson. "System R: A Relational Approach to Database Management." *ACM Transactions on Database Systems*, Vol. 1, No. 2, June 1976, 97–137.

[Astrahan 80] Astrahan, M. M., M. W. Blasgen, D. D. Chamberlin, J. N. Gray, W. F. King, B. G. Lindsay, R. A. Lorie, J. W. Mehl, T. G. Price, G. R. Putzolu, M. Schkolnick, P. G. Selinger, D. R. Slutz, I. L. Traiger, B. Wade, and R. A. Yost. "A History and Evaluation of System R." *Communications of the ACM*, Vol. 24, No. 10, Oct. 1981, 632–46.

[Boyce 73] Boyce, R. F., and D. D. Chamberlin. *Using a Structured English Query Language as a Data Definition Facility*. IBM Research Report RJ-1318. San Jose, CA: IBM Research Laboratory, December 1973.

[Chamberlin 74] Chamberlin, D. D., and R. F. Boyce. "SEQUEL: A Structured English Query Language." *Proceedings of the ACM SIGFIDET Workshop on Data Description, Access, and Control*, 249–64. Ann Arbor, MI: ACM, May 1974. (Note: SIGFIDET was the precursor to SIGMOD, the ACM Special Interest Group on Management of Data.)

[Chamberlin 76] Chamberlin, D. D., M. M. Astrahan, K. P. Eswaran, P. P. Griffiths, R. A. Lorie, J. W. Mehl, P. Reisner, and B. W. Wade. "SEQUEL 2: A Unified Approach to Data Definition, Manipulation, and Control." *IBM Journal of Research and Development*, Vol. 20, No. 6, Nov. 1976, 560–75. (Errata in Vol. 21, No. 1, Jan. 1977)

[Chamberlin 80] Chamberlin, D. D. "A Summary of User Experience with the SQL Data Sublanguage." *Proceedings of the International Conference on Data Bases*, 181–203. London: Heyden & Son, Ltd. July 1980.

[Chamberlin 81] Chamberlin, D. D., M. M. Astrahan, W. F. King, R. A. Lorie, J. W. Mehl, T. G. Price, M. Schkolnick, P. G. Selinger, D. R. Slutz, B. W. Wade, and R. A. Yost. "Support for Repetitive Transactions and Ad-Hoc Queries in System R." *ACM Transactions on Database Systems*, Vol. 6, No. 1, March 1981, 70–94.

[Codd 70] Codd, E. F. "A Relational Model of Data for Large Shared Data Banks." *Communications of the ACM*, Vol. 13, No. 6, June 1970, 377–87.

[Codd 71a] Codd, E. F. "A Data Base Sublanguage Founded on the Relational Calculus." *Proceedings of the 1971 ACM SIGFIDET Workshop on Data Description, Access, and Control*. New York: ACM, Nov. 1971.

[Codd 71b] Codd, E. F. "Relational Algebra," *Database Systems*. Courant Computer Science Symposium. New York: Prentice Hall, 1971.

[Codd 90] Codd, E. F. *The Relational Model for Database Management: Version 2*. Reading, MA: Addison-Wesley, 1990.

[Date 92] Date, C. J. "The Default Values Approach to Missing Information." In C. J. Date and Hugh Darwen, *Relational Database Writings 1989–1991*. Reading, MA: Addison-Wesley, 1992.

[Date 95] Date, C. J. *Introduction to Database Systems,* sixth ed. Reading, MA: Addison-Wesley, 1995.

[Reisner 75] Reisner, P., R. F. Boyce, and D. D. Chamberlin. "Human Factors Evaluation of Two Data Base Query Languages: SQUARE and SEQUEL." *Proceedings of the AFIPS National Computer Conference*, p. 447. Anaheim, CA: AFIPS Press, May 1975.

[Selinger 79] Selinger, P G., M. M. Astrahan, D. D. Chamberlin, R. A. Lorie, and T. G. Price. "Access Path Selection in a Relational Database Management System." *Proceedings of the ACM SIGMOD Conference*. New York: ACM, June 1979.

[Stonebraker 76] Stonebraker, M., G. Held., P. Kreps, and E. Wong "The Design and Implementation of Ingres." *ACM Transactions on Database Systems*, Vol. 1, No. 3, Sept. 1976, 189–222.

[Todd 75] Todd, S. J. P. "The Peterlee Relational Test Vehicle—A System Overview," *IBM Systems Journal*, Vol. 15, No. 4, 1976.

[X/Open 92] *CAE Specification: Structured Query Language (SQL)*. Document No. C201. Berkshire, England: X/Open Company, Ltd., August 1992.

Basics

Today's database applications implement a wide variety of user interfaces. Some applications present their users with forms to fill in; others provide various graphic tools for construction of database queries and updates. Somewhere below the surface of many seemingly disparate systems, however, is a common interface: SQL, the Structured Query Language. SQL has become the standard representation for queries against relational data and for interchange of these queries between clients and servers and between different database systems. Because SQL is a well-defined standard that has been implemented by many vendors, applications based on SQL are relatively portable from one system to another.

This chapter covers the basics of how to use SQL to access and manipulate data. V2 allows you to use SQL in two ways: by embedding SQL statements in application programs written in one of several host programming languages, or by executing SQL statements directly using an interactive user interface. Both of these modes of use provide access to the same language features, and both are described in this chapter.

The host programming languages supported by V2 are C, C++, COBOL, FORTRAN, and REXX. This book focuses on the C and C++ host languages because of their popularity on personal computer and workstation platforms. In this chapter, we will discuss how to embed SQL statements in C and C++ programs, and how to precompile these programs so that an optimal access plan is selected for each SQL statement before the program is executed. The precompilation approach avoids the overhead of access-path selection at run time. Precompilation also allows a user to "encapsulate" a program that operates on the database in some specific way, and to allow other users to execute the program without granting them a general ability to manipulate the database.

The simplest interface supported by V2 for interactive users is the Command Line Processor (CLP), which simply allows you to type SQL statements on a command line and displays the result on your screen. In addition to SQL statements, the CLP allows you to execute various database administration commands. This chapter describes how to use the CLP. Of course, in addition to the CLP, users of V2 can choose among a variety of graphic and other user interfaces supported on top of SQL by query products available from IBM and other vendors.

The basic tasks that are discussed in this chapter include

- Retrieving, inserting, updating, and deleting data
- Designing a database and creating tables and views
- Using the transaction concept to ensure data consistency
- Controlling access to data by using the authorization subsystem

Since this chapter is about basics, most of the features discussed here are not new. At the end of the chapter, there is a section describing which of these features are new in V2. Experienced users of V1 may wish to skip to this section and then selectively read about the new features that interest them. The material in this chapter serves as the foundation on which later chapters build to describe the advanced features of V2.

2.1 TABLES

In a relational database, all data is stored in *tables*, which consist of rows and columns. Each table has a name, and within a table, each column has a name. There is no ordering maintained among the rows of a table (but rows can be retrieved in an order determined by their values). One of the defining characteristics of a relational database is that all information in the database is represented by values that are stored in tables. No information is encoded in the form of physical structures such as indexes, pointers, connections, or orderings. Of course, all these physical structures, and others, can be used by the system to optimize its performance. But all these performance aids remain just that—internal devices that bear no essential information and are not part of the data model with which users interact.

The separation of access aids from the logical data model has several important consequences:

- Users can express their queries in a simple, high-level language that makes applications easy to develop.
- System administrators don't need to anticipate in advance exactly how the database will be used, since indexes and other structures can be added as usage patterns change without impacting existing applications.
- The system has an opportunity to choose the optimum access plan for any given query, based on the access aids that are available when the query is executed.

- The data model does not have a bias that makes some questions (those that correspond to physical access paths) easier to ask than other similar questions.

The tables that are physically stored in a database are called *base tables*. Most relational database systems, including V2, allow users to define additional tables, called *views*, that are derived in some way from the base tables. A view might be defined to omit some data from a base table, or to combine two base tables, or to contain only summary data. In V2, views can be defined using the same syntax that is used to write queries against base tables. (Views are discussed in more detail in Section 2.8.)

2.1.1 Example Database

In order to illustrate the use of SQL to manipulate data in tables, this chapter will use an example database consisting of four tables that might be used to manage a parts warehouse for a small company. The sample queries used in this chapter are based on these tables and have been tested using the sample data shown below.

Our sample warehouse needs to keep track of all the different kinds of parts used by the company, each of which has a unique part number. A table called PARTS is used to record information about each type of part, including its description and the quantity of that type of part that are currently on hand and on order.

PARTS

PARTNO	DESCRIPTION	QONHAND	QONORDER
P207	Gear	75	20
P209	Cam	0	10
P221	Big Bolt	650	200
P222	Small Bolt	1250	0
P231	Big Nut	0	200
P232	Small Nut	1100	0
P250	Big Gear	5	3
P285	Wheel	350	0
P295	Belt	0	25

The warehouse needs to maintain its inventory by ordering new parts when supplies get low. For this purpose, it maintains a list of suppliers, in a table named SUPPLIERS as shown below.

SUPPLIERS

SUPPNO	NAME	ADDRESS
S51	ABC Parts Company	123 Industrial Way, Cleveland OH
S53	Parts Are We	800 River Drive, Yonkers NY
S54	Quality Parts	3820 Bayview St., Seattle WA
S58	Superfast Parts	22500 Airport Blvd., Miami FL
S59	Joe's Scrap Heap	975 Country Club Lane, Boston MA
S61	Partco Inc.	650 Stony St., Dallas TX
S99	Parts Is Parts	500 Scenic Drive, Modesto CA

When ordering a new supply of parts, the warehouse manager generally wants to obtain each type of part at the lowest available price. However, occasionally he receives a rush order for parts that are needed within a certain period of time. In order to manage the process of ordering parts, the warehouse database contains a QUOTATIONS table that lists the parts that are available from the various suppliers, as well as the price and response time in days offered by each supplier for each part.

The QUOTATIONS table records prices in an Integer column as a number of cents (for example, the number 2995 represents $29.95). SQL has a Decimal datatype that might be a more natural choice for representing prices, but Decimal data cannot be exchanged efficiently with a C program because the C language has no equivalent datatype. Representing money values in Integer form is an example of one way to deal with this problem; other techniques are discussed later in the book.

The warehouse also needs to keep track of the orders for new parts that are currently pending. This is done by means of a table named ORDERS, which records the supplier number, part number, and quantity for each order, as well as the date on which the order was placed.

QUOTATIONS

SUPPNO	PARTNO	PRICE	RESPONSETIME
S51	P207	950	45
S51	P209	1250	10
S53	P207	2995	30
S53	P285	3250	21
S54	P209	2500	18
S54	P222	75	7
S54	P285	5500	25
S54	P295	1900	14
S58	P207	?	33
S58	P221	35	10
S58	P222	20	10
S58	P231	25	10
S58	P232	10	10
S61	P207	2995	28
S61	P221	30	15
S61	P222	15	15
S61	P231	20	15
S61	P232	5	15

ORDERS

SUPPNO	PARTNO	QUANTITY	ORDERDATE
S53	P207	20	1996-6-15
S51	P209	10	1996-6-20
S61	P221	200	1996-7-01
S61	P231	200	1996-7-01
S54	P295	25	1996-6-28

2.2 NAMES AND SCHEMAS

Databases are full of things that have names. As we have seen, V2 stores all data in tables, and each table has a name. Other database objects have names, too, including familiar objects such as views, as well as new kinds of objects introduced by V2 such as functions and triggers. A name is a string of up to eighteen characters, beginning with a letter.

Normally, when you type a name, the system automatically folds all lower-case characters to uppercase. Thus, for example, the names TABLE1 and table1 and Table1 are all equivalent. If, for some reason, you wish to use a name that contains lowercase letters, blanks, or special characters, you can do so if you enclose the name in double quotes, as in "My Table". Quoted names are interpreted by the system exactly as they are written, so "My Table" and "my table" are different names. A quoted name may also be the same as an SQL keyword such as SELECT or FROM, though this can lead to some confusing queries.

If you were creating a table named PAYROLL, it would be burdensome to have to search the database to find out whether some other user has already created a table with the same name. It would be even worse if you purchased some database application that creates a PAYROLL table and were unable to use it because of a naming conflict. For these reasons, V2 provides a method called *qualified names*, which enables you to distinguish the names that you create from names created by other users and applications.

A qualified name is a two-part name. The second part is the name of the object, while the first part, or qualifier, is used to distinguish objects that would otherwise have duplicate names. The qualifier of an object is usually the userid of the user who created the object. Thus, for example, user Smith might have a table named SMITH.PAYROLL, and user Jones might have a table named JONES.PAYROLL. In V1, recognizing this convention, the qualifier of a name was referred to as its *creator*.

V2, following the lead of the ANSI/ISO SQL Standard, takes a more general-ized view of qualified names. In V2, the qualifier of a name is referred to as its *schema name*, in recognition of the fact that it may not always represent the creator of the object. You may wish to use schema names as a way of classify-ing your tables into categories. For example, you might create two tables named RESEARCH.PAYROLL and PRODUCT.PAYROLL. A packaged applica-tion might use a schema name to distinguish its tables and views from the tables and views of other applications. In this book, I sometimes use the term *schema* as though it were a collection of objects. For example, I might say that the RESEARCH schema contains the tables RESEARCH.PAYROLL, RESEARCH.PROJECTS, and RESEARCH.EQUIPMENT.

Schema names must begin with a letter and are limited to eight characters in length. Like object names, schema names are folded to uppercase unless they are enclosed in double quotes, in which case they are interpreted exactly as written. Whenever an unqualified (single-part) name is used, the system provides an implicit schema name that is the same as the userid against which authorization is currently being checked.[1] This userid is called the *current authid*. For static SQL in an application program, the current authid is the userid of the user who bound the program. For dynamic SQL and interactive user interfaces like the CLP, the current authid is the userid of the user who is running the program or interacting with the interface. Thus, for example, users Smith and Jones can each refer to their respective tables simply as PAY-ROLL, but Jones must refer to Smith's table by its fully qualified name, SMITH.PAYROLL.

V2 places certain limitations on the use of schema names. If you wish to create an object whose schema name is not the same as your userid, you must have database administration authority. And no user, even a database administrator, is allowed to create an object whose schema name begins with the letters "SYS," because these schema names are reserved for system use.[2] In particular, the system uses the schemas SYSIBM, SYSCAT, and SYSSTAT for system catalog tables and views, and SYSFUN for a collection of system-provided scalar functions. In the future, additional schemas beginning with the letters SYS may be used by the system for other purposes.

In the syntax diagrams used throughout this book, since names are used so often, we will not explicitly represent the fact that the names of tables, views, and other objects can be qualified by schema names. Instead, we will use the diagram below to define the syntax of a name that can be used for many different kinds of objects.

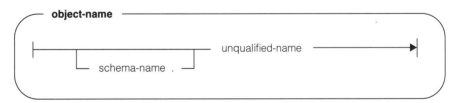

---

1. Actually, for functions and datatypes, the process of resolving an implicit schema name is somewhat more complex, as you will see in Chapter 4.
2. To avoid impacting existing V1 applications, these rules are not enforced for the types of objects that can be created by the V1 system, namely tables, indexes, packages, and views. Nevertheless, these rules are good guidelines for writing portable applications, and they are enforced for the new types of objects introduced by V2, such as aliases, functions, datatypes, and triggers.

When using an object name, remember that the schema name is limited to eight characters and the unqualified name is limited to eighteen characters, and that either may be enclosed in double quotes. Object names having the above syntax may be represented in any of the following ways on syntax diagrams:

alias-name

type-name

function-name

index-name

table-name

view-name

trigger-name

2.3 BASIC SQL DATATYPES

Each item of data stored in a V2 database has a specific datatype, such as Integer or Char(12). The datatype of a given item determines its range of values and the set of operators and functions that apply to it. Each datatype has its own internal representation. Every column of a V2 table has a datatype, specified when the table was created, that applies to all the items stored in that column.

The datatypes that you can use in your database depend on a decision that was made at the time the database was created. The CREATE DATABASE command has options called CODESET and TERRITORY that identify the language in which data will be stored in the new database. V2 uses these options to select a *code page* for the database. For example, a database used for storing English-language data in the United States might use code page 850, but a database used for storing Japanese data might use code page 932. All data stored in the database uses the same code page. The code page determines how bit patterns are used to represent characters. In a single-byte code page such as 850, each character is represented by one byte. In a double-byte code page such as 932, on the other hand, some characters are represented by one byte and other characters are represented by two bytes. A database that uses a single-byte code page is called a *single-byte database*, and a database that uses a double-byte code page is called a *double-byte database*.

Table 2-1 shows the basic datatypes that can be used in a single-byte database.[3] Some of these datatypes have parameters, which means that when you

---

3. In addition to the basic datatypes listed in Table 2-1, a single-byte database may contain *large-object* datatypes and *distinct* datatypes, both of which are discussed in Chapter 4.

TABLE 2-1: Basic Single-byte SQL Datatypes

Datatype	Description
Smallint	16-bit integer
Integer	32-bit integer
Decimal(p,s)	Decimal number with precision p and scale s. Precision is the total number of digits; scale is the number of digits to the right of the decimal point. `Numeric(p,s)` may be used as a synonym for `Decimal(p,s)`. If omitted, precision defaults to 5 and scale defaults to 0.
Double	64-bit ("double-precision") floating point number. `Float` and `Double Precision` may be used as synonyms for `Double`.
Char(n)	Fixed-length character string of length n characters. n cannot exceed 254. If omitted, n defaults to 1.
Varchar(n)	Varying-length character string of maximum length n characters. n cannot exceed 4000. If n is greater than 254, the following operators (discussed later in this chapter) cannot be used with this datatype: GROUP BY, ORDER BY, DISTINCT, and any set operator other than UNION ALL.
Date	Consists of a year, month, and day.
Time	Consists of an hour, minute, and second.
Timestamp	Consists of a year, month, day, hour, minute, second, and microsecond.

TABLE 2-2: Basic Double-Byte SQL Datatypes

Datatype	Description
Graphic(n)	Fixed-length string of n double-byte characters. n cannot exceed 127.
Vargraphic(n)	Varying-length string of up to n double-byte characters. n cannot exceed 2000. If n is greater than 127, the following operators (discussed later in this chapter) cannot be used with this datatype: GROUP BY, ORDER BY, DISTINCT, and any set operator other than UNION ALL.

use the datatype, you must provide some additional information such as a length or precision.

In a double-byte database, you can still use all the datatypes described in Table 2-1, but strings of type Char(n) and Varchar(n) may contain mixed data (mixtures of single-byte and double-byte characters). In addition, in a double-byte database, the datatypes shown in Table 2-2 may be used for pure double-byte strings.[4]

2.4 QUERIES

One of the most common and most basic tasks that a database system needs to perform is to retrieve information from the database. An SQL statement that retrieves some information is called a *query*. A query searches the tables that are stored in the database to find the answer to some question. The answer is expressed in the form of a set of rows, which is called the *result set* of the query.[5] Even if the result of a query is a single value, think of it as a result set consisting of one row and one column. Of course, the result set of a query may be empty.

The simplest form of a query in SQL scans one of the stored tables, searching for rows that satisfy some *search condition*, and for each such row selecting the values that are desired. For example, the following query finds the price and response time offered by supplier number S54 in supplying part number P209:

```
SELECT price, responsetime
FROM   quotations
WHERE  suppno = 'S54'
AND    partno = 'P209';
```

This example illustrates the SELECT - FROM - WHERE format of a basic SQL query. The FROM clause names the table to be searched, the WHERE clause specifies a search condition that is used for finding the desired row(s), and the SELECT clause specifies the information to be retrieved from each row.

Sometimes a query contains another query inside itself. When this happens, we refer to the contained query as a *subquery*. For example, a query might use a subquery to specify some values to be used in a search condition. In general, a subquery may return multiple values; but in the special case that a subquery returns a single value, we refer to it as a *scalar subquery*. The exam-

---

4. Large-object datatypes and distinct datatypes also exist for double-byte databases and are discussed in Chapter 4.

5. Since the result of a query may contain duplicate rows, the term *result multiset* might be more mathematically accurate; but the term *result set* is in more common usage.

ples that follow illustrate many uses for subqueries. (Subqueries are discussed further in Chapter 3.)

2.4.1 Expressions

One of the basic building blocks of SQL queries is the *expression*. An expression is simply a value that can be selected or computed. In the sample query above, the column names `price`, `responsetime`, `suppno`, and `partno` are expressions, as are the constants `'S54'` and `'P209'`. More complex expressions can be constructed by using arithmetic operators, as in `qonhand+qonorder`, or string concatenation, as in `name || address`. Expressions are used in SELECT clauses to specify the values to be retrieved and in WHERE clauses to specify the values used in the search condition. In general, an expression consists of one or more operands, connected by unary or binary operators. The operands that can be used in SQL expressions are as follows:

1. *Column names.* Examples: `price`, `description`. When a query involves more than one table, it is sometimes necessary to qualify a column name by a table name or variable to make it clear which column is being referred to. A qualified column name looks like `quotations.price` or `x.description`. When you write a multitable query, it is a good practice to qualify all the column names.

2. *Constants.* In SQL, constants can take any of the following forms:

   a. Integer constants consist simply of an optional sign and some digits. Examples: `29, -5`

   b. Decimal constants include a decimal point. Examples: `29.5, -3.725`

   c. Floating-point constants use an exponential notation. Examples: `1.875E5, -62E-13`

   d. Character-string constants are enclosed in single quotes. Example: `'Niagara Falls'`. If it is necessary for a constant to contain a quote character, it is represented by two successive quote characters, as in `'Bobbie''s boat'`. The datatype of a quoted-string constant is considered to be Varchar.

   e. String constants using double-byte character sets are enclosed in single quotes and prefixed by the letter G or N (these two prefixes are equivalent). Examples:

   > G`'百聞は一見にしかず'`
   > N`'早起きは三文の徳'`

   The datatype of such a constant is considered to be Vargraphic. Of course, the number of bytes in a double-byte string constant must be an even number.

TIP: G-type and N-type constants can be used only inside SQL statements, never in host language code. Each host programming language has its own way to represent double-byte strings, such as the L-type constants of C and C++, which can be used in host language code but not in SQL statements.

f. Hexadecimal notation can be used in a string constant prefixed by the letter X. Examples: X'FFFF', X'12AB907F'. The letters A through F may be used in hexadecimal constants, in either upper- or lowercase. A hexadecimal constant must always have an even number of hex digits (packed two per byte). Although it contains binary data, a hexadecimal constant is considered to have the datatype Varchar. Note that the string constant '12' is a two-byte constant containing the ASCII codes for the characters "1" and "2," whereas the hex constant X'12' is a one-byte constant containing the bit pattern 00010010.

g. Dates and times can be represented using character-string constants in any of several prescribed formats. Examples:

The date December 25, 1995, can be represented in any of these ways:

   '1995-12-25'
   '12/25/1995'
   '25.12.1995'

The time 1:50 p.m. can be represented in any of these ways:

   '13.50.00' or '13.50'
   '13:50:00' or '13:50'
   '1:50 PM'

The timestamp denoting exactly 12 noon on January 5, 2001, can be represented in any of these ways:

   '2001-01-05-12.00.00.000000'
   '2001-01-05-12.00.00'

3. *Host variables.* If your SQL statement is embedded in a program written in C or some other host programming language, variables declared in the host program can be used in your SQL expressions. In order to distinguish them from column names, host variables are prefixed by a colon. Examples: :x, :deadline. (Host variables are described in more detail in Section 2.7.1.)

4. *Functions.* V2 provides a long list of functions that accept one or more arguments and compute some result. Examples: length(address) returns the length of the character string in the address column; substr(description, 1, 5) returns the first five characters of the description column.

Certain functions operate on a collection of values derived from a column of a table, and compute a scalar result such as the average or sum of the values in the column; these are called *column functions*. (Column functions are discussed in Section 2.4.5.)

All the built-in functions provided by V2 are listed in Appendix B. As we will see in Chapter 4, V2 allows users to create additional functions of their own.

5. *Labelled durations*. When doing arithmetic with dates and times, a length of time (called a *duration*) can be represented by a numeric expression followed by a label indicating the time units, such as 5 DAYS or 1 HOUR. The labels that can be used in this way include the singular and plural forms of the following words: YEARS, MONTHS, DAYS, HOURS, MINUTES, SECONDS, and MICROSECONDS.

TIP: The only place where a labelled duration can be used is in an addition or subtraction where the other operand is a date, time, or timestamp. For example, suppose that you need to find out whether a date named ORDERDATE is more than ten days old. The first expression below is a valid way to make this test, but the second expression is not valid because the labelled duration is not used directly in the subtraction operation.

```
orderdate + 10 DAYS < CURRENT DATE     -- valid expression
CURRENT DATE - orderdate > 10 DAYS     -- invalid expression
```

6. *Special registers*. V2 maintains a set of *special registers*, whose values describe the environment in which your SQL statement is being executed. For example, CURRENT DATE represents the date on which the statement is being executed, CURRENT SERVER represents the name of the database in which the statement is being executed, and USER represents the userid of the user who is connected to the database and executing the statement. (A complete list of special registers is given in Appendix A.)

7. *CASE expressions*. A CASE expression computes a value that is based on finding which of several conditions is true. The following is an example of a CASE expression whose value is a character string:

```
CASE
    WHEN weight < 100 THEN 'Light'
    WHEN weight BETWEEN 100 AND 200 THEN 'Medium'
    WHEN weight > 200 THEN 'Heavy'
END
```

(CASE expressions are discussed further in Section 3.2.)

8. *CAST expressions*. A CAST expression is used to convert a value to a desired datatype. The following is an example of a CAST expression that converts a value from the PRICE column to the datatype Decimal(8,2):

```
CAST (price AS Decimal(8,2))
```

(CAST expressions are discussed further in Section 3.1.)

9. *Subqueries*. A scalar subquery (that is, a subquery that returns a single value) may be used inside an expression wherever a value may be used. (Scalar subqueries are discussed further in Section 3.4.)

Expressions can be constructed by combining the various operands listed above, using the following operators:

1. *Arithmetic operators.* +, -, *, and /. The + and - operators can be used either as unary (prefix) operators or as binary (infix) operators. Examples:

   ```
   qonhand+qonorder
   price*qonorder
   -price
   ```

2. *Concatenation operator.* The || operator concatenates two strings, resulting in a new string. Example: `name || address`. The word `concat` is equivalent to the || operator, as in `name concat address`.

3. *Parentheses.* When arithmetic expressions are evaluated, unary plus and minus are applied first, followed by multiplication and division (left to right), followed by addition and subtraction (left to right). Parentheses can be used to modify this order and to introduce as many levels of nested expressions as you like.

The following are two examples of expressions:

- The number of parts available to be used weekly over the next year might be expressed as `(qonorder+qonhand)/52`.

- The name and address of a supplier, concatenated together and limited to 50 characters, might be expressed as `substr(name || address, 1, 50)`.

2.4.2 Datetime Arithmetic

When arithmetic operators are used with the datatypes that represent dates and times, special rules apply. In order to understand these rules, we need to discuss the concept of a *duration*. Each of the datetime datatypes (Date, Time, and Timestamp) has an associated duration. A duration is not a datatype in its own right, but simply a specialized use of the Decimal datatype, as follows:

- A *date duration* is a Decimal(8,0) number that represents the period of time between two Date values, in format YYYYMMDD.

- A *time duration* is a Decimal(6,0) number that represents the period of time between two Time values, in format HHMMSS.

- A *timestamp duration* is a Decimal(20,6) number that represents the period of time between two Timestamp values, in format YYYYMMDDHHMMSS.ZZZZZZ (the ZZZZZZ portion represents microseconds.)

Since durations are really Decimal values, they can be used in exactly the same ways as other Decimal values (for example, they can be stored in Deci-

TABLE 2-3: Arithmetic Operations on Dates, Times, and Timestamps

First Operand Datatype	Operator	Second Operand Datatype	Result Datatype
Date	+ or −	Date duration	Date
Time	+ or −	Time duration	Time
Timestamp	+ or −	Timestamp duration	Timestamp
Date	−	Date	Date duration
Time	−	Time	Time duration
Timestamp	−	Timestamp	Timestamp duration

mal columns and represented by Decimal constants). Durations may be positive or negative. Durations are exceptional only because they can participate in certain addition and subtraction operations with Dates, Times, and Timestamps. These operations, which are the only arithmetic operations permitted on the datetime datatypes, are shown in Table 2-3.

The following are some examples of expressions that use datetime arithmetic:

- The number of years, months, and days remaining in the century, expressed as a duration (a decimal number of form YYMMDD), can be computed as follows: `'1999-12-31' - CURRENT DATE`

- The date on which we expect an order of parts to arrive might be expressed by using a labelled duration, as follows: `orderdate + responsetime DAYS`

2.4.3 Search Conditions

As we saw in the simple query example on page 48, SQL statements often scan through the rows of a table, applying some search condition to find the rows that qualify for further processing. The search condition is a logical test that can be applied to each row, resulting in one of three truth values: TRUE, FALSE, or UNKNOWN. If the search condition evaluates to TRUE, the row is accepted for further processing (for example, it might become part of the result set of a query, or it might be updated or deleted if the search condition is used in an SQL UPDATE or DELETE statement). If the search condition evaluates to FALSE or UNKNOWN, the row is not accepted for further processing.

AND

	T	F	?
T	T	F	?
F	F	F	F
?	?	F	?

OR

	T	F	?
T	T	T	T
F	T	F	?
?	T	?	?

NOT

T	F
F	T
?	?

Figure 2-1: Truth Tables for Three-Valued Logic

A search condition might evaluate to UNKNOWN for a given row because the row contains null values, which are used to represent missing or inapplicable information. For example, if the price is missing from a particular quotation, the `price` column in the row representing that quotation will contain a null value and the search condition `price > 1000` will evaluate to UNKNOWN for that row. In general, whenever a null value is used in an expression, the result of the expression is null, and whenever a null value is compared to another value (even another null value!), the result is the UNKNOWN truth value.

A search condition might consist of a single test such as `price > 1000`, or a combination of individual tests connected by the logical connectives AND, OR, and NOT, such as `price < 1000  OR  responsetime < 10  AND  NOT suppno = 'S54'`. Each of the individual tests in a search condition is called a *predicate*. The truth value of the search condition for a given row is found by combining the truth values of the individual predicates, using the truth tables shown in Figure 2-1, in which "?" represents the UNKNOWN truth value.

When combining predicates to evaluate a search condition, NOT operators have highest precedence, followed by AND operators, and OR operators have lowest precedence. Of course, parentheses can be used to modify the precedence of these operators. In order to provide the system with opportunities for optimization, no promises are made about the order in which predicates will be evaluated within a group of equal precedence.

V2 supports many different kinds of predicates. The diagrams below show the syntax of the various kinds of predicates and how these predicates can be combined to form search conditions.

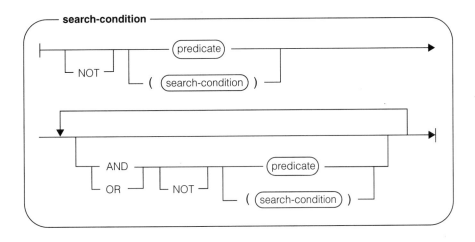

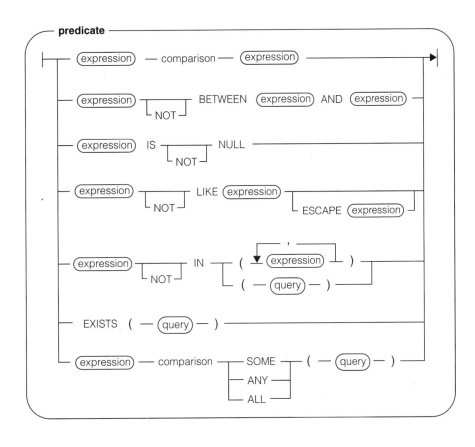

All expressions used in predicates are constructed according to the rules in Section 2.4.1. The individual types of predicates supported by **V2** are explained below.

1. *Simple comparison predicate.* Any two expressions may be compared, using the comparison operators =, <, <=, >, >=, and <>. The <> operator means "not equal." The expressions being compared must have compatible datatypes. (Of course, the CAST notation can be used to convert one datatype into another.) The result of a comparison predicate is UNKNOWN if either expression is null.

   The meaning of > and the other comparison operators for character strings is determined by the collating sequence that was declared at database creation time.[6] Collating sequences are generally defined to be insensitive to upper- and lowercase. (For example, 'cat' < 'DOG' and 'CAT' < 'dog' are both true.)

   Examples:
   ```
   price > 1000
   name <> 'Safeco'
   ```

2. *BETWEEN predicate.* The meaning of expression1 BETWEEN expression2 AND expression3 is the same as the meaning of expression1 >= expression2 AND expression1 <= expression3.

   The meaning of expression1 NOT BETWEEN expression2 AND expression3 is the same as the meaning of expression1 < expression2 OR expression1 > expression3.

   Example:
   ```
   :request BETWEEN qonhand AND qonhand+qonorder
   ```

   TIP: Note that x BETWEEN y AND z does not have the same meaning as x BETWEEN z AND y. In fact, if the value of z is greater than the value of y, the latter predicate can never be true.

3. *IS NULL predicate.* The IS NULL predicate never returns the UNKNOWN truth value. If the expression used in an IS NULL predicate evaluates to null, the predicate is TRUE; otherwise the predicate is FALSE. The meaning of expression1 IS NOT NULL is the same as the meaning of NOT (expression1 IS NULL).

---

6. However, if one of the operands comes from a table column that was created with the FOR BIT DATA property, the string comparison is done as a byte-by-byte binary comparison.

Example:

```
address IS NULL
```

4. *LIKE predicate.* A LIKE predicate is a very powerful way of searching for a given pattern inside a character string. The general form of the predicate is as follows (optional phrases are indicated by square brackets):

```
match-expression [NOT] LIKE pattern-expression
   [ESCAPE escape-expression]
```

The match-expression can be of any single- or double-byte character-string datatype. The pattern-expression must be of a compatible string datatype and has certain additional restrictions: it cannot include a column name, and its length cannot exceed 4000 bytes. Typically, the pattern-expression is a short constant string.

The basic idea of a LIKE predicate is to compare the match-expression with the pattern-expression. But in performing the comparison, certain characters in the pattern-expression are considered to have special meanings:

- The underscore character (_) represents any single character.
- The percent sign (%) represents any string of zero or more characters.

Thus, for example, the following predicate is TRUE for any address that contains the words "New York":

```
address LIKE '%New York%'
```

Similarly, the following predicate is TRUE for any four-character part number that begins with P and ends with 2:

```
partno LIKE 'P__2'
```

The optional ESCAPE clause specifies a single character (called the *escape character*), which, when preceding a % or _ character in the pattern, causes the % or _ character to represent itself rather than to be interpreted as a special character. Thus, for example, the following predicate is TRUE for any description that contains the string "10% solution":

```
description LIKE '%10/% solution%' ESCAPE '/'
```

5. *IN predicate.* An IN predicate is useful for testing whether a given value is included in a list of values. For example, the following predicate is TRUE if the given supplier number matches any of a list of five specific values:

```
suppno IN ('S51', 'S52', 'S53', 'S54', 'S55')
```

The values on the right side of an IN predicate can be provided by a list of literals, as in the above example, or by a subquery that evaluates to a single column of values. For example, the following predicate is TRUE if the given supplier number matches that of any supplier number who supplies part number P221:

```
suppno IN
    (SELECT suppno
     FROM quotations
     WHERE partno = 'P221')
```

6. *EXISTS predicate.* An EXISTS predicate contains a subquery and evaluates to TRUE if the result of the subquery contains at least one row. If the subquery returns no rows, the EXISTS predicate is FALSE. An EXISTS predicate never evaluates to UNKNOWN.

In the following example, the predicate is TRUE if there exists some supplier in the QUOTATIONS table who supplies part number P221:

```
EXISTS
    (SELECT suppno
     FROM quotations
     WHERE partno = 'P221')
```

Many interesting examples of EXISTS predicates involve *correlated subqueries*, which will be discussed in Section 3.3.

7. *Quantified comparison predicate.* Like a simple comparison predicate, a quantified comparison predicate uses one of the six comparison operators =, <, <=, >, >=, and <>. Like an IN predicate, it compares a single value with a list of values returned by a subquery. The unique thing about a quantified comparison predicate is that it includes one of the keywords SOME, ANY, or ALL. The keywords SOME and ANY indicate that the predicate is true if the comparison holds for at least one element in the list. The keyword ALL indicates that the predicate is true if the comparison holds for all elements in the list (or if the list is empty).

The following example predicate is TRUE if the price in variable :p is less than all the prices quoted for part number P207:

```
:p < ALL
       (SELECT price
        FROM quotations
        WHERE partno = 'P207'
        AND price IS NOT NULL)
```

TIP: The phrase `price IS NOT NULL` guards against quotations with null prices, which would otherwise force the <ALL predicate to be always false.

The following example shows how several predicates can be combined by AND, OR, and NOT operators to form a search condition:

```
( partno IN ('P205', 'P207', 'P209')
  OR description LIKE '%Gear%' )
AND qonhand + qonorder <= 10
```

2.4.4 Joins

We have seen how a simple SQL query can scan a single table and select the rows that satisfy some search condition. Often, however, we need to find the answer to a question that involves a relationship among multiple tables. A query that expresses this kind of question is called a *join*.

In a join query, the FROM clause names not just one table, but a list of all the tables participating in the join, separated by commas. Conceptually, the system forms all possible combinations of rows from the tables listed in the FROM clause, and for each combination it applies the search condition. In a join query, the search condition usually specifies some relationship between the rows to be joined. For example, we might join rows from the PARTS table with rows from the QUOTATIONS table that have matching part numbers. This predicate, called a *join condition*, might be expressed as follows:

```
parts.partno = quotations.partno
```

Since more than one table in a join may have a common column name, a column name used in a join query must sometimes be prefixed by a table name to avoid ambiguity, as in the example above. Column names that are unique among the tables being joined do not require such a prefix (but qualifying all column names by table names, even when it's not required, may make the query easier to understand).

The following is an example of a join that lists the part number, description, and price of all parts supplied by supplier number S51:

```
SELECT parts.partno, parts.description, quotations.price
FROM parts, quotations
WHERE parts.partno = quotations.partno
AND quotations.suppno = 'S51';
```

If a row from one of the participating tables never satisfies the join condition (for example, a PARTS row has no matching QUOTATIONS row or vice versa), that row will not appear in the result of the join. Section 3.7 discusses techniques for expressing an alternative kind of join, called an *outer join*, that retains rows from one table that have no matching rows in the other table.

If the search condition contains no predicates that specify a relationship between the rows of the tables in the join, all possible combinations of rows from these tables will be returned, even though the rows may be completely unrelated. This type of query is called a *Cartesian product*; it is expensive to execute and rarely produces a meaningful result.

It is possible to write a query in which a table is joined to itself. The table name is repeated two or more times in the FROM clause, indicating that the join consists of combinations of two or more rows from the same table. Because the table name is not unique in such a query, each table in the FROM clause must be given a unique identifier, called a *correlation name*. A correlation name can be used anywhere in the query as a prefix to a column name that uniquely identifies the row to which the column belongs. In the following query, the QUOTATIONS table is joined to itself, using correlation names x and y. The query finds pairs of quotations for the same part in which the prices differ by more than a factor of two:

```
SELECT x.partno, x.suppno, x.price, y.suppno, y.price
FROM quotations x, quotations y
WHERE x.partno = y.partno
AND y.price > 2 * x.price;
```

Note that the above example has two join conditions, one relating the two rows by PARTNO and the other by PRICE. In general, a query may have many join conditions.

2.4.5 Column Functions

As noted above, a large set of functions are shipped with the V2 product. Most of these functions are *scalar functions*, such as length and substr, that take one or more scalar parameters and return a scalar result. Some of the built-in functions, however, are *column functions,*[7] which operate on a set of values and reduce it to a single scalar value. The names of the built-in column functions are avg, count, min, max, stdev, sum, and variance.[8] (All of these functions are described in Appendix B.)

When a column function is invoked with an argument expression such as qonorder+qonhand, the set of values passed to the function consists of the argument expression evaluated for each row that satisfies the search condition. For example, the following query finds the total number of bolts that are on hand or on order, including all kinds of bolts:

```
SELECT sum(qonorder + qonhand)
FROM parts
WHERE description LIKE '%Bolt%'
```

The syntax for invoking a column function is as follows:

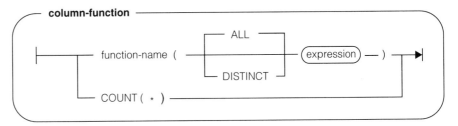

The syntax diagram shows that an invocation of a column function looks like an invocation of a scalar function, with two exceptions:

1. The argument of the function may be preceded by the keyword DISTINCT. This keyword causes duplicate values to be eliminated from the argument set before the function is applied. If DISTINCT is omitted or if ALL is specified, duplicate values are not eliminated before applying the function.

2. The column function count can be invoked with an asterisk in place of its argument, indicating that the function returns the number of rows in its argument set (that is, the number of rows that satisfy the search condition).

Column functions—except count(*)—ignore null values in their argument sets.

---

7. Terminology in this area is not uniform. The term *column function* is used in IBM documentation. The ANSI/ISO SQL92 Standard refers to this type of function as a *set function.* The term *aggregate function* is also used in the literature.

8. The stdev and variance column functions are supported beginning with DB2 Version 2.1.1.

The following queries illustrate applications of column functions:

- Find the maximum and minimum non-null price quotations for part number P207.

```
SELECT max(price), min(price)
FROM quotations
WHERE partno = 'P207';
```

- Find the number of quotations for part number P207, regardless of whether the price quoted (or any other column, apart from PARTNO) is null.

```
SELECT count(*)
FROM quotations
WHERE partno = 'P207';
```

- Find the number of quotations for part number P207 that have non-null prices.

```
SELECT count(price)
FROM quotations
WHERE partno = 'P207';
```

- Find the number of different non-null prices that have been quoted for part number P207.

```
SELECT count(DISTINCT price)
FROM quotations
WHERE partno = 'P207';
```

2.4.6 Grouping

As shown above, column functions operate on sets of values and return scalar results. Rather than applying a column function to a whole table, it is sometimes desirable to divide a table into groups of related rows and to apply a column function to each group separately. This can be accomplished by a feature of SQL called *grouping*.

Grouping permits a table to be conceptually divided into groups of rows with matching values in one or more columns (called the *grouping columns*), which are listed in a GROUP BY clause. When a query contains a GROUP BY clause, each row in the result set represents one group. In such a query, each column name in the SELECT clause must be either one of the grouping columns or must be an argument of a column function. For example, the following query finds the maximum, minimum, and average quoted price for each part:

```
SELECT partno, max(price), min(price), avg(price)
FROM quotations
GROUP BY partno;
```

For the purpose of forming groups, the null value is considered to be a value like any other. Thus, for example, if a table is grouped by PARTNO, all the rows having a null value for PARTNO will be in the same group.

The WHERE clause of a query serves as a filter that is applied before the forming of groups, retaining only those rows that satisfy the search condition. For example, the following query finds the average and minimum price for each part, considering only quotations that have a response time of less than 30 days:

```
SELECT partno, avg(price), min(price)
FROM quotations
WHERE responsetime < 30
GROUP BY partno;
```

It is also possible to apply a qualifying condition to the groups themselves, retaining only those groups that satisfy some condition. This is done by a HAVING clause that is written after the GROUP BY clause. The HAVING clause contains a search condition in which each predicate tests some group property involving a column function or a grouping column. For example, the following query lists the maximum and minimum prices for various parts, considering only those parts that have at least three quotations and for which the maximum price is more than twice the minimum price:

```
SELECT partno, max(price), min(price)
FROM quotations
GROUP BY partno
HAVING count(*) >= 3
AND max(price) > 2 * min(price);
```

A query can contain both a WHERE clause and a HAVING clause. The WHERE clause is applied first as a filter on rows; then the groups are formed and the HAVING clause is applied as a filter on groups. For example, the following query finds part numbers for which we have at least two quotations from different suppliers, each with a response time of less than 30 days:

```
SELECT partno
FROM quotations
WHERE responsetime < 30
GROUP BY partno
HAVING count(DISTINCT suppno) >= 2;
```

It is possible (though unusual) for a query to have a HAVING clause but no GROUP BY clause. In this case, the entire table is treated as one group. If the search condition in the HAVING clause is true for the table as a whole, the SELECT clause (which must consist only of column functions and constants) is evaluated and returned; otherwise the query returns the empty set.

2.4.7 Query Blocks

Now that you understand several specific features of SQL, you are ready to put them together into a unit called a *query block*.[9] A query block is the basic unit of the SQL language that operates on one or more database tables, performing join, grouping, projection, and selection operations to distill these tables into a derived table, which can then be delivered to the user or used for further processing. The syntax of a query block is on the following page.

The clauses of the query block are discussed below, in the order in which they are conceptually applied. (Of course, the system is allowed to execute the query block using any method that leads to an equivalent result.)

1. The first step in processing a query block is to form a Cartesian product of all the tables named in the FROM clause. A Cartesian product consists of all possible combinations of rows taken from the respective tables. Of course, if only one table is named, the FROM clause simply generates all the rows of that table. (Remember that this is a conceptual description of query processing and does not necessarily correspond to the way a query block would really be executed. If the optimizer is smart, it will probably find some way to avoid actually computing a Cartesian product of two or more tables.)

If any table is given a correlation name in the FROM clause, that correlation name replaces the table name for use elsewhere in the query. In other words, if the FROM clause contains the phrase parts as x, then in other parts of the

---

9. Terminology in this area is not uniform. The language unit that I call a "query block" is referred to as a *subselect* in the IBM documentation and as a *query specification* in the ANSI/ISO SQL Standard.

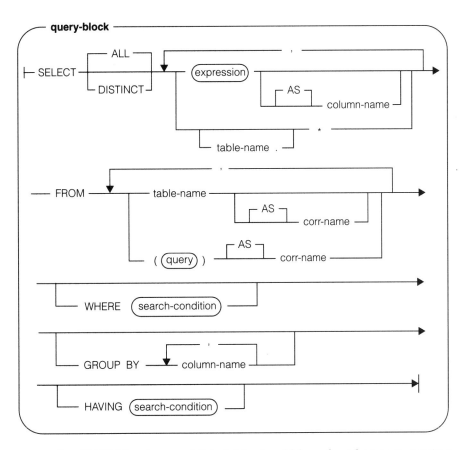

query, the PARTNO column of this table should be referred to as `x.partno` rather than as `parts.partno`.

In place of an actual database table, a FROM clause may contain a query that derives a table. Any use of a query inside of another query is called a *subquery*, and this particular kind of a subquery is called a *table expression*. (Table expressions are discussed in more detail in Section 3.5.) When a table expression is used in a FROM clause, a correlation name *must* be provided to give a name to the derived table. (The column names of the derived table are provided by the subquery itself.)

2. The next step is to apply the search condition in the WHERE clause as a filter to the rows generated by the FROM clause. Only those rows for which the search condition is TRUE (not UNKNOWN) survive for further processing. If no WHERE clause is provided, all the rows survive. If more than one table was named in the FROM clause, the WHERE clause will probably include some join predicates that specify the desired relationships among the tables.

3. The next step is to form the surviving rows into groups according to the grouping columns named in the GROUP BY clause. Within each group, all the rows have matching values of the grouping columns. Of course, the column names in the GROUP BY clause may be prefixed by a table name or correlation name, as in x.partno. A GROUP BY clause may contain only column names, not more general expressions (but techniques for grouping by general expressions are discussed in Section 3.5).

For the purpose of forming groups, null is considered a value. (For example, if the GROUP BY clause specifies a single column, all rows having a null value in the grouping column will be placed in the same group.)

4. After groups have been formed, the search condition in the HAVING clause is applied as a filter to the groups. Only those groups for which the search condition is TRUE are retained for further processing. If the query block has no HAVING clause, all the groups are retained. If the query block has a HAVING clause but no GROUP BY clause, the HAVING search condition applies to the whole query block, which returns the empty table if the search condition is not TRUE.

Each column reference in a HAVING clause must be one of the following:

- A reference to one of the grouping columns
- An argument of a column function
- A correlated reference to a column defined in a higher-level query block that contains this query block as a subquery

5. Finally, the SELECT clause is applied to the rows or groups that have survived to this point. From these rows or groups, the SELECT clause selects the specific columns or expressions that are to be used in the final result of the query block.

If the query block contains a GROUP BY or HAVING clause, all the column references in the SELECT clause must either refer to grouping columns or be used as arguments to column functions. The result of the query block contains one row per group.

If the query block does not contain a GROUP BY or HAVING clause, the SELECT clause must conform to one of the following rules:

- No column functions may be used. In this case, the result of the query block contains one row for each of the rows that satisfies the WHERE clause.
- Alternatively, *all* column references in the SELECT clause may be used as arguments to column functions. In this case, the result of the query block contains exactly one row.

Each expression in the SELECT clause may be given a name that serves as its "column name" in the result of the query block. For example, the SELECT clause might contain the phrase qonorder+qonhand AS totalsupply.

An asterisk appearing in a SELECT clause means "all columns." An asterisk appearing prefixed by a table name or correlation name means "all the columns of the indicated table." For example, if the FROM clause specifies that the QUOTATIONS table is to be joined to itself by the phrase FROM quotations q1, quotations q2, then the SELECT clause might contain the phrase q1.* with the meaning, "all the columns of the row designated by the correlation name q1."

The result of the query block can be thought of as a table whose columns are the expressions in the SELECT clause and whose rows are the rows or groups that are generated and retained by the other clauses. Duplicate rows are not eliminated from the result of the query block unless the keyword DISTINCT is specified in the SELECT clause.

The following example includes all of the clauses that can be used in a query block. It lists the minimum quoted price for various parts, considering only quotations that have a response time of less than thirty days, and including only parts that have at least two such quotations.

```
SELECT i.partno, min(q.price) AS lowprice
FROM parts i, quotations q
WHERE i.partno = q.partno
AND q.responsetime < 30
GROUP BY i.partno
HAVING count(*) >= 2;
```

2.4.8 Queries and Literal Tables

The result of evaluating a query block is a table, possibly containing some duplicate rows (unless SELECT DISTINCT was specified in the query block). SQL permits the results of several query blocks to be combined using the operators UNION, INTERSECT, and EXCEPT, optionally modified by the keyword ALL. The definition of these operators, applied to two tables, T1 and T2, is as follows:

- T1 UNION T2 is a table consisting of all the rows that are either in T1 or in T2, with duplicate rows eliminated.

- T1 UNION ALL T2 is a table consisting of all the rows that are either in T1 or in T2, with duplicate rows preserved. (For example, if a given row occurs three times in T1 and two times in T2, it will occur five times in T1 UNION ALL T2.)

- T1 INTERSECT T2 is a table consisting of all the rows that are common to both T1 and T2, with duplicate rows eliminated.

- T1 INTERSECT ALL T2 is a table consisting of all the rows that are in both T1 and T2. The number of occurrences of a given row in T1 INTERSECT ALL T2 is the minimum of its number of occurrences in T1 and in T2. (For example, if a given row occurs three times in T1 and two times in T2, it will occur two times in T1 INTERSECT ALL T2.)

- T1 EXCEPT T2 is a table consisting of all the rows that are in T1 but not in T2, with duplicate rows not considered significant. (For example, if a given row occurs three times in T1 and two times in T2, that row will not occur at all in T1 EXCEPT T2. If a given row occurs three times in T1 and zero times in T2, that row will occur once in T1 EXCEPT T2.)

- T1 EXCEPT ALL T2 is a table consisting of all the rows of T1 that do not have a corresponding row in T2, with duplicates considered significant. (For example, if a given row occurs three times in T1 and two times in T2, that row will occur once in T1 EXCEPT ALL T2.)

I will use the term *query* to denote an expression whose result is a table.[10] A query block is a simple form of a query. A query may also be composed of multiple query blocks, combined by the operators UNION, INTERSECT, and EXCEPT. Of course, the partial results being combined by these operators must have the same number of columns, and the datatypes of their corresponding columns must be compatible. (The detailed rules for datatype compatibility and for determining the datatypes of the result columns are given in Section 4.6.)

When two tables are combined by UNION, INTERSECT, or EXCEPT, whenever two corresponding columns of the input tables have the same name, this name is preserved in the result column. If the corresponding columns of the input tables do not have the same name, the result column is unnamed.

In evaluating a query, INTERSECT operators take precedence over UNION and EXCEPT operators, and operators with the same precedence are executed from left to right. Of course, parentheses may be used to modify the order of execution. The syntax of a query is on the following page.

---

10. Here again, terminology is not uniform. The language unit that I call a "query" is referred to as *fullselect* in the IBM documentation and as a *query expression* in the ANSI/ISO SQL Standard.

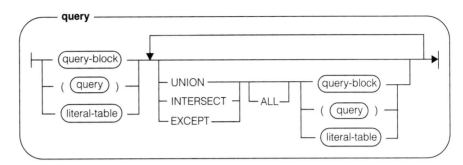

The syntax diagram above shows that the building blocks of a query are query blocks and *literal tables*. A literal table is a collection of one or more rows whose values are contained directly in the query. A literal table begins with the keyword VALUES and contains an expression (or the word NULL) for each of its column values, as shown in the following syntax:

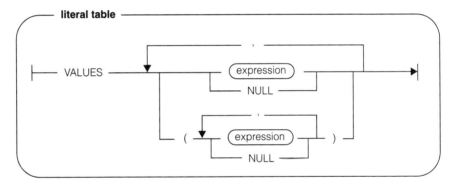

Parentheses are used around each row of a literal table; however, if the literal table has only one column, the parentheses can be omitted. This potentially confusing feature is illustrated in the following examples:

1. VALUES (`Bob`, `Carol`), (`Ted`, `Alice`), (`John`, `Mary`) is a literal table containing three rows of two columns each, as follows:

Bob	Carol
Ted	Alice
John	Mary

2. VALUES (`'Bob'`), (`'Ted'`), (`'John'`) is a literal table containing three rows of one column each.

3. VALUES `'Bob'`, `'Ted'`, `'John'` is exactly equivalent to example 2. Both examples 2 and 3 produce the following table:

Bob
Ted
John

4. VALUES (`'Bob'`, `'Ted'`, `'John'`) is a literal table containing one row of three columns, as follows:

| Bob | Ted | John |

TIP: Because of the danger of confusion between examples 3 and 4, you would be well advised to enclose each row in your literal table inside parentheses, even if the row consists of a single column.

All the values in a given column of a literal table must have compatible datatypes (for example, a column might consist of character strings or of numeric values, but not of character strings mixed with numeric values). (The detailed rules for datatype compatibility in literal tables are given in Section 4.6.) It is not permitted for *all* the values in any column of a literal table to be null, unless one of them is given an explicit datatype by a CAST expression (discussed in Section 3.1).

Queries that use set operators and literal tables can sometimes express questions that would be difficult to express in other ways, as illustrated by the following examples.

• This very simple query finds all the suppliers who currently have no quotations on record:

```
    SELECT suppno
    FROM suppliers
EXCEPT
    SELECT suppno
    FROM quotations;
```

- This query lists the names and addresses of all the suppliers who can supply part number P207 for less than $10.00, including two additional suppliers who did not qualify by the normal criteria:

```
SELECT name, address
FROM suppliers
WHERE suppno IN
    (SELECT suppno
     FROM quotations
     WHERE partno = 'P207'
     AND price < 1000)
UNION
    VALUES('Uncle Bill', 'P.O.Box 1117, Fresno, CA'),
          ('Repo City', '650 First St., Buffalo, NY');
```

An SQL query is a very powerful mechanism for deriving a table from tables stored in the database and from constants and host variables. A query can be used as an SQL statement in its own right, or it can be used as a subquery inside a higher-level SQL statement. For example:

- A query can be used inside a predicate, as shown in the syntax diagram for *predicate* on page 55.
- A query can be used in a FROM clause, as shown in the syntax diagram for *query-block* on page 65.
- A query can be used in the definition of a view, as shown in the syntax diagram for *create-view-statement* on page 136.

A query, by itself, does not impose any ordering on the rows of the result set. Indeed, when a query is used as a subquery, its result set is considered to be unordered. When a query is used in a *select-statement* (see page 72) or in a *cursor-declaration* (see page 101), the enclosing statement can provide an ORDER BY clause that imposes an ordering on the rows of the result set before delivering them to a user or to an application program.

2.4.9 SELECT Statement

When a query is used as a top-level SQL statement, we call it a *SELECT statement*. A SELECT statement can be submitted to an interactive interface such as the CLP, which will execute it and display the result. In addition to the normal query clauses, a SELECT statement may have an additional clause that is meaningful only for top-level queries. That clause is called an *ORDER BY clause* and is used to impose an ordering on the result set, controlling the order in which the result rows are displayed. The syntax of a SELECT statement is as follows:

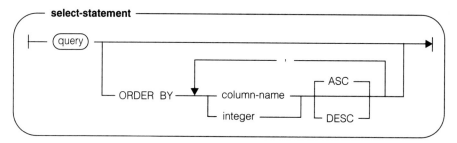

The result set of a query can be ordered by the values of one or more of its columns, in either ascending or descending order. Each of the columns in the ORDER BY clause must correspond to one of the expressions in the SELECT clause. These expressions can be identified in several ways, as shown in the following examples.

- If a simple column name is selected, that column name can be used in the ORDER BY clause. The following query lists all the quotations for part number P231 that have a response time of less than ten days, in order by price from the least expensive to the most expensive.

```
SELECT suppno, price
FROM quotations
WHERE partno = 'P231'
AND responsetime < 10
ORDER BY price;
```

- A column name in the SELECT clause that is qualified by a table name or correlation name can also appear in the ORDER BY clause, just as it appears in the SELECT clause. The following example joins three tables to make a master list of the parts that are supplied by various suppliers. The rows of the result set are ordered alphabetically by the name of the supplier, and secondarily ordered by part number.

```
SELECT s.name, q.partno, q.price, i.description
FROM suppliers s, quotations q, parts i
WHERE s.suppno = q.suppno
AND q.partno = i.partno
ORDER BY s.name, q.partno;
```

- An expression in the SELECT clause that is not a simple column name can be given a name by using the keyword AS, and this name can be used in the ORDER BY clause. The following query lists parts in descending order by the total number of each part that is on hand or on order.

```
SELECT partno, qonorder+qonhand AS totalq
FROM parts
ORDER BY totalq DESC;
```

- If an expression in a SELECT clause is not given a name, it can be referred to in the ORDER BY clause by an integer that represents its ordinal position in the SELECT clause. The following query lists the parts that are currently out of stock, in descending order by their average prices.

```
SELECT partno, avg(price)
FROM quotations
WHERE partno IN
    (SELECT partno
     FROM parts
     WHERE qonhand = 0)
GROUP BY partno
ORDER BY 2 DESC;
```

- When a SELECT statement includes multiple query blocks, remember that the ORDER BY clause is a property of the statement as a whole, not of any individual query block. The following query produces an ordered list of supplier numbers for suppliers who either have an order pending for part number P221 or who can supply this part in ten days or less:

```
SELECT suppno
FROM orders
WHERE partno = 'P221'
UNION ALL
    SELECT suppno
    FROM quotations
    WHERE partno = 'P221'
    AND responsetime <= 10
ORDER BY suppno;
```

2.4.10 VALUES Statement

If you have sharp eyes, you may have noticed that a literal table is a form of a query and that a query can stand alone as a SELECT statement. Therefore, it is possible that a SELECT statement might consist simply of a literal table. We will refer to this special case of a SELECT statement as a *VALUES statement*, since it begins with the word VALUES. If you execute a VALUES statement using the CLP, the system will evaluate all the expressions in your statement and display the literal table. For example, you might type the following statement (try it!):

```
VALUES ('Carter', '1976', 'Democrat'),
       ('Reagan', '1980', 'Republican');
```

The above example is not very useful, since you had to type in all the values to be displayed. For a more useful example, suppose that you need to know the value of one of the special registers, such as CURRENT DATE or CURRENT FUNCTION PATH. It is awkward to write a SELECT statement to retrieve this value, because the special register is not contained in any table. You could choose a random table and type, for example, SELECT CURRENT DATE FROM parts; but this query would display the current date once for every part in the PARTS table, which is probably not what you want. The solution to the problem is to use a VALUES statement to display a "table" containing nothing but the special register that you need. For example, typing the following statement at the CLP prompt will cause the current date to be displayed:

```
VALUES (CURRENT DATE);
```

TIP: You can invoke the CLP from your operating system prompt by typing db2 followed by the SQL statement you want to execute. But you must be careful about special characters. For example, the following command will result in a syntax error:

```
db2 VALUES (CURRENT DATE);
```

The reason for the syntax error is that the operating-system shell is interpreting the parentheses rather than sending them to the CLP. You can execute the SQL statement correctly by enclosing it in single or double quotes, as in the following example:

```
db2 "VALUES (CURRENT DATE)";
```

Another reason to use VALUES as a stand-alone SQL statement is in order to invoke a function. The built-in functions such as substr and avg are not very interesting to invoke, unless you need to use them in a query. But V2 provides a way (described in Section 4.4) for users to create new functions of their own, implemented by C programs. Such a user-defined function might interact with the outside world in some way such as sending a message or writing in a file. Suppose that someone has written a user-defined function called `place-Order(partno, quantity)` that actually sends a message to a supplier ordering a given quantity of a given part. Since `placeOrder` is defined as an SQL function, it can be invoked from an SQL statement—perhaps in the body of a trigger that has discovered a low inventory level. But what kind of SQL statement should we use to invoke the function? The problem is similar to that of examining a special register, since the function (like the special register) does not reside in a table.

In some cases, a SELECT is the appropriate kind of statement to use for invoking a function. For example, if you wish to order 100 units of every part in the PARTS table that has less than 100 units on hand, you might write:

```
SELECT placeOrder(partno, 100)
FROM parts
WHERE qonhand < 100;
```

The above statement will result in the placing of some number of orders, between zero and the total number of rows in the PARTS table. But suppose you want to place exactly one order, for 500 units of part number P285. You need a way to call the `placeOrder` function exactly once, independently of the content of any table in the database. This is accomplished by the following VALUES statement, which you can submit to the CLP or embed in a program:

```
VALUES (placeOrder('P285', 500));
```

TIP: You must be very careful where you invoke a function that has side effects, such as `placeOrder` in the above examples, to make sure your function is executed a predictable number of times. In general, a function invoked in a VALUES statement will be executed exactly once, and a function invoked in the SELECT clause of a query block will be executed once for each row returned by the query block. But you should avoid calling a function with side effects in a query that involves SELECT DISTINCT, or a column function, or a join, or a set operator such as UNION, since these operations can make the number of function calls unpredictable. For the same reason, you should avoid calling a function with side effects in the WHERE or HAVING clause of any query.

2.5 DATA MODIFICATION

The SQL statements for modifying data are INSERT, UPDATE, and DELETE. Each of these statements makes extensive use of the building blocks already discussed, such as expressions, subqueries, and literal tables.

2.5.1 INSERT Statement

The purpose of an INSERT statement is to insert one or more rows into a table or view. The rows to be inserted can be specified as a literal table or can be derived from the database by means of a query. The syntax of an INSERT statement is as follows:

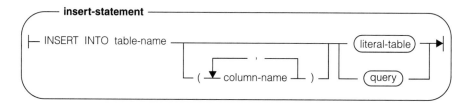

Users of SQL are familiar with the use of a VALUES clause to insert a single row into a table, as in the following example:

```
INSERT INTO quotations(suppno, partno, price, responsetime)
    VALUES ('S59', 'P227', 175, 8);
```

Since V2 allows an INSERT statement to contain a literal table, the VALUES clause in an INSERT statement is no longer limited to a single row, and it may contain expressions as well as constants. Furthermore, when a literal table is used in an INSERT statement, a value inside the literal table may consist simply of the word DEFAULT, indicating "the default value for the target column" (the default value of a column, if any, being determined when a table is created). Some of these features are illustrated by the example below, which inserts two rows into the ORDERS table, using a default value (the current date) for the ORDERDATE column:

```
INSERT INTO orders(suppno, partno, quantity, orderdate)
   VALUES ('S59', 'P227', 100, DEFAULT),
          ('S59', 'P231', 250, DEFAULT);
```

Columns for which no values are provided by an INSERT statement receive default values. For this reason, the INSERT statement in the following example is equivalent to the one in the previous example:

```
INSERT INTO orders(suppno, partno, quantity)
   VALUES ('S59', 'P227', 100),
          ('S59', 'P231', 250);
```

If an INSERT statement contains a query, that query is evaluated and the resulting rows are inserted into the target table. For example, if we create a table named INACTIVE with a column named SUPPNO, we might use the following statement to populate this table with all the suppliers who currently have no quotations on file:

```
INSERT INTO INACTIVE(suppno)
   SELECT suppno
   FROM suppliers
EXCEPT
   SELECT suppno
   FROM quotations;
```

If a query inside an INSERT statement contains a reference to the table into which data is being inserted, the INSERT statement is said to be *self-referencing*. The query in a self-referencing INSERT statement is completely evaluated before any rows are inserted.

The target of an INSERT statement may be either a table or a view. Inserting rows into a view has the effect of inserting rows into the table on which the view is based. Of course, the view must be updatable, and the rows being inserted must satisfy any constraints that are in effect for the table and/or the view (constraints are discussed in Section 5.1). If any error is encountered during execution of an INSERT statement (for example, some constraint is violated by the 100th row to be inserted), the statement is rolled back and no rows are inserted.

An INSERT statement may optionally list the columns of the target table for which values are provided. Omitting the column list is the same as specifying all the columns of the target table, in their natural order. Of course, if the target of the INSERT statement is a view, values can be inserted only into those columns that correspond directly to columns of the underlying table. For any column into which values can be inserted, omitting the column from the list is the same as specifying DEFAULT as the value to be inserted.

2.5.2 UPDATE Statement

The purpose of an UPDATE statement is to modify the values of one or more rows in a table or view. The syntax of an UPDATE statement is as follows:[11]

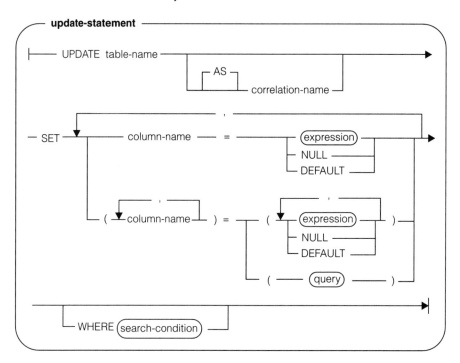

An UPDATE statement applies its SET clause to each row of the named table for which the search condition in the WHERE clause is TRUE. If the UPDATE statement has no WHERE clause, the SET clause is applied to all the rows in the named table.

The SET clause contains one or more *assignments*. Each assignment is executed by computing the value(s) on the right-hand side of the equal sign and assigning them to the column(s) named on the left-hand side of the equal sign. The value to be assigned may be specified by an expression (possibly containing a subquery), by the keyword NULL, or by DEFAULT, which indicates that the column is to be assigned its default value. For example, the following UPDATE statement assigns new values to the PARTS row for part number P207.

---

11. A variation of this syntax, called a *positioned UPDATE statement*, is described in Section 2.7.11.

```
UPDATE parts
SET description = NULL,
    qonhand = 100,
    qonorder = DEFAULT
WHERE partno = 'P207';
```

As each row is updated, all the expressions on the right-hand sides of the assignments are evaluated before any of the updates are applied. Thus, for example, the following statement could be used to interchange the values of qonorder and qonhand for a given part:

```
UPDATE parts
SET qonorder = qonhand,
    qonhand = qonorder
WHERE partno = 'P207';
```

The target of an UPDATE statement may be either a table or a view. Updating a view has the effect of updating the table on which the view is based. Of course, if the target is a view, it must be an updatable view and the columns to be updated must correspond directly to columns of the underlying table. (Rules for defining updatable views are described in Section 2.8.)

It is possible that one of the updates specified by an UPDATE statement may violate some constraint, such as a check constraint or referential integrity constraint (described in Section 5.1). If this or any other error is encountered during execution of an UPDATE statement, the statement is rolled back and no rows are updated.

If a subquery is used in an UPDATE statement, either in the WHERE clause or in the SET clause, that subquery is evaluated before any rows are updated. If such a subquery contains a reference to the table that is being updated, the UPDATE statement is said to be *self-referencing*. All subqueries in self-referencing UPDATE statements (even correlated subqueries!) see the table in its original state, before any updates are applied.

Whenever a subquery is used on the right-hand side of an assignment, that subquery must return at most one row. The value(s) of that row are assigned to the respective column(s) on the left-hand side of the assignment. If the subquery returns no rows, the columns on the left-hand side of the assignment are assigned null values. The use of a subquery on the right-hand side of an assignment is a powerful feature, particularly when the subquery is correlated to the table being updated, as illustrated in the following example. In this example, supplier number S53 has guaranteed to provide the lowest price and the shortest response time for all the parts that it supplies. The following

UPDATE statement modifies the rows of the QUOTATIONS table to reflect this policy:

```
UPDATE quotations AS X
SET (price, responsetime) =
        (SELECT min(price), min(responsetime)
         FROM quotations
         WHERE partno = X.partno)
WHERE suppno = 'S53';
```

When one of the columns being updated by an UPDATE statement participates in a unique index or is part of a primary key, the uniqueness of the index or key is enforced after each row is updated. This may mean that the UPDATE statement will be rolled back because of a temporary uniqueness violation that would have been resolved if the statement were allowed to continue. Since temporary uniqueness violations depend on the order in which rows are updated, it cannot always be predicted whether an UPDATE statement will succeed or fail. For example, suppose that column COL1 is the primary key of table TAB1 and contains the values 1, 2, 3, 4, and 5. Consider the following update:

```
UPDATE TAB1
SET COL1 = COL1 + 1;
```

If the system happens to update the rows of TAB1 in ascending order of primary key values, this statement will fail because the update of the first row will cause a uniqueness violation. On the other hand, if the system happens to update the rows in descending order of primary key values, the statement will succeed.

2.5.3 DELETE Statement

The purpose of a DELETE statement is to delete one or more rows from a table or view. Deleting rows from a view has the effect of deleting rows from the table on which the view is based. The syntax of a DELETE statement is as follows:[12]

---

12. A variation of this syntax, called a *positioned DELETE statement*, is described in Section 2.7.11.

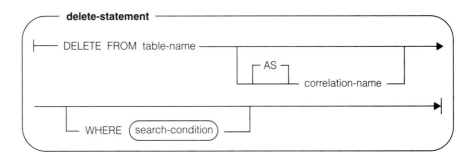

The action of a DELETE statement is simple: those rows of the named table or view for which the search condition is TRUE are deleted from the database. If the WHERE clause is omitted, all the rows of the named table or view are deleted.

If the search condition of a DELETE statement contains a subquery that references the table from which rows are being deleted, that subquery is evaluated before any rows are deleted. A DELETE statement containing such a subquery is said to be *self-referencing.*

It is possible that deletion of one of the rows specified by a DELETE statement may violate some constraint, such as a referential integrity constraint (described in Section 5.1). If this or any other error is encountered during execution of a DELETE statement, the statement is rolled back and no rows are deleted.

The following example statement deletes supplier number S59 from the SUPPLIERS table:

```
DELETE FROM suppliers WHERE suppno = 'S59';
```

The use of a correlation name in a DELETE statement is a powerful feature that permits a subquery in the search condition to specify some specific property of the row that is being deleted. For example, the following statement deletes all suppliers who currently have no quotations on file:

```
DELETE FROM suppliers AS X
WHERE NOT EXISTS
   (SELECT partno
    FROM quotations
    WHERE suppno = X.suppno);
```

The use of a correlation name in UPDATE and DELETE statements is a product extension supported by V2 that is not a part of the ANSI/ISO SQL92 Standard (though it is under consideration for the future SQL3 Standard). The following statement is another example of the use of this feature. This statement deletes all the quotations whose price is more than twice the average quoted price for the same part. Note that this is a self-referencing DELETE statement, and that therefore the set of quotations to be deleted will effectively be computed before any quotations are actually deleted.

```
DELETE FROM quotations AS X
WHERE price >
   (SELECT 2 * avg(price)
    FROM quotations
    WHERE partno = X.partno);
```

2.6 USING THE COMMAND LINE PROCESSOR

We have discussed five basic SQL statements: SELECT, VALUES, INSERT, UPDATE, and DELETE. Together, these five statements are called *data manipulation statements*. These and other SQL statements can be executed using an interactive interface such as the CLP or can be embedded in a program written in some host programming language. This section describes the basics of how to use the CLP. (More information about the CLP can be found in the *DB2 Command Reference.*)

As noted in Chapter 1, the CLP is the basic tool provided by V2 for interactively executing SQL statements and system commands. The CLP can take its input either from the keyboard or from a file, and can direct its output either to your display or to a file. The CLP is invoked by typing the command db2 at your operating system prompt or, if your operating system has a graphic user interface, by double-clicking on the "Command Line Processor" icon in the "DB2" group.

The three forms of the db2 command are as follows:

1. If you follow the word db2 with an SQL statement or system command, the CLP will execute that statement or command and display the result. For example, to direct the CLP to connect to a database named finance, you might type:

   db2 connect to finance

   When using the CLP in this mode, you must remember that the operating system shell is processing your input before sending it to the CLP. Therefore, if you use any characters that are considered special characters by the operating system, such as *, >, or <, you should enclose your input in single or double quotes, as in the following example:

```
db2 "select * from accounts"
```

2. If you follow the word db2 with the option -f filename, the CLP will take its input from the named file, processing all the commands in the file one after another. For example, the following command directs the CLP to process all the statements in the file named monday.clp:

```
db2 -f monday.clp
```

3. If you simply type db2 followed by neither the -f option nor a command, the CLP will go into interactive mode and will prompt you to enter SQL statements or commands, one at a time, at the keyboard. The simplest form of the db2 command is as follows:

```
db2
```

While the CLP is executing in interactive mode, it prompts you for input by means of a prompt that looks like this:

```
db2 =>
```

In addition to SQL statements and database system commands, you can use the CLP to execute operating system commands. Simply prefix the operating system command with an exclamation mark when you include it in a CLP input file or type it in response to the CLP prompt. For example, the following line in a CLP input file would execute the operating system echo command:

```
!echo Monthly Summary
```

TIP: When you are using the CLP to execute a series of SQL statements in a file, the !echo command can be used to generate text into the output stream, perhaps to serve as labels on the results of your queries.

The CLP will not be able to access any data until the database server has been started. The server can be started by a db2start command, which can be executed by a suitably authorized user either at the CLP prompt or at the operating system prompt, or by double-clicking on the "Start DB2" icon in your operating system's graphic user interface.

In a typical CLP session, the first thing you will probably want to do is connect to a database. If you have defined an operating system environment variable named DB2DBDFT, the CLP will automatically connect to the database named in this variable at the beginning of your session. Alternatively, you can simply execute the statement CONNECT TO dbname. Refer to the database by its *alias*—that is, the name by which it is known in the database catalog at your node. Your client system will handle the details of finding where the database resides and establishing a session with the appropriate server machine using the appropriate protocols. All you need to do is enter SQL statements and commands to interact with the database as though it were present on your local machine.

In a CLP session, you are not limited to interacting with a single database. Whenever you execute the statement CONNECT TO dbname, the CLP establishes a connection with the new database named in your command. You can switch back and forth among several databases, executing SQL statements in each. (The CONNECT command is discussed in more detail in Section 2.9.2.)

If you specify the -t option when you invoke the CLP, you must terminate each SQL statement or command with a semicolon. This option is convenient when your statements and commands span more than one input line, as is often the case. The SQL examples in this book are terminated by semicolons, as if they were entered in a CLP session with the -t option.

When you are finished with a CLP session, you should end the session by a TERMINATE command. This command terminates your database connections and shuts down the CLP cleanly.

TIP: A CLP session can be ended by either a TERMINATE command or a QUIT command. The QUIT command is not recommended, because it does not terminate the database connection and it leaves a background process active on the client machine. Under certain circumstances, the database connection and background process left behind after QUIT can interfere with stopping the database server.

2.6.1 SQLCODE and SQLSTATE

The execution of each SQL statement results in two codes—SQLCODE and SQLSTATE—that indicate the success or failure of the statement and identify the type of error encountered, if any. SQLCODE is an integer code that has long been used by the DB2 product family, and SQLSTATE is a newer five-character code that is defined by the ANSI/ISO SQL Standard. In general, a zero SQLCODE denotes normal execution, a negative SQLCODE denotes an error, and a positive SQLCODE denotes a warning or condition of interest such as "no rows were updated." SQLCODE and SQLSTATE are different ways of encoding the same information, but applications that use SQLSTATE will be more portable to other database systems, because SQLSTATE is defined by the SQL Standard.

When you are running the CLP in interactive mode, whenever an SQL statement fails, the CLP displays the SQLSTATE along with a short message describing the error. The message starts with a message identifier from which the SQLCODE can be deduced. For example, an attempt to query a nonexistent table results in SQLCODE -204 and SQLSTATE 42704, and the following message is displayed:

```
SQL0204N  "CHAMBERL.T99" is an undefined name.  SQLSTATE=42704
```

You can get more information about a specific SQLCODE or SQLSTATE by using "?" as a CLP command. "?" followed by a five-digit SQLSTATE displays information about that SQLSTATE, and "?" followed by a message identifier displays a more detailed version of the given message. For example, either of the following CLP commands might be used to get more information about the message above:

```
? 42704;
? SQL0204N;
```

You can also get more information about a specific message by looking it up by its message identifier in the *DB2 Messages Reference*.

2.6.2 Command Line Processor Options

The -f option that directs the CLP to accept input from a file is just one of several options that control the behavior of the CLP. Each of these options has a one-letter name. Some of them can be simply turned on or off, while others can be set to a particular value such as a filename. In the db2 command that starts a CLP session, an option can be turned off by prefixing its letter with a + sign, or turned on by prefixing its letter with a – sign, optionally followed by a value. For example, the following command invokes the CLP with the "c" option turned off, the "v" option turned on, and the "f" option set to the value "infile":

```
db2 +c -v -f infile
```

Each of the CLP options has a default setting. These system-defined defaults can be overridden in the following three ways:

1. If you have defined an operating system environment variable named DB2OPTIONS, the options defined in this variable supersede the system-defined defaults.

2. A db2 command can specify options for a particular CLP session, overriding the defaults defined by the system or specified by DB2OPTIONS.

3. Once a CLP session has begun, the options can be changed by means of the UPDATE COMMAND OPTIONS command.

Table 2-4 summarizes the options that are recognized by the CLP. For each flag, the system-defined default is shown in boldface type.

TABLE 2-4: Command Line Processor Options

Option	Value
–a	After each statement, a structure called SQLCA is displayed, containing codes that summarize the result of executing the statement.
+a	The SQLCA structure is not displayed.
–c	A COMMIT is automatically performed after each SQL statement (making your changes permanent and visible to other users).
+c	No automatic COMMIT is performed. You must execute an explicit COMMIT statement to make your changes permanent and visible to other users.
–ec	SQLCODE is displayed after each SQL statement (used mainly with +o).
–es	SQLSTATE is displayed after each SQL statement (used mainly with +o).
+e	No return code is displayed after executing an SQL statement from the operating system command line.
–f filename	The CLP takes its input from the given file. The filename may be either absolute (a path-name) or relative (to the current directory).
+f	The CLP takes its input from standard input (usually your keyboard).
–l filename	All commands and SQL statements are logged in the named file, appending them to the existing content of this file, if any. Each command or statement is logged with the time of its execution (but the results of queries are not included in the log).
+l	Commands and SQL statements are not logged.
–o	Output (query results and messages) is displayed on standard output (usually your display).
+o	Output is not displayed on standard output.
–p	The CLP prompt is displayed before entry of each interactive command.
+p	No prompt is displayed.

TABLE 2-4: *(Continued)*

Option	Value
–r filename	Results of queries are saved in the named file.
+r	Query results are not saved.
–s	If an error is encountered during execution of a statement, the CLP stops and exits to the operating system.
+s	If an error is encountered during execution of a statement, the CLP continues to the next statement.
–t	The statement termination character is set to a semicolon. Input lines are concatenated together until a semicolon is encountered, and the result is handled as one statement.
–td$x$	The statement termination character is set to x, which may be any character. For example, option -td$ indicates that input lines are to be concatenated together until a $ character is encountered, and the result is to be handled as one statement. This option is useful when the semicolon character is needed for use inside an SQL statement.
+t	There is no statement termination character. Each line is considered to be a statement, unless it ends with a space followed by a backslash ("\").
–v	All statements and commands are echoed to standard output before they are executed.
+v	Statements and commands are not echoed.
–w	Warning messages resulting from execution of SQL statements (such as "string truncated") are displayed.
+w	Warning messages are suppressed and not displayed.
–z filename	Both query results and error messages are saved in the named file.
+z	Query results and error messages are not saved.

During a CLP session, any of the CLP options can be changed by means of a command with the following syntax:

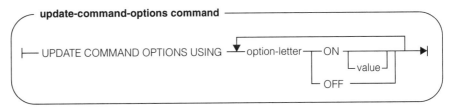

update-command-options command

For example, the following command turns autocommit off, turns verify mode on, and directs all query results and error messages into a file named `outfile.txt`:

```
UPDATE COMMAND OPTIONS USING c OFF v ON z ON outfile.txt;
```

At any time during a CLP session, you can see the current settings of the command options by typing the following command:

```
LIST COMMAND OPTIONS;
```

2.6.3 Comments

According to the SQL92 Standard, any SQL statement can contain one or more comments and each comment begins with two hyphens and extends to the end of the line. Comments have no effect on the processing of the SQL statement. The CLP, however, places an additional requirement on comments: each comment must be on a line by itself. The following example shows an SQL statement containing two comments, only one of which is acceptable to the CLP:

```
SELECT suppno, price
FROM quotations
-- This comment is accepted by the CLP
WHERE partno = 'P231'    -- This comment is not
AND responsetime < 10;
```

In the SQL examples in this book, I have taken the liberty of writing SQL92-style comments on some of the lines of SQL, wherever these comments seemed to be helpful in clarifying the examples. If you want to execute the examples using the CLP, you will need to modify them so that each comment is on a separate line.

2.6.4 Getting Help When You Need It

At any time during a CLP session, you can use the HELP command to browse the online documentation that is provided with your V2 system. To obtain help about a given subject, simply type HELP followed by a word or phrase, such as the following:

```
HELP CREATE TRIGGER;
```

The system will open a window to display the relevant page from one of the online manuals. If you do not specify any word or phrase, or if no specific help is found for the word or phrase you specified, the system will open a window on the table of contents of the *DB2 SQL Reference*. You can use the online help facility to browse through manuals, perform content searches, and follow hypertext links.

Also during a CLP session, you can get a list of system commands by typing "?", or the syntax of a specific command by typing "?" followed by the name of the command. This form of help does not apply to SQL statements such as SELECT and UPDATE, but only to system commands such as CREATE DATABASE (which are discussed in Chapter 8). For example, you might ask for the syntax of the CREATE DATABASE command by typing the following:

```
? create database;
```

TIP: If you are running the CLP with a semicolon as your statement terminator, you must end every CLP command with a semicolon, including "?" commands.

2.7 EMBEDDING SQL IN APPLICATION PROGRAMS

Now that we have discussed how to execute SQL statements using the CLP, we are ready to discuss how to embed the same statements in programs written in a host programming language. The host programming languages supported by V2 are C, C++, COBOL, FORTRAN, and REXX. This section discusses how SQL statements can be embedded in C and C++ programs. For information about how to embed SQL statements in the other host languages, see the *DB2 Application Programming Guide*.

As described in Section 1.2.4, a C program with embedded SQL statements (sometimes called an SQC file) is first processed by an SQL precompiler. All SQL statements in the program must be prefixed by EXEC SQL to enable the precompiler to find them. Each SQL statement ends with a semicolon and may occupy more than one line in the SQC file. The precompiler processes all the SQL statements, replacing them with pure C statements that call the database manager. The precompiler also prepares for each of the SQL statements in the original SQC program a *section*, which encapsulates a plan for executing the statement. At run time, when the C program calls the database manager to execute a given SQL statement, the database manager loads and executes one of the sections. All of the sections that encapsulate the SQL statements in a given program are collectively called a *package*. The SQL precompiler produces a package for each program that it processes, and stores the packages in the database.

SQL statements embedded in C programs may contain SQL-style comments, which begin with two hyphens and extend to the end of the line. Unlike the CLP, the SQL precompiler does not require each comment to be on a line by itself. Outside of SQL statements, of course, comments must use the normal C syntax.

A character-string constant inside an SQL statement can be continued on the next line of your application program by using the line-continuation character (a backslash), as in the following example:

```
EXEC SQL DELETE FROM parts
WHERE description LIKE '%Surplus%\
Equipment%';
```

Database applications written in C and C++ should always include the following C preprocessor statement:

```
#include <sqlenv.h>
```

The header file sqlenv.h (found in sqllib/include), and the other header files that it includes in turn, contain declarations of the structures, functions, and constants that your program will need to interact with the database.

TIP: Since the SQL precompiler is usually invoked before the C preprocessor, it is a good practice to make the SQL statements in your program independent of C preprocessor facilities such as #define and #include. If your SQL statements require material to be included from another file, you can use an INCLUDE statement that is processed by the SQL precompiler, as in the following example:

```
EXEC SQL INCLUDE 'myfile.sqc';
```

2.7.1 Host Variables

Section 2.4.1 discussed how expressions in SQL statements can be built from primitive operands such as constants and column names. One of these primitive operands is a *host variable*, which is the name of a variable declared in the program in which the SQL statement is embedded. The name of a host variable is distinguished from the name of a database column by a colon prefix. For example, the expression x+y represents the value of column x added to the value of column y, but the expression x+:y represents the value of column x added to the content of host variable y. When a variable is used to retrieve a value from the database into the host program, it is called an *output host variable*. On the other hand, when a variable is given a value by the host program and this value is used by an SQL statement, the variable is called an *input host variable*. The following examples show how input host variables can be used in data manipulation statements. Note that each statement begins with the prefix EXEC SQL to mark it for processing by the SQL precompiler.

- Insert a new row into the SUPPLIERS table from input host variables.

```
EXEC SQL
    INSERT INTO SUPPLIERS(suppno, name, address)
        VALUES (:suppno, :sname, :saddr);
```

- Update the price and response time of a specific quotation, based on values in input host variables.

```
EXEC SQL
    UPDATE quotations
    SET price = :newprice,
        responsetime = :newresponse
    WHERE suppno = :suppno
    AND partno = :partno;
```

TIP: Since database columns and host variables are not in the same name space, you can name your host variables after the columns with which they compare or exchange data. This practice can be useful in remembering how your host variables are used.

As a general rule, a host variable used in an SQL statement should be a simple identifier without any host language modifiers such as subscripts. For example, :x is a valid host variable reference, but :x[5] or :x.salary or :x->salary are not valid for use in an SQL statement. The only host language operator that can be applied to a host variable in an SQL statement is the dereference operator (such as :*x), and it may be used only if the host variable is declared to be a pointer type (see Appendix E for the syntax for declaring pointers).

When exchanging values between the database and a host program, we need to solve the problem of how to represent null values. This problem arises because SQL datatypes (such as Integer) allow null values, but host programming–language datatypes (such as long in C) do not. V2 (and all the other DB2 products) solve this problem by allowing each host variable to be associated with a second, auxiliary variable called an *indicator variable*. The main purpose of the indicator variable is to represent null values. A negative indicator variable (usually, by convention, –1) represents a null value. If a host variable is associated with a zero or positive indicator variable, it represents a non-null value. (Positive indicator variables are used with output host variables to indicate the original lengths of retrieved strings before truncation.)

In SQL expressions, each host variable may optionally be followed by its indicator variable. Both variables are prefixed by colons, and the indicator variable may be identified by the keyword INDICATOR, as shown in the following syntax:

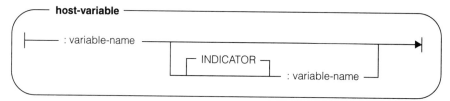

If a host variable has no indicator variable, it cannot be used to represent null values. Any attempt to retrieve a null value into such a variable will result in an error condition.

The UPDATE statement in the example above might be revised by associating indicator variables with the input variables for the new price and new response time, as shown below. This revised example allows the host program to represent null values for prices and response times.

```
EXEC SQL    -- Note price and responsetime may be null
    UPDATE quotations
    SET price = :newprice :indic1,
        responsetime = :newresponse :indic2
    WHERE suppno = :suppno
    AND partno = :partno;
```

2.7.2 The SQL Declare Section

All variables used in a C or C++ program must be declared so that they can be processed properly by the compiler. In addition, the declarations of host variables that are used in SQL statements must be marked for processing by the SQL precompiler. These requirements are met by an *SQL Declare Section*, which must be included in every C or C++ program that contains embedded SQL statements (similar requirements exist for other host languages, except REXX). The SQL Declare Section must contain a declaration for each host variable and indicator variable that is used in any SQL statement in the program.

As a general rule, the SQL Declare Section contains declarations written in host language syntax. Each SQL datatype is associated with a host language datatype that is used for exchanging values between host programs and the database. The C datatypes that correspond to the basic SQL datatypes are shown in Table 2-5.

TABLE 2-5: C Datatypes Corresponding to Basic SQL Datatypes

SQL Datatype	C Datatype
Smallint and indicator variables	`short`
Integer	`long`
Decimal(p,s)	(no C equivalent)
Double	`double`
Char(n)	`char[n+1]` (null-terminated)

Varchar(n)	`char[n+1]` (null-terminated)
	 or
	 `struct`
	    `{`
	    `short length;`
	    `char data[n];`
	    `}`

Date	`char[11]`
Time	`char[9]`
Timestamp	`char[27]`
Graphic(n)	`wchar_t[n+1]` (null-terminated)

Vargraphic(n)	`wchar_t[n+1]` (null-terminated)
	 or
	 `struct`
	    `{`
	    `short length;`
	    `wchar_t data[n];`
	    `}`

TIP: Although there is no C-language equivalent for the Decimal datatype, you can exchange Decimal values with a C program by converting them either to character strings or to floating-point values. These conversions can be done by using built-in functions: the `char` and `decimal` functions can be used to convert between the Decimal and Char datatypes, and the `double` and `decimal` functions can be used to convert between the Decimal and Double datatypes.

In addition to the datatypes listed in Table 2-5, V2 supports some datatypes for handling large objects. Declaration of host variables for exchanging values using these datatypes involves some special considerations, which are discussed in Section 4.1.2.

You may have multiple SQL Declare Sections in your C program. Each Declare Section must be at some location in your program where C declarations are valid, and must be contained between the statements EXEC SQL BEGIN DECLARE SECTION and EXEC SQL END DECLARE SECTION. The SQL precompiler will remove these bracketing statements and leave the variable declarations in their original place in your C program. The SQL Declare Section must occur before any SQL statements that use the host variables that it declares.

The variables declared in the SQL Declare Section obey the usual scoping rules when used in C statements. However, the SQL precompiler considers host variables to be global to all SQL statements in the program (compilation unit). Therefore, the name of each variable declared in an SQL Declare Section must be unique in the program.

The only statements allowed within an SQL Declare Section are declarations of variables having one of the C datatypes shown in Table 2-5 (or one of the large-object datatypes discussed in Section 4.1.2). Inside an SQL Declare Section embedded in a C program, you may use either C-style comments (which begin with /* and end with */) or SQL-style comments (which begin with - - and end with a line break).

The following is an example of an SQL Declare Section that might be embedded near the top of a C program. As you can see, inside the SQL Declare Section, the names of host variables are not prefixed by colons.

```
EXEC SQL BEGIN DECLARE SECTION;
    long qonhand, qonorder, threshold;   /* Integers   */
    char suppno[4];                       /* Char(3)    */
    char partno[5];                       /* Char(4)    */
    char orderdate[11];                   /* Date       */
    struct
        {
        short length;
        char data[50];
        } sname, saddr;                   /* Varchar(50) */
    short indic1=0, indic2=0, indic3=0;   /* Indicators  */
EXEC SQL END DECLARE SECTION;
```

Inside an SQL Declare Section, declarations must obey the following rules:

- The names of host variables must not exceed 30 characters in length and must not begin with the characters EXEC or SQL.

- A declaration may include a storage class specification such as static or extern.

- Multiple variables can be declared and initialized on a single line. However, variables can be initialized only by "=" notation, not by "( )" notation, as in the following examples:

```
int x = 7;   /* OK           */
int x(7);    /* not accepted */
```

(More details about the syntax of host variable declarations can be found in Appendix E.)

2.7.3 Exchanging Double-Byte Strings

The Graphic and Vargraphic datatypes are used to store character data in which the character encodings are larger than one byte, as in the case of many Asian languages. As shown in Table 2-5, the C datatype used to exchange Graphic and Vargraphic data is an array of type wchar_t.

Two different formats are used for representing double-byte data:

- In *multibyte format* (sometimes called *DBCS format*), each character is encoded in two bytes. This format is always used inside the database for storing Graphic and Vargraphic data.

- In *wide-character format*, each character is encoded as a wchar_t, which is defined by your C compiler and which may be two or four bytes. The IBM CSet++ compiler (in the header file stddef.h) defines wchar_t as a two-byte datatype (unsigned short). Wide-character format is not used inside the database, but it is used by many C and C++ compilers. Compilers often provide libraries of functions for manipulating strings in wide-character format. The wide-character string library is declared in wstring.h and includes functions such as wstrcpy, wstrcat, wstrlen, and many others. C and C++ compilers also recognize L-type literals such as the one below, and represent them using wide-character format.

  L"三つ子の魂百まで"

  Since multibyte format is used inside the database but many compiler facilities are based on wide-character format, you may wish your graphic data to be converted from multibyte to wide-character format when it is fetched into an output variable, and to be converted from wide-character to multibyte format when it is read from an input variable. If you specify the precompiler option WCHARTYPE CONVERT, the system will perform these conversions for you automatically. If you specify the precompiler option WCHARTYPE NOCONVERT or allow this option to default, no automatic conversions will be performed, and all input and output variables will be processed in multibyte format (two bytes per character, regardless of the declared size of wchar_t.)

If you precompile your program with WCHARTYPE NOCONVERT (the default), you can explicitly convert between multibyte and wide-character formats in both directions, using the C functions `mbstowcs` and `wcstombs`. For more information about double-byte data, see the *DB2 Application Programming Guide* or the *National Language Support Reference Manual*, IBM Publication No. SE09-8002.

TIP: Remember that C and SQL have different ways of expressing double-byte literals (constant strings of double-byte characters). An L-type literal in C code looks like `L"double-byte data"` and is represented in wide-character format. An SQL double-byte literal looks like `G'double-byte data'` or `N'double-byte data'` and is represented in multibyte format. When initializing a double-byte variable in an SQL Declare Section, use an L-type literal and perform conversions as necessary.

2.7.4 Return Codes and Messages

When your application program is running, each SQL statement that is executed returns a status code and possibly some additional information. The information is returned in a structure called an SQLCA, which is declared (in the header file `sqlca.h`) as follows:

```
struct sqlca
    {
    unsigned char sqlcaid[8];      /* eye-catcher: "SQLCA" */
    long          sqlabc;          /* length of SQLCA      */
    long          sqlcode;         /* result code          */
    short         sqlerrml;        /* length of msg tokens */
    unsigned char sqlerrmc[70];    /* message tokens       */
    unsigned char sqlerrp[8];      /* diagnostic data      */
    long          sqlerrd[6];      /* row counts           */
    unsigned char sqlwarn[11];     /* warning flags        */
    unsigned char sqlstate[5];     /* standard result code */
    };
```

The meaning of the fields inside the SQLCA structure is as follows:

`sqlcaid`: Contains the string "SQLCA   ".

`sqlabc`: Contains 136, the length in bytes of the SQLCA structure.

`sqlcode`: Contains a code indicating the result of executing an SQL statement. In general, zero indicates normal execution, negative codes indicate error conditions, and positive codes indicate special conditions such as "data not found." Codes returned in this field are product-specific and may have different meanings for different database products. The meanings of the codes returned by V2 are documented in the *DB2 Messages Reference*.

sqlerrml: Contains the actual length of the data contained in the sqlerrmc field.

sqlerrmc: Contains zero or more tokens, separated by X'FF', that provide specific information to be used with the error message that corresponds to a given return code. For example, if the return code indicates "table not found in database," the sqlerrmc field will contain the name of the table that was not found.

sqlerrp: Contains diagnostic information that is not meaningful to the user.

sqlerrd: An array of six integers containing additional diagnostic information. Two integers in this array contain information that is meaningful to the user:

sqlerrd[2] (the third integer in the array) contains the number of rows that were modified by an INSERT, DELETE, or UPDATE statement.

sqlerrd[4] (the fifth integer in the array) contains the number of rows that were modified by triggers or by enforcement of foreign key constraints (discussed in Section 5.1).

sqlwarn: An array of characters, normally blank, that are set to "W" if certain warning conditions occur. The following warning conditions are defined:

sqlwarn[0] is set to "W" if any of the other warning characters are set to "W."

sqlwarn[1] indicates that a character string value was truncated on retrieval.

sqlwarn[2] indicates that some of the values passed to a column function were null (these values are ignored).

sqlwarn[3] indicates that the number of values retrieved from the database was not equal to the number of host variables provided to receive them.

sqlwarn[4] indicates that an UPDATE or DELETE statement does not include a WHERE clause and will therefore affect all the rows of a table.

sqlwarn[6] indicates that the result of a date calculation was adjusted to avoid an impossible date, such as February 31.

sqlstate: An array of five characters that indicates the result of executing an SQL statement. The five-character sqlstate codes are defined by the ANSI/ISO SQL92 Standard, so they are more portable from one database product to another than are the numeric codes used in sqlcode. The first two characters of the sqlstate identify an *error class* such as "syntax error," and are uniform across all SQL implementations that conform to the Standard. The last three characters of the sqlstate identify an *error subclass*, which may be implementation-dependent.

The easiest way to declare an SQLCA structure in your application program is to use the following statement:

```
EXEC SQL INCLUDE SQLCA;
```

This statement includes the definition of the SQLCA structure into your program, and also declares one instance of this structure with the name sqlca. Thus, you can refer to the various parts of the structure using qualified names such as sqlca.sqlcode and sqlca.sqlstate[0]. In addition, since the field sqlca.sqlcode is used a lot, the INCLUDE SQLCA statement defines a shorthand name, SQLCODE, as equivalent to sqlca.sqlcode.

The easiest way to obtain the detailed error message that corresponds to the codes inside a given SQLCA structure is to use a utility routine named sqlaintp. This routine takes an SQLCA structure and returns a null-terminated character string containing the message associated with the codes in that structure, complete with the sqlerrmc tokens inserted into the message in the proper places, ready for display. The interface to this utility routine (declared in the header file sql.h) is as follows:

```
int sqlaintp
    (
    char *buffer,            /* message buffer                 */
    short buff_size,         /* size of message buffer         */
    short line_width,        /* desired line width             */
    struct sqlca *sqlca      /* to be decoded into a message   */
    );
```

The first parameter to sqlaintp is a pointer to a buffer that you have allocated for receiving the decoded message. The second parameter indicates the size of the buffer, and the third parameter indicates how you would like the message to be formatted (maximum number of characters between line breaks). Most messages will fit into a buffer of 512 bytes. A positive return code from sqlaintp indicates the length of the message, and a negative return code indicates that no message could be returned for the given codes.

TIP: Remember that you can use the "?" command of the CLP to display the full message associated with any given SQLCODE or SQLSTATE, as described in Section 2.6.1.

2.7.5 WHENEVER Statement

Each time your application program executes an SQL statement, a code indicating the outcome of the statement is returned in the SQLCA structure. To guard against errors, you will probably want to check the content of the SQLCA after each statement is executed. To make it easy for you to perform these checks, the SQL precompilers (for all languages except REXX) provide a facility called a WHENEVER statement.

Although the WHENEVER statement is prefixed by EXEC SQL like other SQL statements, it is not an executable statement. Instead, it causes the precompiler to automatically generate code in your program to check the SQLCA after each SQL statement. The generated code will cause your program either to branch to some indicated label or to continue normal execution, depending on the content of the SQLCA. The syntax of a WHENEVER statement is as follows:[13]

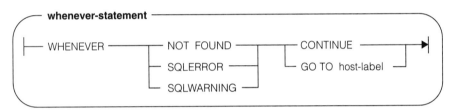

You can have as many WHENEVER statements as you like, and you can put them anywhere in your program. The behavior of your program after execution of each SQL statement is determined as follows:

- If the SQL statement is successful (SQLCODE = 0), control passes to the next statement in your program.

- If the SQL statement returns SQLCODE +100, indicating that no data rows were found to satisfy your request, the previous WHENEVER NOT FOUND statement in your program (in statement-listing order, not necessarily in execution order) is effective. This SQLCODE might be returned by a FETCH, UPDATE, or DELETE statement, or by a "single-row SELECT" statement (described in Section 2.7.10).

- If the SQL statement returns any other positive SQLCODE or any warning condition, the previous WHENEVER SQLWARNING statement in your program (again, in listing order) is effective.

---

13. The prefix EXEC SQL is omitted from this and other syntax diagrams. However, this prefix is required on all SQL statements embedded in host programs.

- If the SQL statement returns any negative SQLCODE, indicating an error condition, the previous WHENEVER SQLERROR statement in your program (in listing order) is effective.

The WHENEVER statement that is effective, according to the above rules, will cause your program to either continue normal execution or branch to the label indicated in the GO TO clause of the WHENEVER statement. The GO TO clause simply contains a label of a host language statement, optionally prefixed by a colon. If no WHENEVER statement is effective for the condition indicated in the SQLCA structure, the default behavior is CONTINUE.

Using WHENEVER statements, you can define up to three routines for handling exceptional conditions at any given point in your program: one for errors, one for warnings, and one for "not found" conditions. Inside these handlers is a good place to call the `sqlaintp` utility routine to retrieve the message associated with the codes that are found in the SQLCA structure.

The following lines of code might be embedded in a C program to define the actions desired when exceptional conditions are detected:

```
EXEC SQL WHENEVER NOTFOUND GO TO end_of_loop;
EXEC SQL WHENEVER SQLERROR GO TO print_message;
EXEC SQL WHENEVER SQLWARNING CONTINUE;
```

TIP: If you intend a WHENEVER statement to apply only to a specific part of your program (such as a function or subroutine), you must limit its scope by another WHENEVER statement at the end of the section to which it applies. Remember that WHENEVER is not an executable statement, but is interpreted by the SQL precompiler. The precompiler does not understand the scoping rules of your host language, and it assumes that each WHENEVER statement applies until another WHENEVER statement is encountered in your program listing for the same condition.

2.7.6 Cursor Declarations

INSERT, DELETE, and UPDATE statements are relatively simple to embed in application programs—they execute, possibly modifying the content of the database, and return an SQLCA structure indicating what happened. But embedded queries are more complex, because they need to return data to the application program, and the number of rows to be returned is usually not known in advance. In order to write a program that retrieves data from a database, you need a mechanism that specifies the rows to be retrieved and then fetches these rows into your program, one at a time. This mechanism is called a *cursor*.

A cursor is like a name that is associated with a query. A *cursor declaration* is used to declare the name of the cursor and to specify its associated query. Three statements, called OPEN, FETCH, and CLOSE, operate on cursors. An OPEN statement prepares the cursor for retrieval of the first row in the result set. A FETCH statement retrieves one row of the result set into some designated variables in the host program. After each FETCH statement, the cursor is said to be *positioned* on the row of the result set that was just fetched. FETCH statements are usually executed repeatedly until all the rows of the result set have been fetched (this condition is indicated by SQLCODE +100 and SQL-STATE 02000). A CLOSE statement releases any resources used by the cursor when it is no longer needed (if needed again, the cursor can be reopened).

The syntax of a cursor declaration is as follows (see also "Dynamic Cursor Declaration" on page 433):

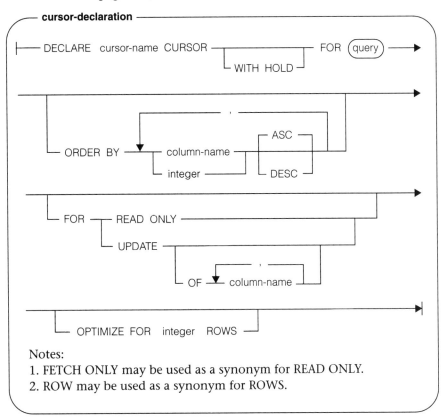

Notes:
1. FETCH ONLY may be used as a synonym for READ ONLY.
2. ROW may be used as a synonym for ROWS.

A cursor declaration declares the name of the cursor (which must be different from all other cursor names in the same program), and associates it with a particular query. The syntax of a query is given on page 69. The cursor declaration does not specify where the results of the query are to delivered—that's the job of the FETCH statement.

A query used in a cursor declaration may include some host variables. For example, the following example associates the cursor name c1 with a query that finds parts in the PARTS table for which the quantity on order is greater than an input host variable named :threshold.

```
EXEC SQL DECLARE c1 CURSOR FOR
    SELECT partno, qonhand, qonorder
    FROM parts
    WHERE qonorder > :threshold
    ORDER BY partno;
```

TIP: It's bad form for a query in an application program to use the phrase SELECT * to indicate that all the columns of a table are to be retrieved. This is because, if the table is later expanded with an additional column, the program will have no host variable into which to receive the new column, and so will be unable to accept delivery of "all the columns." However, such a program will continue to run, retrieving the values of all the columns that were present when the program was bound.

A cursor declaration may contain the following optional clauses:

ORDER BY: This clause, like the ORDER BY clause in a SELECT statement, specifies the order in which the rows of the result set are to be delivered. If no ORDER BY clause is provided, the rows are delivered in a system-determined order that may not be the same from one execution to the next. (For an explanation of the ORDER BY clause, see Section 2.4.9.)

WITH HOLD: This clause causes the cursor to remain open after a COMMIT statement. COMMIT statements, discussed in Section 2.9.1, are used to make database changes permanent. Ordinarily, all open cursors are closed by a COMMIT statement. The WITH HOLD option allows multiple COMMIT statements to be executed while a cursor remains open.

FOR READ ONLY: This clause declares that you do not intend to use the cursor for a *positioned UPDATE* or *positioned DELETE* statement. These statements, described in Section 2.7.11, can be used to update or delete the row on which a cursor is positioned. However, if a cursor is to be used in this way, certain query processing methods are ruled out. Declaring your cursor FOR READ ONLY signals the system that it is free to use any method for processing the query associated with the cursor. This may result in better performance for your query. If you declare a cursor FOR READ ONLY and then use it in a positioned UPDATE or DELETE statement, an error condition will result.

FOR UPDATE: This clause is used to declare the columns that you plan to update by means of positioned updates that refer to this cursor. This information is useful to the query optimizer. If you specify FOR UPDATE but do not list the columns to be updated, the optimizer will assume that you may apply a positioned update to any (or all) columns of the result set. If a cursor definition includes an ORDER BY clause, it may not also include a FOR UPDATE clause.

OPTIMIZE FOR *n* ROWS: This clause advises the query optimizer that you expect to fetch only *n* rows of the result set associated with this cursor. This may affect the method used to process your query. If you omit this clause, the optimizer will assume that you plan to fetch the entire result set.

The following example declares a cursor that will be used to retrieve certain rows from the PARTS table and that may be used for a positioned update of the QONORDER column. The FOR UPDATE clause tells the optimizer that it would be a bad idea to process this query by scanning over the PARTS table using the QONORDER index, since the ordering of rows in this index may change as the column is updated.

```
EXEC SQL DECLARE c2 CURSOR FOR
    SELECT partno, qonhand, qonorder
    FROM parts
    WHERE qonhand < 100
    FOR UPDATE OF qonorder;
```

 TIP: It is a good practice for all your cursor declarations to include either a FOR UPDATE clause (if you plan to use positioned updates or deletes with the cursor) or a FOR READ ONLY clause (if you do not plan to use positioned statements). This makes your intentions explicit and gives the system the best opportunity to optimize the performance of your query.[14]

2.7.7 OPEN Statement

An OPEN statement prepares a cursor for fetching the rows in the result set. Any input variables in the query associated with the cursor are bound (their values are examined and used) when the cursor is opened. As long as the cursor is open, it has a *position* in the result set of the query. This position may be *on* a row, or *before* or *after* a row. The OPEN statement positions the cursor before the first row of the result set.

---

14. If you don't follow this advice, and declare a cursor without specifying either FOR UPDATE or FOR READ ONLY, the status of your cursor depends on a precompiler option. If you precompile your program with the option LANGLEVEL MIA, the system will assume that your cursor can be used for a positioned update of any column (unless it is not updatable for one of the reasons listed in Section 2.7.11). If you precompile with the option LANGLEVEL SAA1 or with no LANGLEVEL option, the system will assume that your cursor is FOR READ ONLY.

The syntax of an OPEN statement is as follows (see also "Dynamic Open Statement" on page 433):

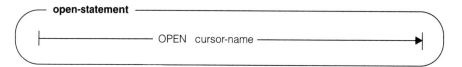

Example:

```
EXEC SQL OPEN c1;
```

2.7.8 FETCH Statement

A FETCH statement fetches the row of the result set that is next after the current position of the cursor and delivers it into the host variables listed. The cursor named in the FETCH statement must be open. If there is no row after the current position of the cursor, the FETCH statement returns SQLCODE +100 (SQLSTATE 02000), and the host variables are unchanged. The position of the cursor is advanced to be *on* the row that was just fetched.

The syntax of a FETCH statement is as follows (see also "Dynamic Fetch Statement" on page 433):

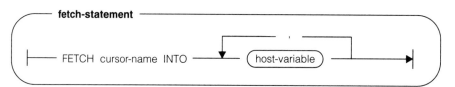

Example:

```
EXEC SQL FETCH c1
INTO :partno :indic1, :qonhand :indic2, :qonorder :indic3;
```

The host variables used in a FETCH statement must be type-compatible with the values that are fetched into them (for a summary of compatibility rules, see Section 4.6). If any of the columns of the result set allow null values, the host variables associated with these columns must have indicator variables.

Depending on the access plan chosen by the optimizer, the result of the query associated with a cursor may be completely materialized and saved in a temporary table at the time when the first row is fetched, or it may be materialized one row at a time in response to individual FETCH statements. If the result is materialized in a temporary table, it will not reflect database changes that occur after the first fetch; on the other hand, if the result set is materialized as each row is fetched, it will reflect such changes. Since the optimizer reserves the right to choose how the query will be processed, whether the result is materialized at first fetch time cannot, in general, be predicted.

When character-string data is fetched into a host variable of type `char[n]` or `wchar_t[n]`, truncation may take place if the host variable is not large enough to hold the fetched value. The `sqlwarn[1]` flag in the SQLCA structure and the indicator (if any) provided with the host variable are used together to provide a warning when truncation occurs, according to the following rules:[15]

1. If the fetched value, including its null terminator, fits into the host variable (for example, a column value of type Char(5) is fetched into a host variable of type `char[6]`):

   The value is copied into the host variable with a null terminator.

   `sqlcode` is set to zero, and `sqlstate` is set to "00000".

   `sqlwarn[1]` is set to blank.

   The indicator variable, if any, is set to zero.

2. If the fetched value fits into the host variable, but there is no room for the null terminator (for example, a column value of type Char(5) is fetched into a host variable of type `char[5]`):

   The value is copied into the host variable with no null terminator.

   `sqlcode` is set to zero, and `sqlstate` is set to "01004".

   `sqlwarn[1]` is set to "N".

   The indicator variable, if any, is set to zero.

3. If the fetched value is too long to fit into the host variable (for example, a column value of type Char(5) is fetched into a host variable of type `char[4]`):

   The host variable is filled with as many bytes of the fetched value as will fit, not including a null terminator.

   `sqlcode` is set to zero, and `sqlstate` is set to "01004."

   `sqlwarn[1]` is set to "W."

   The indicator variable, if any, is set to the original length of the fetched value, before truncation.[16]

---

15. These rules assume that your application has been precompiled with the option LANGLEVEL SAA1, which is the default. An alternative set of truncation rules, invoked by the option LANGLEVEL MIA, is described in the *DB2 Application Programming Guide*.

16. For large-object datatypes (described in Section 4.1), the original length of the string is not returned in the indicator variable.

2.7.9 CLOSE Statement

A CLOSE statement closes a cursor and releases any resources that it may be holding, such as a temporary copy of the result set. If a closed cursor is later reopened, its input variables are rebound, its query is reexecuted, and the cursor is positioned before the first row of the new result set.

The syntax of a CLOSE statement is as follows:

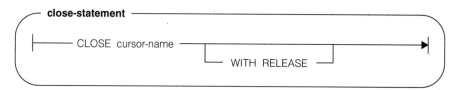

Example:

```
EXEC SQL CLOSE c1;
```

The optional phrase WITH RELEASE tells the system that it can release any read-locks that are associated with this cursor.[17] This is meaningful only if you are using an isolation level of *Repeatable Read* (RR) or *Read Stability* (RS), as described in Section 2.9.1. These isolation levels cause the system to acquire locks on the rows that you fetch, to guarantee that if you close the cursor and reopen it later, the rows will be unchanged. These locks are ordinarily held until the end of a transaction, but you can release them earlier by closing a cursor WITH RELEASE.

2.7.10 Single-Row SELECT and VALUES Statements

As we have seen, the usual way to retrieve data from the database into a host program is to write a query specifying the data to be retrieved, declare a cursor for the query, open the cursor, and fetch the rows of the result set into host variables. In some cases, however, you may know that the result of your query consists of a single row. For example, if your query invokes a column function such as SUM or AVG (and does not have a GROUP BY clause), it will always return exactly one row of data. In a case like this, it seems unnecessary to declare a cursor, open it, fetch one row, and then close the cursor.

V2 provides a shortcut method for retrieving the result of a query into a list of host variables when the query is known to return no more than one row.

---

17. The WITH RELEASE clause on a CLOSE statement is supported beginning with DB2 Version 2.1.1.

The method is called a *single-row SELECT statement* (or, if the query consists of a literal table, a *single-row VALUES statement*).

A single-row SELECT statement is simply a query block, with an INTO clause following the SELECT clause to specify the host variables into which the result is to be delivered. The query block is executed, and if the result is a single row, the row is delivered into the host variables in the INTO clause. If the result set of the query is empty, SQLCODE +100 and SQLSTATE 02000 are returned and the host variables are unchanged. If the result set consists of more than one row, an error results.

A single-row VALUES statement is a literal table consisting of a single row, followed by an INTO clause that specifies the host variables into which the row is to be delivered. A single-row VALUES statement might be used, for example, to retrieve the current date and time into host program variables. Like a single-row SELECT, a single-row VALUES statement raises an error if the literal table contains more than one row. A literal table used in a single-row VALUES statement cannot contain a NULL column, unless the null value is given an explicit datatype by a CAST expression (discussed in Section 3.1).

Of course, single-row SELECT and single-row VALUES statements can be used only by embedding them in host programs, prefixed by EXEC SQL. The syntax of the single-row statements is shown on the next page.

The following example finds the total number of gears on hand and on order, and delivers these numbers into two host variables with null indicators. If there are no rows in the PARTS table whose descriptions satisfy the LIKE predicate, the column functions will return null values.

```
EXEC SQL
    SELECT sum(qonhand), sum(qonorder)
    INTO :gearsonhand :indic1, :gearsonorder :indic2
    FROM parts
    WHERE description LIKE '%Gear%';
```

The following example retrieves the current date and time into two host variables:

```
EXEC SQL
    VALUES(CURRENT DATE, CURRENT TIME)
    INTO :today, :rightnow;
```

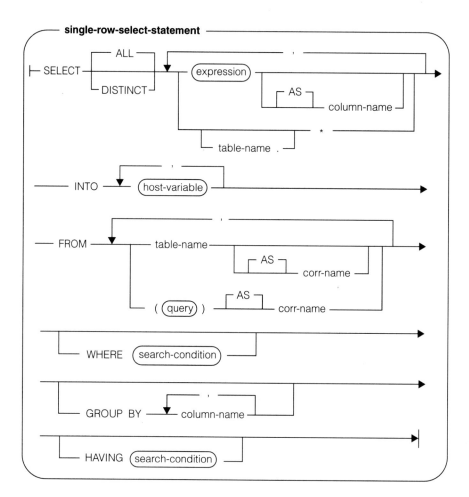

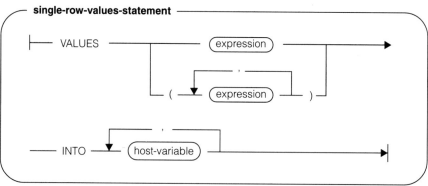

2.7.11 Positioned UPDATE and DELETE Statements

In addition to their use in retrieving query results into host programs, cursors can play a role in updating and deleting rows of data in the database. A special form of the UPDATE statement, called a *positioned UPDATE statement*, can be used to update exactly one row in the database, based on the position of a cursor. In a positioned update, instead of a search condition, the WHERE clause contains the phrase "CURRENT OF" followed by a cursor name. The statement updates the single row on which the named cursor is positioned. Similarly, the DELETE statement has a special form called a *positioned DELETE statement*, which names a cursor in the WHERE clause and deletes the single row on which this cursor is positioned.

Apart from their method of finding the row to be updated or deleted, positioned UPDATE and DELETE statements behave exactly the same as UPDATE and DELETE statements that contain a search condition. In fact, rather than drawing a special syntax diagram for the positioned statements, we will simply refer to the syntax diagrams for the UPDATE statement on page 78 and for the DELETE statement on page 81. To convert these diagrams into syntax diagrams for positioned UPDATE and DELETE statements, simply replace the WHERE clause with the following "positioned" WHERE clause:

The following are some examples of positioned statements. (Remember that the prefix EXEC SQL is required before any statement that is embedded in a host program.)

- Update the row of the QUOTATIONS table on which the cursor C10 is positioned.

```
EXEC SQL
   UPDATE quotations
   SET price = 900,
       responsetime = 14
   WHERE CURRENT OF c10;
```

- Delete the row of the SUPPLIERS table on which the cursor C20 is positioned.

```
EXEC SQL
   DELETE FROM suppliers
   WHERE CURRENT OF c20;
```

When the row on which a cursor is positioned is deleted, the cursor's position becomes "before" the next row of the result set (or, if there is no next row, "after" the last row of the result set). Note that a positioned delete is one way (but not the only way) in which the row on which a cursor is positioned might be deleted.

In order to be used in a positioned UPDATE or DELETE statement, a cursor must meet certain requirements. Some of these requirements pertain to the cursor itself, and some pertain to the query that is associated with the cursor (in its DECLARE CURSOR statement), which we will refer to as the *cursor query*. The purpose of these requirements is to make sure that the current row of the cursor uniquely identifies a row in the database that can be updated or deleted. The requirements are as follows:

1. The cursor query must have exactly one table or view in its FROM clause, and this must be the same table or view that is named in the positioned UPDATE or DELETE statement. If it is a view, it must not be a read-only view (defined in Section 2.8.4).

2. The cursor query may not contain any of the following features, which make it impossible to identify a unique row in the database that corresponds to the current row of the cursor:

   - DISTINCT, GROUP BY, HAVING, or ORDER BY
   - A column function such as AVG, MAX, MIN, SUM, COUNT, STDEV, or VARIANCE
   - A set operator such as UNION, INTERSECT, or EXCEPT, with or without the ALL option

3. The cursor must be open and positioned on a row.

4. The cursor declaration should include a FOR UPDATE clause.[18] In the case of a positioned update, the FOR UPDATE clause must include the names of the columns to be updated (or it may omit the column list, implicitly applying to all columns).

---

18. This is a piece of friendly advice rather than an absolute requirement. If your program was precompiled with the LANGLEVEL MIA option, a positioned update or delete can be applied to a cursor that was not declared FOR UPDATE. However, the safest and most efficient thing to do is to declare your cursor FOR UPDATE whenever you plan to use positioned statements.

2.7.12 Using Cursors with the Command Line Processor

Since one of the purposes of a cursor is to deliver the rows of a query result, one at a time, into host program variables, you might expect cursors to be used only in application programs with embedded SQL. Surprisingly, however, the CLP can be used to execute cursor declarations, OPEN, FETCH, and CLOSE statements, and positioned updates and deletes. Of course, when one of these statements is submitted to the CLP, it is not prefixed by EXEC SQL, and it may not contain any host variables.

Using a cursor in an interactive CLP session gives you an opportunity to examine the result of a query, one row at a time, updating the rows as you examine them. It can also be useful to debug some cursor logic by running it in the CLP before embedding it in an application program. In the following example, we use the CLP to examine the rows of the PARTS table and to update one of the rows after examining it:

```
UPDATE COMMAND OPTIONS USING c OFF;
DECLARE c1 CURSOR FOR
    SELECT partno, qonhand, qonorder
    FROM parts
    FOR UPDATE OF qonorder;
OPEN c1;
FETCH c1;
FETCH c1;
FETCH c1;
UPDATE parts
    SET qonorder = qonorder + 25
    WHERE CURRENT OF c1;
CLOSE c1;
COMMIT;
```

TIP: All operations on a cursor—including DECLARE, OPEN, FETCH, and CLOSE—must take place within a single transaction, unless the cursor is declared WITH HOLD. Therefore, in order to use cursors in the CLP, you must either declare them WITH HOLD or turn off the "autocommit" feature, which places each statement in its own transaction. In the above example, we have turned autocommit off by using an UPDATE COMMAND OPTIONS statement. When you have turned autocommit off, you must end your own transaction by a COMMIT or ROLLBACK statement. This is the purpose of the last statement in the above example. (Transactions are discussed in Section 2.9.1.)

2.7.13 Compound SQL

When an application program runs on a client machine, each SQL statement is ordinarily sent in a separate message to the server machine to be executed. To reduce message traffic and improve efficiency, V2 provides a way for a program to wrap two or more SQL statements into a bundle and send the bundle to the server in a single message. The bundle is called a *compound SQL statement*. Compound statements can be used to improve the performance of applications that need to perform several related updates without interacting with the database during the update sequence.

Compound SQL statements always have the *static* property, which means that the values of all the input host variables in the individual SQL statements are bound before any of the statements are executed. This means that host variables cannot be used to pass information from one individual statement to another inside a compound SQL statement. The reason for this restriction is obvious: the values of host variables do not change until the end of the compound statement, because results are not returned to the client machine by the individual statements inside the compound statement. If more than one of the individual statements assigns a value to the same host variable, the host variable retains the last value that was assigned to it.

The programmer who writes a compound SQL statement must specify whether the statement is *atomic* or *not atomic*. If it is atomic, all the individual statements inside the compound statement are rolled back if any individual statement fails. If it is not atomic, then changes made by successful statements within the compound statement remain effective even if other statements in the same compound statement are not successful. Atomic compound statements are accepted by V2 servers but not by other database servers reached by DRDA connections.

The syntax of a compound SQL statement is as follows:

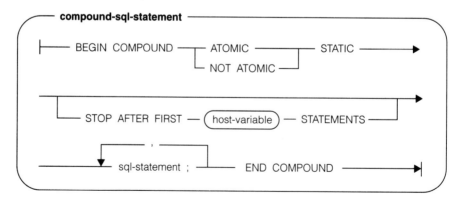

Example:

```
EXEC SQL
  BEGIN COMPOUND ATOMIC STATIC
    INSERT INTO orders(suppno, partno, quantity, orderdate)
      VALUES(:s, :p, :q, CURRENT DATE);
    UPDATE parts
      SET qonorder = qonorder + :q
      WHERE partno = :p;
  END COMPOUND;
```

Compound SQL statements may not be nested inside each other. Dynamic SQL statements (PREPARE, DESCRIBE), operations on cursors (OPEN, FETCH, CLOSE), and statements that affect database connections (CONNECT, RELEASE) are not allowed inside compound statements. A compound statement may contain a COMMIT as its last individual statement, but it may not contain a ROLLBACK. (The COMMIT and ROLLBACK statements are discussed in Section 2.9.1.)

As shown in the above syntax diagram, an application program can specify that only a certain number of the individual statements within a compound statement are to be executed, providing this number in a host variable in a STOP AFTER clause.

Like all SQL statements embedded in host programs, a compound SQL statement returns an SQLCA structure indicating its outcome. If one or more of the individual statements within the compound statement returns an error or warning condition, the errors and warnings are combined inside the SQLCA structure using a scheme described in the *DB2 SQL Reference*.

2.7.14 Example Program PARTS1: Ordering Parts

As an example of embedded SQL, we will write a C program that interacts with users to process requests for parts, using the tables in our warehouse database. Our program prompts the user for a description of the parts needed. It then finds all part numbers that meet this description and, for each such part number, asks the user how many parts are needed and how soon they are needed. If the need can be met by parts that are in stock, the program simply updates its records accordingly. If, on the other hand, it is necessary to order a new supply, the program finds the supplier who can supply the parts within the required time limit at minimum cost and places an order with this supplier. After finding and processing all the parts that meet the user's description, the program prompts the user for another part description.

The PARTS1 program on page 114 consists of nine steps.

Steps for Example Program PARTS1: Ordering Parts

STEP 1: The program embeds the required header file `sqlenv.h`, which provides declarations for the symbols, structures, and interfaces used in embedded SQL.
The file `sqlenv.h` is found in the directory `sqllib/include`, and it in turn
embeds several other header files found in the same directory. In our example,
we also use the statement `INCLUDE SQLCA`, which declares a structure named
`sqlca` to contain return codes.

STEP 2: The SQL Declare Section contains host language declarations of all host variables used in embedded SQL statements, using the C-language datatypes listed
in Table 2-5. Also at the beginning of the program, we declare a cursor named
C1 to represent a query on the PARTS table. Each time this cursor is opened, it
binds the value of the input variable `:userdescrip` and finds all the parts
that match this description (using a LIKE predicate to allow for approximate
matches). Since we plan to use this cursor for a positioned update, it includes
a FOR UPDATE clause.

Code for Example Program PARTS1: Ordering Parts

```
/*
**   STEP 1: Include some header files
*/
#include <stdlib.h>
#include <string.h>
#include <stdio.h>
#include <sqlenv.h>

EXEC SQL INCLUDE SQLCA;

void main()
   {
   /*
   **   STEP 2: Declare some host variables and a cursor
   */
   EXEC SQL BEGIN DECLARE SECTION;
      char  dbname[9] = "partsdb";   /* name of database              */
      char  partno[5];               /* part number                   */
      long  qonhand;                 /* quantity on hand              */
      long  qonorder;                /* quantity on order             */
      long  qneeded;                 /* quantity needed               */
      long  rneeded;                 /* response time needed (days)   */
      long  shortfall;               /* qty. needed minus qty. available */
      long  bestprice;               /* best qualifying price for part */
      short priceIndicator;          /* -1 (null) if no qualifying quotes */
      char  bestsuppno[4];           /* supplier no. with best price  */
      char  userdescrip[21];         /* user's description of part    */
      char  actualdescrip[21];       /* actual description of part    */
      char  msgbuffer[500];          /* buffer for DB2 error message  */
      short moreToDo = 1;            /* 1 until program is ready to exit */
   EXEC SQL END DECLARE SECTION;

   EXEC SQL DECLARE C1 CURSOR FOR
      SELECT partno, description, qonhand, qonorder
      FROM parts
      WHERE description LIKE '%' || :userdescrip || '%'
      FOR UPDATE OF qonhand, qonorder;
```

STEP 3: The WHENEVER statement specifies the label to which control will pass in the event of an unexpected return code from an SQL statement. After establishing this error handler, we are ready to connect to the PARTS database and to prompt the user for a description of the first part needed.

STEP 4: The While-loop will execute as long as the user keeps responding to the prompt with more part descriptions. Each time the user enters a new part description, we open cursor C1 and fetch the first part that meets the new description. We use a LIKE predicate in searching for part descriptions, so if the user enters "Wheel" we might find parts with descriptions such as "Small Wheel," "Red Wheel," and "Wheel Cover." If no matching part is found, the FETCH statement returns SQLSTATE 02000.

STEP 5: For each part that matches the user's description, we prompt the user for the number needed and the deadline. We then compute the "shortfall": the amount by which the number of parts needed exceeds the number of parts that are on hand. If there is no shortfall, we simply update the PARTS table (using a positioned update) to indicate that the requested parts have been removed from the warehouse. A more sophisticated version of the program might try to meet the user's needs from orders that have already been placed for the desired part but that have not yet arrived, taking into account the expected delivery times of these orders.

```
/*
**  STEP 3: Establish an error-handler and connect to the database
*/
EXEC SQL WHENEVER SQLERROR GO TO badnews;

EXEC SQL CONNECT TO :dbname;

printf("\nEnter one-word description of parts needed:");
scanf("%s", userdescrip);

/*
**  STEP 4: For each description entered by the user, open the
**  cursor and fetch the matching parts
*/
while (moreToDo)
   {
   EXEC SQL OPEN C1;

   EXEC SQL FETCH C1
      INTO :partno, :actualdescrip, :qonhand, :qonorder;

   if (!strncmp(sqlca.sqlstate, "02000", 5))
      {
      printf("Sorry, no parts meet that description.\n");
      }

   /*
   **  STEP 5: For each matching part, prompt the user for how
   **  many are needed and how soon
   */
   while(strncmp(sqlca.sqlstate, "02000", 5))
      {
      printf("\nPart number %s is a %s.\n", partno, actualdescrip);
      printf("Enter quantity needed and how soon (in days): ");
      scanf("%d %d", &qneeded, &rneeded);

      if (qneeded > 0)
         {
         shortfall = qneeded - qonhand;

         if (shortfall <= 0)
            {
            EXEC SQL
               UPDATE parts
               SET qonhand = qonhand - :qneeded
               WHERE CURRENT OF C1;
```

STEP 6: If the parts on hand are not enough to meet the user's needs, we need to place an order for more parts. In this step, we find the minimum price in the QUOTA-TIONS table from any supplier who can supply the kind of part needed within the designated time. If no qualifying quotation exists (the minimum price is null), we print a message and prompt the user for another part description.

STEP 7: At this point, we know that we need to place an order for parts, and we know the lowest price that meets our requirements. It is time to generate the order. One complication remains: it's possible that the lowest price might be available from more than one supplier. In this step, we arbitrarily choose the supplier with the lowest supplier number, among all the suppliers who are tied for lowest price. We print a message indicating the order to be placed, and we insert a record of this order into the ORDERS table. We also update the PARTS table (using a positioned update) to reflect the new parts that are on order.

As an exercise for the reader, how could the SELECT statement in Step 7 be modified so that, if several qualifying quotations are tied for lowest price, the statement chooses the quotation with the fastest response time? (Remember that more than one quotation might be tied for both lowest price and fastest response.)

```
        printf("\nYour request has been filled from inventory.\n");
        }

else
    {
    /*
    **   STEP 6: Find the minimum-cost supplier
    */
    EXEC SQL
        SELECT min(price) into :bestprice :priceIndicator
        FROM quotations
        WHERE partno = :partno
        AND responsetime <= :rneeded;

    if (priceIndicator < 0)
        {
        printf("\nSorry, no supplier can fill your request.\n");
        }
    else
        {
        /*
        **   STEP 7: Generate an order and update the database
        */
        EXEC SQL
          SELECT min(suppno) into :bestsuppno
          FROM quotations
          WHERE partno = :partno
          AND price = :bestprice
          AND responsetime <= :rneeded;

        printf("Place an order with supplier  %s ", bestsuppno);
        printf("for part %s, quantity %d\n", partno, shortfall);
        EXEC SQL
          INSERT INTO orders
          VALUES(:bestsuppno, :partno, :shortfall, CURRENT DATE);

        EXEC SQL
          UPDATE parts
          SET qonorder = qonorder + :shortfall
          WHERE CURRENT OF C1;
        }   /* end of case where a good quotation is found */

    }   /* end of case where an order is needed */

}   /* end of case where qneeded > 0 */
```

STEP 8: After processing all the rows returned by cursor C1 (that is, all the parts that meet the user's description), we close the cursor and commit our database changes, making them permanent. We then prompt the user for another part description and provide the opportunity to exit from the program.

STEP 9: The label badnews identifies the handler for unexpected return codes from SQL statements. This handler uses the sqlaintp utility routine to retrieve the message associated with the failing SQL statement, and then prints the message. For example, if the PARTS1 package were to be deleted from the database for some reason, the program would print the following message:

```
Unexpected return code from DB2.
Message: SQL0805N  Package "YOURNAME.PARTS1" was not found.
SQLSTATE=51002
```

```
            EXEC SQL FETCH C1
                INTO :partno, :actualdescrip, :qonhand, :qonorder;

            }   /* end of loop while matching parts are found */

        /*
        **  STEP 8: Close the cursor, commit the updates, and prompt
        **  the user for a new part description
        */
        EXEC SQL CLOSE C1;

        EXEC SQL COMMIT;

        printf("\nEnter description of next part, or Q to quit: ");
        scanf("%s", userdescrip);
        if (!strcmp(userdescrip, "Q"))
            {
            moreToDo = 0;
            printf("Goodbye, come back soon!\n");
            }

        }   /* end of loop while more to do */

    EXEC SQL CONNECT RESET;
    return;

badnews:
    /*
    **  STEP 9: Handler for bad return codes.
    **  Retrieves and prints an error message.
    */
    printf("Unexpected return code from DB2.\n");
    sqlaintp(msgbuffer, 500, 70, &sqlca);
    printf("Message: %s\n", msgbuffer);
    return;

    }       /* end of main */
```

2.7.15 Compiling, Binding, and Executing Application Programs

You can prepare an application program to run on V2 by using the Software Developer's Kit (SDK), either on a server machine or on a client machine. The process of preparing a program for execution consists of several steps, as discussed in Section 1.2.4 and illustrated by Figure 1-6. In this section, we will discuss how these steps might be applied to the PARTS1 program in Section 2.7.14. As usual, our example is based on the C host language; similar steps apply to other programming languages and are described in the manual called *DB2 Software Developer's Kit: Building Your Applications* for your platform.

1. Of course, the first step in creating an application is to write the program. We will assume that the program described in Section 2.7.14 exists in a file named parts1.sqc.

2. In order to install your program for use with a particular database, it is first necessary to connect to the database. Suppose that the database that you plan to use is named SUPPLIES. You might use the following command to connect to this database:

   ```
   db2 CONNECT TO supplies;
   ```

   (The CONNECT command is described further in Section 2.9.2.)

3. Next, you need to invoke the V2 precompiler to scan your program for embedded SQL statements and to generate an optimized access plan for each statement. This might be done by the following command:

   ```
   db2 PREP parts1.sqc;
   ```

   The PREP command has many options, which are documented in the *DB2 Command Reference*. When invoked with no options, as in the example above, it produces a *package* containing the access plans for the SQL statements in your program and stores the package in the database to which you are connected. The precompiler also generates a pure C-language file named parts1.c, based on your parts1.sqc file, with the SQL statements replaced by calls that will cause DB2 to execute the plans contained in the package.

   The process of generating a package for your program is called *binding* the program. During binding, all the names of tables and other objects in your program are resolved to specific objects in the database. If your SQL statements contain syntactic errors, or if your program attempts to access objects that do not exist in the database, binding will be unsuccessful and you will receive some error messages.

If you want the precompiler to generate a bind file as well as a package for your program, you can invoke it using the BINDFILE option, as in the following example:

```
db2 PREP parts1.sqc BINDFILE PACKAGE;
```

In addition to the package and the C program, this command will produce a file named `parts1.bnd` that can be used later to rebind your program without invoking the precompiler (rebinding is discussed in Section 2.7.16).

TIP: Invoking the precompiler with the BINDFILE option will suppress the production of a package unless you also specify the PACKAGE option.

4. After precompiling your program, the next step is to compile the resulting C program and link it together with other programs or library functions to make an executable file. Your application may consist of several C files, each containing its own embedded SQL statements. The files can be precompiled and compiled separately and then linked together. Of course, exactly one of the files must contain a `main()` function.

Since the file generated by the precompiler is a pure C program, it can be compiled and linked by the same methods that you usually use for handling C programs. The specific commands for these tasks depend on the compiler and operating system platform that you are using. The following are examples of how you might compile and link your program. For more information about compiling and linking, consult your compiler documentation or *DB2 Software Developer's Kit: Building Your Applications* for your platform.

- *If you are using the IBM CSet++ compiler under AIX:*

  Your compiler needs access to the include files (such as `sqlenv.h`) that are needed for interfacing with the database. These are usually installed in the directory `/usr/lpp/db2_02_01/include`. Similarly, the linker needs access to the database libraries that are usually installed in the directory `/usr/lpp/db2_02_01/lib`. The following commands might be used to compile and link the program `parts1.c`:

  ```
  xlC -I/usr/lpp/db2_02_01/include -c parts1.c
  xlC -o parts1 parts1.o -ldb2 -L/usr/lpp/db2_02_01/lib
  ```

- *If you are using the IBM CSet++ or VisualAge compiler under OS/2:*

  To enable the compiler and linker to find the necessary include files and database libraries, you should include the following commands in your CONFIG.SYS file or in some command file that you execute before compiling database applications:

  ```
  set INCLUDE=%DB2PATH%\include;%INCLUDE%
  set LIB=%DB2PATH%\lib;%LIB%
  ```

The following commands might be used to compile and link the program parts1.c:

```
icc -C+ -O- -Ti+ parts1.c
link386 /NOI /DEBUG /ST:32000 /PM:VIO parts1.obj ,,,db2api;
```

- *If you are using the Microsoft Visual C++ compiler under Windows NT:*

  To enable the linker to find the necessary database libraries, you should include the following command in your CONFIG.SYS file or in some .BAT file that you execute before compiling database applications:

  ```
  set LIB=%DB2PATH%\lib;%LIB%
  ```

  The following commands might be used to compile and link the program parts1.c:

```
cl -Z7 -Od -c -W2 -D_X86=1 -DWIN32 -I%DB2PATH%\include parts1.c
link -debug:full -debugtype:cv -out:parts1.exe parts1.obj db2api.lib
```

5. After you have precompiled, compiled, and linked your program, it is ready to run. Like any other application, it can be invoked simply by typing its name on the operating system command line, as follows:

```
parts1
```

TIP: V2 provides command files that can be used to simplify the process of "building" (precompiling, compiling, and linking) your application programs. You should take a look at these files and decide whether they are helpful in your environment. Before using the command files, you may need to edit them to delete the reference to util.o, a utility program that is used in some of the programming examples shipped with V2. The command files are described in *DB2 Software Developer's Kit: Building Your Applications* and are found in the following places:

- Under AIX, the shell script sqllib/samples/c/bldxlc can be used for building C programs, and sqllib/samples/c/bldcset can be used for building C++ programs.

- Under OS/2, the command file sqllib\samples\c\bldcspp2.cmd can be used for building C++ programs and can be modified and used for building C programs.

- Under Windows NT, the file sqllib\lib\bldcspp2.bat can be used for building C++ programs and can be modified and used for building C programs.

2.7.16 Rebinding Packages

The package that is stored in the database for your program contains the best access plan that the system could find for your SQL statements at the time your program was bound. However, over a period of time, database changes may occur that would lead to a different access plan if your program were to be bound again. These changes fall into the following general categories:

1. A package may contain access plans that make use of certain physical structures such as indexes. If an index is dropped that is used by a given package, that package is marked *invalid* and its access plans are automatically replaced by new access plans the next time the package is invoked. This process, called *implicit rebind,* is transparent to the user except for a slight delay caused by generating the new plans and possibly for a change in the performance of the application.

   The loss of an index used by a package is not too serious, because the optimizer will always be able to find an alternate access plan that does not require the missing index. However, a package may be more severely affected if one of the tables it accesses is dropped or one of the privileges it depends on is revoked. If one of these events should occur, the system will mark the package invalid and will attempt to implicitly rebind it when it is next invoked. If the table or privilege has not been restored, the implicit rebind will fail and the application program will receive an error code each time it tries to execute an SQL statement.

2. It is also possible that, after your package is created, a new index might be created that would improve the performance of your program. The system will *not* automatically detect this condition and revise your package to take advantage of the new index. If you wish your package to take advantage of the latest indexes, you must explicitly rebind it, using one of the methods described below.

3. Some of the SQL statements in your program may contain calls to scalar functions such as `length` or to column functions such as `avg`. As we will see in Chapter 4, V2 allows users to write functions of their own that can be used in SQL statements in the same way as the system-provided functions. In fact, the system allows several functions to be created with the same name but different argument datatypes, such as `foo(Integer)` and `foo(Float)`. When a

program is bound, a process called *function resolution* finds the actual functions that most closely match the function calls in the program and uses these functions in the access plan for the program. However, if one of the functions selected is a user-defined function, it is possible that this function may later be dropped. If this happens, the package is placed into an *inoperative* state. An inoperative package cannot be used until it is explicitly rebound, using one of the methods described below. Explicitly rebinding a package repeats the function-resolution process, possibly choosing different functions from those originally selected. For example, if the function foo(Integer) is dropped, the system might select an alternative function foo(Float) and invoke it by promoting the argument. However, the system will not perform this kind of substitution unless you explicitly rebind your package. This policy, called *conservative binding semantics*, protects you against unexpected changes in the behavior of a program.

There are three ways to explicitly rebind a package, which are summarized below. In order to use any of these methods, you must be connected to the database in which the package is bound.

1. The fastest and most straightforward way to explicitly rebind a package is by using the REBIND command. The REBIND command takes only one parameter: the name of the package to be rebound. It does not require the existence of a bind file. It operates directly on the package that is stored in the database, which contains a copy of the original SQL statements from which it was created. These statements are rebound into a new package, using exactly the same options that were in effect when the package was last bound. In the rebind process, all table and function names are resolved from scratch and new access plans are generated for all the SQL statements in the package. The following is an example of a REBIND command for the parts1 program:

   ```
   REBIND parts1
   ```

2. If you created a bind file when you precompiled your program, you can use the BIND command to rebind this file. You might choose to use BIND rather than REBIND if you want to change one of the options with which your program was bound, such as its isolation level (discussed in Section 2.9.1). The following is an example of a BIND command that might be used to change the isolation level of the parts1 program:

   ```
   BIND parts1 ISOLATION RS
   ```

3. If you make any changes to the source code of your program, you must invoke the precompiler again, as in the following example:

```
PREP parts1.sqc
```

The following is a summary of the reasons why you might choose to explicitly rebind a package using one of the above three methods:

- To take advantage of new indexes created since your package was bound.

- To take advantage of the latest statistics gathered on database tables, which might have changed their size or distribution in such a way that a different access plan would be optimal.

- To explicitly perform function resolution in order to take advantage of a new user-defined function created since your package was bound, or to rescue your package from an inoperative state due to the dropping of a user-defined function.

- To avoid the delay in invoking your application that would occur if you allowed an invalid package to be automatically rebound by the system.

- To change one or more of the options with which your package was bound, such as its isolation level.

TIP: You can list all the packages in the database that belong to you, as well as their current state of validity (valid, invalid, or inoperative) by typing the command LIST PACKAGES to the CLP.

2.7.17 Embedding SQL Statements in C++ Programs

Since C++ is a superset of C, all the techniques used to embed SQL statements in C programs can be used in C++ programs also. In fact, the same precompiler (invoked by the same PREP command) is used to process both C and C++ programs with embedded SQL statements. The convention for filename extensions used by the V2 precompiler is shown in Table 2-6.

When you declare a C++ class, you can declare the data members of the class as host variables by including them in an SQL Declare Section inside the class definition. You can then write SQL statements inside the member functions of the class, using the host variables that are data members of that class. Each time such a host variable is used in an SQL statement, it is implicitly qualified by the "this" pointer that identifies the object whose member function is being executed.

The use of SQL statements in the member functions of a C++ class is illustrated by the example C++ program named PARTS2. This program defines a class named Request. Each instance of the Request class represents a request

TABLE 2-6: Filename Convention for C and C++ Programs

File	Extension Under OS/2 and Windows NT	Extension Under AIX and Other Unix Platforms
C program with embedded SQL (input to precompiler)	.sqc	.sqc
Pure C program (output of precompiler)	.c	.c
C++ program with embedded SQL (input to precompiler)	.sqx	.sqC
Pure C++ program (output of precompiler)	.cxx	.C

for a certain number of parts with a given part number. Since the member functions of the Request class need to interact with the database, the data members of the Request class (partno and qneeded) are placed inside an SQL Declare Section.

The Request class has a member function named howSoon(), which returns an integer indicating how soon the request can be satisfied. If the desired parts are already on hand, howSoon() returns zero. If the parts can be ordered, howSoon() returns the minimum response time for the given part available from any supplier. If the part number is unknown or no quotations exist for it, howSoon() returns –1. In order to compute its return value, how-Soon() contains two SQL statements that query the PARTS and QUOTA-TIONS tables. The howSoon() member function uses the data members of the Request class (implicitly qualified by the "this" pointer) as host variables, and also declares some additional host variables in an SQL Declare Section of its own.

The Request class also has another member function named howMuch(), which returns an integer indicating the minimum cost of the requested parts (zero if they are already on hand, –1 if no price quotations are available for the given part number). Like the howSoon() function, howMuch() has its own SQL Declare Section and contains SQL statements that query the PARTS and QUO-TATIONS tables using data members of the Request class as host variables.

Example C++ Program PARTS2: Processing Requests for Parts

```cpp
#include <stdlib.h>
#include <string.h>
#include <sqlenv.h>
#include <iostream.h>

EXEC SQL INCLUDE SQLCA;

class Request
   {

   // private data members:
   EXEC SQL BEGIN DECLARE SECTION;
      char partno[5];      // part number of part needed
      long qneeded;        // quantity of part needed
   EXEC SQL END DECLARE SECTION;

public:                             // methods

   Request(char *p, long q)      // constructor method
      {
      strncpy(partno, p, 5);
      qneeded = q;
      }

   long howSoon()                 // minimum time to get parts
      {
      EXEC SQL BEGIN DECLARE SECTION;
         long qonhand1;
         long mintime;
      EXEC SQL END DECLARE SECTION;

      EXEC SQL
         SELECT qonhand INTO :qonhand1
         FROM parts WHERE partno = :partno;
      if (SQLCODE != 0) return -1;
      if (qonhand1 >= qneeded) return 0;

      EXEC SQL
         SELECT min(responsetime) INTO :mintime
         FROM quotations WHERE partno = :partno;
```

```
        if (SQLCODE != 0) return -1;
        else return mintime;
        }                  // end of howSoon method

    long howMuch()                     // minimum cost of parts
        {
        EXEC SQL BEGIN DECLARE SECTION;
            long qonhand2;
            long minprice;
        EXEC SQL END DECLARE SECTION;

        EXEC SQL
            SELECT qonhand INTO :qonhand2
            FROM parts WHERE partno = :partno;
        if (SQLCODE != 0) return -1;
        if (qonhand2 >= qneeded) return 0;

        EXEC SQL
            SELECT min(price) INTO :minprice
            FROM quotations WHERE partno = :partno;
        if (SQLCODE != 0) return -1;
        else return minprice * qneeded;
        }          // end of howMuch method

    };          // end of class Request

void main()
    {
    long time, cost;
    Request *rq1;

    EXEC SQL CONNECT TO partsdb;

    // Create a Request object
    rq1 = new Request("P231", 5);

    // Invoke the howSoon and howMuch methods of the Request object
    time = rq1->howSoon();
    cost = rq1->howMuch();
    cout << endl << "Request 1:" << endl;
    if (time < 0 || cost < 0)
        cout << "    Sorry, I have no information about that part number"
            << endl;
```

```
else cout << "   Min time is " << time
          << " days, Min. cost is " << cost << " dollars" << endl;

EXEC SQL COMMIT;

EXEC SQL CONNECT RESET;
return;

}         // end of main()
```

2.8 DATA DEFINITION

The *data definition statements* of SQL are those statements that create and destroy database objects such as tables. Some data definition statements also alter the structure of an existing object, as in adding a column to a table. This chapter discusses data definition statements that operate on the following kinds of objects:

- *Tables*, which contain all the information stored in the database
- *Aliases*, which are alternative names for tables
- *Views*, which are "virtual" tables that are derived in some way from the real stored tables
- *Indexes*, which help the system to access data quickly, provide an ordering on the rows of a table, and enforce the uniqueness of the values in a table

This chapter also briefly discusses a subject called *normalization*, which provides some guidelines for good table design.

The system automatically maintains a set of tables, called *catalog tables*, that contain descriptions of all the objects in the database. Data definition statements automatically cause updates to these tables. (The catalog tables are described in Appendix D.)

TIP: Data definition statements can be executed either via the CLP or by embedding them in application programs. However, data definition statements embedded in application programs can lead to some confusing situations. As an example, consider a C program containing SQL statements to create a table and insert some data into the table. When processing this program, the precompiler will try to generate an access plan for the INSERT statement but will fail, because the table does not yet exist. As a general rule, an object cannot be created and used in the same program without using one of the dynamic SQL techniques described in Chapter 6. To keep things simple, it is best to keep data definition statements separate from your application programs and to execute them using the CLP.

2.8.1 CREATE TABLE Statement

Since tables are the basic objects that are used to store information in V2, the most fundamental data definition statement is the CREATE TABLE statement. The basic job of a CREATE TABLE statement is to specify the name of the table to be created and the names and datatypes of all its columns. In addition, the statement can optionally specify that certain columns of the table do not accept null values and that one or more columns constitute the *primary key* of the table. Primary key columns never accept null values, and the values of the primary key columns uniquely identify a row of the table.

In addition to the "basic" features described above, a CREATE TABLE statement can control the placement of the table in physical storage and can specify constraints on the data values to be stored in the table. Discussion of these CREATE TABLE features is deferred until Chapter 5. For now, I will give examples of the CREATE TABLE statements that might be used to create the tables in our sample database. Using these examples as templates and choosing datatypes from Table 2-1 and Table 2-2, you can create simple tables of your own. If you want to "peek ahead" at the full syntax for CREATE TABLE, it can be found on page 335.

```
CREATE TABLE parts
   (partno Char(4) NOT NULL PRIMARY KEY,
    description Varchar(20),
    qonhand Integer,
    qonorder Integer);
CREATE TABLE quotations
   (suppno Char(3) NOT NULL,
    partno Char(4) NOT NULL,
    price Integer,
    responsetime Integer,
    PRIMARY KEY (suppno, partno) );
CREATE TABLE orders
   (suppno Char(3) NOT NULL,
    partno Char(4) NOT NULL,
    quantity Integer,
    orderdate Date);
```

```
CREATE TABLE suppliers
   (suppno Char(3) NOT NULL PRIMARY KEY,
    name Varchar(35),
    address Varchar(35) );
```

As you can see from the examples, a CREATE TABLE statement contains a parenthesized list of column names with a datatype specified for each column. If a column does not accept null values, the phrase NOT NULL is specified after its datatype. An optional PRIMARY KEY clause identifies the columns that constitute the primary key of the table. Every column that is identified as part of the primary key must also have a NOT NULL designation (though you might suppose that the system could figure this out for itself).

If the table name in a CREATE TABLE statement is unqualified, the new table is given a schema name equal to the current authid. A table can also be given an explicit schema name, as in the following example, which creates a table in the ACCOUNTS schema:

```
CREATE TABLE accounts.receivable
   (invoiceno Char(6) NOT NULL PRIMARY KEY,
    customername Varchar(20),
    address Varchar(50),
    amountdue Decimal(8,2) NOT NULL,
    datebilled Date NOT NULL,
    datedue Date NOT NULL);
```

When you create a table, a description of the table is stored in the system catalog table named TABLES and descriptions of its columns are stored in the catalog table named COLUMNS.

2.8.2 ALTER TABLE Statement

A column can be added to an existing table by an ALTER TABLE statement. Any existing rows in the table receive a default value for the new column. The ALTER TABLE statement can also be used to add or delete constraints on the values that can be stored in the table. As in the case of CREATE TABLE, an example of an ALTER TABLE is given here, but a detailed discussion of this statement is deferred until Chapter 5, by which time you will have a better understanding of constraints. (If you want to peek ahead, the syntax for an ALTER TABLE statement is shown on page 341.)

Suppose that, after creation of the ACCOUNTS.RECEIVABLE table above, our accounting department decides to add a column named STATUS to the table. This might be done by the following statement:

```
ALTER TABLE accounts.receivable
    ADD COLUMN status Varchar(18);
```

All existing rows in the ACCOUNTS.RECEIVABLE table at the time when the ALTER TABLE statement is executed receive null values for the new STATUS column, since no other default value was specified by the ALTER TABLE statement. (Default values and other features of the ALTER TABLE statement are discussed further in Section 5.2.2.)

2.8.3 Aliases

Suppose that you need to develop a new application program that operates on the PARTS table. During the development process you might need to run the program against a test table without interfering with the production data in your real parts inventory. Then, when the program is debugged and ready to go into production, you would like to easily switch the program to operate on the real PARTS table. Even after a program is in production, you may sometimes need to change the table on which the program operates, without changing the logic of the program.

Of course, you can always edit your source program and change all its table names. But this process is time-consuming and prone to error. V2 provides a better way, called *aliases*, to control the table on which a program operates. An alias is simply a table name that substitutes for another table name, called the *target* of the alias. Whenever an alias is used in an SQL statement, it is equivalent to using the target name. Since an alias can be easily changed from one target to another, programs that use aliases are easily redirected from one table to another.

As an example, suppose that your database contains two tables named TEST.PARTS and PRODUCT.PARTS. You can create an alias whose target is one of these tables, as follows:

```
CREATE ALIAS parts FOR test.parts;
```

You might write an application program that contains references to the name PARTS. When you bind your program to the database, the name PARTS will be interpreted as an alias and resolved to the target table TEST.PARTS. When you are ready to put your program into production, you can redefine the target of the alias, using the following statements:

```
DROP ALIAS parts;
CREATE ALIAS parts FOR product.parts;
```

No change is necessary in the source code of your program, but before the program can begin to operate on the production table, it must be rebound. You can rebind your program explicitly, using the REBIND command, or you can allow the rebind to occur implicitly. The system knows that your program uses an alias, and when the target of that alias changes, the system will automatically rebind your program to the new target the next time it is used.

The syntax of a CREATE ALIAS statement is as follows:

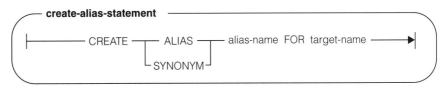

The target of an alias may be a real table, a view, or another alias. In fact, an alias can be defined even if its target does not exist at all! An alias simply declares the equivalence of the alias-name and the target-name. When an alias is referenced in an SQL statement, the target must exist and must be appropriate in the context where it is used. If the target of an alias is another alias, it is resolved through as many levels as necessary to reach a real table or view.

In a CREATE ALIAS statement, both the alias-name and the target-name may be either qualified or unqualified. Any unqualified names are given an implicit schema name equal to the current authid. Thus all the following are valid statements:

```
CREATE ALIAS t1 FOR t2;
CREATE ALIAS s3.t3 FOR t4;
CREATE ALIAS t5 FOR s6.t6;
CREATE ALIAS s7.t7 FOR s8.t8;
```

All the aliases that are currently defined are recorded in the catalog table named TABLES. Each row of TABLES that represents an alias has the code "A" in the TYPE column; it records the alias-name in columns TABSCHEMA and TABNAME, and the target-name in columns BASE_TABSCHEMA and BASE_TABNAME. Thus, if the four aliases above were defined by user Jones, they would be represented by four rows in TABLES, as shown in Figure 2-2.

TABSCHEMA	TABNAME	TYPE	BASE_TABSCHEMA	BASE_TABNAME
JONES	T1	A	JONES	T2
S3	T3	A	JONES	T4
JONES	T5	A	S6	T6
S7	T7	A	S8	T8

Figure 2-2: Examples of Aliases in the TABLES Catalog Table

2.8.4 Views

One of the nice things about a relational database is that, even when they are sharing data, all users do not need to look at the data in the same way. Some users can operate directly on the real tables that are stored in the database, while other users operate on *views*, which are virtual tables derived in some way from the real tables. For example, several users may be sharing a table of data about employees. One user might see only those employees who report to her; another user might see all the employees but none of their salaries; and a third user might see only the average salary of each department. Views such as these are an aid to application development and provide a valuable degree of control over access to data.

A query returns a table that is derived in some way from data in the database, and that is exactly what a view is. SQL was perhaps the first language to exploit this fact and to make creating a view as easy as writing a query. To create a view in SQL, one needs only to write the query that defines the view and to specify the names of the columns of the view (if they cannot be derived from the query). The syntax of the CREATE VIEW statement in V2 is shown below. (See page 69 for the syntax of a query.)

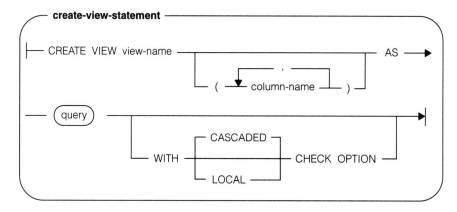

The view name in a CREATE VIEW statement may be either qualified or unqualified; if unqualified, it is given a default schema name equal to the current authid (the userid who bound the program, for static SQL, or the userid who is currently running, for dynamic SQL).

The column names of the view are listed after the view name. The list of column names can be omitted if all the column names can be derived from the query that defines the view (for example, if each column is either given a name in the SELECT clause of the query or is derived directly from a column of an underlying table). Of course, a query used in a CREATE VIEW statement cannot contain any references to host program variables, since the view definition must stand by itself, independent of any host program.

The following are some examples of views defined on our example database:

- The view FAST_QUOTES contains all the quotations whose response time is less than ten days.

```
CREATE VIEW fast_quotes AS
    SELECT suppno, partno, price, responsetime
    FROM quotations
    WHERE responsetime < 10;
```

- The view LOW_PRICES lists the minimum price quoted for each part.

```
CREATE VIEW low_prices(partno, minprice) AS
    SELECT partno, min(price)
    FROM quotations
    GROUP BY partno;
```

- The view OLD_ORDERS joins three tables to list all the orders that are more than two months old, including the name of the supplier and the description of the part. The column names of the view are derived from the column names of the underlying tables.

```
CREATE VIEW old_orders AS
    SELECT o.partno, o.quantity, o.orderdate,
            s.name, p.description
    FROM orders AS o, suppliers AS s, parts AS p
    WHERE s.suppno = o.suppno
    AND p.partno = o.partno
    AND o.orderdate + 2 MONTHS < CURRENT DATE;
```

- It is often useful to define a view based on the special register USER. For example, the following view includes information from the system catalog about the tables and views that have been created by the user of the view:

```
CREATE VIEW mytables AS
    SELECT tabschema, tabname
    FROM syscat.tables
    WHERE definer = USER;
```

- The query that defines a view need not access the database at all. The following view is based on a literal table:

```
CREATE VIEW collarsizes(numeric, descriptive) AS
    VALUES (14, 'Small'), (15, 'Medium'), (16, 'Large');
```

A view can be defined by a query that operates on real tables, on other views, or on some mixture of tables and views. When an SQL statement references a view, the definition of that view is "merged" into the SQL statement to form a new effective statement that is processed against the database. Since all operations on views are ultimately mapped into operations on real tables, the columns of the view inherit their characteristics (such as datatype and NOT NULL) from the columns of the underlying tables. Like real tables, the virtual tables defined by views have no intrinsic ordering of their rows; but a SELECT statement that retrieves rows from a view can contain an ORDER BY clause that specifies a desired ordering.

Read-Only Views

Because of their structure, some views are *read-only* while others are *updatable*. Read-only views can only be queried, but updatable views can also be used in INSERT, UPDATE, and DELETE statements. In general, a view is updatable if each row in the view can be uniquely mapped onto one row of a real table. This makes it possible for the system to map insertions, deletions, and updates on the view into the same operations on the underlying table. If any of the following query features is used in a view definition at the outermost level (that is, not in a subquery), the view is read-only:

- VALUES, DISTINCT, GROUP BY, HAVING, or any column function
- A join
- Any reference to a read-only view
- UNION, INTERSECT, or EXCEPT (except that views defined using UNION ALL can be used in UPDATE and DELETE statements, if their corresponding columns have exactly the same datatypes, including lengths and default values)

Subject to the above limitations, a view name can be used in place of a table name in any SELECT, INSERT, DELETE, UPDATE, DECLARE CURSOR, or CREATE VIEW statement. In the syntax diagrams for these statements, *table-name* should be interpreted as "the name of a table or view."

The definition of each view is stored in the catalog table named VIEWS. In addition, since views can be used in most of the places that tables can be used, each view is also described in the TABLES catalog table and the columns of each view are described in the COLUMNS catalog table.

CHECK Option

Suppose that you execute the following statement, using the FAST_QUOTES view described above:

```
INSERT INTO fast_quotes(suppno, partno, price, responsetime)
    VALUES ('S51', 'P221', 3000, 20);
```

This is an interesting statement, because it inserts a row representing a quotation with a response time of 20 days into a view whose definition includes only quotations with response times of less than ten days. What happens to the row? The FAST_QUOTES view does not include any query features that would make it read-only, so the system is quite able to insert the specified row into the underlying QUOTATIONS table. But if the INSERT were immediately followed by a query against the FAST_QUOTES view, the new row would not be seen. This raises a question of policy: Should a view support insertions and updates whose results are not visible through the view?

V2 allows the creator of each view to answer this policy question by means of a feature called the *check option*. If a view is created with the check option, each row that is inserted or updated using the view must satisfy the view definition. If any row inserted or updated by an SQL statement fails to satisfy the view definition, all the changes made by the SQL statement are rolled back and the statement has no effect. A view defined with the check option is called a *symmetric view*, because everything that can be inserted into it can also be retrieved from it.

As you can see from the syntax diagram on page 136, the check option has two forms: *cascaded* and *local*. The difference between these two forms is meaningful only when a view is defined on top of another view. If a view called VIEW1 is defined by a query on another view called VIEW2, we will refer to VIEW2 as an *underlying view*. When VIEW1 is defined with a *local* check option, operations on VIEW1 must satisfy the definitions of VIEW1 and of all underlying views that also have a check option; however, they need not satisfy the definitions of underlying views that do not have a check option. On the other hand, when VIEW1 is defined with a *cascaded* check option, all

operations on VIEW1 must satisfy the definitions of VIEW1 and of all underlying views, regardless of whether they have a check option or not. If a CRE-
ATE VIEW statement simply specifies WITH CHECK OPTION, the default is a
cascaded check option. If no check option is specified at CREATE VIEW time,
no checking is performed.

Inoperative Views

A view is defined by a query that, in general, contains references to one or
more tables, views, or aliases. We will refer to the tables, views, and aliases that
are used in the definition of a view V as the *underlying objects* of V. When a
view is defined, the system checks the privileges of the view definer on the
underlying objects and grants to the definer the appropriate privileges on the
view. For example, if the view definer is authorized to perform SELECT and
INSERT statements on the table that underlies a view, and if the view is not
read-only because of its definition, then the definer will receive SELECT and
INSERT privileges on the view as well.

It is interesting to consider what happens to a view if one of its underlying
objects disappears or if the definer of the view loses a privilege on an underlying object. In V1, such an event would cause the view to be dropped and its
definition to be lost. Sometimes, however, this policy seems more heavy-
handed than necessary. For example, suppose that the definition of an alias is
changed from one table to another. It seems unfortunate, and even dangerous, for this event to cause the system to completely forget about the definitions of any views that reference the alias. Similarly, if some user U
temporarily loses a privilege on some table T and then regains it, it seems
unfortunate for the system to forget the definitions of all views defined by
user U that reference table T.

V2 has adopted a somewhat gentler policy regarding views that depend on
some object or privilege that has gone away. In V2, such a view has a special
status, called *inoperative*. The definition of an inoperative view is retained in
the VIEWS catalog table, with its inoperative status indicated by the column
VALID = 'X'. Any SQL statement that operates on an inoperative view (except
to drop it or recreate it) will result in an error message. However, a user can
restore an inoperative view to normal status by retrieving its definition from
the VIEWS catalog table and using this definition in a new CREATE VIEW
statement. The following SQL statement can be used to retrieve from VIEWS
the definitions of all inoperative views that were defined by the current user:

```
SELECT viewschema, viewname, seqno, text
FROM syscat.views
WHERE valid = 'X'
AND definer = USER
ORDER BY viewschema, viewname, seqno;
```

When a CREATE VIEW statement is executed that creates a view with the same schema name and view name as an existing inoperative view, the new view replaces the inoperative view. This is an exception to the general rule that a view cannot be defined if its name duplicates the name of a view that already exists. Since all privileges held on a view are revoked when a view becomes inoperative, the definer of the view must grant these privileges again after recreating the inoperative view. The definition of an inoperative view can be removed from the VIEWS catalog table in the usual way, by a DROP VIEW statement.

2.8.5 Indexes

An *index* is an access aid that can be created on a table, using one or more columns of the table as the *key columns* of the index. An index can serve the following purposes:

1. It provides a fast way to find rows of the table, based on their values in the key columns. Indexes can greatly improve the performance of queries that search for a particular column value or range of values.

2. It provides an ordering on the rows of the table, based again on the key-column values. The ordering can be ascending or descending on each column. The ordering property of an index is useful in processing queries with ORDER BY and GROUP BY clauses, and in some kinds of join algorithms. Of course, you can execute a query that includes an ORDER BY or GROUP BY that is not supported by an index—the system will simply sort the data as needed to process your query.

3. An index can optionally enforce the uniqueness of its key columns, meaning that no two rows of the table are allowed to have the same values for the key columns.

You can create as many indexes on a table as you like, using various combinations of columns as keys. However, each index carries a certain cost. Part of the cost is paid in space, since each index replicates its key values and occupies some space on disk. Another part of the cost is paid in update performance, since each update to a column must be reflected in all the indexes that use that column as a key. Finding the optimum set of indexes to maintain in your database is an art that you will learn by experience. Fortunately, the data independence of the relational model allows you to add and drop indexes as usage patterns change, without recoding your applications. The optimizer will find a way to process your queries, exploiting the indexes that exist at the time each query is executed.

In a pure relational system, the presence or absence of an index would have absolutely no effect on the behavior of programs or data, other than a possible impact on performance. In V2, for historical reasons, this is not quite true. In V2, if you wish to enforce the uniqueness of the values in a particular column or set of columns, you can do so in only two ways: by creating a unique index on the column(s), or by declaring the column(s) to be a primary key. For example, if you declare SERIALNO to be the primary key of the EMPLOYEE table, but you wish the system to enforce the uniqueness of SOCSECNO also, you must create a unique index on SOCSECNO. It would perhaps be more elegant to declare the uniqueness of SOCSECNO in some declarative syntax and let the system decide whether to use an index to enforce the uniqueness rule—and indeed the SQL92 Standard provides such a declarative syntax. But in V2, uniqueness is always enforced by an index, and users are allowed to create indexes for this purpose. (The system automatically creates an index to support each primary key, and you can tell that the system is using an index in this way by looking at the SYSTEM_REQUIRED column of the INDEXES catalog table.)

Indexes are created by the CREATE INDEX statement, which has the following syntax:

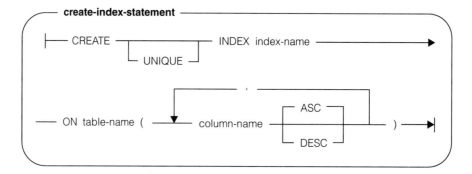

Examples:

```
CREATE INDEX i1 ON suppliers(name);
CREATE UNIQUE INDEX i2 ON quotations(partno, suppno);
CREATE INDEX i3 ON quotations(partno ASC, price DESC);
```

The keywords ASC and DESC denote ascending and descending order, respectively.

There are certain limitations on the creation of indexes. An index may not have more than 16 key columns, and the sum of the lengths of the key columns (including a small allowance for system overhead) may not exceed 255 bytes.

If you attempt to create a unique index on a set of columns that already contains nonunique values, the index creation will fail.

TIP: After creating an index, you should use the RUNSTATS command (described in Section 8.6.2) to collect statistical information that will enable the optimizer to make best use of the index.

2.8.6 Dropping Objects

Tables, views, and other kinds of objects can be removed from the database by means of a DROP statement. The diagram below shows the syntax for dropping various kinds of objects, both those we have discussed in this chapter and others, such as distinct types and triggers, which are discussed in later chapters. In addition to the options shown in this diagram, there is a DROP statement for user-defined functions that has a slightly different syntax and is discussed separately in Section 4.4.12.

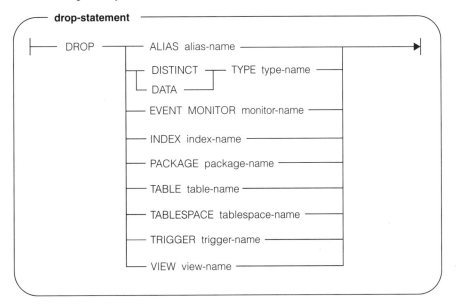

Examples:

```
DROP TABLE accounts.receivable;
DROP VIEW overdue;
DROP PACKAGE payroll;
```

As usual, if an object name in a DROP statement does not have an explicit schema name, it is given an implicit schema name equal to the current authid. Of course, built-in objects such as the system catalog tables cannot be dropped.

TABLE 2-7: Catalog Tables Containing Comments on Various
Types of Objects

Type of Object	Catalog Table Containing Comments
Alias	TABLES
Column of a table or view	COLUMNS
Constraint	TABCONST
Datatypes	DATATYPES
Functions	FUNCTIONS
Index	INDEXES
Package	PACKAGES
Table or view	TABLES
Tablespace	TABLESPACES
Trigger	TRIGGERS

When you drop an object such as a table, view, or index, you may affect other objects that depend on the object you have dropped. For example, if you drop a table that is used in a view definition, that view definition will no longer be valid, and if you drop an index that is being used by a package, that package must be rebound before it can be executed. In some cases, the system will automatically repair the dependent object (for example, a package that depends on a dropped index will automatically be rebound to use some other access plan). In other cases, dropping an object causes dependent objects to be dropped also (for example, dropping a table automatically drops all indexes defined on that table). In still other cases, you are not allowed to drop an object if other objects are depending on it. Since dependency is a complex subject that involves some types of objects not yet discussed in this book, its discussion is deferred until Chapter 5.

2.8.7 Commenting on Objects

Many of the system catalog tables that describe various objects in a V2 database contain a column named REMARKS in which you can enter an explanatory comment of up to 254 characters. Table 2-7 summarizes the types of objects that you can comment on and the names of the catalog tables in which the comments are stored. Some of these types of objects, such as constraints, datatypes, tablespaces, and triggers, are discussed in later chapters.

The catalog tables—which are really views of underlying tables—are found in the SYSCAT schema. (For details about catalog tables, see Appendix D.)

Comments on various types of objects can be entered into the catalog tables by means of the COMMENT statement, shown in the syntax diagram below. In each case, the text of the comment must be a string constant of no more than 254 characters. As you can see from the diagram, COMMENT ON TABLE is used to enter a comment for either a table or a view, and there is a special form of the COMMENT statement that can be used to comment on several columns of a table or view at once. In addition to the options shown on the syntax diagram, there is a COMMENT statement for functions that has a slightly different syntax and is discussed in Section 4.4.13.

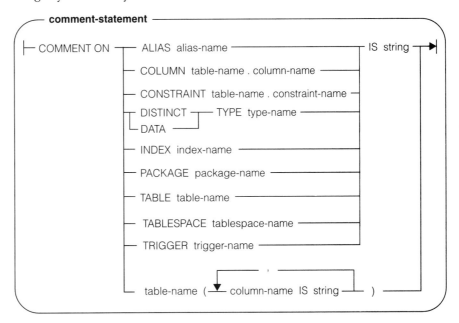

Examples:

```
COMMENT ON PACKAGE finance.payroll
   IS 'Salary schedule effective 1-1-96';
COMMENT ON COLUMN quotations.responsetime
   IS 'Response time in days';
COMMENT ON quotations
   ( price IS 'Price in cents, 100 = one dollar',
     responsetime IS 'Response time in days' );
```

2.8.8 Normalization

Books have been written about how to arrive at a well-designed set of tables to represent a given collection of data. In fact, books have been written about just one aspect of this problem, which is called *normalization*. Normalization is the process of designing tables in such a way that each "fact" is represented exactly once. It is important to avoid multiple representations of the same fact, not only to save storage, but to avoid possible inconsistencies in the database. In this section, we present a brief introduction to the concept of normalization.

Any attempt to avoid redundant representation of facts depends crucially on what we consider to be a fact. In order to discuss this subject, we will examine a fragment of our sample database. Consider the following three columns of the PARTS table:

PARTS

PARTNO	DESCRIPTION	QONHAND
P207	Gear	75
P208	Gear	50
P281	Wheel	100
P285	Wheel	75

It is part of the semantics of this table, understood by those who use it, that part numbers uniquely identify parts. In other words, for a given part number, there can be only one description, and only one quantity on hand, at a given time. We will say that a part number *determines* the description and the quantity on hand. In our sample table, PARTNO is the only column that determines another column. For example, the DESCRIPTION column does not determine PARTNO, because a description of "Gear" is associated with more than one part number.

When a column or set of columns determines another column or set of columns, we say that a *functional dependency* exists, and we describe the functional dependency using an arrow notation, as shown in Figure 2-3.

The columns on the left side of the arrow in a functional dependency are collectively called the *determinant*, and the columns on the right side of the arrow are called the *dependent*. It is important to understand that a functional dependency is a statement about the semantics of the data and that it holds for all time. In other words, the functional dependency described above doesn't just indicate that "each part number has only one description right

$$PARTNO \longrightarrow \{ DESCRIPTION, QONHAND \}$$

Figure 2-3: A Functional Dependency

now." Instead, it promises that "no part number will ever have more than a single description." For this reason, it is not possible to deduce functional dependencies by looking at the content of a table—the dependencies must be known a priori, as part of the raw material of the database design.

You are familiar with the term *primary key*, which denotes a column or set of columns that does not permit duplicate values. Since a primary key can have no duplicates, any primary key value uniquely identifies a row of the table; in other words, the primary key column(s) *determine* all the columns of the table. Actually, a table may have more than one set of columns that have the property of determining all the columns of the table. Each set of columns that has this property (and contains no column that is not essential to having this property) is called a *candidate key*, regardless of whether it is declared as a primary key. In the PARTS table in our example database, PARTNO is the only candidate key.

To continue our discussion of keys and normalization, consider the following columns of the QUOTATIONS table:

QUOTATIONS

SUPPNO	PARTNO	PRICE
S53	P207	2995
S53	P208	3250
S54	P208	4000
S54	P281	1900

In this table, given a supplier number and a part number, we can find the price (if any) offered by that supplier for that part. This means that the PRICE column is functionally dependent on the combination of the SUPPNO and PRICE columns. We might represent this functional dependency as shown in Figure 2-4. (Actually, since the determinant always trivially determines itself, we could include the SUPPNO and PARTNO columns on the right side of the arrow as well.)

$$\{ \text{SUPPNO, PARTNO} \} \longrightarrow \text{PRICE}$$

Figure 2-4: A Functional Dependency with a Two-Column Determinant

The QUOTATIONS table has only one candidate key—that is, only one minimal set of columns that determines all the columns of the table. This candidate key is SUPPNO and PARTNO, which is also the determinant in Figure 2-4.

The PARTS and QUOTATIONS tables have an important property in common: the only functional dependency that exists in each table is the dependency of all the columns of the table on the candidate key. To understand the importance of this property, let's look at a table that doesn't have the property. Consider a database design in which the contents of the PARTS and QUOTATIONS tables are combined into a single table called INVQUOTES, as shown below:

INVQUOTES

PARTNO	DESCRIPTION	QONHAND	SUPPNO	PRICE
P207	Gear	75	S53	2995
P208	Gear	50	S53	3250
P208	Gear	50	S54	4000
P281	Wheel	100	S54	1900
P285	Wheel	75	?	?

The functional dependencies in the INVQUOTES table are shown in Figure 2-5 (again, we have omitted repeating the left side of each dependency on the right side).

$$\text{PARTNO} \longrightarrow \{ \text{DESCRIPTION, QONHAND} \}$$

$$\{ \text{PARTNO, SUPPNO} \} \longrightarrow \{ \text{DESCRIPTION, QONHAND, PRICE} \}$$

Figure 2-5: Functional Dependencies in the INVQUOTES Table

A close look at the INVQUOTES table reveals that it has some obnoxious properties. For example, the fact that part number P208 is a Gear is represented twice. Indeed, this fact will be represented again (redundantly) each time a new price quote for that part is added to the table. This redundant representation of facts is both wasteful of storage and awkward when the table is updated. For example, if the description of part number P208 were to change from a Gear to a Cogwheel, it would be necessary to find and update *all* the places where this fact is represented.

The INVQUOTES table has other shortcomings as well. Since part number P285 has no price quotes at present, we have been forced to use nulls in the SUPPNO and PRICE columns for this part. This means that we can't find the number of price quotes available for a given part by simply counting the number of rows with the given part number. Worse, it means that when the first quote arrives for part number P285, we need to insert this fact into the table by updating an existing row rather than by inserting a new row. It is awkward and asymmetrical to be forced to handle the first quote for a given part differently from other quotes.

If supplier number S53 were to withdraw its quote to supply part number P207, we would be confronted with another problem. Ordinarily a quote is deleted from the table by deleting the row that represents it; but since supplier number S53 is the only supplier for part number P207, if we delete that row, we will lose the information that part number P207 is a Gear and that we have 75 of them on hand. Thus, in order to prevent loss of information, we need to treat the deletion of the last quote for a given part as another special case in which we insert null values into the SUPPNO and PRICE columns.

By now, we should be convinced that the INVQUOTES table shown above is an example of bad table design. Our common sense tells us that the problem is caused by the redundant representation of facts. The theory of normalization is an attempt to codify our common sense into a set of rules for good table design. A number of *normal forms* have been defined as guidelines for good table design. We will discuss only one of these, named *Boyce-Codd Normal Form* (BCNF) because it was jointly defined by Raymond Boyce, coinventor of SQL, and E. F. Codd, inventor of the relational data model. BCNF can be defined, somewhat informally, as follows:

> *A table is in Boyce-Codd Normal Form if and only if every determinant in the table is a candidate key.*

It is easy to see that the INVQUOTES table is not in BCNF, because it contains a functional dependency in which the determinant is not a candidate key for the table. The offending functional dependency is as follows:

PARTNO ──────▶ { DESCRIPTION, QONHAND }

This functional dependency is at the heart of what is wrong with the INV-QUOTES table: it is the "fact" that is represented redundantly in multiple rows of the table. The solution to the anomalies associated with the INVQUOTES table is to break out the functional dependency whose determinant is PARTNO into a table of its own. This leads us back to the original design in which PARTS and QUOTATIONS are two separate tables, each of which is in BCNF.

In a nutshell, the process of reducing a table to BCNF involves listing the functional dependencies among the columns of each table and, if any dependencies are found in which the determinant is not a candidate key, splitting that dependency out into a table of its own. A description of some other normal forms, and a discussion of normalization in greater depth, can be found in any standard textbook on database management, such as one of the following:

- *An Introduction to Database Systems*, 6th ed. by C. J. Date (Addison-Wesley, 1995)

- *Database: Principles, Programming, Performance* by Patrick O'Neil (Morgan Kaufmann, 1994)

- *Fundamentals of Database Systems*, 2nd ed. by Ramez Elmasri and Shamkant B. Navathe (Benjamin/Cummings, 1994)

- *Database System Concepts*, 2nd ed. by Henry F. Korth and Abraham Silberschatz (McGraw-Hill, 1991)

2.9 PROTECTING DATA CONSISTENCY

Protecting stored data is an essential function of a database system. V2 protects data in three quite different ways:

1. Protection for *data security* is provided by the authorization subsystem, which is discussed in Section 2.10. The authorization subsystem protects data against being accessed or modified by unauthorized users.

2. Protection for *data integrity* is provided by constraints and triggers, which are discussed in Chapter 5. These features protect the database against insertions, deletions, or updates that would result in invalid data values.

3. Protection for *data consistency* is provided by the concept of *transactions*, which are discussed in this section. Transactions prevent lost updates, inconsistent data values, and conflicts among multiple concurrent users.

2.9.1 Transactions

Suppose that you drive up to an automatic teller machine, insert your bank card, and instruct the machine to transfer $100 from your savings account to your checking account. Following your instructions, the machine makes two updates to the bank database: first, it subtracts $100 from your savings balance; then, it adds $100 to your checking balance. You drive to a ticket agency and write a $100 check for some concert tickets, confident that the money you transferred will cover your check.

Although you usually don't think about it, your bank's database system is protecting you against some nasty surprises. Suppose, for example, that just after the $100 was subtracted from your savings account, the power failed and your checking account was never credited. I'm sure you would prefer that the bank treat your money transfer as "all or nothing" and guarantee that if any part of the database update is done, then all parts are done. This desirable property of a database interaction is called *atomicity*.

You would also be unhappy if you discovered that, after the teller machine accepted your money transfer and printed a record of it, a power failure at the bank caused all the updates to disappear and the $100 to revert back to your savings account, ultimately causing your check to bounce. You have a right to expect that, once you have received confirmation of an update, the update will not disappear. This desirable property of a database interaction is called *durability*.

Most database systems, including V2, provide guarantees of atomicity and durability by using a concept called a *transaction*. A transaction is simply a set of interactions between an application and the database that the database views as a single unit of work (in fact, the V2 documentation uses the term *unit of work* rather than the more common term *transaction*). A transaction is implicitly begun when any data in the database is read or written. All subsequent reads and writes by the same application are considered to be part of the same transaction, until the application executes either a COMMIT statement or a ROLLBACK statement, which ends the transaction. A COMMIT statement causes all the database changes made by the transaction to become permanent, with guarantees of atomicity and durability. A ROLLBACK causes all the database changes made by the transaction to be undone and the database to be restored to its state before the transaction began. As long as a transaction is in progress and has not been committed or rolled back, the changes that it makes to the database are considered tentative and not yet reliable.

In addition to atomicity and durability, V2 transactions provide you with another desirable property called *isolation*. This property deals with preventing anomalies that might result from interference among multiple users who are interacting with the database at the same time. Here are some examples of possible anomalies that might result from a lack of isolation:

1. Suppose that you ask your ticket agency to list all the performances of the Metropolitan Opera for the spring season, and you get a list of four performances. You ask for tickets to all of them, but when you receive the tickets, you discover that another performance has been added and you have to pay for five tickets. This is called the *phantom row anomaly*, because a piece of data has appeared where you were told that no data existed.

2. Suppose that you ask your ticket agency for the price of tickets to a concert and are told that the price is $35. You decide to buy some tickets, but after you make your decision you discover that the price has gone up to $50. This is called the *nonrepeatable read anomaly*, because you have accessed the same piece of data twice and found different values.

3. Suppose that you scan a list of planned concerts and see that Willie Nelson will be performing in your town next summer. But when you try to buy a ticket, you find out that the list was only tentative and that the concert was never really scheduled. This is called the *dirty read anomaly*, because you were allowed to read information before it was reliable.

4. Suppose that you ask your ticket agency if any tickets are available for a Bruce Springsteen concert, and the agency replies that one ticket is left. A short time later, I ask my agency if any tickets are left for the same concert and get the same reply. You and I both try to buy the ticket. Your agency prints a ticket and updates the available tickets to zero; then my agency does the same thing. This is called the *lost update anomaly*, because two users have updated the same piece of data and one of the updates has been lost.

Ideally, you would like to avoid all these anomalies. Unfortunately, however, there is a cost associated with this: while you are making up your mind what tickets to buy, the system must prevent all other users from buying tickets, or updating ticket prices, or changing the concert schedule. This limits the *concurrency* of the database, which is the ability of the system to provide service to multiple users at the same time. V2 allows application designers to control the trade-off between isolation and concurrency, by specifying an *isolation level* for each transaction. The following four isolation levels are supported:[19]

1. *Repeatable Read (RR).* This is the highest level of isolation, and it prevents all the anomalies described above. A transaction running with RR isolation acquires a lock on all data that it reads, preventing other transactions from updating any of this data until it has committed or rolled back. Thus, if a

---

19. Terminology in this area is somewhat nonuniform. The ANSI/ISO SQL Standard recognizes the same four isolation levels as V2, but it uses different names for them, as follows: V2 "Repeatable Read" corresponds to ANSI "Serializable"; V2 "Read Stability" corresponds to ANSI "Repeatable Read"; V2 "Cursor Stability" corresponds to ANSI "Read Committed"; and V2 "Uncommitted Read" corresponds to ANSI "Uncommitted Read."

program reads the same piece of data twice in the same transaction with an isolation level of RR, it is guaranteed to see the same value (or absence of a value!). If an RR-level transaction reads a lot of data, the concurrency of the database can be severely limited.

2. *Read Stability (RS).* This isolation level guarantees that if a transaction reads the same row twice, it will have the same value, but it does not prevent new rows from appearing during the course of a transaction. An RS-level transaction has a smaller impact on concurrency than an RR-level transaction, and it is protected from nonrepeatable read anomalies but not from phantom row anomalies.

3. *Cursor Stability (CS).* This isolation level guarantees only that a row of a table will not change while your transaction has a cursor positioned on that row. This means that you can read data by fetching from a cursor, then update the current row of that cursor without danger that someone else has updated the row since you read it. If you execute the same query more than once in a CS-level transaction, you may get different answers, but at least each answer will contain data that was committed at the time you read it. CS-level transactions are protected against dirty reads and lost updates, but not against phantoms and nonrepeatable reads. Obviously, the CS level of isolation provides much less protection and has much less impact on concurrency than the levels described above.

4. *Uncommitted Read (UR).* This is the lowest level of isolation and provides the least amount of protection against the isolation anomalies. UR-level transactions have virtually no effect on concurrency. Since a UR-level transaction can read data that is in an inconsistent state (for example, it may see the debit to your savings account but not the credit to your checking account), this isolation level is usually used only in statistical surveys or other applications where perfect accuracy is not required.

Table 2-8 summarizes the isolation levels and their protection against the types of anomalies described above.[20] A YES entry indicates that the given anomaly is possible at the given isolation level.

The PREP and BIND commands have a parameter that controls the isolation level for all transactions executed by the program that is being bound. The parameter consists of the word ISOLATION followed by the abbreviation of the desired level: RR, RS, CS, or UR. The default isolation level, both for application programs and for CLP sessions, is Cursor Stability (CS). During a CLP session, if no transaction is in progress and you are not connected to a

---

20. Table 2-8 assumes that both of the interfering transactions are running at the given isolation level. Interactions between two transactions running at different isolation levels are somewhat more complicated. The "Lost Update" column also assumes that the transactions use positioned (cursor-based) updates.

TABLE 2-8: Anomalies Seen at Various Levels of Isolation

	Phantom	**Nonrepeatable Read**	**Dirty Read**	**Lost Update**
Repeatable Read (RR)	NO	NO	NO	NO
Read Stability (RS)	YES	NO	NO	NO
Cursor Stability (CS)	YES	YES	NO	NO
Uncommitted Read (UR)	YES	YES	YES	NO

database, you can change your isolation level for future transactions by a command such as the following:

```
CHANGE ISOLATION TO RS;
```

The CLP has a feature called *autocommit* that automatically ends a transaction and commits updates after each SQL statement. This feature is turned on by default if you invoke the CLP without any explicit options. (You can also change the default by an entry in your db2cli.ini file.) During a CLP session, if you wish to execute transactions consisting of more than one SQL statement, you can turn off the autocommit feature by the following statement:

```
UPDATE COMMAND OPTIONS USING C OFF;
```

COMMIT and ROLLBACK

As noted above, a transaction is implicitly begun whenever any data is read or written, and is ended by a COMMIT or ROLLBACK statement. These statements may be embedded in an application program or executed via an interactive interface such as the CLP. The syntax of the COMMIT and ROLLBACK statements is shown on the next page.

COMMIT causes all database changes made by the current transaction to become permanent and visible to other transactions running at isolation level RR, RS, or CS. ROLLBACK cancels all database changes made by the current transaction and restores the rows modified by this transaction to their state before the transaction was begun. Both COMMIT and ROLLBACK cause all open cursors to be closed, except that cursors declared WITH HOLD are not closed by a COMMIT statement.

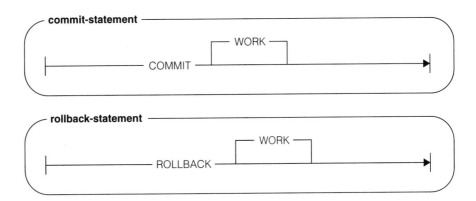

The system implements transaction semantics by acquiring and holding *locks* on the various data items that you read or write. For example, if you read a row in an RR-level transaction, the system must hold a lock that prevents any other user from updating that row until the end of your transaction. These locks are acquired automatically as your transaction runs, and you do not need to be aware of them unless your transaction gets into a *deadlock* condition in which it is unable to acquire the locks that it needs in order to proceed. In this case, your transaction will automatically be rolled back to the last commit point and you will receive a code indicating a rollback due to deadlock (SQLCODE –911, SQLSTATE 40001). Any SQL statement that reads or updates the database might result in this code.

TIP: Using short transactions with frequent COMMIT statements reduces your chance of being caught in a deadlock and rolled back.

LOCK TABLE

If you know in advance that you will be reading or updating a whole table, you can save the system the overhead of acquiring many individual locks on the rows of the table by using an SQL statement that locks the whole table at once. You can lock a table in SHARE mode, which allows other transactions to read the table but prevents them from modifying it, or in EXCLUSIVE mode, which prevents other transactions from reading or modifying the table (except that UR-level transactions are allowed to read the table). If you acquire an explicit lock on a table, the lock is held until the end of the transaction in which it is acquired. The syntax for explicitly locking a table is as follows:

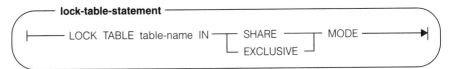

Example:

```
LOCK TABLE quotations IN SHARE MODE;
```

Locks are automatically released at the end of each transaction, except for locks that are acquired by an open cursor that was declared WITH HOLD; these locks are held until the end of the transaction in which the cursor is closed.

 TIP: A good reference book for learning more about transactions is *Transaction Processing: Concepts and Techniques,* by Jim Gray and Andreas Reuter (Morgan Kaufmann, 1993).

2.9.2 Database Connections

Before leaving the topic of transactions, we need to discuss the closely related concept of a *database connection*. Before any access to data is possible, your application program or query interface must be connected to a database. In general, your application may be running on a client machine and the database may be located on a different server machine. During the course of an application program or query session, it may be necessary to connect to more than one database.

A database connection can be established explicitly by a CONNECT statement, such as CONNECT TO dbase1. You can also cause V2 to connect to a database automatically. This is done by setting the environment variable DB2DBDFT to the name of the default database you wish to use. If this environment variable is defined, V2 will establish an *implicit connection* to the default database at the beginning of each application or CLP session. Of course, you can override the implicit connection by using an explicit CONNECT statement. The following are examples of how you might define dbase1 as your default database for implicit connections:

- If you are running under AIX and using the K-shell, place the following command in your .profile file:

  ```
  export DB2DBDFT=dbase1
  ```

- If you are running under OS/2 or Windows NT, place the following command in your CONFIG.SYS file or type the command in the window in which your program is invoked:

  ```
  set DB2DBDFT=dbase1
  ```

```
                    ┌ CONNECT TO dbase1;
                    │
                    │  ...(Reads and updates against dbase1)...
                    │
  (Application is   │  COMMIT;
  connected to     ⟨
  dbase1)           │  ...(More reads and updates against dbase1)...
                    │
                    │  COMMIT;
                    │
                    └ CONNECT TO dbase2;
                    ┌
                    │  ...(Reads and updates against dbase2)...
  (Application is   │
  connected to     ⟨  COMMIT;
  dbase2)           │
                    └ DISCONNECT ALL;
```

Figure 2-6: Example of Type 1 Connections

V2 provides two types of database connections: Type 1 and Type 2. If you are using Type 1 connections, each transaction is confined to a single database, so you must end a transaction before connecting to a new database. If you are using Type 2 connections, a transaction can connect to multiple databases, possibly on different servers, and can commit or roll back its changes to all these databases at the same time. A transaction that uses Type 2 connections is sometimes called a *distributed unit of work*. For application programs, the choice between Type 1 and Type 2 connections is made when the program is precompiled, by including the option CONNECT 1 or CONNECT 2 on the PREP command (the default is CONNECT 1). For a CLP session, the choice between Type 1 and Type 2 connections can be made by the SET CLIENT command (discussed in Section 8.2.3).

 TIP: Each program must be precompiled in the database in which it executes SQL statements. Thus, an application containing a distributed unit of work must be precompiled in multiple databases. In order to avoid errors during precompilation, split your application up into several source files, each of which accesses a single database, and precompile each source file in the database that it accesses. You can then compile the source files and link them together into a single executable program. To precompile a source file in a given database, connect to that database before executing the PREP command.

Figure 2-6 shows a typical sequence of statements executed by an application using Type 1 connections. Each CONNECT statement terminates the current database connection and establishes a new one. Each transaction operates on a single database and must be ended, either by COMMIT or by ROLLBACK, before a new database connection can be established. The final DISCONNECT ALL statement leaves the application unconnected to any database. Each SQL statement that accesses data is directed to the database named in the most recent CONNECT statement.

Figure 2-7 shows a typical sequence of statements executed by an application using Type 2 connections, which permit multiple connections to be acquired within the same transaction. In the example, the application connects to dbase1, then to dbase2, and then to dbase1 again before committing its first set of updates. As before, each SQL statement is directed to the database named in the most recent CONNECT statement. However, using Type 2 connections, multiple databases can participate in the same transaction. Each COMMIT or ROLLBACK statement applies to all the modifications made by the current transaction, in all the databases to which it is connected. The database connections are retained until they are explicitly terminated by a RELEASE or DISCONNECT statement. The RELEASE statement tells the system that the connection to a specific database can be terminated at the end of the current transaction (of course, the database connection cannot be terminated before the end of the transaction, because the database may contain uncommitted updates). The statements provided by V2 for controlling database connections are described in the following sections.

CONNECT

The syntax of the CONNECT statement is as follows:

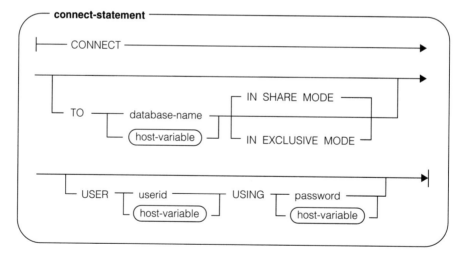

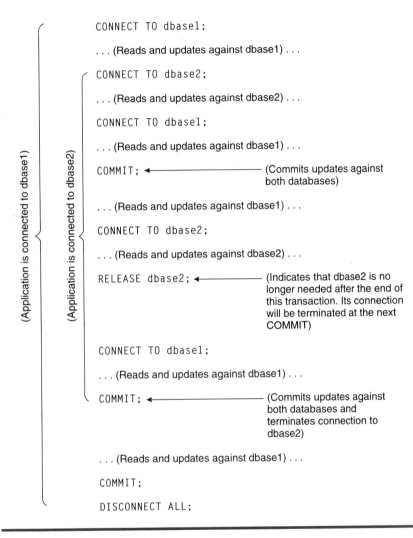

Figure 2-7: Example of Type 2 Connections

Example:

```
CONNECT TO dbase1;
```

When using Type 1 connections, the CONNECT statement terminates the previous database connection, if any. When using Type 2 connections, the CONNECT statement retains the previous connection, acquires a new connection if necessary, and directs subsequent SQL statements to the database named in the new connection.[21] An application cannot be connected to the same database more than once at the same time, even if it is using Type 2 connections (however, this restriction does not apply to CLI applications, as described in Chapter 6).

The phrase IN EXCLUSIVE MODE prevents other users from connecting to this database while you are connected to it. The default SHARE MODE makes no such restriction. As we will see in Section 2.10.2, you must be authorized to connect to a database, but no additional authorization is required to connect in exclusive mode. Obviously, you should think carefully before connecting to a database in exclusive mode, because you are denying other users access to the database. If you try to connect to a database in exclusive mode when some other users are already connected to it, your CONNECT statement will fail.

The USER and USING phrases provide a userid and password that are passed to the server machine for authentication, if your database installation performs authentication on the server machine. If your installation performs authentication on the client machine, the USER and USING phrases can be omitted. The way in which authentication is done is specified at the time your database system is installed.

If the CONNECT statement has no operands (that is, it consists only of the word CONNECT), it returns information about the current database connection. If such a CONNECT statement is executed by a program, the connection information is returned in the SQLERRP field of the SQLCA structure; if it is executed using the CLP, the connection information is displayed to the user.

CONNECT RESET

The syntax of the CONNECT RESET statement is as follows:

connect-reset-statement

CONNECT RESET

If your application is using Type 1 connections, CONNECT RESET commits the current transaction and ends the current connection. If your application is using Type 2 connections, CONNECT RESET retains the current connection, acquires a connection to the default database defined by the environment

---

21. This description assumes that your application was precompiled with the option SQL-RULES DB2, which is the default. If the precompile option SQLRULES STD was specified, a different syntax is used for reactivating a previously established connection. For example, rather than the statement `CONNECT TO dbase1`, you would use the statement `SET CONNECTION dbase1`. This alternate syntax is derived from the SQL92 Standard.

variable named DB2DBDFT, and directs subsequent SQL statements to the default database.

DISCONNECT

The syntax of the DISCONNECT statement is as follows:

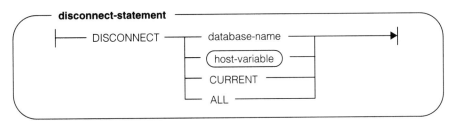

Example:

```
DISCONNECT dbase1;
```

A DISCONNECT statement can be used only when no transaction is in progress (that is, when no reading or writing of the database has taken place since the last COMMIT or ROLLBACK). It disconnects the application from a named database, or from the currently connected database, or from all databases.

RELEASE

The syntax of the RELEASE statement is as follows:

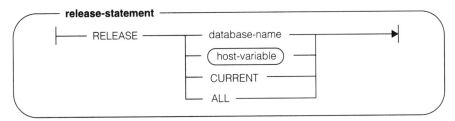

Example:

```
RELEASE dbase1;
```

A RELEASE statement is similar to a DISCONNECT statement, except that it is used inside a transaction to mark one or more database connections as ready to be terminated at the end of the current transaction. The actual connections are terminated by the next COMMIT statement (but not by a ROLLBACK statement). The connections to be terminated may be of either Type 1 or Type 2.

Precompiler Options

As noted previously, an application uses Type 2 connections if it is precompiled with the option CONNECT 2. When an application is using Type 2 connections, the exact meanings of COMMIT and ROLLBACK are determined by another precompiler option named SYNCPOINT, which can take the following values:

1. SYNCPOINT ONEPHASE (this is the default). This option means that although a transaction can connect to multiple databases, it can modify data in only one of them. If a transaction attempts to modify data in more than one database, an error will result.

2. SYNCPOINT TWOPHASE. Using this option, a transaction can modify data in all the databases to which it is connected. When the transaction ends by a COMMIT or ROLLBACK, all the changes to all the databases are committed or rolled back together. In this option, the database manager cooperates with a transaction manager that uses a two-phase commit protocol to ensure that either all the databases commit or all the databases roll back. If the transaction attempts to commit its changes but one of the databases is unable to commit successfully, all the databases will be rolled back by the transaction manager. For this purpose, V2 provides a transaction manager of its own, or can cooperate with another transaction manager such as CICS. For more information on transaction managers, see the *DB2 Administration Guide*.

If you plan to use the built-in transaction manager of V2 to coordinate your distributed transactions, you must set a database manager configuration parameter named TM_DATABASE. This parameter names the database in which the transaction manager is to keep records on the progress of the transaction. You can use any database for this purpose, including (but not limited to) the databases that participate in the distributed transaction. You can see the current setting of the database manager configuration parameters by the following CLP command:

```
GET DATABASE MANAGER CONFIGURATION;
```

The following command might be used to set the TM_DATABASE configuration parameter to the value center, indicating that the database named center is to be used for managing distributed transactions:

```
UPDATE DATABASE MANAGER CONFIGURATION
    USING TM_DATABASE center;
```

TIP: When you update your database manager configuration parameters, the new parameters do not become effective until both the database server and the client are restarted. To restart the server, execute DB2STOP and DB2START commands. If the CLP is running on a client machine, stop it by a TERMINATE command (not a QUIT command; it is not strong enough) and restart it to make the new configuration parameters effective.

3. SYNCPOINT NONE. Like TWOPHASE, this option allows a transaction to modify data in multiple databases and transmits a COMMIT or ROLLBACK to all the connected databases at the end of the transaction. Unlike TWOPHASE, however, this option does not employ a commit protocol to ensure that the COMMIT is successful in all the databases. With SYNCPOINT NONE, it is possible that the changes made by the transaction will be committed in some of the connected databases and will fail to commit in others. Since atomicity is one of the main properties that defines a transaction, the SYNCPOINT NONE option does not provide a true distributed transaction.

In addition to CONNECT and SYNCPOINT, two other precompiler options influence the detailed behavior of Type 2 database connections. The DISCONNECT option allows connections to be automatically terminated at the end of a transaction, and the SQLRULES option modifies the syntax of the CONNECT statement. These options, and a variation of the CONNECT statement called SET CONNECTION, are described in more detail in the *DB2 SQL Reference*.

Using Type 2 Connections with the CLP

The CLP initially provides the options CONNECT 1 and SYNCPOINT ONEPHASE. If you wish to use Type 2 connections with the CLP, you can change its connection options by using a command called SET CLIENT, as in the following example:

```
SET CLIENT CONNECT 2 SYNCPOINT TWOPHASE;
```

Following this command, you can use the CLP to connect to and update multiple databases within the same transaction. (The SET CLIENT command is discussed further in Section 8.2.3.)

TIP: When using Type 2 connections with the CLP, don't forget to turn off the autocommit feature by using the statement UPDATE COMMAND OPTIONS USING C OFF. At the end of your CLP session, use the TERMINATE command to end all your database connections.

2.10 AUTHORIZATION

As stated in Section 2.9, protecting data against unauthorized access and modification is one of the essential tasks of a database management system. V2 accomplishes this task by means of a system of *authorities* and *privileges*. In this section, we will examine the various types of authorities and privileges and how they are created and used.

An *authority* is a general right to perform certain kinds of administrative actions. Some authorities apply at the level of a V2 product installation (called a DB2 *instance*), which may manage multiple databases. Other authorities apply to a specific database. Authorities are generally (with some exceptions) held by *groups* of users rather than by individuals. The concept of a *group* is defined and managed by the operating system on which V2 is running—for example, in AIX, users can be placed into groups by the *System Management Interface Tool* (SMIT), and in OS/2, groups are managed by the *User Profile Management* tool (UPM).

A *privilege* is a specific right to perform certain kinds of actions on a specific object within a database, such as a table or view. Privileges can be held either by individual users or by groups.

2.10.1 Instance-Level Authorities

There are three authorities that apply at the level of a DB2 instance and therefore span all the databases managed by that instance. Each of these instance-level authorities is held by a group, and the names of the groups holding these authorities are recorded in the database manager configuration file. The names of the groups holding the instance-level authorities can be seen by executing the following command:

```
GET DATABASE MANAGER CONFIGURATION;
```

The three instance-level authorities are listed below.

1. *System Administration authority.* In general, authorities and privileges are granted from one user to another, forming a treelike structure of grants. The root of this tree is the System Administration, or SYSADM, authority, which is the highest authority recognized by V2. It is held by a group and confers on members of that group the ownership of all V2 resources and the ability to execute any V2 command, including the ability to confer or revoke all the other authorities and privileges.

   The group holding SYSADM authority for a given V2 instance is determined at the time the system is installed. Because of the sensitive nature of this authority, it is advisable to create a group specifically for this purpose. A new userid should also be created at product installation time, to be the owner of the V2 instance (remember that more than one instance of the product can be installed on the same machine). Operating system facilities are used to create the system administration group and the instance owner userid, and to make sure that the instance owner userid belongs to the system administration group as its principal group. Other userids can be added to the system administration group, in addition to the instance owner.

The instance owner userid must be specified as part of the V2 installation process. The home directory of the instance owner becomes the installation site for the product, and the members of the principal group to which the owner belongs become the holders of SYSADM authority for the product instance. The name of this group is recorded in the database manager configuration parameter named SYSADM_GROUP.

2. *System Control authority.* System Control, or SYSCTRL, is an instance-level authority that conveys the right to control system resources. For example, a holder of SYSCTRL authority can create and destroy databases and tablespaces (units of physical storage in which data resides).

Although a holder of SYSCTRL controls the resources used by the database manager, SYSCTRL does not automatically include the right to read or modify the actual data that is stored in databases. Access to data requires DBADM authority or one of the more specific privileges.

The name of the group holding SYSCTRL authority is recorded in the database manager configuration parameter named SYSCTRL_GROUP. During installation of a V2 instance, no group is given SYSCTRL authority; it is up to the system administrators to decide whether they wish to share authority in this way. Any member of the system administration group can specify the name of the group to be given SYSCTRL authority, by using a command such as the following:

```
UPDATE DATABASE MANAGER CONFIGURATION
    USING SYSCTRL_GROUP goodguys;
```

The system commands for which SYSCTRL is the minimum required authority are listed below. (Descriptions of these commands can be found in Chapter 8.) In addition to the commands in this list, holders of SYSCTRL authority can execute any command that is available to a holder of SYSMAINT authority.

CREATE, ALTER, and DROP TABLESPACE

CATALOG and UNCATALOG for nodes and databases

CREATE and DROP DATABASE

FORCE APPLICATION

RESTORE to a new database

3. *System Maintenance authority.* System Maintenance, or SYSMAINT, is an instance-level authority that conveys the right to perform maintenance operations such as starting and stopping the DB2 server, backing up and restoring databases, and operating the database monitor. Like SYSCTRL, SYSMAINT does not include the right to read or modify the data that is stored in databases.

The name of the group holding SYSMAINT authority is recorded in the database manager configuration parameter named SYSMAINT_GROUP, which is set to null during system installation. Any member of the system administration group can specify the name of the SYSMAINT group by using a command such as the following:

```
UPDATE DATABASE MANAGER CONFIGURATION
    USING SYSMAINT_GROUP hackers;
```

The system commands for which SYSMAINT is the minimum required authority are listed below. (Descriptions of these commands can be found in Chapter 8.)

UPDATE DATABASE CONFIGURATION

BACKUP and RESTORE for an existing database

ROLLFORWARD

DB2START and DB2STOP

GET, RESET, and UPDATE MONITOR SWITCHES

2.10.2 Database-Level Authorities

Database-level authorities apply to a specific database rather than to an instance of the DB2 product. Each of these authorities is recorded in the catalog table named DBAUTH, in the database to which the authority applies. The user who creates a database automatically receives a full set of database-level authorities on the new database; this user can then grant database-level authorities selectively to other users or groups by means of the GRANT statement, which is discussed in Section 2.10.6. Database-level authorities are important to users who need to develop new database applications. They are as follows.

1. *Database Administration (DBADM) authority.* DBADM authority conveys the right to access and modify all the objects within a given database, including tables, indexes, views, packages, and everything else that is stored there. It also includes the right to grant any privilege on a specific object in the database to any user. A holder of DBADM can also grant the other database-level authorities (but not DBADM itself) to other users.

2. *BINDADD authority.* This authority conveys the right to create packages in the database by precompiling and/or binding application programs. The user who

binds a program receives CONTROL privilege on the resulting package.

3. *CONNECT authority.* This authority conveys the right to connect to the database, using the SQL CONNECT statement.

4. *CREATETAB authority.* This authority conveys the right to create tables in the database. The creator of a table receives CONTROL privilege on the table.

5. *CREATE_NOT_FENCED authority.* This authority conveys the right to create user-defined functions that operate within the address space of the database. These functions are called *nonfenced functions*. Great care must be taken when creating a nonfenced function, because the database is not protected against damage that might be caused by errors in these functions. (User-defined functions are described in Section 4.4.)

2.10.3 Table and View Privileges

In general, privileges convey the right to perform a specific action on a specific object. For the privileges described in this section, the object to which the action applies is a table or a view. All table and view privileges are recorded in the catalog table named TABAUTH. Table and view privileges may be held by individual users and/or groups of users.

Table and view privileges are granted and revoked by means of SQL GRANT and REVOKE statements, which are described in Section 2.10.6. In order to grant any privilege on a table or view, a user must hold SYSADM authority, DBADM authority, or the CONTROL privilege on the object in question. The privileges that apply to tables and views are as follows.

1. *CONTROL privilege.* CONTROL is like a "master" privilege—it includes all the privileges that are applicable to a given table or view. (ALTER, INDEX, and REFERENCES privileges apply only to tables; INSERT, DELETE, and UPDATE apply only to tables and updatable views.) The CONTROL privilege also includes the right to grant any applicable privilege on a table or view to other users or groups, the right to drop the table or view, and the right to update the statistics that apply to a table by means of the RUNSTATS command (described in Section 8.6.2).

   The creator of a table automatically receives CONTROL privilege on it. The creator of a view receives CONTROL privilege on it only if he or she holds CONTROL privilege on all the tables on which the view is defined.

2. *ALTER privilege.* Conveys the right to change the definition of a table, using the ALTER TABLE statement; to comment on a table, using the COMMENT statement; or to attach triggers to a table, using the CREATE TRIGGER statement (described in Section 5.3).

3. *DELETE privilege.* Conveys the right to delete rows from the table or updatable view.

4. *INDEX privilege.* Conveys the right to create indexes on the table.

5. *INSERT privilege.* Conveys the right to insert rows into the table or updatable view.

6. *REFERENCES privilege.* Conveys the right to create and drop foreign key constraints in other tables, referencing this table as the parent table. (Foreign key constraints are discussed in Section 5.1.)

7. *SELECT privilege.* Conveys the right to retrieve data from the table or view, using the SELECT statement, or to use the table or view in a subquery.

8. *UPDATE privilege.* Conveys the right to update rows of the table or updatable view.

In order to create a view, a user must hold SELECT or CONTROL privilege on all the tables that are used in the definition of the view. The creator of a view receives SELECT privilege on the view, and also receives CONTROL privilege on the view if he or she holds CONTROL privilege on all the underlying tables. In addition, if the view is not read-only because of its definition, the definer of the view receives the same INSERT, DELETE, and UPDATE privileges on the view that he or she holds on the underlying table.

When a privilege on a table or view is revoked, all privileges that are derived from the revoked privilege are revoked also. For example, if a user has created a view V1 based on table T1, and that user loses the UPDATE privilege on table T1, the UPDATE privilege on view V1 will be lost also.

2.10.4 Index Privileges

There is only one privilege that applies to indexes: the CONTROL privilege, which conveys the right to drop the index. The CONTROL privilege is automatically given to the user who creates an index. It may be held by individual users and/or groups of users. In order to grant the CONTROL privilege on an index, a user must hold SYSADM or DBADM authority. The holders of the CONTROL privilege on various indexes are recorded in the catalog table named INDEXAUTH.

2.10.5 Package Privileges

The privileges described in this section apply to packages, which are created by precompiling and/or binding an application program. The package encapsulates all the SQL statements in the program, including an optimized plan for executing each statement. All package privileges are recorded in the catalog table named PACKAGEAUTH. Package privileges may be held by individual users and/or groups of users.

Package privileges are granted and revoked by means of GRANT and REVOKE statements, which are described in Section 2.10.6. In order to grant any package privilege, a user must hold SYSADM authority, DBADM authority, or the CONTROL privilege on the package in question. The privileges that apply to packages are as follows.

1. *CONTROL privilege.* The CONTROL privilege is like a "master" privilege that includes the EXECUTE and BIND privileges, as well as the right to grant these privileges to others. It also includes the right to drop the package. The CONTROL privilege is automatically given to the user who creates a package. In order to create a package, a user must hold all the privileges necessary to execute the SQL statements that are included in the package.

2. *EXECUTE privilege.* This privilege conveys the right to execute a package by executing the application program from which the package was bound. A user holding EXECUTE privilege on a package can execute it even if he or she does not hold the privileges needed to execute the individual statements inside the package. This provides a useful form of *encapsulation* of privileges. For example, the personnel manager of a company, who holds the privilege to update employee records, might create a package by binding an application program that updates salaries in a particular way. The personnel manager might then grant the EXECUTE privilege on this package to a clerk, who can then run the application even though he does not hold the general privilege to update employee records. In effect, the manager has granted to the clerk an encapsulated privilege to update salaries in a particular way, under the control of the application program.

TIP: In order to create a package that encapsulates a particular privilege, a user must hold that privilege explicitly as an individual user (not by reason of the privilege being granted to a group or to PUBLIC).

3. *BIND privilege.* This privilege conveys the right to rebind a package, using the PREP, BIND, or REBIND command. Rebinding a package may be necessary in case the package has become invalid due to changes in the database. When a package is rebound, a new package is created for it based on the latest indexes, view definitions, table statistics, and other information found in the database. In order to rebind a package, a user must hold not only the BIND privilege for the package, but also the privileges needed to execute the individual SQL statements found in the package.

2.10.6 GRANT and REVOKE Statements

Database-level authorities, and all privileges, can be granted by a user to another user, or to a group, by means of the GRANT statement. Privileges can also be revoked by the REVOKE statement. As shown in the syntax diagram below, the GRANT and REVOKE statements have very similar syntax.

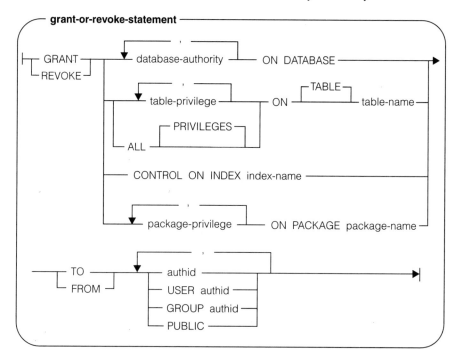

Examples:

```
GRANT DBADM ON DATABASE TO overton;
GRANT CONNECT, CREATETAB, BINDADD ON DATABASE TO spatz;
GRANT SELECT, INSERT, DELETE, UPDATE ON test.table1
    TO tester1, tester2;
GRANT BIND, EXECUTE ON PACKAGE program5 TO PUBLIC;
REVOKE ALL PRIVILEGES ON table1 FROM USER badguy;
REVOKE CONTROL ON INDEX i1 FROM smith, jones;
```

The following notes apply to GRANT and REVOKE statements:

- Keywords must be used in the proper combinations: "GRANT . . . TO . . ." and "REVOKE . . . FROM . . ."
- The names of the authorities and privileges (CONTROL, CONNECT, SELECT, EXECUTE, and so on) can be chosen from the lists in Sections 2.10.2 through 2.10.5.

TABLE 2-9: Authorizations Required to Execute GRANT and REVOKE Statements

If you hold . . .	You can grant and revoke . . .		
	DBADM	Any database-level authority or any CONTROL privilege	Any privilege on the specific object except CONTROL
SYSADM	Yes	Yes	Yes
DBADM	No	Yes	Yes
CONTROL on a specific object	No	No	Yes, but you can only revoke those privileges that you granted

- When granting or revoking table or view privileges, the term "ALL PRIVI-LEGES" means "all privileges (except the CONTROL privilege) that are applicable to the given object." For example, ALL PRIVILEGES on a table includes SELECT, INSERT, DELETE, UPDATE, ALTER, INDEX, and REFERENCES, but ALL PRIVILEGES on a view includes only SELECT, INSERT, DELETE, and UPDATE.

- The authid(s) to which the grant or revoke applies are eight-character identifiers for users or groups that are known to your operating system. You need to use the keyword USER or GROUP only when referring to an authid that is defined both as a user and as a group. If an authid identifies a user or a group but not both, the system will figure out which kind of identifier it is.

- Privileges and authorities that are granted to PUBLIC can be exercised by any user, including users who have no explicit privileges or authorities, and including new userids that may be created after the grant is made. It is often useful to grant CONNECT authority to PUBLIC, allowing any user to connect to the database. DBADM authority cannot be granted to PUBLIC.

- Of course, a user can execute a GRANT or REVOKE statement only if that user is properly authorized. Table 2-9 summarizes the authorization requirements of GRANT and REVOKE statements.

2.10.7 Authorization Checking

The userid against which authorization is checked for a given SQL statement is called the *authid* for that statement. The authid for a static SQL statement in an application program is that of the user who bound the package for that program. This enables a user who holds certain privileges to encapsulate these privileges in a package that uses the privileges only in a certain way, and to grant to other users the right to execute the package without granting the privileges on which the package is based. For dynamic SQL statements, on the other hand, the authid is always the userid of the current user. Dynamic SQL statements include all statements executed via the CLP and all statements executed by the Call Level Interface (CLI) or Embedded Dynamic SQL facilities (described in Chapter 6).

The time at which a privilege is checked depends on the type of the SQL statement. Authorization is checked at bind time for static SELECT, INSERT, DELETE, UPDATE, and VALUES statements, and at run time for all other types of statements. Table 2-10 summarizes the authorization-checking rules for various types of SQL statements.

Privileges that are granted to groups or to PUBLIC are not taken into account when binding a package. That is, when binding a package that contains static SQL statements, the binder of the package must explicitly (as an individual) hold the privileges required to execute the static SQL statements.

Table 2-11 summarizes the privileges that are required to execute the statements and commands that are discussed in this chapter. The SYSADM and DBADM authorities are also sufficient to execute any statement or command in the table, even in the absence of any other authority or privilege. (Authorization is also discussed in the context of the CREATE TABLE statement in Section 5.2.1, the ALTER TABLE statement in Section 5.2.2, and the CREATE TRIGGER statement in Section 5.3.1.)

TABLE 2-10: Authorization-Checking Rules for Static and Dynamic SQL Statements

Type of Statement	Static SQL	Dynamic SQL
Data manipulation statements (SELECT, INSERT, UPDATE, DELETE, and VALUES)	Checked against binder of program, at bind time	Checked against current user, at run time
All other SQL statements	Checked against binder of program, at run time	Checked against current user, at run time

TABLE 2-11: Privileges Required to Execute Various SQL Statements

In order to execute . . .	An authid must hold . . .
BIND command	BINDADD authority for the database, if the package does not yet exist; or BIND or CONTROL privilege for an existing package. In addition, the authid must hold all the privileges required by the static SQL statements contained in the package.
COMMENT statement	CONTROL privilege on the object that is being commented on. Alternatively, you can comment on an alias, datatype, function, or trigger if your authid matches the schema name of the object, or on a view if your authid matches the DEFINER of the view in the VIEWS catalog table.
CONNECT statement	CONNECT authority for the database in question.
CREATE INDEX statement	INDEX or CONTROL privilege on the table that is being indexed.
CREATE VIEW statement	SELECT or CONTROL privilege on all the tables and views that are referenced in the view definition.
DELETE statement	DELETE or CONTROL privilege on the table or view from which rows are to be deleted, and SELECT or CONTROL privilege on all tables or views that are used in subqueries.
DROP statement	CONTROL privilege on the object that is being dropped. Alternatively, you can drop an alias, datatype, function, or trigger if your authid matches the schema name of the object, or a view if your authid matches the DEFINER of the view in the VIEWS catalog table.
INSERT statement	INSERT or CONTROL privilege on the table or view into which rows are to be inserted, and SELECT or CONTROL privilege on all tables or views that are used in subqueries.
LOCK TABLE statement	SELECT or CONTROL privilege on the table to be locked.
PREP command	BINDADD authority for the database, if the package does not yet exist, or BIND or CONTROL privilege for an existing package. In addition, the authid must hold all the privileges required by the static SQL statements contained in the package.
REBIND command	BIND privilege on the package.
SELECT statement, or any query used in a cursor declaration	SELECT or CONTROL privilege on all the tables and views referenced in the query and its subqueries.
UPDATE statement	UPDATE or CONTROL privilege on the table or view to be updated, and SELECT or CONTROL privilege on all tables and views that are used in subqueries.
VALUES statement	SELECT or CONTROL privilege on any tables or views referenced in subqueries.

2.11 SUMMARY OF NEW FEATURES IN THIS CHAPTER

This has been a chapter about the basic features of V2, most of which are shared with V1, the predecessor product. Nevertheless, some of the features discussed are new in V2, and these are listed below. In scanning this list, keep in mind that these are only the enhancements to the basic features of the product, as discussed in this chapter. The areas in which V2 offers major new functional enhancements, including advanced query features, datatypes and functions, triggers, constraints, and the Call Level Interface (CLI), will be discussed in the following chapters.

2.11.1 Query Enhancements

- A new VALUES statement is provided for evaluating expressions that do not contain a table reference, as in the following example:

```
VALUES (CURRENT TIME);
```

- The VALUES clause is expanded to specify a literal table that can be used wherever a subquery can be used. The following is an example of a literal table containing two rows of two columns each:

```
VALUES('Uncle Bill', 'P.O.Box 1117, Fresno, CA'),
       ('Repo City', '650 First St., Buffalo, NY');
```

- Expressions in a SELECT clause can be given names, and these names can be used in an ORDER BY clause, as in the following example:

```
SELECT partno, qonhand + qonorder AS totalq
FROM parts
ORDER BY totalq;
```

- Many new built-in functions are provided. These functions, which are listed in Appendix B, include two new column functions, stdev and variance, as well as all the scalar functions defined by the Open Database Connectivity (ODBC) interface, and various other new functions.

- An ESCAPE clause in the LIKE predicate enables fuzzy searching for patterns that contain the percent and underscore characters.

- An IN predicate is no longer limited to a list of constants but may contain expressions such as

```
SELECT suppno, partno
FROM orders
WHERE year(orderdate)
    IN (year(CURRENT DATE), year(CURRENT DATE) - 1);
```

- Several new special registers such as CURRENT TIMEZONE have been added. All the special registers are listed in Appendix A.

- The keyword DISTINCT can now be used more than once in a SELECT clause. Also, the argument of a DISTINCT column function can now be an expression, as in the following example:

```
SELECT count(DISTINCT description),
       count(DISTINCT qonhand + qonorder)
FROM parts;
```

- COUNT can be used without DISTINCT to count the number of non-null values in a column, as in:

```
SELECT count(address) FROM suppliers;
```

- A literal string can now be written in a hexadecimal format such as X'CCFF'.

- The optional word AS can be used before a correlation name in a FROM clause, and INDICATOR can be used before an indicator variable.

2.11.2 Enhancements to INSERT, UPDATE, and DELETE

- INSERT, UPDATE, and DELETE statements are now allowed to contain subqueries that reference the same table that is being modified by the statement. The subqueries are evaluated before the modifications are performed.

- An INSERT statement may insert multiple rows, including rows containing expressions, as in the following example:

```
INSERT INTO orders(suppno, partno, quantity, orderdate)
    VALUES ('S59', 'P227', 100, CURRENT DATE + 2 DAYS),
           ('S59', 'P231', 250, CURRENT DATE + 5 DAYS);
```

- An UPDATE statement may use a subquery in a SET clause to assign values to one or more columns, as in the following example:

```
UPDATE quotations AS X
SET (price, responsetime) =
        (SELECT min(price), min(responsetime)
         FROM quotations
         WHERE partno = X.partno)
WHERE suppno = 'S53';
```

- A DELETE statement may contain a correlated subquery, as in the following example:

```
DELETE FROM quotations AS X
WHERE price >
   (SELECT 2 * avg(price)
    FROM quotations
    WHERE partno = X.partno);
```

2.11.3 Enhancements to Views

- A view can now have a cascaded check option that applies not only to the view itself but also to all lower-level views on which the view is defined.

- Views based on UNION ALL can now be used in UPDATE and DELETE statements.

- Views are no longer limited to 255 columns (but the old 255-column limit still applies to base tables).

- A view definition that is no longer valid is retained in the VIEWS catalog table, where it can be easily retrieved and recreated.

2.11.4 Enhancements to Transactions

- A transaction can now connect to and modify multiple databases (distributed unit of work).

- A new isolation level, Read Stability (RS), has been added.

2.11.5 Enhancements to Authorization

- Two new authorities have been added for use in system administration: SYS-CTRL and SYSMAINT.

- The GRANT statement can now specify whether a privilege is being granted to an individual user or to a group.

2.11.6 Removal of Limitations

- The number of table references in an SQL statement, formerly limited to 15, is now limited only by the amount of memory on your machine.
- The number of predicates in an SQL statement, formerly limited to 300, is now limited only by the amount of memory on your machine.
- The maximum length of a correlation name has been increased from 8 characters to 18 characters.

2.11.7 Other New Features

- Aliases (alternative names for tables) can now be created and used to easily redirect applications from one table to another.
- Users are now allowed to provide comments to be stored in the system catalog tables for several additional types of objects—including indexes and packages—and to comment on several columns of a table in a single statement.
- Compound SQL statements can now be specified NOT ATOMIC, meaning that failure of one individual statement does not roll back the entire compound statement. A compound statement can also specify how many of its individual statements are to be executed.
- A new REBIND command is provided for rebinding a package that is already in the database. The REBIND command does not require the existence of a bind file.

Query Power

H ave you ever wanted to know which department in your company has the highest average salary? Or how to fly from Oshkosh to Oslo in the minimum number of flights? Or what fraction of your company's accidents last year were caused by chain saws? This is the chapter in which you will learn to answer these and other important questions, each in a single SQL statement, using powerful new query features supported by V2.

The essence of a database system is its ability to retrieve information. The query features introduced by V2 greatly increase the expressive power of SQL and remove a number of long-standing limitations of the language. The language enhancements supported by V2 encompass most of the query features of the SQL92 Standard, as well as a number of additional features that are not included in the Standard.

Many of the new features introduced in this chapter involve subqueries. SQL has always supported the concept of a subquery, which is a query used inside of another query to compute some intermediate result. However, the original SQL has frequently been criticized because of the rules and limitations it placed on the use of subqueries. In V1, for example, the result of a subquery was a derived table, but the columns of the derived table did not always have names and the derived table could not in general be used in the same ways as a real table or view. These rules and limitations have been eliminated in the SQL92 Standard and in the V2 system. The result is a language with greatly improved orthogonality and expressive power compared with the original SQL.

One of the most powerful new features of V2 is its support for recursive queries, which involve searching the database repeatedly until some desired goal is reached. Recursive queries enable SQL to be used for whole new categories of database applications, such as finding all the descendants of a given person, all the components of a given assembly, or all the paths to a given destination. The V2 syntax for recursive queries enables you to search for all solutions to a given problem or for the optimum solution according to some criterion that you define.

In Chapter 2, we discussed basic SQL features that were supported by V1 except where noted otherwise. In Chapter 3, the convention is the opposite: everything discussed in this chapter is new in V2 except simple subqueries.

3.1 CAST EXPRESSIONS

Programming languages use the term *cast* to refer to the process of changing a value from one datatype to another, as in *casting* an Integer value into the Decimal datatype. V2 supports several built-in functions, such as `decimal`, `integer`, `float`, and `date`, that have the effect of casting their operands into specific datatypes. In some cases, casting a value into a given datatype may change the value itself. For example, any Integer can be cast into a Decimal without changing its value, but casting a Decimal value into the Integer datatype may result in truncation of its fractional part.

In addition to the built-in functions that have the effect of casting, V2 supports a new casting notation that is defined by the SQL92 Standard. The new notation has the following syntax:

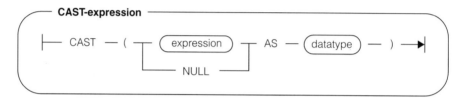

The *expression* in a CAST expression is constructed according to the rules in Section 2.4.1. (The syntax for a datatype is given on page 339.)

In order for a CAST to be successful, the target datatype must be well defined, including its length, scale, and precision, if any. The safest thing to do is to specify these properties explicitly, as in the following examples:

```
CAST (c1+c2 AS Decimal(8,2))
CAST (name || address AS Varchar(255))
```

If you omit the length and precision from a Decimal target datatype, it is assumed to be Decimal(5,0). A Char target datatype with no specified length is assumed to be Char(1), and a Graphic target datatype with no specified length is assumed to be Graphic(1). Other target datatypes with missing lengths result in error conditions. Of course, if the value used in a CAST expression cannot be converted to the target datatype, an error results.

If you cast a string-type value into a target datatype that has a longer length, the value will be padded with blanks. If you cast a string-type value into a target datatype that has a shorter length, the value will be truncated and you will receive a warning message if any of the truncated characters were nonblank.

Casting is sometimes useful when a value of a particular datatype is needed as the parameter of a function. For example, the built-in function `substr`

TABLE 3-1: Valid Uses of the CAST Expression

Source Datatype	Target Datatype
Smallint, Integer, Decimal, Double	Smallint, Integer, Decimal, Double
Char, Varchar, Long Varchar, Clob	Char, Varchar, Long Varchar, Clob, Blob
Graphic, Vargraphic, Long Vargraphic, Dbclob	Graphic, Vargraphic, Long Vargraphic, Dbclob, Blob
Char, Varchar	Smallint, Integer, Decimal, Date, Time, Timestamp, Vargraphic
Smallint, Integer, Decimal	Char
Date, Time, Timestamp	Char, Varchar
Date	Date
Time	Time
Timestamp	Date, Time, Timestamp
Blob	Blob

expects integers as its second and third parameters. If, for some reason, you wish to use floating-point values x and y (after truncating their fractional parts) as parameters of substr, you can do so as follows:

```
substr(string1, CAST(x AS Integer), CAST(y AS Integer))
```

Table 3-1 summarizes the built-in casts that are supported by V2. In each row of the table, any of the source datatypes is castable into any of the target datatypes. Of course, if the source datatype is Char or Varchar and the target datatype is a numeric datatype or datetime datatype, the source value must be a character-string representation of some valid target-type value; otherwise, an error will occur during the conversion. The datatypes Blob, Clob, and Dbclob are "large-object" datatypes, which are discussed in Section 4.1.

TIP: You may sometimes find it useful to cast a value into its own datatype in order to change its length, precision, or scale. For example, if a column named ELEVATION has a datatype of Decimal(8,3), you might truncate the fractional part of the values in this column in a query by using an expression such as the following:

```
CAST(elevation AS Decimal(5,0))
```

CAST expressions allow the keyword NULL to be used in ways that were not possible in V1. For example, V1 did not allow NULL to be used in a SELECT clause, because the word NULL, standing by itself, does not indicate the datatype of the null value that is intended. Thus, V1 had no way of knowing whether the word NULL represented a null Integer, a null Varchar, or some other type of null value, each of which has a different representation. The CAST notation of V2 provides a way to specify the datatype of a null value, allowing the word NULL to be used wherever a typed value is needed.

As an example of casting null values, suppose that our database contains the following two tables:

STUDENTS

SOLDIERS

Suppose that our company considers all students and soldiers to be prospective customers, and wishes to define a view named PROSPECTS that contains a combined list of all the students and soldiers. Students will appear in the view with a real school but a null service, and soldiers will appear in the view with a real service but a null school. This view might be defined as follows:

```
CREATE VIEW prospects(name, school, service) AS
    SELECT name, school, CAST(NULL AS Varchar(20))
    FROM students
UNION
    SELECT name, CAST(NULL AS Varchar(20)), service
    FROM soldiers;
```

The CAST expressions are essential to the definition of the PROSPECTS view, since they provide the datatype information that enables null values to participate in the UNION. The use of NULL in a CAST expression is also helpful in expressing an outer-join query, as will be seen in Section 3.7.

CAST expressions are very useful in dealing with user-defined types and functions, which are discussed in Chapter 4. For example, suppose that you have defined a datatype called Sex, with a representation of Char(1), and another datatype called Height, with a representation of Double. You might create a user-defined function called normalWeight(Sex, Height), and you might invoke your function using a CAST notation as in the following example:

```
normalWeight(CAST('M' AS Sex), CAST(66 AS Height))
```

(A specialized use of the CAST notation called a *typed parameter marker* is discussed in Section 6.1.4.)

3.2 CASE EXPRESSIONS

Often, a database designer will choose to conserve space by using some short encoding for the values in a database column. When retrieving values from the column, however, an application might prefer to display the actual meanings of the values rather than their short codes. This is a simple example of what can be accomplished using a powerful new V2 feature called a *CASE expression*.

3.2.1 Simple Form

A CASE expression evaluates to a scalar value and can be used wherever you can use an expression such as x + y or foo(x). CASE is often used in a SELECT clause, in a WHERE clause, or in the SET clause of an UPDATE statement. In its simplest form, a CASE expression evaluates to one of several *result expressions*, depending on the value of a *test expression*.

To illustrate the simple form of the CASE expression, consider the following table that contains a list of military officers:

OFFICERS

NAME	STATUS	RANK	TITLE

The STATUS column is an integer code that represents various possibilities, such as "Active," "Reserve," and "Retired." The following query might be used to list the officers together with the descriptive text represented by their status codes:

```
SELECT name,
    CASE status
        WHEN 1 THEN 'Active Duty'
        WHEN 2 THEN 'Reserve'
        WHEN 3 THEN 'Special Assignment'
        WHEN 4 THEN 'Retired'
        ELSE 'Unknown'
    END AS status
FROM officers;
```

The syntax of the simple form of a CASE expression is as follows:

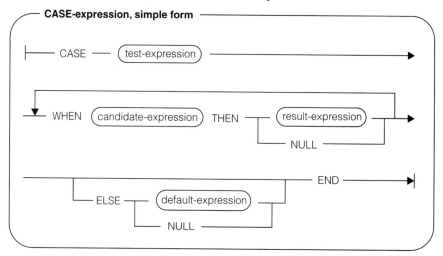

In this syntax diagram, the symbols *test-expression, candidate-expression, result-expression*, and *default-expression* all represent general expressions, constructed according to the rules described in Section 2.4.1.

The value of a simple CASE expression is the value of the first result expression whose corresponding candidate expression is equal to the test expression. If the test expression does not match any of the candidate expressions, the value of the CASE expression is the default expression, or NULL if no default has been specified. When writing a CASE expression, you must make sure that the datatypes of all the candidate expressions are compatible with the datatype of the test expression and that the datatypes of all the result expressions and the default expression are compatible with each other.

As another example of a simple CASE expression, consider a motor vehicle application that needs to compute license fees for various kinds of vehicles. The application is based on the following table:

VEHICLES

LICENSE	RENEWAL_DATE	TYPE	WEIGHT	NWHEELS

Suppose that, according to the law, fees for cars are based on their weight, fees for trucks are based on their number of wheels, and motorcycles are charged a flat fee. The following query might perform the proper fee computation for each vehicle due for renewal, based on its type:

```
SELECT license,
    CASE type
        WHEN 'Car' THEN 0.05 * weight
        WHEN 'Truck' THEN 25.00 * nwheels
```

```
        WHEN 'Motorcycle' THEN 35.00
        ELSE NULL
    END AS fee
 FROM vehicles
 WHERE year(renewal_date) <= 1996;
```

3.2.2 General Form

The CASE expression also has a more general form, which consists of a set of search conditions, each paired with a result expression. The search conditions can contain any kind of predicate, or even multiple predicates connected by AND, OR, and NOT. The value of the CASE expression is the result expression corresponding to the first search condition that evaluates to TRUE. If none of the search conditions is TRUE, the value of the CASE expression is the default expression, or NULL if no default is provided. The syntax of this form of CASE expression is as follows:

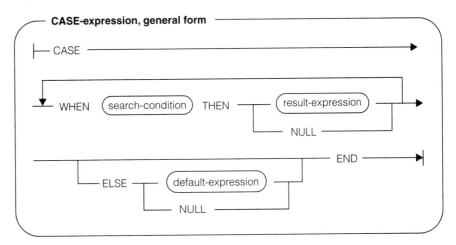

The syntax of a search condition is given on page 55. As in the simple form of CASE, *result-expression* and *default-expression* represent general expressions constructed according to the rules described in Section 2.4.1.

As an example of the general form of a CASE expression, suppose that a certain county maintains a list of properties within the county, using the following table:

PROPERTIES

PARCELNO	CITY	AREA	TAXRATE

If the property tax rate for the county changes to a system based on the area of each property, the tax rate column might be updated as follows:

```
UPDATE properties
SET taxrate =
   CASE
       WHEN area < 10000 THEN .05
       WHEN area < 20000 THEN .07
       ELSE .09
   END;
```

A CASE expression can be used to avoid dividing by zero when computing some result. Suppose that a company keeps records on all its machines in the following table:

MACHINES

SERIALNO	TYPE	YEAR	HOURS_USED	ACCIDENTS

The following query computes the average accident rate for each type of machine in the database, taking care not to divide by zero in case there are machines that have never been used:

```
SELECT type,
   CASE
       WHEN sum(hours_used) > 0
           THEN sum(accidents)/sum(hours_used)
       ELSE NULL
   END AS accident_rate
FROM machines
GROUP BY type;
```

CASE expressions make certain types of queries easy to write and efficient to execute that would otherwise be very difficult or costly. For example, using the MACHINES table above, suppose that we want to know the fraction of all accidents that involve machines of type "chain saw." Using a CASE expression, we can find the answer to this question in a single pass over the MACHINES table, by writing the following query:

```
SELECT sum(CASE
               WHEN type = 'chain saw' THEN accidents
               ELSE 0e0
           END) / sum(accidents)
FROM machines;
```

TIP: The constant "0e0" in the above example is a floating-point zero. We use a floating-point zero rather than an integer zero to force the computation to be done in floating point. If the constant were expressed as "0", the computation would be done in integer arithmetic, and, since the result is a fraction, it would be rounded to zero.

CASE expressions can sometimes be used to compute simple functions. You might choose to use a CASE expression rather than a function call to improve the portability of your application or to avoid the overhead of calling an external function. For example, the absolute value function, which is provided by V2 in the SYSFUN schema, can be simulated by a CASE expression. The expression abs(x) is equivalent to the following expression:

```
CASE
    WHEN x >= 0 THEN x
    ELSE -x
END
```

As an example of the use of CASE to compute absolute values, suppose that I am looking for a college and I think the ideal size for a college is about 8,000 students. My database contains the following table:

COLLEGES

NAME	STATE	ENROLLMENT

The following query lists all the colleges in Colorado and Utah, in order by how close their enrollment is to 8,000 (that is, the college whose enrollment is closest to 8,000 is first on the list):

```
SELECT name, enrollment,
    CASE
        WHEN enrollment >= 8000 THEN enrollment - 8000
        ELSE 8000 - enrollment
    END AS difference
FROM colleges
WHERE state IN ('CO', 'UT')
ORDER BY difference;
```

We will end our discussion of CASE with an example of how one CASE expression can be nested inside another. Suppose that our database contains a table of new hires and their starting dates, as shown on the next page.

HIRES

NAME	STARTDATE

Our legal department has decided that each employee will receive vested rights in the company pension plan on the last day of the month that contains that employee's fifth service anniversary. The following query computes the month, day, and year on which each of the new hires will receive vested rights (note the use of the new built-in function mod to detect leap years):

```
SELECT name,
       month(startdate) AS vestmonth,
       CASE
          WHEN month(startdate) IN (4, 6, 9, 11) THEN 30
          WHEN month(startdate) = 2 THEN
             CASE
                WHEN mod(year(startdate)+5, 4) = 0 THEN 29
                ELSE 28
             END
          ELSE 31
       END as vestday,
       year(startdate) + 5 AS vestyear
FROM hires;
```

TIP: V2 imposes one limitation on the use of CASE expressions. If a CASE expression is used in a SELECT clause, in a VALUES clause (literal table), or in an IN-predicate, then no search condition in that CASE expression may contain a subquery. It may seem arbitrary, but that's the rule.

3.2.3 RAISE_ERROR Function

V2 supports a new built-in function named raise_error, which is particularly useful inside CASE expressions. The raise_error function, as its name implies, aborts the processing of the current SQL statement and raises an error condition. It rolls back all database changes caused by the current SQL statement but leaves the current transaction in progress, so the user or application program can still choose to commit or roll back the other statements in the transaction.

The raise_error function takes two character-string parameters: an SQL-STATE and a message string. The SQLSTATE must be a string of exactly five uppercase letters or digits. The SQLSTATE specified in the call to raise_error is returned to the application program in the SQLCA structure, along with an SQLCODE of –438. In choosing an SQLSTATE to represent a user-defined error condition, you should avoid values that have been reserved by IBM or by the

SQL92 Standard. You can easily avoid conflicts by choosing an SQLSTATE whose first character is a digit between 7 and 9 or a letter between I and Z, inclusive.[1] The second parameter of `raise_error` is a message string of up to 70 characters, which is returned to the application program in the SQLERRMC field of the SQLCA structure.

To illustrate the use of `raise_error` inside a CASE statement, we will return to the PROPERTIES table used in Section 3.2.2. A recent election has raised the tax rate for some of the cities in our county. The PROPERTIES table can be updated to reflect the new tax rates by the following statement, which returns SQLSTATE 70007 if an unexpected city is encountered in the table:

```
UPDATE properties
SET taxrate =
    CASE city
        WHEN 'San Jose' THEN taxrate
        WHEN 'Santa Clara' THEN taxrate + .005
        WHEN 'Campbell' THEN taxrate + .005
        WHEN 'Los Gatos' THEN taxrate + .008
        ELSE raise_error('70007',
            'Parcel ' || parcelno || ' has unknown city')
    END;
```

TIP: A `raise_error` function is compatible with any datatype. For example, a `raise_error` function can be used inside a CASE expression whose result expressions are of type Integer, Varchar, or any other datatype. But if you use a `raise_error` function in a way that requires it to have a datatype of its own (for example, in a CASE expression where *every* result expression is a call to `raise_error`), you must provide an explicit datatype by a CAST expression such as CAST(`raise_error`('77777', 'Bad News') AS Integer). The actual value returned by `raise_error` is the null value.

3.2.4 NULLIF and COALESCE Functions

Among the built-in scalar functions of V2, there are two functions that behave like special kinds of CASE expressions: `nullif` and `coalesce`. The `nullif` function is a shorthand notation for a CASE expression that returns a null value if its first parameter is equal to its second parameter; otherwise, it returns its first parameter. This function is sometimes useful in cases where a designated value such as −1 has been used as a do-it-yourself encoding for null values. For example, `nullif`(salary, -1) is a shorthand notation for the following expression:

---

1. Certain other values for SQLSTATE are also permitted and are described in the *DB2 SQL Reference*.

```
CASE
    WHEN salary = -1 THEN NULL
    ELSE salary
END
```

The coalesce function takes a variable number of parameters and returns the first of its parameters that has a non-null value (if all parameters are null, the result is null). All the parameters passed in a given call to coalesce must have compatible (but not necessarily identical) datatypes (for example, the parameters might have various numeric datatypes such as Integer, Decimal, and Float). The datatype of the result of a call to coalesce is the "greatest" of the input datatypes (that is, the datatype to which all the input datatypes can be promoted). For example, if we call coalesce(x, y, z) where x is a null Integer, y is the Decimal value 5.7, and z is a null value of type Double, the result will have datatype Double and value 5.7. (For a more complete description of how datatypes are handled by the coalesce function, see Section 4.6.2.)

As an example of the use of coalesce, consider the OFFICERS table introduced in Section 3.2.1, which has columns RANK and TITLE. The following query might be used to print the names and ranks of all the officers in certain status categories, substituting title for rank when rank is null:

```
SELECT name, coalesce(rank, title) AS rank_or_title
FROM officers
WHERE status IN (1, 2, 3);
```

In this query, the expression coalesce(rank, title) might be considered to be a shorthand for the following CASE expression:

```
CASE
    WHEN rank IS NOT NULL THEN rank
    ELSE title
END
```

The coalesce function can also be called by the name value, for compatibility with V1 and other members of the DB2 product family. For example, the expression value(rank, title) is equivalent to the expression coalesce(rank, title).

TIP: It is important not to confuse the value function with the VALUES keyword that is used to construct a literal table, as discussed in Section 2.4.8. Because of the danger of confusion between value and VALUES, and because the function name coalesce is used in the SQL92 Standard, you would be wise to use the name coalesce rather than value in your function calls.

3.3 SUBQUERIES

Since SQL was first introduced, it has had the concept of a subquery: a query enclosed in parentheses and used inside some SQL statement. To explore the use of subqueries, we will use a database of employees and departments, containing the following tables:

EMP

NAME	DEPTNO	JOB	MANAGER	RATING

SALARY	BONUS	STARTDATE

DEPT

DEPTNO	DEPTNAME	BUDGET	LOCATION

Suppose that we need to find the names and salaries of all the employees who work in Menlo Park. This could be accomplished by the following query:

```
SELECT name, salary
FROM   emp
WHERE  deptno IN
  (SELECT deptno
   FROM   dept
   WHERE  location = 'Menlo Park');
```

This query contains a subquery that finds all the departments located in Menlo Park, and this set is then used in the outer-level query to find all the employees who work in these departments. In this example, the subquery can be completely evaluated before the outer-level query is begun. However, there is another kind of subquery, called a *correlated subquery*, that is evaluated once for every row of the table used in the outer-level query. You can tell that a subquery is correlated because it contains an identifier, called a *correlation name*, that represents a row of the outer-level query. The correlation name is defined in the FROM clause of the outer-level query, optionally preceded by the keyword AS. The following is an example of a correlated subquery, using correlation name x, that finds employees whose salary is more than 10% of their department budget:

```
SELECT name, salary
FROM   emp AS x
WHERE  salary >
  (SELECT 0.1 * budget
   FROM   dept
   WHERE  deptno = x.deptno);
```

You might think of this query as being processed as follows: "For each row x in the EMP table, evaluate the subquery to find the budget of x's department, then compare one-tenth of this budget to x's salary." (Of course, the optimizer reserves the right to process this query in some other equivalent way.)

In the above example, the subquery returns a single value, called a *scalar* (in this case, one-tenth of a department budget). In the previous example, the subquery returned a set of values of the same datatype (department numbers), which we might think of as a table consisting of a single column. A subquery might also return a table consisting of many rows and columns, as in the following example of a subquery inside an INSERT statement:

```
CREATE TABLE artists(name Varchar(30),
                     deptno Char(3),
                     salary Decimal(8,2));
INSERT INTO artists
   (SELECT name, deptno, salary
    FROM   emp
    WHERE  job = 'Artist');
```

In general, the user who writes a subquery must make sure that its result fits properly into the context of the statement in which it is used; otherwise, an error will result.

Whenever a column name is used in an SQL statement, the system must *resolve* the name to a column of a particular table. Subqueries introduce some complications into the rules for resolving names. If a column name appears in a subquery, the system attempts to interpret it as a column of one of the tables in the FROM clause of the subquery. If none of these tables has a column with the given name, the system looks at the next higher-level query block that contains the subquery and attempts to resolve the column name among the tables in its FROM clause. This process continues through successively higher-level query blocks until a table is found that contains a column with the given name. Of course, a correlation name can be used to force the resolution of the column to a particular table. If a column name cannot be resolved unambiguously, an error results. The following example repeats the query that finds employees whose salary is more than 10% of their department budget, writing the query in a different way this time to illustrate the resolution of column names. In the subquery inside this example, BUDGET is interpreted as a column of DEPT, but SALARY is interpreted as a column of EMP (since the table in the FROM clause of the subquery has no SALARY column).

```
SELECT name, salary
FROM   emp
WHERE  deptno IN
  (SELECT deptno
   FROM   dept
   WHERE  salary > 0.1 * budget);
```

V2 has introduced some new features, based on the SQL92 Standard, that greatly increase the power of subqueries. In order to understand these new features, you must first understand two principles of programming language design, called *closure* and *orthogonality*, and how they have been applied in V2.

3.3.1 Closure

The principle of *closure* states that the objects that are computed by expressions in a language should be the same types of objects that serve as input to those expressions. For example, the familiar arithmetic operators +, –, *, and / have the closure property because they operate on numbers and they produce numbers as their result (actually, the division operator violates closure if its second operand is zero). Closure is an important property, because it allows the result of one operator to be used as input to another operator. We will need this property if we wish to make general use of subqueries inside SQL statements.

The basic objects on which SQL operates are tables with named columns. In order for the closure property to hold, the result of an SQL query should also be a table with named columns. In general, the result of an SQL query is a table, but some of the columns of the table may have no obvious name, since they may contain some computed result like avg(salary) or salary + bonus. This has always been a problem when users need their output to be ordered by some computed result, since the computed result has no name that can be used in the ORDER BY clause. DB2 has solved this problem by allowing integers to be used in the ORDER BY clause, representing the position of the desired column in the SELECT list, as in the following example, which makes a list of employees in order of their combined salary and bonus:

```
SELECT name, salary + bonus
FROM emp
ORDER BY 2;
```

V2 introduces a more elegant solution to this problem, which preserves the closure property. In V2, each expression in a SELECT list can be given a name (optionally preceded by the keyword AS), which serves as a "column name" in the result set. This "column name" can be used in an ORDER BY clause, and it will also be used as a label by the CLP when displaying the result of the query. For example, the query in the previous example could be rewritten as follows:

```
SELECT name, salary + bonus AS pay
FROM emp
ORDER BY pay;
```

Ordinarily, column names are case-insensitive (that is, folded to uppercase) and contain no blanks. If you wish, however, you may name your output columns using *delimited identifiers,* which are strings enclosed in double quotes. Delimited identifiers are case-sensitive and may contain blanks or SQL keywords. For example, you might make the previous example more descriptive by writing it as follows:

```
SELECT name AS "Employee Name",
       salary + bonus AS "Total Pay"
FROM emp
ORDER BY "Total Pay";
```

A subtle point to remember when you generate your own column names is that these names apply to the *result* of a query or subquery, and therefore cannot be used inside the query or subquery in which they are defined. For example, the above query defines "Total Pay" as the name of one of its result columns. This name can be used in an ORDER BY clause or in an outer-level query. However, it would be incorrect to use the name inside this query, in a WHERE or GROUP BY or HAVING clause. If you wish your query result to be formed into groups based on some expression such as salary + bonus, you must use a technique called a *table expression*, which is described in Section 3.5.

The naming of output columns in a SELECT list is useful both in outer-level queries and in subqueries. As we have seen, generated column names in outer-level queries are useful for ordering output and for making more descriptive output labels. In a subquery, generated column names are important for preserving the closure property so that the result of the subquery can be used in the outer query just as if it were a table.

3.3.2 Orthogonality

SQL has always placed some limitations on the places in which a subquery could be used. For example, subqueries have been allowed in INSERT statements and in WHERE clauses subject to certain rules, but they have not been permitted in SELECT clauses, in FROM clauses, or in the SET clause of an UPDATE statement. The rules governing usage of subqueries have been rightly criticized by Chris Date, Hugh Darwen, and others as a violation of the principle of *orthogonality,* which states that the features of a language should be independent of each other and should interact in regular and predictable ways. Applying this principle to subqueries suggests that a subquery that returns a table should be usable wherever a table is expected, and that a subquery that returns a scalar should be usable wherever a scalar is expected. Indeed, these are the rules governing usage of subqueries in the SQL92 Standard, and they have been implemented in V2, as is shown in the next two sections.

3.4 SCALAR SUBQUERIES

An *expression* represents a scalar value, constructed from primitive parts such as column names, constants, host variables, functions, and special registers, as described in Section 2.4.1. In V2, wherever an expression can be used, you can also use a subquery that returns a scalar value (that is, one row with exactly one column). When a subquery is used in a place where a scalar is expected, it is called a *scalar subquery.* If a scalar subquery returns more than one row or more than one column, an error results. If a scalar subquery returns zero rows, its result is interpreted as the null value (no error results in this case, unless the context where the scalar subquery is used does not permit null values for some reason).

Many of the uses of subqueries that were permitted in V1 involved scalar subqueries. However, the new level of orthogonality supported by V2 permits scalar subqueries to be used in places that were not accepted by V1, as I will show by some examples.

The first scalar subquery example finds the names and locations of departments in which the average bonus is greater than the average salary.

```
SELECT d.deptname, d.location
FROM   dept AS d
WHERE (SELECT avg(bonus)
       FROM   emp
       WHERE  deptno = d.deptno)
     > (SELECT avg(salary)
       FROM   emp
       WHERE  deptno = d.deptno)
```

The above query would not have been accepted by V1, which did not permit more than one subquery in a predicate. V1 also did not permit subqueries in a SELECT clause, as illustrated by the next example, which lists the department numbers, names, and maximum salaries of all the departments located in Sausalito.

```
SELECT d.deptno, d.deptname,
          (SELECT max(salary)
           FROM    emp
           WHERE   deptno = d.deptno) AS maxpay
FROM    dept AS d
WHERE   d.location = 'Sausalito';
```

In the above example, any department in Sausalito that has no employees will appear in the result set with a null value for its maximum salary. Note that this is different from the example below, which expresses a similar query as a join. In the join formulation of the query, departments in Sausalito that have no employees do not appear in the result set at all.

```
SELECT d.deptno, d.deptname, max(e.salary) AS maxpay
FROM dept AS d, emp AS e
WHERE d.deptno = e.deptno
AND d.location = 'Sausalito'
GROUP BY d.deptno, d.deptname;
```

In our next example, we assume the existence of the following table, which contains planned pay raises for employees based on their job and rating:

SALARYPLAN

JOB   RATING   RAISE

Using the SALARYPLAN table, we will update the salaries of employees in department no. A74 by applying the appropriate pay raises. This is done by using a scalar subquery in the SET clause of an UPDATE statement.

```
UPDATE emp AS e
SET salary = salary + (SELECT raise FROM salaryplan p
                       WHERE p.job = e.job
                       AND p.rating = e.rating)
WHERE deptno = 'A74';
```

It is interesting to consider what the above UPDATE statement will do if some employee has a job and/or rating that is not found in the SALARYPLAN table. The scalar subquery will return no result, which will be interpreted as a null value; when this null value is added to the employee's current salary, the salary will become null! If this is not the behavior we desire, we can guard against it by modifying the UPDATE statement as follows:

```
UPDATE emp AS e
SET salary = salary +
                coalesce((SELECT raise FROM salaryplan p
                          WHERE p.job = e.job
                          AND p.rating = e.rating), 0)
WHERE deptno = 'A74';
```

The following points should be clear from the examples above:

1. Interesting uses of scalar subqueries often involve correlation names.

2. Scalar subqueries pose many challenges for attractive indentation of your SQL code.

3.5 TABLE EXPRESSIONS

In all of the examples above, the subquery was used in place of a scalar value. But we know that a subquery can also return a table consisting of many rows and columns. Such a subquery is called a *table expression*, and it can be used in a FROM clause where the name of a table is expected.

The FROM clause of a SELECT statement lists the table(s) on which the query operates. Each table listed in the FROM clause can optionally be given a correlation name, which serves as the name of the table within the current query. We have seen how correlation names are used in correlated subqueries. They are also useful in cases where it is necessary to join a table to itself, as in the famous query "Find employees who earn more than their managers." In this query, we join the EMP table to itself as though it were two different tables named e and m:

```
SELECT e.name, e.salary, m.name, m.salary
FROM   emp AS e, emp AS m
WHERE  e.manager = m.name
AND    e.salary > m.salary
```

V2 allows a table expression (subquery) to be used in place of a table name in a FROM clause. The table expression participates in the query just as though it were a real table in the database. The table expression must be enclosed in parentheses and followed by an AS clause that gives it a table name. The column names of the virtual table can be specified in the SELECT clause of the subquery itself.

Suppose that, for the purposes of a particular query on the EMP table, we would like to consider only employees whose job is "Plumber," to treat the SALARY and BONUS columns as though they were combined into a single column named PAY, and to treat the STARTDATE column as though it contained only a year rather than an actual date. In other words, we would like to write a query against a table expression derived from EMP that has the following structure:

PLUMBERS

NAME	PAY	STARTYEAR

The following query uses such a table expression to list the name, combined pay, and starting year of all plumbers whose pay is less than $50,000. Note how the table expression is given both a table name (PLUMBERS) and a set of column names (NAME, PAY, STARTYEAR).

```
SELECT name, pay, startyear
FROM (SELECT name,
             salary + bonus AS pay,
             year(startdate) AS startyear
      FROM emp
      WHERE job = 'Plumber') AS plumbers
WHERE pay < 50000;
```

In the example above, it was not really necessary to use a table expression, since the predicates and column definitions in the subquery could have been moved to the outer-level query. However, in some cases, table expressions allow you to express queries that could not have been expressed otherwise. One such case arises when you want to form a table into groups based on some computed value such as salary + bonus or year(startdate). SQL allows only column names to appear in a GROUP BY clause, so it would not accept either of the above expressions. But you can accomplish the same purpose by computing the desired grouping value inside a subquery and then using a GROUP BY clause in the outer-level query. For example, the following query groups employees by their starting year and prints the average pay of each group:

```
SELECT startyear, avg(pay)
FROM (SELECT name,
             salary + bonus AS pay,
             year(startdate) AS startyear
      FROM emp) AS emp2
GROUP BY startyear;
```

A table expression might also do some grouping of its own. For example, a query might wish to view the EMP table as though it contained the total pay of the employees in each department. The next two examples use a table expression, based on the EMP table, that has the following structure:

PAYROLL

DEPTNO   TOTALPAY

The following example finds the departments whose total pay is greater than $200,000:

```
SELECT deptno, totalpay
FROM (SELECT deptno, sum(salary) + sum(bonus) AS totalpay
      FROM emp
      GROUP BY deptno) AS payroll
WHERE totalpay > 200000;
```

The following example shows how a table expression can be joined to a real table in the database. It finds the names and locations of departments whose total pay is greater than half their budget.

```
SELECT dept.deptname, dept.location
FROM dept,
      (SELECT deptno, sum(salary) + sum(bonus) AS totalpay
       FROM emp
       GROUP BY deptno) AS payroll
WHERE dept.deptno = payroll.deptno
AND payroll.totalpay > 0.5 * dept.budget;
```

TIP: It may be worth mentioning why we wrote sum(salary) + sum(bonus) in the above example rather than sum(salary + bonus). The reason has to do with null values. If an employee has, for example, a well-defined salary but a null bonus, we want the salary of that employee to participate in our computation. The expression sum(salary) + sum(bonus) computes the two sums independently, taking into account all non-null salaries and bonuses. The expression sum(salary + bonus), on the other hand, includes an employee's salary and bonus in the sum only if both salary and bonus are non-null.

3.6 COMMON TABLE EXPRESSIONS

Suppose that we need to find the department that has the highest total pay. This query is difficult because it involves two levels of aggregation: first, we need the sum function to combine individual employees' pay into totals by department; then, we need the max function to find the greatest of all the department totals. In V1, such a query could be expressed only by creating a view and then writing a query that uses the view, as shown below. Note the similarity between the view and the table expression that was used in the previous examples.

```
CREATE VIEW payroll(deptno, totalpay) AS
    SELECT deptno, sum(salary) + sum(bonus)
    FROM emp
    GROUP BY deptno;

SELECT deptno
FROM payroll
WHERE totalpay =
    (SELECT max(totalpay)
     FROM payroll);
```

It is awkward to be forced to create a view in order to express a query. We are required to think of a name that does not conflict with the names of existing views, and we must remember to drop the view when we no longer need it. The database system is forced to do some work to enter the view into the system catalog tables, even if it is needed only for processing a single query. It would be both more elegant and more efficient if we could express the query above in a single statement without defining a view.

Examining the SELECT statement above, we see that it uses the PAYROLL view in two places. We might consider replacing each of these references to PAYROLL with a table expression whose definition is the same as that of the view. This would result in the following query:

```
SELECT deptno
FROM (SELECT deptno, sum(salary) + sum(bonus) AS totalpay
      FROM emp
      GROUP BY deptno) AS payroll1
WHERE totalpay =
  (SELECT max(totalpay)
    FROM (SELECT deptno, sum(salary) + sum(bonus) AS totalpay
          FROM emp
          GROUP BY deptno) AS payroll2);
```

This query, while it is valid in V2, has some disadvantages. First, it seems inelegant to repeat the same table expression twice in the same query. Even worse, each of the table expressions will be evaluated independently, which is inefficient and may lead to inconsistencies if some other user is updating the EMP table during the time when our query is running (if the isolation level of our query is not RR). What we would really like to do is to define the table expression once, give it a name, and use the name as often as we like in a query, without creating a permanent view. This is exactly the function that is provided in V2 by a feature called *common table expressions*.

A common table expression takes the form of a WITH clause at the beginning of an SQL statement. The syntax of the WITH clause is similar to that of a view definition, as shown below.

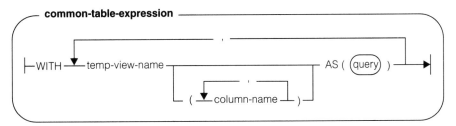

A common table expression defines one or more temporary views that are only effective during the processing of the current SQL statement. The temporary views defined in the WITH clause can be used as often as you like inside the statement. Regardless of how often you use them, each temporary view will be evaluated only once, so there is no possibility of your SQL statement seeing inconsistent data. Using a common table expression, we can rewrite our query that finds the department with the greatest total pay as follows:

```
WITH payroll(deptno, totalpay) AS
  (SELECT deptno, sum(salary) + sum(bonus)
    FROM emp
    GROUP BY deptno)
SELECT deptno
FROM payroll
WHERE totalpay =
  (SELECT max(totalpay)
    FROM payroll);
```

Queries that need to perform multiple levels of aggregation occur surprisingly often. Here's another example that finds the department with the most employees, also handled nicely by a common table expression:

```
WITH staff(deptno, headcount) AS
   (SELECT deptno, count(*) FROM emp GROUP BY deptno)
SELECT deptno, headcount
FROM    staff
WHERE   headcount =
   (SELECT max(headcount) from staff);
```

As we have seen, a common table expression behaves like a view that is defined only for the duration of a single SQL statement, saving both the user and the system the work of creating and dropping an actual view. A common table expression also has another advantage over an actual view: its definition can contain a reference to a host program variable. A real view definition can never contain a host variable, because the view is not limited to being used by a specific program. A common table expression, however, is used only within a specific SQL statement, and if that SQL statement is embedded in a program, then it has access to the host language variables declared in that program. To illustrate this, we will modify the previous example to find the department that has the most employees whose jobs match the job contained in program variable x:

```
WITH staff(deptno, headcount) AS
   (SELECT deptno, count(*)
    FROM emp
    WHERE job = :x
    GROUP BY deptno)
SELECT deptno, headcount
FROM staff
WHERE headcount =
   (SELECT max(headcount) from staff);
```

Common table expressions are used mainly in queries that need to use the same table expression more than once. It's even possible to write a query that joins a table expression to itself. This is done by using a common table expression and giving it a different correlation name each time it is used, as in the following example. This example finds pairs of departments in which the average salary of one department is more than twice the average salary of the other.

```
WITH deptavg(deptno, avgsal) AS
   (SELECT deptno, avg(salary)
    FROM emp
    GROUP BY deptno)
SELECT d1.deptno, d1.avgsal, d2.deptno, d2.avgsal
FROM deptavg AS d1, deptavg AS d2
WHERE d1.avgsal > 2 * d2.avgsal;
```

We have seen that a view can be defined using either a SELECT clause or a VALUES clause. This rule applies not only to permanent views but also to temporary views defined using common table expressions. In the following example, we define a common table expression (temporary view) named VITAL, which contains a list of pairs of departments and jobs that are vital to our company; the example then joins this temporary view to the EMP table to find the names of employees whose department number and job are found on the list.

```
WITH vital(deptno, job) AS
    (VALUES('A29', 'Machinist'),
           ('J16', 'Fork Lift Operator'),
           ('M07', 'Welder'))
SELECT e.name
FROM emp e, vital v
WHERE e.deptno = v.deptno
AND e.job = v.job;
```

A common table expression (WITH clause) can be used only in the following places:

1. In a top-level query (SELECT statement), as in all the examples above.

2. In a SELECT nested immediately inside a CREATE VIEW statement. Thus, the query in the previous example could be turned into a permanent view named VITALEMP as follows:

```
CREATE VIEW vitalemp(name) AS
    WITH vital(deptno, job) AS
        (VALUES('A29', 'Machinist'),
               ('J16', 'Fork Lift Operator'),
               ('M07', 'Welder'))
    SELECT e.name
    FROM emp e, vital v
    WHERE e.deptno = v.deptno
    AND e.job = v.job;
```

3. In a SELECT nested immediately inside an INSERT statement. Thus, the results of the above query could be inserted into an existing table named VITALEMP as follows:

```
INSERT INTO vitalemp(name)
    WITH vital(deptno, job) AS
        (VALUES('A29', 'Machinist'),
               ('J16', 'Fork Lift Operator'),
               ('M07', 'Welder'))
```

```
SELECT e.name
FROM emp e, vital v
WHERE e.deptno = v.deptno
AND e.job = v.job;
```

TIP: A WITH clause is not allowed in a single-row SELECT statement. Therefore, if you embed a query in an application program and that query uses a common table expression, you must use a cursor to fetch the result of the query, even if you know that the result consists of a single row.

3.7 OUTER JOIN

Imagine that we are responsible for a university database containing the following tables:

TEACHERS

NAME	RANK
Ms. Redding	Assoc. Prof.
Mr. Glenn	Assist. Prof.
Ms. Barnes	Full Prof.
Mrs. Plummer	Assoc. Prof.

COURSES

QUARTER	SUBJECT	TEACHER	ENROLLMENT
Fall 96	Math 101	Mr. Glenn	40
Fall 96	English 280	Ms. Redding	30
Fall 96	Science 580	Ms. Redding	33
Fall 96	Physics 405	Mrs. Plummer	28
Fall 96	Latin 237	Mr. Glenn	20
Fall 96	German 130	Staff	31
Winter 96	French 140	Ms. Barnes	(null)

At the beginning of a quarter, our university might need to print a master list of all the teachers (including their ranks) and the courses they teach in the current quarter (including their enrollments). This can be done by a join query, as follows:

```
SELECT t.name, t.rank, c.subject, c.enrollment
FROM teachers AS t, courses AS c
WHERE t.name = c.teacher
AND c.quarter = 'Fall 96';
```

The result of the query above will not include the names of teachers who are not teaching any classes in the "Fall 96" quarter, nor any classes being taught in that quarter whose teachers are not listed in the TEACHERS table. But the university administration might reasonably wish either or both of these kinds of data to be included in the master list. This kind of requirement gives rise to a kind of a query called an *outer join*.

An outer join always involves a join of two tables, which we will refer to as the *left table* and the *right table*. An outer join is different from a conventional, or "inner" join, because it includes rows that have no "partners"—that is, rows from the left table that have no matching rows in the right table, or vice versa. There are three kinds of outer-join queries:

1. A *left outer join* includes rows from the left table that have no matching values in the right table, such as teachers who are not teaching any courses. These rows are given null values for the missing course data.

2. A *right outer join* includes rows from the right table that have no matching values in the left table, such as courses that have no teacher. These rows are given null values for the missing teacher data.

3. A *full outer join* includes both kinds of rows. In our example, it would include both teachers that have no courses and courses that have no teachers, supplemented by null values as needed.

Outer joins were difficult to express in V1, because V1 did not allow NULL to appear in a SELECT clause. As noted in Section 3.1, the CAST notation of V2 provides a way to specify the datatype of a null value, allowing NULL to be used in SELECT clauses and other places where typed values are needed. For example, a query might use the following clause to specify both the name and the datatype of a column of null values in its result set:

```
SELECT name, rank, CAST(NULL AS Varchar(20)) AS subject
```

Another V2 feature that is useful in expressing outer joins is the common table expression. In the following example, we will construct the full outer join of the TEACHERS and CLASSES table for the Fall 1996 quarter, using three common table expressions. The first common table expression, named `innerjoin`, expresses the conventional or inner join of the two tables. The second table expression, named `teacher_only`, finds the teachers who are not teaching any courses in Fall 1996, and uses `innerjoin` in its definition. The third table expression, named `course_only`, finds courses offered in Fall 1996 that have no matching teacher in the TEACHERS table, also using the `innerjoin` expression. The full outer join can then be expressed as a UNION ALL of the three common table expressions, supplemented by nulls as needed.

```
WITH
    innerjoin(name, rank, subject, enrollment) AS
        (SELECT t.name, t.rank, c.subject, c.enrollment
         FROM teachers AS t, courses AS c
         WHERE t.name = c.teacher
         AND c.quarter = 'Fall 96'),
    teacher_only(name, rank) AS
        (SELECT name, rank
         FROM teachers
         EXCEPT ALL
         SELECT name, rank
         FROM innerjoin),
    course_only(subject, enrollment) AS
        (SELECT subject, enrollment
         FROM courses
         WHERE quarter = 'Fall 96'
         EXCEPT ALL
         SELECT subject, enrollment
         FROM innerjoin)

SELECT name, rank, subject, enrollment
FROM innerjoin

UNION ALL

SELECT name,
       rank,
       CAST(NULL AS Varchar(20)) AS subject,
       CAST(NULL AS Integer) AS enrollment
FROM teacher_only

UNION ALL
```

```
SELECT CAST(NULL AS Varchar(20)) AS name,
       CAST(NULL AS Varchar(20)) AS rank,
       subject,
       enrollment
FROM course_only;
```

The result of this outer-join query is as follows:

NAME	RANK	SUBJECT	ENROLLMENT
Mr. Glenn	Assist. Prof.	Math 101	40
Mr. Glenn	Assist. Prof.	Latin 237	20
Mrs. Plummer	Assoc. Prof.	Physics 405	28
Ms. Redding	Assoc. Prof.	English 280	30
Ms. Redding	Assoc. Prof.	Science 580	33
Ms. Barnes	Full Prof.	(null)	(null)
(null)	(null)	German 130	31

— From innerjoin (rows 1–5)
← From teacher_only (Ms. Barnes row)
← From course_only (German 130 row)

Of course, if only the left outer join is needed, the course_only common table expression can be eliminated from the above query, and if only the right outer join is needed, the teacher_only expression can be eliminated.

TIP: The EXCEPT ALL and UNION ALL operators in the example above ensure that duplicate rows are represented properly in the query result. If EXCEPT or UNION were used instead of the ALL versions of these operators, duplicate rows in one table with no matching row in the other table would be condensed into a single row in the result set.

For a certain class of outer joins, there is an alternative method of expression that you might consider. If you need to express a left outer join in which you are sure that each row of the left table is associated with at most one row of the right table, you can express the outer join by using scalar subqueries in the SELECT clause. For example, in our university database, suppose that we wish to express a left outer join of COURSES and TEACHERS, in which each course is listed with the name and rank of its teacher, using a null rank if the teacher is not found in the TEACHERS table. This left outer join can be expressed as follows:

```
SELECT c.subject, c.teacher,
       (select rank from teachers where name = c.teacher)
FROM courses c;
```

3.8 RECURSION

Section 3.6 showed how a common table expression (WITH clause) can be used to define a temporary view for use inside a single SQL statement. Common table expressions have another powerful feature, called *recursion*, that we have not yet discussed. A common table expression is *recursive* if it uses itself in its own definition. Recursion is very powerful, because it allows certain kinds of questions to be expressed in a single SQL statement that would otherwise require the use of a host program. Recursive queries can also be tricky to write and have the possibility of placing the system into a loop, so you will need to carefully follow certain rules when using recursion.

I will begin with a simple example. Suppose that we have a table of federal employees, with the following structure:

FEDEMP

NAME	SALARY	MANAGER

Suppose that we wish to find the names and salaries of employees in the FEDEMP table whose manager is Hoover and whose salary is greater than $100,000. This is easily done by the following (nonrecursive) query:

```
SELECT name, salary
FROM fedemp
WHERE manager = 'Hoover'
AND salary > 100000;
```

The problem becomes harder if we wish to find the employees who earn more than $100,000 and who have Hoover anywhere in their management chain. To express this question, we need a recursive query. A recursive query can be written by following these rules:

1. Define a common table expression, using a WITH clause. The common table expression computes a temporary view, which in our example will be named AGENTS. The common table expression must be defined as a UNION ALL (not a regular UNION, and not any other set operation) between two parts:

   a. The first part of the UNION ALL, called the *initial subquery*, is a conventional subquery that does not involve recursion. In processing a recursive query, the system evaluates the initial subquery first. In our example, the initial subquery finds all the employees who report directly to Hoover.

b. The second part of the UNION ALL, called the *recursive subquery*, is a subquery that adds more rows to the temporary view, based somehow on the rows that are already there. In writing the recursive subquery, you must be careful to define how the new rows are related to the old rows, and you must make sure that the query has a way to stop when it has found all the necessary rows. In our example, the recursive subquery adds to the AGENTS view the employees who are managed by employees who are already in the view. The system will stop adding new rows to the view when it reaches the set of employees who are not managers. The recursive subquery is subject to the following rules:

- It may not contain any column function, SELECT DISTINCT, GROUP BY, or HAVING clause.

- It may contain a reference to the common table expression in which it is embedded, but it may not contain a lower-level subquery that has such a reference.

- Each column of the recursive subquery must be assignment-compatible with (and not longer than) the corresponding column of the initial subquery.

TIP: You may need to cast one or more columns of the initial subquery to match the datatypes and lengths of the corresponding columns of the recursive subquery. Try this technique if your recursive query fails with SQLCODE –344 or SQLSTATE 42825.

2. After the WITH clause has defined a temporary view, use the view in a SELECT statement to express the original question. In our example, the temporary view named AGENTS consists of all employees who have Hoover anywhere in their management chain, and the query that follows it selects those employees in the view whose salary is greater than $100,000.

The query that solves our problem may be written as follows:

```
WITH agents(name, salary) AS
    ((SELECT name, salary       -- Initial Subquery
      FROM    fedemp
      WHERE   manager = 'Hoover')
    UNION ALL
      (SELECT f.name, f.salary  -- Recursive Subquery
       FROM    agents AS a, fedemp AS f
       WHERE   f.manager = a.name))
SELECT name                     -- Final Query
FROM    agents
WHERE   salary > 100000;
```

In visualizing the processing of this query, it is important to realize that each time the recursive subquery is executed, when it reads the temporary view AGENTS, it sees only the rows that were added to this view by the previous iteration of the recursive subquery. Thus, for example, the first evaluation of the recursive subquery adds to AGENTS all the employees whose manager-once-removed is Hoover, the second evaluation adds those employees whose manager-twice-removed is Hoover, and so on. The system keeps on evaluating the recursive subquery until no more rows are added to the temporary view. As you will see, it is necessary to be careful to make sure the system does not keep looping forever.

In Section 3.6, we learned that common table expressions (WITH clauses) can be used in queries, view definitions, and INSERT statements. WITH clauses that involve recursion can be used in exactly the same ways. If a recursive query is used inside a CREATE VIEW statement, it defines a recursive view. Similarly, if a recursive query is used in an INSERT statement, its result is inserted into the target table. Use of recursion inside an INSERT statement can be a powerful technique for generating synthetic tables. For example, suppose that I would like to generate a table named NUMBERS with columns named COUNTER and RANDOM. The COUNTER column will contain all the integers from 1 to 1,000, and the RANDOM column will contain random integers between 1 and 1,000. This table can be created and populated by the following statements (note the use of recursion in the INSERT statement):

```
CREATE TABLE numbers (counter Integer, random Integer);
INSERT INTO numbers(counter, random)
    WITH temp(n) AS
        (VALUES(1)                      -- Initial Subquery
      UNION ALL
        SELECT n+1 FROM temp        -- Recursive Subquery
        WHERE n < 1000)
    SELECT n, integer(rand()*1000)
    FROM temp;
```

Synthetic data generated by recursive INSERT statements has many uses. For example, the data generated by the example above might be used as input to a statistical experiment requiring 1,000 random integers. With some creative use of the char and translate functions, you can generate random string data as well.

3.8.1 Recursion with Computation

In the example of searching for federal employees, the problem was simply one of exploring a hierarchy (all the employees below Hoover) and printing all the rows that satisfy some condition (salary greater than $100,000). There is a more interesting class of problems that perform some computation while recursively exploring a data space. I will illustrate this class of problems with a classic recursive example called the "parts explosion problem."

Suppose that an aircraft manufacturer maintains a table of all the parts used in a certain kind of airplane and the subparts from which each part is assembled. A fragment of the data in this table is shown below. By looking at the data, we can see that each wing has one aileron, each aileron has two hinges, each hinge has four rivets, and so on.

COMPONENTS

PART	SUBPART	QTY
wing	strut	5
wing	aileron	1
wing	landing gear	1
wing	rivet	100
strut	rivet	10
aileron	hinge	2
aileron	rivet	5
landing gear	hinge	3
landing gear	rivet	8
hinge	rivet	4

Another way of looking at this data is to draw a graph in which each node represents some part used in the airplane. The nodes are connected by lines that are labelled with numbers, representing how many of each kind of subpart are needed to assemble each part. By looking at the graphic representation of this data in Figure 3-1, we see that the components database is not a strict hierarchy as was the employee database in the previous example. For example, hinges are used in both ailerons and landing gear, and many parts use rivets. The mathematical name for this kind of data is a *directed acyclic graph*. The term *acyclic* means that the graph has no cycles (no part is a component of itself).

Suppose that, due to a national rivet shortage, we receive an urgent question from top management: What is the total number of rivets used in a wing? This question requires us to recursively explore all the components used in a wing, to discover how many rivets are used at each level of the assembly. But we cannot simply add up the number of rivets used at each level—we must also take into account how many times each subassembly is used in a wing.

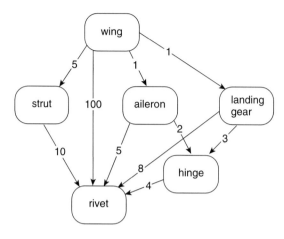

Figure 3-1: Graphic Representation of Parts and Components

For example, a hinge needs four rivets, but a wing needs five hinges (two in the aileron and three in the landing gear).

To write our recursive query, we will follow the same rules used in the previous example. We begin by writing a common table expression, or temporary view, consisting of an initial subquery and a recursive subquery connected by UNION ALL. The name of the temporary view is WINGPARTS, and each row in the view describes some component of a wing and the quantity of that component used for some specific purpose in the wing (for example, the number of hinges used in the landing gear). The initial subquery lists the parts that are directly used in assembling the wing, and the recursive subquery lists the parts that are used in lower-level subassemblies inside the wing. The acyclic nature of the database provides us with a stopping rule, since the recursion will stop when it gets to primitive parts like rivets that have no subparts.

The initial WITH clause of our query, which defines the temporary view that we need, may be written as follows:

```
WITH wingparts(subpart, qty) AS
  ((SELECT subpart, qty                  -- Initial
    FROM components                      -- Subquery
    WHERE part = 'wing')
  UNION ALL
    (SELECT c.subpart, w.qty * c.qty     -- Recursive
    FROM wingparts w, components c        -- Subquery
    WHERE w.subpart = c.part));
```

We might visualize the temporary view WINGPARTS as shown in the table below. The solid lines through the table have no significance other than to help us visualize "first-generation subparts," "second-generation subparts," "third-generation subparts," and so on.

WINGPARTS

SUBPART	QTY	
strut	5	(direct usage)
aileron	1	(direct usage)
landing gear	1	(direct usage)
rivet	100	(direct usage)
rivet	50	(from struts)
hinge	2	(from aileron)
rivet	5	(from aileron)
hinge	3	(from landing gear)
rivet	8	(from landing gear)
rivet	8	(from aileron hinges)
rivet	12	(from landing gear hinges)

Note that a subpart such as a rivet may appear multiple times in the view, and that each row represents the total number of that subpart needed for some particular usage. For example, one row indicates a usage of 50 rivets due to five struts with ten rivets each. Note also that the elimination of duplicate rows from this temporary view would be quite harmful to our computation!

Using the temporary view defined above, it is easy to write queries to solve the rivet problem and to answer other similar questions. Shown below are two queries that use the WINGPARTS expression, and the result of each (remember that WINGPARTS must be defined separately in each query):

1. Find the total number of rivets used in a wing.

```
WITH wingparts(subpart, qty) AS
  ((SELECT subpart, qty              -- Initial
    FROM components                  -- Subquery
    WHERE part = 'wing')
  UNION ALL
    (SELECT c.subpart, w.qty * c.qty  -- Recursive
     FROM wingparts w, components c   -- Subquery
     WHERE w.subpart = c.part))
  SELECT sum(qty) AS qty
  FROM wingparts
  WHERE subpart = 'rivet';
```

Result:

QTY
183

2. List all the subparts used to assemble a wing, with the total number of each.

```
WITH wingparts(subpart, qty) AS
   ((SELECT subpart, qty                -- Initial
     FROM components                    -- Subquery
     WHERE part = 'wing')
   UNION ALL
     (SELECT c.subpart, w.qty * c.qty   -- Recursive
      FROM wingparts w, components c     -- Subquery
      WHERE w.subpart = c.part))
SELECT subpart, sum(qty) AS qty
FROM wingparts
GROUP BY subpart;
```

Result:

SUBPART	QTY
strut	5
aileron	1
landing gear	1
hinge	5
rivet	183

3.8.2 Recursive Searching

An important class of computer applications involves searching for a solution (usually the *best* solution according to some criterion) to a problem. Searching applications are often recursive, and I will illustrate such an application by searching a database of airline flights.

Suppose that a client has arrived at our travel agency and requested that we find for her the least expensive way to fly from San Francisco to New York. Because of membership in a frequent flyer club, our client wishes to travel only on HyFlier Airlines, which has the route map shown in Figure 3-2 (numbers represent the cost of a one-way flight):

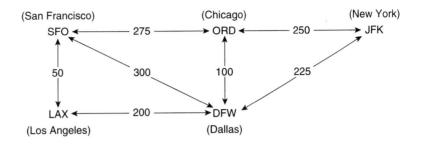

Figure 3-2: Airline Route Map

We can see by looking at the route map that this database is not an acyclic graph as in the previous example. The data contains cycles, which make it possible to fly around in circles indefinitely. As we will see, it is necessary to be alert to this cyclic property in order to provide our query with a "stopping rule."

The data in the HyFlier route map might be represented in a relational database by the following table:

FLIGHTS

FLIGHTNO	ORIGIN	DESTINATION	COST
HY120	DFW	JFK	225
HY130	DFW	LAX	200
HY140	DFW	ORD	100
HY150	DFW	SFO	300
HY210	JFK	DFW	225
HY240	JFK	ORD	250
HY310	LAX	DFW	200
HY350	LAX	SFO	50
HY410	ORD	DFW	100
HY420	ORD	JFK	250
HY450	ORD	SFO	275
HY510	SFO	DFW	300
HY530	SFO	LAX	50
HY540	SFO	ORD	275

For our initial attempt to solve the client's problem, we will write a recursive query that finds ways to fly from San Francisco (SFO) to New York (JFK). The example query below uses the same template as the previous recursive examples. It defines a temporary view called TRIPS that consists of a UNION ALL between an initial subquery and a recursive subquery. The initial subquery finds all the cities that can be reached from San Francisco in a single flight. The recursive subquery finds all the cities that can in turn be reached from these cities, and, for each city reached, it records the route and the total cost. Finally, from the set of trips computed by the recursive view, we write a query that selects the trips ending in New York.

Our first try at writing a recursive query for this problem might be as follows:

```
WITH trips(destination, route, totalcost) AS
   ((SELECT destination, destination, cost      -- Initial
     FROM flights                               -- Subquery
     WHERE origin = 'SFO')
   UNION ALL
     (SELECT f.destination,                      -- Recursive
             t.route || ',' || f.destination,    -- Subquery
             t.totalcost + f.cost
     FROM trips t, flights f
     WHERE t.destination = f.origin))
 SELECT route, totalcost                         -- Final
 FROM trips                                      -- Query
 WHERE destination = 'JFK';
```

Unfortunately, the "first try" query above has two problems. The first problem is that it violates the rule that the columns of the recursive subquery must not be longer than the corresponding columns of the initial subquery. The second column selected by the initial subquery is destination, which we will assume to have datatype Char(3). The second column selected by the recursive subquery is an expression, t.route || ',' || f.destination, which is a character string that grows longer on each invocation of the recursive subquery. The system needs some advice from us about how long this column can grow, so that it can assign the proper datatype to the second column of the temporary view. Let's allow the column to grow to a length of 20 characters, allowing plenty of room for interesting routes. By casting the second column to the datatype Varchar(20) in both the initial subquery and the recursive subquery, we can comply with the length rule and also give the system the information it needs about the correct length for this column. The changes we need to make are as follows:

- In the initial subquery, replace the second destination column by CAST(destination AS Varchar(20)).
- In the recursive subquery, replace t.route || ',' || f.destination by CAST(t.route || ',' || f.destination as Varchar(20)).

The second problem with our "first try" query is more serious: the query will not stop until the system runs out of resources. The reason why the query will not stop on its own is that it does not specify how far a given trip should be explored before it becomes no longer interesting. For example, in processing the query above, the system might consider a trip that flies from San Francisco to Dallas, then to Chicago, then to San Francisco again, then to Los Angeles, then back to San Francisco again, and so on, indefinitely. In order to rule out such trips, we need to think carefully about how we decide that a given trip has been explored far enough that no further extensions should be added to it.

Suppose that you are explaining to another person how to put flight segments together to find the cheapest trip from San Francisco to New York, building up various candidate trips by adding one flight at a time. You might use the following rules to decide whether it is reasonable to add a given flight segment to a given trip:

1. Don't consider any flight segments whose destination is San Francisco, because that is where we started.

2. Don't consider any flight segments whose origin is New York, because that is our final destination.

3. Don't consider any trips that have more than three flight segments.

These commonsense rules are fairly easy to add to our recursive query. In the example below, we add the stopping rules and also add the requirement that among all the trips to New York, we wish to choose the least expensive.

```
WITH trips(destination, route, nsegs, totalcost) AS
  ((SELECT destination,                -- Initial subquery
          CAST(destination AS Varchar(20)),
          1,
          cost
    FROM flights
    WHERE origin = 'SFO')
  UNION ALL
  (SELECT f.destination,               -- Recursive subquery
          CAST(t.route || ',' || f.destination
                          AS Varchar(20)),
          t.nsegs + 1,
          t.totalcost + f.cost
```

```
        FROM trips t, flights f
        WHERE t.destination = f.origin
        AND f.destination <> 'SFO'          -- Stopping rule 1
        AND f.origin <> 'JFK'               -- Stopping rule 2
        AND t.nsegs < 3 ))                  -- Stopping rule 3
SELECT route, totalcost                     -- Final query
FROM trips
WHERE destination = 'JFK'
AND totalcost =                             -- Find minimum cost
    (SELECT min(totalcost)
     FROM trips
     WHERE destination = 'JFK');
```

This query may seem intimidating, but it is really quite simple. To see how it works, we will first look at how the system might evaluate the temporary view named TRIPS. First, the system places into TRIPS all the flights that originate in San Francisco. Then, it constructs new trips by adding flights to existing trips, subject to the constraints that no trip can go back to San Francisco, continue beyond New York, or contain more than three flights. Each new trip is constructed from an old trip by adding one to the number of flight segments, concatenating the new destination onto the trip's route, and adding the new flight cost to the trip cost. The resulting table will contain some strange trips. For example, a valid trip might consist of flights from San Francisco to Los Angeles, then to Dallas, then back to Los Angeles again—not a promising start for a trip to New York. We might like to add some more commonsense rules for constructing trips, such as "Don't add any flight segment that goes to a city that we have already visited on this trip." But this rule can't be expressed without using a lower-level subquery inside the recursive subquery, which is not allowed, so we will have to get along without it. The temporary view TRIPS constructed during the processing of this query might be visualized as shown on the following page.

We might visualize a recursive computation by a graph like the one in Figure 3-3, which shows how the temporary view TRIPS is computed by starting with some flights selected by the initial subquery and then adding additional flights by repeatedly executing the recursive subquery.

After evaluating the TRIPS view, the system proceeds to evaluate the main SELECT statement in the query above, which searches the TRIPS view for trips whose destination is JFK and whose total cost is equal to the minimum total cost of any trip to JFK. In our example database, the result of this query is the single row shown below:

ROUTE	TOTALCOST
LAX, DFW, JFK	475

TRIPS

DESTINATION	ROUTE	NSEGS	TOTALCOST
DFW	DFW	1	300
ORD	ORD	1	275
LAX	LAX	1	50
JFK	DFW, JFK	2	525
LAX	DFW, LAX	2	500
ORD	DFW, ORD	2	400
DFW	LAX, DFW	2	250
DFW	ORD, DFW	2	375
JFK	ORD, JFK	2	525
DFW	DFW, LAX, DFW	3	700
DFW	DFW, ORD, DFW	3	500
JFK	DFW, ORD, JFK	3	650
LAX	LAX, DFW, LAX	3	450
JFK	LAX, DFW, JFK	3	475
ORD	LAX, DFW, ORD	3	350
LAX	ORD, DFW, LAX	3	575
JFK	ORD, DFW, JFK	3	600
ORD	ORD, DFW, ORD	3	475

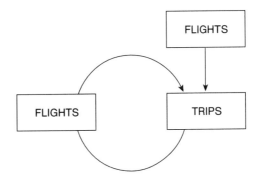

Figure 3-3: A Recursive Computation

If our client is unhappy that the cheapest trip to New York involves three flights, it is easy to modify our query to select the "best" trip according to a different criterion. For example, to find the trip(s) that reach New York with the minimum number of flights, we would simply replace the part of our statement labelled "Final query" with the following:

```
SELECT route, totalcost           -- Final query
FROM trips
WHERE destination = 'JFK'
AND nsegs =                       -- Find fewest flights
    (SELECT min(nsegs)
     FROM trips
     WHERE destination = 'JFK');
```

In our example database, the result of our query would then include the following two trips, which are tied for the minimum number of flights:

ROUTE	TOTALCOST
DFW, JFK	525
ORD, JFK	525

One of the strengths of the V2 approach to recursion is that it is not limited to a single initial subquery or a single recursive subquery. You are allowed to write a query that contains more than one initial subquery and more than one recursive subquery, as long as all the subqueries are connected by UNION ALL and follow the rules that we have discussed. This technique gives you great power to solve complex recursive problems.

To illustrate the use of multiple recursive subqueries, we will consider an extension to the airline route problem discussed above. Suppose that, in addition to HyFlier Airlines, our client is willing to consider trip segments on her favorite railroad, FastTrack Railways. The route map for FastTrack is represented in our database by a table with the following structure:

TRAINS

TRAINNO	ORIGIN	DESTINATION	COST

Our client now asks us to find the minimum-cost trip from San Francisco to New York, in which the segments of the trip can be either by plane or train. Our basic approach to solving this problem will be the same as before, but we

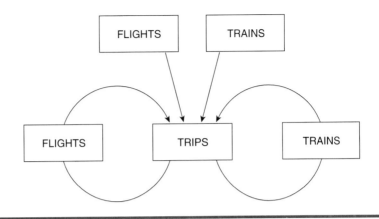

Figure 3-4: A Computation with Multiple Recursive Subqueries

will use two initial subqueries: one to find flights originating in San Francisco and another to find train trips originating in San Francisco. We will also use two recursive subqueries: one to add additional flights to possible trips and another to add additional trains to possible trips. We might visualize the resulting computation by the graph in Figure 3-4.

The query that performs the computation in Figure 3-4 is very similar to the query that corresponds to Figure 3-3. In addition to two initial and two recursive subqueries, this query adds another new feature: it computes a "plan" for each trip by concatenating together a string of flight numbers and train numbers. This plan is needed, for example, so our client will know whether to travel from Dallas to Chicago by air or by rail. The resulting query is as follows:

```
WITH trips(destination, route, plan, nsegs, totalcost) AS
  ( (SELECT destination,            -- Initial subquery #1
            CAST(destination AS Varchar(20)),
            CAST(flightno AS Varchar(20)),
            1,
            cost
    FROM flights
    WHERE origin = 'SFO')
  UNION ALL
    (SELECT destination,            -- Initial subquery #2
            CAST(destination AS Varchar(20)),
            CAST(trainno AS Varchar(20)),
            1,
            cost
    FROM trains
    WHERE origin = 'SFO')
```

```
        UNION ALL
          (SELECT f.destination,              -- Recursive subquery #1
                  CAST(t.route || ',' || f.destination
                                          AS Varchar(20)),
                  CAST(t.plan || ',' || f.flightno
                                          AS Varchar(20)),
                  t.nsegs + 1,
                  t.totalcost + f.cost
            FROM trips t, flights f
            WHERE t.destination = f.origin
            AND f.destination <> 'SFO'      -- Stopping rule 1
            AND f.origin <> 'JFK'           -- Stopping rule 2
            AND t.nsegs < 3 )               -- Stopping rule 3
        UNION ALL
          (SELECT x.destination,              -- Recursive subquery #2
                  CAST(t.route || ',' || x.destination
                                          AS Varchar(20)),
                  CAST(t.plan || ',' || x.trainno
                                          AS Varchar(20)),
                  t.nsegs + 1,
                  t.totalcost + x.cost
            FROM trips t, trains x
            WHERE t.destination = x.origin
            AND x.destination <> 'SFO'      -- Stopping rule 1
            AND x.origin <> 'JFK'           -- Stopping rule 2
            AND t.nsegs < 3 )               -- Stopping rule 3
          )                                 -- End of WITH clause
    SELECT route, plan, totalcost           -- Final query
    FROM trips
    WHERE destination = 'JFK'
    AND totalcost =
       (SELECT min(totalcost)               -- Find minimum cost
        FROM trips
        WHERE destination = 'JFK');
```

Recursive queries are very powerful, and not hard to write after you learn the rules. In writing your own recursive queries, you will stay out of trouble if you remember these guidelines:

1. Begin your query with a table expression that is a UNION ALL of one or more initial subqueries and one or more recursive subqueries.

2. Each initial subquery must be nonrecursive (its definition must not depend on the table expression in which it is embedded).

3. A recursive subquery may make use of the table expression in which it is embedded (but it may not include any lower-level subqueries that do so).

4. A recursive subquery may not contain any column function, SELECT DISTINCT, GROUP BY, or HAVING.

5. The columns of the recursive subqueries must be assignment-compatible with (and not longer than) the corresponding columns of the initial subqueries.

6. The recursive subqueries must specify how each new row is computed from the rows that already exist. If the data contains cycles, the recursive subqueries must also include a stopping rule to make sure the query terminates (such as a limit on the number of iterations).

7. Write your final query, making use of the recursive table expression and adding any additional predicates that are needed (for example, to find the best of several solutions).

TIP: When you run a recursive query, you may receive a warning message, "A recursive common table expression may contain an infinite loop" (SQLCODE +347, SQLSTATE 01605). This message will not interfere with the correct processing of your query (unless, of course, it actually contains an infinite loop). The system is simply warning you that recursive queries sometimes need stopping rules. Since the system is not very good at predicting whether a given query will terminate, you may receive this warning even though you have provided a correct stopping rule. Try not to be annoyed by this; the system has your best interests at heart.

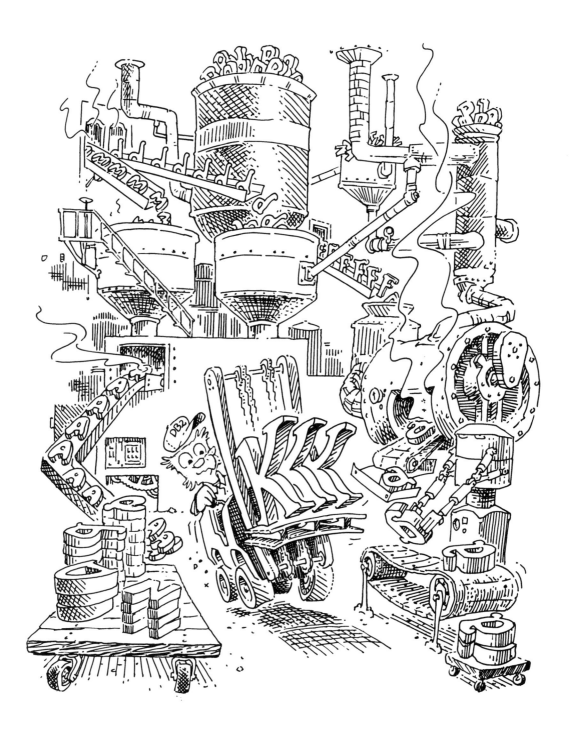

4 Datatypes and Functions

A recurring criticism of traditional database systems has been their poverty of datatypes and functions. The first relational systems typically provided only a few built-in datatypes, such as integers and strings, and a few built-in functions, such as `substr` and `avg`. These datatypes and functions are useful for storing and processing small objects with simple behavior, such as bank balances. Increasingly, however, database applications are requiring the storage and manipulation of objects that are very large (such as images, drawings, audio, and video) and/or have complex behavior (such as the components of an engineering design).

In the past few years, a number of object-oriented database systems have been developed to support the growing requirement for storage of large and complex objects. These systems typically provide their users with facilities to define new datatypes by combining simple datatypes together into complex structures. Users can also define complex behavior for objects by writing new functions in some programming language and associating these new functions with their new datatypes.

Relational database systems are based on the principle that users should access data by means of a high-level language, such as SQL, that is independent of the physical access paths or algorithms used to retrieve and manipulate the data. This principle, called *data independence*, allows the system to automatically choose the best access plan for a given query, even though such a query may not have been anticipated in the database design. Data independence also enables system administrators to add and drop indexes and other access aids in response to changing usage patterns without impacting running applications (except by affecting their performance). Another aspect of data independence is support for multiple views of data—for example, an application might be given a data view that contains salary values averaged by job code without exposing individual salaries.

The principle of data independence is as important today as ever. Furthermore, there is a growing realization that the traditional advantages of relational systems are not in any way incompatible with a rich and extensible system of datatypes and functions. In fact, some new database systems are beginning to appear, called *extended relational* or *object-relational* systems, that combine a high-level query language and multiple views of data with ability to define new datatypes and functions for storage of complex objects. Compared with conventional relational systems, object-relational systems increase the value of stored data by capturing more of its semantic meaning. Part of this semantic meaning is carried in the definitions of datatypes and functions, created by users to model the objects in their application domain. Another important part of the semantic meaning of data is carried in a set of constraints and triggers that protect the integrity of the data and implement its active behavior.

The ANSI/ISO SQL Standard has recognized the importance of the trend toward capturing data semantics by the various kinds of constraints that can be specified in SQL92 and by several features that are under consideration for SQL3, including triggers, user-defined datatypes and functions, and inheritance.

In the subtitle of this book, V2 is referred to as an "object-relational system." This term is used because, in the design of V2, IBM has included many features for capturing data semantics and has set a clear direction for the product to evolve toward support for the object-oriented paradigm. For modelling complex objects, V2 provides an extended set of built-in datatypes and also allows users to define new datatypes and functions of their own. These facilities are described in this chapter. V2 also provides an extensive set of facilities for representing the semantics of data objects using constraints and triggers, which are described in Chapter 5. Many V2 features, including user-defined datatypes, functions, and triggers, are under consideration by ANSI and ISO but are not yet formally a part of the SQL Standard.

It is clear that V2 does not represent the end of the object-oriented evolution of DB2, but only the beginning. One direction this evolution might take is toward support for indexes and other access paths based on user-defined functions. Other such directions are represented by object-oriented SQL extensions currently being discussed by ANSI and ISO committees, such as abstract datatypes, inheritance, and collection types.

4.1 LARGE OBJECTS

Today's multimedia applications depend on storage of many types of large data objects, such as scanned documents, medical images, and audio messages. V1 provided datatypes called Long Varchar and Long Vargraphic for the storage of objects up to 32K bytes in size, with certain limitations (for example, only certain types of predicates could be applied to these datatypes). V2 provides an improved facility for storing much larger objects, consisting of three new datatypes with the following names:

1. *Blob (Binary Large Object).* The Blob datatype can contain up to two gigabytes (2^{31}–1 bytes) of binary data. Blobs cannot be assigned to or compared with values of any other datatype.

2. *Clob (Character Large Object).* The Clob datatype can contain up to two gigabytes (2^{31}–1 bytes) of single-byte character data. Like other character-string datatypes, a Clob has a code page associated with it (indicating, for example, that its contents are encoded using the Swedish character set). Clobs can be assigned to and compared with values of other character-string datatypes (Char, Varchar, and Long Varchar).

3. *Dbclob (Double-Byte Character Large Object).* The Dbclob datatype can contain up to one gigacharacter (two gigabytes, or 2^{31}–2 bytes) of double-byte character data. You can use this datatype only if your database was configured for double-byte data at database creation time. A Dbclob is associated with a double-byte code page such as Japanese. Dbclobs can be assigned to or compared with values of other double-byte string datatypes (Graphic, Vargraphic, and Long Vargraphic).

These three new datatypes are referred to generically as *Large Objects* (LOBs). Although the older Long Varchar and Long Vargraphic datatypes are still supported, this book focuses mainly on the new LOB datatypes, because we expect that they will be the preferred datatypes for new applications. The capabilities of the new LOB datatypes are a superset of the capabilities of Long Varchar and Long Vargraphic.

The design of the new LOB datatypes is based on the fact that it is quite expensive to move large objects from one place to another in memory. For this reason, every effort has been made to minimize this kind of movement. In addition to their large size, the LOB datatypes are distinguished from conventional datatypes by the following special features:

1. When a LOB is stored in a table, the table entry is actually a descriptor that points to the LOB value, which is stored elsewhere. Users can configure their databases with separate units of physical storage called *tablespaces* for holding LOB values so that they will not interfere with the clustering of tables. (Tablespaces are described in more detail in Section 8.1.1.)

2. LOBs can be manipulated in user programs by means of *locators*, which represent the value of a LOB without actually containing the LOB data. By manipulating these locators, application programs can defer and sometimes even avoid actually materializing the LOB in the program.

3. By means of a feature called a *file reference*, programs can input LOB data directly into the database from a file, or fetch LOB data directly from the database into a file, without passing the data through memory buffers in the application program.

4. For each LOB-type column in a table, the creator of the table can specify independently whether changes to that column are to be recorded in the system log. A user might choose to turn off logging for a LOB-type column to improve performance and to avoid the possibility of log overflow. Columns that are not logged are still guaranteed transaction semantics, and updates to these columns can be committed or rolled back in the usual way. However, if a column is not logged, it cannot participate in forward recovery (reexecution of completed transactions after a media failure). (Forward recovery is discussed in Section 8.4.)

4.1.1 Creating LOB Columns

To store LOB data in a database, you simply create a table having a column of one of the LOB datatypes, using the familiar CREATE TABLE and ALTER TABLE statements. Some examples of these statements were given in Section 2.8, and their complete syntax is discussed in Section 5.2. A CREATE TABLE or ALTER TABLE statement might define a LOB-type column using the following syntax:

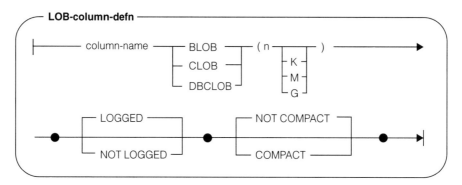

The following are some examples of statements that create tables or add columns to tables using the above syntax:

```
CREATE TABLE phonemail
    (origin      Varchar(18),
     addressee   Varchar(18),
     arrival     Timestamp,
     message     Blob(10M) NOT LOGGED COMPACT);    -- audio

CREATE TABLE graduates
    (name        Varchar(30),
     address     Varchar(200),
     degree      Varchar(50),
     grad_date   Date,
     photo       Blob(5M) NOT LOGGED COMPACT,       -- image
     thesis      Clob(500K) NOT LOGGED COMPACT);    -- text
```

```
CREATE TABLE design
    (partno       Char(18),
     last_updated Timestamp,
     updated_by   Varchar(30),
     drawing      Blob(2M) LOGGED);        -- CGM graphics

ALTER TABLE student ADD COLUMN transcript Clob(5K) LOGGED;
```

All the LOB datatypes are varying-length types, like Varchar and Vargraphic. When declaring a column of a LOB datatype, you must declare its maximum length, which can be anywhere in the range from one byte to two gigabytes. The maximum length can be declared as a simple integer representing a number of bytes (double-byte characters, in the case of a Dbclob), or as an integer followed by one of the following suffixes:

K: kilobytes (2^{10} or 1,024 bytes)

M: megabytes (2^{20} or 1,048,576 bytes)

G: gigabytes (2^{30} or 1,073,741,824 bytes; 2G is interpreted as 2^{31}–1)

You may be wondering why it is necessary to declare the maximum length of the data to be stored in a LOB-type column. Actually, there are two reasons why this information may be helpful:

1. When you fetch data from a column into your application program, you will need to allocate a buffer big enough to hold the data. If you know that the data is limited to, say, 50K bytes, you can allocate just the right amount of memory.

2. Inside each row that contains a LOB-type value is a descriptor that points at the actual data. The maximum length of this descriptor depends on the maximum length of the data; it varies from 72 bytes for a LOB of less than 1K up to 316 bytes for a LOB of maximum size 2G. In any given table, the total size of all the columns, including the descriptors of the LOB columns, cannot exceed 4,005 bytes. So, if you know that the data in a given column will never be larger than a certain limit, you can improve clustering and leave room for more columns by declaring the maximum size.

Of course, if neither of the considerations above is important to you, you can declare all your LOB-type columns to have a maximum length of 2G, retaining the maximum flexibility for storing large objects.

When creating a LOB-type column, you have two choices to make that do not apply to columns of other datatypes. These choices are as follows:

1. *COMPACT or NOT COMPACT.* This option allows you to control a space-time trade-off in storage of the LOB data in your column. If you specify COMPACT, the LOB data will occupy minimum space on disk, but there may be a performance penalty for any update that increases the size of a LOB. If you specify

NOT COMPACT, some extra space will be allocated to allow the LOB values room to grow. The default is NOT COMPACT.

2. *LOGGED or NOT LOGGED.* This option allows you to control whether updates to your column are recorded in the system log. In making this decision, you will need to consider the size of your LOB data, how valuable it is, and how easily it can be reconstructed.

If you choose LOGGED (the default), the LOB data in this column is treated exactly like all other data. Whenever the column is updated, the new value is recorded in the system log. This provides the maximum protection for the data, but for obvious reasons it is costly both in terms of time and disk space. In fact, since the maximum size of the log is currently limited to 2 gigabytes, and a single LOB value can occupy this much space, it is not practical to choose the LOGGED option for very large LOB columns. It is an error to specify LOGGED for a column larger than one gigabyte, and it is probably unwise to specify LOGGED for columns larger than ten megabytes.

If you choose NOT LOGGED for a column, changes to the column are not recorded in the system log, but another part of the recovery system, called *shadowing*, remains in effect. When an update is applied to a NOT LOGGED column, both the new pages and the original ("shadow") pages are retained until the end of the transaction. Shadowing enforces transaction consistency for your data (that is, the COMMIT and ROLLBACK statements apply to shadowed data, and when you invoke the RESTART command after a failure, your shadowed data will be restored to a transaction-consistent state).

The feature that you forego by specifying NOT LOGGED for a column is the ability, after a media failure, to reapply all the changes that have been made to that column since the last media backup. A media backup can be made by the BACKUP command, and the database can be restored from a media backup by the RESTORE command. After restoring the database from a media backup, all committed transactions can be reapplied by the ROLLFORWARD command. This process, called *forward recovery*, relies on the system log and is effective only for logged columns. If a column was created with the NOT LOGGED option, any updated values in this column will be lost (set to binary zeros) during the execution of ROLLFORWARD. (The commands for backup and recovery of databases are discussed further in Section 8.4.)

4.1.2 Declaring Large-Object Variables in C and C++

When you write an application program for V2, you will probably need to declare some variables that exchange values with the database, either for input or for output. These variables must be declared in a special part of your program called the *SQL Declare Section*, as described in Section 2.7.2. Each SQL datatype (except Decimal) has a corresponding C-language datatype that you

TABLE 4-1: C Datatypes Corresponding to Long Varchar
and Long Vargraphic

SQL Datatype	C Datatype
Long Varchar(n)	```struct{short length;char data[n];}```
Long Vargraphic(n)	```struct{short length;wchar_t data[n];}```

can use in the SQL Declare Section to declare variables for exchanging values
of that datatype (for example, the C datatype corresponding to the SQL Integer datatype is `long`). The C-language datatypes corresponding to the basic
SQL datatypes are summarized in Table 2-5.

V2 continues to support the old-style large-object datatypes named Long
Varchar and Long Vargraphic, introduced by V1. Long Varchar can be used to
represent character strings up to 32K bytes in length, and Long Vargraphic can
be used to represent double-byte strings up to 16K characters in length. The
C-language datatypes corresponding to these V1 datatypes, for use in the SQL
Declare Section, are shown in Table 4-1.

Declarations of variables to exchange the new LOB-type values supported by
V2 require some new syntax in the SQL Declare Section. Rather than pure host
language syntax, these declarations use a new syntax that is recognized and
translated by the SQL precompiler. When declaring such a variable, you should
use the phrase `SQL TYPE IS` followed by a LOB-type just as you would write it
in a CREATE TABLE statement, such as `CLOB(32K)` or `BLOB(1M)`. The type
name is then followed by the name of the variable you are declaring. The precompiler automatically translates your declaration into a declaration of the
proper host language datatype for exchanging the kind of data you specified.
The examples in Table 4-2 illustrate the LOB datatypes you can use inside an
SQL Declare Section and the corresponding C-language declarations that are
generated by the precompiler. Of course, the variable names x, y, and z and the
lengths shown here are only examples that would be replaced by lengths and
variable names of your choice.

TABLE 4-2: Declarations Generated by the C Precompiler for LOB Datatypes

If you write . . .	The C precompiler will generate . . .

SQL TYPE IS BLOB(1K) x;	struct x_t
	{
	    unsigned long length;
	    char data[1024];
	} x;

SQL TYPE IS CLOB(1M) y;	struct y_t
	{
	    unsigned long length;
	    char data[1048576];
	} y;

SQL TYPE IS DBCLOB(1K) z;	struct z_t
	{
	    unsigned long length;
	    wchar_t data[1024];
	} z;

The datatype wchar_t, generated from a Dbclob declaration, is an implementation-defined C datatype used to represent a double-byte character. It is defined in the header file stddef.h, provided with your C compiler. Thus, the declaration SQL TYPE IS DBCLOB(1K) would allocate space for 1,024 double-byte characters (occupying 2,048 bytes of storage if your compiler defines wchar_t as a two-byte datatype).

The format used for strings of type Long Vargraphic and Dbclob in input and output host variables is affected by the precompiler option WCHARTYPE. If your program is precompiled with the option WCHARTYPE CONVERT, all double-byte strings are exchanged in wide-character format, which is compatible with the wide-character string library provided by your C compiler in wstring.h. If you precompile your program with the option WCHARTYPE NOCONVERT or accept the default option, double-byte strings are exchanged in multibyte format. Your compiler provides functions named wcstombs and mbstowcs to convert double-byte strings between the two formats.

You are allowed to specify a C storage class such as static or extern on your declaration, and you may also use the C notations * (indicating a pointer) and & (indicating a reference). You may declare multiple variables in a single statement, and you may mix LOB-type declarations with other declarations in the same SQL Declare Section. (Additional details about declarations of LOB-type host variables can be found in Appendix E.)

V2 provides macros named SQL_BLOB_INIT, SQL_CLOB_INIT, and SQL_DBCLOB_INIT for initializing variables of LOB datatypes. These macros take a string and use it to initialize both the length and data parts of a LOB structure. Use of the initializing macros is illustrated in the example below:

```
EXEC SQL BEGIN DECLARE SECTION;
    static SQL TYPE IS CLOB(100K)
                    *p1, c1 = SQL_CLOB_INIT("Hello");
EXEC SQL END DECLARE SECTION;
```

The precompiler will translate the code above into the following C declarations:

```
static struct
    {
    unsigned long length;
    char data[102400];
    } *p1, c1 = SQL_CLOB_INIT("Hello");
```

Note that in the example above, 100K bytes of memory have been allocated for variable c1, but variable p1 is only a pointer (its data buffer must be allocated separately). The C compiler will expand the macro used to initialize variable c1 as follows:

```
c1 = {sizeof("Hello")-1, "Hello"}
```

You may be wondering why special syntax is used for the declaration of LOB-type host variables, rather than allowing you to write your own host language declarations as you do for other datatypes. There are two reasons for this change:

1. V2 recognizes the convenient K, M, and G length-notations, translating them into numbers that are acceptable to C. For example, 100K is translated into 102400.

2. You may have noticed that Blob and Clob SQL datatypes share the same host language datatype. The special syntax in the declaration tells the database system whether your variable should be treated as a Blob or as a Clob.

You can use your LOB-type variables for exchanging data with the database in the usual way. If an indicator variable is used with an output LOB-type variable, the indicator variable will be set negative if the output value is null. However, if a LOB-type output value is truncated because the length of the output variable is too short (indicated by SQLSTATE 01004), the indicator variable is *not* set to the original length of the output value (as in the case of other string datatypes).

I will illustrate the use of LOB-type host variables by a simple application program named MOVIE. This program operates on a table with the following structure:

MOVIES

TITLE   CAST   REVIEW

The TITLE and CAST columns of the MOVIES table have datatype Varchar(100), and the REVIEW column has datatype Clob(50K). The MOVIE application program exchanges data with the REVIEW column using two Clob-type host variables named review and newreview.

First, the program places a new movie review in the newreview variable, taking care to set both the length and data fields of the structure. It then uses newreview as an input variable in an SQL UPDATE statement, adding the new review to the database.

Next, the program declares a cursor and uses it to retrieve all the reviews in the database for movies starring Steve McQueen. The reviews are retreived into the output variable review. Since Clob-type data does not include a null terminator, the program must use the length field of the review structure to indicate the length of each review and must generate its own null terminator before printing each review.

Example Program MOVIE: Processing Movie Reviews

```
#include <stdio.h>
#include <string.h>
#include <sqlenv.h>

void main()
   {
   EXEC SQL INCLUDE SQLCA;

   EXEC SQL BEGIN DECLARE SECTION;
       char dbname[9] = "moviedb";        /* name of database          */
       char msgbuffer[500];               /* buffer for DB2 error message */
       char title[100];                   /* for Varchar data          */
       char cast[100];                    /* for Varchar data          */
       SQL TYPE is CLOB(50K) review;      /* output Clob structure     */
       SQL TYPE is CLOB(50K) newreview;   /* input Clob structure      */
       short indicator1, indicator2;      /* indicator variables       */
   EXEC SQL END DECLARE SECTION;
```

```
EXEC SQL WHENEVER SQLERROR GO TO badnews;

EXEC SQL CONNECT TO :dbname;

strcpy (newreview.data, "Bullet is a pretty good movie.");
newreview.length = strlen(newreview.data);
indicator1 = 0;

EXEC SQL
    UPDATE movies
    SET review = :newreview :indicator1
    WHERE title = 'Bullet';

EXEC SQL COMMIT;

EXEC SQL DECLARE c1 CURSOR FOR
    SELECT title, review
    FROM movies
    WHERE cast LIKE '%Steve McQueen%';

EXEC SQL WHENEVER NOT FOUND GO TO close_c1;

EXEC SQL OPEN c1;

while (1)
    {
    EXEC SQL FETCH c1 INTO :title, :review :indicator2;

    /* Provide your own null terminator */
    review.data[review.length] = '\0';

    printf("\nTitle: %s\n", title);
    if (indicator2 < 0)
       printf("No review available\n");
    else
       printf("%s\n", review.data);
    }

close_c1:
  EXEC SQL CLOSE c1;
  return;
```

```
badnews:
   printf("Unexpected return code from DB2.\n");
   sqlaintp(msgbuffer, 500, 70, &sqlca);
   printf("Message: %s\n", msgbuffer);
   }      /* End of main */
```

4.1.3 Locators

A very powerful feature of the new LOB datatypes, which distinguishes them from Long Varchars and other implementations of large objects, is the concept of a *locator.* Locators arose out of the observation that it is quite expensive to move large objects back and forth between the database and an application program. If a program is manipulating large objects, it is desirable to defer the actual movement of bits from the database into the program as long as possible and to move only those bits that are really needed. If the program is able to specify exactly what manipulations it needs to do, it may be possible in many cases to perform the manipulations entirely in the database without ever delivering the large object to the application program.

A locator is a value that can be used in an application program to represent the value of a large object without actually containing the bytes of the large object. By manipulating locators, a program can perform operations on large objects while these objects remain inside the database system. In this way, the program can often avoid allocating the storage to hold a large object and paying the cost of moving the large object between the database and the application.

A locator variable is a variable that is declared in the SQL Declare Section of an application program to hold a locator. In each host programming language, there is a datatype designated for locator variables. For example, in C, the datatype of a locator variable is long. However, not just any long variable in the SQL Declare Section can be used as a locator variable. Locator variables must be distinguished from long variables used for input and output of Integer data; furthermore, Clob locator variables must be distinguished from Blob locator variables and from Dbclob locator variables.

A special syntax is used to notify the precompiler of the intended use of a locator variable. Inside an SQL Declare Section, any of the following phrases will be recognized by the precompiler and translated into the datatype used for locators in your host language:

```
SQL TYPE IS BLOB_LOCATOR
SQL TYPE IS CLOB_LOCATOR
SQL TYPE IS DBCLOB_LOCATOR
```

For example, in the SQL Declare Section of a C program, the declaration

```
extern SQL TYPE IS CLOB_LOCATOR loc1, loc2, loc3;
```

would be translated by the precompiler as follows:

```
extern long loc1, loc2, loc3;
```

Locator variables can be used in any SQL statement wherever an input or output variable of a LOB datatype can be used. If a LOB-type value is fetched into a locator variable, the variable is set to contain a locator that represents the LOB value. This variable can then be used in SQL statements exactly as though it contained the actual LOB value. For example, it can be used as an input variable in an SQL UPDATE statement or passed as an argument to a LOB function such as `posstr`. Whenever a locator variable is used in an SQL statement, the database system operates on the LOB-type value that is represented by that locator. The LOB-type value itself is held inside the database server and is not transferred into the application program.

In order to understand the power of locators, it is important to remember the following:

1. A locator represents a constant value. There is no way to change the value of the object that a locator represents (but, of course, it is possible to use the locator to compute another object with a different value, represented by a different locator).

2. Inside the database server, each locator corresponds to a *recipe* for assembling a LOB-type value from fragments that are stored in various places. Whenever possible, manipulations of LOBs are performed, not by manipulating the actual data, but by manipulating the recipes. For example, if two large objects are to be concatenated, a new recipe is created that includes copies of the recipes for the two original objects (which may, in turn, contain fragments copied from earlier recipes). The concatenation operation is performed entirely by manipulating the recipes rather than by touching the actual content of the large objects. If the result of the concatenation is fetched into a locator variable, the variable gets a new locator representing the new recipe.

3. The actual content of a large object is moved on only two occasions: when the object is assigned to a host language variable of a LOB datatype (not a locator datatype), or when the object is assigned to a column of a database table. Intermediate results of large-object expressions (for example, the results of `concat` and `substr` operations) are never materialized until the final assignment.

Locator variables are often used as arguments of functions that manipulate strings. This is the most efficient way to manipulate large-object data because it postpones actual movement of the data as long as possible. Shown below are some examples of functions that are useful for manipulating LOB-type data (for details of these and other functions, see Appendix B). Since all the locators are host language variables, their names are prefixed by colons.

- Two strings can be concatenated by the concat function or by the || operator. In the following examples, we concatenate two large objects that are represented by locators:

  ```
  concat(:clobloc1, :clobloc2)
  :clobloc1 || :clobloc2
  ```

- The length function returns the length of its argument. This example finds the length of a large object:

  ```
  length(:clobloc1)
  ```

- The posstr function returns the starting position of the first instance of a pattern inside a string. This function is particularly useful for finding a pattern inside a large object and can be used with either character-string or binary data. This example finds the location of the word "Experience" within a large object represented by a locator named resumeloc:

  ```
  posstr(:resumeloc, 'Experience')
  ```

- The substr function returns a substring of its argument. This function is very useful for snipping a relevant part out of a large object. This example returns a substring of length 200 characters, beginning at character offset 1,200 within the large object represented by clobloc1:

  ```
  substr(:clobloc1, 1200, 200)
  ```

Since locator variables can be used both as input and as output variables, it is possible (and often useful) to compute one locator from another without any reference to a database table. For example, suppose that locator variable loc1 contains a locator that represents a Clob value. You may wish to find, in this Clob value, the 100-byte substring beginning with the first occurrence of "Rosebud." Since the actual Clob value resides in the database server, you need the help of the database system. But you do not need to access any particular table in the database (indeed, the value represented by the locator in variable loc1 may not be stored in any table). This is a perfect application for the new VALUES statement supported by V2, which might create a new locator for the desired value in variable loc2, as follows:

```
EXEC SQL VALUES
    substr(:loc1, posstr(:loc1, 'Rosebud'), 100) INTO :loc2;
```

Once a locator has been fetched into a locator variable, it remains valid until the end of the transaction in which it was fetched. The value represented by the locator will never change, even if the underlying columns from which it was computed are updated or deleted. However, there is a way in which you can notify the system that you are no longer using a locator, so that the system can release the resources represented by that locator. This is done by a new SQL statement, FREE LOCATOR, which has the following syntax:

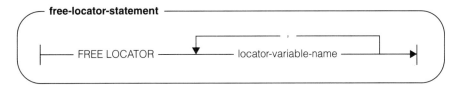

Example:

```
EXEC SQL FREE LOCATOR :loc1, :loc2;
```

It is advisable to use the FREE LOCATOR statement if you are fetching locators inside a loop and, after completing each iteration of the loop, you have no further use for the locator fetched during that iteration. Before fetching another locator into your locator variable, free the previous locator so that the database system no longer needs to keep track of it. The system cannot free a locator automatically when you fetch another locator into the same variable, because it does not know whether you have made a copy of the locator in another variable.

The following example illustrates how an application program can manipulate large objects by operating on their locators without ever "taking delivery" on the actual underlying data. Suppose we have a table that describes a set of plays used by a repertory company, with the following columns:

PLAYS

The TEXT column is a Clob containing the actual text of the play. The following program might be used to scan through the text of a play, replacing each instance of the word "colour" with "color," without ever reading any of the actual text into the application program (in practice, the program would need to search more carefully for various combinations of upper- and lower-case). Note how the program creates a series of locators that represent partial results, freeing each locator when it is no longer needed.

Example Program PLAY: Revising a Play

```c
#include <stdio.h>
#include <string.h>
#include <sqlenv.h>

void main()
  {
  EXEC SQL INCLUDE SQLCA;

  EXEC SQL BEGIN DECLARE SECTION;
      char dbname[9] = "playdb";          /* name of database           */
      char msgbuffer[500];                /* buffer for DB2 error message */
      SQL TYPE IS CLOB_LOCATOR loc1, loc2;
      long n;
  EXEC SQL END DECLARE SECTION;

  EXEC SQL WHENEVER SQLERROR GO TO badnews;

  EXEC SQL CONNECT TO :dbname;

  EXEC SQL SELECT text into :loc1
          FROM plays
          WHERE title = 'As You Like It';

  EXEC SQL VALUES posstr(:loc1, 'colour') INTO :n;

  while (n > 0)
      {
      EXEC SQL VALUES substr(:loc1, 1, :n-1) || 'color'
                      || substr(:loc1, :n+6) INTO :loc2;
      /*
      ** Free the old locator and keep the new one.
      */
      EXEC SQL FREE LOCATOR :loc1;
      loc1 = loc2;
      EXEC SQL VALUES posstr(:loc1, 'colour') INTO :n;
      }
  /*
  ** No data moved yet; only a series of locators has been created.
  */

  EXEC SQL UPDATE plays SET text = :loc1
          WHERE title = 'As You Like It';
```

```
    /*
    ** Now the new text is assembled according to the final recipe
    ** and assigned to the database table.
    */

    EXEC SQL COMMIT;
    return;

badnews:
    printf("Unexpected return code from DB2.\n");
    sqlaintp(msgbuffer, 500, 70, &sqlca);
    printf("Message: %s\n", msgbuffer);
    }     /* End of main */
```

The example program above computes, using locator variable loc1, a recipe for replacing all instances of "colour" with "color" in the text of the play. Each time the body of the while-loop is executed, one more instance of the text replacement is added to the recipe. But no data is ever delivered into the application program and no bits are actually moved until the final statement, which applies the recipe to update the table in the database.

TIP: Remember that the statement FREE LOCATOR <variable> applies to the locator that is contained in the variable, not to the variable itself. If you have made copies of a locator, freeing any one of the copies frees (and invalidates) all the copies. Thus, for example, it would be a mistake to write EXEC SQL FREE LOCATOR :loc2 after the statement loc1 = loc2 in the example program above.

4.1.4 File References

In many cases, a LOB-type value may be so large that you would prefer to move it directly from a file into the database, or from the database into a file, without allocating memory buffers to hold it in your application program. This is made possible by a special declaration, called a *file reference declaration*, in the SQL Declare Section of your program. A file reference is a structure that contains the name of a file and certain other information about how the file is to be used to exchange large objects with the database. Inside the SQL Declare Section, special syntax is used to identify a variable as a file reference and to indicate whether the file will be used to exchange values of datatype Blob, Clob, or Dbclob. In place of a datatype, any of the following phrases are recognized by the precompiler and translated into the appropriate structure used for representing a file reference in your host language:

```
SQL TYPE IS BLOB_FILE
SQL TYPE IS CLOB_FILE
SQL TYPE IS DBCLOB_FILE
```

For example, in the SQL Declare Section of a C program, the declaration

```
SQL TYPE IS CLOB_FILE f1;
```

would be translated by the precompiler as follows (I have added the comments for clarity):

```
struct
  {
    unsigned long name_length;    /* length of filename   */
    unsigned long data_length;    /* length of data in file */
    unsigned long file_options;   /* denote usage of file  */
    char          name[255];      /* filename             */
  } f1;
```

After declaring a file reference in your SQL Declare Section, it is your job to fill in the name of the file and its intended usage. The name of the file, denoted by the `name` and `name_length` fields of the structure, may be either an absolute path name such as `/u/clinton/games/marbles.txt` or a relative path name such as `games/marbles.txt`. The filename represents the name of a file on the client machine (not on the database server). The intended usage of the file is denoted by the `file_options` field, which you must set to one of the codes shown in Table 4-3.

The C-language declarations of these codes and of the file reference structure (named `sqlfile`) can be found in the header file `sqllib/include/sql.h`.

After you have declared a file reference variable in your SQL Declare Section and filled in the appropriate fields of the reference structure, you can use the file reference variable in an SQL statement exactly as though it were a LOB-type variable. If you have set `file_options` to SQL_FILE_READ, you can use the file reference variable in an input role such as in a predicate, an INSERT statement, the SET clause of an UPDATE statement, or the argument of a function. If you have set `file_options` to SQL_FILE_CREATE, SQL_FILE_OVER-WRITE, or SQL_FILE_APPEND, codes, you can use the file reference variable in an output role such as SELECT INTO or FETCH INTO. If you use a file reference variable in an output role, the system will write a LOB-type value into the designated file and will set the `data_length` field of the file reference structure to the length of the file after output, in bytes. A file reference variable can be used together with an indicator variable, which is used to denote null values in the usual way.

When you use a Dbclob file reference as an input or output variable to exchange double-byte strings, the data is always exchanged in multibyte format (not wide-character format). In other words, Dbclob file references always use the format specified by the precompiler option WCHARTYPE NOCONVERT.

TABLE 4-3: File Option Codes for LOB File References

Code	Meaning
SQL_FILE_READ (numeric value = 2)	The content of the file is treated as an input LOB-type value.
SQL_FILE_CREATE (numeric value = 8)	A new file is created with the given name and used to receive a LOB-type output value. If the file already exists, an error results.
SQL_FILE_OVERWRITE (numeric value = 16)	An output LOB-type value is fetched into the named file, replacing its previous content. If the file does not exist, it is created.
SQL_FILE_APPEND (numeric value = 32)	An output LOB-type value is appended to the named file. If the file does not exist, it is created.

As an example of a file reference variable used for output, we will write a piece of code to fetch a student's photograph from a database table into a file. Suppose that our database contains a table with the following structure:

STUDENTS

STUDENTNO   NAME   POSITION   PHOTO

If the PHOTO column has datatype Blob(1M), the following code fragment might be used to search the table for a student whose position is "President," and to fetch that student's photograph into a file named president.photo:

```
EXEC SQL BEGIN DECLARE SECTION;
    SQL TYPE IS BLOB_FILE photoFile;
    short ind;
EXEC SQL END DECLARE SECTION;

strcpy(photoFile.name, "president.photo");
photoFile.name_length = strlen(photoFile.name);
photoFile.file_options = SQL_FILE_OVERWRITE;

EXEC SQL SELECT photo INTO :photoFile :ind
    FROM students WHERE position = 'President';
```

After execution of the statements above, SQLSTATE will be set to "00000," if a Blob was successfully written into the designated file; "02000," if no student

was found with a position of "President"; or "21000," if more than one student was found with that position. If the PHOTO column of the selected student was null, the `ind` variable will be negative. If a Blob was written into the
file, `photoFile.data_length` will be set to the length of the file.

As an example of a file reference variable used for input, we will write a program fragment to update a database of advertising copy. Suppose that our
database contains a table named ADVERTISING with a column named COPY
of datatype Clob(200K). Our legal department has advised us to attach a disclaimer to all advertising copy for our "Speedster" product. The disclaimer is
contained in a file named `speedlimit.txt`. The following code fragment
might be used to attach this disclaimer to all the appropriate entries in the
ADVERTISING table:

```
EXEC SQL BEGIN DECLARE SECTION;
    SQL TYPE IS CLOB_FILE disclaimer;
EXEC SQL END DECLARE SECTION;

strcpy(disclaimer.name, "speedlimit.txt");
disclaimer.name_length = strlen(disclaimer.name);
disclaimer.file_options = SQL_FILE_READ;

EXEC SQL UPDATE advertising
        SET copy = copy || :disclaimer
        WHERE copy LIKE '%Speedster%';
```

It is important to note that both of the examples above exchange potentially
large amounts of data with the database without allocating any memory buffers for transferring the data.

4.1.5 Limitations of LOB Datatypes

Certain limitations apply to the use of LOB-type data, regardless of whether it
is represented by a locator, a file reference, or a conventional variable. These
limitations are summarized below. All the limitations (except the last one)
apply to the older Long Varchar and Long Vargraphic datatypes as well as to
LOBs.

1. LOB-type data cannot be used in predicates that perform direct comparisons.
    This includes predicates that use operators =, <>, <, <=, >, >=, IN, or BETWEEN.
    Rather than using a direct comparison, many applications search for LOB-type
    data using a LIKE predicate,[1] as in the following examples:

---

1. The first operand of a LIKE predicate may have a LOB datatype. The second operand
(the pattern) may not have a LOB datatype unless the first operand is a Blob; in this case,
the pattern may be a Blob if its length is 4,000 bytes or less.

```
... WHERE clob1 LIKE '%Gilligan%'
... WHERE clob1 LIKE :hostvar2
```

2. LOB-type columns cannot be used in any context that requires comparing two column values for equality or for ordering. This includes SELECT DISTINCT, COUNT(DISTINCT), GROUP BY, ORDER BY, PRIMARY KEY, and FOREIGN KEY.

3. LOB-type columns cannot be used with any column function such as `max` or `min`.

4. LOB-type columns cannot be used as operands of INTERSECT, EXCEPT, or UNION (other than UNION ALL).

5. Clob-type data cannot be compared or assigned to Dates, Times, or Timestamps (even though other character-string datatypes can be compared and assigned to datetime datatypes). Furthermore, Clobs cannot be passed as arguments to functions that expect a character-string encoding of a Date or Time, such as `date`, `time`, `timestamp`, `day`, `hour`, `month`, and `year`.

6. Indexes cannot be created on LOB-type columns.

7. LOB-type data cannot be exchanged between client (Application Requestor) and server (Application Server) machines using the DRDA (Distributed Relational Database Architecture) protocol. This means that if you are connected to a database that resides on a DRDA server, you will not be able to exchange any LOB values with that database (unless you cast the values into some other datatype).

 TIP: If the actual length of a LOB is less than 4,000 bytes, you can get around most of the above restrictions by casting the LOB into a Varchar or Vargraphic datatype.

4.1.6 Example Program SCHOLAR: Processing Scholarship Applications

As a final example of the power of LOB datatypes, locators, and file references, we will write a program to process student scholarship applications. Suppose that all the scholarship applications we have received have been entered into a table with the following structure:

APPLICANTS

NAME	DATERECEIVED	STATUS	APPLICATION

APPLICATION is a column of datatype Clob(100K), in which our data-entry department has recorded each application in a predefined format. Each application consists of several parts. One part is the student's transcript, recorded in a standard 1,000-byte format beginning with the characters "*TRAN-SCRIPT*." In a later part of the application is an essay, beginning with the characters "*ESSAY*" and continuing until the end of the application.

The task of our program is to search through all the applications received in 1996 whose status is "OK." Among these applications, we need to find the one with the "best" transcript, and we need to retrieve that transcript and its accompanying essay into a file. To help in this process, we will assume the existence of a user-defined function that can compare two transcripts in our standard format and decide which is "better." This function is assumed to have the following interface:

```
int compareTranscripts (char *t1, char *t2);
/* returns 1 if first transcript is better, else returns 2 */
```

Naturally, we prefer to fetch only the minimum data that is needed for processing each application. Even though an application can contain up to 100K bytes and may include a photograph and several supporting letters, we will locate and fetch only the 1,000-byte transcript from each application. After choosing the best transcript, we will copy the corresponding essay directly into a file without allocating any memory buffers for it in our application. To accomplish these objectives, we will use locators, file references, and some LOB functions such as posstr and substr. The storage used by our program to hold application data is limited to two 1,000-byte buffers, one to hold a transcript being considered and another to hold the best transcript seen so far. Note how the program frees each locator when it is no longer needed.

Example Program SCHOLAR: Processing Scholarship Applications

```c
#include <stdio.h>
#include <string.h>
#include <sqlenv.h>

int compareTranscripts(char *t1, char *t2);

int main()
    {
    EXEC SQL BEGIN DECLARE SECTION;
        char dbname[9] = "mydb";
        char candidate[30], winner[30];
        long transPosn, essayPosn;
        char thisTranscript[1000], bestTranscript[1000];
```

```
      SQL TYPE IS CLOB_LOCATOR loc1, bestLoc;
      SQL TYPE IS CLOB_FILE winningFile;
      char msgbuffer[500];
EXEC SQL END DECLARE SECTION;

EXEC SQL INCLUDE SQLCA;

int justStarting = 1;

EXEC SQL DECLARE c1 CURSOR FOR
      SELECT name, application FROM applicants
      WHERE year(datereceived) = 1996 AND status = 'OK';

EXEC SQL WHENEVER SQLERROR GOTO errorExit;

EXEC SQL CONNECT TO :dbname;

EXEC SQL OPEN c1;

while (1)
    {
      EXEC SQL FETCH c1 INTO :candidate, :loc1;    /* Next application */
      if (SQLCODE == 100) break;                   /* No more appl'ns  */

      /*
      ** Fetch the transcript portion of this application
      */
      EXEC SQL
        VALUES(posstr(:loc1, '*TRANSCRIPT*')) INTO :transPosn;

      EXEC SQL
        VALUES(substr(:loc1, :transPosn, 1000)) INTO :thisTranscript;

      if (justStarting == 1)
        {
        /*
        ** First transcript we've looked at is automatically best so far
        */
        memcpy(bestTranscript, thisTranscript, 1000);
        bestLoc = loc1;
        justStarting = 0;
        strcpy(winner, candidate);
        }
```

```
   else
     {
     if (compareTranscripts(bestTranscript, thisTranscript) == 2)
        {
        /*
        ** The current transcript replaces the previous best one
        */
        memcpy(bestTranscript, thisTranscript, 1000);
        EXEC SQL FREE LOCATOR :bestLoc;
        bestLoc = loc1;
        strcpy(winner, candidate);
        }
     else
        {
        /*
        ** Don't need this locator anymore.
        */
        EXEC SQL FREE LOCATOR :loc1;
        }
     }
  }          /* End of while-loop over applications */

EXEC SQL CLOSE c1;

if (justStarting == 1)
   printf("No qualifying applications were found.\n");
else
   {
   /*
   ** Find the position of the essay in the winning application
   */
   EXEC SQL VALUES(posstr(:bestLoc, '*ESSAY*')) INTO :essayPosn;

   /*
   ** Prepare the file reference for fetching the winning application
   */
   strcpy(winningFile.name, "winner.txt");
   winningFile.name_length = strlen(winningFile.name);
   winningFile.file_options = SQL_FILE_OVERWRITE;

   /*
   ** Copy winning transcript and essay into file
   */
```

```
    EXEC SQL VALUES(:bestTranscript || substr(:bestLoc, :essayPosn))
              INTO :winningFile;

    printf("The winner is %s\n", winner);
    }

  EXEC SQL COMMIT;
  return 0;

errorExit:
  printf ("Unexpected return code from DB2.\n");
  sqlaintp(msgbuffer, 500, 70, &sqlca);
  printf ("Message: %s\n", msgbuffer);

  EXEC SQL COMMIT;
  return -1;

}       /* end of main() */
```

After execution of this program, if at least one qualifying application was found, the "best" transcript and the essay that accompanies it can be found in the file named `winner.txt` in the directory from which the program was executed.

4.2 DISTINCT TYPES

As discussed in Section 2.3, each item of data stored in V2 has a specific datatype that determines its representation and the operations that apply to it. The built-in datatypes of V2 include the basic datatypes listed in Table 2-1 and Table 2-2, plus the large-object datatypes discussed in Section 4.1 (Long Varchar, Long Vargraphic, Blob, Clob, and Dbclob).

In building a database, you may decide to use one of the built-in datatypes in a specialized way; for example, you may use the Integer datatype to represent ages, or the Decimal(8,2) datatype to represent amounts of money, or the Double datatype to represent geometric angles. When you do this, you may have certain rules in mind about the kinds of computations that make sense on your data. For example, it may make sense to add or subtract two amounts of money, but it may not make sense to multiply two amounts of money, and it almost surely makes no sense to add or compare an age to an amount of money.

V2 provides a way for you to declare such specialized usages of datatypes and the rules that go with them. The system then enforces the rules, by performing only the kinds of computations and comparisons that you have declared to be reasonable for your data. For example, if you were to write a query that involves adding an age to an amount of money, the query would fail with an error message. In other words, the system guarantees the *type-safety* of your queries.

4.2.1 Creating Distinct Types

The way to declare a specialized use of data in V2 is to create a new datatype of your own, called a *distinct type*, to supplement the system's built-in datatypes. Each distinct type shares a common internal representation with one of the built-in datatypes, called its *base type*. Despite this common representation, the distinct type is considered to be a separate datatype, distinct from all others (hence the name). The following example statements create distinct types named Sex, Money, Geometry.Angle, and Video, which take their internal representations from various built-in datatypes:

```
CREATE DISTINCT TYPE Sex AS Char(1) WITH COMPARISONS;
CREATE DISTINCT TYPE Money AS Decimal(8,2) WITH COMPARISONS;
CREATE DISTINCT TYPE Geometry.Angle
                AS Double WITH COMPARISONS;
CREATE DISTINCT TYPE Video AS Blob(100M);
```

An instance of a distinct type is considered comparable only with another instance of the same distinct type. For example, if M1 is a column of type Money and D1 is a column of type Decimal(8,2), then m1 + d1 and m1 > d1 are not valid expressions—an SQL statement containing such an expression would fail with an error message.

The phrase WITH COMPARISONS serves as a reminder that instances of the new distinct type can be compared with each other, using six comparison operators: =, <, <=, >, >=, and <>. The meanings of the comparison operators applied to instances of the distinct type are the same as if they were applied to instances of the base type. Furthermore, since the system automatically knows how to compare instances of a distinct type, you can apply the language elements ORDER BY, GROUP BY, and DISTINCT to columns of a distinct type, and you can create a unique or nonunique index on a column of a distinct type. However, since comparisons, indexes, ORDER BY, GROUP BY, and

DISTINCT are not supported for LOB datatypes, neither are they supported for distinct types based on LOB datatypes (and when you create such a distinct type, you should omit the phrase WITH COMPARISONS).

The syntax of a CREATE DISTINCT TYPE statement is as follows:

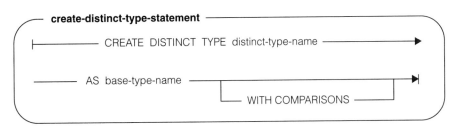

create-distinct-type-statement

CREATE DISTINCT TYPE distinct-type-name

AS base-type-name WITH COMPARISONS

The following facts are important to remember about the CREATE DISTINCT TYPE statement:

- The distinct-type name may be qualified by a schema name. The schema name may not begin with the letters SYS. If the schema name is omitted, it defaults to the userid of the user who is creating the distinct type. Whenever you are using a distinct type, you should add the schema name of the distinct type to your function path (described in Section 4.3).

- The distinct-type name must not be the same as the name of any built-in datatype or any other distinct type in the same schema. The name BOOLEAN is also prohibited as the name of a distinct type—it is reserved for a possible future built-in datatype.

- The base-type name must be the name of a built-in datatype. If it is qualified by a schema name, the schema name must be SYSIBM.

- If the base type takes a length or precision and scale (such as Char(n) or Decimal(p,s)), the values of these parameters must be fixed. If you omit the length of a Char base type, it is assumed to be Char(1); if you omit the precision and scale of a Decimal base type, it is assumed to be Decimal(5,0).

- The distinct-type name must not include any specification of length or precision and scale (since these are inherited from the base type).

- No authorization is required to execute a CREATE DISTINCT TYPE statement, unless a schema name is specified that is different from the current authid; in this case, either SYSADM or DBADM authority is required.

- The phrase WITH COMPARISONS is required if the base type is not a large-object datatype; if the base type is Blob, Clob, Dbclob, Long Varchar, or Long Vargarphic, the phrase WITH COMPARISONS is tolerated with a warning message, even though comparisons are not supported.

Each distinct type is recorded in a system catalog table called DATATYPES, which has the following columns (among others):

TYPESCHEMA, TYPENAME: The name of the distinct type.

SOURCESCHEMA, SOURCENAME: The name of the datatype on which the distinct type is based.

REMARKS: A descriptive comment, usually supplied by the user who created the distinct type.

You can place a comment in the REMARKS column of the DATATYPES catalog table by using the COMMENT statement described in Section 2.8.7. Here's an example:

```
COMMENT ON DISTINCT TYPE Money
    IS 'Signed dollar amounts less than $1 million';
```

After you have created a distinct type, you can use it in a CREATE TABLE or ALTER TABLE statement just as you would use a built-in datatype, as in the following examples. Note that since column names and datatype names are not in the same name space, a column is allowed to have the same name as its datatype.

```
CREATE TABLE employees
    (empno  Char(5),
     deptno Char(3),
     name   Varchar(20),
     sex    Sex,
     salary Money);
ALTER TABLE employees
    ADD bonus Money;
```

If you have a distinct type that is no longer needed, you can drop it by using the DROP statement described in Section 2.8.6. But before dropping a distinct type you should make sure that it is not used in any table or view or as a parameter of any function. (For more information about finding objects that depend on a distinct type, see Section 5.5.2.) Here are some examples of statements that drop distinct types:

```
DROP DISTINCT TYPE Video;
DROP DISTINCT TYPE Geometry.Angle
```

Of course, the built-in datatypes (which are in the SYSIBM schema) cannot be dropped.

4.2.2 Casting Functions

When you create a distinct type, two casting functions are automatically created, to convert between the distinct type and its base type. For example, if you create a distinct type Age based on Integer, the system automatically generates casting functions named age(Integer) and integer(Age). Using these casting functions, you can freely convert a distinct-type value to its base type and vice versa. For example, if AGE1 and AGE2 are columns of type Age, which is based on Integer, and no "+" operator is defined for the Age datatype, the expression age1 + age2 would be an error, but the expression age(integer(age1) + integer(age2)) would be correct. This expression would be your way of telling the SQL compiler, "I know what I'm doing, and I want to add together these two Ages as though they were Integers." The casting functions between distinct types and their base types are very efficient (in fact, you might say they cost nothing), because the base type and the distinct type share the same representation, so no real work is needed to convert from one to the other.

The name of the casting function that converts a base-type value into a distinct type is the same as the name of the distinct type, and the casting function is created in the same schema as the distinct type. For example, if the distinct type Age in the COMPANY schema is based on Integer, its casting function (also in the COMPANY schema) is as follows:

```
age(Integer) returns Age
```

The age casting function in this example can be invoked on any value that can be promoted to Integer datatype by the normal rules of argument-promotion (described in Section 4.6.1). For example, if C1 is a Smallint column and C2 is a Double column, age(c1) is valid (because Smallint is promotable to Integer) but age(c2) is not valid (because Double is not promotable to Integer).[2]

The name of the casting function that converts a distinct-type value into its base type is derived from the name of the base type, as shown in Table 4-4. This casting function is also generated in the same schema as the distinct type. For example, if Money in the COMPANY schema is based on Decimal(8,2), it has a system-generated casting function named decimal, also in the COMPANY schema, that takes Money as a parameter and returns Decimal(8,2).

---

2. If a distinct type is defined on Smallint, casting functions are automatically created to cast both Smallint and Integer values into the distinct type. This is necessary because constants such as 25 and -9 are always considered to be of type Integer. Suppose, for example, that Hatsize is a distinct type based on Smallint. Then the expression hatsize(8) could be used to convert a constant Integer into a Hatsize even though Integer is not the base type. For a similar reason, a Varchar instance can be cast into a distinct type based on Char (since character constants are considered to be of type Varchar), and a Vargraphic instance can be cast into a distinct type based on Graphic (because double-byte constants are considered to be of type Vargraphic).

TABLE 4-4: Names of System-Generated Casting Functions

Base Type	Casting Function
Smallint	`smallint`
Integer	`integer`
Decimal(p,s) or Numeric(p,s)	`decimal`
Float or Double or Double Precision	`double`
Char(n)	`char`
Varchar(n)	`varchar`
Long Varchar	`long_varchar`
Clob(n)	`clob`
Graphic(n)	`graphic`
Vargraphic(n)	`vargraphic`
Long Vargraphic	`long_vargraphic`
Dbclob(n)	`dbclob`
Blob(n)	`blob`
Date	`date`
Time	`time`
Timestamp	`timestamp`

When a distinct type is based on a datatype such as Char or Varchar that has a length parameter, the distinct type specifies (explicitly or by default) a fixed length, and the casting functions convert between instances of the distinct type and instances of the base type with the specified length. For example, suppose the distinct type Address is defined, based on Char(32). The following casting functions are automatically generated:

```
address(Char(32)) returns Address
char(Address) returns Char(32)
```

If a base-type value with a different length, such as Char(20) or Char(50), is passed to a casting function, its length is adjusted according to the rules for assignment to a host variable (for example, Char(20) would be padded with blanks to Char(32), and Char(50) would be truncated to Char(32) with a warning message). Similar rules apply to the casting functions for distinct types based on Decimal datatypes, which have a fixed precision and scale.

The casting functions that are created along with a distinct type can be invoked either by their names (like any other function) or by using the CAST notation described in Section 3.1. For example, if the distinct type Money is defined on the base type Decimal(8,2), either of the following expressions could be used to cast a Decimal constant into the Money type:

```
money(1234.50)
CAST(1234.50 AS Money)
```

Similarly, if SALARY is a database column of type Money, either of the following expressions could be used to cast a salary value into the Decimal base type:

```
decimal(salary)
CAST(salary AS Decimal(8,2))
```

The CAST notation can also be used to convert a distinct-type value into a form of its base type that has a different length and/or precision and scale. For example, consider the following expression:

```
CAST(salary AS Decimal(10,4))
```

This expression invokes the casting function `decimal(salary)`, resulting in a value of type Decimal(8,2), then adjusts the precision and scale of the result to conform to the desired type Decimal(10,4).

4.2.3 Using Distinct Types

Distinct types are useful tools for protecting the type-safety of a program. They can be used to make sure that different types of data are not combined in ways that do not make sense, such as comparing a Height to a Weight, even though both Height and Weight may be based on floating-point numbers.

It is important to remember that, although casting functions are automatically defined between each distinct type and its base type, you must invoke these casting functions explicitly if you wish to compare a distinct-type value with a base-type value. Furthermore, constants are always considered to be base-type values—for example, 21 is considered to be an Integer, and 'Green' is considered to be a Varchar(5). Therefore, to compare a distinct-type value to a constant, you must perform an explicit cast. For example, if MYAGE is a column of type Age, the expression `myage > 21` is a type error, but `myage > age(21)` is correct, as is `integer(myage) > 21`.

When a distinct type is created, the only operations that are automatically defined on it are casting between the distinct type and its base type in both directions, and comparisons between two values of the distinct type (provided the base type is not a large-object datatype). Other operations that may apply to the base type, such as arithmetic operators, are not automatically inherited by the distinct type. It is probably not very useful to define a distinct type whose only operations are casting and comparison. Therefore, V2 provides a way for you to enhance the semantics of your distinct type, either by inheriting some of the operations of the base type or by defining new operations of your own.

In order to understand the behavior of a distinct type, it is important to realize that the system considers all arithmetic operators such as + and * to be *functions*. For example, the + operator for Integers is considered to be a function (named "+") that takes two Integers as arguments and returns another Integer (the sum of its arguments). You can even use a functional notation to invoke an arithmetic operator—just remember to enclose the name of the function in double quotes (this tells the system that the symbol "+" is being used as a name). For example, the following two queries are exactly equivalent:

```
SELECT qonhand + qonorder
FROM parts WHERE partno = 'P207';
```

```
SELECT "+"(qonhand, qonorder)
FROM parts WHERE partno = 'P207';
```

The built-in datatypes of V2 come with a collection of built-in functions that operate on them. Some of these functions implement operators such as the arithmetic operators on numeric datatypes and the concatenate (||) operator on string datatypes. Other built-in functions include scalar functions, such as length and substr, and column functions, such as sum and avg. After creating a distinct type, you can specify that the distinct type inherits some or all of the functions that operate on its base type. This is done by creating new functions, called *sourced functions*, that operate on the distinct type and duplicate the semantics of built-in functions that operate on the base type. For example, you might specify that your distinct type Weight inherits the arithmetic operators + and -, and the column functions sum and avg, from its base type Float. By selectively inheriting the semantics of the base type, you can make sure that programs do not perform operations that make no sense, such as multiplying two weights, even though the underlying base type supports multiplication.

You can also go beyond mere inheritance of base-type functions and give your distinct type some semantics of its own. This is done by creating some *external functions*, written in a host programming language, that operate on your distinct type. Since you implement these functions yourself, they can do anything you want. If you use an operator such as "+" as the name of your external function, you can invoke your function using infix notation (such as weight1 + weight2). In this way, you can define specialized meanings for arithmetic operations on your distinct type. But you are not limited to the existing operators—you can create an external function with any name and behavior that you like. For example, you might create a function named complement(Angle) that returns another Angle, or a function named zipcode (Address) that returns Char(5). (The process of creating sourced functions and external functions is discussed in Section 4.4.)

4.2.4 Assigning Distinct Types

We use the term *assignment* for the process of giving a new value to an entry in a database table or to a host variable. We refer to the value that is being assigned as the *source* of the assignment and to the database entry or host variable that is receiving the new value as the *target* of the assignment. In SQL, assignment can occur in the following ways:

1. An entry in a table can be assigned a new value by an UPDATE statement, as in:

```
UPDATE employees SET bonus = 1250.00 WHERE empno = '12345';
```

2. A new row can be inserted into a table, assigning new values to each of its columns, as in:

```
EXEC SQL
    INSERT INTO budget
    VALUES('Supersonic Wind Tunnel', 1996, :funds, :mgr);
```

3. A query (or FETCH statement) can deliver a value into a host variable, as in:

```
EXEC SQL
    SELECT bonus INTO :bonus
    FROM employees WHERE empno = '12345';
```

4. An assignment statement (SET statement) can be used in the body of a trigger. (Triggers and assignment statements are discussed in Section 5.3.)

In all these cases, the target is receiving a new value that is computed from an expression that may contain database columns and/or host language variables. If the datatype of the target is the same as the datatype of the value that is being assigned to it, the assignment is straightforward. The built-in datatypes have a set of rules for what happens when a value is assigned to a target of a different datatype, which might be summarized as follows:

1. Numeric datatypes (Smallint, Integer, Decimal, and Double) may be assigned freely to one another (however, loss of precision or a run-time error condition may occur if the source value cannot be represented in the target datatype).

2. Character-string datatypes (Char, Varchar, Long Varchar, and Clob) may be assigned freely to one another (however, padding, truncation, or a run-time error condition may occur, depending on the relative lengths of the source and the target).

3. Graphic-string datatypes (Graphic, Vargraphic, Long Vargraphic, and Dbclob) may be assigned freely to one another (again, various run-time exceptions may occur, depending on their lengths).

4. A Char or Varchar containing a valid representation of a Date may be assigned to a Date target and vice versa. Similarly, a Char or Varchar containing a valid representation of a Time may be assigned to a Time target and vice versa, and a Char or Varchar containing a valid representation of a Timestamp may be assigned to a Timestamp target and vice versa.

Since V2 allows users to define their own distinct types, some extension to the assignment rules is necessary to cover the cases where the source and/or target of an assignment is a distinct type. Since each distinct type is generally considered to be comparable only to itself, one approach might be to require an explicit casting function to be invoked whenever a distinct type is assigned to or from another datatype. The problem with this "strict typing" approach lies with host variables. Since the host programming languages such as C and COBOL have no way to declare variables of distinct types, all host variables have base types. (More precisely, they have the programming language data-types that correspond to base types; for example, the C datatype `long` corresponds to the base type Integer.) So when a distinct-type data value is fetched into (or inserted from) a host variable, the "strict typing" approach would require the programmer to use an explicit casting function. This rule would cause some serious problems for certain kinds of applications. For example, consider a program that is prompting its user for ad hoc SQL queries, executing them, and displaying the results. Suppose the user types the query `SELECT * FROM students`. The program needs to fetch values from the STUDENTS table into host variables for display, but if these values have distinct types, it is very difficult to insert casting functions into the query.

In order to make applications easier to develop, V2 has adopted the policy of automatically invoking a cast function when a distinct-type value is assigned to a base-type target and vice versa. In order to see how this policy works, consider the following specific kinds of assignments:

1. If the target of the assignment is a database column of some distinct type DT, the source expression must also be of type DT or must be convertible to DT by using a system-generated casting function. In other words, the datatype of the source expression must be the base type of DT or some other base type that is promotable to the base type of DT using the argument promotion rules shown

in Figure 4-5 in Section 4.6. For example, a column of type Money that is based on Decimal(8,2) can be assigned a value of type Money, Decimal, or Integer, since Integer is promotable to Decimal, but it may not be assigned a value of type Double, since Double is not promotable to Decimal. The system automatically invokes the appropriate casting function to carry out the assignment.

2. If the target of the assignment is a database column of some base type but the source expression has a distinct type DT, the target type must be the base type of DT. For example, a column of type Decimal(8,2) (or even Decimal with a different precision and scale) can be assigned a value of type Money. Once again, the system automatically invokes the appropriate casting function when performing the assignment.

3. If the target of the assignment is a host variable and the source expression has a distinct type DT, the assignment is carried out in a two-step process. In Step 1, the source value is converted from DT to the base type of DT, using the system-provided casting function. In Step 2, the resulting base type is assigned to the host variable, using the normal assignment rules for base types. The reason for separating these steps is that, in general, Step 1 is carried out at the server machine and Step 2 is carried out at the client machine. Thus, for example, a Money value might be assigned to a host variable of type double, by first casting Money to Decimal(8,2) and then assigning the Decimal(8,2) value to the double variable, which is permitted by the assignment rules. As in the previous cases, the system performs the type conversions automatically.

For some more examples of automatic casting on assignment, consider a geometry application. Suppose that Angle is a distinct type with a base type of Double, TRIANGLES is a table having a column named VERTEX of type Angle, and :v is a host language variable of type Double. Then, all of the following examples are valid assignments:

```
EXEC SQL
    SELECT vertex INTO :v FROM triangles WHERE color = 'Red';
    /* Assignment to host variable; calls double(Angle) */

EXEC SQL
    INSERT INTO triangles(color, vertex) VALUES ('Blue', :v);
    /* Assignment to Angle column; calls angle(Double)  */

UPDATE triangles SET vertex = 45.5 WHERE color = 'Green';
    /* Assignment to Angle column; calls angle(Double)  */
    /* Decimal constant 45.5 is promoted to Double,      */
    /* then cast to Angle by calling function            */
```

4.3 FUNCTION PATH

Before proceeding any further with our discussion of user-defined datatypes and functions, we need to discuss the concept of *function path*. Since V2 allows users to create their own datatypes and functions, it is possible that multiple datatypes and/or functions may be created with the same name. For example, you might develop or purchase a specialized set of datatypes and functions for solving tax problems and keep them in a schema named TAX96. At the same time, you might develop, or purchase from another source, another set of datatypes and functions for managing investments and install them in a schema named INVEST. These two schemas might each contain a datatype named Money or a function named `monthlyPayment`.

If you call a function using a name such as `monthlyPayment(x,y)` that does not include a schema name, and multiple functions with this name that all accept the parameter types of your call exist in different schemas, the system must decide which function you intend to invoke. The same problem can occur with datatype names. The process of choosing a specific function or datatype to satisfy a given reference is called *function resolution* or *type resolution*.

You can always include an explicit schema name when you refer to a function or datatype, as in `tax96.Money` or `invest.monthlyPayment`. But there are some reasons why you might prefer to use unqualified names, including the following:

1. Fully qualified names are long and hard to remember.

2. It's better for applications not to depend on the schemas in which their datatypes and functions are installed. For example, if you replace your TAX96 package with a new upward-compatible package named TAX97, you would prefer not to have to edit all your existing applications and change the schema name of every datatype and function from TAX96 to TAX97.

The mechanism provided in V2 for resolving datatypes and functions without requiring fully qualified names is the function path. Despite its name, the function path applies to datatypes as well as to functions. It is a sequence of schema names that will be searched, in order, whenever an unqualified (that is, schemaless) datatype name or function name is encountered. An unqualified datatype name resolves to the first matching datatype that is found on the path. The process of resolving an unqualified function name is somewhat more complex because it involves the *signature* of the function—that is, the datatypes of its parameters. (Function resolution is discussed in more detail in Section 4.4.5.)

For static SQL statements, the function path is determined by an optional FUNCPATH parameter on the PREP or BIND command that bound the application program, which specifies the list of schemas on the path. For example, the following command might be used to precompile a program named NAV-IGATE with a particular function path:

```
PREP navigate FUNCPATH maps, geometry, sysibm
```

Schema names used in the FUNCPATH parameter are automatically folded to uppercase by the system unless they are enclosed in double quotes. The default function path for static SQL is SYSIBM, followed by SYSFUN, followed by the userid under which the program is being precompiled or bound. SYSIBM and SYSFUN are the schemas containing all the built-in functions, and SYSIBM is the first schema on the default path in order to minimize the time spent by the SQL compiler in searching for built-in functions.

TIP: In the FUNCPATH parameter of a PREP or BIND command, USER is not recognized as a keyword representing the current userid. If you want to specify your own userid as a schema name in the function path for PREP or BIND, you must spell it out explicitly.

4.3.1 SET CURRENT FUNCTION PATH Statement

For dynamic SQL (including CLI), the function path is taken from a special register called CURRENT FUNCTION PATH. When a program begins to execute, the initial value of CURRENT FUNCTION PATH is SYSIBM, followed by SYSFUN, followed by the content of the USER special register (the userid of the user who is running the program). During execution of a program, the current function path register can be changed by an SQL statement with the following syntax:

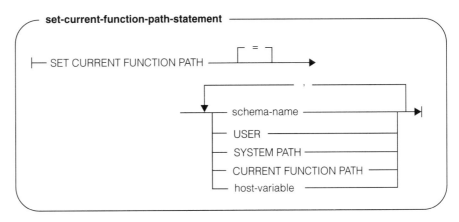

A SET CURRENT FUNCTION PATH statement can be either static or dynamic. In either case, it affects only the resolution of names in dynamic SQL statements that are executed after the SET CURRENT FUNCTION PATH is executed.

In a SET CURRENT FUNCTION PATH statement, schema names need not be enclosed in quotes unless they contain blanks or special characters or are the same as keywords. Schema names not enclosed in quotes are folded to uppercase (however, the content of a host variable is not folded to uppercase). The keywords that can be included in the path specification are interpreted as follows:

- USER represents the userid of the user who is running the program (not necessarily the same as the user who precompiled or bound the program).
- SYSTEM PATH represents the pair of schemas SYSIBM and SYSFUN (the part of the default path that contains system-provided functions).
- CURRENT FUNCTION PATH represents the function path that was in effect before the SET CURRENT FUNCTION PATH statement was executed. This is useful, for example, if you wish to keep the path intact and add a new schema to the end of it.

The following are examples of SET CURRENT FUNCTION PATH statements:

```
SET CURRENT FUNCTION PATH = USER, tax97, SYSTEM PATH;
SET CURRENT FUNCTION PATH = chem, physics, user;
SET CURRENT FUNCTION PATH = CURRENT FUNCTION PATH, maps;
```

TIP: A SET CURRENT FUNCTION PATH statement does not modify the database and therefore is not subject to rollback. For example, if you set your function path to a new value and then roll back your transaction, your function path will still retain the new value.

Like all special registers, the current function path can be examined using an SQL statement such as the following:

```
VALUES(CURRENT FUNCTION PATH);
```

The result of this VALUES statement is the current function path with each schema name enclosed in double quotes. For example, if the first SET CURRENT FUNCTION PATH statement above had been executed by user HILLARY, the result of the VALUES statement above would be "HILLARY","TAX97","SYSIBM","SYSFUN".

TIP: Remember that a SET CURRENT FUNCTION PATH inside an application program does not affect the resolution of datatypes or function calls in *static* SQL statements. However, it may affect the resolution of datatypes and function calls in *dynamic* statements executed by this program.

Since all the built-in datatypes and many important functions are found in the SYSIBM schema, V2 would be very hard to use if SYSIBM were not on your function path. For this reason, every function path is required to include SYSIBM. If you specify a path that does not include SYSIBM, either in a PREP or BIND command or in a SET CURRENT FUNCTION PATH statement, the system will implicitly add SYSIBM to the beginning of the path, before the other schemas. (Placing SYSIBM at the beginning of the path allows applications that use only built-in functions to avoid any performance degradation that might be caused by searching for user-defined functions with the same name.) Of course, if you specify SYSIBM on your path in some position other than the first schema, the system will respect your wishes. The string returned by VALUES(CURRENT FUNCTION PATH) does not include the implicit SYSIBM schema (if any) that was added to your path.

The function path is used for resolving references to datatypes and functions, but not for resolving references to other objects such as tables, views, indexes, and aliases. Unqualified names of objects other than functions and datatypes have an implicit qualifier equal to the userid who bound the program (for static SQL) or the userid who is running the program (for dynamic SQL). For example, the unqualified table name RESULTS, in a static SQL statement in a program bound by user SMITH, is interpreted as SMITH.RESULTS, independently of the function path.

TIP: Whenever you are manipulating objects of a distinct type, the schema name of the distinct type should be on your function path, because the comparison operators of the distinct type are considered to be functions that are in the same schema as the distinct type. Thus, for example, if you have created a distinct type named Weight in the VEHICLES schema, a comparison of two Weight values such as `weight1 = weight2` is valid only if the VEHICLES schema is on your function path.

4.4   USER-DEFINED FUNCTIONS

In a V2 system, the functions that are available for use in SQL statements fall into the following general categories:

1. *Built-in functions.* Some functions are built into the code of the V2 system. These functions are found in the SYSIBM schema, and include the following:

   - Arithmetic and string operators: +, -, *, /, ||
   - Scalar functions: substr, concat, length, days, and so on
   - Column functions: avg, count, min, max, stdev, sum, variance

   In addition to the built-in functions in the SYSIBM schema, many other functions are shipped with V2, in the SYSFUN schema. Although these functions are shipped with the system, they are not implemented directly by system code. Instead, they are implemented as preinstalled external functions, using the same facilities that are available to users to define functions of their own. In practice, as long as both SYSIBM and SYSFUN are on your function path, there is no distinction in usage between the SYSIBM and SYSFUN functions.

2. *System-generated functions.* These functions are automatically generated when a distinct type is created and are found in the same schema as the distinct type. System-generated functions include casting functions and comparison operators for the distinct type.

3. *User-defined functions.* These functions are created explicitly by users, using a statement called CREATE FUNCTION, which names the new function and specifies its semantics. User-defined functions can be further classified into two subcategories:

   a. *Sourced functions.* A sourced function duplicates the semantics of another function, called its *source function.* A sourced function can be an operator, a scalar function, or a column function. Sourced functions are particularly useful for allowing a distinct type to selectively inherit the semantics of its base type.

   b. *External functions.* An external function is a function that is written by a user in a host programming language. In V2, external functions can be written in C or C++.[3] The CREATE FUNCTION statement for an external function tells the system where to find the code that implements the function. An external function may be an operator or a scalar function but may not be a column function. Furthermore, in V2, an external function may not contain any SQL statements. In other words, an external function may perform any computation you like on the parameters that are passed to it, but it may not access or modify the database.

System-generated functions and user-defined functions are always created in a specific database and can be used only in that database. Within their database, system-generated and user-defined functions can be used in exactly the same ways as built-in functions. System-generated and user-defined functions are available to all users of the database and can be used without any specific authorization. No authorization is required to create a user-defined function, unless the function is being created in a schema that is different from the creator's userid (which requires DBADM or SYSADM authority), or unless the function has the NOT FENCED property (described in Section 4.4.3).

A CREATE FUNCTION statement may be embedded in an application program or executed via an interactive query interface such as the CLP. However, if a CREATE FUNCTION statement is embedded in a program, static SQL statements in that program cannot call the newly created function, since when the program is first bound, the new function will not yet exist (that is, the function will not exist until the program has been executed).

Like many modern programming languages, SQL supports the concept of *function overloading*. This means that several functions may be defined that have the same name, as long as they are in different schemas or take different types of parameters. For example, you can define a function square(Integer) that returns Integer and another function square(Double) that returns Double. When a function call such as square(x) is encountered, the system automatically invokes the proper function for the datatype of the argument. It is easy to see that the built-in functions of V2 are already overloaded, since scalar functions such as length and operators such as + can be applied to many different datatypes. We will sometimes find it necessary to use the term *function family* to refer to a set of functions that share a common name, and *function instance* to refer to one of the functions within a function family.

When you create a new function, you may be starting a new function family or adding a function instance to an existing function family. In either case,

---

3. Actually, an external function can be written in any programming language that follows the C linkage conventions. Using the DataBasic product, an external function can be written in BASIC and provided with a "wrapper" function that enables it to be called using C linkage conventions (see *DataBasic Developer's Guide* for details). All the external function examples in this chapter are written in C.

you must make sure that your new function has a unique *signature*. The signature of a function is the combination of its fully qualified name and all its parameter types. For example, if a function `square(Double)` already exists, you will not be allowed to create another `square(Double)` function in the same schema.

In addition to its name, which it shares with all other functions in the same family, each user-defined function instance has another name called its *specific name*. The specific name of each function instance is unique within its schema. For example, in the MATH schema, we might create a function `square(Integer)` with a specific name of `square1` and another function `square(Double)` with a specific name of `square2`. Specific names are used only to identify a function instance in cases where no arguments are present, such as in dropping a function, commenting on a function, or naming a function as the source of another function. When you invoke a function, you must always use its family name (not its specific name). The function resolution process (to be described later) will resolve the family name to a function instance based on the datatypes of the arguments and the function path.

Every user-defined and system-generated function is described in a system catalog table called FUNCTIONS, which has the following columns:

- FUNCSCHEMA, FUNCNAME: Qualified name of the user-defined function.

- SPECIFICNAME: Specific name of the function (useful for dropping a function instance from an overloaded function family).

- ORIGIN: A one-letter code that identifies the origin of the function as one of the following:
    B: built-in
    S: system-generated
    U: user-defined, sourced
    E: user-defined, external

- TYPE: Specifies whether the function is a scalar function (like `length`) or a column function (like `avg`).

- Various other columns that specify the properties of the function, including the name of the source (for a sourced function) or the name of the file that contains the implementation (for an external function).

Another catalog table, named FUNCPARMS, describes the datatypes of the parameters and the result of each system-generated or user-defined function. This catalog table has one row for each parameter of each function, and an additional row for the result type. (Details of the FUNCTIONS and FUNCPARMS catalog tables are given in Appendix D.)

4.4.1 Creating a Sourced Function

A sourced function is a new function that is based on some other function that already exists, called the source function. When the new function is invoked, its arguments are cast into the parameter types of the source function; the source function is then invoked; and finally, the result of the source function is cast into the result type of the new function.

The process of executing a sourced function is illustrated in Figure 4-1. In this example, Weight is a distinct type based on the built-in Double datatype. Since it makes sense to add two Weights, the definer of the distinct type has created a function "+"(`Weight, Weight`) sourced on the built-in function "+"(`Double, Double`). This causes the Weight type to inherit the semantics of addition from the Double type. When two Weights are added, the system converts them to Double values, adds them together, and converts the result back into a Weight. (Remember that these "conversions" take no time, because a Weight and a Double have the same representation.)

The syntax of a CREATE FUNCTION statement to create a sourced function is on the next page.

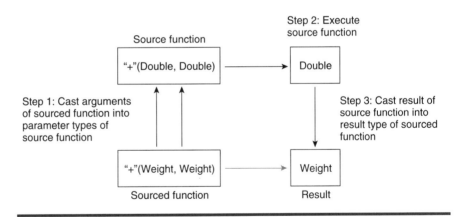

Figure 4-1: Executing a Sourced Function

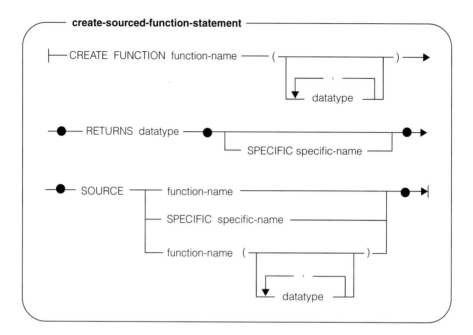

The parts of the CREATE FUNCTION statement for a sourced function are as follows:

1. *Function-name.* This is the name by which the function will be invoked. It may include a schema name, but the schema name may not begin with the letters SYS. If the schema name is omitted, it defaults to the current authid. DBADM or SYSADM authority is required to create a function whose schema name is not the same as the current authid.

   A function name may be an arithmetic operator such as "+" or "*" but when defining such a function you must enclose the function name in double quotes. If the name of a function is the same as an infix operator such as "+" the function can be called using infix notation (such as weight1 + weight2).

   Comparison operators such as "=" and ">" may not be used as the names of functions. SQL keywords that might occur within a predicate (such as AND, OR, NOT, EXISTS, and BETWEEN) are also not valid function names.

2. *(datatype, . . .).* This part of the CREATE FUNCTION statement lists the datatypes of the function parameters. A function may take from 0 to 90 parameters. The parentheses must be present even if there are no parameters. The parameter types may be either built-in datatypes or user-defined (distinct) types.

   If one of the parameter types takes an attribute such as length or scale/ precision, you can either specify the attribute exactly—as in Decimal(8,3)—or use empty parentheses in place of the attribute—as in Decimal( ). Empty parentheses mean "same as the corresponding parameter of the source function." For example, creating a new function named foo(Char()) with a source function bar(Char(5)) effectively specifies the signature of the new function to be foo(Char(5)).

When checking the signature of a function for uniqueness, the system ignores the length, precision, and scale of the function parameters. Thus, for example, schema1.foo(char(10)) and schema1.foo(char(20)) are considered duplicate signatures and cannot both exist.

TIP: When defining the datatypes of your function parameters, be careful to distinguish between empty parentheses, which mean "same as source function," and omitted parentheses, which result in a default value for the missing attribute. For example, if the signature of the new function is specified as foo(Char), its parameter is assumed to have a length of 1, regardless of the parameter of the source function.

3. *RETURNS clause.* This clause specifies the return type of the new function. If the return type takes an attribute such as length or scale/precision, you can either specify the attribute exactly—as in Decimal(8,3)—or use empty parentheses in place of the attribute—as in Decimal( ). Empty parentheses mean "same as the return type of the source function." If the source function returns a datatype of indefinite length, the new function will do the same. In the following example, the parameters and result of both the source function and the new function have indefinite lengths:

```
CREATE FUNCTION "+"(Varchar(), Varchar()) RETURNS Varchar()
    SOURCE concat(Varchar(), Varchar());
```

4. *SPECIFIC clause.* This clause gives a specific name to the new function instance being created. The purpose of the specific name is to provide a unique way to identify a function instance, despite the fact that several function instances can have the same function name.

The specific name must be unique within its schema. If you do not specify a specific name for your function, the system will generate one automatically. The specific name is recorded in the SPECIFICNAME column of the FUNCTIONS catalog table, and can be used to drop the function, to comment on it, or to use it as the source of another function. However, a function can never be invoked by its specific name, but only by its function name.

There is no need to specify a schema for the specific name, since the specific name of a function is implicitly qualified by the same schema as the function name. Since function names and specific names are in different name spaces, the function name and specific name of a function instance can be identical.

5. *SOURCE clause.* This clause identifies your new function as a sourced function and specifies the existing function that will serve as its "source." The source function can be either built-in or user-defined and can be an operator such as "+"; a scalar function such as substr; or a column function such as avg. The source function can be identified in one of three ways:

a. By its function name, with no parameters. This method applies only if the source function is user-defined and only if its name is unique within its schema. You can provide a schema name or omit it, causing the system to search through the function path to find the first schema that contains a function with the given name. If the name of the source function is an operator such as "+" or an SQL keyword, it must be enclosed in double quotes.

b. By its specific name. This method applies only if the source function is user-defined, since built-in functions do not have specific names. You can look up the specific name of any user-defined function in the SPECIFIC column of the FUNCTIONS catalog table. You can provide a specific name that is qualified by a schema name, such as `geometry.cosine`, or you can omit the schema name, causing the system to search through the function path until it finds a function with the given specific name.

c. By its signature (its function name together with the datatypes of its parameters). This is the only way to identify a source function that is a built-in function. As usual, you can provide an explicit schema name or omit the schema name and let the system search for the function on the function path. The rules for identifying a source function by its signature are as follows:

- The system searches for a source function whose parameter types exactly match the datatypes that you specify, without any promotion of types. For example, if you specify `SOURCE  foo(Integer)`, the function `foo(Double)` will not qualify, even though Integer is promotable to Double.

- If the signature includes a datatype that has an attribute such as length or scale/precision, you can either specify the attribute exactly—for example, Decimal(8,3)—or use empty parentheses in place of the attribute—for example, Decimal( ). Empty parentheses match any length or scale/precision. For example, `SOURCE length(Char())` searches for a source function named `length` that takes a Char parameter of any length (as does the built-in `length` function).

TIP: Empty parentheses are not equivalent to omitted parentheses. For example, `SOURCE length(Char)` searches for a source function that takes a Char parameter of default length, which is Char(1). This SOURCE clause would fail to find the system's built-in `length` function. In a SOURCE clause, it is a good rule to always use empty parentheses (never omitted parentheses) for all lengths, precisions, and scales.

After the system has found a source function that matches your SOURCE clause, it applies a *castability test* to the source function. The test requires that each parameter of your new function be castable into the corresponding parameter of the source function and that the result type of the source function be castable into the result type of your new function, as illustrated in Figure 4-1. The most common case is that the parameters and/or result of the new function are distinct types, and the corresponding parameters and/or result of the source function are the base types of those distinct types. If the function identified by your SOURCE clause fails the castability test (for example, its result type is not castable into the result type of the new function), the CREATE FUNCTION statement fails.[4]

The reason for the castability test is obvious: it ensures that the system has a way to do the conversions that it needs to do when the function is called. For example, in Figure 4-1, the system needs to cast the two Weight parameters into Double values and to cast the Double result back into a Weight. Since the cast functions `weight(Double)` and `double(Weight)` were created when the Weight datatype was created, the castability test is satisfied.

4.4.2 Examples of Sourced Functions

As an example of the use of sourced functions, suppose that a distinct type Money has been defined, based on the built-in datatype Decimal(8,2). The Decimal datatype has arithmetic operators +, -, *, and /. We might wish to specify that the Decimal operators + and - are inherited by the Money datatype. This would be done by the following statements:

```
CREATE FUNCTION "+"(Money, Money) RETURNS Money
    SOURCE "+"(Decimal(), Decimal());
CREATE FUNCTION "-"(Money, Money) RETURNS Money
    SOURCE "-"(Decimal(), Decimal());
```

If SALARY and BONUS are two database columns of type Money, the functions above allow us to write expressions such as `salary + bonus` and `salary - bonus`. Of course, since the operators * and / are still undefined for Money, `salary * bonus` is not a valid expression.

Here are some things to notice about the CREATE FUNCTION statements in the above example:

- The operators "+" and "-" are enclosed in quotes to indicate that they are being used as function names.

- The empty parentheses after `Decimal` mean "any precision and scale." In other words, the source function operates on Decimal input parameters of any

---

4. The precise meaning of "castable" is explained in Section 4.6.4.

precision and scale. Of course, the newly created function operates only on input parameters of type Money, which has a well-defined precision and scale.

If it is meaningful to use arithmetic operators between your distinct type and its base type (or some other datatype), you must define these operators explicitly. For example, suppose that you wish to be able to multiply Money values by Integers to make new Money values. This can be accomplished by creating a sourced function, as follows:

```
CREATE FUNCTION "*"(Money, Integer) RETURNS Money
    SOURCE "*"(Decimal(), Integer);
```

This function enables you to write expressions such as money(111.11) * 2. Of course, if you want to write expressions such as 2 * money(111.11), you must define another sourced function with the signature "*"(Integer, Money).

The built-in column functions avg, count, min, max, stdev, sum, and variance do not apply to distinct types unless they are made to do so by means of sourced functions. For example, the following statement causes the Money datatype to inherit the semantics of the avg function from the underlying Decimal datatype:

```
CREATE FUNCTION avg(Money) RETURNS Money
    SOURCE avg(Decimal());
```

Creation of the above function makes the following query valid when the SALARY column is of type Money:

```
SELECT deptno, avg(salary) FROM employees GROUP BY deptno;
```

A new function will be a column function if its source function is a column function. This is independent of the name given to the new function, which may or may not be the same as the name of the source function. It is even possible (though confusing and not recommended) to create a function sourced on a function with a quite different name, as in the following example:

```
CREATE FUNCTION sum(Money, Money) RETURNS Money
    SOURCE "+"(Decimal(), Decimal());
```

In this example, the name sum, which ordinarily denotes a column function, is assigned the semantics of ordinary decimal addition when applied to the

Money datatype. Thus the expression sum(salary, bonus) would be a valid expression with the same meaning as salary + bonus, but sum(salary) would be invalid (unless a unary sum(Money) function is defined separately).

We have illustrated how sourced functions are used for selectively applying to a distinct type the semantics of its base type. However, it is possible to create a new function sourced on any existing function you like, either built-in or user-defined, as long as the argument types of the new function are castable to the argument types of the source function and the result type of the source function is castable to the result type of the new function. For example, the following statement might be used to give a new name to integer addition:

```
CREATE FUNCTION add(Integer, Integer) RETURNS Integer
    SOURCE "+"(Integer, Integer);
```

This statement indicates that, if x and y are of type Integer, the expression add(x,y) has the same meaning as the expression x + y. Of course, the new function name add is not recognized as an infix operator, so x add y would not be a valid expression.

4.4.3 Creating an External Function

An external function is a function whose implementation is written in some host programming language. The ability to create your own external functions is a very powerful feature of V2. Using this feature, you can enhance the usefulness of the built-in datatypes by adding new functions that operate on them, and you can define whatever behavior you wish for your distinct types.

By defining external functions and installing them in your database, you can share these functions among all your database applications, avoiding the necessity to duplicate the code in each application. External functions can also be used in interactive SQL statements, wherever built-in functions can be used.

When external functions are used in predicates, they can provide an important performance advantage, because external functions are executed at the server machine. If a function can be applied to a candidate row at the server machine, it can often eliminate the row from consideration before transmitting it to the client machine, reducing the amount of data that must be passed from server to client.

The syntax of a CREATE FUNCTION statement to create an external function is as follows:

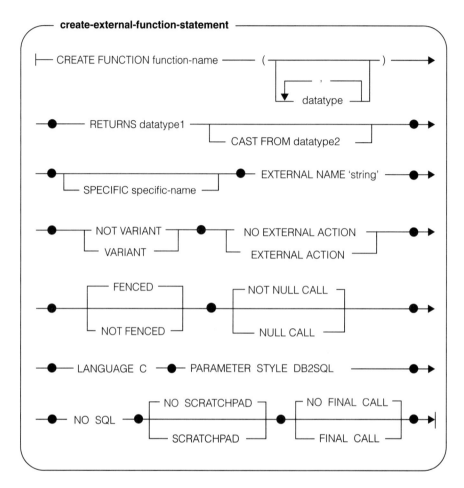

The parts of the CREATE FUNCTION statement for an external function are as follows:

1. *Function-name.* This is the name by which the function will be invoked. It may include a schema name, as in geometry.tangent. The schema name may not begin with the letters SYS. If the schema name is omitted, it defaults to the current authid. DBADM or SYSADM authority is required to create a function whose schema name is not the same as the current authid.

As in the case of sourced functions, the name of an external function may be an arithmetic operator such as "+" but not a comparison operator such as ">" or a keyword used in predicates such as AND, OR, NOT, EXISTS, or BETWEEN. It is also wise to avoid using a datatype name as the name of a function, since it might be confused with the system-generated casting function for that datatype (a user-defined function is *not* considered a casting function by the system just because its name and result type match some datatype).

2. (*datatype, . . .*). This part of the CREATE FUNCTION statement lists the datatypes of the function parameters. A function may take from 0 to 90 parameters. The parentheses must be present even if there are no parameters. The parameter types may be either built-in datatypes or user-defined (distinct) types.

If any parameter of an external function is a string type, its maximum length must be specified explicitly—for example, Char(12), Varchar(25), or Blob(32K). When checking the signature of an external function for uniqueness, the system ignores the length attributes of the function parameters. Thus, for example, `schema1.reverse(Varchar(10))` and `schema1.reverse(Varchar(20))` are considered duplicate signatures and cannot both exist.

As each parameter is passed to the C program that implements the external function, it is converted from an SQL datatype to the corresponding C datatype. A list of the C datatypes corresponding to each of the SQL datatypes is given in Table 4-6 on page 286. None of the parameters of an external function may be of type Decimal, because there is no way to pass a Decimal value to a C program. If you need to pass Decimal data to an external function, you can do so by first changing its datatype to Char or Double, using the built-in cast functions `char(Decimal)` or `double(Decimal)`.

If a function parameter is declared to have a distinct type, it is converted to its base type before being passed to the external function. For example, if Zipcode is a distinct type based on Char(5), a Zipcode parameter is passed to the program that implements the function as though its SQL datatype were Char(5). For this reason, no function parameter may have a distinct type that is based on a Decimal datatype.

TIP: It is not advisable to define a function having a parameter of type Smallint, fixed-length Char, or fixed-length Graphic, because constants and host variables are never interpreted as having these datatypes. For example, the constant 5 is considered to be an Integer, not a Smallint, and the constant 'abc' is considered to have datatype Varchar, not Char. Therefore, if you create a function with a parameter of type Smallint, Char, or Graphic, an explicit cast will be required every time you pass a constant or host variable to your function, as in `foo(Smallint(5))`. Your function will be much more useful if its parameter type is Integer, Varchar, or Vargraphic.

3. *RETURNS clause.* This clause specifies the result type of your function. The result type can be either a built-in or a user-defined datatype. If it is a string type, its maximum length must be specified explicitly.

Of course, since your external function is implemented by a C program, the actual value returned by the C program will have one of the C datatypes shown in Table 4-6 and will be converted into the corresponding SQL datatype as though it were an input host variable.

If the result of your external function is declared to have a distinct type, it is returned by a two-step process that is the reverse of the process used to pass a distinct-type parameter to an external function. The value returned by the C program is converted from a C datatype into an SQL datatype as though it were an input host variable; this SQL datatype is then cast into the desired distinct type using the system-provided casting function. For example, if the declared return type of your function is Zipcode, the C program would return a C datatype of null-terminated char[6], which would be converted into the base SQL datatype of Char(5) and then into the distinct type Zipcode. All these conversions are done automatically, using system-provided casting functions.

If you wish the result type of your function to be different from the datatype returned by the C program that implements the function, you can specify an additional conversion by using a CAST FROM clause. For example, suppose that you want to write an external function named grade_level (Clob(10K)), which examines a piece of text and returns an estimate of its reading difficulty expressed as a Decimal(3,1). The C program that implements your function has no way to return a Decimal value, since there is no C datatype in Table 4-6 that corresponds to Decimal. But the C program can return a Double value, which could then be converted into a Decimal(3,1) by the system. You could call for this conversion to be done by the following statement:

```
CREATE FUNCTION grade_level(Clob(10K))
   RETURNS Decimal(3,1) CAST FROM Double EXTERNAL ... ;
```

4. *SPECIFIC clause.* This clause gives a specific name to the new function instance being created. Like a sourced function, an external function can have a specific name that uniquely identifies it among all the function instances with the same function name. The specific name can be used to drop the function, to comment on it, or to specify it as the source of another function, but it is never used to invoke the function. Functions are always invoked by their function name, which selects a function instance by means of the function resolution process described in Section 4.4.5.

5. *EXTERNAL NAME clause.* This clause identifies your new function as an external function and contains a quoted string that tells the system how to find the C function that serves as its implementation. This C function must be compiled, linked, and placed in a directory on the server machine, from which it can be dynamically loaded by the database system when needed.

The quoted string in the EXTERNAL NAME clause must contain the name of the binary file resulting from compiling and linking the C function, followed by a "!", followed by the name of the entry point in that file that implements the function. The name of the file may be given either as a full path name or as a simple filename that is implicitly found in the `sqllib/function` directory associated with your database.

As an example, suppose that your file named `mortgage` contains a function named `payment` and that you have placed this executable file in the default directory `sqllib/function`. The following clause might be used to register this function with the database system:

```
EXTERNAL NAME 'mortgage!payment'
```

TIP: Since the external name of your function is specified as a quoted string, it is case-sensitive. The external name you specify must exactly match the name of your executable file and entry point, including upper- and lowercase.

6. *VARIANT or NOT VARIANT.* You must declare your function either VARIANT or NOT VARIANT. VARIANT means that your function might return different results from two calls with the same parameters. The database optimizer takes some extra precautions in processing queries that contain variant functions.

A useful example of a variant function is a random-number generator such as the system-provided function `rand`, which returns a random floating-point number between 0 and 1. Suppose that you have a need for random integers between 0 and 100, and you have defined a view that uses `rand` to generate these numbers, as follows:

```
CREATE VIEW random(n) AS
    VALUES integer(rand() * 100);
```

Each time you use this view, you expect it to contain a different random integer between 0 and 100. You would expect the following query to return either a random integer less than 50 or no result at all:

```
SELECT n
FROM random
WHERE n < 50;
```

But if the above query is processed using two separate calls to the `rand` function, the random number returned by the query may or may not be less than 50. To prevent this anomaly, `rand` is declared to have the VARIANT property. If you create a function like `rand` whose result can vary from one call to another with the same parameters, you must also declare it to be VARIANT.

7. *EXTERNAL ACTION or NO EXTERNAL ACTION.* This clause is also mandatory, and it specifies whether your function performs some action that affects the world outside the database. For example, you might write a function that sends mail to someone, writes into a file, or sets off an alarm. Of course, you

want the number of invocations of such a function to be predictable—for example, if the function is used once in a SELECT list, it should be invoked exactly once for each row returned by the query. The EXTERNAL ACTION clause alerts the database optimizer to the existence of these functions, so that it will not modify a query in a way that changes the number of calls to such a function.

TIP: In addition to using the EXTERNAL ACTION clause, you must be careful where you invoke a function with side effects in order to make sure it is executed a predictable number of times. As a general rule, it is safe to invoke such a function in a VALUES statement or in the SELECT clause of a query that does not involve DISTINCT, a column function, a join, or a set operator such as UNION.

8. *FENCED or NOT FENCED.* The FENCED option specifies that your function must always be run in an address space that is separate from the database. This causes a performance penalty but protects the integrity of the database against accidental or malicious damage that might be inflicted by the function. This clause is optional, and the default is FENCED.

An unfenced function runs in the same address space as the database and can damage the integrity of your data. In order to create an unfenced function, you must possess either SYSADM or DBADM authority, or a database-level authority called CREATE_NOT_FENCED, which can only be granted by someone with SYSADM or DBADM authority, as described in Section 2.10.2. You can see who has been authorized to create unfenced functions by looking in the NOFENCEAUTH column of the DBAUTH catalog table.

It is strongly suggested that you run your functions in fenced mode until they are very well tested. You may wish to declare a function as FENCED at first and later convert it to NOT FENCED when you have confidence that it is working correctly. To do this, you must drop the function and recreate it with a new CREATE FUNCTION statement.

9. *NULL CALL or NOT NULL CALL.* This clause controls what happens when your function is invoked with a null value as one of its arguments. Many functions follow the convention that, if any argument is null, the function returns a null value. If your function follows this convention, you can specify NOT NULL CALL. In this case, the system will never pass a null argument to your function; instead, if a null argument is detected, the system will automatically consider the result of the function to be null. This convention makes your function easier to write, because it does not need to test its input parameters for nulls. It also improves performance by avoiding a function call whenever an argument is null. Of course, a function can still return a null value, even if it is created with a NOT NULL CALL specification.

This clause is optional, and its default is NOT NULL CALL.

TIP: If you are writing a function mainly to cause some side effect such as logging events in a file, you will probably want to specify NULL CALL rather than accepting the default of NOT NULL CALL.

10. *LANGUAGE C.* This mandatory clause specifies that the function is written in a programming language that obeys the C linkage conventions. At present, only the C linkage conventions are supported. For this reason, if your function implementation is written in C++, you should specify `extern "C"` as part of your function declaration in the implementation file.

11. *PARAMETER STYLE DB2SQL.* This mandatory clause identifies the conventions that are used by the database in calling your external function. These conventions, which are described in Section 4.4.6, deal with issues such as how null values are represented and how error conditions are reported. At present, only the parameter style named DB2SQL is supported.

12. *NO SQL.* This mandatory clause specifies that your external function contains no SQL statements. At present, external functions are not allowed to access the database.

13. *SCRATCHPAD or NO SCRATCHPAD.* If a function is created with the SCRATCHPAD option, that function is provided with a "scratchpad" area in memory that it can use to preserve information from one function invocation to the next. Scratchpad functions are discussed in Section 4.4.9. The default is NO SCRATCHPAD.

14. *FINAL CALL or NO FINAL CALL.* When a function is used in an SQL statement, the function may be called multiple times during the processing of the statement, depending on how it is used. For example, a function used in a WHERE clause might be called once for each row of the table being queried. If the function is created with the FINAL CALL option, the function is called one extra time (the "final call") at the end of processing the SQL statement. A special parameter is passed to the function body to distinguish the final call from the other calls. The final call can be used for "cleanup" purposes, such as freeing memory allocated by the function body. The FINAL CALL option is often used with the SCRATCHPAD option and is also discussed in Section 4.4.9. The default is NO FINAL CALL.

If a sourced function is defined whose source is an external function, the VARIANT, EXTERNAL ACTION, FENCED, NULL CALL, SCRATCHPAD, and FINAL CALL properties of the external function are inherited by the sourced function.

TIP: If your CREATE FUNCTION statement was not successful, check for missing clauses. All the following clauses are required on a CREATE FUNCTION statement for an external function:

```
RETURNS
EXTERNAL NAME
VARIANT or NOT VARIANT
EXTERNAL ACTION or NO EXTERNAL ACTION
LANGUAGE C
NO SQL
PARAMETER STYLE DB2SQL
```

At this point, you may be wondering why the CREATE FUNCTION statement has so many mandatory clauses that do not provide you with any real choices. For example, why should you be required to specify NO SQL when external functions can never contain SQL statements, or PARAMETER STYLE DB2SQL when no other parameter style is supported? A similar question might be asked about the CREATE DISTINCT TYPE statement, which requires the phrase WITH COMPARISONS, even though there is no way to create a distinct type on a non-LOB base type without comparison functions. In both cases, the answer has to do with standards. At the time when V2 was being designed, discussions were underway in ANSI and ISO committees about adding user-defined datatypes and functions to the SQL Standard. Since these discussions were still in progress, it was impossible to predict exactly what the standard syntax would eventually look like. For example, the standards committees might settle on a parameter-passing convention that is different from that adopted by V2. For this reason, the designers of V2 decided to include in the CREATE FUNCTION and CREATE TYPE statements some required phrases that identify the parameter-passing convention and other details of the V2 implementation. These phrases protect your applications against any change in default behavior that might be required by a future version of the SQL Standard.

4.4.4 Example of an External Function

In the following example, we create an external function that computes a person's normal weight, based on sex and height. Sex might be a distinct type based on Char(1), and Height might be a distinct type based on Double. The function returns a value of type Weight, which might be a distinct type based on Double.

```
CREATE FUNCTION medical.normalWeight(Sex, Height)
    RETURNS Weight
    EXTERNAL NAME 'medical!nweight'
    NOT VARIANT
```

```
NO EXTERNAL ACTION
LANGUAGE C
PARAMETER STYLE DB2SQL
NO SQL;
```

An external function can be used in an SQL statement in exactly the same way as a built-in function. No special authorization is required to call an external function, even if it was created by another user.

For an example of how the `normalWeight` function created above might be used, suppose that our database contains the following table:

PATIENTS

SOCSECNO   NAME   SEX   HEIGHT   WEIGHT

Suppose that the SEX, HEIGHT, and WEIGHT columns of the PATIENTS table have datatypes of Sex, Height, and Weight, respectively. Suppose further that the following sourced function has been defined that allows us to multiply a floating-point value times a Weight to get another Weight:

```
CREATE FUNCTION "*"(Double, Weight) RETURNS Weight
    SOURCE sysibm."*"(Double, Double);
```

The following query might be used to find all the patients in the table whose weight is less than 80% of their normal weight:

```
SELECT name, weight,
        medical.normalWeight(sex, height) AS normal
FROM patients
WHERE weight < 0.8 * medical.normalWeight(sex, height);
```

4.4.5 Function Resolution

When a function is called in an SQL statement, the function may be referred to either by its fully qualified name (such as `medical.normalWeight`) or by its unqualified name (such as `normalWeight`). If an unqualified name is used, V2 automatically searches through the schemas on your function path to find an applicable function. A function is considered applicable to a given call if its function name matches the call and if the arguments of the call are "promotable" to the parameters of the function. This means that the datatype of each function parameter must either match the datatype of the corresponding call argument, or it must be found by starting with the call-argument type and moving to the right along one of the promotion paths shown in Figure 4-2.

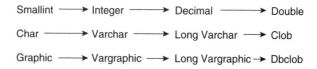

Figure 4-2: Valid Datatype Promotions for Function Arguments

The built-in datatypes Blob, Date, Time, and Timestamp, and any user-defined datatypes, do not appear in any of the promotion diagrams above, and therefore they require an exact match between call-argument type and function-parameter type. The length, precision, and scale of a datatype are not considered in finding an applicable function, but after the function has been selected, the length, precision, and/or scale of the call arguments are converted to those of the function parameters. For example, if column C3 has a datatype of Char(3), and user-defined function udf.foo has a parameter of datatype Char(5), then the call foo(c3) might invoke udf.foo after padding the value of C3 with blanks to a length of five characters.

If you call a function by its unqualified name, it is possible that more than one applicable function may be found on the function path. Even if you qualify the function name by a schema name, it is possible that more than one applicable function may be found in the given schema. In either case, the system chooses the "best" applicable function, considering the parameters from left to right and using the path as a tiebreaker. This process is called *function resolution*. Conceptually, the function resolution process consists of the following steps:

1. First, find the set of all applicable functions. Each of these functions has the correct function name and number of parameters, and all the call-argument types are promotable to the corresponding function-parameter types, and the schema of the function is either on the path or named in the function call.

2. Next, consider each call argument, from left to right. For each argument, eliminate all the functions that are not the "best available" match for that argument. In this context, "best" means "farthest to the left on the promotion diagram in Figure 4-2." For example, if the call is foo(Integer, Date), and the applicable functions are foo(Decimal, Date) and foo(Double, Date), then the function foo(Decimal, Date) has a "better" match for the first argument, so foo(Double, Date) is eliminated from further consideration. Remember that length, precision, and scale of function arguments are ignored during function resolution.

3. After considering all the arguments, if more than one function remains, all the remaining functions must have the same set of parameter types and must therefore be in different schemas. In this case, select the function whose schema is earliest on the path.

TABLE 4-5: Function Resolution Rules for Static and Dynamic SQL Statements

Type of Statement	Static SQL	Dynamic SQL
Data manipulation statements (SELECT, INSERT, UPDATE, DELETE, and VALUES)	Functions resolved at bind time, using path specified as PREP or BIND option	Functions resolved at run time, using CURRENT FUNCTION PATH special register
All other SQL statements	Functions resolved at run time, using path specified as PREP or BIND option	Functions resolved at run time, using CURRENT FUNCTION PATH special register

TIP: During function resolution, a host language variable such as `char x[11]` is always interpreted as having datatype Varchar, not Char or Date. Thus, in resolving the function call `foo(:x)`, the system will look for a function `foo(Varchar)`, not `foo(Char)` or `foo(Date)`. If you wish your host variable to be interpreted as a Char or Date, you must use an explicit cast, as in `foo(char(:x))` or `foo(date(:x))`.

As a general rule, function calls in static data manipulation statements are resolved when their program is bound, whereas function calls in dynamic statements are resolved at run time. The details are given in Table 4-5 (note the similarities between Table 4-5 and Table 2-10).

When a program is bound, all of its function calls that occur in static data manipulation statements are resolved, as shown in Table 4-5. After the program is bound, the system guarantees that it will continue using the same function instances, even if a better-matching function instance is created and even if the program is automatically rebound (for example, when an index is dropped). However, if you explicitly rebind your program by using a BIND or REBIND command, the function resolution process will start over from scratch, and the best applicable function at that time will be selected. If the function instance to which a program has been bound is dropped, the program goes into an "inoperative" state in which it cannot be used until it is explicitly rebound. This policy, called *conservative binding semantics*, guarantees that once your program is bound, its behavior will not change without an explicit action on your part (an explicit rebind).

TIP: SQLCODE –440 (SQLSTATE 42884) indicates that the system was unable to find any applicable function for one of your function calls. If you receive this code, check your current function path to make sure that it includes the schema containing the desired function. Next, check the arguments of your function call to make sure their datatypes match (or are promotable to) the datatypes of the function parameters.

4.4.6 Implementing an External Function

Suppose you wish to define an external function, written in C, that takes n parameters and returns a result. The actual function body that you write in C will need more than n parameters. Some of these C parameters will be used to indicate that null values are being passed to the external function, one C parameter will be used for returning the result of the function, and other C parameters will be used for special purposes such as returning error codes.

We will illustrate the conventions for exchanging parameters and results with user-defined functions by writing an example function named addWeeks, which takes a Date and an Integer that represents a number of weeks and returns a new Date computed by adding the given number of weeks to the given Date. This might be a useful function, since V2 does not recognize a constant such as "5 WEEKS" as a valid duration. Since dates are not a native datatype in C, this example will give us an opportunity to see how conversion is done between SQL datatypes and host language datatypes. For complete generality, we will write our function to accept and process null values rather than using the simpler NOT NULL CALL convention.

The SQL statement that might be used to register our example function is as follows:

```
CREATE FUNCTION addWeeks(Date, Integer)
    RETURNS Date
    EXTERNAL NAME 'datefns!addWeeks'
    NOT VARIANT
    NO EXTERNAL ACTION
    NULL CALL
    LANGUAGE C
    PARAMETER STYLE DB2SQL
    NO SQL;
```

This statement declares to the database a function named addWeeks that can be used in any SQL statement. The function takes a Date and an Integer as parameters and returns a Date. Since this function is invoked from an SQL statement, of course its parameters and result have SQL datatypes, not C datatypes. In our example, we will refer to this function as the "SQL Function," even though we understand that it is not written in SQL.

The CREATE FUNCTION statement above promises that we will implement the SQL function by creating a C file named datefns that contains a function named addWeeks, compiling and linking this file, and placing the resulting binary file in the sqllib/function directory on our server machine. We could have placed the binary file in any desired directory on the server machine, as long as the CREATE FUNCTION statement tells the database system where to find it by a full path name. Several C functions can be contained in a single binary file, and the C functions need not have the same names as

```
funcname (

        input SQL parameters,          /* IN */

        return value,                  /* OUT */

        input null indicators,         /* IN */

        return null indicator,         /* OUT */

        SQLSTATE,                      /* OUT */

        SQL function name,             /* IN */

        specific name,                 /* IN */

        error message,                 /* OUT */

        scratchpad,                    /* IN */

        final call indicator           /* IN */

        ) ;
```

Figure 4-3: Parameter Conventions for External Functions

the SQL functions they support, as long as the mapping between SQL functions and C functions is declared in CREATE FUNCTION statements.

Of course, the C function that underlies our SQL function must have parameter types and result types that are recognized by the C language, not by SQL. We need a convention for mapping the parameters and result of the SQL function onto the parameters and result of the C function. All the parameters of the C function are pointers to storage that is managed by the database. If the function is declared FENCED, this storage is in an address space that is isolated from the database itself, so errors in the C function cannot damage the database; however, if the function is declared NOT FENCED, the C function can damage the database by storing bad data through the pointers that are passed to it as parameters. For this reason, users are strongly advised to use FENCED functions, at least until the functions have been thoroughly tested.

Figure 4-3 summarizes the parameters of a C function that serves as the implementation of an external SQL function. Each parameter is labelled "IN" (meaning that it provides input data to the function body) or "OUT" (meaning that it carries information returned by the function body).

The details of the V2 convention for passing parameters to a C function that implements an SQL function are as follows (assuming that N is the number of parameters of the SQL function):

1. The first N parameters of the C function are pointers to the N parameters of the SQL function, converted to their corresponding host language datatypes according to the rules for assignment of SQL datatypes to host variables. The objects pointed at are copies of the actual parameters, so the C function cannot modify its actual input parameters by using these pointers.

If the datatype of a parameter is a distinct type, the parameter is first converted into the base type on which the distinct type is defined, then it is converted into the host language datatype that corresponds to that base type. For example, suppose that the distinct types Age and Sex are defined on the base types Integer and Char(1), respectively. If an external function avgHeight (Age, Sex) is defined, its parameters will be converted from an Age and a Sex into an Integer and a Char(1), and will then be converted into the C-language datatypes that correspond to an Integer and a Char(1), as defined in Table 4-6.

In our example, the Date and Integer parameters of the SQL function are passed to the C function using datatypes char[11] and long, respectively. The SQL datatypes that can be passed to C functions, and their corresponding C datatypes, are summarized in Table 4-6. For each of these C datatypes, there is a symbolic type name declared in the header file sqllib/include/sqludf.h, which you may prefer to use rather than spelling out the full C declaration.

TABLE 4-6: Datatypes Used for Passing Parameters to External Functions[5]

SQL Datatype	Symbolic Type Name in sqludf.h	Underlying Datatype as Seen by C Program
Smallint	SQLUDF_SMALLINT	short
Integer	SQLUDF_INTEGER	long
Decimal(p,s)	(none)	No equivalent in C. You can't pass Decimal data to an external function. As an alternative, you can convert the parameter to a Char datatype by using the char(Decimal) function, or to a Double datatype by using the double(Decimal) function.
Double	SQLUDF_DOUBLE	double
Char(n)	SQLUDF_CHAR	char[n+1] (null-terminated)

---

5. The similarities between Table 4-6 and Table C-1 in Appendix C are, of course, intentional.

TABLE 4-6 *(Continued)*

SQL Datatype	Symbolic Type Name in sqludf.h	Underlying Datatype as Seen by C Program
Varchar(n) (not for bit data)	SQLUDF_VARCHAR	char[n+1] (null-terminated)

Varchar(n) FOR BIT DATA	SQLUDF_VARCHAR_FBD	struct
		{
		  unsigned short length;
		  char data[n];
		}

Long Varchar	SQLUDF_LONG	struct
		{
		  unsigned short length;
		  char data[n];
		}

Graphic(n) and Vargraphic(n)	SQLUDF_GRAPH, SQLUDF_VARGRAPH	wchar_t[n+1] (null-terminated)

Long Vargraphic	SQLUDF_LONGVARG	struct
		{
		  unsigned short length;
		  wchar_t data[n]
		}
		(Note: Length is denoted in two-byte units.)

Date	SQLUDF_DATE	char[11], null-terminated, in format 'yyyy-mm-dd'
Time	SQLUDF_TIME	char[9], null-terminated, in format 'hh.mm.ss'
Timestamp	SQLUDF_STAMP	char[27], null-terminated, in format 'yyyy-mm-dd-hh.mm.ss.nnnnnn'

Blob(n) and Clob(n)	SQLUDF_BLOB, SQLUDF_CLOB	struct
		{
		  unsigned long length;
		  char data[n];
		};

Dbclob(n)	SQLUDF_DBCLOB	struct
		{
		  unsigned long length;
		  wchar_t data[n];
		};
		(Note: Length is denoted in two-byte units.)

When double-byte data (SQL datatype Graphic, Vargraphic, Long Vargraphic, or Dbclob) is exchanged with an external function, it is always exchanged in multibyte format (not wide-character format). In other words, parameters and results of external functions always use the format specified by the precompiler option WCHARTYPE NOCONVERT.

2. The next parameter of the C function is a pointer to the place where the return value should be stored. The C datatype that should be stored at this location is the C datatype that corresponds (in Table 4-6) to the declared SQL datatype of the return value, before any casting. For example, if the return value is declared as Date, the C function should store a null-terminated char[11] value in the indicated position, since null-terminated char[11] is the C datatype that corresponds to the SQL datatype Date. The casting of the return value into its final datatype of Date is done by the database system; the C function need not be concerned with this process, except to provide a return value that can be validly cast into a Date. Of course, the database system has provided only enough storage to hold a return value of the declared datatype; attempting to return a longer value is one of the ways in which an unfenced function can cause a lot of trouble.

3. The next N parameters of the C function are null indicators for the N parameters of the SQL function. Each of these parameters is a pointer to a value whose C datatype is short, containing 0 if the corresponding SQL parameter is not null, or –1 if the corresponding SQL parameter is null. These parameters are always present, even if the function has been declared with the NOT NULL CALL property (of course, in such a case, all the indicator values would be zero on every call).

4. The next parameter is a pointer to the place where the C function should store the null indicator of the return value. The C datatype of this indicator is short, and it should be set to zero if the return value is not null, or to –1 if the return value is null. Even if the function has been declared with the NOT NULL CALL property, it might have a need to generate a null result, so it is important to set this indicator properly.

5. The next parameter is a pointer to the place where the C function should store the five-digit SQLSTATE generated by the function. The C datatype of the SQLSTATE is char[6], and it is initialized to 00000 with a null terminator before the C function is called. Since 00000 denotes a normal return, the C function need not set the SQLSTATE explicitly unless an error or warning is encountered. SQLSTATE codes 01H00 through 01H99 have been reserved for user-generated warning conditions, and 38600 through 38999 have been reserved for user-generated error conditions. If the C function generates one of these codes, it will be used as the SQLSTATE to be returned by the SQL statement that invoked the function. If the C function generates any SQLSTATE other than one of the reserved codes, the SQLSTATE returned by the invoking SQL

statement will be 39001. Certain other SQLSTATEs can also result from invocation of a user-defined function (for example, if the C function terminates abnormally, the SQLSTATE is set to 38503).

6. The next parameter of the C function is a pointer to a storage area of type `char[28]`, containing the fully qualified name of the SQL function (such as `YOURNAME.ADDWEEKS`), with a null terminator. This parameter makes it possible for several SQL functions to be implemented by the same C function, using this parameter to distinguish which SQL function is desired by each invocation.

7. The next parameter of the C function is a pointer to a storage area of type `char[19]`, containing the specific name of the SQL function, with a null terminator. Like the previous parameter, this parameter can be useful when a single C function is used to implement several SQL functions. Remember that every user-defined function has a specific name in addition to its family name, even if the specific name is system-generated.

8. The next parameter of the C function is a pointer to a place where the C function may store up to 70 characters of message text, followed by a null terminator. If the SQLSTATE returned by the function is nonzero, this message text will be copied into the `sqlerrmc` field of the SQLCA control block. The `sqlerrmc` field consists of a series of "tokens." The first token is set to the function name, the second token to the specific name of the function, and the third token to the message text returned by the function. The message text may be truncated if necessary to fit into the `sqlerrmc` field.

9. The next parameter is present only if the function was defined with the SCRATCHPAD option. It is a pointer to the memory area provided for the function, to preserve information from one function invocation to the next function invocation within the same SQL statement. The datatype of the parameter is `struct  sqludf_scratchpad*` (this structure is declared in `sqllib/include/sqludf.h`). Scratchpad functions are discussed in Section 4.4.9.

10. The next parameter is present only if the function was defined with the FINAL CALL option. It is a pointer to a `long` variable that is set equal to –1 on the first call to a function during processing of an SQL statement, to +1 on the "final call," and to 0 on all other calls to the function. The FINAL CALL option is discussed in Section 4.4.9.

When writing a program to implement your user-defined function, you should observe the following rules:

• Your program should be *reentrant* (that is, it should not use any static variables). This enables your function to be invoked by several different users at the same time without interference.

- If your program allocates any dynamic memory, it should free the memory before returning. The only exception to this rule is in the case of a *scratchpad function*, which may allocate memory on one invocation and free it on another, as described in Section 4.4.9.

- Your program should return to its caller by a `return` statement. It should never call the operating system `exit` function. Since all exchanging of values between the program and the database system is accomplished by parameters, the return datatype of the C function should be `void`.

- Your program should not attempt to read from the standard input stream (for example, by `scanf`) or write to the standard output stream (for example, by `printf`). These streams are not available to your program, because it is executed on the server machine in a process that is not connected to your keyboard or display. Your program may, however, read and write files on the server machine.

- If your function implementation is written in C++, you should specify `extern` "C" as part of your function declaration in the implementation file. This will ensure that your function is made available for linking by the name you gave it rather than by a "mangled" name chosen by the C++ compiler. If possible, avoid using an overloaded C++ function name (otherwise, you will need to follow special procedures documented in *DB2 Software Developer's Kit: Building Your Applications*).

TIP: When debugging the implementation of a user-defined function, you may find it helpful for your function to write a trace of its actions in a file on the server machine. But if your function writes into a file, that file must be authorized for writing by any user; if your function creates a file, the directory in which the file is created must be authorized for writing by any user. Remember that your function is executed under a dummy process on the server machine, *not* under your own userid.

4.4.7 Example: The "addWeeks" Function

In the previous section, we discussed a function named `addWeeks` that adds a given number of weeks to a given date and returns another date. This function could be used in queries such as the following, which lists all the parts that have been ordered within the last four weeks:

```
SELECT partno, quantity, orderdate
FROM orders
WHERE addWeeks(orderdate, 4) > CURRENT DATE;
```

Using the parameter-passing conventions described in the previous section, we can implement the `addWeeks` function as follows:

Example Function: addWeeks

```c
#include <stdio.h>
void addWeeks
   (
   char  *dateIn,         /* 1st input parameter, char[11], null-term. */
   long  *weeksIn,        /* 2nd input parameter, long                 */
   char  *dateOut,        /* return value, char[11], null-terminated   */
   short *nullDateIn,     /* 1st input parameter, indicator variable   */
   short *nullWeeksIn,    /* 2nd input parameter, indicator variable   */
   short *nullDateOut,    /* return value, indicator variable          */
   char  *sqlstate,       /* returned SQLSTATE, char[6], null-term.    */
   char  *fnName,         /* family name of fn, char[28], null-term.   */
   char  *specificName,   /* specific name of fn, char[19], null-term. */
   char  *message         /* message area, char[70], null-terminated   */
   )

   {
   /*
   ** The following array tells us how many days are in each month.
   */
   const int monthDays[] = {31, 28, 31, 30, 31, 30,
                            31, 31, 30, 31, 30, 31};
   int year, month, day, conversions, daysThisMonth;

   /*
   ** If either input is null, return a null result.
   ** (This function could have specified "not null call".)
   */
   if (*nullDateIn || *nullWeeksIn)
     {
     *nullDateOut = -1;
     return;
     }

   /*
   ** Convert input date string into year, month, and day
   ** Return error code if conversion fails.
   */
   conversions = sscanf (dateIn, "%4d-%2d-%2d", &year, &month, &day);
   if (conversions != 3)
     {
     strcpy (sqlstate, "38601");
     strcpy (message, "Bad date");
     return;
     }
```

```
/*
** Check the input parameters for sanity
*/
if (year < 0 || month < 0 || month > 12
      || day < 0 || day > monthDays[month-1] || *weeksIn < 0)
  {
   strcpy (sqlstate, "38602");
   strcpy (message, "Bad input");
   return;
  }


/*
** Add up the days, then roll into months and years as needed.
*/
day = day + 7 * *weeksIn;
daysThisMonth = monthDays[month-1];
if (month == 2 && year % 4 == 0)
   daysThisMonth++;   /* leap year */
while (day > daysThisMonth)
  {
   day = day - daysThisMonth;
   month++;
   if (month > 12)
     {
      year++;
      month = 1;
     }
   daysThisMonth = monthDays[month-1];
   if (month == 2 && year % 4 == 0)
      daysThisMonth++;   /* leap year */
  }

/*
** Convert the date back into string form for output
*/
sprintf(dateOut, "%4.4d-%2.2d-%2.2d\0", year, month, day);
*nullDateOut = 0;

return;
}
```

4.4.8 Installing an External Function

The file containing the C source code for your external function may have any name you like and may contain more than one function body. As shown in the example above, the source code can include header files such as <stdio.h> and can reference standard C functions such as sprintf(). Before the database system can use your external function, you must compile it and link it. The steps in this process depend on your operating system platform, as described below. More details about installing external functions can be found in the manual entitled *DB2 Software Developer's Kit: Building Your Applications* for your platform.

Installing Under AIX

If your database system is running under AIX, you should use the following steps to install an external function:

1. Create a separate file, called an *export file*, containing a list of the functions that are implemented by your source program. Your program is said to "export" these functions (that is, it makes them available for dynamic loading). Create the export file in the same directory as your source code file and give it the same filename, with an extension of .exp. For example, if your datefns.c file contains source code for two functions named addWeeks and subWeeks, you will need a separate file named datefns.exp, containing the following lines:

   ```
   #! datefns export file
   addWeeks
   subWeeks
   ```

2. Compile and link the file containing the source code for your function. V2 provides a script named bldxlcudf for this purpose, which can be found in the directory sqllib/samples/c. To invoke the script, copy it to some directory that is on your path and type its name followed by the name of your source code file (without extension). For example, type the following command to compile the functions in datefns.c:

   ```
   bldxlcudf datefns
   ```

   The bldxlcudf script will compile and link your program and will generate an executable file (named datefns in the example). If you experience any problems in this step, it may be necessary to edit the bldxlcudf script and adjust some of its compiler or linker options according to your local environment.

3. Place the executable file (datefns in the example) into the appropriate directory on the server machine. By default, the executable file should be placed in the directory sqllib/function. If this is done, your CREATE FUNCTION statement need not include a path name (for example, it can specify EXTERNAL NAME 'datefns!addWeeks'). Alternatively, your executable file can be placed in some other directory on the server machine, and your CREATE

FUNCTION statement can specify a full path name for the file (for example, `EXTERNAL NAME '/usr/udflib/datefns!addWeeks'`).

4. Make your file executable by other users. This can be done by a command such as the following:

```
chmod a+x datefns
```

5. "Register" your external function by executing a CREATE FUNCTION statement in each database where the function will be used. The CREATE FUNCTION statement can be executed either before or after the function is compiled.

Installing Under OS/2 or Windows NT

If your database system is running under OS/2 or Windows NT, you should use the following steps to install an external function:

1. Create a separate file, called a *module definition file*, containing a list of the functions that are implemented by your source program. Your program is said to "export" these functions (that is, it makes them available for dynamic loading). Create the module definition file in the same directory as your source code file, and give it the same filename, with an extension of `.DEF`. For example, if your `DATEFNS.C` file contains source code for two functions named `addWeeks` and `subWeeks`, you will need a separate file named `datefns.def`, containing the following lines:

```
LIBRARY DATEFNS
EXPORTS addWeeks
EXPORTS subWeeks
```

2. Compile and link the file containing the source code for your function. V2 provides a command file named `bldcs2ud` for this purpose that can be found in the directory `sqllib\samples\c`. With minor editing, this command file can be used to compile and link functions written in either C or C++ (read the comments in the command file for instructions). To invoke the command file, copy it to some directory that is on your path and type its name followed by the name of your source code file (without extension). For example, type the following command to compile the functions in `DATEFNS.C`:

```
bldcs2ud datefns
```

The `bldcs2ud` command file will compile and link your program and will generate an executable file (named `DATEFNS.DLL` in the example). If you experience any problems in this step, it may be necessary to edit the `bldcs2ud` command file and adjust some of its compiler or linker options according to your local environment.

3. Place the DLL file (`DATEFNS.DLL` in the example) into the appropriate directory on the server machine. By default, the DLL file should be placed in a directory that is included in the LIBPATH statement in the `CONFIG.SYS` file on the server machine. If this is done, your CREATE FUNCTION statement need not include a path name (for example, it can specify EXTERNAL NAME 'datefns!addWeeks'). Alternatively, your DLL file can be placed in some other directory on the server machine, and your CREATE FUNCTION statement must then specify a full path name for the file (for example, EXTERNAL NAME 'C:\udflib\datefns!addWeeks').

4. "Register" your external function by executing a CREATE FUNCTION statement in each database where the function will be used. The CREATE FUNCTION statement can be executed either before or after the function is compiled.

 TIP: Regardless of your operating system platform, you should be very careful to protect the executable file that implements your external function against unauthorized tampering. The database does not protect this file and will execute it whenever your function is invoked. If your function implementation is replaced by another executable file, it could potentially do something harmful.

4.4.9 Scratchpad Functions

A scratchpad function is an external function that needs to preserve some information between one function call and the next. If the phrase SCRATCHPAD is included in the CREATE FUNCTION statement, the function body is provided with a 100-byte "scratchpad" area in which it may write any data that it chooses. The data in the scratchpad is preserved between function calls, so each invocation of the function can see the data stored by the last invocation. The data in the scratchpad is preserved only during the processing of a given SQL statement, not between SQL statements. For example, if a scratchpad function foo is used in the SQL statement SELECT foo(c1) FROM t1, the function foo is executed once for each row of table T1, and the scratchpad data is preserved across all these function invocations. But if the same SQL statement is executed a second time, it receives a new scratchpad. If a function is used multiple times in the same SQL statement, each use of the function receives its own separate scratchpad.

If a function was created with the SCRATCHPAD option, every invocation of the function is passed a parameter containing a pointer to the scratchpad area. The datatype of the parameter is struct sqludf_scratchpad*. The declaration of the scratchpad structure, which can be found in sqllib/include/sqludf.h, is as follows:

```
struct sqludf_scratchpad
   {
   unsigned long  length;      /* length of data area   */
   char           data[100];   /* initialized to all \0 */
   };
```

As you can see in the above declaration, the scratchpad contains 100 bytes that the function implementation can use as it sees fit. If the function needs to preserve more than 100 bytes of data between invocations, it can allocate additional memory (using `malloc`) and keep a pointer to the additional memory in the scratchpad.

The scratchpad area is initialized to binary zeros before the first function call in each SQL statement. The function body can test for zeros to detect the first call, or it can use the FINAL CALL option, which causes a parameter to be passed to the function containing −1 on initial call, +1 on final call, and 0 on all other calls within an SQL statement. The "final call" is a special call made to the function body after the SQL statement has been processed.[6] If the function body needs to allocate memory, it should be written with the FINAL CALL option and it should free the allocated memory on the final call. Since the final call takes place after processing of the SQL statement, its input and output parameters (other than the `calltype` parameter that identifies the final call) are not meaningful.

Perhaps the simplest example of a scratchpad function is a function that simply counts the number of times it has been invoked within an SQL statement. Since all the data stored by this function fits into the scratchpad, it does not need to allocate memory or to use the FINAL CALL option. The function relies on the fact that its scratchpad will be initialized to binary zeros before the first call within each SQL statement. The body of the function might be written as follows:

```
#include <stdlib.h>
#include "sqludf.h"

void seqno
    (
    long  *returnValue,      /* return value, an integer   */
    short *returnNull,       /* return indicator variable  */
    char  *sqlstate,         /* returned SQLSTATE, char[6] */
    char  *fnName,           /* family name of fn, char[28] */
    char  *specificName,     /* specific fn name, char[19] */
    char  *message,          /* message area, char[70]     */
    struct sqludf_scratchpad *scratchpad   /* in sqludf.h */
    )
```

---

6. If the SQL statement containing the function is a query that is being processed by means of a cursor, the "final call" takes place at the time the cursor is closed (either by a CLOSE statement or by end of transaction).

```
{
long *p;
p = (long *)(scratchpad->data);  /* point at pad data   */
*p = (*p)+1;             /* increment counter inside pad */
*returnValue = *p;       /* return the counter value      */
*returnNull = 0;
return;
}
```

The seqno function is registered in the database by the following statement (assuming that the executable file has been placed in the default directory sqllib/function). Note that the function is created with the VARIANT option, indicating that it does not return the same result every time it is called.

```
CREATE FUNCTION seqno() RETURNS Integer
    EXTERNAL NAME 'seqno!seqno'
    SPECIFIC seqno
    VARIANT
    NO SQL
    NO EXTERNAL ACTION
    LANGUAGE C
    FENCED
    PARAMETER STYLE DB2SQL
    SCRATCHPAD;
```

You might use the seqno function defined above in a query to automatically generate a sequence number for each row of the result set. For example, suppose that all the candidates in a mayoral election and the dates on which they declared their candidacy are recorded in a table with the following structure:

CANDIDATES

NAME	PARTY	DECLARE_DATE

The following query will list all the candidates, with a sequence number for each indicating the order in which they entered the race:

```
SELECT seqno() AS seqno, name, party, declare_date
FROM   candidates
ORDER BY declare_date;
```

TIP: Scratchpad functions are not recommended for use inside constraints or triggers (described in Chapter 5) or inside correlated subqueries. This is because a given SQL statement may cause a constraint, trigger, or correlated subquery to be executed multiple times. The system guarantees to initialize your scratchpad only once, at the beginning of the outermost SQL statement. Scratchpad functions used inside constraints, triggers, or correlated subqueries may not be properly initialized.

4.4.10 Example: The "nthbest" Function

The next example of a scratchpad function is based on a table of employees having the following structure:

EMPLOYEES

NAME   JOB   SALARY

Suppose that you need to search this table to find the engineer with the third highest salary. This is a surprisingly difficult query to express in standard SQL. An initial attempt at writing such a query might look like this:

```
SELECT name, salary
FROM    employees e
WHERE   job = 'Engineer'
AND 2 =
   (SELECT count(*)
    FROM    employees
    WHERE   job = 'Engineer'
    AND     salary > e.salary);
```

On close inspection, this query has two serious problems. The first problem is performance: the correlated subquery will do an enormous amount of work to find the answer to such a simple question. But the more serious problem is that the query will not find the right answer if there are duplicates among the engineers' salaries. For example, consider the case when two engineers are tied for second place in the salary ordering. In this case, the above query will always return the empty set.

Another approach to this problem is to write a query that selects engineers in descending order by their salaries, and then fetch only the first three engineers in the result set. That solution is not very elegant, and it requires the database system to do lots of unnecessary work, sorting all the engineers in order by their salaries even though you will fetch only the top three. A much better solution would be to make a single scan over the engineers, somehow remembering the third highest salary seen so far as you go along. After the scan is complete, you will have the salary of the third highest-paid engineer, which you can then use to fetch all the engineers who have that salary (remember, there may be duplicates).

Implementing the "scan and remember" solution described above provides an interesting example of a user-defined function that uses the SCRATCHPAD and FINAL CALL options. We will write a general-purpose function called nthbest that can be used to find the nth largest integer in a set of integers (we chose the name nthbest because it is short, hoping to avoid a discussion of whether largest is necessarily best).[7]

Viewed as an SQL function, nthbest will take two parameters. The first parameter is a value from the set being scanned, and the second parameter is n, the rank of the desired value within the set. The nthbest function is designed to be called repeatedly within an SQL statement, examining a set of values one at a time. The second parameter, which defines the desired rank, is meaningful only on the first call to the function within an SQL statement. Each time it is called, the nthbest function returns the nth largest value that it has seen so far; if fewer than n values have been seen, it returns null. Thus, in a series of calls to find the nth largest value, nthbest will first return n null values, followed by a nondecreasing series of values that culminates in the desired value. By using nthbest inside a max function, the final (correct) value can be isolated from the others and returned as the result of the query. For example, the third highest engineer's salary can be found by the following query:

```
SELECT max(nthbest(salary, 3))
FROM   employees
WHERE  job = 'Engineer';
```

The above query can be used as a subquery to find the actual engineer(s) who earn the third highest salary, as follows:

```
SELECT name, deptno, salary
FROM   employees
WHERE  job = 'Engineer'
AND    salary =
    (SELECT max(nthbest(salary,3))
     FROM    employees
     WHERE   job = 'Engineer');
```

The implementation of the nthbest function is given in the example below and described in the following series of steps.

---

7. The nthbest function in this example operates on Integer values, and we assume that salaries are represented as Integers; of course, a similar nthbest function could be written for Decimal or Money or any other datatype that supports comparison operators.

Steps for Example Function: nthbest

STEP 1:   The first step in implementing `nthbest` is to decide how to use the scratch-pad. Since we don't know how many values we will need to store (after all, someone may ask for the 5,000th largest value), we will need to allocate memory for our list of the n largest values. In the scratchpad, we will record the desired rank, the number of values we have seen so far, and a pointer to an array of up to n values in which we will keep a sorted list of the highest values we have seen. We declare these three variables in the form of a structure called `myPad`, which we will overlay on the scratchpad provided by the system.

STEP 2:   The parameters to the body of the `nthbest` function include a pointer to the system-provided scratchpad area and an integer indicating the type of the call (first, middle, or final). The function body uses the scratchpad pointer to over-lay its own `myPad` structure on top of the scratchpad.

Code for Example Function: nthbest

```c
#include <string.h>
#include "sqlenv.h"
#include "sqludf.h"

/*
**   STEP 1: Define a structure to overlay on the scratchpad.
*/
typedef struct
   {
   long  desiredRank;     /* rank of the desired value         */
   long  valuesStored;    /* how many values are in the array  */
   long *bigValues;       /* array of the biggest values so far */
   } myPad;

/*
**   STEP 2: Declare the parameters of the function implementation.
*/
void nthbest
   (
   long  *inValue,        /* 1st input parameter, an integer value      */
   long  *inRank,         /* 2nd input parameter, rank of desired value */
   long  *outValue,       /* result, the value with the desired rank    */
   short *inValueNull,    /* 1st input parameter, null indicator        */
   short *inRankNull,     /* 2nd input parameter, null indicator        */
   short *outNull,        /* return value, null indicator               */
   char  *sqlstate,       /* returned SQLSTATE, char[6], null-term.     */
   char  *fnName,         /* family name of fn, char[28], null-term.    */
   char  *specificName,   /* specific name of fn, char[19], null-term.  */
   char  *message,        /* message area, char[70], null-term.         */
   struct sqludf_scratchpad *scratchpad,     /* declared in sqludf.h    */
   long  *calltype        /* -1 = first call, 0 = normal, 1 = last call */
   )

   {
   myPad *p;              /* overlay this pointer on the scratchpad */
   long least, temp;      /* working variables                      */
   int i;                 /* loop counter                           */

   p = (myPad *)(scratchpad->data);
```

STEP 3: On the first call to nthbest, the function body allocates enough memory to hold the n largest integers in the set to be scanned. Before doing this, of course, it tests the parameter n to make sure it is positive and not null.

STEP 4: On the final call, the function frees the memory that was allocated on the first call. There is no need to examine the input parameters or to return any result on the final call.

STEP 5: On every call except the final call, a new input value is passed to the function. If this value is not null, the function inserts it into its proper position in the array of stored values.

```
/*
**  STEP 3: On first call, allocate space for storing the top n values.
*/
if (*calltype == -1)   /* first call */
   {
   if (*inRankNull != 0 || *inRank <= 0)
      {
      strcpy (sqlstate, "38601");
      strcpy (message, "Bogus rank");
      return;
      }
   p -> desiredRank = *inRank;
   p -> valuesStored = 0;
   p -> bigValues = (long *)malloc(*inRank * 4);
   }


/*
**  STEP 4: On final call, free the allocated space.
*/
if (*calltype == 1)  /* last call */
   free(p->bigValues);


/*
**  STEP 5: On first or middle call, add the current value to the
**  set of stored values if it is among the n highest values seen.
*/
if (*calltype < 1)     /* first or middle call */
   {
   if (*inValueNull == 0)
      {
      least = *inValue;
      for (i = 0; i < p->valuesStored; i++)
         {
         if (p->bigValues[i] < least)
            {
            temp = least;                    /* exchange */
            least = p->bigValues[i];    /* exchange */
            p->bigValues[i] = temp;      /* exchange */
            }
         }
      if (p->valuesStored < p->desiredRank)
         {
         p->valuesStored++;
         p->bigValues[p->valuesStored - 1] = least;
         }
      }
```

STEP 6: If fewer than n values have been seen, the function returns null; otherwise, it returns the nth-largest value stored in its array (since the array is of size n, this is the smallest value in the array).

The following SQL statement might be used to register the nthbest function in the database system as an external function. Note that we declare the function to be VARIANT because two function calls with the same parameters do not always return the same result. Scratchpad functions are likely to be VARIANT, because their results often depend on the state of the scratchpad as well as on their input parameters.

```
CREATE FUNCTION nthbest(Integer, Integer)
          -- candidate value, desired rank --
    RETURNS Integer
          -- value having desired rank --
    EXTERNAL NAME 'nthbest!nthbest'
    VARIANT
    NO SQL
    NO EXTERNAL ACTION
    LANGUAGE C
    FENCED
    PARAMETER STYLE DB2SQL
    SCRATCHPAD
    FINAL CALL;
```

```
    /*
    **  STEP 6: Return the nth highest value seen so far
    **  (or null if less than n values have been seen.)
    */
    if (p->valuesStored < p->desiredRank)
        {
        *outNull = -1;            /* array not full, return null value */
        return;
        }
    else
        {
        *outValue = p->bigValues[p->desiredRank - 1];
        *outNull = 0;
        return;                   /* return value having desired rank */
        }
    }       /* end of first or middle call */
}
```

4.4.11 Using External Functions with Distinct Types

The power of distinct types and external functions is most evident when these two features are used together. As an example of the interaction of distinct types and functions, we will define two distinct types and create external functions to convert between them.

Suppose that you work for a multinational company that produces some products in the United States and other products in France. The dimensions of the American products are recorded in feet, and the dimensions of the French products are recorded in meters. Your company has defined two distinct types, Feet and Meters, both based on the built-in Double datatype, for use in its product database. The following statements show how these distinct datatypes could be used to create and populate tables containing all the American and French products respectively:

```
CREATE DISTINCT TYPE Feet
   AS Double WITH COMPARISONS;
```

```
CREATE DISTINCT TYPE Meters
   AS Double WITH COMPARISONS;
```

```
CREATE TABLE us_products
   (name Varchar(20),
    size Feet);
```

```
CREATE TABLE french_products
   (name Varchar(20),
    size Meters);
```

```
INSERT INTO us_products VALUES
   ('Widget', 3),
   ('Wadget', 5);
```

```
INSERT INTO french_products VALUES
   ('Gadget', 0.5),
   ('Gizmo', 1.5);
```

The system provides casting functions between each distinct type and its base type, but it does not provide casting functions between Feet and Meters. To make the distinct types more useful, your database administrator writes external functions to convert between Feet and Meters in both directions. The CREATE FUNCTION statements for these conversion functions, and their implementations, are shown below. The functions are created with the NOT NULL CALL feature to simplify their implementations.

```
CREATE FUNCTION feet(Meters)
   RETURNS Feet
   EXTERNAL NAME 'units!feet'
   NOT VARIANT
   NO EXTERNAL ACTION
   NOT NULL CALL
   LANGUAGE C
   PARAMETER STYLE DB2SQL
   NO SQL;
```

```
CREATE FUNCTION meters(Feet)
   RETURNS Meters
   EXTERNAL NAME 'units!meters'
   NOT VARIANT
   NO EXTERNAL ACTION
   NOT NULL CALL
   LANGUAGE C
   PARAMETER STYLE DB2SQL
   NO SQL;
```

```
void feet
   (
     double *metersIn,
     double *feetOut,
     short  *nullIn,
     short  *nullOut,
     char   *sqlstate,
     char   *fnName,
     char   *specificName,
     char   *message
   )
   {
     *feetOut = *metersIn * 3.28;
     *nullOut = 0;
   }
```

```
void meters
   (
     double *feetIn,
     double *metersOut,
     short  *nullIn,
     short  *nullOut,
     char   *sqlstate,
     char   *fnName,
     char   *specificName,
     char   *message
   )
   {
     *metersOut = *feetIn / 3.28;
     *nullOut = 0;
   }
```

Your company would like to publish two catalogs, each listing all the products and their countries of origin. The first catalog, for use in the United States, should have all its dimensions in feet, and the second catalog, for use in France, should have all its dimensions in meters. The two catalogs correspond to two views of the database that might be defined as follows:

```
CREATE VIEW                              CREATE VIEW
  us_catalog(name, size, country)          french_catalog(name, size, country)
  AS                                       AS
    SELECT name, size, 'USA'                 SELECT name, size, 'France'
    FROM us_products                         FROM french_products
  UNION ALL                                UNION ALL
    SELECT name, feet(size), 'France'        SELECT name, meters(size), 'USA'
    FROM french_products;                    FROM us_products;
```

A sales representative in France might issue the following query against the French catalog view to find all the products having a size less than one meter, in order to meet a customer's specifications.

```
SELECT *
FROM french_catalog
WHERE size < meters(1);
```

Based on the sample data listed above, the result of this query is as follows:

```
NAME                    SIZE                    COUNTRY
------------------      ----------------------  -------
Gadget                  +5.00000000000000E-001  France
Widget                  +9.14634146341463E-001  USA
```

4.4.12 Dropping a Function

A user-defined function can be dropped from the system by means of a DROP FUNCTION statement, which is a variation of the DROP statement described in Section 2.8.6. The syntax of the DROP FUNCTION statement is as follows:

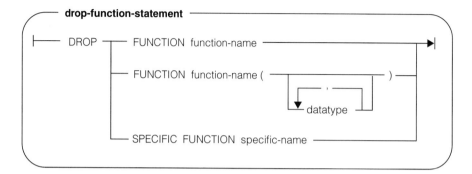

Dropping a function deletes the function from the system catalog tables, but it does not physically remove the executable file that implements the function from the directory where it resides.

As you can see from the syntax diagram above, there are three ways in which a DROP statement can identify the function instance to be dropped:

1. The function can be identified by its function name if there is only a single function instance with this name. If the schema name is omitted, it is considered to be the current authid.

   Example: `DROP FUNCTION geometry.cosine;`

2. The function can be identified by its signature—that is, its name and the datatypes of all its parameters. If the schema name is omitted, it is considered to be the current authid. The function name and list of parameter types must uniquely identify a function instance. The parameter types must be an exact match for the function to be dropped, except that the length or precision/scale of a datatype can be represented by empty parentheses, meaning "any." For example, `Char()` would match a Char parameter of any length, but it would not match a Varchar parameter.

   Examples: `DROP FUNCTION addWeeks(Date, Integer);`

   `DROP FUNCTION payroll.raise(Char(), Double);`

 TIP: Remember that `Char` without any parentheses denotes a Char datatype of default length, which is Char(1); similarly, `Decimal` without any parentheses denotes Decimal(5,0). Thus, `DROP FUNCTION foo(Char())` drops a function named `foo` that takes a Char parameter of any length, but `DROP FUNCTION foo(Char)` drops a function named `foo` only if its parameter is Char(1).

3. The function can be identified by its specific name. This is the name given in the "specific name" clause of the CREATE FUNCTION statement when this function instance was created (or, if no specific name was supplied by the user, one was assigned by the system). Specific names are guaranteed to be unique within a schema. If the schema is omitted, it is considered to be the current authid.

   Example: `DROP SPECIFIC FUNCTION geometry.area1;`

In order to execute a DROP FUNCTION statement, the current authid must be equal to the schema name of the function to be dropped, or it must possess the DBADM or SYSADM privilege. No one (not even a system administrator) is allowed to drop a function whose schema name is SYSIBM. Similarly, no one is allowed to drop the casting functions that are automatically created by the system for each distinct type.

A function instance cannot be dropped if it is currently used in a view definition, in a constraint or trigger, or as the "source" of another function instance. In all of these cases, the DROP FUNCTION statement will fail. Usage of a function instance in views, constraints, and triggers is recorded in the system catalog tables named VIEWDEP, CONSTDEP, and TRIGDEP. Usage of a function instance as the source of another function instance is recorded in the FUNCTIONS catalog table.

Usage of a function instance by a program will not cause a DROP FUNCTION statement to fail. If a function instance that is used by a program is dropped, the program's package is marked "inoperative" and cannot be used again until it is explicitly rebound. When the package is rebound, another applicable function instance will be chosen by the function resolution algorithm if one is available.

4.4.13 Commenting on a Function

Each user-defined function (but not the built-in functions) is described by an entry in the system catalog table named FUNCTIONS. Like many catalog tables, FUNCTIONS allows you to add a descriptive comment by using the COMMENT statement, described in Section 2.8.7. However, the syntax for commenting on functions has some special features, as shown in the following diagram:

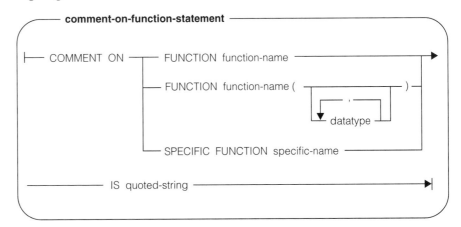

The three ways of identifying the function to which the comment applies correspond exactly to the three ways of identifying a function in a DROP FUNCTION statement, described in Section 4.4.12. The authorization requirements for the COMMENT ON FUNCTION statement are also the same as those for DROP FUNCTION. The content of the quoted string in the COMMENT statement is entered into the REMARKS column of the FUNCTIONS catalog table.

Examples:

```
COMMENT ON FUNCTION addWeeks(Date, Integer) IS
   'Second operand must be positive';
COMMENT ON FUNCTION nthbest IS
   'Returns nth-largest value so far.
    Wrap in MAX() to get global nth-largest';
COMMENT ON SPECIFIC FUNCTION seqno IS
   'Counts the number of times it is called';
```

TIP: Notice that the CLP does not mind if your quoted string spans more than one line. The CLP treats line breaks within a character-string constant as though they were blanks.

4.5 STEPS TOWARD OBJECTS

The power of large objects, user-defined functions, and distinct types becomes most evident when these features are used together. Large objects provide the ability to store objects in the database that have a complex internal state. User-defined functions provide the ability to associate a complex behavior with these objects. Finally, distinct types provide the ability to combine user-defined state and behavior into a first-class datatype. Taken together, these features represent a significant step toward support of the object-oriented paradigm. As the DB2 product evolves, it might reasonably be expected to take additional steps in the same direction, such as providing support for true abstract datatypes with inheritance and polymorphism, and support for access plans based on user-defined functions.

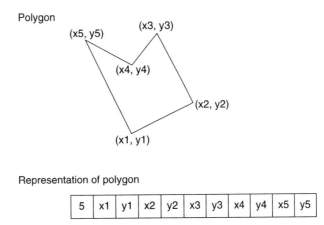

Figure 4-4: A Polygon and Its Representation

4.5.1 Example: A Polygon Datatype

I will illustrate the synergy among large objects, user-defined functions, and distinct types by creating a datatype named Polygon. Polygons are useful in many applications, such as architecture, urban planning, VLSI design, and computer graphics.

The first step in creating a Polygon datatype is to choose a representation for Polygon data. In our example, we will represent a Polygon by an Integer that represents its degree, followed by a series of floating-point number pairs that represent the coordinates of its vertices in counterclockwise order. The Integer and the series of coordinates (of type Double) are packed together into a Blob, as illustrated in Figure 4-4. Since in V2 an Integer occupies four bytes and a Double occupies eight bytes, a Polygon of degree n can be represented by a Blob of length $16n + 4$.

The declaration of Polygon as an SQL datatype can be accomplished by the following statement:

```
CREATE DISTINCT TYPE Polygon AS Blob(16004);
```

The above statement permits Polygons of degree up to 1,000 to be created; of course, no space is wasted if the Polygon has fewer than 1,000 sides. We do not include the phrase WITH COMPARISONS, because comparison operators are not supported on the Blob base type.

Before we can use the Polygon datatype, we need to have some way of creating an instance of a Polygon. This will be done by means of a *constructor function*, which creates a Polygon from a collection of simpler datatypes. The Polygon datatype might have many constructor functions, which create various types of Polygons from various different inputs. In this example, we will discuss one example of a Polygon constructor, which creates a three-sided Polygon (a triangle) from parameters that represent the coordinates of the vertices. The signature of this constructor function is as follows:

```
triangle(Double, Double, Double, Double, Double, Double)
    RETURNS Polygon;
```

In order for Polygon to be a useful datatype, we will need to create some functions that implement Polygon behavior. A great many such functions can be imagined, of which we will list only a few:

```
degree(Polygon) returns Integer;
area(Polygon) returns Double;
perimeter(Polygon) returns Double;
rotate(Polygon, Double) returns Polygon;
intersect(Polygon, Polygon) returns Polygon;
```

We will discuss in detail the implementation of two Polygon functions, namely the `triangle` constructor and the `perimeter` function. Both of these functions will be implemented in a single C source file named `polygon.c`. We will make use of the NOT NULL CALL convention, declaring that the output of each function is null if any of its inputs are null, so that our function implementations need not be concerned with nulls. The following SQL statements are used to "register" our functions with the system (if we plan to use our functions in more than one database, we must execute the following statements while connected to each database):

```
CREATE FUNCTION
    triangle(double, double, double, double, double, double)
        --    x1,     y1,     x2,     y2,     x3,     y3
    RETURNS Polygon
    EXTERNAL NAME 'polygon!triangle'
    NOT VARIANT
    NO EXTERNAL ACTION
    FENCED
    NOT NULL CALL
    LANGUAGE C
    NO SQL
    PARAMETER STYLE DB2SQL;
```

```
CREATE FUNCTION
    perimeter(Polygon)
        RETURNS Double
        EXTERNAL NAME 'polygon!perimeter'
        NOT VARIANT
        NO EXTERNAL ACTION
        FENCED
        NOT NULL CALL
        LANGUAGE C
        NO SQL
        PARAMETER STYLE DB2SQL;
```

The function bodies are written using the parameter-passing conventions discussed in Section 4.4.6. The content of the implementation file, polygon.c, is shown below. This file contains the bodies of the triangle and perimeter functions, and it also contains a definition of a C structure named Pgon that can be overlaid on a Blob in order to interpret the Blob as a Polygon.

Example Program: Polygon

```c
#include <stdlib.h>      /* Standard C library          */
#include <sqludf.h>      /* UDF-related declarations     */
#include <math.h>        /* needed for sqrt function     */
#include <string.h>      /* needed for strcpy function   */

/**********************************************************************
**   The following structure will be overlaid on the data area of a Blob  *
**   to represent a Polygon.                                            *
**********************************************************************/

struct Pgon
    {
    long  degree;
    double  coord[1];    /* actually an array of many coordinates */
    };
```

```
/**********************************************************************
**              CONSTRUCTOR FUNCTION FOR TRIANGLES                   *
**       Triangle(x1, y1, x2, y2, x3, y3) returns Polygon            *
**********************************************************************/

void triangle( double           *x1,       /* IN:  vertex 1, x-coord.  */
               double           *y1,       /* IN:  vertex 1, y-coord.  */
               double           *x2,       /* IN:  vertex 2, x-coord.  */
               double           *y2,       /* IN:  vertex 2, y-coord.  */
               double           *x3,       /* IN:  vertex 3, x-coord.  */
               double           *y3,       /* IN:  vertex 3, y-coord.  */
               struct sqludf_lob *poly,    /* OUT: Polygon in a Blob   */
               short            *x1null,    /* IN:  indicator (ignored) */
               short            *x2null,    /* IN:  indicator (ignored) */
               short            *x3null,    /* IN:  indicator (ignored) */
               short            *x4null,    /* IN:  indicator (ignored) */
               short            *x5null,    /* IN:  indicator (ignored) */
               short            *x6null,    /* IN:  indicator (ignored) */
               short            *nullout,   /* OUT: indicator           */
               char             *sqlstate,  /* OUT: result code         */
               char             *fnname,    /* IN:  generic fn name      */
               char             *specname,  /* IN:  specific fn name     */
               char             *message )  /* OUT: message text        */
{
  struct Pgon *p;          /* overlay a Pgon on the Blob  */
  p = (struct Pgon *)(poly->data);

  /*
  **   Length: 4-byte degree plus six 8-byte coordinates = 52
  */
  poly->length = 52;

  /*
  **   Fill in the degree and the coordinates of the polygon
  */
  p->degree = 3;           /* degree of a triangle is 3   */
  p->coord[0] = *x1;
  p->coord[1] = *y1;
```

```
    p->coord[2] = *x2;
    p->coord[3] = *y2;
    p->coord[4] = *x3;
    p->coord[5] = *y3;

    *nullout = 0;                    /* return null indicator        */
    /*
    **  No need to set sqlstate to 00000 for normal return.
    */

    }        /* end of triangle function */



/*********************************************************************
**                  PERIMETER FUNCTION FOR POLYGONS                 *
**                  Perimeter(Polygon) returns Double               *
*********************************************************************/

void perimeter(struct sqludf_lob *poly,     /* IN:  Polygon in a Blob  */
               double            *perim,     /* OUT: return value       */
               short             *nullin,    /* IN:  indicator (ignored) */
               short             *nullout,   /* OUT: indicator          */
               char              *sqlstate,  /* OUT: result code        */
               char              *fnname,    /* IN:  generic fn name     */
               char              *specname,  /* IN:  specific fn name    */
               char              *message )  /* OUT: message text       */
    {
    int     degree;                          /* degree of polygon       */
    double  startx, starty;                  /* start of line segment   */
    double  endx, endy;                      /* end of line segment     */
    int     i;                               /* loop counter            */
    double  deltax, deltay, lengthSoFar;     /* working variables       */

    struct Pgon *p;                          /* overlay Pgon on the Blob */
    p = (struct Pgon *)(poly->data);

    /*
    **  Check the degree of the polygon for validity
    */
    degree = p->degree;
    if (degree < 1 || degree > 1000)
       {
       strcpy(sqlstate, "38610");            /* return abnormal sqlstate */
       strcpy(message, "Invalid degree");
       return;
       }
```

```
/*
**   Coordinates of point i are in (coord[2*i], coord[2*i+1])
**   where i ranges from 0 to degree-1.
*/
endx = p->coord[2*(degree-1)];          /* last point */
endy = p->coord[2*(degree-1)+1];        /* in polygon */
lengthSoFar = 0;
for (i=0; i<degree; i++)
   {
   startx = endx;
   starty = endy;
   endx = p->coord[2*i];
   endy = p->coord[2*i+1];
   deltax = endx - startx;
   deltay = endy - starty;
   lengthSoFar += sqrt(deltax * deltax + deltay * deltay);
   }
*perim = lengthSoFar;                    /* return value           */
*nullout = 0;                            /* return null indicator   */
strcpy(sqlstate, "00000");               /* return normal sqlstate  */

}      /* end of perimeter function */
```

In addition to the implementation file polygon.c, we need to create an export file named polygon.exp (under AIX) or a module definition file named polygon.def (under OS/2 or Windows NT). The content of the export file is shown below (the module definition file is similar):

```
#! polygon export file
triangle
perimeter
```

To complete the definition of the Polygon object, we compile and link the polygon.c source file, copy the executable file to the sqllib/function directory, and authorize it for execution by any user, following the steps described in Section 4.4.8. Polygon is now a first-class datatype with its own behavior, which is implemented by a set of user-defined functions.

As an example of the use of Polygons, we will consider a real estate application. The following SQL statements create a table named PROPERTIES containing a column of type Polygon, and insert two triangular parcels of property into the table:

```
CREATE TABLE properties
   (parcelno Char(6),
    owner    Varchar(32),
    parcel   Polygon);
```

```
INSERT INTO properties(parcelno, owner, parcel) VALUES
  ('123456', 'John Smith',
      triangle( 500,  600, -400, -500, 1000, -500)),
  ('123457', 'Susan Doe',
      triangle(1100, 1100, 1300, 1100, 1300, 1400));
```

The following query retrieves the parcels that have a perimeter of more than 1,000 (John's parcel qualifies, but Susan's does not):

```
SELECT owner, perimeter(parcel)
FROM   properties
WHERE  perimeter(parcel) > 1000;
```

 TIP: When writing an application program that uses a distinct type such as Polygon that is based on a LOB datatype, you may wish to use locators to avoid actually materializing large objects in your program. Since Polygon is based on Blob, for example, you can use Blob locators in your program to manipulate Polygons. However, if you wish to invoke a function that takes a Polygon as its argument, you must explicitly cast the locator to a Polygon datatype before calling the function. For example, if `loc1` is a host variable of type Blob locator, `perimeter(Polygon(:loc1))` would be a correct function call, but `perimeter(:loc1)` would fail to compile, with the error message "no function having compatible arguments was found."

4.6 DATATYPE CONVERSIONS

There are many reasons, while processing SQL statements, why it might be necessary to convert a value from one datatype into another. Now that we have discussed user-defined datatypes and functions, it may be worthwhile to summarize all the ways in which the system performs datatype conversions. There are four different ways in which datatype conversion is done by V2, and these are summarized below.

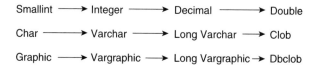

Figure 4-5: Promotion of Function Arguments

4.6.1 Promotion of Function Arguments

Each function, whether built-in or user-defined, has a well-defined list of parameter types. Most of the built-in functions are really families of overloaded functions. For example, the family SYSIBM.LENGTH consists of the built-in functions length(Integer), length(Decimal), length(Char), length (Varchar), length(Date), and many other function instances. User-defined functions may also consist of overloaded families. When a function is called with a set of arguments, the best function instance is selected by the function resolution algorithm described in Section 4.4.5. Then, if the selected function is not a perfect match for the actual arguments, the arguments are promoted to match the parameter types of the function. Only built-in datatypes are promoted, and only in certain predetermined ways. Promotion of arguments is done only by moving to the right along one of the promotion paths shown in Figure 4-5. As a value is promoted, its length, precision, or scale may also be adjusted in order to fit the parameter of the chosen function.

Since the Blob, Date, Time, and Timestamp datatypes, and all distinct types, are not members of any promotion hierarchy, these datatypes are never promoted. When one of these datatypes is used as an argument of a function, the parameter of the selected function instance must be an exact match.

All combining of dissimilar datatypes by arithmetic or concatenation operators is handled by promotion. For example, if x is an Integer and y is a Double, the expression x + y is treated as a call to the function "+"(Double, Double) with promotion of the first argument.

4.6.2 UNION Semantics

The set operations UNION, INTERSECT, and EXCEPT can combine values of different datatypes. When doing so, these operations use conversion semantics similar to the promotion of arguments, but slightly more liberal. All the conversions allowed for promotion of function arguments are also allowed for the set operations, and, in addition, a Char or Varchar value containing a valid representation of a Date, Time, or Timestamp can be converted to a Date, Time, or Timestamp. The datatype conversions supported by UNION,

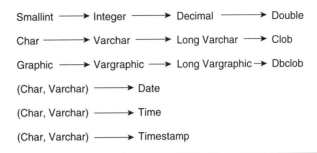

Figure 4-6: UNION Datatype Hierarchies

INTERSECT, and EXCEPT are shown in Figure 4-6. If two datatypes T1 and T2 from the same UNION hierarchy are combined by one of the set operations, the result datatype is either T1 or T2, whichever is farther to the right in the hierarchy. Furthermore, the length of the result datatype is the greater of the input lengths. For example, if a Char(50) and a Varchar(10) are combined by an INTERSECT operation, the result will be a Varchar(50), which is not the same datatype as either of the operands.

Since Blobs and distinct types do not participate in any of these UNION datatype hierarchies, each of these datatypes can be combined only with itself in set operations.

UNION semantics for datatype conversion are also used by a few other datatype-combining operations in the SQL language. These operations are:

1. Computing the result of a `coalesce` function when its operands have different datatypes. For example, if x is a Char(10) and y is a Date, then the result type of `coalesce(x, y)` is a Date, even if the value of x is returned.

2. A CASE expression whose candidate results have different datatypes. For example, consider the following expression:

```
CASE testvalue
    WHEN 1 THEN 100
    WHEN 2 THEN 200.00
    ELSE 3.0E+2
END
```

The result of this expression will be 1.0E+2, 2.0E+2, or 3.0E+2, depending on `testvalue`. The datatype of the result will always be Double, because that is the "greatest datatype" of the candidate results.

3. VALUES expressions. A VALUES expression is like a "literal table." The datatypes of the columns of this table are computed from the component parts of the VALUES expression using UNION semantics. For example, the following VALUES expression behaves like a literal table whose first column is of type Double and whose second column is of type Decimal:

```
VALUES (1, 2.0), (3E3, 4)
```

4.6.3 Assignment

In SQL, assignment can take place in any of the following ways:

- A column can be assigned a value by the SET clause of an UPDATE statement.
- A column can be assigned a value by an assignment (SET) statement in a before trigger (described in Section 5.3.2).
- Values can be inserted into a row by an INSERT statement.
- Values can be delivered into a host variable by a SELECT, FETCH, or VALUES statement.

In Section 4.2.4, we discussed the conversions that can take place when a value is assigned to a target of a different datatype. These conversions are more liberal than those supported by either promotion or UNION, in two respects:

1. Unlike promotions, assignment conversions are bidirectional. That is, a value can be assigned to a target of a "lower" datatype, as in assigning a Float to an Integer. Of course, precision may be lost when values are truncated, and run-time error conditions may occur if a value cannot be represented in the target datatype (for example, if a Double value is out of the range expressible by the Integer datatype).

2. Distinct-type values can be assigned to their base-type targets, and vice versa, with automatic conversion using the system-provided casting functions. When a distinct-type value is assigned to a host variable, it is first converted to its base type, and the base-type value is then assigned to the host variable.

For purposes of assignment, datatypes are treated as a collection of families with assignment in any direction supported inside each family, as shown in Figure 4-7.

4.6.4 Casting

The casting operation is invoked explicitly by the CAST expression discussed in Section 3.1. The following is an example of a CAST expression:

```
CAST (x AS Decimal(8,2))
```

{ Smallint, Integer, Decimal, Double }

{ Char, Varchar, Long Varchar, Clob }

{ Graphic, Vargraphic, Long Vargraphic, Dbclob }

{ (Char or Varchar representation of a Date), Date }

{ (Char or Varchar representation of a Time), Time }

{ (Char or Varchar representation of a Timestamp), Timestamp }

{ (Any distinct type), (The base type of that distinct type) }

Figure 4-7: Assignment Datatype Families

Casting is also invoked implicitly when the arguments of a sourced function are converted to the parameter types of the source function, and the result of the source function is converted to the result type of the sourced function.

The conversions supported by casting are the most liberal of the four forms of datatype conversion. All the conversions supported by assignment are supported, along with certain additional conversions such as casting a numeric value into its character-string representation.

The rules governing castability of one datatype into another are as follows:

1. A distinct type is castable into its base type.

2. The base type of a distinct type is castable into the distinct type. Also, since the casting is performed by a function, any datatype that is promotable to the base type is castable into the distinct type.

3. A distinct type is never castable into another distinct type.[8]

4. Among built-in datatypes, castability is defined by Table 3-1.

---

8. A user can create a function that converts one distinct type into another, such as the feet(Meters) and meters(Feet) examples in Section 4.4.11, but these user-defined functions are not considered to be casting functions and cannot be invoked by using the CAST notation.

Active Data

O ne of the most important trends in database management is the trend toward increasing the semantic content of stored data. Since a database is a resource shared by many applications, any knowledge about data semantics that can be put into the database is knowledge that does not need to be replicated in every application. This knowledge might include rules about what values are valid for a particular column of data, how data values are related to each other, or how an action should be triggered automatically whenever a certain condition is detected. When rules like these are enforced by the database system, stored data becomes more "active," having behavior of its own that goes beyond passively accepting updates from the world outside the database. Active data is more valuable than passive data, because it is richer in semantic content.

We will define an *active data feature* as a mechanism whereby an SQL statement can invoke an action that is not explicitly specified by the SQL statement. V2 includes several active data features, which we will classify into the following two broad categories:

1. *Constraints.* Constraints are rules that govern how data values can change, generally stated in a declarative way. Constraints ensure the validity of data values and may generate values automatically when necessary. Attempts to update the database in a way that violates a constraint will in general be refused. The importance of constraints has been recognized by the "integrity feature" of the ANSI/ISO SQL89 Standard, which includes several kinds of constraints, and by the subsequent SQL92 Standard, which includes some additional kinds.

2. *Triggers.* Triggers are general-purpose automatic actions that are invoked, or "triggered," by certain events such as update of a specific table. In contrast to the declarative nature of constraints, triggers are defined by procedures, consisting of a series of SQL statements to be executed automatically whenever the triggering event is detected. Triggers are very powerful, because they are not limited to predefined actions such as rolling back an offending update. They can be used to enforce global integrity of the database or to invoke complex automatic actions, including interactions with the world outside the database such as placing an order or sending a message. A trigger facility is under consideration for inclusion in the next ANSI/ISO SQL Standard, currently known as SQL3.

This chapter describes all the active data features supported by V2 and includes a comprehensive example of a database design that uses many constraints and triggers. Also, since constraints are properties of database tables, this is the chapter in which the complete syntax of the SQL statements for creating and altering tables is described.

An active database can be very complex and richly interconnected. This chapter describes how multiple constraints and triggers interact when they are activated by the same statement. It also describes how views, triggers, constraints, programs, and other objects depend on each other and how the principle called *conservative binding semantics* prevents your views and application programs from changing their behavior unexpectedly.

5.1 CONSTRAINTS

In V2, each constraint is associated with a specific table in the database and protects the validity of data values in that table. Constraints are associated with base tables only, not with views[1] (though, of course, a constraint on a table protects that table from invalid updates applied through a view). Most types of constraints can have names, which must be unique among all the constraints associated with a particular table. The name of a constraint is used by the system in error messages whenever the constraint is violated, and can also be used in an ALTER TABLE statement to drop the constraint. If you create a constraint and do not give it a name, the system will generate a name for the constraint automatically.

Since each constraint applies to a particular table, constraints are defined as part of a CREATE TABLE statement. After a table has been created, constraints associated with that table can be added or dropped by means of an ALTER TABLE statement. Of course, when a table is dropped, all the constraints associated with it are dropped also.

V2 includes the following six features that can be considered types of constraints, in the sense that they govern or influence the ways in which data values can be modified:

NOT NULL constraints

Column defaults

Unique indexes

Check constraints

---

1. A view feature called the *check option*, discussed in Section 2.8.4, might be considered to be a constraint on a view.

Primary key constraints

Foreign key constraints

5.1.1 NOT NULL Constraints

This very primitive form of constraint specifies that a given column of a table cannot contain a null value. Any INSERT or UPDATE statement that attempts to place a null value in the column will fail.

NOT NULL constraints may not have names. The following is an example of a CREATE TABLE statement that includes a NOT NULL constraint:

```
CREATE TABLE patients (socsecno Char(11) NOT NULL, ...);
```

If a column has a NOT NULL constraint, its entry in the COLUMNS catalog table has the value "N" in the NULLS column.

5.1.2 Column Defaults

When a column is created or added to a table, a default value can be specified for the column. The default value is generated automatically whenever a row that is inserted into the table does not include a specific value for the column. If a new column with a default value is added to a table that has some existing rows, the existing rows are given the default value for the new column.

The syntax of a default clause in a column definition is shown on page 336. The default value specified for a column can be NULL or a constant or special register that is compatible with the datatype of the column. If the datatype of the column is a Blob or a distinct type, the default value can be specified by using a casting function such as `blob(X'00000000')` or `shoesize(8)`. If no explicit default value is specified for a column, its default value is determined according to the rules in Table 5-1.[2]

In the following example of a CREATE TABLE statement, the comments indicate the default values of the four columns. The INSERT statement inserts a row that receives default values for the STATE and CITATIONS columns.

```
CREATE TABLE drivers
    (licenseno Char(8) NOT NULL,          -- No default
     state Char(2) WITH DEFAULT 'CA',     -- Default is 'CA'
     expiration Date,                     -- Default is null
     citations Smallint WITH DEFAULT);    -- Default is zero

INSERT INTO drivers(licenseno, expiration)
    VALUES ('K0123456', '1998-06-15');
```

---

2. Explicit specification of default values is supported beginning with DB2 Version 2.1.1. In previous versions, only system-defined default values were supported.

TABLE 5-1: Default Values for Columns

If the column definition contains . . .	. . . and the datatype of the column is . . .	. . . then the default value of the column is . . .
No DEFAULT clause	(Any datatype)	Null (unless NOT NULL is specified; in this case, the column has no default)
A DEFAULT clause that specifies an explicit default value	(Any datatype)	The value specified in the DEFAULT clause
WITH DEFAULT (but no explicit default value is specified)	Smallint, Integer, Decimal, Double	Zero
	Char, Graphic	Blanks
	Varchar, Long Varchar, Graphic, Long Vargraphic, Clob, Dbclob, Blob	Zero-length string
	Date	The current date when the row is inserted. When a Date column is added to a table, existing rows receive the date January 1, 0001.
	Time	The current time when the row is inserted. When a Time column is added to a table, existing rows receive the time 00:00:00.
	Timestamp	The current timestamp when the row is inserted. When a Timestamp column is added to a table, existing rows receive a timestamp containing the date January 1, 0001 and the time 00:00:00.
	A distinct type	The system-defined default value for the base datatype, cast into the distinct type

The default value for each column can be found in the DEFAULT column of the COLUMNS catalog table.

5.1.3 Unique Indexes

Any column or combination of columns in a table can be declared "unique," meaning that no two rows of the table may have the same value or combination of values in these columns.[3] In V2, this is done by creating a *unique index* on the desired columns. Up to 16 columns, with a combined length of up to 255 bytes, may be included in the index (but none of the columns may have a datatype of Blob, Clob, Dbclob, Long Varchar, or Long Vargraphic). The index enforces uniqueness of the column values and also provides an efficient access path for retrieving rows of the table based on the values of the given columns. Any INSERT or UPDATE statement that attempts to place nonunique values into a set of columns that are covered by a unique index will fail. A unique index can be dropped if enforcement of uniqueness is no longer required.

The following example illustrates creation and dropping of a unique index on a pair of columns:

```
CREATE UNIQUE INDEX i25 ON players(team, position);
DROP INDEX i25;
```

Each index is described by an entry in the INDEXES catalog table. The names of the columns covered by the index are contained in the COLNAMES column, and a value of "U" in the UNIQUERULE column indicates that the index is unique.

5.1.4 Check Constraints

Check constraints are a new feature in V2. Each check constraint can have a name and is attached to a particular table to ensure the validity of its data values. A check constraint contains a predicate (or combination of predicates connected by AND/OR) called a *check condition*. The check condition is enforced to be "not false" (that is, it must evaluate to true or unknown) for every row in the table. Whenever a row of a table is inserted or updated, the check condition is tested for the changed row, and if it is false, the insert or update is rolled back. If multiple rows are inserted or updated by a single SQL statement and a check constraint fails for any of these rows, all changes made by the SQL statement are rolled back and the statement has no effect. When a statement is rolled back because it violates a check constraint, the current transaction remains in progress and other statements within the transaction are not affected.

---

3. For the purpose of determining uniqueness, NULL is treated as an ordinary value.

In V2, the check condition must be some test that can be evaluated by examining a single row of the table to which the check constraint is attached. In other words, the check constraint is like a WHERE clause that refers only to the columns of a single table, with no subqueries or references to special registers. This restriction allows the check condition to be quickly evaluated whenever a row is inserted or updated.

Check constraints are attached to a table as part of a CREATE TABLE or ALTER TABLE statement. The following are examples of valid check constraints on a table with columns JOBCODE, SALARY, and BONUS:

```
CONSTRAINT check1
   CHECK (jobcode IN (10, 20, 30, 40, 50));
CONSTRAINT check2
   CHECK (salary < 100000 AND bonus <= salary);
```

The following is an example of a check constraint that is *not* valid because it cannot be tested by examining a single row:

```
CONSTRAINT check3
   CHECK (salary < (SELECT max(salary) FROM emp));
```

Although check3 in the example above is not a valid check constraint, you can accomplish its purpose by writing a trigger, as described in Section 5.3.

Each check constraint is described by a row in the CHECKS catalog table, which contains the name of the constraint, the name of the table to which it is attached, and the text of the check condition.

TIP: A check constraint may call a user-defined function, and in fact user-defined functions add greatly to the power of check constraints. However, a check constraint may not call a user-defined function that has been defined with the VARIANT, EXTERNAL ACTION, or SCRATCHPAD properties.

5.1.5 Primary Key Constraints

Each table may optionally have one primary key. A primary key is a column or combination of columns that has the combined properties of uniqueness and NOT NULL. A primary key may consist of up to 16 columns, with a combined length of up to 255 bytes. None of the columns in a primary key may have a datatype of Blob, Clob, Dbclob, Long Varchar, or Long Vargraphic. When you declare that a certain set of columns make up the primary key of a table, the system automatically maintains a unique index on that set of columns. You need not create the index explicitly, but V2 does require you to specify NOT NULL separately for each column in the primary key.

There's only one important difference between specifying a primary key for a table and specifying NOT NULL constraints and a unique index on the same set of columns: if a table has a primary key, it can serve as the *parent table* in a referential integrity relationship (as discussed in Section 5.1.6).

You can find the primary key columns for a given table by looking in the COLUMNS catalog table. If a column is part of the primary key for its table, its KEYSEQ value in COLUMNS will indicate its position within the primary key. (For example, a KEYSEQ value of 2 indicates the second column in the primary key.)

Primary keys can be defined for a table as part of a CREATE TABLE statement and can be added or dropped by means of an ALTER TABLE statement. A primary key can be given a name, but there is little reason to do so, because a primary key can be dropped without reference to its name (after all, each table can have only one primary key). The following are examples of CREATE TABLE statements that specify primary keys. (Of course, each primary key specification must be contained in a separate CREATE TABLE statement, since a given table cannot have more than one primary key.)

```
CREATE TABLE patients (socsecno Char(11)
                                NOT NULL PRIMARY KEY,
                       name Varchar(15));

CREATE TABLE quotations (suppno Char(3) NOT NULL,
                         partno Char(4) NOT NULL,
                         price  Integer,
                         PRIMARY KEY (suppno, partno));
```

5.1.6 Foreign Key Constraints

A foreign key constraint specifies a relationship between two tables: the *parent table* and the *child table*. The parent table and child table may be the same table, in which case the table is said to be *self-referencing*. The relationship between the tables, sometimes called a *referential integrity relationship*, is a 1:*n* relationship between the rows of the parent table and the rows of the child table. The relationship is based on matching values between the primary key columns of the parent table and a set of columns in the child table called the *foreign key*. As long as the foreign key constraint is in effect, the system guarantees that, for each row in the child table with a non-null value in all of its foreign key columns, there is a row in the parent table with a matching value in its primary key. Of course, the foreign key and the primary key must have the same number of columns and compatible (but not necessarily identical) datatypes. None of the columns in the foreign key may have a datatype of Blob, Clob, Dbclob, Long Varchar, or Long Vargraphic.

A table may participate in multiple referential integrity relationships, both as a parent and as a child. Each relationship is created by a clause, in a CREATE TABLE or ALTER TABLE statement for the child table, that specifies the foreign key columns and names the parent table to which they refer. It is advisable to give each foreign key a descriptive name, but if you do not specify a name, the system will generate one for you.

As you have seen, the system automatically maintains an index on each primary key. No index is maintained automatically on a foreign key, but you can create such an index, and it's probably wise to do so.

Each referential integrity relationship is recorded by a row in the REFERENCES catalog table that contains the name of the constraint, the names of the parent and child tables, and the sets of columns that are included in the (parent's) primary key and the (child's) foreign key. You can also find the relationships that apply to a particular column by looking in the KEYCOLUSE catalog table, which has an entry for each column that participates in a primary or foreign key.

Foreign key constraints can be illustrated by means of tables named EMP and DEPT, which participate in two referential integrity relationships. Each EMP row represents an employee, and each DEPT row represents a department. We wish to make sure that each employee is in a valid department and has a valid manager. This can be done by specifying two foreign keys for the EMP table, as shown in Figure 5-1. In one of these constraints (the one from MANAGER to EMPNO), the EMP table is self-referencing. The primary and foreign keys can be specified when the respective tables are created (as in the example) or can be added later by ALTER TABLE statements. The constraints in Figure 5-1 guarantee that each non-null DEPTNO value in EMP has a matching DEPTNO value in DEPT and that each non-null MANAGER value in EMP has a matching EMPNO value in EMP. Since we have also specified that DEPTNO and MANAGER in the EMP table are NOT NULL (note that this is not required by the foreign key constraint), we have guaranteed that every employee has both a valid department and a valid manager. (Of course, some departments may have no employees, and some employees may not be anyone's manager.)

You may have noticed that in the CREATE TABLE statements in Figure 5-1, no columns are named in the REFERENCES clauses. The REFERENCES clause names the parent table; the specific columns within the parent table that participate in the relationship need not be named because they are always the primary key columns.

At this point, you may be wondering what happens if an SQL statement attempts to change some data value in a way that would violate a foreign key constraint. I will answer this question by listing all the ways in which the constraint could be violated and explaining what happens in each case.

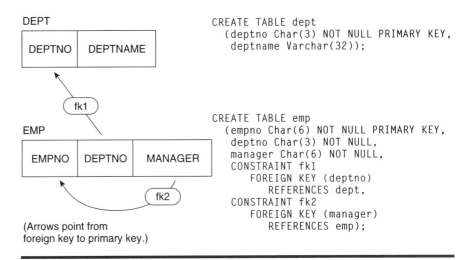

```
CREATE TABLE dept
    (deptno Char(3) NOT NULL PRIMARY KEY,
     deptname Varchar(32));
```

```
CREATE TABLE emp
    (empno Char(6) NOT NULL PRIMARY KEY,
     deptno Char(3) NOT NULL,
     manager Char(6) NOT NULL,
     CONSTRAINT fk1
         FOREIGN KEY (deptno)
             REFERENCES dept,
     CONSTRAINT fk2
         FOREIGN KEY (manager)
             REFERENCES emp);
```

(Arrows point from
foreign key to primary key.)

Figure 5-1: Foreign Key Constraints

1. An SQL statement could try to insert a row into the child table, with a foreign key value that matches no primary key in the parent table. Such an INSERT statement will fail, and all rows inserted by the statement will be rolled back.

2. An SQL statement could try to update a foreign key value in the child table to a new value that matches no primary key in the parent table. Such an UPDATE statement will fail, and all rows updated by the statement will be rolled back.

3. An SQL statement could try to delete a row from the parent table, leaving some unmatched foreign key values in the child table. The user who created the foreign key constraint can choose among the following options to take effect in this case:

ON DELETE CASCADE: The deletion of the parent row succeeds, and all rows of the child table with matching foreign keys are deleted also.

ON DELETE SET NULL: The deletion of the parent row succeeds, and all matching foreign keys in the child table are set to null. (Of course, at least one of the foreign key columns must be nullable.)

ON DELETE NO ACTION: The deletion of the parent row fails, and all changes are rolled back. Constraints with this option are checked *after* all cascaded updates and deletes have taken effect.

ON DELETE RESTRICT: As in the NO ACTION option, the deletion of the parent row fails, and all changes are rolled back. However, constraints with the RESTRICT option are checked *before* cascaded updates and deletes take effect. Therefore, ON DELETE RESTRICT is slightly more restrictive than ON DELETE NO ACTION.

The default behavior of a foreign key constraint is ON DELETE NO ACTION.

4. An SQL statement could try to update a primary key in the parent table in such a way that some foreign key values in the child table would be left unmatched. The user who created the foreign key constraint can choose between the following options to take effect in this case:

ON UPDATE NO ACTION: This option requires that, after the UPDATE statement has been executed, every child row with a non-null foreign key must have *some* matching parent row—but not necessarily the same parent row as the one it had before the UPDATE statement. If this condition is not met, the UPDATE statement fails, and all changes are rolled back.

ON UPDATE RESTRICT: This option requires that, after the UPDATE statement has been executed, every child row with a non-null foreign key must have the *same* matching parent row that it had before the UPDATE statement. Therefore, ON UPDATE RESTRICT is slightly more restrictive than ON UPDATE NO ACTION. For example, an UPDATE statement that causes two rows of the parent table to exchange their primary key values might violate a RESTRICT constraint but will not violate a NO ACTION constraint. If the constraint is violated, the UPDATE statement fails, and all changes are rolled back.

The default behavior of a foreign key constraint is ON UPDATE NO ACTION.

The foreign key behaviors described above help us to understand why the V2 authorization system provides a REFERENCES privilege, by which the owner of a table can control which users are allowed to create foreign keys that reference the table. To illustrate the importance of the REFERENCES privilege, suppose that you are the owner of a table T1. If another user can create a table T2 with a foreign key that references T1, that user can find the set of parent key values that exist in T1 by inserting various child key values into T2 and noting which inserts are successful. The other user can also prevent you from deleting or updating rows in T1 by inserting matching rows into T2 and specifying a foreign key constraint with ON DELETE NO ACTION. For these reasons, users may not create foreign key constraints that reference a table unless they are granted the REFERENCES privilege by the owner of the table.

It is possible to define a chain of referential integrity relationships in which the child table of one relationship is the parent table of the next, as shown in Figure 5-2. In this way, deletion of a row from the "uppermost" parent table may cause deletions and/or updates to propagate through several related tables. For example, in Figure 5-2, deletion of a row from the DIVISION table would cause the matching rows of DEPT to be deleted, which would in turn

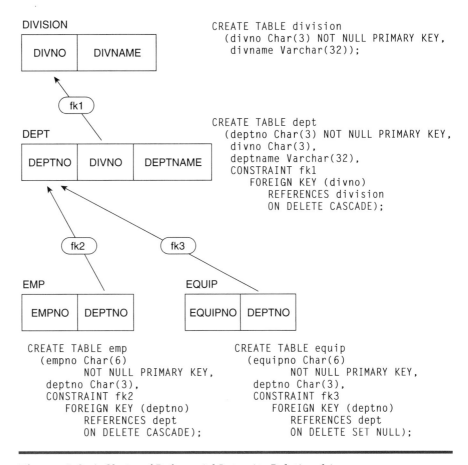

DIVISION

```
CREATE TABLE division
    (divno Char(3) NOT NULL PRIMARY KEY,
    divname Varchar(32));
```

```
CREATE TABLE dept
    (deptno Char(3) NOT NULL PRIMARY KEY,
    divno Char(3),
    deptname Varchar(32),
    CONSTRAINT fk1
        FOREIGN KEY (divno)
            REFERENCES division
            ON DELETE CASCADE);
```

```
CREATE TABLE emp
    (empno Char(6)
        NOT NULL PRIMARY KEY,
    deptno Char(3),
    CONSTRAINT fk2
        FOREIGN KEY (deptno)
        REFERENCES dept
        ON DELETE CASCADE);
```

```
CREATE TABLE equip
    (equipno Char(6)
        NOT NULL PRIMARY KEY,
    deptno Char(3),
    CONSTRAINT fk3
        FOREIGN KEY (deptno)
        REFERENCES dept
        ON DELETE SET NULL);
```

Figure 5-2: A Chain of Referential Integrity Relationships

cause matching rows of EMP to be deleted and matching foreign keys in EQUIP to be set to null. Note that, in this example, the foreign key columns do not have NOT NULL constraints. Therefore, for example, a row of the DEPT table could have a null DIVNO column, but if its DIVNO column contains a non-null value, that value must match some primary key in the DIVISION table.

A *referential cycle* is defined as a chain of referential integrity relationships that is closed on itself, making a table its own descendant. A self-referencing table (such as the EMP table in Figure 5-2) is the simplest example of a referential cycle. Referential cycles involving more than one table were not allowed in V1, but they are allowed in V2 if the DELETE rule is CASCADE.

5.2 CREATING AND DROPPING CONSTRAINTS

Since constraints always apply to a specific table, they are usually specified as part of the process of creating or altering a table, using the CREATE TABLE or ALTER TABLE statement. One exception is a constraint that requires unique values in a set of columns, which is enforced by means of an index and is therefore specified by a CREATE INDEX statement. The basics of the statements for creating and altering tables were described in Chapter 2. This section gives more details about the V2 syntax for these statements, including the features for managing constraints.

The V2 syntax for the CREATE TABLE and ALTER TABLE statements is complex and provides many different ways for doing the same thing. Some of these alternative syntaxes are supported mainly for compatibility with previous versions of DB2 or with other products. This book describes a simplified syntax for CREATE TABLE and ALTER TABLE that provides a consistent and relatively simple way to create and name each kind of constraint. The simplified syntax gives you access to all the features of V2 and is recommended for new applications. However, since V2 is tolerant of other syntactic forms, you should consult the *DB2 SQL Reference* if you are migrating an existing application to V2.

The CREATE TABLE statement allows you to define a constraint either as a *column constraint* or as a *table constraint*. A column constraint is a constraint that applies to a single column of a table and is defined as part of the definition of that column. For example, if an integer column named C1 is the primary key of a given table, that column might be defined by the syntax C1 INTEGER NOT NULL PRIMARY KEY. A table constraint, on the other hand, may involve more than one column of a table. For example, if the primary key of a table includes columns C1 and C2, the definition of the table might contain the following table constraint: PRIMARY KEY (C1, C2).

In the syntax diagrams below, *table-name* represents a two-part name, such as ACCOUNTS.PAYABLE. The first part of the name is a schema name, and the second part identifies the table within the schema. If the schema name is omitted, it defaults to the userid under which the statement is being compiled (for static SQL) or executed (for dynamic SQL). For example, if user SMITH creates a table named T1, the full name of the table becomes SMITH.T1.

Unlike table names, constraint names consist of a single part. Each constraint name must be unique among all the constraints attached to the same table.

5.2.1 **CREATE TABLE Statement**

The userid under which a CREATE TABLE statement is executed (or compiled, if it is a static statement) must hold SYSADM authority, DBADM authority, or both of the following:

- CREATETAB authority on the database in which the table is being created
- If the new table includes any foreign key constraints, CONTROL or REFERENCES privilege on the parent tables of these constraints

The syntax of a CREATE TABLE statement is shown below in several syntax diagrams. For examples of valid CREATE TABLE statements, see the example application in Section 5.4.

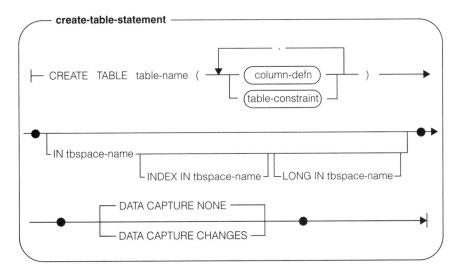

Notes:

- In the syntax diagram, *tbspace-name* represents the name of a tablespace, which is a unit of physical storage. The CREATE TABLE statement allows you to specify the tablespace in which your table will be stored and also allows you to specify separately the tablespaces to be used for indexes and large-object values in your table. You might choose to store indexes and large objects in a different tablespace from the rest of your table to increase the clustering of your data and improve performance. If you omit any tablespace specifications, the system will choose a tablespace for you. (Tablespaces are discussed in Section 8.1.1.)
- The clause DATA CAPTURE CHANGES is necessary if you want changes to your table to be propagated to other databases by the DataPropagator product.

This clause causes special entries to be made in the system log in support of data propagation. If you omit this clause or specify DATA CAPTURE NONE, no special entries are made in the log when changes are made to your table.

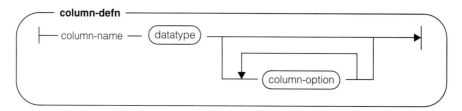

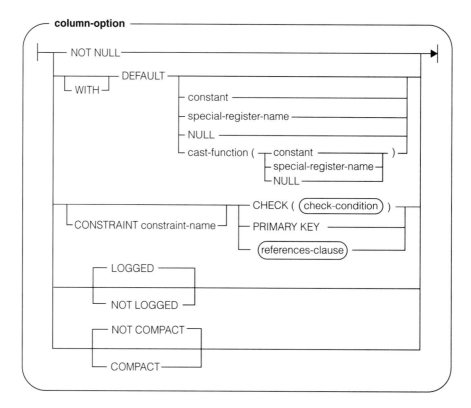

Notes:

- If no explicit default value is specified, the column default value is determined as shown in Table 5-1.[4]

---

4. Specification of explicit column default values is supported beginning with DB2 version 2.1.1.

- If no name is specified for a column constraint, the system will generate a name.

- A *check condition* is any predicate, or combination of predicates connected by AND/OR, that can be evaluated by examining a single row of the table. If a check constraint is specified as a column constraint, it may contain references only to the column to which it applies. For example, CHECK (BONUS < 5000) is a valid column constraint that applies to the BONUS column. CHECK (BONUS < SALARY), on the other hand, must be specified as a table constraint, because it involves more than one column.

- If the PRIMARY KEY option is specified for a column, the NOT NULL option must also be specified for that column.

- The LOGGED/NOT LOGGED and COMPACT/NOT COMPACT options apply only to columns of large-object datatypes (Blob, Clob, Dbclob, and distinct types based on these datatypes). (These options are described in Section 4.1.1.) The default values for these options are LOGGED and NOT COMPACT.

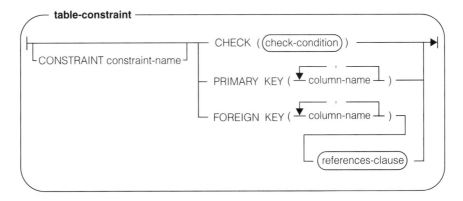

Notes:

- If no name is specified for a table constraint, the system will generate a name.

- A *check condition* is any predicate, or combination of predicates connected by AND/OR, that can be evaluated by examining a single row of the table on which the check constraint is defined.

- If a primary key is specified, all the columns in the primary key must have been declared NOT NULL.

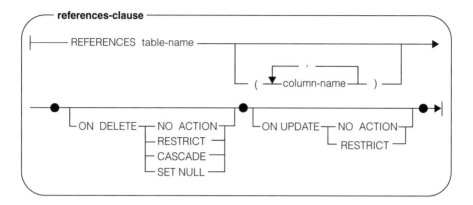

Notes:

- The REFERENCES clause names the parent table of a referential integrity relationship; the referenced columns are always the primary key of the parent table. If column names are included in the REFERENCES clause, they must be the primary key columns of the parent table.

- Default actions are ON DELETE NO ACTION and ON UPDATE NO ACTION.

The syntax of a datatype specification is shown on the following page.

Notes on datatype syntax:

- The maximum length of a Char, Varchar, Blob, or Clob datatype is specified in bytes; the maximum length of a Graphic, Vargraphic, or Dbclob datatype is specified in characters, each of which occupies two bytes.

- In specifying the maximum lengths of Blob and Clob datatypes, the suffixes K, M, and G represent 2^{10} bytes (1 kilobyte), 2^{20} bytes (1 megabyte), and 2^{30} bytes (1 gigabyte), respectively. In specifying the maximum length of a Dbclob datatype, these suffixes have similar meanings but refer to the maximum number of two-byte characters.

- For the Char and Graphic datatypes, the default length is 1.

- For the Decimal datatype, the precision indicates the total number of digits and the scale indicates the number of digits to the right of the decimal point. The default precision is 5 and the default scale is 0.

- The FOR BIT DATA option indicates that a character-string datatype is to be used for storing binary data and is not associated with a particular character set or code page.

- Many of the built-in datatypes have synonyms that can be used in place of their proper names. These synonyms are summarized in Table 5-2.

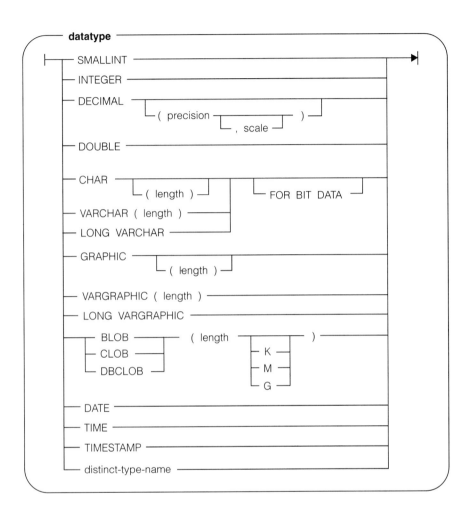

TABLE 5-2: Synonyms for Built-in Datatypes

Type Name	Synonyms
INTEGER	INT
DOUBLE	DOUBLE PRECISION, FLOAT
DECIMAL	DEC, NUMERIC, NUM
CHAR	CHARACTER
VARCHAR	CHARACTER VARYING, CHAR VARYING

TABLE 5-3: System Catalog Tables That Describe Tables, Columns, and Constraints

Catalog Table	Object Described
TABLES	Tables and views
COLUMNS	Columns of tables and views
TABCONST	Constraints and the tables to which they apply
CHECKS	Check constraints
COLCHECKS	Columns that participate in check constraints
REFERENCES	Referential integrity relationships (foreign key constraints)
KEYCOLUSE	Columns that participate in primary keys and foreign keys

The system catalog tables for each database maintain a complete description of all the tables in the database, as well as the columns they contain and the constraints that apply to them. These catalog tables (which are really views of underlying tables) are found in the SYSCAT schema and are described in Appendix D. The catalog tables that describe tables, columns, and constraints are summarized in Table 5-3.

5.2.2 ALTER TABLE Statement

The ALTER TABLE statement is used to add a column to an existing table or to add a constraint to or drop a constraint from an existing table. The userid under which an ALTER TABLE statement is executed (or compiled, if it is a static statement) must hold SYSADM authority, DBADM authority, or all of the following:

- CONTROL or ALTER privilege on the table being altered
- If any foreign key constraints are being added or dropped, CONTROL or REFERENCES privilege on the parent tables of these constraints
- If a primary key is being dropped, CONTROL or ALTER privilege on any descendant tables of the table being altered (that is, any tables that are linked to it by foreign key constraints)

The syntax of an ALTER TABLE statement is shown below. Some of the elements used in the ALTER TABLE syntax diagram are used also by the CREATE TABLE statement and were explained in Section 5.2.1.

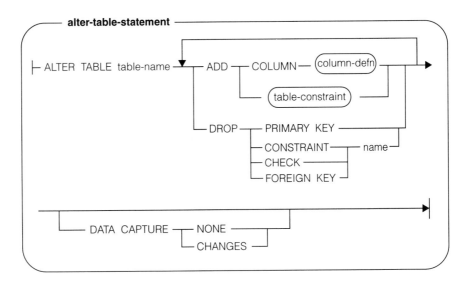

Notes:

- When a column is added to a table and the column definition has the NOT NULL option, it must also have a DEFAULT clause. The default value is used for the value of the new column in the existing rows of the table.

- Adding a primary key, foreign key, or check constraint to a table causes the constraint to be checked against all existing data (unless the table is in Check Pending state); if it fails, the ALTER TABLE is rolled back. (Check Pending state is described in Section 8.5.5.)

- The DATA CAPTURE phrase allows you to turn on and off the saving of special information in the system log in support of data propagation.

The following are examples of valid ALTER TABLE statements:

```
ALTER TABLE equip
    ADD COLUMN description Varchar(20)
    ADD COLUMN value Decimal(8,2);
ALTER TABLE equip
    ADD CONSTRAINT check1 CHECK (value < 500000);
ALTER TABLE equip
    DROP CONSTRAINT check1;
```

TIP: If your ALTER TABLE statement has multiple ADD and DROP clauses, remember that there are no commas between the clauses.

TIP: You can add a primary key constraint to an existing table only if all the columns in the primary key were declared NOT NULL when the table was created. If some of the columns in the desired primary key do not have the NOT NULL property (even if they do not in fact contain any nulls), you are out of luck, since there is no way to add the NOT NULL property to an existing column.

5.3 TRIGGERS

A trigger is like a genie that you can place inside the database, to wake up and do your bidding whenever a certain event takes place. You can tell your genie to wake up and execute a series of SQL statements whenever data is inserted, deleted, or updated in a specific table. Triggers are powerful tools that can be used to enforce the validity of data in ways that cannot be done by a simple constraint. They can also be used to make sure that whenever a certain action occurs in the database, another action automatically occurs. This automatic action can affect any database table or even the world outside the database. Triggers are ideal for keeping audit trails, detecting exceptional conditions, and maintaining relationships in the database.

When you create a trigger, you will need to specify the following parts:

1. *Name.* Like a table, a trigger has a two-part name that includes a schema name. The trigger name must be unique within its schema (not just within the table to which it is attached).

2. *Triggering event.* The triggering event is the event that causes the trigger to be activated. In general, a triggering event is the insertion, deletion, or update of rows in a specific table. If the triggering event is an update, it may apply to all columns of the table or only to specific named columns. A trigger is said to be *attached to* the table named in its triggering event. A trigger is always attached to a real table, not a view. (Of course, if a trigger is attached to a table, it is activated when the table is manipulated through a view defined on it.)

3. *Activation time.* The activation time of a trigger is always either *before* or *after* its triggering event takes place in the database.

The following are some examples of triggering events and activation times:

```
BEFORE INSERT ON books
AFTER DELETE ON voters
AFTER UPDATE ON inventory
AFTER UPDATE OF jobcode, salary ON emp
```

There is no limit on the number of triggers that can be attached to a table. Multiple triggers that have the same triggering event and activation time will be executed in the order of their creation.

4. *Granularity.* The SQL statement that caused the triggering event may insert, delete, or update multiple rows in the database. The definer of the trigger can specify whether the trigger is to be activated only once for such an SQL statement or once for each row that is modified. We will refer to this distinction as the *granularity* of the trigger, and we will refer to the two types of triggers as *statement triggers* and *row triggers*, respectively. The definition of a statement trigger contains the phrase FOR EACH STATEMENT, and the definition of a row trigger contains the phrase FOR EACH ROW. If an SQL INSERT, DELETE, or UPDATE statement operates on a table but modifies zero rows, it may activate a statement trigger but will not activate a row trigger.

As you can see, there are three ways to classify triggers: according to their activation time (*before* or *after*), their trigger event (*insert, delete,* or *update*), and their granularity (*statement* or *row*). A trigger is sometimes referred to by one or more of its properties, as in a *before trigger*, an *after update trigger*, or a *before insert row trigger.*

Before triggers must always be row triggers (before statement triggers are not supported by V2).

5. *Transition variables.* When a trigger is activated, it often needs to make use of information about the specific database change that activated it. For example, an update row trigger may need to see the data values in the updated row, both before and after the update. Similarly, a delete statement trigger may need to see all the rows that were deleted by the triggering statement. This kind of transitional information can be made available to the trigger in the form of *transition variables*. There are four kinds of transition variables:

- The *old row variable* represents the value of the modified row before the triggering event.
- The *new row variable* represents the value of the modified row after the triggering event.
- The *old table variable* represents a hypothetical read-only table containing all the modified rows as they appeared before the triggering event.
- The *new table variable* represents a hypothetical table containing all the modified rows as they appeared after the triggering event.

When defining a trigger, you can define transition variables in an optional REFERENCING clause, giving them any names you like. A trigger definition may include more than one transition variable but at most one variable of each type. In the REFERENCING clauses shown below, the first two examples define row transition variables and the last two examples define table transition variables.

```
REFERENCING NEW AS newrow
REFERENCING OLD AS lastyear NEW AS thisyear
REFERENCING OLD_TABLE AS oldtable
REFERENCING NEW_TABLE AS arrivals
```

Row transition variables may be used in a trigger definition as though they were correlation names. Table transition variables may be used in a trigger definition as though they were table names (but only for the purpose of querying these tables, not for modifying them). For example, using the transition variables defined in the second example above, an after update trigger might refer to salary values before and after the update as oldrow.salary and newrow.salary. Or, using the transition variable defined in the third example above, an after delete trigger might compute the number of rows that were deleted by the subquery (SELECT count(*) FROM oldtable).

For certain types of triggers, only some of the four possible transition variables can be used. For example, insert triggers can use new transition variables but not old transition variables, because a newly inserted row has no old value. For a similar reason, delete triggers can use old transition variables but not new transition variables. Table 5-4 summarizes the types of transition variables that are valid for each type of trigger.

It is interesting to note that old and new table transition variables can be used in an after row trigger. Even though such a trigger is executed once for each modified row, the *set* of rows to be modified is computed (and the old and

TABLE 5-4: Transition Variables Used by Various Types of Triggers

Triggering Event and Activation Time	Row Trigger Can Use . . .	Statement Trigger Can Use . . .
BEFORE INSERT	New row	(Invalid)
BEFORE UPDATE	Old row, new row	(Invalid)
BEFORE DELETE	Old row	(Invalid)
AFTER INSERT	New row New table	New table
AFTER UPDATE	Old row, new row Old table, new table	Old table, new table
AFTER DELETE	Old row Old table	Old table

new table transition variables are defined) before any of the after row triggers are executed.

6. *Trigger condition.* A trigger condition is a test that evaluates to true, false, or unknown. It may contain one or more predicates, much like a WHERE clause (though a trigger condition starts with WHEN instead of WHERE). A trigger condition can include transition variables and subqueries, as in the following examples:

```
WHEN (newrow.salary < oldrow.salary)
WHEN (newrow.salary > (SELECT max(salary)
                       FROM emp
                       WHERE jobcode = newrow.jobcode) )
WHEN (SELECT count(*) FROM oldtable) > 100
```

When the trigger is activated, the trigger body is executed only if the trigger condition is true. For example, the first trigger condition given above specifies that the trigger body should be executed only if the SALARY value after the update is less than the SALARY value before the update. If no trigger condition is specified, the trigger body is executed unconditionally.

7. *Trigger body.* The trigger body consists of one or more SQL statements. Depending on the type of trigger, there may be some restrictions (which we will discuss below) on the types of statements that can be used in the trigger body. If the trigger body contains more than one SQL statement, the statements are enclosed between BEGIN ATOMIC and END and are separated by semicolons. The word ATOMIC indicates that a trigger body behaves like an atomic compound SQL statement (discussed in Section 2.7.13). If any statement in the trigger body fails, the triggering SQL statement and all actions of all triggers activated by that statement are rolled back and an SQLCODE of –723 (SQLSTATE 09000) is returned for the triggering statement. The SQLCODE and SQLSTATE generated by the failing statement (inside the trigger body) are also returned as part of the error message (contained in the SQLERRMC field of the SQLCA structure). Although the triggering statement is rolled back, the current transaction is still considered to be in progress, and the application is free to execute additional statements, commit, or roll back the transaction.

5.3.1 Creating and Dropping Triggers

The syntax of a CREATE TRIGGER statement is shown below. Remember that a trigger name is a two-part name and that its schema name (first part) defaults to the current userid.

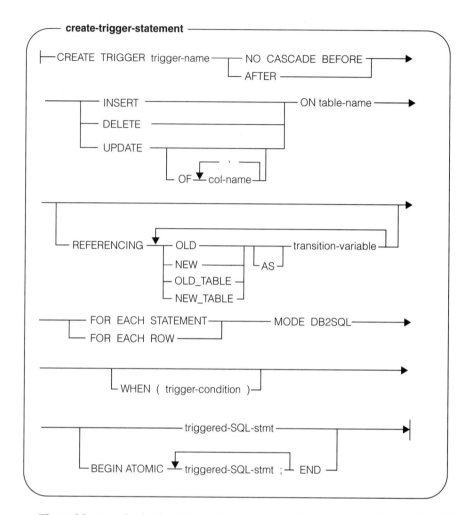

The table to which the trigger is attached (that is, the table in the ON clause) must be a real table (not a view), and it must not be a system catalog table.

The required phrase NO CASCADE in the creation of a before trigger serves as a reminder that a before trigger never activates another before trigger.

The required phrase MODE DB2SQL represents the trigger execution mode currently implemented by V2. This phrase ensures that your existing applications will not be affected if alternative trigger execution modes are added to the product in the future.

The user who executes a CREATE TRIGGER statement must have DBADM authority, SYSADM authority, or all of the following:

- ALTER privilege on the table to which the trigger is attached
- Sufficient privileges to execute all the SQL statements in the trigger body
- SELECT privilege on the table to which the trigger is attached, if the CREATE TRIGGER statement contains any transition variables
- SELECT privilege on all the tables referenced in the trigger condition

SYSADM or DBADM authority is required to create a trigger with a schema name that is not the same as the current authid.

The body of a trigger is always executed under the authority of the user who created the trigger, not the authority of the user who happened to activate it. For example, suppose that user Barney defines a trigger on insert to the PROGRAMS table, which updates a row in the BUDGET table by adding the cost of each new program. In order to define this trigger, Barney must possess UPDATE privilege on the BUDGET table. Now suppose that user Wilma inserts a new entry into the PROGRAMS table. Of course, in order to do this, Wilma must have INSERT privilege on PROGRAMS, but she need not possess UPDATE privilege on BUDGET, even though her action will cause BUDGET to be updated by activating Barney's trigger.

The definition of each trigger is recorded in the system catalog table named TRIGGERS. A descriptive comment can be added to this catalog table by using the COMMENT statement described in Section 2.8.7.

When a trigger is no longer needed, it can be dropped by using the DROP statement described in Section 2.8.6. In order to drop a trigger, a user must possess SYSADM or DBADM authority or must be the owner of the trigger (the user whose userid matches the schema name of the trigger). The following is an example of a statement used to drop a trigger:

```
DROP TRIGGER emp_trig1;
```

Before continuing with our discussion of triggers, we will introduce two special SQL statements that can be used only inside the body of a trigger: the *assignment statement* and the *SIGNAL statement*.

5.3.2 Assignment Statement

Assignment statements are used only in before triggers. The usual purpose of a before trigger is to modify the behavior of an insert or update statement. A before trigger can accomplish this purpose by using an assignment statement to assign values to the columns of the "new row" that is about to be inserted or updated.

An assignment statement begins with the keyword SET and looks much like the SET clause of an UPDATE statement. The syntax of an assignment statement is as follows:

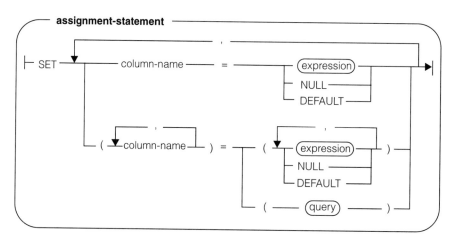

The column names on the left side of the equal sign in an assignment state-ment must match the names of columns in the table to which the trigger is attached. The effect of the assignment statement is to replace the values of the "new row"—that is, the row that is about to be inserted or updated—with the values on the right side of the equal sign. By modifying the values of the "new row," a before trigger can generate missing values automatically or override the values that were provided by the triggering SQL statement.

Since only the "new row" can be modified by an assignment statement, you might suppose that the system would not need any further qualification of the column names on the left side of the assignments. Nevertheless, V2 enforces the following rules:

1. Any before trigger that contains an assignment statement must define a "new row" transition variable.

2. If the trigger defines only a "new row" transition variable, column names in assignment statements (on both sides of the equal sign) may be unqualified and implicitly reference the "new row."

3. If the trigger defines both a "new row" and an "old row" transition variable, all column names in assignment statements (on both sides of the equal sign) must be qualified by a transition variable. Of course, the column names on the left side must be qualified by the "new row" variable.

The values on the right side of the equal sign in an assignment statement are the values that are being assigned to the columns of the new row. General expressions may be used, containing arithmetic operators and functions, either built-in or user-defined. The word DEFAULT represents the default value of the column being assigned. There must be a one-to-one correspon-dence between the values and the columns to which they are being assigned.

If a subquery is used on the right side of the equal sign to generate a list of column values, the subquery must return only a single row. If an assignment statement assigns values to multiple columns, all the right-hand sides are evaluated before any of the assignments are done.

The following are examples of valid assignment statements:

```
SET newrow.startdate = CURRENT DATE;
SET deptno = 'A52', bonus = 1000;
SET salary = (SELECT min(salary)
                FROM emp
                WHERE jobcode = newrow.jobcode);
```

The user who creates a trigger containing an assignment statement must have either SYSADM or DBADM authority or both of the following:

- UPDATE privilege for the columns referenced on the left side of the assignment statement
- SELECT privilege for the columns or tables referenced on the right side of the assignment statement

5.3.3 SIGNAL Statement

The purpose of a SIGNAL statement is to raise an error condition and to roll back the effects of an SQL statement. A SIGNAL statement can be used in either a before trigger or an after trigger. It rolls back the effects of the triggering SQL statement,[5] and also rolls back all the changes caused by triggers and cascading referential integrity relationships invoked by the triggering SQL statement. However, the SIGNAL statement leaves a transaction in progress, so the user or application program can still choose to commit or roll back the other statements in the transaction.

The syntax of a SIGNAL statement is as follows:

---

5. A SIGNAL statement may be executed by a trigger that was activated by another trigger or by a cascading referential integrity action. In this case, the SIGNAL statement rolls back not just the specific event that activated its trigger but also the user's original SQL statement, including all the triggers and cascading actions that it invoked.

The state specified in a SIGNAL statement must be expressed in the form of a character-string literal containing exactly five characters, such as '70ABC'. The five characters must all be digits or uppercase letters. In choosing an SQL-STATE to represent a user-defined error condition, you should avoid values that have been reserved by IBM or by the SQL92 Standard. You can easily avoid conflicts by choosing an SQLSTATE whose first character is a digit between 7 and 9 or a letter between I and Z, inclusive.[6] The message specified by a SIGNAL statement can be any expression that evaluates to a string of up to 70 characters.

When a SIGNAL statement is executed inside the body of a trigger, the triggering SQL statement (and all changes derived from it) are rolled back. The application that executed the triggering statement receives the SQLSTATE specified by the SIGNAL statement and an SQLCODE of –438. The message specified by the SIGNAL statement is also returned to the calling application (in the SQLERRMC field of the SQLCA structure).

The following are examples of valid SIGNAL statements:

```
SIGNAL SQLSTATE '70001' ('No such jobcode');
SIGNAL SQLSTATE 'PRO99'
          ('Invalid project: ' || char(newrow.project) );
```

5.3.4 Before Triggers

As you have seen, one of the ways of classifying triggers involves before triggers, which are activated before the triggering SQL statement is executed, and after triggers, which are activated after the triggering SQL statement is executed. Although before triggers and after triggers are syntactically similar, they are quite different in purpose and in the SQL statements that can be used in their trigger bodies. Before triggers can be thought of as a powerful form of constraint, whereas after triggers often contain more general application logic. Because of these important differences, I discuss before triggers and after triggers separately.

I illustrate before and after triggers by writing some sample triggers that operate on a version of the familiar table named EMP, containing employee records. In this chapter, let us assume that the EMP table contains the following columns:

---

6. Certain other SQLSTATE values are also permitted and are described in the *DB2 SQL Reference*.

EMP

EMPNO	NAME	DEPTNO	JOBCODE	PROJECT	MANAGER	SALARY	BONUS

As you have seen, before triggers are always row triggers. Before triggers are usually used to "condition" data values before they are entered into the database by an INSERT or UPDATE statement. For example, suppose that a given column of a table is subject to a NOT NULL constraint. A before trigger can be used to generate a value for that column whenever data is inserted into the table, using an algorithm that is not limited to the system-provided default value. This kind of data conditioning must be done by a before trigger rather than by an after trigger, because an after trigger would be too late. (By the time an after trigger could be activated, the insert statement would already have failed by violating the constraint.)

TIP: If a column is declared NOT NULL and its default values are generated by a before trigger, the definition of the column must also include a DEFAULT clause. The specified default value will be generated for the column and then overridden by the default value provided by the before trigger. If you specify NOT NULL but omit the DEFAULT clause, the system will not allow a row to be inserted into the table unless it contains an explicit value for the column, and the before trigger will never be activated.

Since before triggers are intended for conditioning of data that is about to be entered into the database, they are not allowed to manipulate the database itself. For this reason, only the following kinds of SQL statements are permitted in the body of a before trigger:

Assignment (SET) statements that modify the "new row"

SELECT

VALUES

SIGNAL

If your trigger needs to update the database in a more general way, using an SQL INSERT, DELETE, or UPDATE statement, you should write an after trigger rather than a before trigger. Since a before trigger never modifies the database directly, the execution of a before trigger can never activate another before trigger (this is the meaning of the required phrase NO CASCADE in the statement that creates a before trigger). However, if a before trigger modifies a column of the new row that was not modified by the original SQL statement, it may enlarge the list of after triggers that will be activated after the statement has been executed.

SELECT and VALUES statements are used in triggers mainly for invoking functions that have some side effect such as sending a message or writing into a file. Often these functions will be user-defined.

 TIP: Suppose that you write a trigger that calls a function that performs some external action such as sending a message. If some statement that activates the trigger is executed and then rolled back, the database system has no way to undo the external action. Therefore, you must use such functions very carefully and provide your own mechanism to generate compensating external actions in the case of a rollback.

I will illustrate before triggers with several examples. The first example illustrates conditioning of data by automatically computing the starting salary and bonus of a newly hired employee, using a separate table of starting pay based on job code. This trigger might be used to enforce a company policy about starting pay, eliminating the necessity to embed this policy in every application program that inserts new employees. Note the use of the "new row" transition variable in the subquery.

```
CREATE TRIGGER emp_trig1
   NO CASCADE BEFORE INSERT ON emp
   REFERENCING NEW AS newrow
   FOR EACH ROW MODE DB2SQL
   SET (salary, bonus) =
     (SELECT salary, bonus
      FROM startingPay
      WHERE jobcode = newrow.jobcode);
```

It is possible for a before trigger to override the values that were provided by the triggering SQL statement. For example, the following before trigger limits salary increases to 50%. Salary increases of less than 50% are applied without modification. In this example, the assignment statement is required to use the "new row" transition variable on the left side of the equal sign (because both "old row" and "new row" transition variables are defined).

```
CREATE TRIGGER emp_trig2
   NO CASCADE BEFORE UPDATE OF salary ON emp
   REFERENCING OLD AS oldrow NEW AS newrow
   FOR EACH ROW MODE DB2SQL
   WHEN (newrow.salary > 1.5 * oldrow.salary)
   SET newrow.salary = 1.5 * oldrow.salary;
```

Of course, before triggers can be used to detect exceptional conditions and roll back SQL statements that attempt to modify the database in anomalous ways. Triggers that detect exceptional conditions are similar to check constraints but are more powerful, because they are not limited to examining the new values of a single row. The following example illustrates a trigger that prevents the deletion of any employee whose importance, as computed by a user-defined function, exceeds a given value. Triggers such as this one can be used to define and enforce corporate policies in a central way that applies to all existing and future applications.

```
CREATE TRIGGER emp_trig3
    NO CASCADE BEFORE DELETE ON emp
    REFERENCING OLD AS oldrow
    FOR EACH ROW MODE DB2SQL
    WHEN (importance(oldrow.jobcode, oldrow.project) > 20)
    SIGNAL SQLSTATE '70010' ('We need this person');
```

At first glance, it seems that a before trigger could be used to generate a primary key automatically whenever a new row is inserted into a table. The automatic generation of primary keys, however, is harder than it looks and cannot in general be done with triggers. To see the problem, consider an ORDERS table with a primary key of ORDERNO. We would like to write a trigger to generate order numbers sequentially as rows are inserted into the table. A first try at such a trigger might be the following:

```
CREATE TRIGGER orders_trig1
    NO CASCADE BEFORE INSERT ON orders
    REFERENCING NEW AS newrow
    FOR EACH ROW MODE DB2SQL
    SET orderno =
        (SELECT max(orderno)
        FROM orders) + 1;
```

This trigger will encounter a problem when the first row is inserted into the empty ORDERS table. The subquery will try to find the maximum order number in the empty table and will return null. The trigger will then attempt to insert an order with a null order number, which will violate the NOT NULL constraint of the primary key. This problem can be fixed by modifying our CREATE TRIGGER statement as follows:

```
CREATE TRIGGER orders_trig2
    NO CASCADE BEFORE INSERT ON orders
    REFERENCING NEW AS newrow
    FOR EACH ROW MODE DB2SQL
    SET orderno =
        COALESCE((SELECT max(orderno)
                    FROM orders) + 1, 1);
```

This trigger will run successfully as long as rows are inserted into the ORDERS table one at a time. However, if an SQL statement attempts to insert more than one order, all the orders inserted by the same statement will receive the same order number, and the primary key constraint will be violated.

5.3.5 After Triggers

Like before triggers, after triggers have triggering events, optional trigger conditions, and trigger bodies. However, after triggers differ from before triggers in the following ways:

1. An after trigger is executed only after the triggering SQL statement, and all its constraints, have been executed successfully. Thus, the after trigger sees the effects not only of the triggering statement but also of all the cascaded updates and deletions caused by any foreign key constraints that are invoked by the triggering statement. If more than one after trigger is activated by a given statement, each trigger can see the effects on the database that are caused by triggers that were activated before it.

2. After triggers can have a granularity of either FOR EACH STATEMENT or FOR EACH ROW.

3. An after trigger is not restricted to modifying the row that triggered it. An after trigger can operate on any table in the database and can contain any of the following kinds of SQL statements:
INSERT
DELETE
UPDATE
SELECT
VALUES
SIGNAL

Since after triggers can modify the database directly, execution of an after trigger can activate other triggers. To guard against loops, the system imposes a limit of 16 levels on the nesting of triggers.

After triggers are often used to implement some desired semantic behavior of stored data. Because there are fewer restrictions on the body of an after trigger, they are more powerful than before triggers. I will illustrate the use of after triggers with several examples.

The first example is a trigger that could be expressed either as a before trigger or as an after trigger. It enforces a policy (sadly, true only for our hypothetical company) that salaries never decrease. Furthermore, whenever an update is detected that attempts to decrease some employee's salary, the trigger invokes a user-defined function called logEvent. This example illustrates how a trigger can interact with the world outside the database. The logEvent function, which is written in C, can take some action such as writing into a file or sending a message (however, you should remember that functions are executed on the server machine, so that is where any actions will take place). In this example, assume that the logEvent function takes three parameters: a string identifying the type of event, a timestamp, and another string that provides additional details. Of course, the user who wrote the logEvent function can define its parameters and its actions in any way desired, using the techniques for defining an external function described in Chapter 4. The trigger in this example uses a VALUES statement when it needs to invoke a function without accessing a table.

```
CREATE TRIGGER emp_trig4
   AFTER UPDATE OF salary ON emp
   REFERENCING OLD AS oldrow NEW AS newrow
   FOR EACH ROW MODE DB2SQL
   WHEN (newrow.salary < oldrow.salary)
   BEGIN ATOMIC
      VALUES (logEvent('Salary decrease',
                         CURRENT TIMESTAMP, oldrow.empno));
      SIGNAL SQLSTATE '70011'
         ('Salary decrease for employee ' || oldrow.empno);
   END
```

The next after trigger example will show how two or more tables can be linked together in such a way that updates to one table automatically trigger updates to another. Assume that the database contains a table named TEMPS that is updated periodically to contain the current temperature at various locations. The TEMPS table contains columns named PLACE and TEMP, and the PLACE column is the primary key. On a typical winter day, the contents of the table might look like this:

TEMPS

PLACE	TEMP
Anchorage	−15
Denver	25
Madison	8
Miami	82
San Francisco	65
Washington	35

We wish to create a trigger that will automatically maintain an auxiliary table, named EXTREMES, that keeps records of the maximum and minimum temperatures ever encountered in each place, as well as the dates on which they occurred. The structure of the auxiliary table is as follows:

EXTREMES

PLACE	HIGHTEMP	HIGHDATE	LOWTEMP	LOWDATE

First, we will create the EXTREMES table and populate it with a row for each place recorded in the TEMPS table. Each row of EXTREMES will initially have nulls for its high and low temperatures and their respective dates. The statements used to create and populate the table are as follows:

```
CREATE TABLE extremes
   (place    Varchar(20) NOT NULL,
    hightemp Integer,
    highdate Date,
    lowtemp  Integer,
    lowdate  Date,
    PRIMARY KEY (place) );
INSERT INTO extremes(place)
   SELECT place FROM temps;
```

Next, we will write a pair of triggers that inspect each update to the TEMPS table and copy the temperature and the current date into the proper cells of the EXTREMES table if a new high or low temperature occurs (or if the relevant cell of EXTREMES contains a null, indicating that no high or low temperature is yet recorded).

```
CREATE TRIGGER temps_trig1
   AFTER UPDATE ON temps
   REFERENCING NEW AS newrow
   FOR EACH ROW MODE DB2SQL
   WHEN (newrow.temp >
            (SELECT hightemp
             FROM    extremes
             WHERE   place = newrow.place)
        OR
          (SELECT hightemp
           FROM extremes
           WHERE place = newrow.place) IS NULL )
   UPDATE extremes
         SET hightemp = newrow.temp,
             highdate = CURRENT DATE
         WHERE place = newrow.place;

CREATE TRIGGER temps_trig2
   AFTER UPDATE ON temps
   REFERENCING NEW AS newrow
   FOR EACH ROW MODE DB2SQL
   WHEN (newrow.temp <
            (SELECT lowtemp
             FROM    extremes
             WHERE   place = newrow.place)
        OR
          (SELECT lowtemp
           FROM extremes
           WHERE place = newrow.place) IS NULL )
   UPDATE extremes
         SET lowtemp = newrow.temp,
             lowdate = CURRENT DATE
         WHERE place = newrow.place;
```

The triggers defined above will maintain the EXTREMES table properly when rows of the TEMPS table are updated, but we still have a problem to solve: what happens when new places are added to the TEMPS table, or when old places are deleted?

When a new place is added to the TEMPS table (by inserting a new row, since PLACE is the primary key), we can make sure the same place is added to the EXTREMES table by creating another trigger. The trigger will insert a row into EXTREMES, using the initial temperature of the new place as both the high and the low temperatures.

```
CREATE TRIGGER temps_trig3
   AFTER INSERT ON temps
   REFERENCING NEW AS newrow
   FOR EACH ROW MODE DB2SQL
   INSERT INTO extremes(place, hightemp, highdate,
                                    lowtemp, lowdate)
      VALUES(newrow.place, newrow.temp, CURRENT DATE,
                     newrow.temp, CURRENT DATE);
```

When a row is deleted from TEMPS, we could choose to keep the corresponding row in EXTREMES or to delete it. If our policy is to delete rows from EXTREMES that have no matching row in TEMPS, we can take advantage of the fact that PLACE is the primary key of TEMPS. The following foreign key constraint will ensure that when a place is deleted from TEMPS, it is also deleted from EXTREMES:

```
ALTER TABLE extremes
   ADD CONSTRAINT fk1 FOREIGN KEY(place) REFERENCES temps
      ON DELETE CASCADE;
```

After triggers are very well suited for maintaining an *audit trail*, or record of updates that have been made to the database. We will consider a very simple example of how a set of after statement triggers could be used to maintain an audit trail for a specific table. Suppose that our database contains a table called ACCOUNTS and that we wish to keep a record of all changes that are made to this table. Suppose further that, in this example, it is sufficient to record the user making the change, the type of the change and when it occurred, and the number of rows that were changed. First, we create an auxiliary table named ACCOUNT_CHANGES in which the changes will be recorded. The structure of this table and the statement that is used to create it are shown below:

ACCOUNT_CHANGES

TYPE	WHEN	BYWHOM	NROWS

```
CREATE TABLE account_changes
   (type   Char(1),
    when   Timestamp,
    bywhom Char(8),
    nrows  Integer);
```

Next, we create a set of three after triggers that link the ACCOUNT_CHANGES table to the ACCOUNTS table in such a way that any changes to ACCOUNTS are automatically journalled in ACCOUNT_CHANGES. Notice that, since these triggers record aggregate changes rather than specific values, they use table transition variables rather than row transition variables. Notice also that the insert and update triggers use new table variables and that the delete trigger uses an old table variable.

```
CREATE TRIGGER account_trig1
    AFTER INSERT ON accounts
    REFERENCING NEW_TABLE AS newtable
    FOR EACH STATEMENT MODE DB2SQL
    INSERT INTO account_changes(type, when, bywhom, nrows)
        VALUES('I', CURRENT TIMESTAMP, USER,
            (SELECT COUNT(*) FROM newtable) );

CREATE TRIGGER account_trig2
    AFTER UPDATE ON accounts
    REFERENCING NEW_TABLE AS newtable
    FOR EACH STATEMENT MODE DB2SQL
    INSERT INTO account_changes(type, when, bywhom, nrows)
        VALUES('U', CURRENT TIMESTAMP, USER,
            (SELECT COUNT(*) FROM newtable) );

CREATE TRIGGER account_trig3
    AFTER DELETE ON accounts
    REFERENCING OLD_TABLE AS oldtable
    FOR EACH STATEMENT MODE DB2SQL
    INSERT INTO account_changes(type, when, bywhom, nrows)
        VALUES('D', CURRENT TIMESTAMP, USER,
            (SELECT COUNT(*) FROM oldtable) );
```

The three triggers shown above will make entries in the ACCOUNT_CHANGES table to record all INSERT, UPDATE, and DELETE statements that apply to the ACCOUNTS table, including statements that did not actually modify any rows (these will result in entries with NROWS = 0).

5.3.6 Recursive Triggers

As we have seen, a trigger body may apply some updates to the database, and these updates may in turn cause more triggers to be executed. If the updates applied by a particular trigger can cause that same trigger to be executed again, we say that the trigger is *recursive*. Great care is needed in writing recursive triggers, because they can easily lead to loops or to statements that are too complex for the system to handle.

We will illustrate recursive triggers by a simple example. Suppose that we decide to record, for each employee in our organization, the total number of other employees that the employee manages, either directly or indirectly. We will add a new column named SPAN to the EMP table for this purpose. A high-level manager might be responsible for a multilevel "tree" of employees, and the total number of employees in this tree will be recorded in the SPAN column for the manager's row in EMP. The following statement might be used to add the desired new column:

```
ALTER TABLE emp ADD COLUMN span Integer WITH DEFAULT;
```

The WITH DEFAULT clause ensures that when new employees are added to the database, they receive an initial SPAN of zero, the system-provided default value for the Integer datatype.

After setting SPAN to the correct value for all our existing employees, we would like to create a series of triggers that will automatically maintain the SPAN column as employees are inserted, deleted, and moved from one manager to another. This might be done by the following triggers (note that we have chosen the ! character as a statement terminator in these examples, since the semicolon is used to separate individual statements inside one of the trigger bodies):

```
CREATE TRIGGER emp_hire
    AFTER INSERT ON emp
    REFERENCING NEW AS newrow
    FOR EACH ROW MODE DB2SQL
    UPDATE emp
        SET span = span + 1
        WHERE empno = newrow.manager!

CREATE TRIGGER emp_quit
    AFTER DELETE ON emp
    REFERENCING OLD AS oldrow
    FOR EACH ROW MODE DB2SQL
    UPDATE emp
        SET span = span - 1
        WHERE empno = oldrow.manager!

CREATE TRIGGER emp_transfer
    AFTER UPDATE OF manager ON emp
    REFERENCING OLD AS oldrow NEW AS newrow
    FOR EACH ROW MODE DB2SQL
    BEGIN ATOMIC
        UPDATE emp
        SET span = span - 1
        WHERE empno = oldrow.manager;
```

```
      UPDATE emp
      SET span = span + 1
      WHERE empno = newrow.manager;
   END!

CREATE TRIGGER emp_propagate
   AFTER UPDATE OF span ON emp
   REFERENCING OLD AS oldrow NEW AS newrow
   FOR EACH ROW MODE DB2SQL
   UPDATE emp
      SET span = span + newrow.span - oldrow.span
      WHERE empno = newrow.manager!
```

To see how this set of triggers is recursive, consider what happens when an employee transfers from one manager to another. The update of the MAN-AGER column activates the trigger named EMP_TRANSFER, which increases the span of the new manager and decreases the span of the old manager. The updates to the SPAN column of the new and old manager, in turn, activate the trigger named EMP_PROPAGATE, which increases the span of the new second-level manager and decreases the span of the old second-level manager. Each time the EMP_PROPAGATE trigger updates the span of a manager, it activates itself again recursively to update the span of the manager at the next level. Since the compiler doesn't know how many levels of management are represented in the database, it generates a program that can handle 16 levels of recursion; if more levels than this are encountered when the statement is executed, a run-time error (SQLSTATE 54038, SQLCODE –724) results.

The reason that recursive triggers are so tricky is that you need to avoid a situation called *multiple recursion*. Multiple recursion occurs when a recursive trigger activates itself more than once, or when a recursive trigger activates more than one other recursive trigger. Whenever V2 encounters an SQL statement that invokes a multiply recursive trigger, it will fail to compile that statement, generating an error message such as "Statement too long or too complex." To see how easy it is to fall into the trap of multiple recursion, let us modify the previous example slightly. Suppose that, instead of recording the manager of each employee, we have a table that records the mother and father of each person. The table also records the total number of descendants of each person, using the following columns:

PERSONS

NAME   MOTHER   FATHER   DESCENDANTS

We would like to write a set of triggers that is activated when a new person is inserted into the table and that automatically adds one to the DESCEN-DANTS column of all the new person's ancestors. Such a set of triggers might be written as follows:

```
CREATE TRIGGER new_mother
    AFTER INSERT ON persons
    REFERENCING NEW AS newrow
    FOR EACH ROW MODE DB2SQL
    UPDATE persons
        SET descendants = descendants + 1
        WHERE name = newrow.mother;

CREATE TRIGGER new_father
    AFTER INSERT ON persons
    REFERENCING NEW AS newrow
    FOR EACH ROW MODE DB2SQL
    UPDATE persons
        SET descendants = descendants + 1
        WHERE name = newrow.father;

CREATE TRIGGER maternal_ancestor
    AFTER UPDATE OF descendants ON persons
    REFERENCING OLD AS oldrow NEW AS newrow
    FOR EACH ROW MODE DB2SQL
    UPDATE persons
        SET descendants = descendants +
            newrow.descendants - oldrow.descendants
        WHERE name = newrow.mother;

CREATE TRIGGER paternal_ancestor
    AFTER UPDATE OF descendants ON persons
    REFERENCING OLD AS oldrow NEW AS newrow
    FOR EACH ROW MODE DB2SQL
    UPDATE persons
        SET descendants = descendants +
            newrow.descendants - oldrow.descendants
        WHERE name = newrow.father;
```

To see why this set of triggers is multiply recursive, consider what happens when a new person is inserted into the table. Insertion of the new person acti-vates the NEW_MOTHER and NEW_FATHER triggers, which update the DESCENDANTS columns of the rows representing the new person's mother and father. The updates caused by these triggers, in turn, invoke the

MATERNAL_ANCESTOR and PATERNAL_ANCESTOR triggers, which update the DESCENDANTS columns of the rows representing the new person's four grandparents. Each of these updates invokes both the MATERNAL_ANCESTOR and PATERNAL_ANCESTOR triggers again, causing 2^n updates to occur at the nth level of the family tree. This exponential explosion of updates is too much for the system to handle, so any INSERT statement on the PERSONS table will fail to compile.

There does exist a way in which the set of triggers above can be rewritten so that it automatically maintains the ANCESTORS column in the PERSONS table without using multiple recursion. Finding this way is left as an exercise for the reader (hint: the method involves combining multiple triggers into a single trigger).

TIP: If you attempt to compile or execute an SQL statement that invokes one or more triggers and you receive the message "The statement is too long or too complex," that is the system's way of telling you that the statement, together with all the triggers that it invokes, exceeds the resources of the compiler. Examine the statement carefully, list all the triggers that it might invoke, and make sure that none of these triggers is multiply recursive. If you are sure that no multiply recursive triggers are invoked, you can sometimes get the statement to compile by increasing the database configuration parameters named APPLHEAPSZ, PCKCACHESZ, and STMTHEAP, which govern the amount of memory space available to the compiler. (Database configuration parameters are discussed in Section 8.3.4.) The statement in the following example specifies values for these configuration parameters in the database named MYDB, setting each configuration parameter to twice its default value:

```
UPDATE DATABASE CONFIGURATION FOR mydb
    USING APPLHEAPSZ 256 PCKCACHESZ 72 STMTHEAP 4096;
```

5.3.7 Comparing Constraints and Triggers

It is worth taking a moment at this point to consider the relative advantages of constraints and triggers for enforcing database rules. In general, it is better to use a constraint than to write a trigger that enforces the same rule, for the following reasons:

- Constraints are written in a less procedural way than triggers and give the system more opportunities for optimization.

- Constraints, unlike triggers, are enforced at the time of their creation for all existing data in the database.

- Constraints protect data against being placed into an invalid state by any kind of statement, whereas each trigger applies only to a specific kind of statement such as an update or delete.

On the other hand, triggers are more powerful than constraints and are able to enforce many rules that cannot be enforced by constraints. For example, any rule that requires knowledge of both "before" and "after" states, such as "salaries never decrease," requires the use of a trigger.

5.3.8 Interactions Among Constraints and Triggers

When using constraints and triggers, you should be aware of the order in which they will be enforced or executed during the processing of an SQL statement. A single INSERT, DELETE, or UPDATE statement may modify many rows of data. Each of these rows may be subject to a list of constraints and triggers. The sequence of events for an SQL statement that modifies multiple rows of a table is as follows:

1. The values of "old" transition variables are bound before any modifications are made to the data. These transition variables will not change during processing of the statement.

2. Before triggers are activated, in the order of their creation. The before triggers may modify the "new row" values that are about to be applied to the database.

3. The actual insertions, deletions, or updates (possibly modified by before triggers) are applied to the database, and constraints are checked. If any constraint is found to be violated, the statement is rolled back and has no effect. At the conclusion of this step, the database is in a *consistent state* (meaning that all constraints are enforced and all cascaded updates and deletions resulting from referential integrity relationships have taken place).

   Any constraint requiring uniqueness of column values (such as a primary key constraint or a unique index) is enforced as each individual row is updated. As an example of the consequences of this row-by-row enforcement, consider an SQL statement that adds one to every entry in a column named SERIALNO, which is declared to be a primary key. If duplicate SERIALNO values are generated during the row-by-row processing of the statement, the statement will fail, even though all the SERIALNO values would once again be unique if the statement were allowed to execute to completion. Thus, in some cases, an UPDATE statement may succeed or fail depending on the order in which rows are processed.

4. The values of "new" transition variables are bound after the statement has been executed and all its constraints checked, but before any after triggers have been executed.

5. Finally, the relevant after triggers are applied, in the order of their creation. Each after statement trigger is executed exactly once (even if no rows were modified). Each after row trigger is executed once for each row that was modi-

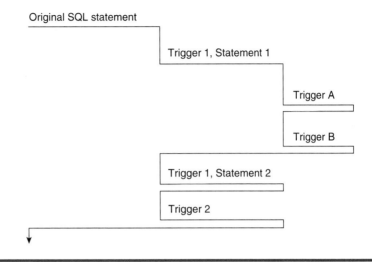

Figure 5-3: An Example of Trigger Activation Order

fied, either by the original statement or by a foreign key constraint with the CASCADE or SET NULL option.

An after trigger may contain SQL statements and may update the database. Each after trigger can see the effects on the database caused by other triggers that have executed previously.

Since the body of an after trigger consists of a series of SQL statements, each of these statements may, in turn, invoke constraints and triggers of its own. Each SQL statement inside a trigger is executed independently, using the same sequence of events listed here. A consequence of this design is that the database is enforced to be in a consistent state after the execution of each individual SQL statement inside a trigger body (and, of course, after the completion of the trigger itself).

The example in Figure 5-3 may help to visualize the execution order of statements in after triggers. In this example, an original SQL statement has activated after triggers named Trigger 1 and Trigger 2 (listed in the order of their creation). Inside Trigger 1 are two SQL statements, and the first of these statements activates Trigger A and Trigger B (again, listed in the order of their creation). The execution order of the original statement and the four triggers is shown in this figure in the form of a "path."

5.4 DESIGNING AN ACTIVE DATABASE

In this section, we will learn about the use of constraints and triggers by walking through the process of creating a database that uses many active data features as well as some user-defined datatypes and functions. Our database will serve a mail-order business that purchases items from suppliers and fills orders from customers. We will not write all the application programs needed by the business, but we will define a set of tables, constraints, and triggers that encapsulate certain policies that underlie the operation of the business.

The SQL statements that create the database for the mail-order business are shown in the STORE example program. The tables used in the STORE example are shown in Figure 5-4 and described further in the steps of the example program.

The STORE example contains SQL statements that could be placed in a file and submitted to the CLP for processing. Some of the statements create triggers whose bodies, in turn, contain multiple SQL statements separated by semicolons. Therefore it is necessary to choose a different delimiter character to separate the top-level SQL statements in the file. In the STORE example, we have used the "!" character for this purpose. The delimiter character for top-level SQL statements is declared to the CLP when the file is submitted for execution, as in the following command:

```
db2 -td! -f store.sql
```

TIP: The declared delimiter is interpreted by the CLP as ending an SQL statement only if it is the last character on a line. Thus, "!" can be used as a delimiter in the STORE example even though it occurs inside some of the CREATE FUNCTION statements, as long as any use of "!" inside a statement does not occur at the end of a line.

CUSTOMERS

| CUSTNO | CUSTNAME | ADDRESS | BALANCEDUE | CREDITLIMIT |

SUPPLIERS

| SUPPLIERNO | SUPPLIERNAME | ADDRESS | AMOUNTOWED |

INVENTORY

| ITEMNO | ITEMNAME | SUPPLIERNO | QUANTITYONHAND | UNITSALEPRICE |

| QUANTITYONORDER | UNITORDERPRICE | ORDERTHRESHOLD | MINIMUMORDER |

PURCHASES

| ORDERDATE | ORDERTIME | SUPPLIERNO | ITEMNO | QUANTITYORDERED |

| DATERECEIVED | QUANTITYRECEIVED | UNITPRICE |

SALES

| SALEDATE | SALETIME | CUSTNO | ITEMNO | QUANTITYSOLD | UNITPRICE | TOTALSALE |

Figure 5-4: Tables Used in the STORE Example

Steps for Example Program STORE: An Active Database

STEP 1: Before creating any tables for our business, we need to decide whether our application will need to define any distinct types. An obvious example of a specialized type of data used in business applications is Money. We have a choice of base datatypes to use for the underlying representation of Money. Perhaps the best fit is a Decimal datatype such as Decimal(8,2), but there is a problem with this datatype: since there is no equivalent of a Decimal datatype in C, we cannot pass Decimal data to a user-defined function written in C. To get around this limitation, we will define a Money datatype that uses Integer as its base datatype, and we will adopt the convention that Money is represented as an integer number of cents (for example, the integer 500 represents $5.00). Using this convention with a signed 32-bit integer as a base datatype allows us to represent amounts of money up to several millions of dollars, which will be sufficient for this application.

When we define a distinct type named Money for our business application, we also need to define the operators and functions that apply to the Money datatype. In this example, we decide that it is meaningful to add and subtract Money amounts, to multiply and divide Money amounts by integers, and to find the sum or maximum of a set of Money amounts, using the corresponding operators on the Integer base datatype. Other operators, such as multiplying Money by Money, will not be permitted. The SQL statements for defining the Money datatype and its operators and functions are shown in Step 1 of the example program.

STEP 2: In Step 2, we begin the process of defining our business database by creating the tables that represent our external contacts: customers and suppliers. We create a table called CUSTOMERS that records each customer's name, address, balance due, and credit limit. We also create a table called SUPPLIERS that records the name and address of each supplier, as well as the amount currently owed to that supplier by our store. The CUSTOMERS table has a CHECK constraint that requires each customer's credit limit to be greater than or equal to zero (unlike balance due, which is allowed to be negative if the customer has a credit balance).

Code for Example Program STORE: An Active Database

```
--
-- STEP 1:
--
CREATE DISTINCT TYPE Money AS Integer WITH COMPARISONS!

CREATE FUNCTION "+"(Money, Money) RETURNS Money
    SOURCE sysibm."+"(Integer, Integer)!

CREATE FUNCTION "-"(Money, Money) RETURNS Money
    SOURCE sysibm."-"(Integer, Integer)!

CREATE FUNCTION "*"(Money, Integer) RETURNS Money
    SOURCE sysibm."*"(Integer, Integer)!

CREATE FUNCTION "/"(Money, Integer) RETURNS Money
    SOURCE sysibm."/"(Integer, Integer)!

CREATE FUNCTION max(Money) RETURNS Money
    SOURCE sysibm.max(Integer)!

CREATE FUNCTION sum(Money) RETURNS Money
    SOURCE sysibm.sum(Integer)!

--
-- STEP 2:
--
CREATE TABLE customers
  (custno     Char(6) NOT NULL PRIMARY KEY,
   custname   Varchar(20),
   address    Varchar(20),
   balanceDue Money,
   creditLimit Money,
   CONSTRAINT check1
      CHECK (creditLimit >= Money(0)) )!

CREATE TABLE suppliers
  (supplierno   Char(4) NOT NULL PRIMARY KEY,
   suppliername Varchar(20),
   address      Varchar(20),
   amountOwed   Money)!
```

STEP 3: Next, we create a table called INVENTORY to record the stock of items held in our warehouse. Each row in the INVENTORY table represents a particular type of item. In each row we record the name of the item, the quantity that is on hand and on order, and the supplier from which we order the item. We record the unit sale price and the unit order price for the item and hope that the former is larger than the latter. Our policy is to reorder a new supply of each item when its quantity on hand falls below a certain threshold, and we record the order threshold and the minimum order quantity separately for each type of item. Since we wish our database to be normalized, we do not repeat the details of the suppliers in the INVENTORY table but simply use the supplier number as a key and declare a referential integrity relationship between the INVENTORY and SUPPLIERS tables. We may need to delete a supplier from the SUPPLIERS table while some items from that supplier remain in our inventory, so we declare a delete rule of SET NULL for the referential integrity relationship. (If a supplier is deleted, the SUPPLIERNO column in the corresponding rows of the INVENTORY table is set to null.)

STEP 4: Next, we create a table to record the details of the purchases we have made from our suppliers. Each row in the PURCHASES table represents an order for a certain kind of item placed with a certain supplier on a certain date and time. The table has columns named ORDERDATE and ORDERTIME, which we declare to be NOT NULL WITH DEFAULT so that the date and time will be generated automatically when rows are inserted into the table.

When a shipment of merchandise arrives from a supplier, we update the corresponding row of the PURCHASES table, entering the date received and quantity received. (Since we have some business experience, we allow for the fact that the quantity received may not be the same as the quantity ordered.)

We declare referential integrity relationships between the PURCHASES table and both the SUPPLIERS and INVENTORY tables. Since we really do not want to delete a supplier or an inventory item while an order is outstanding for that item, we will accept NO ACTION semantics (the default) for the delete rules of these relationships. Before a supplier or an inventory item can be deleted, we will need to remove all corresponding rows from the PURCHASES table.

```
--
-- STEP 3:
--
CREATE TABLE inventory
  (itemno          Char(7) NOT NULL PRIMARY KEY,
   itemname        Varchar(20) NOT NULL,
   supplierno      Char(4),
   quantityOnHand  Integer,
   unitSalePrice   Money,
   quantityOnOrder Integer,
   unitOrderPrice  Money,
   orderThreshold  Integer,
   minimumOrder    Integer,
   CONSTRAINT ifk1
      FOREIGN KEY (supplierno) REFERENCES suppliers
      ON DELETE SET NULL,
   CONSTRAINT check1
      CHECK (quantityOnHand >= 0
      AND quantityOnOrder >= 0
      AND orderThreshold >= 0
      AND minimumOrder >= 0) )!


--
-- STEP 4:
--
CREATE TABLE purchases
  (orderDate        Date NOT NULL WITH DEFAULT,
   orderTime        Time NOT NULL WITH DEFAULT,
   supplierno       Char(4),
   itemno           Char(7),
   quantityOrdered  Integer,
   dateReceived     Date,
   quantityReceived Integer,
   unitPrice        Money,
   CONSTRAINT pfk1
      FOREIGN KEY (supplierno) REFERENCES suppliers,
   CONSTRAINT pfk2
      FOREIGN KEY (itemno) REFERENCES inventory,
   CONSTRAINT check1
      CHECK (quantityOrdered > 0
      AND quantityReceived >= 0),
   CONSTRAINT check2
      CHECK (dateReceived >= orderDate) )!
```

STEP 5: In this step, we create a table to record the most important thing that happens in our business: sales. As in the PURCHASES table, we give the SALES table columns to record the date and time of each sale and declare these columns NOT NULL WITH DEFAULT so the dates and times will be generated automatically. The SALES table also records the customer and item numbers, quantity sold, unit price, and the total monetary amount of the sale.

Since a sale involves both a customer and some type of item from our inventory, we declare referential integrity relationships between the SALES table and both the CUSTOMERS and INVENTORY tables. These relationships (foreign key constraints) will cause a transaction to be rolled back if it attempts to insert a sales record for a customer or an item that does not exist.

The five tables in our database and their referential integrity relationships (foreign keys) are shown in Figure 5-5. The labels on the arrows represent the names of foreign key constraints.

STEP 6: After creating the tables, we are ready to create some triggers that operate on the tables. We need to design these triggers carefully, since they represent and enforce the policies of our business. A properly designed set of triggers can make applications easier to develop and can protect the integrity of our data.

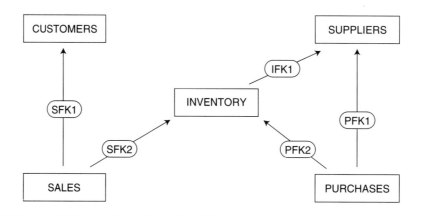

Figure 5-5: Tables and Referential Integrity Relationships in the STORE Database

```
--
-- STEP 5:
--
CREATE TABLE sales
  (saleDate      Date NOT NULL WITH DEFAULT,
   saleTime      Time NOT NULL WITH DEFAULT,
   custno        Char(6),
   itemno        Char(7),
   quantitySold Integer,
   unitPrice     Money,
   totalSale     Money,
   CONSTRAINT sfk1
      FOREIGN KEY (custno) REFERENCES customers,
   CONSTRAINT sfk2
      FOREIGN KEY (itemno) REFERENCES inventory,
   CONSTRAINT check1
      CHECK (quantitySold > 0) )!


--
-- STEP 6:
--
CREATE TRIGGER pt1
  NO CASCADE BEFORE INSERT ON purchases
  REFERENCING NEW AS newrow FOR EACH ROW
  MODE DB2SQL
  BEGIN ATOMIC
     SET (newrow.unitPrice, newrow.supplierno) =
            (SELECT unitOrderPrice, supplierno
             FROM inventory
             WHERE itemno = newrow.itemno);
  END!

CREATE TRIGGER pt2
  AFTER INSERT ON purchases
  REFERENCING NEW AS newrow FOR EACH ROW
  MODE DB2SQL
  BEGIN ATOMIC
     UPDATE inventory
        SET quantityOnOrder = quantityOnOrder + newrow.quantityOrdered
        WHERE itemno = newrow.itemno;
  END!
```

Our first trigger, PT1, will make it easy to insert new orders into the PUR-CHASES table. We want users and application programs to be able to insert rows into PURCHASES by specifying only the item number and the quantity ordered. The ORDERDATE and ORDERTIME columns will default to the current date and time, and trigger PT1 will automatically fill in the supplier number and unit price for the desired item by looking them up in the INVENTORY table. It is necessary to copy the supplier number and unit price from INVENTORY into the new row of PURCHASES, in order to maintain a proper record of the order in case the preferred supplier or unit price of this item changes in the future. Since PT1 modifies the row that is about to be inserted, it is a before insert trigger.

Also in this step, we write an after insert trigger that propagates information from the PURCHASES table to the INVENTORY table. When a new order is inserted into PURCHASES, trigger PT2 updates the quantity on order of the corresponding item in INVENTORY.

STEP 7: When the items that we ordered finally arrive from the supplier, someone will update the DATERECEIVED and QUANTITYRECEIVED columns of the appropriate row in PURCHASES. Trigger PT3, created in this step, is an after trigger that is activated by update of the QUANTITYRECEIVED column. The trigger is designed to carry out some additional actions that are necessary when supplies are received. It performs two automatic updates: it updates the INVENTORY table to reflect the arrival of the new items, and it updates the SUPPLIERS table to reflect the amount that we owe to the supplier for the shipment (based on the actual quantity received, not the quantity ordered).

STEP 8: In this step, we create a trigger to implement our policy on reordering supplies. Whenever there is a change in the quantity on hand or the order threshold for a given item in the INVENTORY table, trigger IT1 decides whether a new supply of the item needs to be ordered. It automatically generates an order if the sum of the quantity on hand and the quantity already on order for the given item is less than the order threshold.

The process of generating an order for new supplies involves interactions with both the database and the external world. Trigger IT1 interacts with the database by inserting a row into the PURCHASES table (as we saw in Step 6, this will activate two other triggers, PT1 and PT2). Trigger IT1 also interacts with the external world by calling a function named logOrder. logOrder is a user-defined function, written in C, that does whatever is necessary to make the new order effective, such as printing a purchase order on the proper form. The trigger passes to the logOrder function all the information that it needs, including the name and address of the supplier, the item number and name, and the quantity and unit price of the order.

```
--
-- STEP 7:
--
CREATE TRIGGER pt3
  AFTER UPDATE OF quantityReceived ON purchases
  REFERENCING NEW AS newrow FOR EACH ROW
  MODE DB2SQL
  BEGIN ATOMIC
      UPDATE inventory
        SET quantityOnHand = quantityOnHand + newrow.quantityReceived,
            quantityOnOrder = quantityOnOrder - newrow.quantityReceived
        WHERE itemno = newrow.itemno;
      UPDATE suppliers
        SET amountOwed = amountOwed +
              newrow.unitPrice * newrow.quantityReceived
        WHERE supplierno = newrow.supplierno;
  END!


--
-- STEP 8:
--
CREATE FUNCTION logOrder
    (Date,  Time,  Varchar(32),  Varchar(64),
        -- order date, order time, supplier name, supplier address,
    Char(7),  Varchar(30),  Integer,  Money)
        -- item number, item name, quantity, unit price
    RETURNS Integer
        -- not used
    NOT VARIANT
    NO SQL
    EXTERNAL ACTION
    LANGUAGE C
    FENCED
    PARAMETER STYLE DB2SQL
    EXTERNAL NAME 'storefun!logorder'!
```

The SQL statement to create the logOrder function is also shown in this step (of course, it must precede the creation of the trigger). The phrase EXTERNAL ACTION is included in the CREATE FUNCTION statement, because the function takes an action visible to the world outside the database. The body of the logOrder function must be written in C, compiled, and installed in the proper directory before the trigger can be used. The logOrder function is declared to return an Integer, since all user-defined functions are required to return some value; however, the return value is ignored by trigger IT1.

TIP: In a CREATE FUNCTION statement, it is helpful to give each function parameter a descriptive name, such as "Supplier address," in addition to its datatype. Since the CREATE FUNCTION syntax does not include parameter names, these names must take the form of comments. In V2, each comment inside an SQL statement must be preceded by two hyphens and must be on a line by itself.

STEP 9: This step implements our store policy on what to do about customers who exceed their credit limit. We wish to refuse any update to the balance owed by a customer that would exceed that customer's credit limit; furthermore, we wish to print a report for review by our credit office whenever such an update is attempted. First, we create an external function called logLimit, which prints the credit report (the body of this function must be written separately). Next, we create a trigger named CT1, which detects credit violations, invokes the logLimit function, and rolls back the offending update. We need to write this trigger carefully. It would not be wise to simply roll back the update whenever the new balance due is greater than the customer's credit limit, since that rule might prevent a customer who has somehow exceeded his credit limit from making a payment. We need to include a test in the WHEN clause that compares the old and new balance due and executes the body of the trigger only if the balance due is increasing. The trigger body rolls back the update that triggered it (but not the effects of other statements in the same transaction), and it generates an SQLSTATE of 70001 and the message "Credit limit exceeded."

We might consider implementing the credit policy in this step by means of a check constraint such as CHECK (balanceDue < creditLimit). However, if expressed in this way, the constraint would prevent a customer's credit limit from being lowered to an amount less than his current balance, which our store might choose to do under certain circumstances. Also, expressing the policy in the form of a trigger gives us an opportunity to call a user-defined function that generates a credit warning report.

```
    CREATE TRIGGER it1
       AFTER UPDATE OF quantityOnHand,
                       orderThreshold ON inventory
       REFERENCING NEW AS newrow FOR EACH ROW
       MODE DB2SQL
       WHEN (newrow.quantityOnHand + newrow.quantityOnOrder
               < newrow.orderThreshold)
       BEGIN ATOMIC
          INSERT INTO purchases(itemno, quantityOrdered)
             VALUES (newrow.itemno, newrow.minimumOrder);
          VALUES(logOrder(CURRENT DATE,
                          CURRENT TIME,
                          (SELECT suppliername
                              FROM suppliers
                              WHERE supplierno = newrow.supplierno),
                          (SELECT address
                              FROM suppliers
                              WHERE supplierno = newrow.supplierno),
                          newrow.itemno,
                          newrow.itemname,
                          newrow.minimumOrder,
                          newrow.unitOrderPrice ) );
       END!


--
-- STEP 9:
--
CREATE FUNCTION logLimit
   (Date, Time, Char(6), Money, Money)
         -- date, time, customer number, credit limit, amount owed
   RETURNS Integer
         -- not used
   NOT VARIANT
   NO SQL
   EXTERNAL ACTION
   LANGUAGE C
   FENCED
   PARAMETER STYLE DB2SQL
   EXTERNAL NAME 'storefun!loglimit'!
```

STEP 10: In this step, we attach some triggers to the SALES table. Trigger ST1 makes it easy to insert a new row into SALES, by automatically filling in the UNIT-PRICE and TOTALSALE columns of the new row (looking up the UNITPRICE value in the INVENTORY table). Thus, a new SALES row might be inserted with information only in the CUSTNO, ITEMNO, and QUANTITYSOLD columns; values for SALEDATE and SALETIME will default to the current date and time, and values for UNITPRICE and TOTALSALE will be generated by the trigger ST1.

Also in this step, we create trigger ST2, which makes sure that, whenever a sale is recorded, the customer's balance due is updated accordingly and the items sold are subtracted from the quantity on hand in the INVENTORY table. Note that the action of this trigger might cascade to activate other triggers as well. For example, if this sale would cause a customer to exceed his credit limit, trigger CT1 will generate a warning report and roll back the statement. Similarly, if this sale results in the quantity on hand of an item falling below its order threshold, trigger IT1 will be activated and will generate a new order for the item. It is also worth noting that if the quantity sold is more than the entire quantity on hand for this item, trigger ST2 will update the quantity on hand in the INVENTORY table to a value less than zero and the statement will be rolled back by check constraint CHECK1 in the INVENTORY table.

The order of the SQL statements in the body of trigger ST2 is important. We want to update the customer's balance due before we update the inventory table, because updating the customer's balance due results in a credit check that could roll back the statement if the customer's credit limit is exceeded. We want the credit check to be completed before we update the inventory table (which could result in placing a new order for supplies that would prove unnecessary if the customer has insufficient credit).

```
CREATE TRIGGER ct1
   AFTER UPDATE OF balanceDue ON customers
   REFERENCING OLD AS oldrow NEW AS newrow FOR EACH ROW
   MODE DB2SQL
   WHEN (newrow.balanceDue > oldrow.balanceDue
      AND newrow.balanceDue > newrow.creditLimit)
   BEGIN ATOMIC
      VALUES(logLimit(CURRENT DATE,
                      CURRENT TIME,
                      newrow.custno,
                      newrow.creditLimit,
                      newrow.balanceDue));
      SIGNAL SQLSTATE '70001' ('Credit Limit Exceeded');
   END!

--
-- STEP 10:
--
CREATE TRIGGER st1
   NO CASCADE BEFORE INSERT ON sales
   REFERENCING NEW AS newrow FOR EACH ROW
   MODE DB2SQL
   BEGIN ATOMIC
      SET (newrow.unitPrice, newrow.totalSale) =
          (SELECT unitSalePrice, unitSalePrice * newrow.quantitySold
           FROM inventory
           WHERE itemno = newrow.itemno);
   END!

CREATE TRIGGER st2
   AFTER INSERT ON sales
   REFERENCING NEW AS newrow FOR EACH ROW
   MODE DB2SQL
   BEGIN ATOMIC
      UPDATE customers
         SET balanceDue = balanceDue + newrow.totalSale
         WHERE custno = newrow.custno;
      UPDATE inventory
         SET quantityOnHand = quantityOnHand - newrow.quantitySold
         WHERE itemno = newrow.itemno;
   END!
```

STEP 11: This step is an attempt to do some automatic fine-tuning of our system for ordering new supplies. Since it takes about a month for a new order of supplies to arrive, we do not want our inventory of any item to fall below about one month's sales for that item. Therefore, whenever we find that the quantity sold of a given item in the last month is greater than the order threshold for that item, it is probably time to increase the ordering threshold and possibly the minimum order quantity as well. This policy is implemented by trigger ST3, which automatically increases both the ordering threshold and the minimum order quantity by 25% and generates a report (by calling the user-defined function logSales) that will be reviewed and approved by our purchasing manager. We show the CREATE FUNCTION statement for logSales, another function with EXTERNAL ACTION, whose C implementation must be compiled separately.

The body of trigger ST3 contains two SQL statements: the first updates the database and the second contains several scalar subqueries that retrieve values to be passed to logSales. These SQL statements are executed sequentially, and the second statement can see the database updates made by the first statement.

```
--
-- STEP 11:
--
CREATE FUNCTION logsales
    (Date,  Time,  Char(7),  Varchar(30),
            -- date, time, item number, item name,
    Integer,  Integer,  Integer)
            -- quant. sold last month, new order threshold, new order quant.
    RETURNS Integer
            -- not used
    NOT VARIANT
    NO SQL
    EXTERNAL ACTION
    LANGUAGE C
    FENCED
    PARAMETER STYLE DB2SQL
    EXTERNAL NAME 'storefun!logsales'!

CREATE TRIGGER st3
    AFTER INSERT ON sales
    REFERENCING NEW AS newrow FOR EACH ROW
    MODE DB2SQL
    WHEN ((SELECT SUM(quantitySold)
           FROM sales
           WHERE itemno = newrow.itemno
           AND saleDate + 1 MONTH > CURRENT DATE )
          >
          (SELECT orderThreshold
           FROM inventory
           WHERE itemno = newrow.itemno) )
    BEGIN ATOMIC
      UPDATE inventory
        SET orderThreshold = orderThreshold * 1.25,
            minimumOrder = minimumOrder * 1.25
        WHERE itemno = newrow.itemno;
      VALUES (logsales(CURRENT DATE, CURRENT TIME, newrow.itemno,
                        (SELECT itemname FROM inventory
                            WHERE itemno = newrow.itemno),
                        (SELECT SUM(quantitySold) FROM sales
                            WHERE itemno = newrow.itemno
                            AND saleDate + 1 MONTH > CURRENT DATE ),
                        (SELECT orderThreshold FROM inventory
                            WHERE itemno = newrow.itemno),
                        (SELECT minimumOrder FROM inventory
                            WHERE itemno = newrow.itemno) ) );
    END!
```

STEP 12: This step represents an afterthought on the part of our marketing department. Someone in marketing wants to keep a record of the total amount of purchases by each customer in the current calendar year. This data may be used to identify big spenders for special mailings and promotional offers. We implement this last-minute addition to the database by altering the CUSTOMERS table, adding a new column to record the total sales this year, and by creating the trigger ST4 to update this column whenever a new sale is recorded.

Figure 5-6 shows a graphic representation of all the triggers created in the STORE example. Each trigger is represented by an arrow with its tail on the table to which the trigger is attached and its head(s) on the table(s) that are modified by the trigger. When designing an active database, it is a good idea to draw a "trigger graph" like this one and to look for cycles. Investigate each cycle in the trigger graph to make sure that it cannot lead to a trigger invoking itself in an infinite loop. In Figure 5-6, for example, the apparent loops between triggers IT1 and PT2 and between IT1 and PT3 should be investigated, as well as the self-loops represented by CT1, ST1, and PT1. In each case, the triggers involved are written in such a way that they avoid infinite recursion.

This figure shows us that quite a complex series of actions can result from a simple database update. For example, the series of actions on page 384 might result from the insertion of a new row into the SALES table (the levels of indentation represent how the action of one trigger results in firing another trigger).

```
--
-- STEP 12:
--
ALTER TABLE customers
   ADD COLUMN salesThisYear Money!

CREATE TRIGGER st4
   AFTER INSERT ON sales
   REFERENCING NEW AS newrow FOR EACH ROW
   MODE DB2SQL
   BEGIN ATOMIC
      UPDATE customers
         SET salesThisYear =
            ( SELECT sum(totalSale)
              FROM sales
              WHERE custno = newrow.custno
              AND year(saleDate) = year(CURRENT DATE) )
         WHERE custno = newrow.custno;
   END!
```

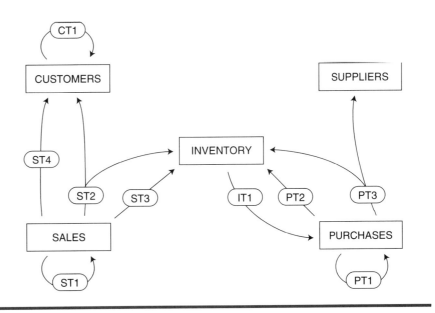

Figure 5-6: A Graph of Triggers in the STORE Database

1. ST1 conditions the new SALES row by filling in its UNITPRICE and TOTAL-SALE columns.

2. ST2 updates the CUSTOMERS table (increasing BALANCEDUE) and the INVENTORY table (decreasing QUANTITYONHAND).

   a. CT1 rolls back the statement if the customer's credit limit is exceeded.

   b. IT1 inserts a new order into PURCHASES if more supplies are needed.

      - PT1 conditions the new PURCHASES row by filling in the SUPPLIERNO and UNITPRICE columns.

      - PT2 updates the INVENTORY table (increasing QUANTITYONORDER).

3. If this sale represents a new high in monthly sales for some item, ST3 updates the INVENTORY table, increasing the THRESHOLD and MINIMUMORDER columns for this item. (If the THRESHOLD is increased to a value greater than QUANTITYONHAND, this could lead to firing triggers IT1, PT1, and PT2 again.)

4. ST4 updates the CUSTOMERS table (increasing SALESTHISYEAR).

5.5 BINDING AND DEPENDENCIES

Features of V2 such as constraints and triggers go a long way toward capturing the semantics of objects that are stored in the database. As these features are implemented, it becomes increasingly true that the behavior of an SQL statement may depend on things that are outside the statement itself, such as constraints, triggers, views, and functions. For example, if a trigger is added to a table that is updated by an SQL statement, the behavior of the SQL statement may change. This is an example of a *dependency* of one object on another. Now that this book has discussed all the kinds of objects implemented by V2, it is time to have a general discussion of dependencies.

The example questions below illustrate some of the kinds of dependencies that can exist among various objects in a database. The questions and answers are followed by a discussion of the general rules governing dependencies.

- Suppose that you create a view on Monday, but on Tuesday one of the tables that underlies the view is dropped. What happens to the view? *Answer*: The view becomes "inoperative" and cannot be used until it is explicitly recreated.

- Suppose that you bind an application program on Wednesday, but on Thursday a new index is created that would be helpful to your program. Will the program take advantage of the new index? *Answer*: No, not until the program is rebound.

- Suppose that after you bind an application program that inserts data into a table, a check constraint is added to the table. Is your existing program subject to the new check constraint? *Answer*: Yes, its package will automatically be modified to incorporate the new constraint.

- Suppose that, after you create a trigger that encapsulates one of the rules of your business, someone tries to drop a function that is used by your trigger. What happens? *Answer*: The function cannot be dropped as long as the trigger exists.

The topic of dependencies is closely related to the topic of *binding*. Before any SQL statement (including the definition of a view, constraint, or trigger) can be used, each unqualified name used in the statement must be resolved to some specific object (table, function, and so on) in the database. We use the term *binding* to describe the process of finding the specific object that corresponds to each unqualified name in an SQL statement. For example, the unqualified table name SALARYPLAN might be bound to the specific table ADMIN.SALARYPLAN when it occurs in an application prepared under the ADMIN userid; or the unqualified function name area might be bound to the specific function geometry.area when it is used in a particular view.

After a name has been bound to a particular object, it is possible that changes may occur in the database that could potentially affect the binding. For example, after the function name area has been bound to the specific function geometry.area, another function named area could be created in a schema that is earlier in the user's function path than geometry. Or, the specific function geometry.area could be dropped and no longer be available for use. We use the term *binding semantics* to describe how an object behaves after all its names have been bound. The term applies to every kind of persistent object, such as a view or program, whose definition contains an unqualified name.

5.5.1 Conservative Binding Semantics

The general approach taken by V2 to the issue of binding is called *conservative binding semantics*. This term means that, after an object is bound, its behavior will not change unpredictably. For example, if you compile an application program that invokes a user-defined function called payIncrease, you can be confident that the program will not suddenly begin using a different payIncrease function unless you take an explicit action.[7] Having stated the

---

7. Of course, we are assuming here that you have protected the executable file that implements your function against unauthorized tampering, using the protection features of your file system.

general principle, we will now examine the binding semantics of some specific kinds of objects.

The binding semantics of views are easy to describe. All the names contained in a view definition are bound to specific objects in the database at the time when the CREATE VIEW is executed. After this time, the bindings of the names never change. If a new function, alias, or other object is created later that would have been chosen if the view were rebound, the new object is ignored, even in applications that are compiled after the creation of the new object. If an object (function, table, alias, and so on) to which a view has been bound is dropped, the view becomes *inoperative*. This means that the view definition is retained in the VIEWS catalog table, but the view cannot be used until it is explicitly recreated by a new CREATE VIEW statement. The view definition is retained in order to help you recreate the view after the dropped object has been replaced with a replacement object of the same name. If a view is inoperative, creating a new view with the same name is not considered a naming conflict; instead, the inoperative view definition is replaced. The following query retrieves the names and definitions of all the inoperative views in schema S1:

```
SELECT viewname, seqno, text
FROM syscat.views
WHERE viewschema = 'S1' AND valid = 'X'
ORDER BY viewname, seqno;
```

The binding semantics of triggers are the same as those of views. Like a view, a trigger can become inoperative if some object that it depends on is dropped. The definition of an inoperative trigger is maintained in the TRIGGERS catalog table, so that a user can retrieve the definition and use it in a new CREATE TRIGGER statement. The following query can be used to fetch the definitions of all inoperative triggers in schema S1:

```
SELECT trigname, text
FROM syscat.triggers
WHERE trigschema = 'S1' and valid = 'X'
ORDER BY trigname;
```

The binding semantics of programs are also conservative but are somewhat more complex than those of views and triggers. When a program is bound, a specific plan is generated for executing each SQL statement in the program, and all these plans are stored in the database in the form of a *package*. After binding a program, we do not want its behavior to change, but we do not insist that each statement always be executed using the original plan. For example, if an index that was used in the original plan for some statement is dropped, the statement can still be executed by choosing a different (but functionally equivalent) plan. Therefore, if some object that a program uses is dropped, the package for that program can become either *invalid* or *inoperative*. If an index that a package uses is dropped, the package is marked *invalid*, and the system automatically generates a new plan for executing the package the next time it is used. This process is called *implicit rebind* and is invisible to users except for performance: there may be a slight delay when the automatic rebind occurs, and the performance of the program may change due to the new access plan. On the other hand, if a function that a package uses is dropped, the package is marked *inoperative* and can no longer be executed until it is explicitly rebound. This protects the users of the application from unexpected changes in its behavior. An inoperative package can be rebound using the PREP, BIND, or REBIND commands. The status of each package is stored in the PACKAGES catalog table. The following query can be used to list all the packages that are invalid or inoperative:

```
SELECT pkgschema, pkgname, valid
FROM syscat.packages
WHERE valid = 'N' OR valid = 'X';
```

TIP: When a package is implicitly rebound, the implicit rebind takes place within the scope of the first transaction executed by the package. If the first transaction is rolled back, the implicit rebind will be rolled back also. In fact, if a package always rolls back its first transaction, that package can never be implicitly rebound.

5.5.2 Types of Dependencies

The binding semantics of views, programs, and other objects are enforced by recording *dependencies* in the system catalog tables. A dependency exists whenever the definition of some object (called the *depending object*) refers to some other object (called the *underlying object*). Dependencies can be classified into four semantic categories, according to what happens when the underlying object is dropped.

R = *Restrict semantics*. As long as the dependency exists, users are not allowed to drop the underlying object.

C = *Cascade semantics*. When the underlying object is dropped, the dependent object is automatically dropped also.

A = *Automatic revalidation semantics*. When the underlying object is dropped, the dependent object is marked *invalid* and is automatically revalidated on its next use, selecting the best replacement for the object that was dropped.

X = *Inoperative semantics.* When the underlying object is dropped, the dependent object is marked *inoperative.* An inoperative object cannot be used until a user takes some explicit action to restore it to an operative state. However, the definition of the inoperative object remains in the catalog tables as an aid to restoring the object.

Table 5-5 summarizes all the kinds of dependencies that are recorded in V2. Like the catalog tables, Table 5-5 includes only *immediate* dependencies. Of course, these dependencies may propagate; for example, if a program is dependent on a view, and the view is dependent on a privilege (held by the view definer), then loss of that privilege by the view definer will have an effect on the program, even though the dependency of the program on the privilege is not recorded directly.

In Table 5-5, the codes R, C, A, and X denote the four types of dependency semantics. The numbers in parentheses refer to the notes that follow the table.

TABLE 5-5: Types of Dependencies of One Object on Another

Depending Object	Underlying Object									
	Table	View	Alias	Index	Function Instance	Datatype	Constraint	Trigger	Privilege	Tablespace
Program	A(3)	A	A	A	X		A(4)	A(4)	A	
Table						R				C(5)
View	X	X	X		R				X	
Alias (6)										
Index	C									
Function Instance					R	C				
Datatype (1)										
Constraint	C				R		C(2)			
Trigger	X	X	X		R				X	

Notes:

1. Distinct types have no dependencies, because they are always based on built-in datatypes, which cannot be dropped.

2. A foreign key constraint is dependent on a primary key constraint in the parent table, with Cascade semantics.

3. A program is dependent, not only on the tables that it manipulates directly, but also on tables that it manipulates indirectly through views, aliases, triggers, or foreign key constraints.

4. If a program operates on a particular table, the package generated for the program will include all the constraints and triggers that were defined on that table at the time the program was bound. If constraints or triggers are added to or deleted from that table, the program will be invalidated (and automatically rebound on next use). This type of dependency is recorded as a dependency of the program on the table, not on the individual constraints and triggers.

5. Dropping a tablespace causes all tables that are completely contained within the tablespace to be dropped. But if a table spans more than one tablespace, none of its tablespaces can be dropped as long as the table exists.

6. Aliases have no dependencies. It is permissible for an alias to be defined on a table that does not exist.

Since all of the various kinds of dependencies are recorded in the catalog tables, you can write queries to find all the objects that depend on a given object or to find all the objects that a given object depends on. The main catalog tables that are used to record dependencies are the following:

- CONSTDEP records dependencies of constraints on other objects.
- PACKAGEDEP records dependencies of packages on other objects.
- TRIGDEP records dependencies of triggers on other objects.
- VIEWDEP records dependencies of views on other objects.

Dependencies are also recorded in certain other catalog tables that are used mainly for other purposes; for example, the COLUMNS catalog table records the datatype of each column, which represents a dependency of a table or view on a datatype.

The following are some examples of queries that might be used to find dependencies. (More information about catalog tables can be found in Appendix D.)

- Find all the objects that are depended on by the trigger named SECURITY.HIRETRIGGER:

```
SELECT bschema, bname, btype
FROM syscat.trigdep
WHERE trigschema = 'SECURITY'
AND trigname = 'HIRETRIGGER';
```

- Find all the table columns and view columns that use the distinct datatype Money:

```
SELECT tabschema, tabname, colname
FROM syscat.columns
WHERE typename = 'MONEY';
```

- Find all the functions that take parameters or return results of type Money:

```
SELECT DISTINCT funcschema, funcname
FROM syscat.funcparms
WHERE typename = 'MONEY';
```

TIP: Since SQL folds all (nonquoted) names to uppercase, you should use an uppercase name when searching for an object (type, function, table, and so on) in the catalog tables, unless you know that the object you are searching for was explicitly created with a (quoted) lowercase name.

Dynamic SQL

SQL is a language that can be used in many different ways. We have seen how SQL statements can be embedded in programs written in a host programming language such as C. These statements, called *static SQL,* are analyzed and prepared for execution by the V2 precompiler, so when the application program runs it needs only to invoke a preoptimized access plan for each SQL statement. However, it is not always possible to anticipate in advance exactly what SQL statements an application program may need to execute. Therefore, some means is needed for a program to generate SQL statements at run time and present them to the database system to be executed. This approach to processing SQL statements is called *dynamic SQL.*

In exchange for run-time flexibility, of course, dynamic SQL applications must pay a performance penalty, since their SQL statements cannot be optimized in advance. The cost of analyzing each SQL statement and choosing an optimal access plan is repeated each time a dynamic SQL application is run, whereas in static SQL this cost is incurred only once, when the application is precompiled.

Another issue that you may wish to consider in choosing between static and dynamic SQL is the stability of your application. A static SQL application is encapsulated in a package whose behavior will not change without explicit action on your part. A dynamic application, on the other hand, is processed "from scratch" each time it is run, which means that its behavior may differ from one run to the next as changes are made to the database, such as the addition of new user-defined functions.

V2 provides two separate facilities for handling dynamic SQL statements, called the Call Level Interface (CLI) and Embedded Dynamic SQL. The functionalities of CLI and Embedded Dynamic SQL are very similar. Each facility provides a way for application programs to submit dynamically computed SQL statements to the database system at run time. In each facility, the process of parsing an SQL statement and choosing an optimal access plan for it is called *preparing* the statement.

Both CLI and Embedded Dynamic SQL separate the process of preparing a statement from the process of executing it, allowing a statement to be prepared once and executed many times using different data values. For example, an UPDATE statement might be prepared to update a particular table and then executed once for each row to be updated. In this approach, the cost of parsing and optimizing the SQL statement is incurred only once, when the statement is prepared, rather than on each execution.

When a dynamic SQL statement is being prepared for execution, some of its data values may not yet be available. For example, we may know that we want to update the EMPLOYEES table and change the SALARY of the row with a certain EMPNO. But the particular values of EMPNO and SALARY to be used may not be available at prepare time and indeed may change from one execution of the statement to the next. Missing data values in a dynamic SQL statement can be represented by question marks, which are called *parameter markers*. Before a prepared statement can be executed, real data values must be substituted for all its parameter markers. This is done by *binding* each parameter marker to a host variable, so that the value of the parameter marker is taken from the content of the variable at execution time.

This chapter examines the two dynamic SQL facilities, CLI and Embedded Dynamic SQL, and shows how each facility allows application programs to prepare SQL statements for execution, to bind their parameter markers, and to execute the statements. To illustrate the use of dynamic SQL and to compare the two facilities, we will write some application programs using both CLI and Embedded Dynamic SQL.

6.1 CALL LEVEL INTERFACE

The Call Level Interface (CLI) is one of the two facilities provided by V2 for processing dynamic SQL statements—that is, statements that are presented to the database system for the first time when the application program is running. However, there are some reasons why you might choose to write your application using CLI, even if your SQL statements are known in advance. One such reason is that CLI allows you to avoid the precompilation step. Instead of a precompiler, CLI relies on a set of function calls that can be embedded in a C program and compiled by a conventional C compiler. By linking your program to the V2 CLI library, you have access to all the SQL facilities of the system. Furthermore, since the CLI functions conform to a standard that is widely implemented, your CLI application is portable to a variety of database products. Since there is no need to precompile your application, you can distribute it in the form of object code. Users of your application can run it on their own databases without having access to source code and without needing to "bind" the application to each database on which it will be used.

If you have decided to write a dynamic (rather than static) SQL application, you still need to decide whether to use the CLI or Embedded Dynamic SQL. CLI offers several advantages over Embedded Dynamic SQL, which might be summarized as follows:

1. Portability. CLI, originally defined by Microsoft, the X/Open Company, and the SQL Access Group, has recently been adopted as an International Standard (ISO/IEC 9075-3: "SQL Call-Level Interface"). The V2 implementation of CLI is compatible with the widely used Microsoft version called Open Database Connectivity (ODBC). V2 provides full support for ODBC Level 1 and also supports most of the functions of ODBC Level 2. Therefore, your applications written for V2 using the CLI interface will be portable to other database systems, and many ODBC applications written for other database systems are portable to V2. CLI programs contain no references to system-specific control blocks such as SQLCA and SQLDA.

2. As noted above, CLI applications do not require a precompiler. Therefore, they can be distributed in the form of object code and do not need to be bound to each database on which they are used.

3. CLI applications, unlike Embedded Dynamic SQL applications, can connect to the same database multiple times and can independently commit transactions in each database connection. This facility is useful in developing applications with graphic user interfaces that use multiple windows.

4. In keeping with its strategy of system independence, CLI provides a set of function calls that can be used to access system catalog tables in a standard way. Most relational systems maintain a set of catalog tables containing information about the database and its users, but the form of these catalog tables may vary from one system to another. Using CLI functions, you can access some of this catalog data in a portable way, including information about the tables and columns in the database, primary and foreign keys, and user privileges. Of course, the V2 catalog tables contain a lot of additional information that can be accessed directly by SQL statements but is not accessible via the system-independent CLI catalog functions.

5. CLI supports a function called `SQLExtendedFetch()`, which can be used to retrieve multiple rows from the database into an array in your application program with a single call, avoiding the overhead of fetching the rows one at a time. Similarly, using the function `SQLParamOptions()`, an application can execute an SQL statement multiple times with a single CLI call, using an array of input variables.

6. CLI supports a large number of datatype conversions. For example, data of any SQL datatype can be fetched into a C variable of datatype `char[]`. The data is automatically converted from its SQL datatype (perhaps Double or Timestamp) into a character-string representation. Its rich set of datatype conversions makes CLI well adapted to writing programs to support interactive query interfaces.

7. V2 supports some CLI functions (such as `SQLGetSubString()`) that make it easy to manipulate large objects in the form of locators, postponing the actual materialization of the objects as long as possible. These functions are IBM extensions (not a part of the standard ODBC interface) and are not available using Embedded Dynamic SQL.

8. CLI, unlike Embedded Dynamic SQL, supports compound SQL statements (which enable several SQL statements to be sent from client to server in a single flow, reducing execution time and network traffic).

9. Client programs written in CLI can invoke stored procedures that return multiple result sets (as described in Section 7.2.3).

A complete description of CLI is given in the *DB2 Call Level Interface Guide and Reference*. Many examples of CLI applications are provided with the V2 system and can be found in the directory `sqllib/samples/cli`.

6.1.1 Handles

In order to read and write CLI programs, you need to understand the concept of a *handle*. A handle is simply a C variable of type `long` that represents some information that is being managed for you "behind the scenes" by the CLI implementation. CLI supports the following three types of handles:

1. An *environment handle* represents the global state of your application. Your CLI program will need to allocate an environment handle at the beginning and free it at the end, but otherwise it will make little use of the environment handle.

2. A *connection handle* represents the connection of your application to a particular database. Your program can be connected to multiple databases, or multiple times to the same database, using a separate connection handle for each connection. You will use connection handles to commit and roll back transactions in various databases and to control aspects of your database connections such as isolation level.

3. A *statement handle* represents the execution state of an SQL statement. Your program can allocate multiple statement handles and can reuse each one repeatedly to process many SQL statements (one at a time, of course). A statement handle is a powerful object that combines the information that a static SQL program would find in structures called SQLCA (return codes and messages), SQLDA (datatypes and bindings to host variables), and cursors (current position within a set of rows). Since all this information is represented by a statement handle, your program no longer needs to manage these (rather messy) data structures directly. Instead, your program uses CLI function calls to execute an SQL statement and to retrieve information about the statement using its handle. A statement handle can be used in the following ways:

- It can retrieve error codes and messages pertaining to the execution of the statement.
- It can find out whether the statement was a query and, if so, the datatypes of the columns in the result set.
- It can tell the system where to deliver the results of a query, and it can fetch the rows of the result set one at a time.
- Like a cursor, it can maintain a position on a "current" row in the result set and can provide a name (called a *cursor name*) that can be used by other SQL statements to update or delete the current row.

It is your job to allocate one environment handle, one or more connection handles, and one or more statement handles, and to free these handles when they are no longer needed. You will use these handles in all the CLI function calls in your program.

6.1.2 Configuring CLI

A configuration file named db2cli.ini can be used to specify various options that control the behavior of CLI. Each of these options has a system-wide default that applies if the option is not included in the configuration file. In addition, many of the options can be overridden by individual CLI commands. For example, the system-wide default for the transaction isolation level is Cursor Stability (CS). A given machine may have a db2cli.ini file that establishes a different default isolation level for all CLI applications run on that machine. But an individual CLI application can have the last word about the isolation level of a specific database connection by using the function SQLSetConnectOption().

The db2cli.ini file is found in the sqllib directory of a V2 system running on OS/2, in the sqllib\win directory of a system on Windows, and in the sqllib/cfg directory of a UNIX-based system.

Some of the options that can be specified in the db2cli.ini file are listed below. (For a more complete list, see the *DB2 Call Level Interface Guide and Reference*.)

AUTOCOMMIT controls whether a commit is automatically performed after each SQL statement is executed. The system-wide default is to turn auto-commit ON.

CONNECTTYPE controls the type of database connections acquired by CLI applications. The system-wide default is Type 1, which permits connection to only one database at a time.

CURSORHOLD controls whether open cursors remain open when a COMMIT statement is executed. The system-wide default is to hold cursors open across commit points. Applications that do not need this feature can improve performance by turning it off.

DB2OPTIMIZATION controls the optimization level used in processing SQL statements by CLI applications. The system-wide default is Level 5. (Optimization levels are discussed in Section 8.6.1.)

TXNISOLATION controls the isolation level for CLI transactions. The system-wide default is Cursor Stability (CS).

6.1.3 Summary of CLI Functions

It is important to remember that CLI is not a new query language—it is simply an interface that an application program can use to submit SQL statements for processing. Your database queries and updates are still written in SQL and "wrapped" in CLI function calls. CLI neither adds to nor subtracts from the power of SQL. The CLI function calls handle details like connecting to the database, fetching query results into program variables, and committing or rolling back your transaction.

The following is a list of all the CLI functions supported by V2, organized into categories of related functions. A complete description of all the parameters of these functions is beyond the scope of this book, but can be found in the *DB2 Call Level Interface Guide and Reference*. The functions marked with an asterisk in the list below are V2 extensions that are not a part of ODBC and that may therefore limit the portability of your application.

- Functions for allocating and freeing handles:

  SQLAllocEnv() allocates an environment handle.

  SQLAllocConnect() allocates a connection handle.

  SQLAllocStmt() allocates a statement handle.

  SQLFreeEnv() frees an environment handle.

  SQLFreeConnect() frees a connection handle.

  SQLFreeStmt() frees a statement handle.

- Functions for controlling database connections:

  SQLConnect() connects your application program to a particular database.

  SQLDriverConnect() connects your application program to a particular database, after prompting the user for certain information such as userid and password.

  SQLDisconnect() closes a database connection.

  SQLSetEnvAttr() controls options such as connection type for all database connections within the scope of an environment handle.

  SQLGetEnvAttr() retrieves the current value of an option set by SQLSetEnvAttr().

SQLSetConnectOption() controls options such as isolation level or auto-commit for a specific database connection.

SQLGetConnectOption() retrieves the current value of a database connection option.

SQLSetConnection()* is used to specify which database connection is used by static SQL statements embedded in a CLI program.

- Functions for preparing an SQL statement for execution and obtaining a description of the result:

    SQLPrepare() prepares a statement for execution.

    SQLNumResultCols() returns the number of columns in the result set if the prepared statement was a query.

    SQLDescribeCol() describes a particular column in the result set.

    SQLColAttributes() retrieves one specific attribute of a column in the result set, such as its name, datatype, or length.

    SQLSetColAttributes()* informs the system that the attributes of a column are known and need not be retrieved from the database server.

    SQLNativeSql() accepts an SQL statement and returns it, translated into the "native" form that would be sent to the database server. This translation process is used to remove local system dependencies from SQL statements. The translated statement is returned but not executed.

- Functions for handling parameter markers:

    SQLNumParams() returns the number of parameter markers in a prepared SQL statement.

    SQLBindParameter() binds a parameter marker to a host program variable. An earlier version of this function named SQLSetParam() is also supported for use by older applications.

    SQLParamData(), SQLPutData(), and SQLCancel() can be used together to send large parameter values from a CLI program to the database system, a piece at a time.

- Functions for executing an SQL statement and testing its result:

    SQLExecute() executes a statement that was previously prepared.

    SQLExecDirect() prepares and executes a statement in one step.

    SQLRowCount() returns the number of rows that were inserted, deleted, or updated by a statement.

    SQLError() returns information about errors encountered while processing a statement.

    SQLGetSQLCA()* returns the SQLCA structure that results from processing a statement. Most of the information in the SQLCA can also be obtained by SQLError() and SQLRowCount().

SQLSetStmtOption() controls certain options pertaining to the execution of a statement, such as a limit on the number of rows to be returned in the result set.

SQLGetStmtOption() retrieves the current value of a statement option.

- Functions for handling the result of a query:

    SQLBindCol() tells CLI where to deliver the values for one column in the result set and what kind of type conversion to perform on the column values. If the datatype of the column is Blob, Clob, or Dbclob, SQLBind-Col() can specify that the system deliver the column value in the form of a locator rather than materializing the actual value.

    SQLFetch() fetches one row of the result set into the host program locations specified by SQLBindCol().

    SQLExtendedFetch() fetches multiple rows of the result set into one or more arrays in your program.

    SQLGetData() fetches a single column value from the current row of the result set and can be used to fetch large data values in pieces.

    SQLSetCursorName() associates a cursor name with a statement handle, for use in positioned deletes and updates. If you do not supply a cursor name for a statement handle, the system will generate one.

    SQLGetCursorName() returns the cursor name associated with a statement handle.

- Functions that are useful in handling large objects:

    SQLGetLength()* returns the length of a string value. This function is useful for measuring the length of a large object that is represented by a locator.

    SQLGetSubString()* returns a portion of a LOB-type string value that is represented by a large-object locator. The result can be either a materialized string or another locator. This function is useful for postponing the materialization of a large object as long as possible.

    SQLGetPosition()* returns a number representing the position of one string inside another. The string to be searched must be represented by a locator, and the string to be found may be represented by either a locator or a literal. This function is useful for searching for patterns of bits or characters within a large object.

    SQLBindFileToParam()* is used to bind a parameter marker in an SQL statement to a file containing a large object. The content of the file is substituted for the parameter marker when the SQL statement is executed.

    SQLBindFileToCol()* is used in fetching the result of a query. It directs the system to deliver the values of a particular large-object column into a file rather than into a program variable.

- Functions for managing transactions:

    SQLTransact() can be used to commit or abort a transaction. A CLI application can group several database connections inside the same transaction, or it can have a separate transaction for each database connection, committing or aborting these transactions independently. Note that in CLI, transaction commit and abort are accomplished by function calls rather than by SQL statements. Also note that the autocommit option, controlled by your db2cli.ini file and by SQLSetConnectOptions(), automatically commits every SQL statement as soon as it is executed. The autocommit option is turned on by default, and you must turn it off if you wish to control your own transactions.

- Functions for querying the system catalog tables (each of these functions executes a query, whose result can then be retrieved using SQLFetch() and the other functions that operate on result sets):

    SQLTables() lists the names of tables (including views and aliases) that are stored in a given database.

    SQLColumns() lists the names and datatypes of the columns in a specified table.

    SQLForeignKeys() lists the names of columns used in the foreign keys of a table.

    SQLPrimaryKeys() lists the names of columns used in the primary key of a table.

    SQLSpecialColumns() lists columns that participate in either a primary key or a unique index.

    SQLStatistics() returns information about the number of rows in a table and about the indexes that are maintained on a table.

    SQLTablePrivileges() lists the privileges that you hold on various tables in the database.

    SQLColumnPrivileges() lists the privileges that you hold on various columns in the database.

    SQLProcedures() lists the stored procedures in a given database, relying on information in the DB2CLI.PROCEDURES catalog table described in Appendix D. (For more information about stored procedures, see Chapter 7.)

    SQLProcedureColumns() lists the input and output parameters associated with a stored procedure.

- Functions for obtaining information about available databases and servers:

  SQLDataSources() lists the databases that are available for your program to use.

  SQLGetInfo() returns general information about the functionality of the database system to which the CLI program is connected.

  SQLGetFunctions() returns information about the specific CLI functions that are supported by a given database server; you can use this information to make your application more portable.

  SQLGetTypeInfo() returns information about the datatypes supported by a particular database.

- Functions that are used for handling sets of input and output values:

  SQLParamOptions() binds a parameter marker to a host program array so that a given SQL statement can be executed multiple times using an array of parameter values.

  SQLMoreResults() is used to advance from one result set to the next when an SQL query has been executed multiple times using an array of parameters. Within each result set, individual rows may be fetched using SQLFetch(). SQLMoreResults() is also used to advance from one result set to the next when multiple result sets are returned by a stored procedure (as described in Section 7.2.3).

6.1.4 Typed Parameter Markers

As noted earlier in this chapter, a parameter marker is used to denote a data value that is not known at the time when a dynamic SQL statement is being prepared for execution. Parameter markers are represented by question marks and can be used in SQL statements executed either by CLI or by Embedded Dynamic SQL. A parameter marker represents a single data value and may be used anyplace where a host variable could be used. A parameter marker may not take the place of a table name, column name, or SQL keyword. In the following dynamic SQL statement, the two question marks represent missing values for a salary and an employee number, which must be provided by binding the parameter markers to host variables before the statement is executed:

```
UPDATE employees SET salary = ? WHERE empno = ?
```

Since V2 is a strongly typed system, it needs to know the datatype of each value used in an SQL statement during compilation. If a value is represented by a constant or a host variable, the system can easily infer its datatype from the appearance of the constant or the declared datatype of the host variable. But if the value is represented by a parameter marker, inferring its datatype is more difficult. If the parameter marker is being compared to a value of a known datatype (as in the predicate empno = ?) or inserted into a column of known datatype (as in the assignment salary = ?), the system can infer its datatype from context. But in other cases, the system must rely on the user to declare the datatype of the parameter marker, using a notation called a *typed parameter marker*. The syntax of a typed parameter marker is as follows:

Although it resembles a call to a casting function, a typed parameter marker is not a function call. It is a "promise" by the application programmer that a value of the named datatype (or a value that can be converted to that datatype) will be substituted for the parameter marker when the statement is executed.[1] The SQL compiler will rely on this promise while preparing the SQL statement for execution. Let us consider a case in which the type information in a typed parameter marker is critical to the compilation process.

Suppose that a statement being prepared for execution contains a function call with a parameter marker as one of its arguments, such as payraise(?). Because V2 allows overloaded functions, a user may have defined several payraise functions—perhaps payraise(Varchar(10)), payraise(Double), and payraise(Date). Since function resolution is based on the datatype of the argument, the system will not be able to choose which function to invoke for payraise(?) and will return an error code. However, function selection will be successful if the function argument is a typed parameter marker, as in the example payraise(CAST(? AS Double)). In this case, the system will select the function payraise(Double), relying on the user's promise that a value of datatype Double will be provided when the statement is executed. At execution time, if the parameter is bound to a host variable whose datatype corresponds to the SQL datatype Double (or to some datatype that can be converted to Double, such as Integer), the statement will execute successfully. If, on the other hand, the parameter is bound to a host variable

---

1. If the named datatype is a distinct type, the value provided at execution time must have (or be convertible to) the base datatype of that distinct type.

that is incompatible with Double, the programmer's "promise" is broken and an error results.

It is a good general policy that all parameter markers used as function arguments should be typed. Since V1 supported only a fixed set of built-in functions, it was sometimes able to infer the datatype of an untyped parameter marker passed to a specific function. For example, the built-in `substr` function knows that its second argument must be an Integer. For compatibility with V1, these special cases are still supported in V2. However, it is good coding practice to use typed parameter markers when passing a parameter marker to a function, regardless of whether the function is built-in or user-defined.

6.1.5 Example Program LOADER1: A Bulk Loader

Let us illustrate the use of CLI and parameter markers by writing two example programs. Each of the examples will be written using both CLI and Embedded Dynamic SQL, so that you can compare these two interfaces side by side. Each of the examples will use dynamically computed SQL statements that could not be executed by a static SQL program.

Example LOADER1 is a bulk loader program. It uses dynamic SQL because the name of the table to be loaded is not known at compile time. In this simple example, the names and datatypes of the columns are fixed, but in a more complex general-purpose table loader, these datatypes could be read or computed dynamically.

For this example, let us imagine that we work at a laboratory that needs to record a series of experiments in a database. Each experiment consists of a series of trials, and each trial consists of a name and a value. The data from each experiment is recorded in a file. Each file contains the name of the experiment and the number of trials, followed by the name and value of each trial in the experiment. The data from each experiment needs to be loaded into a two-column table, using the name of the experiment as the name of the table. Our loader program reads the name of the experiment and the number of trials, and creates a table to hold the data. In our example, the tables created by the loader program always have two columns—the first column has name TRIALNAME and datatype Varchar(18), and the second has name TRIAL-VALUE and datatype Double.

VEGETABLES

TRIALNAME	TRIALVALUE
Eggplant	28.35
Okra	16.92
Rhubarb	14.86
Zucchini	25.07

FISH

TRIALNAME	TRIALVALUE
Carp	8.35
Flounder	6.08
Perch	5.29
Smelt	7.70

Figure 6-1: Example Tables Created by LOADER1

After creating the table, our loader program reads the experimental data in the form of a sequence of names and values, then loads the data into the table. The LOADER1 program reads its input data from standard input, which could be piped from a file or from another program.

Figure 6-1 shows an example of two tables that might be created and loaded by LOADER1, containing the results of two experiments named VEGE-TABLES and FISH.

By preparing an INSERT statement containing parameter markers and then executing it repeatedly, the LOADER1 program incurs the cost of parsing and analyzing the INSERT statement only once. The program consists of a series of steps, which are explained below and labelled in the example code.

Steps for Example Program LOADER1: A Bulk Loader Using CLI

STEP 1: Declare variables. Since a CLI program does not pass through a precompiler, there is no need for an SQL Declare Section such as you would find in a static SQL program. We simply declare our variables using normal C syntax. To ensure the portability of our program, it is wise to use a set of datatypes that are defined in the header file sqlcli1.h rather than native C datatypes. For example, the defined type SQLHSTMT represents the C datatype used for a statement handle (probably long), and the defined type SQLDOUBLE represents the C datatype used to hold a double-precision floating-point value (probably double). The header file sqlcli1.h also includes declarations of the CLI functions that we will need to call.

TIP: The type SQLCHAR is defined in sqlcli1.h as unsigned char. Some C and C++ compilers are sensitive to the difference between the datatypes char* and unsigned char*. If you are using one of these compilers and you have declared some variables of type SQLCHAR* or SQLCHAR[], you will need to cast these variables into the char* type before using them in places where a char* is expected, such as in the arguments of C functions strcat and strlen.

STEP 2: Allocate an environment handle. This directs CLI to set aside an area of memory that it will use to record the state of our application as long as it is running.

Code for Example Program LOADER1: A Bulk Loader Using CLI

```
#include "sqlcli1.h"
#include <stdlib.h>
#include <string.h>
#include <stdio.h>

void errorExit(SQLHENV henv, SQLHDBC hdbc, SQLHSTMT hstmt, char *place);

int main()
    {
    /*
    **   STEP 1: Declare variables
    */
    SQLHENV henv;                       /* environment handle        */
    SQLHDBC hdbc;                       /* connection handle         */
    SQLHSTMT hstmt;                     /* statement handle          */

    SQLCHAR dbname[] = "labdb";         /* name of database          */
    char qstring[80];                   /* holds an SQL statement    */
    char tablename[19];                 /* table to be created       */
    char trialname[19];                 /* name of one trial         */
    SQLINTEGER indicator1;              /* indicator for trialname   */
    SQLDOUBLE trialvalue;               /* value of one trial        */
    SQLINTEGER indicator2;              /* indicator for trialvalue  */

    SQLRETURN rc;                       /* return code               */
    SQLINTEGER ntrials;                 /* no. of trials in expt.    */
    SQLINTEGER baddata;                 /* set to 1 if bad data found */
    SQLINTEGER i;                       /* iteration variable        */

    /*
    **   STEP 2: Allocate environment handle
    */
    SQLAllocEnv(&henv);
```

STEP 3: Allocate a connection handle. If we plan to have multiple database connections (to the same or different databases), we will need multiple connection handles. Each connection handle has a set of properties such as isolation level and autocommit that govern the way in which our application will connect to a database. Autocommit is a particularly important connection option, because it determines whether each SQL statement is automatically committed after execution. The default value of autocommit (unless overridden by an entry in our `db2cli.ini` configuration file) is ON. In this example program, since we prefer to control our own commits and rollbacks, we turn autocommit OFF.

STEP 4: Connect to the database. Using the `SQLConnect()` function, we can connect to any database in the system database directory. If the server to which we wish to connect is performing authentication, we need to provide a valid userid and password at connect time. The constant SQL_NTS is used to indicate that the database name is passed in the form of a null-terminated string.

STEP 5: Allocate a statement handle. This handle will be used to execute many SQL statements, one after another.

STEP 6: Read the name of the experiment and the number of trials.

STEP 7: Construct and execute an SQL statement to create a table. In this simple example, the name of the table is determined by the name of the experiment, and the names and datatypes of the columns are known in advance. Of course, a more complex loader program could read or compute the number of columns to be created, as well as their names and datatypes, and could construct its CREATE TABLE statement accordingly.

We construct our CREATE TABLE statement as an ordinary character string. According to our laboratory rules, the value of a trial can be null, but the name of a trial is never null, so we include the phrase NOT NULL in the definition of the TRIALNAME column. The CLI function `SQLExecDirect()` causes our dynamic CREATE TABLE statement to be prepared and executed in one step, returning a code that indicates success or failure. In case of failure, we will pass the current context (the three handles and a notation of where the error occurred) to a routine called `errorExit`, which is discussed later.

STEP 8: Prepare an INSERT statement. Now that the table has been created, we are ready to insert data into the table, using an INSERT statement for each row. But since we plan to insert many rows, we don't want each INSERT statement to be a "surprise" that the system needs to parse and analyze from scratch. It's far more efficient to prepare a "prototype" INSERT statement in which the data values are represented by parameter markers (question marks). Once prepared, the statement can be executed as many times as we like without reinvoking the system parser and optimizer. Remember that parameter markers can only be used to substitute for missing data *values*, not for table names, column names, or keywords.

```
/*
**   STEP 3: Allocate connection handle and turn off autocommit option.
**   (Warning: the default is autocommit ON.)
*/
SQLAllocConnect(henv, &hdbc);
SQLSetConnectOption(hdbc, SQL_AUTOCOMMIT, SQL_AUTOCOMMIT_OFF);


/*
**   STEP 4: Connect to database
*/
rc = SQLConnect(hdbc, dbname, SQL_NTS,
                      NULL, SQL_NTS,
                      NULL, SQL_NTS);
if (rc != SQL_SUCCESS)
   errorExit(henv, hdbc, SQL_NULL_HSTMT, "Connecting to database");


/*
**   STEP 5: Allocate statement handle
*/
SQLAllocStmt (hdbc, &hstmt);


/*
** STEP 6: Read name of experiment and number of trials
*/
scanf ("%18s %d\n", tablename, &ntrials);


/*
**   STEP 7: Construct and execute a CREATE TABLE statement
*/
strcpy (qstring, "CREATE TABLE ");
strcat (qstring, tablename);
strcat (qstring,
          " (trialname Varchar(18) NOT NULL, trialvalue Double)" );
rc = SQLExecDirect (hstmt, (SQLCHAR *)qstring, SQL_NTS);
if (rc != SQL_SUCCESS)
   errorExit(henv, hdbc, hstmt, "Executing Create Table");


/*
**   STEP 8: Prepare an INSERT with two parameter markers
*/
strcpy (qstring, "INSERT INTO ");
strcat (qstring, tablename);
strcat (qstring, " VALUES (?, ?)" );
rc = SQLPrepare(hstmt, (SQLCHAR *)qstring, SQL_NTS);
if (rc != SQL_SUCCESS)
   errorExit(henv, hdbc, hstmt, "Preparing Insert statement");
```

STEP 9: Bind variables to parameter markers. Before the prepared INSERT statement can be executed, it is necessary to tell the system where to find the missing data values. This is done by calls to SQLBindParameter() that associate each parameter marker with two host variable addresses: one that contains the actual data, and another "indicator" variable. The indicator variable is used to indicate a null value by the code SQL_NULL_DATA (–1). If the variable being bound to the parameter marker contains a non-null character string, the indicator variable contains the length of the string, or the code SQL_NTS (–3) which means "null-terminated string."

As part of the binding process, the SQL datatype of the parameter and the C datatype of the host variable to which it is bound must both be specified, so that the system can provide any necessary conversions. Each time the prepared statement is executed, the system will take a new data value (or null) from the host variables that are bound to each of the parameter markers.

STEP 10: Read and insert the data. Now that the parameter markers are bound to variables, we can execute a loop that reads input data into the bound variables and executes the prepared INSERT statement repeatedly. We also check the input data for validity, and if it appears invalid, we set a "bad data" flag and break out of the loop. Each trial is represented by three input values, which are read by scanf: the trial name, the trial value, and a code that is set to 0 for a valid trial value or –1 for a null value. This code is used in indicator2 (the indicator variable of the TRIALVALUE column), and indicator1 (the indicator variable of the TRIALNAME column) is set to SQL_NTS to indicate a null-terminated string. The INSERT is executed by calling SQLExecute() and passing the handle of the prepared statement. The return code indicates success or failure, and we call our errorExit routine in case of failure.

```
/*
**   STEP 9: Bind host variables to the parameter markers
*/
SQLBindParameter(hstmt,
            1,                          /* first parameter marker     */
            SQL_PARAM_INPUT,            /* input parameter            */
            SQL_C_CHAR,                 /* datatype of host variable  */
            SQL_VARCHAR,                /* SQL datatype               */
            18,                         /* max length of input data   */
            0,                          /* not used in this call      */
            (SQLPOINTER)trialname,      /* address of host variable   */
            18,                         /* size of input buffer       */
            &indicator1 );              /* null or length indicator   */

SQLBindParameter(hstmt,
            2,                          /* second parameter marker    */
            SQL_PARAM_INPUT,            /* input parameter            */
            SQL_C_DOUBLE,               /* datatype of host variable  */
            SQL_DOUBLE,                 /* SQL datatype               */
            0,                          /* not used in this call      */
            0,                          /* not used in this call      */
            (SQLPOINTER)&trialvalue,    /* address of host variable   */
            8,                          /* size of input buffer       */
            &indicator2 );              /* null or length indicator   */

/*
**   STEP 10: Execute the INSERT statement for each input data record
*/
baddata = 0;
indicator1 = SQL_NTS;               /* trialname is never null */
for (i=0; i<ntrials && baddata == 0; i++)
   {
   rc = scanf("%18s %1f %d\n", trialname, &trialvalue, &indicator2);
   if (rc != 3 || (indicator2 != 0 && indicator2 != SQL_NULL_DATA))
      {
      baddata = 1;   /* bad input data */
      break;
      }
   rc = SQLExecute(hstmt);
   if (rc != SQL_SUCCESS)
      errorExit(henv, hdbc, hstmt, "Executing Insert statement");
   }
```

STEP 11: Commit or roll back. After completion of the loop, it is time to commit or roll back our transaction. If bad input data was discovered, we will roll back all database changes, including the creation of the table; otherwise we will commit our changes. In CLI, transactions are committed or rolled back by the SQLTransact() function rather than by an SQL statement. It is important to remember that we can control our own commits and rollbacks only because we turned off the autocommit option in Step 3.

STEP 12: Clean up. The orderly completion of our CLI program requires us to "clean up" by disconnecting from the database and freeing the resources represented by the statement handle, the connection handle, and the environment handle.

```
/*
**  STEP 11: Commit (or roll back if bad data was found)
*/
if (baddata)
   {
   rc = SQLTransact(henv, hdbc, SQL_ROLLBACK);
   if (rc != SQL_SUCCESS)
      errorExit(henv, hdbc, SQL_NULL_HSTMT, "Rollback due to bad data");
   printf ("Bad input data, transaction rolled back.\n");
   rc = -1;
   }
else
   {
   rc = SQLTransact(henv, hdbc, SQL_COMMIT);
   if (rc != SQL_SUCCESS)
      errorExit(henv, hdbc, SQL_NULL_HSTMT, "Commit");
   printf ("Data loaded successfully\n");
   rc = 0;
   }

/*
**  STEP 12: Clean up
*/
SQLFreeStmt(hstmt, SQL_DROP);        /* free statement handle   */
SQLDisconnect(hdbc);                 /* disconnect from database */
SQLFreeConnect(hdbc);                /* free connection handle   */
SQLFreeEnv(henv);                    /* free environment handle  */
exit(rc);

}    /* end of main */

void errorExit(SQLHENV henv, SQLHDBC hdbc, SQLHSTMT hstmt, char *place)
   {
   SQLCHAR sqlstate[SQL_SQLSTATE_SIZE + 1];
   SQLINTEGER sqlcode;
   SQLSMALLINT msglength;
   SQLCHAR msgbuffer[SQL_MAX_MESSAGE_LENGTH + 1];

   printf ("\nSQL error at %s, transaction rolled back.\n", place);
```

STEP 13:   Analyze errors. The errorExit routine is called whenever the return code of a CLI function indicates that the function was not successful. This is often caused by an error in the SQL statement that the CLI function is trying to execute. For example, if the CREATE TABLE statement attempts to create a table whose name is the same as that of an existing table, the SQL statement will fail and the SQLExecDirect() function will return the code SQL_ERROR. The job of the errorExit routine is to find and print more details about why the statement failed. This is done by repeatedly calling the SQLError() function, passing the handle associated with the failed statement. Each call to SQL-Error() will return an SQLCODE, an SQLSTATE, and an error message. When there are no more messages to be retrieved, SQLError()will return the code SQL_NO_DATA_FOUND.

STEP 14:   Roll back and clean up. If an error was encountered partway through the loading process, we would like to roll back all the database changes we have made so far. This is accomplished by a call to SQLTransact(), followed by calls to disconnect from the database and to free the handles.

6.1.6 Example Program QUERY1: A Query Interface

The second CLI example illustrates how a CLI program can interactively accept queries from a user and execute them, displaying results of various datatypes. This is the way in which interactive interfaces such as the CLP are implemented. A true interactive query interface is quite a complex program, so we will make some simplifying assumptions for the purpose of this example. We will accept only queries whose result is a single column of datatype Double or Clob. I chose these two datatypes in order to illustrate the handling of different types of data; of course, our program could be extended to handle multiple columns and additional datatypes.

```
/*
**   STEP 13: Retrieve error codes and messages
*/
while ( SQLError(henv, hdbc, hstmt, sqlstate, &sqlcode,
           msgbuffer, SQL_MAX_MESSAGE_LENGTH+1, &msglength)
   == SQL_SUCCESS )
   {
   printf("    SQLCODE = %d, SQLSTATE = %s\n", sqlcode, sqlstate);
   printf("    MESSAGE: %s\n", msgbuffer);
   }

/*
**   STEP 14: Roll back and clean up
*/
SQLTransact(henv, hdbc, SQL_ROLLBACK); /* roll back transaction   */
SQLDisconnect(hdbc);                   /* disconnect from database */
SQLFreeConnect(hdbc);                  /* free connection handle   */
SQLFreeEnv(henv);                      /* free environment handle  */
exit(-2);
}
```

Our program will prompt the user to enter an SQL statement, and it will then execute the SQL statement and display the result. Since the program is intended only as a query interface, we will detect and roll back any attempt to update the database. The user can cause the program to terminate by entering a null query (empty input line). The program consists of several steps, which are explained below and labelled in the example code.

As in the case of the bulk loader example, the query interface example is repeated using both CLI and Extended Dynamic SQL, so that these two approaches can be compared side to side on the same application.

Steps for Example Program QUERY1: A Query Interface Using CLI

STEP 1: Declare variables. As in example LOADER1, we use the types defined in `sqlcli1.h` rather than native C datatypes to enhance the portability of our program. In this simple example, we know that all query results will consist of a single column and that its datatype will be either Double or Clob. Therefore, we declare buffers to hold results of these two datatypes. To illustrate how Clobs can be handled in CLI programs, we will first fetch Clob data in the form of a locator and then use the locator to fetch the first 10 characters of the Clob (obviously, this can be extended to fetch any desired substring). Thus, our buffers for fetching results consist of a Double, a Clob locator, an 11-character array to hold the Clob substring, and an indicator variable to represent null values.

Code for Example Program QUERY1: A Query Interface Using CLI

```c
#include <stdlib.h>
#include <string.h>
#include <stdio.h>
#include "sqlcli1.h"

void errorExit(SQLHENV henv, SQLHDBC hdbc, SQLHSTMT hstmt, char *place);

int main()
   {
   /*
   **   STEP 1: Declare variables
   */
   SQLHENV henv;                     /* environment handle              */
   SQLHDBC hdbc;                     /* connection handle               */
   SQLHSTMT hstmt1;                  /* 1st statement handle            */
   SQLHSTMT hstmt2;                  /* 2nd statement handle            */
   SQLHSTMT hstmt3;                  /* 3rd statement handle            */
   SQLRETURN rc;                     /* return code                     */

   SQLCHAR dbname[9] = "yourdb";     /* name of database                */
   char qstring[100];                /* buffer for SQL query            */

   SQLDOUBLE  answerDouble;          /* answer buffer (if type is DOUBLE) */
   SQLINTEGER answerLocator;         /* answer locator (if type is CLOB)  */
   SQLCHAR answerString[11];         /* answer buffer (if type is CLOB)   */
   SQLINTEGER actualLength;          /* length of returned CLOB substring */
   SQLINTEGER nullindicator;         /* set to -1 if answer is null       */
   SQLINTEGER four = 4;              /* constant used in SQLBindParameter() */

   SQLSMALLINT ncols;                          /* no. of columns in result set */
   SQLCHAR colname[SQL_MAX_ID_LENGTH+1]; /* name of result column        */
   SQLSMALLINT colnamelen;                     /* actual length of column name */
   SQLSMALLINT coltype;                        /* datatype of result column    */

   SQLCHAR sqlstate[SQL_SQLSTATE_SIZE+1];                /* result sqlstate  */
   SQLINTEGER sqlcode;                                   /* result sqlcode   */
   SQLCHAR msgbuffer[SQL_MAX_MESSAGE_LENGTH+1];          /* error msg buffer */
   SQLSMALLINT msglength;                  /* actual length of error message */
```

STEP 2: Allocate an environment handle and a connection handle and turn off the autocommit option. This enables us to control our own commits and rollbacks. This program is intended to be a query interface, and we will force a rollback if a user attempts to execute a statement that modifies the database.

STEP 3: Connect to the database. This call to SQLConnect() illustrates how we can check the return code after each CLI function call and invoke a routine named errorExit to retrieve and display messages in the event of an error. To save space in our example code, we will not repeat this return code check after each CLI call.

STEP 4: Allocate three statement handles. We need a separate statement handle for each statement that will be "active" at the same time. For example, hstmt1 will maintain a cursor position while hstmt2 fetches a substring and hstmt3 frees a Clob locator.

STEP 5: Get an SQL statement from the user. We prompt the user to enter a statement and read it into the qstring buffer.

```
/*
**   STEP 2: Allocate environment and connection handles.
**   Turn off autocommit option (warning: default is autocommit ON).
*/
SQLAllocEnv(&henv);
SQLAllocConnect(henv, &hdbc);
SQLSetConnectOption(hdbc, SQL_AUTOCOMMIT, SQL_AUTOCOMMIT_OFF);

/*
**   STEP 3: Connect to database, test return code.
**   Similar checks for errors could be added to all CLI calls
**   but have been omitted for brevity.
*/
rc = SQLConnect(hdbc, dbname, SQL_NTS,
                        NULL, SQL_NTS,   /* provide userid, if needed   */
                        NULL, SQL_NTS);  /* provide password, if needed */
if (rc != SQL_SUCCESS)
   errorExit(henv, hdbc, SQL_NULL_HSTMT, "Connecting to database");

/*
**   STEP 4: Allocate three statement handles
*/
SQLAllocStmt (hdbc, &hstmt1);
SQLAllocStmt (hdbc, &hstmt2);
SQLAllocStmt (hdbc, &hstmt3);

/*
**   STEP 5: Get an SQL statement from the user
*/
printf("\nEnter a query, or empty string to quit:\n");
gets(qstring);
```

STEP 6: Execute the statement. At this point, we do not have a clue as to whether qstring contains a valid SQL statement or what kind of a statement it might be. To find the answer to these questions, we begin by examining the return code from SQLExecDirect(), which will be one of the following:

SQL_ERROR: This code indicates that qstring does not contain a valid SQL statement. We call SQLError() to retrieve and display the diagnostic messages, and prompt the user to enter another statement.

SQL_NO_DATA_FOUND: Surprisingly, this code does not indicate that the SQL statement was a query with an empty result set. Instead, it indicates that the statement was a valid UPDATE or DELETE statement that didn't happen to update or delete any rows. Since the database was not modified by the statement, there's no harm done, and we simply print a message and prompt the user to enter another statement.

SQL_SUCCESS or SQL_SUCCESS_WITH_INFO: These codes indicate that the SQL statement executed successfully, possibly with one or more informational messages. We print the messages, if any, and continue with our analysis of the result.

STEP 7: The next step in our analysis is to check the number of columns in the result set by calling the CLI function SQLNumResultCols(). This gives us an important clue about the SQL statement that was just executed. If the number of result columns is zero, the statement was not a query. This means that the user has successfully executed an SQL statement that was not a query, but we don't know what it was—it might even have modified the database. Since our program is a query-only interface, we will roll back the last statement and prompt the user to enter another statement.

If the number of columns in the result set is greater than one, the user will need to wait for a more sophisticated query interface than this example. We simply print a message and prompt for the next statement.

STEP 8: If the number of columns in the result set is exactly one, we know that the SQL statement was a successful one-column query. The next step is to obtain the name of the column and its datatype by calling the CLI function SQL-DescribeCol(), and to print the name of the column. We can then branch according to the datatype of the column. If the datatype of the column is a distinct type, SQLDescribeCol() retrieves the base datatype corresponding to that distinct type; the name of the distinct type can then be obtained by a call to SQLColAttributes(). Our simple example handles only a single column of type Double or Clob, but it would not be hard to extend the program to handle multiple columns of multiple datatypes.

```
while (strlen(qstring)>0)
   {
   /*
   **   STEP 6: Execute the statement and check return code
   */
   rc = SQLExecDirect (hstmt1, (SQLCHAR *)qstring, SQL_NTS);
   if (rc == SQL_NO_DATA_FOUND)
      printf("Your statement had no effect on the database.\n");
   if (rc == SQL_ERROR || rc == SQL_SUCCESS_WITH_INFO)
      {
      printf("Result of processing your SQL statement:\n");
      while ( SQLError(henv, hdbc, hstmt1, sqlstate, &sqlcode,
                  msgbuffer, SQL_MAX_MESSAGE_LENGTH+1, &msglength)
         == SQL_SUCCESS )
         {
         printf("   SQLCODE: %d, SQLSTATE: %s\n", sqlcode, sqlstate);
         printf("   MESSAGE: %s\n", msgbuffer);
         }
      }
   if (rc == SQL_SUCCESS || rc == SQL_SUCCESS_WITH_INFO)
      {
      /*
      **   STEP 7: Check the number of columns in the result set
      */
      rc = SQLNumResultCols(hstmt1, &ncols);
      if (ncols == 0)
         {
         printf("Your statement was not a valid query.\n");
         printf("Any updates have been rolled back.\n");
         SQLTransact(henv, hdbc, SQL_ROLLBACK);
         }
      else if (ncols > 1)
         printf("The result set has more than one column.\n");
      else
         {
         /*
         **   STEP 8: Get the column name and datatype, then
         **   print the column name
         */
         rc = SQLDescribeCol(hstmt1, 1, colname, SQL_MAX_ID_LENGTH,
                  &colnamelen, &coltype, NULL, NULL, NULL);
         printf("%s\n", colname);
         printf("-----------------\n");
```

STEP 9: If the datatype of the result column is SQL_DOUBLE, we need to fetch and display a column of double-precision floating-point numbers. In CLI, we do not need to explicitly open a cursor to fetch a result set. After a query has been executed, its statement handle automatically serves as a cursor on the result set and need not be explicitly opened.

In order to fetch answer values, we must first tell CLI where to deliver them. The SQLBindCol() function binds our buffer named answerDouble, and its indicator variable, to the first column of the result set. Then, each time we call SQLFetch(), one answer value is fetched into the answer buffer and the indicator variable. We continue fetching values and displaying them as long as we get successful return codes from SQLFetch(). If the user's SQL statement was a valid query with an empty result set, the first SQLFetch() will return a code of SQL_NO_DATA_FOUND. When we run out of results, we are ready to prompt the user for the next SQL statement.

STEP 10: If the datatype of the result column is SQL_CLOB, we need to fetch and display a column of Clob-type data. In this example program, we demonstrate the manipulation of Clobs by first fetching each Clob in the form of a locator, then using the locator to materialize the first 10 bytes of the Clob value into a buffer. First, we bind a variable of type SQLINTEGER (and an indicator variable) to the first column of the result set and indicate by a code that we wish to retrieve values in locator form. Each call to SQLFetch() delivers the locator of the next Clob value.

```
switch(coltype)
   {
   case SQL_DOUBLE:
      /*
      **   STEP 9: Fetch a column of Double-type answers
      **   and display them
      */
      SQLBindCol(hstmt1, 1, SQL_C_DOUBLE,
                        &answerDouble, 0, &nullindicator);
      rc = SQLFetch(hstmt1);
      if (rc == SQL_NO_DATA_FOUND)
         printf("Result set is empty.\n");
      else while (rc == SQL_SUCCESS
                     || rc == SQL_SUCCESS_WITH_INFO)
         {
         if (nullindicator==SQL_NULL_DATA) printf("(Null)\n");
         else printf("%f\n", answerDouble);
         rc = SQLFetch(hstmt1);
         }
      break;      /* end of SQL_DOUBLE case */

   case SQL_CLOB:
      /*
      **   STEP 10: Fetch a column of Clob-type answers
      **   in Locator form
      */
      SQLBindCol(hstmt1, 1, SQL_C_CLOB_LOCATOR,
                        &answerLocator, 0, &nullindicator);
      rc = SQLFetch(hstmt1);
      if (rc == SQL_NO_DATA_FOUND)
         printf("Result set is empty.\n");
      else while (rc == SQL_SUCCESS
                     || rc == SQL_SUCCESS_WITH_INFO)
         {
         if (nullindicator==SQL_NULL_DATA) printf("(Null)\n");
```

STEP 11: Once we have fetched a locator, we can use it in one or more calls to SQLGet-SubString() to materialize any desired subset of the actual Clob value. Notice that we need to use our second statement handle for the call to SQLGetSubString(), because the first statement handle is still "active," maintaining a cursor position in the result set.

STEP 12: After printing the Clob value, we don't need its locator anymore, so we free it, using our third statement handle to execute a FREE LOCATOR statement. Since the parameter of the FREE LOCATOR statement is always bound to the same host variable, the call to SQLBindParameter() could have been taken out of the loop and executed only once at the beginning of the program (but we have left it here for clarity).

```
else    /* Clob value is not null */
   {
   /*
   **   STEP 11: For each Clob, use its locator to
   **   fetch the first 10 characters of the answer
   */
   SQLGetSubString
      (hstmt2,                 /* 2nd stmt handle    */
       SQL_C_CLOB_LOCATOR,     /* source type        */
       answerLocator,          /* source locator     */
       1,                      /* starting position  */
       10,                     /* how many chars     */
       SQL_C_CHAR,             /* target type        */
       answerString,           /* target buffer      */
       11,                     /* size of buffer     */
       &actualLength,          /* returned length    */
       &nullindicator );       /* null indicator     */

   printf("%s ...\n", answerString);

   /*
   **   STEP 12: Free the Clob locator.   The
   **   SQLBindParameter could be taken out of the loop
   */
   SQLBindParameter
      (hstmt3,                 /* 3rd stmt handle    */
       1,                      /* parameter number   */
       SQL_PARAM_INPUT,        /* input parameter    */
       SQL_C_CLOB_LOCATOR,     /* C type of parm     */
       SQL_CLOB_LOCATOR,       /* SQL type of parm   */
       0,                      /* not used here      */
       0,                      /* not used here      */
       &answerLocator,         /* addr. of locator   */
       0,                      /* not used here      */
       &four);                 /* length of locator  */

   SQLExecDirect
      (hstmt3, (SQLCHAR *)"FREE LOCATOR ?", SQL_NTS);
   }
```

STEP 13: Using statement handle hstmt1, we now fetch the next Clob value in the form of a locator.

STEP 14: This simple example demonstrates the handling of two datatypes; obviously it could be extended to handle other datatypes as well by adding more cases to the switch statement.

STEP 15: The call to SQLFreeStmt() with a code of SQL_CLOSE tells CLI to close the cursor associated with the first statement handle, but to retain the handle for executing another statement. We are now ready to prompt the user for another SQL statement and return to the top of the loop.

STEP 16: When the user has indicated (by entering a null line) that there are no more queries to be processed, we end our transaction, release our various handles, and exit from the program.

```
                         /*
                         **  STEP 13: Fetch the next Clob value in Locator form
                         */
                         rc = SQLFetch(hstmt1);
                         }
                  break;    /* end of SQL_CLOB case */

             default:
                /*
                **  STEP 14: Other datatypes could be added here
                */
                printf("Answer datatype %d is not DOUBLE or CLOB\n",
                                                      coltype);
                break;    /* end of default case */

       }            /* end of switch on coltype              */
     }            /* end of case where result set has 1 column */
   }          /* end of processing a successful query        */

  /*
  **  STEP 15: Close the cursor and get the next query
  */
  SQLFreeStmt(hstmt1, SQL_CLOSE);
  printf("\nEnter a query, or empty string to quit:\n");
  gets(qstring);
  }    /* end of while-loop that processes queries */

/*
**  STEP 16: Commit the transaction and clean up
*/
printf("\nGoodbye, have a nice day.\n");

SQLTransact(henv, hdbc, SQL_COMMIT);    /* end the transaction     */
SQLFreeStmt(hstmt1, SQL_DROP);          /* free statement handle   */
SQLFreeStmt(hstmt2, SQL_DROP);          /* free statement handle   */
SQLDisconnect(hdbc);                    /* disconnect from database */
SQLFreeConnect(hdbc);                   /* free connection handle  */
SQLFreeEnv(henv);                       /* free environment handle */
return (0);
}    /* end of main */
```

STEP 17: All our CLI calls should check their return codes and invoke an error-handling routine if necessary (though we have omitted most of these calls for brevity). In this example, the error handler prints the place at which the error was detected; retrieves and prints all the available error codes and messages; and finally rolls back the transaction, disconnects from the database, and exits.

6.2 EMBEDDED DYNAMIC SQL

Embedded Dynamic SQL is the second method by which SQL statements may be generated and submitted for execution at run time. It is an older interface than CLI, but its power is approximately the same. You might choose to use Embedded Dynamic SQL rather than CLI for a dynamic application for one of the following reasons:

1. It supports host programming languages other than C.

2. It is more consistent in style with static SQL, and therefore you may prefer to use it in applications that mix dynamic and static SQL statements.

```
void errorExit(SQLHENV henv, SQLHDBC hdbc, SQLHSTMT hstmt, char *place)
   {
   SQLCHAR sqlstate[SQL_SQLSTATE_SIZE + 1];
   SQLINTEGER sqlcode;
   SQLSMALLINT msglength;
   SQLCHAR msgbuffer[SQL_MAX_MESSAGE_LENGTH + 1];

   printf ("\nSQL error at %s\n", place);

   /*
   **   STEP 17: Retrieve error codes and messages.
   **   Then roll back, clean up, and exit.
   */
   while ( SQLError(henv, hdbc, hstmt, sqlstate, &sqlcode,
              msgbuffer, SQL_MAX_MESSAGE_LENGTH+1, &msglength)
      == SQL_SUCCESS )
      {
      printf("   SQLCODE = %d, SQLSTATE = %s\n", sqlcode, sqlstate);
      printf("   MESSAGE: %s\n", msgbuffer);
      }

   SQLTransact(henv, hdbc, SQL_ROLLBACK); /* roll back transaction   */
   SQLDisconnect(hdbc);                   /* disconnect from database */
   SQLFreeConnect(hdbc);                  /* free connection handle   */
   SQLFreeEnv(henv);                      /* free environment handle  */
   exit(-2);
   }
```

3. Embedded Dynamic SQL programs tend to be somewhat more compact than equivalent CLI programs, partly because they do not require a separate function call to bind each parameter marker.

4. You may simply prefer the EXEC SQL notation or find it more familiar than the function-call notation of CLI.

The basic tasks to be accomplished by Embedded Dynamic SQL are the same as those of CLI: to prepare an SQL statement for execution, to obtain a description of the result if the prepared statement was a query, to execute a prepared statement with real values substituted for its parameter markers, and to fetch the result of a query, one row at a time. While CLI accomplished these tasks by means of function calls, Embedded Dynamic SQL accomplishes them by means of a special set of SQL statements that can be embedded in host programs and processed by the V2 precompiler.

6.2.1 Embedded Dynamic Statements

Embedded Dynamic SQL consists of four statements: PREPARE, DESCRIBE, EXECUTE, and EXECUTE IMMEDIATE. In addition, some options are added to the OPEN and FETCH statements in support of dynamic SQL queries.

Embedded Dynamic SQL statements make heavy use of *descriptors*. A descriptor is a data structure that contains a description of the datatypes used in one row of data. A descriptor may also indicate the column names associated with a row of data and may contain pointers to the data values themselves. The data structure used for a descriptor in an Embedded Dynamic SQL statement is called an SQLDA and is described in Section 6.2.3.

PREPARE

The purpose of PREPARE is to prepare an SQL statement, contained in a host variable, for execution. The syntax of a PREPARE statement is as follows:

prepare-statement

PREPARE statement-name — INTO descriptor — FROM host-variable

The host variable must be a character string containing an SQL statement. This statement is compiled by V2 and prepared for execution, but it is not executed. The statement name can be any identifier and is used in a later DESCRIBE, EXECUTE, or OPEN statement. The SQL statement being prepared may not contain any host variables, but it may contain one or more parameter markers, represented by question marks, which represent values to be supplied later, when the statement is executed. The parameter markers may be given explicit datatypes by using the CAST notation as described in Section 6.1.4. The descriptor, if provided, is used for obtaining a description of the result of the statement, if it is a query.

Examples of PREPARE statements:

```
PREPARE s1 FROM :mystatement;
PREPARE q1 INTO :mysqlda FROM :myquery;
```

DESCRIBE

The purpose of a DESCRIBE statement is to obtain a description of the datatypes in the result set of a query that has been prepared. A DESCRIBE statement is similar to the "INTO descriptor" clause of a PREPARE statement. Its syntax is as follows:

Example:

```
DESCRIBE q1 INTO :mysqlda;
```

Unlike the other Embedded Dynamic SQL statements, DESCRIBE can be executed from the CLP. If you type DESCRIBE followed by a query, the CLP will display a list of the datatypes and column names in the result set of your query. For example, you can obtain a list of the column names and datatypes in the FUNCTIONS catalog table by executing the following statement during a CLP session:

```
DESCRIBE SELECT * FROM syscat.functions;
```

EXECUTE

The EXECUTE statement executes a previously prepared SQL statement, substituting the values in the host variable list or descriptor for the parameter markers (question marks) in the prepared statement. The host variable list (or the descriptor) must provide exactly one value for each parameter marker. The datatypes of the values provided must be compatible with the declared types of the parameter markers; if the parameter markers are untyped, the values must have datatypes appropriate for their context. The syntax of an EXECUTE statement is as follows:

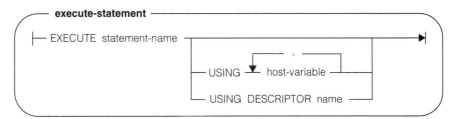

V1 had a limitation that an SQL statement must be prepared and executed within the same transaction. In V2, this limitation has been removed. Once prepared for execution, an SQL statement can be executed repeatedly, in multiple transactions, as long as the application remains connected to the database.

If a prepared SQL statement is a SELECT or VALUES statement, it cannot be executed by an EXECUTE statement, because the EXECUTE statement provides no way to return a result set. In order to obtain the result of a dynamically prepared SELECT or VALUES statement, it is necessary to declare a cursor for the statement and to apply OPEN and FETCH statements to the cursor.

Examples of EXECUTE statements:

```
EXECUTE s1;
EXECUTE s2 USING :x, :y :yindicator, :z :zindicator;
EXECUTE s3 USING DESCRIPTOR :mysqlda;
```

EXECUTE IMMEDIATE

An EXECUTE IMMEDIATE statement prepares an SQL statement for execution and executes it immediately, combining the functions of the PREPARE and EXECUTE statements. The host variable must contain a valid SQL statement that is not a SELECT or VALUES statement and that contains no parameter markers. The syntax of an EXECUTE IMMEDIATE statement is as follows:

Example:

```
EXECUTE IMMEDIATE :mystatement;
```

Dynamic Cursor Declaration

Embedded Dynamic SQL provides a means for obtaining results of dynamically prepared queries (SELECT or VALUES statements). This is done by declaring a cursor on the result of the prepared statement and by using special options of the OPEN and FETCH statements.

A cursor can be associated with the result of a query that has been (or will be) dynamically prepared, by means of a *dynamic cursor declaration,* which has the following syntax:

The statement name used in a dynamic cursor declaration should also be used in a PREPARE statement. After the PREPARE statement has been executed, if the prepared statement is a query, the dynamic cursor can be used in dynamic OPEN and FETCH statements to obtain the result of the query. If WITH HOLD is specified, the cursor can remain open across transaction boundaries.

Example of a dynamic cursor declaration:

```
DECLARE c1 CURSOR FOR q1;
```

Dynamic OPEN

A dynamic OPEN statement executes a previously prepared query (SELECT or VALUES statement), substituting the values in the host variable list or descriptor for the parameter markers (question marks) in the prepared query. The host variable list (or the descriptor) must provide exactly one value for each parameter marker, and the datatypes of these values must be compatible with the declared datatypes of the parameter markers or must be appropriate in the contexts where the parameter markers are used.

The cursor named in a dynamic OPEN statement must be associated (by a dynamic cursor declaration) with a prepared query. The dynamic OPEN statement opens a cursor on the result of the prepared query and positions the cursor before the first row of the result set. Rows of the result set can then be fetched using dynamic FETCH statements.

The syntax of a dynamic OPEN statement is as follows:

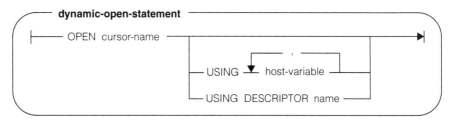

Examples:

```
OPEN c1;
OPEN c1 USING :x, :y :yindicator, :z :zindicator;
OPEN c1 USING DESCRIPTOR :mysqlda;
```

Dynamic FETCH

A dynamic FETCH statement advances the cursor to the next row of the result set and fetches it into a set of host variables or into a descriptor. The named cursor must be open, and the number of host variables (or entries in the descriptor) must match the number of columns in the result set. If the result set is empty or the cursor is positioned on or after the last row of the result set, the dynamic FETCH statement returns SQLCODE +100 (SQLSTATE 02000).

The syntax of a dynamic FETCH statement is as follows:

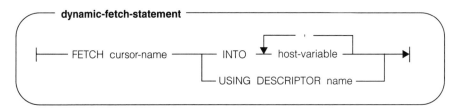

Examples:

```
FETCH c1 INTO :x :xindicator, :y :yindicator;
FETCH c1 USING DESCRIPTOR :mysqlda;
```

If a SELECT statement or a VALUES statement is executed using Embedded Dynamic SQL, that statement may not include an INTO clause. This restriction comes from the fact that, unlike static SQL, Embedded Dynamic SQL cannot handle both input and output host variables in the same statement. To illustrate the restriction, consider the following valid static SQL statement:

```
EXEC SQL SELECT salary INTO :x FROM emp WHERE name = :y;
```

In order to write an equivalent statement using Embedded Dynamic SQL, we would need to use a cursor (even though only a single result value is expected). The result would look like this:

```
char qstring[] = "SELECT salary FROM emp WHERE name = ?";
EXEC SQL PREPARE q1 FROM :qstring;
EXEC SQL DECLARE c1 CURSOR FOR q1;
EXEC SQL OPEN c1 USING :y;
EXEC SQL FETCH c1 INTO :x;
EXEC SQL CLOSE c1;
```

6.2.2 Example Program LOADER2: A Bulk Loader

Example LOADER2 is a bulk loader program, the same loader that we wrote using CLI in Section 6.1.5. You can refer to that section for a complete description of the application. To summarize it here, we need to read the name of a table from the input stream and create a two-column table with the given name and with columns named TRIALNAME and TRIALVALUE; then we need to read a series of names and values from the input stream and load them into the table. To accomplish these tasks, we will dynamically generate a CREATE TABLE statement and execute it, then we will prepare an INSERT statement containing parameter markers and execute it once for each row to be loaded. The following steps explain the statements in the program listing. By comparing these steps with the corresponding steps in example LOADER1, you can get a good understanding of the difference between CLI and Embedded Dynamic SQL. Depending on your programming style, you may find that an Embedded Dynamic SQL program is more concise than an equivalent CLI program.

In the LOADER2 example, all parameter markers are bound to host program variables. (For an example of how parameter markers can be bound using descriptors, see the QUERY2 example program in Section 6.2.6.)

Steps for Example Program LOADER2: A Bulk Loader Using Embedded Dynamic SQL

STEP 1: Declare variables. Since Embedded Dynamic SQL uses a precompiler, it requires that all program variables to be used in SQL statements be declared in an SQL Declare Section.

STEP 2: Include the SQL Communication Area (SQLCA). SQLCA is a structure containing the return codes and messages that result from executing SQL statements. It is declared in the header file sqlca.h.

STEP 3: Set up an error exit. You can specify a label to which control will be transferred whenever an SQL statement fails to execute successfully. In our case, we will ask the system to branch to errorExit whenever an error is detected.

Code for Example Program LOADER2: A Bulk Loader Using Embedded Dynamic SQL

```c
#include <sqlenv.h>
#include <stdlib.h>
#include <string.h>
#include <stdio.h>

int main()
   {
   /*
   **   STEP 1: Declare variables
   */
   EXEC SQL BEGIN DECLARE SECTION;
      char dbname[9] = "labdb";      /* name of database              */
      char qstring[80];              /* holds an SQL statement        */
      char tablename[19];            /* name of experiment            */
      char trialname[19];            /* name of one trial in expt.    */
      double trialvalue;             /* value of one trial in expt.   */
      short indicator;               /* indicator variable for trialvalue */
      char  msgbuffer[500];          /* buffer for DB2 error message  */
   EXEC SQL END DECLARE SECTION;

   int rc;                           /* return code                   */
   int ntrials;                      /* no. of trials in expt.        */
   int baddata;                      /* set to 1 if bad data found    */
   int i;                            /* iteration variable            */

   /*
   **   STEP 2: Include SQLCA
   */
   EXEC SQL INCLUDE SQLCA;           /* SQL Communication Area        */

   /*
   **   STEP 3: Set up an error exit
   */
   EXEC SQL WHENEVER SQLERROR GOTO errorExit;
```

STEP 4: Connect to the database. For this purpose, we can use a static SQL statement, passing the name of the database in a program variable.

STEP 5: Read the name of the experiment and the number of trials.

STEP 6: Construct and execute a CREATE TABLE statement. The name of the table comes from input, and the names and datatypes of the columns are known in advance. Of course, a more general-purpose loader program could be written in which the column names and datatypes are also controlled by program input.

   The EXECUTE IMMEDIATE statement, like the `SQLExecDirect()` function of CLI, prepares and executes our CREATE TABLE statement in a single step.

STEP 7: Prepare an INSERT statement. As in the CLI example, our INSERT statement will contain two parameter markers (question marks) so that we can execute the statement repeatedly with different data values.

STEP 8: Read and insert the data. The CLI step of binding parameter markers to variables is accomplished by the USING clause on the EXECUTE statement, which lists the variables whose values are to be substituted, in order, for the parameter markers in the statement. For any parameter marker that represents a nullable value, we must provide both a program variable and a null indicator. Thus, the clause `USING :trialname, :trialvalue :indicator` binds variables to two parameter markers: `:trialname` for the first marker, and `:trialvalue :indicator` for the second marker.

   As in example LOADER1, our program tests its input for validity, and if bad input data is encountered, it sets the `baddata` flag and breaks out of the input loop. Remember that if the SQL statement being executed fails for any reason, control will transfer to `errorExit`.

```
/*
**  STEP 4: Connect to the database
*/
EXEC SQL CONNECT TO :dbname;

/*
** STEP 5: Read name of experiment and number of trials
*/
scanf ("%18s %d\n", tablename, &ntrials);

/*
**  STEP 6: Construct and execute a CREATE TABLE statement
*/
strcpy (qstring, "CREATE TABLE ");
strcat (qstring, tablename);
strcat (qstring,
          " (trialname Varchar(18) NOT NULL, trialvalue Double)" );
EXEC SQL EXECUTE IMMEDIATE :qstring;

/*
**  STEP 7: Prepare an INSERT with two parameter markers
*/
strcpy (qstring, "INSERT INTO ");
strcat (qstring, tablename);
strcat (qstring, " VALUES (?, ?)" );
EXEC SQL PREPARE s1 FROM :qstring;

/*
**  STEP 8: Execute the INSERT statement for each input data record
*/
baddata = 0;
for (i=0; i<ntrials && baddata == 0; i++)
   {
   rc = scanf("%18s %lf %d\n", trialname, &trialvalue, &indicator);
   if (rc != 3 || (indicator != 0 && indicator != -1))
      {
      baddata = 1;    /* bad input data */
      break;
      }
   EXEC SQL EXECUTE s1 USING :trialname, :trialvalue :indicator;
   }
```

STEP 9: Commit or roll back. After completion of the loop, it is time to commit or roll back our transaction. If bad input data was discovered, we will roll back all database changes, including the creation of the table; otherwise we will commit our changes. We can use static SQL statements for these purposes.

STEP 10: Clean up. Since Embedded Dynamic SQL has no "handles" to release as CLI does, all we need to do is disconnect from the database.

STEP 11: Analyze errors. In this program, `errorExit` is not a separate procedure but simply a label for some statements that retrieve and print an error message, roll back the transaction, and exit. Note that the error-handling code executes WHENEVER SQLERROR CONTINUE before executing ROLLBACK, to avoid branching back to itself and looping in case the ROLLBACK is not successful.

```
    /*
    **   STEP 9: Commit (or roll back if bad data was found)
    */
    if (baddata)
        {
        EXEC SQL ROLLBACK;
        printf ("Bad input data, transaction rolled back.\n");
        rc = -1;
        }
    else
        {
        EXEC SQL COMMIT;
        printf ("Data loaded successfully\n");
        rc = 0;
        }

    /*
    **   STEP 10: Clean up
    */
    EXEC SQL CONNECT RESET;
    exit(rc);

errorExit:
    /*
    **   STEP 11: Handle SQL error conditions by
    **   retrieving and printing an error message
    */
    printf("\nSQL error, transaction rolled back.\n");
    sqlaintp(msgbuffer, 500, 70, &sqlca);
    printf("Message: %s\n", msgbuffer);

    EXEC SQL WHENEVER SQLERROR CONTINUE;
    EXEC SQL ROLLBACK;
    EXEC SQL CONNECT RESET;
    exit(-2);
    }    /* end of main */
```

6.2.3 The SQLDA Descriptor

Several of the Embedded Dynamic SQL statements use a *descriptor* for passing datatypes and/or values between the application program and the database. In each case, the descriptor used is a structure called an SQLDA. An SQLDA is a data structure that can describe the datatypes, lengths, and values of a variable number of data items. Such a descriptor is more flexible than a list of host variables, because it can be dynamically configured for different numbers and types of data items. This dynamic capability is important, for example, in writing a user-interface program to collect and process ad hoc queries, since the number of columns and the datatypes of the columns will be different in each query result.

Programs that need to use descriptors can obtain a declaration of the SQLDA structure by means of the following statement:

```
EXEC SQL INCLUDE SQLDA;
```

This statement causes the following declarations to be included in your program:

1. A type definition for the SQLDA structure

2. Type definitions for structures named sqlvar and sqlvar2, which occur inside the SQLDA structure

3. Definition of a macro named SQLDASIZE(n), which computes the size in bytes of an SQLDA structure having n entries; this macro is useful in allocating memory space to hold an SQLDA structure

An SQLDA descriptor consists of a fixed-size header, followed by a variable number of entries called sqlvars, as shown in Figure 6-2. The content of the entries varies with the type of statement (FETCH, DESCRIBE, and so on), but in general, each entry contains a description of one host variable or one table column. Since each descriptor can contain a different number of entries, it is your responsibility to use the generic type definitions obtained from EXEC SQL INCLUDE SQLDA to allocate space for each descriptor needed by your particular application.

The header of the descriptor contains an "eye-catcher" field containing the characters "SQLDA" and three integers named sqldabc, sqln, and sqld. The sqldabc and sqln fields are set at the time that the descriptor is allocated, indicating the size of the descriptor in bytes and its total number of entries. These numbers are fixed for the life of the descriptor. The sqld field, on the other hand, indicates how many of the entries are currently in use to describe

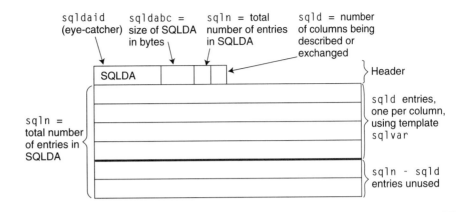

Figure 6-2: Overall Structure of an SQLDA Descriptor

columns or host variables for a particular SQL statement. The value of `sqld` can change from one statement to another, but it must always remain less than or equal to `sqln`.

The content of the `sqlvar` entries depends on the usage of the descriptor, as follows:

1. If the descriptor is used in a PREPARE or DESCRIBE statement, each `sqlvar` entry describes one column of a query result. The `sqlvar` indicates the datatype of the column, its maximum length, and the name of the column (if any).

2. If the descriptor is used in an OPEN, FETCH, EXECUTE, or CALL statement, each `sqlvar` entry is used to exchange one data value with the database (an input value in the case of OPEN and EXECUTE, an output value in the case of FETCH, or a bidirectional value in the case of CALL). The `sqlvar` indicates the datatype of the value and the address and length of the buffer allocated by the host program to contain the value. It may also contain the address of the indicator variable that is used to represent null values.

The `sqltype` field of an `sqlvar` entry is used to indicate the datatype of the entry. (The typecodes used in this field are listed in Appendix C.)

The basic structures of the SQLDA and `sqlvar`, as described above, are the same for all products in the DB2 family. However, the new features of V2 have required some extensions to be made in the way that descriptors are used. These changes were necessary for the following reasons:

1. The length field in an `sqlvar` entry occupies only two bytes, which is not large enough to describe the length of a LOB-type value.

2. Some way is needed to describe the datatype of a column when that datatype is user-defined. Built-in datatypes can be indicated by predefined typecodes, but for user-defined (distinct) types, it is necessary to return the actual name of the datatype. This requires more space than is available in an `sqlvar` entry.

For these reasons, the designers of V2 have introduced the concept of a "double-size" SQLDA, which is used whenever it is necessary to describe or exchange data that includes LOB types or distinct types. A double-size SQLDA contains *two* entries for each data value: an `sqlvar` entry and an `sqlvar2` entry. A double-size SQLDA can be distinguished from a single-size SQLDA because it contains the character "2" in byte 7 of its eye-catcher field, as shown in Figure 6-3. All the `sqlvar` entries come first, followed by all the `sqlvar2` entries. The `sqlvar2` entries are used to contain the information that will not fit into the `sqlvar` entries: the lengths of LOB-type data and the datatype names of distinct-type data. The `sqln` and `sqld` fields still indicate the total number of entries in the descriptor and the number of columns being described, respectively. But the relationship between these two numbers is different: in a double-size SQLDA, `sqld` cannot be more than half `sqln`.

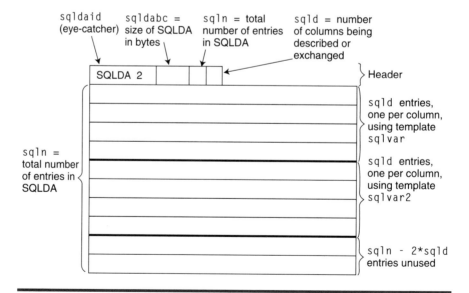

Figure 6-3: A "Double-Size" SQLDA Descriptor

The information pertaining to the nth column (or the nth data value) in a double-size descriptor is found in two entries: entry number n (type `sqlvar`) and entry number `sqld` + n (type `sqlvar2`). The second of these entries contains meaningful information only if the datatype of the column (or value) is a LOB datatype or distinct type. The actual content of the `sqlvar2` entry depends on the usage of the descriptor, as follows:

1. If the descriptor is used in a PREPARE or DESCRIBE statement, each `sqlvar2` entry describes the maximum length of the corresponding column (if it is a LOB datatype) and/or the datatype of the column (if it is a distinct type). The datatype is spelled out as a fully qualified name such as "`geometry.triangle`."

2. If the descriptor is used in an OPEN, FETCH, EXECUTE, or CALL statement, each LOB-type data value being exchanged has an `sqlvar2` entry that contains two pieces of length information: the length of the buffer that holds the value and a pointer to a buffer containing the actual length of the value itself.

The C declarations for the SQLDA, `sqlvar`, and `sqlvar2` structures are found in `sqllib/include/sqlda.h` and are given below:

```
struct sqlda
{
    char           sqldaid[8];             /* Eye-catcher = 'SQLDA    '       */
    /***********************************************************************/
    /* The 7th byte has special meaning.  If it is '2', this means there */
    /* are twice as many sqlvars as there are host variables or columns. */
    /***********************************************************************/
    long           sqldabc;                /* SQLDA size in bytes=16+44*SQLN */
    short          sqln;                    /* Number of SQLVAR elements      */
    short          sqld;                    /* # of columns or host vars.     */
    struct sqlvar  sqlvar[1];              /* First SQLVAR element           */
};

struct sqlvar                              /* Variable Description            */
{
    short          sqltype;                /* Typecode                       */
    short          sqllen;                 /* Length of data value           */
    char           *sqldata;               /* Pointer to data value          */
    short          *sqlind;                /* Pointer to Null indicator      */
    struct sqlname sqlname;                /* Variable name                  */
};
```

```
struct sqlvar2                          /* Variable Description        */
{
   union sql8bytelen  len;              /* 8-byte length, 4 bytes used now */
   char               *sqldatalen;      /* Pointer to 4-byte length buffer */
   struct sqldistinct_type sqldatatype_name;   /* Distinct type name    */
};

union sql8bytelen
{
  long            reserve1[2];     /* Reserved for future 8-byte lengths. */
  long            sqllonglen;      /* This is what is currently used       */
};

struct sqldistinct_type                 /* Name of distinct type       */
{
   short          length;          /* Name length [1..27]             */
   char           data[27];        /* Name of distinct type           */
   char           reserved1[3];    /* Reserved                        */
};
```

6.2.4 Using an SQLDA in a PREPARE or DESCRIBE Statement

The SQLDA descriptor is used in PREPARE and DESCRIBE statements to investigate the "shape" of a query result—that is, the number of columns in the result set and the datatypes and names (if any) of the columns. In order to do this, you must first allocate a descriptor of the proper size. For this purpose, you can use the macro SQLDASIZE(n), which computes the size (in bytes) of an SQLDA structure containing n entries.

You should allocate a descriptor containing at least 2n entries, where n is the maximum number of columns in any result set that you expect to DESCRIBE. (If you are sure that no result set will ever contain a LOB datatype or a distinct type, you need only n entries rather than 2n.)

The following example allocates memory for a descriptor containing 50 entries and sets the values of the fields sqln (total number of entries) and sqldabc (total size in bytes).

```
short numEntries = 50;
short bytesNeeded = SQLDASIZE(numEntries);
struct sqlda *daptr;
daptr = (struct sqlda *)malloc(bytesNeeded);
daptr->sqln = numEntries;
daptr->sqldabc = bytesNeeded;
```

TABLE 6-1: Return Codes from PREPARE and DESCRIBE Statements

SQLCODE	SQLSTATE	Meaning
+236	01005	Your descriptor was too small, and the result set contains no LOBs or distinct types. The number of columns in the result set is returned in `sqld`. You must allocate a new descriptor containing at least this many entries and try again.
+237 +238 +239	01594 01005 01005	Your descriptor was too small, and the result set contains some LOBs and/or distinct types. The number of columns in the result set is returned in `sqld`. You must allocate a new descriptor containing at least twice this many entries and try again.

After you execute a PREPARE or DESCRIBE statement, you should examine the resulting SQLCODE (or SQLSTATE) to make sure that your descriptor was big enough to hold the result. If your descriptor was too small, you will get one of the return codes listed in Table 6-1.

The following code fragment illustrates the process of examining a descriptor after a DESCRIBE statement and reallocating a larger descriptor if necessary.

```
short entriesNeeded, bytesNeeded;
entriesNeeded = 0;
/* assume daptr points at an SQLDA structure */
EXEC SQL DESCRIBE s1 INTO :*daptr;
if (SQLCODE == 236)
    entriesNeeded = daptr->sqld;
if (SQLCODE == 237 || SQLCODE == 238 || SQLCODE == 239)
    entriesNeeded = 2 * daptr->sqld;
if (entriesNeeded > 0)
    {                    /* old SQLDA was too small */
    free(daptr);
    bytesNeeded = SQLDASIZE(entriesNeeded);
    daptr = (struct sqlda *)malloc(bytesNeeded);
    daptr->sqln = entriesNeeded;
    daptr->sqldabc = bytesNeeded;
    EXEC SQL DESCRIBE s1 INTO :*daptr;
    }
```

After your PREPARE or DESCRIBE statement has executed successfully, the seventh byte of the sqldaid field will contain the character "2" if the descriptor is "double-size." The following macros have been defined (in sqlda.h) to make it easy to examine (and set) the character that indicates "double-size":

GETSQLDOUBLED(daptr): Evaluates to 1 if daptr points to a double-size descriptor; otherwise evaluates to 0.

SETSQLDOUBLED(daptr, newvalue): Sets the double-size indicator character of the given descriptor to a new value. To indicate a double-size descriptor, use SETSQLDOUBLED(daptr, SQLDOUBLED). To indicate a single-size descriptor, use SETSQLDOUBLED(daptr, SQLSINGLED).

The details of the descriptor structures returned by PREPARE and DESCRIBE are shown in Figure 6-4. The sqlvar entries indicate the names and datatypes of all the columns in the result set, using the typecodes listed in Appendix C. For every column that is a distinct type, the sqlvar2 entry contains the full name of the distinct type and the sqlvar entry contains the typecode of the underlying base datatype. Since distinct types have the same representation as their underlying base datatype, the sqltype in the sqlvar entry can be used to indicate the proper type of variable for exchanging data with the distinct-type column.

The sqllen field of an sqlvar entry indicates the maximum length, in bytes, of the data value described by the entry, for all datatypes except Decimal and the LOB datatypes. For the Decimal datatype, the sqllen field contains the precision (first byte) and scale (second byte) of the data value. The precision and scale can be retrieved separately as shown in the following example (assuming that daptr points to an SQLDA whose nth entry describes a Decimal value):

```
precision = ((char *)&(daptr->sqlvar[n].sqllen))[0];
scale     = ((char *)&(daptr->sqlvar[n].sqllen))[1];
```

For LOB datatypes, the sqllen field of sqlvar is set to zero, and the maximum length of the data value is indicated in the len.sqllonglen field of sqlvar2. Two macros have been provided (in sqlda.h) to help you examine (and set) the "long-length" information in an sqlvar2 entry. Because of the alignment of the long-length data, you should use these macros rather than accessing the long-length field directly. The macros are as follows:

GETSQLDALONGLEN(daptr, n): Evaluates to the four-byte long-length field of the sqlvar2 entry that corresponds to the nth column in the given descriptor.

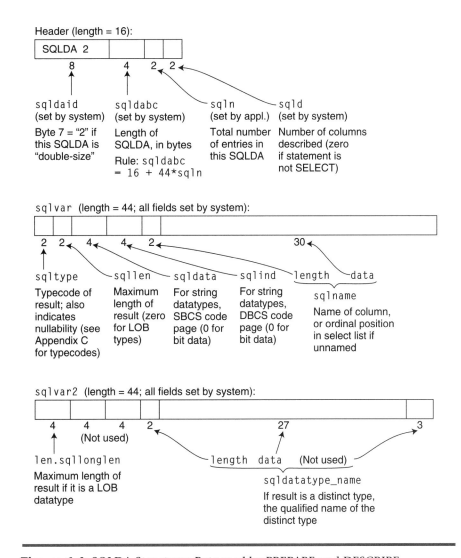

Figure 6-4: SQLDA Structures Returned by PREPARE and DESCRIBE Statements

SETSQLDALONGLEN(daptr, n, length): Sets the long-length field of the sqlvar2 entry that corresponds to the nth column in the given descriptor. Use this macro to indicate the length of the data buffer you have allocated for input or output of a LOB-type value.

6.2.5 Using an SQLDA in an OPEN, FETCH, EXECUTE, or CALL Statement

Another use of an SQLDA descriptor is for actual exchange of data between an application program and the database. In an OPEN or EXECUTE statement, the values being exchanged are input values that are being substituted for the parameter markers in a statement that was previously prepared. In a FETCH statement, the values being exchanged are output values that are being delivered into variables or buffers in the application program. These buffers might have been allocated on the basis of information returned by a previous PREPARE or DESCRIBE statement. In a CALL statement, data is being exchanged in both directions between a stored procedure and a client program. (Stored procedures are discussed in Chapter 7.)

The details of the SQLDA structures used in OPEN, FETCH, EXECUTE, and CALL statements are shown in Figure 6-5.

The `sqlname` field of the `sqlvar` structure has a specialized meaning in a CALL statement: a name consisting of four bytes of binary zeros indicates that the data value is a binary string and that no code page conversion should be done on the value when it is exchanged between a client program and a stored procedure. If an SQLDA is being used to exchange binary strings (such as Varchar FOR BIT DATA) in a CALL statement, the sixth byte of its `sqldaid` field should be set to a "+" character. (The use of a CALL statement to exchange data between a client program and a stored procedure is discussed in Section 7.2.1.)

As usual, the `sqlvar2` entries in the descriptor are used to carry information about LOB-type data values. When used in OPEN, FETCH, EXECUTE, and CALL statements, the `sqlvar2` entries contain two pieces of length information:

1. The length of the buffer allocated for input or output of the LOB-type value is carried in `sqlvar2.len`. This length information should be examined and set by the GETSQLDALONGLEN and SETSQLDALONGLEN macros described previously.

2. The actual length of an individual LOB-type value is carried in an eight-byte buffer pointed to by `sqlvar2.sqldatalen`. This pointer allows you to manage the actual-length information for LOB-type data separately from the value itself. If the pointer is set to NULL, the actual-length information is carried in the first eight bytes of the LOB-type value itself. The following macros have been provided (in `sqlda.h`) for getting and setting the actual-length pointer:

    GETSQLDALENPTR(daptr, n): Returns the actual-length pointer from the `sqlvar2` entry that corresponds to the nth column in the given descriptor.

    SETSQLDALENPTR(daptr, n, lenptr): Sets the actual-length pointer in the `sqlvar2` entry that corresponds to the nth column in the given descriptor.

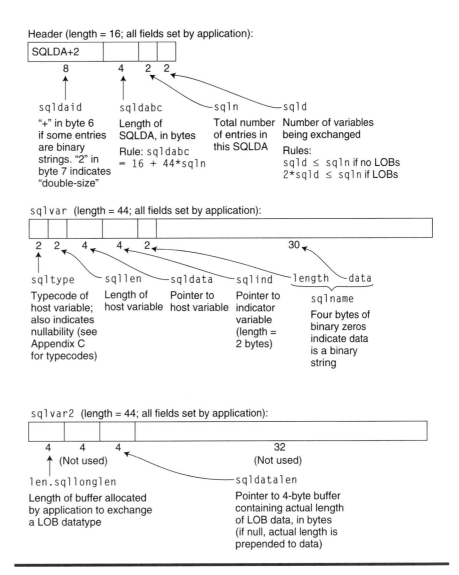

Figure 6-5: Use of an SQLDA Descriptor in OPEN, FETCH, EXECUTE, and CALL Statements

Before a descriptor returned by a DESCRIBE statement can be used in a FETCH statement, the following information must be added to the descriptor for each value to be fetched:

- The address into which the data is to be fetched
- The length of the buffer allocated at this address to receive the data
- The address of the null indicator variable (if any)

The task of preparing a descriptor for use in a FETCH statement consists of allocating buffers of the proper size and placing their addresses and lengths in the proper fields of the descriptor. For columns that permit null values (indicated by odd-numbered typecodes), a two-byte null indicator variable must be allocated as well as a buffer to receive the column value. The size of the buffer required for each column is indicated in the `sqlvar.sqllen` field for that column, unless the datatype of the column is Decimal or a LOB datatype. Thus, the following code fragment will allocate buffers of the proper size for all columns except those containing Decimal or LOB-type data (assume that `daptr` points to a descriptor returned by a DESCRIBE statement):

```
for (i = 0; i < daptr->sqld; i++)
   {
   daptr->sqlvar[i].sqldata =
           (char *)malloc(daptr->sqlvar[i].sqllen);
   if (daptr->sqlvar[i].sqltype % 2 == 1)
      daptr->sqlvar[i].sqlind = (short *)malloc(2);
   }
```

 TIP: Don't forget to set the `sqlind` pointer for all nullable columns. If you leave this pointer uninitialized, the system will attempt to store through it anyway and your program will probably crash.

For some types of data, you have a certain amount of flexibility in the type of buffer that you use for data exchange. For example, if DESCRIBE returns a typecode of 448 (indicating Varchar) for a given column, you can leave the typecode as 448 and exchange the data in length-prefix form, or change the typecode to 460 and exchange the data in null-terminated form (be sure to allocate an extra byte for the null terminator).

LOB-type columns provide the greatest amount of flexibility in how data can be exchanged. For example, suppose that, after a DESCRIBE statement, `daptr` points to a descriptor in which the fifth entry has an `sqltype` code of 408, indicating a non-nullable Clob-type column. You can prepare to fetch the values in this column in any of the following ways:

1. Find the maximum length of the column by using the GETSQLDALONGLEN macro, allocate a memory buffer of at least this size, and place its address in the corresponding `sqlvar.sqldata` field. Use the SETSQLDALENPTR macro to indicate where you want the actual-length information to be delivered. Your code might look like this:

```
int n = 5;                              /* (use the actual column number)     */
int maxLen;                             /* max. length of Clob column         */
char *buffPtr;                          /* points at buffer for data          */
long *actLenPtr;                        /* points at buffer for actual length */
sqlvar *var1Ptr;                        /* sqlvar entry for this column        */
var1Ptr = (sqlvar *) &(daptr->sqlvar[n]);
maxLen = GETSQLDALONGLEN(daptr, n);       /* get max. length of column  */
buffPtr = (char *)malloc(maxLen);         /* allocate data buffer       */
var1Ptr->sqldata = buffPtr;               /* set addr. of data buffer   */
actLenPtr = (long *) malloc(sizeof(long)); /* allocate length buffer    */
SETSQLDALENPTR(daptr, n, actLenPtr);      /* set addr. of length buffer */
```

Now this column is ready for FETCH. After each FETCH, the data will be in `*buffPtr` and its actual length will be in `*actLenPtr`.

2. Allocate a Clob file-reference structure (`struct sqlfile`, declared in `sql.h`) and put its address in the `sqlvar.sqldata` pointer for the given column. Change `sqlvar.sqltype` from SQL_TYP_CLOB (408) to SQL_TYP_CLOB_FILE (808), indicating that the data should be delivered to a file. Fill in the file-reference structure with the name of the file where you want the Clob output to be delivered. Each FETCH statement will then replace (or append) the file with a new Clob value. Your code might look like this:

```
int n = 5;                              /* (use the actual column number)      */
struct sqlfile  *fileRefPtr;            /* points at a file-reference structure */
sqlvar *var1Ptr;                        /* sqlvar entry for this column         */
var1Ptr = (sqlvar *) &(daptr->sqlvar[n]);
fileRefPtr = (sqlfile *) malloc(sizeof(sqlfile)); /* allocate file ref  */
strcpy(fileRefPtr->name, "clobfile.txt");         /* initialize file ref */
fileRefPtr->name_length = strlen(fileRefPtr->name);
fileRefPtr->file_options = SQL_FILE_APPEND;   /* append data to file   */
var1Ptr->sqltype = SQL_TYP_CLOB_FILE;         /* requested output type */
var1Ptr->sqldata = (char *)fileRefPtr;        /* addr. of file ref     */
var1Ptr->sqllen = SQL_LOBFILE_LEN;            /* size of file ref      */
```

Now this column is ready for FETCH. Each FETCH will append a new Clob to the output file named `clobfile.txt` and will return the new length of the file in `fileRefPtr->data_length`.

3. Allocate a Clob locator (you can use the C type `long`) and put its address in the `sqlvar.sqldata` pointer for the given column. Change `sqlvar.sqltype` from SQL_TYP_CLOB (408) to SQL_TYP_CLOB_LOCATOR (964), indicating that you want to receive a locator rather than the actual data. After each FETCH, you will have a locator that you can use to manipulate the Clob-type data without actually retrieving the bits. Your code might look like this:

```
int n = 5;                              /* (use the actual column number) */
long *locatorPtr;                       /* points at buffer for locator   */
sqlvar *var1Ptr;                        /* sqlvar entry for this column    */
var1Ptr = (sqlvar *) &(daptr->sqlvar[n]);
locatorPtr = (long *) malloc(sizeof(long));  /* allocate locator buffer   */
var1Ptr->sqltype = SQL_TYP_CLOB_LOCATOR;     /* requested output type     */
var1Ptr->sqldata = (char *)locatorPtr;       /* addr. of locator buffer   */
var1Ptr->sqllen = sizeof(long);              /* length of locator buffer  */
```

Now this column is ready for FETCH. After each FETCH, a new locator will be in `*locatorPtr`. After you have fetched a locator, you can use the locator to fetch part or all of the actual Clob value. One way to do this is by using a VALUES statement as shown below. When you no longer need the locator, free it by using a FREE LOCATOR statement.

```
EXEC SQL BEGIN DECLARE SECTION;
    SQL TYPE IS CLOB_LOCATOR locator1;
    char clobValue[101];
EXEC SQL END DECLARE SECTION;

locator1 = *locatorPtr;

/* Fetch first 100 bytes of Clob */
EXEC SQL VALUES(substr(:locator1, 1, 100)) INTO :clobValue;

/* Free locator when no longer needed */
EXEC SQL FREE LOCATOR :locator1;
```

 TIP: In the above example, the actual locator is copied from `*locatorPtr` into a variable with a declared type of CLOB_LOCATOR. This was done in order to provide an argument of the proper type for the `substr` function.

6.2.6 Example Program QUERY2: A Query Interface

As an example of how to use an SQLDA descriptor, let us write an interactive query interface program using Embedded Dynamic SQL. The following program, QUERY2, is functionally equivalent to the CLI example program named QUERY1 in Section 6.1.6. It is revealing to compare these two programs side by side.

Remember that the purpose of our simple query interface example is to obtain an SQL statement from an interactive user, execute the statement, and display the results. As before, we will keep the program simple by handling only queries and by requiring that the result set be a single column of datatype Double or Clob.

Steps for Example Program QUERY2: A Query Interface Using Embedded Dynamic SQL

STEP 1: Declare variables. In Embedded Dynamic SQL, all variables used for database interactions must be declared in an SQL Declare Section.

STEP 2: Allocate an SQLDA descriptor for our queries. In this example, we require that all result sets have a single column, so we can predict the necessary size of the SQLDA in advance. Our SQLDA must contain two `sqlvar` entries, because two entries are needed to describe a single column of type Clob. If the number of columns in the result set were unknown, we would need to allocate a descriptor using the techniques described in Section 6.2.4. After allocating the SQLDA, we turn on its "doubled" flag and make it describe its own length by setting its `sqln` field to 2.

Code for Example Program QUERY2: A Query Interface Using Embedded Dynamic SQL

```c
#include <stdlib.h>
#include <string.h>
#include <stdio.h>
#include <sqlenv.h>

EXEC SQL INCLUDE SQLCA;

int main()
    {
    /*
    **   STEP 1: Declare variables
    */
    EXEC SQL BEGIN DECLARE SECTION;
        char dbname[9] = "yourdb";    /* name of database              */
        char  qstring[100];           /* buffer for SQL query          */
        double answerDouble;          /* answer data (if type is DOUBLE) */
        SQL TYPE IS CLOB_LOCATOR
                    answerLocator;    /* answer locator (if type is CLOB) */
        char answerString[11];        /* answer buffer (if type is CLOB) */
        short nullindicator;          /* set to -1 if answer is null   */
        char  msgbuffer[500];         /* buffer for DB2 error message  */
    EXEC SQL END DECLARE SECTION;

    char *colnameptr;                 /* name of result column         */
    short colnamelen;                 /* actual length of column name  */
    short coltype;                    /* type of result column         */

    struct sqlda  *sqldaptr;          /* points to allocated sqlda     */

    /*
    **   STEP 2: Allocate an SQLDA containing two SQLVARs.
    **   (Remember, we need two SQLVARs to describe a single CLOB column.)
    */
    sqldaptr = (struct sqlda*) malloc( SQLDASIZE(2) );
    sqldaptr->sqln = 2;
    SETSQLDOUBLED(sqldaptr, SQLDOUBLED);
```

STEP 3: Connect to the database.

STEP 4: Establish a way for handling errors. In general, if an error is detected in processing a user's SQL statement, we want to display the error code and then
prompt the user for another query. The WHENEVER statement causes this to
happen by telling the system to go to the bottom of the query loop whenever
an error is encountered. Unexpected errors in the SQL statements that we
build into the program will be handled in the same way as user errors.

STEP 5: Prompt the user for an SQL statement and read it into the qstring buffer.

STEP 6: Prepare the query and get a description of the result set. The PREPARE and
DESCRIBE statements could have been combined into a single PREPARE INTO
statement. If the user's input was not a valid SQL statement, the program will
automatically branch to the nextquery label. On the other hand, if the input
was a valid SQL statement, we can learn something about it by examining the
sqld field of the descriptor. If sqld is equal to zero, the statement was a valid
statement but not a query, so we need to roll back any updates that might
have been made to the database. If sqld is greater than zero, it indicates the
number of columns in the result set. If this number is greater than one, we
print an error message and prompt for the next query.

```
/*
**   STEP 3: Connect to database and check return code
**   (provide userid and password, if needed)
*/
EXEC SQL CONNECT TO :dbname;
if (SQLCODE != 0)
   {
   printf("Error in connecting to database\n");
   exit(1);
   }

/*
**   STEP 4: Establish a way for handling errors
*/
EXEC SQL WHENEVER SQLERROR GO TO nextquery;

/*
**   STEP 5: Get an SQL statement from the user
*/
printf("\nEnter a query, or empty string to quit:\n");
gets(qstring);

while (strlen(qstring)>0)
   {
   /*
   **   STEP 6: Prepare the query and get a description
   **   of the result set
   */
   EXEC SQL PREPARE Q1 FROM :qstring;

   EXEC SQL DESCRIBE Q1 into :*sqldaptr;

   if (sqldaptr->sqld == 0)
      {
      printf("Your statement was not a valid query.\n");
      printf("Any updates have been rolled back.\n");
      EXEC SQL ROLLBACK;
      }
   else if (sqldaptr->sqld > 1)
      printf("The result set has more than one column.\n");
```

STEP 7: Once we have established that the user's input was a valid single-column query, we can print the name of the column, which is found in the `sqlname` field of the first `sqlvar` entry in the descriptor.

STEP 8: In order to fetch the result set, it is necessary to open a cursor. The cursor will maintain a position in the result set as we fetch it, row by row. The explicit opening of a cursor is necessary in Extended Dynamic SQL but not in CLI, since a CLI statement handle serves as an implicit cursor.

After opening the cursor, we branch according to the datatype of the result column, which is found in the `sqltype` field of the first `sqlvar` entry in the descriptor.

STEP 9: If the datatype of the result column is SQL_TYP_NFLOAT (nullable double-precision float), we need to fetch and display a column of floating-point numbers. The first step is to place the addresses of our Double-type answer buffer and indicator variable into the SQLDA descriptor. Then, each time we execute a FETCH statement, one answer value is fetched into the buffer. We continue fetching and displaying values (checking the indicator variable for nulls) until we receive an SQLCODE of 100, indicating that the end of the result set has been reached.

```
else   /* sqld is exactly 1 */
   {
   /*
   **   STEP 7: Print the column name
   */
   colnamelen = sqldaptr->sqlvar[0].sqlname.length;
   colnameptr = sqldaptr->sqlvar[0].sqlname.data;
   printf("%*.*s\n", colnamelen, colnamelen, colnameptr);
   printf("------------------\n");


   /*
   **   STEP 8: Open a cursor on the result set
   */
   EXEC SQL DECLARE C1 CURSOR FOR Q1;
   EXEC SQL OPEN C1;

   coltype = sqldaptr->sqlvar[0].sqltype;
   switch(coltype)
      {
      case SQL_TYP_NFLOAT:
         /*
         **   STEP 9: Fetch a column of Double-type answers
         **   and display them
         */
         sqldaptr->sqlvar[0].sqldata = (char *) &answerDouble;
         sqldaptr->sqlvar[0].sqllen = 8;
         sqldaptr->sqlvar[0].sqlind = &nullindicator;
         EXEC SQL FETCH C1 USING DESCRIPTOR :*sqldaptr;
         if (SQLCODE == 100)
            printf("Result set is empty.\n");
         else while (SQLCODE == 0)
            {
            if (nullindicator == -1) printf("(Null)\n");
            else printf("%f\n", answerDouble);
            EXEC SQL FETCH C1 USING DESCRIPTOR :*sqldaptr;
            }
         break;    /* end of DOUBLE case */
```

STEP 10: If the datatype of the result column is SQL_TYP_NCLOB (nullable Clob), we
need to fetch and display a column of Clob-type data. As in the CLI version of
this example program, we will fetch each Clob in the form of a locator, then
use the locator to fetch the first 10 bytes of the actual Clob value. The first step
is to place the address of our answerLocator variable into the descriptor,
along with a code indicating that we wish to retrieve values in locator form.
Each FETCH delivers another locator into our program variable.

STEP 11: Once we have fetched a locator, we can use it to fetch the first 10 characters
(or any desired substring) of the Clob value, using a VALUES statement. After
we are finished with each locator, we free it so that the database system does
not need to maintain it until the end of the transaction.

Note that the VALUES and FREE LOCATOR statements are *static* SQL, not
dynamic SQL, because we know at compile time exactly what they need to do.

STEP 12: This simple example has demonstrated the handling of two datatypes; obviously, it could be extended to handle other datatypes as well by adding more
cases to the switch statement.

```
case SQL_TYP_NCLOB:        /* nullable CLOB */
   /*
   **   STEP 10: Fetch a column of Clob-type answers
   **   in Locator form
   */
   sqldaptr->sqlvar[0].sqltype = SQL_TYP_NCLOB_LOCATOR;
   sqldaptr->sqlvar[0].sqldata = (char *) &answerLocator;
   sqldaptr->sqlvar[0].sqllen = 4;
   sqldaptr->sqlvar[0].sqlind = &nullindicator;
   EXEC SQL FETCH C1 USING DESCRIPTOR :*sqldaptr;
   if (SQLCODE == 100)
      printf("Result set is empty.\n");
   else while (SQLCODE == 0)
      {
      if (nullindicator == -1) printf("(Null)\n");
      else
         {
         /*
         **   STEP 11: For each Clob, use its locator to fetch
         **   and display the first 10 characters of the answer.
         **   Don't forget to free each locator before fetching
         **   the next one.
         */
         EXEC SQL VALUES(substr(:answerLocator, 1, 10))
                    INTO :answerString;
         printf("%s ...\n", answerString);
         EXEC SQL FREE LOCATOR :answerLocator;
         }
      EXEC SQL FETCH C1 USING DESCRIPTOR :*sqldaptr;
      }
   break;    /* end of CLOB case */

default:
   /*
   **   STEP 12: Other datatypes could be added here
   */
   printf("Answer datatype %d is not DOUBLE or CLOB\n",
                                               coltype);
}      /* end of switch on coltype */
```

STEP 13:   After fetching and displaying the result set, we close the cursor. The same cursor will be reopened to fetch the result of the next query.

STEP 14:   This is the place to which control passes after a result set has been displayed or whenever an SQL error is encountered. At this point in the program, we display any error message that may be pending, prompt the user to enter another SQL statement, and return to the top of the query loop.

STEP 15:   When the user has indicated (by entering a null line) that there are no more queries to be processed, we end our transaction, disconnect from the database, and exit from the program.

```
    /*
    **   STEP 13: Close the cursor
    */
    EXEC SQL CLOSE C1;

    }        /* end of processing a successful query */

nextquery:
    /*
    **   STEP 14: Print error codes, if any, and get the next query
    */
    if (SQLCODE < 0)
      {
      printf("Result of processing your SQL statement:\n");
      sqlaintp(msgbuffer, 500, 70, &sqlca);
      printf("Message: %s\n", msgbuffer);
      }

    printf("\nEnter a query, or empty string to quit:\n");
    gets(qstring);
    }    /* end of while-loop that processes queries */

printf("\nGoodbye, have a nice day.\n");

/*
**   STEP 15: Commit the transaction and clean up
*/
EXEC SQL WHENEVER SQLERROR CONTINUE;
EXEC SQL COMMIT;
EXEC SQL CONNECT RESET;
return (0);

}    /* end of main */
```

Stored Procedures

Normally, when an application program is running on a client machine, each SQL statement is sent separately from the client to the server machine, and each result is returned separately. Sometimes, however, a piece of work can be identified that involves relatively heavy database activity but relatively little user interaction. In such a case, it may make sense to install this piece of work on the server machine in the form of a *stored procedure* that can be invoked by a single message from the client machine, thus reducing message traffic and improving application performance.

A complete stored-procedure application includes two parts: the stored procedure itself, which runs on the server machine, and the client program, which runs on the client machine. Stored-procedure applications have the restrictions that all input data must be passed from the client program to the stored procedure at invocation time, and result data can be returned to the client program only when the stored procedure is completed. No interactions between the client program and the stored procedure are permitted during execution of the stored procedure. For example, a client program might accumulate a collection of database updates and pass them to a stored procedure to be applied as a batch, with a return code indicating whether the entire batch was applied successfully or rolled back due to a failure.

You can build and use stored procedures in the following ways:

1. Using the facilities that are provided with the V2 product, you can write a stored procedure in any of the host programming languages supported by V2: C, C++, COBOL, FORTRAN, or REXX. You can then invoke the stored procedure from a client program by using a CALL statement. CALL can be used as a static SQL statement or can be invoked from a CLI program using functions such as SQLPrepare() and SQLExecute(). Stored procedures written for V1 can also be invoked by function calls using the older Database Application Remote Interface (DARI).

2. You can use an IBM product named DataBasic that is closely related to V2 to develop, test, and install a stored procedure using the BASIC programming language. Stored procedures written in DataBasic can be invoked by client programs written in BASIC or in other host languages. DataBasic provides facilities that simplify the process of installing a stored procedure and exchanging data between the stored procedure and the client program.

This chapter examines how a stored-procedure application might be implemented using the C programming language, then it discusses how the same example application might be developed using the facilities of DataBasic. Information about writing stored procedures in other host languages can be found in the *DB2 Application Programming Guide*. Several examples of stored procedures written in C are provided with the V2 system, in the directory sqllib/samples/c.

7.1 THE SERVER SIDE

A stored procedure is simply an application program, installed on your server machine, that follows certain conventions for exchanging data with a client program. An SQLDA data structure (described in Section 6.2.3) is used both for passing input data to the stored procedure and for returning results. An SQLCA structure (described in Section 2.7.4) is used for returning codes and messages to the client program to indicate the success or failure of the stored procedure. This section discusses how to write stored procedures using the C host programming language.

When written according to V2 conventions, a stored procedure takes four parameters, but it really uses only two of them,[1] which are pointers to SQLDA and SQLCA structures. The declaration of such a stored procedure might look as follows:

```
int STORPROC(
        void         *dummy1,      /* not used        */
        void         *dummy2,      /* not used        */
        struct sqlda *exchange_da, /* input and output */
        struct sqlca *out_sqlca    /* output only     */
        );
```

The parameter named exchange_da above is a pointer to an SQLDA structure that is used to pass data in both directions between the client program and the stored procedure. When the stored procedure is invoked, the SQLDA contains a description (including datatypes, lengths, and buffer addresses) of all the data values to be exchanged in both directions. Input values are available to the stored procedure in the buffers pointed to by the SQLDA. The stored procedure returns values to the client program by copying them into the buffers pointed to by the SQLDA (of course, these values must conform to the datatypes and lengths indicated by the SQLDA) and by copying a set of return codes into the SQLCA structure provided by the out_sqlca parameter. The SQLCA and SQLDA structures are allocated by the client program.

The stored procedure does not connect to the database itself, but relies on the database connection already established by the client. The stored procedure

---

1. The two unused parameters are left over from a stored procedure calling convention used in V1 called DARI, which is described in Section 7.2.4.

can execute SQL statements but not statements such as CONNECT that would affect its database connection. When its job is done, the stored procedure must copy any information to be returned to the client program into the SQLDA and SQLCA structures passed to it as parameters. The stored procedure then returns one of two integer codes: SQLZ_HOLD_PROC, indicating that the procedure should be retained in memory to improve the performance of subsequent invocations, or SQLZ_DISCONNECT_PROC, indicating that no further invocations are expected and the procedure should be removed from memory. These return codes, which are defined in sql.h, affect only the handling of the stored procedure on the server machine and are not returned to the client program.

TIP: The process of creating and installing a stored procedure is simpler if you follow certain conventions. For maximum simplicity and portability, the source code file for your stored procedure should contain exactly one function whose name is the same as the filename, and this name should be eight characters or less and all uppercase. For example, you might create a file named SERVER1.sqc containing the source code for the function SERVER1. These rules are stricter than necessary for some environments, but they will help you to avoid unpleasant surprises. For example, you can't call a stored procedure with a lowercase name from certain client platforms.

7.1.1 Example Program SERVER1: A Stored Procedure for a Bank

As an example, let us write a stored procedure for use by a bank. Suppose that our bank has automatic teller machines distributed in many locations. Each teller machine has a list of accounts and is capable of functioning autonomously for a period of time, accepting deposit and withdrawal transactions against the accounts on its list. Periodically, each teller machine connects to the central database stored on the bank's server machine and invokes a stored procedure named SERVER1, which updates the central database to record a batch of deposits and withdrawals processed by the teller machine.

This example illustrates one way to solve a problem that often arises when dealing with stored procedures: finding a way to pass a large collection of input data to the stored procedure. In our example, the client program needs to pass a variable-length list of account numbers and net changes. We will accomplish this by packing the list of account numbers and net changes into a Blob and passing to the stored procedure an SQLDA that points to the Blob.

In our simplified example, the stored procedure interacts only with the following table:

BANK.ACCOUNTS

ACCTNO	BALANCE

The code for the stored procedure is given in example SERVER1 and is explained in detail below.

Steps for Example Program SERVER1: Stored Procedure, Server Side

STEP 1: The stored procedure uses the INCLUDE SQLCA statement to get a local copy of an SQLCA structure that will capture the return codes of SQL statements executed inside the stored procedure. It also declares other host language variables that will be needed during execution. The stored procedure does not need to connect to a database, since it uses the database connection established by its client program.

STEP 2: The stored procedure unpacks its input parameters from the SQLDA structure and interprets them as follows: The first entry of the SQLDA points to an integer that indicates the number of accounts to be updated. The second entry points to a Blob that is really a list of updates, each expressed as a pair of integers containing an account number and a net change. The stored procedure loops over the list of updates, extracting the account numbers and net changes and applying them to the database by an SQL UPDATE statement. The loop counts the number of updates that were successful and exits when the list is exhausted or an update fails.

Code for Example Program SERVER1: Stored Procedure, Server Side

```c
#include <stdio.h>
#include <memory.h>
#include <sqlenv.h>

int SERVER1(
     void         *dummy1,         /* not used                  */
     void         *dummy2,         /* not used                  */
     struct sqlda *exchange_da,    /* for input and output      */
     struct sqlca *out_sqlca       /* sqlca for return codes    */
     )
   {
   /*
   **   STEP 1: Declare a local SQLCA and some host variables
   */
   EXEC SQL INCLUDE SQLCA;

   EXEC SQL BEGIN DECLARE SECTION;
      long acctno;          /* account number to be updated        */
      long netchange;       /* net change in this account's balance */
   EXEC SQL END DECLARE SECTION;

   long n_updates;          /* total no. of accounts to update     */
   long counter;            /* how many accts updated so far       */
   long *p;                 /* current position inside BLOB         */

   /*
   **   STEP 2: Get updates from the exchange SQLDA and apply them to the
   **   database.  The SQLDA has two SQLVAR entries, used as follows:
   **   1. (Integer) on input:  the number of accounts to be updated
   **                on output: no. of accounts processed successfully
   **   2. (Blob)    on input:  vector of (acct. no, net change) pairs
   **                on output: set to null (don't return unnecessary data)
   */

   n_updates = *(long *)(exchange_da->sqlvar[0].sqldata);
   p = (long *)(exchange_da->sqlvar[1].sqldata);
   p++;     /* skip over length in first four bytes of Blob */
```

STEP 3: After exiting from the loop, the stored procedure compares the number of successful updates with the total number of updates requested. If these numbers are equal, the stored procedure commits the transaction; otherwise it rolls back all changes. The stored procedure runs in the same transaction as the client program that invoked it, so any commit or rollback executed by the stored procedure applies to updates performed by the client since the previous commit or rollback, as well as to updates performed by the stored procedure itself. If necessary, a stored procedure can execute a series of several transactions.

STEP 4: The stored procedure sends the number of successful updates back to the client program by copying it into the first entry of the exchange SQLDA (since this SQLDA is used for both input and output, the original number of requested updates is overridden). This number enables the client program to find the first invalid update for diagnostic purposes. By convention, the client program knows that all changes were rolled back if any updates failed. The stored procedure also sets the null indicator of the second SQLDA entry to –128, which means that its data is used for input only and need not be copied back to the client program.

STEP 5: The stored procedure copies its local SQLCA into the one provided by the client program before returning. It then returns the code SQLZ_HOLD_PROC, which indicates that it expects to be called again and should be retained in main memory.

```
for (counter = 0; counter < n_updates; counter++)
   {
   acctno = *p;
   p++;
   netchange = *p;
   p++;

   EXEC SQL UPDATE bank.accounts
           SET balance = balance + :netchange
           WHERE acctno = :acctno;

   if (SQLCODE != 0) break;
   }

/*
**   STEP 3: If all updates were successful, commit work;
**   otherwise roll back
*/
if (counter == n_updates)
    EXEC SQL COMMIT;
 else
    EXEC SQL ROLLBACK;

/*
**   STEP 4: Copy counter into output SQLDA.  Set the second SQLDA
**   entry indicator to -128 (no need to return all the
**   account data).
*/

*(long *)(exchange_da->sqlvar[0].sqldata) = counter;
*(short *)(exchange_da->sqlvar[1].sqlind) = -128;

/*
**   STEP 5: Copy local SQLCA into return SQLCA and return
*/
memcpy((char *)out_sqlca, (char *)&sqlca, sizeof(struct sqlca));
return (SQLZ_HOLD_PROC);
}
```

7.1.2 Rules for Implementing Stored Procedures

When writing the program that implements a stored procedure, you must observe the following rules:

1. A stored procedure must return to its caller (it must never call the `exit` function to terminate its process).

2. A stored procedure must not execute any SQL statements (such as CONNECT) that would change its database connection. The stored procedure must rely on the database connection established by the client program.

3. A stored procedure cannot execute an SQL COMMIT or ROLLBACK statement if it is called by a client program using a Type 2 database connection (distributed transaction).

TIP: If called by a client program using a Type 1 database connection, a stored procedure can commit or roll back. But remember that this commit or rollback applies to the transaction begun by the client program and may have undesired effects, such as closing cursors and releasing LOB locators in the client program.

4. Since a stored procedure runs in background mode, it cannot display output on a screen using `printf`. It may, however, write into a file on the server machine.

5. If a stored procedure sets the `sqlind` field of an SQLDA entry to –128, the data in that entry will not be returned to the client program. When using this technique, make sure that the client program provides a null indicator variable to receive the –128 code.

6. If your function implementation is written in C++, you should specify `extern` "C" as part of your function declaration in the implementation file. This will ensure that your function is made available for linking by the name you gave it rather than by a "mangled" name chosen by the C++ compiler. If possible, avoid using an overloaded C++ function name (otherwise, you will need to follow special procedures documented in *DB2 Software Developer's Kit: Building Your Applications*).

7. Parameters of LOB datatypes (Blob, Clob, and Dbclob) can be exchanged only between V2 clients and V2 servers (not with servers on other platforms reached by the DRDA protocol).

8. If you pack binary data into a Blob, the data will be exchanged "as is" between client and server. If, for example, the representation of integers is different between the client and server platforms, the transformation from one representation to the other (such as byte reversal) is the responsibility of the stored procedure itself.

9. If you exchange data strings between client and server using datatypes Char, Varchar, Long Varchar, Clob, Graphic, Vargraphic, Long Vargraphic, or Dbclob, the system will perform a transformation between the code page of the client application and that of the database. If the client application and the database are using different code pages, this transformation will damage any binary information packed inside the strings.[2]

10. When double-byte data (SQL datatype Graphic, Vargraphic, Long Vargraphic, or Dbclob) is exchanged with a stored procedure, it is always exchanged in multibyte format (not wide-character format). In other words, parameters and results of stored procedures always use the format specified by the precompiler option WCHARTYPE NOCONVERT. For more information about handling double-byte data inside stored procedures, see the *DB2 Application Programming Guide*.

7.1.3 Installing a Stored Procedure

Before you can use a stored procedure, you must install it on a server machine. The installation process is very similar to the process of "building" (precompiling, compiling, and binding) an application program. Before you can start the installation process, you must make sure that all the tables used by the stored procedure exist in the database in which the stored procedure will be installed. In our bank example, the table BANK.ACCOUNTS must be created before the stored procedure can be installed. The process of installing a stored procedure takes place on the server machine and varies with the platform on which the server is running, as described below.

TIP: If you have trouble installing and running a stored procedure, it is possible that your node type is not compatible with stored procedures or that your database manager configuration parameters are not set properly. You can check both of these conditions by the command db2 get database manager configuration. The resulting display should identify your node type as "Database server with local and remote clients" and should list the values of the configuration parameters KEEPDARI as YES and MAXDARI as a positive number. The default values of KEEPDARI = YES, MAXDARI = 200 are acceptable. (Information about how to set database manager configuration parameters can be found in Section 8.3.4 and in the *DB2 Administration Guide*.)

---

2. However, you can inhibit code-page conversion for a given entry in an SQLDA by setting the seventh byte of the sqldaid field to the "+" character and setting the sqlname field of the given entry to four bytes of binary zeros.

Installing Under AIX

1. Create a separate file, called an *export file*, containing the name of the function that implements your stored procedure. This function is "exported" (made available for dynamic loading) by your stored procedure source file. Create the export file in the same directory with the stored procedure source file and give it the same filename, with an extension of .exp. For example, if your file SERVER1.sqc contains source code for the function SERVER1, you will need a separate file named SERVER1.exp, containing the following lines:

   ```
   #! SERVER1 export file
   SERVER1
   ```

2. Build (precompile, compile, and link) the stored procedure. V2 provides a script named bldxlcsrv for building stored procedures written in C and another script named bldcsetsrv for building stored procedures written in C++. Both scripts can be found in the directory sqllib/samples/c. Each script takes four parameters: the name of the stored procedure, the name of the database in which it is to be installed, and the userid and password under which it is to be installed. For example, you might type the following command to install the C stored procedure named SERVER1 in the database named bankdb:

   ```
   bldxlcsrv SERVER1 bankdb yourname yourpwd
   ```

   The script will connect to the indicated database and will precompile, compile, and link your stored procedure, producing an executable file (named SERVER1 in our example).

   TIP: The bldxlcsrv and bldcsetsrv scripts contain a command to link your stored procedure to an IBM-supplied utility program named util that is used in some of the programming examples that are shipped with V2. You are not required to use the util program when writing a stored procedure. If you are not using util, edit the bldxlcsrv and bldcsetsrv scripts to remove the reference to util.o. If you wish to use util, you must compile util.c (found in sqllib/samples/c) and place the resulting file util.o in some directory on your link path.

3. Place the executable file (SERVER1 in our example) into the appropriate directory on the server machine. The usual practice is to place the executable file into the directory sqllib/function. If this is done, a client program can invoke the stored procedure by using its name (SERVER1) in an SQL CALL statement. If the executable file is placed into some other directory, its full path name must be specified in the CALL statement.

   If your stored procedure is very well debugged and you wish to allow it to run in the same address space as the database engine for maximum performance, you can place its executable file into the directory sqllib/function/unfenced.

This type of installation, called an *unfenced stored procedure*, exposes your database to possible damage caused by a faulty or malicious stored procedure. Before using an unfenced stored procedure, you should read the section "Working with Not-Fenced Stored Procedures" in the *DB2 Application Programming Guide*.

Since your stored procedure will be executed on the server machine under a userid belonging to the database system, you must make your stored procedure file executable by userids other than your own. This can be done by a command such as the following:

```
chmod a+x SERVER1
```

4. If you wish other users to be able to use your stored procedure, grant to them the EXECUTE privilege on your stored procedure's package. The following example statement allows any user to execute the stored procedure named SERVER1:

```
GRANT EXECUTE ON PACKAGE SERVER1 TO PUBLIC;
```

Installing Under OS/2 or Windows NT

1. Create a separate file, called a *module definition file*, containing the name of the function that implements your stored procedure. This function is "exported" (made available for dynamic loading) by your stored procedure source file. Create the module definition file in the same directory with the stored procedure source file and give it the same filename, with an extension of .DEF. For example, if your file SERVER1.SQC contains source code for the function SERVER1, you will need a separate file named SERVER1.DEF, containing the following lines:

```
LIBRARY SERVER1
EXPORTS SERVER1
```

2. Build (precompile, compile, and link) the stored procedure. V2 provides a command file named bldcs2sr in sqllib\samples\c for building stored procedures written in C++, and this file can be easily modified (following directions given in comments inside the file) to build stored procedures written in C. The command file takes four parameters: the name of the stored procedure, the name of the database in which it is to be installed, and the userid and password under which it is to be installed. For example, you might type the following command to install the stored procedure named SERVER1 in the database named bankdb:

```
bldcs2sr SERVER1 bankdb yourname yourpwd
```

The command file will connect to the indicated database and will precompile, compile, and link your stored procedure, producing a Dynamic Link Library (named SERVER1.DLL in our example).

3. Place the Dynamic Link Library (SERVER1.DLL in our example) into the appropriate directory on the server machine. The usual practice is to place the DLL file into the directory %DB2PATH%\function. If this is done, a client program can invoke the stored procedure by using its name (SERVER1) in an SQL CALL statement. If the DLL file is placed into some other directory, its full path name must be specified in the CALL statement.

If your stored procedure is very well debugged and you wish to allow it to run in the same address space as the database engine for maximum performance, you can place its DLL file into the directory %DB2PATH%\function\unfenced. This type of installation, called an *unfenced stored procedure*, exposes your database to possible damage caused by a faulty or malicious stored procedure. Before using an unfenced stored procedure, you should read the section "Working with Not-Fenced Stored Procedures" in the *DB2 Application Programming Guide*.

4. If you wish other users to be able to use your stored procedure, grant to them the EXECUTE privilege on your stored procedure's package. The following example statement allows any user to execute the stored procedure named SERVER1:

```
GRANT EXECUTE ON PACKAGE SERVER1 TO PUBLIC;
```

7.1.4 The Stored Procedure Catalog Table

The Call Level Interface (CLI) provides two functions that enable an application program to list the stored procedures that are available at a given server: SQLProcedures(), which returns a list of stored procedures, and SQLProcedureColumns(), which returns a description of the input and output parameters of a given stored procedure. However, in order for these functions to work properly, all the stored procedures installed on a given server must be listed in a catalog table called DB2CLI.PROCEDURES.

Unlike the catalog tables in the SYSCAT schema, DB2CLI.PROCEDURES is not automatically created and maintained by the system. Instead, it must be manually created and maintained by a database administrator. It is the database administrator's responsibility to make sure that the contents of DB2CLI.PROCEDURES accurately reflect the stored procedures that are available on a given V2 server.

V2 provides some help for the database administrator in the form of the following two CLP scripts, which can be found in sqllib/misc:

• STORPROC.DDL contains the SQL statements needed to create the DB2CLI.PROCEDURES table and to grant SELECT privilege on it to all users. A database administrator may also decide to grant INSERT, DELETE, and UPDATE privileges on DB2CLI.PROCEDURES to certain users or to all users.

- STORPROC.XMP contains examples of SQL statements that insert entries into DB2CLI.PROCEDURES to describe stored procedures. These examples can be modified to insert a description of a new stored procedure that is being installed in your database.

(The structure of the DB2CLI.PROCEDURES catalog table is described in Appendix D.)

7.2 THE CLIENT SIDE

An application program running on a client machine can invoke a stored procedure on a server machine by means of an SQL CALL statement. The CALL statement causes an SQLDA structure to be passed from the client program to the stored procedure, and the same SQLDA structure is returned to the client program at the conclusion of the stored procedure. Since the SQLDA is exchanged in both directions by the client program and stored procedure, it can be used both for input parameters and for returning results. (The content of an SQLDA structure is described in Section 6.2.3.)

7.2.1 The CALL Statement

When invoking a stored procedure with a CALL statement, you can specify the name of the stored procedure either in the CALL statement itself or in a host variable named in the CALL statement. You can create your own SQLDA structure to be passed to the stored procedure, using the DESCRIPTOR syntax shown below, or you can provide a list of host variables. If you provide a list of host variables, V2 will automatically pack them into an SQLDA structure, saving you the trouble of filling in all the fields of the SQLDA. The host variables you specify can be used for passing data in both directions between the client program and the stored procedure.

Like any SQL statement, the CALL statement implicitly assigns return codes and messages to the SQLCA structure declared in the calling program. In the case of a CALL statement, the content of the SQLCA is determined by the SQLCA structure returned by the stored procedure.

The syntax of a CALL statement is as follows:

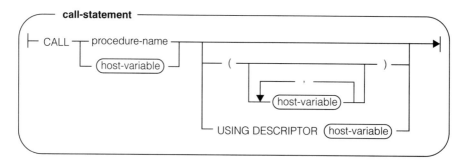

Although CALL is an SQL statement, it is subject to certain restrictions. It can be used in a host language program as a static SQL statement, and it can be invoked from a CLI program using the functions SQLExecDirect() or SQLPrepare() and SQLExecute(). However, a CALL statement cannot be executed from the CLP or by using Embedded Dynamic SQL statements such as PREPARE and EXECUTE.

When using a CALL statement, the arguments passed to the stored procedure must be host variables, not constants. The host variables may have null indicators. For example, the following statement is incorrect:

```
EXEC SQL CALL proc1(7, NULL);
```

The intent of the statement above is accomplished by the following correct statements:

```
x = 7;
xind = 0;
y = 0;
yind = -1;
EXEC SQL CALL proc1(:x :xind, :y :yind);
```

TIP: Make sure your client program and stored procedure agree on which of their exchanged variables have null indicators. If a stored procedure attempts to return a null value when no indicator variable has been provided, it will probably crash. When indicator variables are used, both the client program and the stored procedure should set their values explicitly.

If you use the DESCRIPTOR form of a CALL statement and provide your own SQLDA structure, and if one or more of the entries in your SQLDA contains binary data (such as Varchar FOR BIT DATA), you must set the sixth byte of the sqldaid field to the "+" character (rather than its normal blank charac-

ter), and you must set the `sqlname` fields of the binary data entries to four
bytes of binary zeros. (The use of an SQLDA in CALL statements is described
further in Section 6.2.5.)

There are no special requirements for installation of a client program that
uses the CALL statement; you can simply precompile it, bind it to the database, and invoke it as you would any application program.

CLIENT1A, shown below, is an example of a client program that exercises
the SERVER1 stored procedure using an SQL CALL statement.

Example Program CLIENT1A: A Client Program Using CALL

```
#include <stdlib.h>
#include <stdio.h>
#include <sqlenv.h>

int main()
   {

   EXEC SQL BEGIN DECLARE SECTION;
      long n_updates_req;                   /* no. of updates requested   */
      long n_updates;                       /* no. of successful updates  */
      SQL TYPE IS BLOB(8000) update_list;   /* list of update pairs       */
      long *p;                              /* points inside update_list  */
      char dbname[9] = "bankdb";            /* name of database           */
      short indicator = 0;                  /* indicator (not null)       */
   EXEC SQL END DECLARE SECTION;

   EXEC SQL INCLUDE SQLCA;                  /* local return code structure */

   /*
   **   Collect a series of account updates.
   **   To exercise the stored procedure, we will make up 5 updates.
   **   Each update consists of a pair of integers: (acct. no., net change)
   */
   n_updates = n_updates_req = 5;           /* five updates requested     */
   update_list.length = 40;                 /* 10 integers, 4 bytes each  */
   p = (long *)(update_list.data);          /* p points to the first update */
   p[0] = 1; p[1] = +150;                   /* specify first update       */
   p[2] = 2; p[3] = -75;                    /* specify second update      */
   p[4] = 3; p[5] = -100;                   /* specify third update       */
   p[6] = 4; p[7] = +90;                    /* specify fourth update      */
   p[8] = 5; p[9] = -20;                    /* specify fifth update       */
```

```
/*
**  Connect to the database.
*/
EXEC SQL CONNECT TO :dbname;
if (SQLCODE != 0)
    {
    printf("\nError in connecting to database.\n");
    printf("SQLCODE = %d, SQLSTATE = %5.5s\n", SQLCODE, sqlca.sqlstate);
    }

/*
**  Call the stored procedure, passing an Integer and a Blob
**  as host variables.  These host variables are automatically
**  packed into an SQLDA structure and used for both input and output.
*/
EXEC SQL CALL SERVER1(:n_updates, :update_list :indicator);

if (SQLCODE == 0)
    {
    /*
    **  The number of successful updates is returned in n_updates.
    **  Compare this to the number we requested.
    */
    if (n_updates == n_updates_req)
        {
        printf("\nStored procedure was successful.\n");
        printf("Number of accounts updated = %d\n", n_updates);
        }
    else
        {
        printf("\nError encountered after updating %d accounts.\n",
                n_updates);
        printf("All updates have been rolled back.\n");
        }
    }
else
    {
    printf("\nUnexpected error in stored procedure.\n");
    printf ("   SQLCODE = %d, SQLSTATE = %5.5s\n",
                                 SQLCODE, sqlca.sqlstate);
    }

EXEC SQL CONNECT RESET;

}        /* end of main */
```

7.2.2 Calling a Stored Procedure from a CLI Client

In Section 6.1, we discussed the advantages of using the Call Level Interface (CLI) to invoke SQL from a host language program. In a stored-procedure application, CLI can be used either in the stored procedure or in the client program, or in both.

CLIENT1B, shown below, is an example of a client program that was written using CLI and that invokes the SERVER1 stored procedure. Like CLIENT1A, it uses a CALL statement to invoke the stored procedure. The CALL statement is prepared for execution by the SQLPrepare() function; its parameters are bound to specific variables by the SQLBindParameter() function; and it is executed by the SQLExecute() function.

Example Program CLIENT1B: A CLI Client

```
#include "sqlcli1.h"
#include <stdlib.h>
#include <string.h>
#include <stdio.h>

void errorExit(SQLHENV henv, SQLHDBC hdbc, SQLHSTMT hstmt, char *place);

int main()
    {
    SQLHENV henv;                    /* environment handle             */
    SQLHDBC hdbc;                    /* connection handle              */
    SQLHSTMT hstmt;                  /* statement handle               */

    SQLCHAR dbname[] = "bankdb";     /* name of database               */
    char qstring[80];                /* holds an SQL statement         */

    SQLINTEGER n_updates_req;        /* no. of updates requested       */
    SQLINTEGER n_updates;            /* no. of successful updates      */
    char update_list[8000];          /* list of update pairs           */
    long *p;                         /* points inside update_list      */
    SQLINTEGER indicator1;           /* indicator variable for n_updates   */
    SQLINTEGER indicator2;           /* indicator variable for update_list */

    SQLRETURN rc;                    /* return code                    */
```

```
/*
**   Allocate environment, connection, and statement handles
**   and establish a database connection.
*/
SQLAllocEnv(&henv);
SQLAllocConnect(henv, &hdbc);

rc = SQLConnect(hdbc, dbname, SQL_NTS,
                      NULL, SQL_NTS,
                      NULL, SQL_NTS);
if (rc != SQL_SUCCESS)
   errorExit(henv, hdbc, SQL_NULL_HSTMT, "Connecting to database");

SQLAllocStmt (hdbc, &hstmt);

/*
**   Collect a series of account updates.
**   To exercise the stored procedure, we will make up 5 updates.
**   Each update consists of a pair of integers: (acct. no., net change)
*/
n_updates = n_updates_req = 5;    /* five updates requested           */
p = (long *)update_list;          /* p points to the Blob length field */
*p = 40;                          /* set length of Blob to 40         */
p++;                              /* now p points to the Blob data    */
p[0] = 1; p[1] = +150;            /* specify first update             */
p[2] = 2; p[3] = -75;             /* specify second update            */
p[4] = 3; p[5] = -100;            /* specify third update             */
p[6] = 4; p[7] = +90;             /* specify fourth update            */
p[8] = 5; p[9] = -20;             /* specify fifth update             */

/*
**   Prepare a CALL statement with two parameter markers.
*/
strcpy (qstring, "CALL SERVER1(?, ?)");
rc = SQLPrepare(hstmt, (SQLCHAR *)qstring, SQL_NTS);
if (rc != SQL_SUCCESS)
   errorExit(henv, hdbc, hstmt, "Preparing CALL statement");
```

```
/*
**   Bind host variables to the parameter markers.
*/
SQLBindParameter(hstmt,
            1,                            /* first parameter marker     */
            SQL_PARAM_INPUT_OUTPUT,       /* used for input and output  */
            SQL_C_LONG,                   /* datatype of host variable  */
            SQL_INTEGER,                  /* SQL datatype               */
            0,                            /* not used in this call      */
            0,                            /* not used in this call      */
            (SQLPOINTER)&n_updates,       /* address of host variable   */
            4,                            /* length of buffer           */
            &indicator1 );                /* null or length indicator   */

SQLBindParameter(hstmt,
            2,                            /* second parameter marker    */
            SQL_PARAM_INPUT,              /* used for input only        */
            SQL_C_BINARY,                 /* datatype of host variable  */
            SQL_BLOB,                     /* SQL datatype               */
            8000,                         /* max length of input data   */
            0,                            /* not used in this call      */
            (SQLPOINTER)update_list,      /* address of host variable   */
            8000,                         /* length of buffer           */
            &indicator2 );                /* null or length indicator   */

/*
**   Execute the CALL statement.
*/
indicator1 = 0;            /* length of an integer is implicit */
indicator2 = 40;           /* 10 binary integers, 4 bytes each */

rc = SQLExecute(hstmt);
if (rc != SQL_SUCCESS)
   errorExit(henv, hdbc, hstmt, "Executing CALL statement");

/*
**   Check results.
**   The number of successful updates is returned in n_updates.
**   Compare this to the number we requested.
*/
if (n_updates == n_updates_req)
   {
   printf("\nStored procedure was successful.\n");
   printf("Number of accounts updated = %d\n", n_updates);
   }
```

```
else
   {
   printf("\nError encountered after updating %d accounts.\n",
          n_updates);
   printf("All updates have been rolled back.\n");
   }

/*
** Clean up
*/
SQLFreeStmt(hstmt, SQL_DROP);              /* free statement handle    */
SQLDisconnect(hdbc);                       /* disconnect from database */
SQLFreeConnect(hdbc);                      /* free connection handle   */
SQLFreeEnv(henv);                          /* free environment handle  */
exit(rc);

}    /* end of main */

void errorExit(SQLHENV henv, SQLHDBC hdbc, SQLHSTMT hstmt, char *place)
   {
   SQLCHAR sqlstate[SQL_SQLSTATE_SIZE + 1];
   SQLINTEGER sqlcode;
   SQLSMALLINT msglength;
   SQLCHAR msgbuffer[SQL_MAX_MESSAGE_LENGTH + 1];

   printf ("\nSQL error at %s, transaction rolled back.\n", place);

   /*
   ** Retrieve error codes and messages.
   */
   while ( SQLError(henv, hdbc, hstmt, sqlstate, &sqlcode,
             msgbuffer, SQL_MAX_MESSAGE_LENGTH+1, &msglength)
      == SQL_SUCCESS )
      {
      printf("   SQLCODE = %d, SQLSTATE = %s\n", sqlcode, sqlstate);
      printf("   MESSAGE: %s\n", msgbuffer);
      }
```

```
/*
**   Roll back and clean up.
*/
SQLTransact(henv, hdbc, SQL_ROLLBACK); /* roll back transaction    */
SQLDisconnect(hdbc);                   /* disconnect from database */
SQLFreeConnect(hdbc);                  /* free connection handle   */
SQLFreeEnv(henv);                      /* free environment handle  */
exit(-2);
}
```

7.2.3 Returning Multiple Result Sets

There is one useful feature of stored procedures that is available only to client programs that are written using CLI: the ability for the stored procedure to return multiple result sets. If a client program is written using static SQL, it can receive results from a stored procedure only in the program variables or SQLDA structure that is passed via the CALL statement. But a client program written using CLI has another means of receiving results from a stored procedure, which can be used to retrieve one or more result sets, each containing many rows of data.

A stored procedure can return multiple result sets to a CLI client simply by opening a cursor on each result set and leaving the cursors open when it returns to the client program. If a CLI client invokes a stored procedure that leaves a cursor open, the client can retrieve the data associated with the open cursor by means of CLI functions such as SQLNumResultCols(), SQL-DescribeCol(), SQLBindCol(), and SQLFetch(), using the statement handle that was used to execute the CALL statement that invoked the stored procedure. If more than one cursor was left open by the stored procedure, the first rows retrieved are the rows associated with the first cursor opened by the stored procedure. The end of the first result set is indicated by a return code of SQL_NO_DATA_FOUND from the SQLFetch() function. When a result set has been exhausted, the client can advance to the next result set (associated with the next cursor opened by the stored procedure) by calling the CLI function SQLMoreResults(). SQLFetch() and related functions can then be used to retrieve the rows in the next result set. After the last result set has been exhausted, further calls to SQLMoreResults() return the code SQL_NO_DATA_FOUND, indicating that no more result sets are available.

TIP: If you are writing a stored procedure that returns a set of rows, you should think about whether it could be replaced by a user-defined function. Stored procedures that return sets of rows are sometimes used for applying "filters" to data that are difficult or impossible to express in SQL. But if such a "filter" can be implemented by a user-defined function, it can be executed by the database engine, and the qualifying rows can be delivered directly to the application program. This method is more efficient than using a stored procedure, because it avoids the need to materialize many data rows that do not pass the filter.

7.2.4 Database Application Remote Interface (DARI)

In V1, stored procedures were invoked by means of an interface called the Database Application Remote Interface, or DARI. In DARI, a client application invokes a stored procedure by calling a function named `sqleproc`, which takes the following five parameters:

- The name of the stored procedure to be invoked
- A pointer to a character string containing input data for the stored procedure
- A pointer to an SQLDA structure containing input data for the stored procedure
- A pointer to an SQLDA structure in which the stored procedure should return output data
- A pointer to an SQLCA structure in which the stored procedure should place return codes

The `sqleproc` function invokes the stored procedure named by its first parameter and passes its other four parameters to the stored procedure. This is the reason why stored procedures have four parameters.

In V2, `sqleproc` has been replaced by the SQL CALL statement, which passes a single SQLDA structure to the stored procedure. This SQLDA structure is used for both input and output data, replacing the two SQLDA structures and the input character string of the DARI interface. Unlike `sqleproc`, the CALL statement can be used to invoke stored procedures on other DB2 platforms such as DB2 for MVS.

Stored procedures that were written for V1 can still be used on V2 systems, but since they were written according to the DARI interface, they must still be invoked by calling `sqleproc`. For this reason, `sqleproc` is still supported in V2. (For more information about DARI and `sqleproc`, see Appendix D of the *DB2 Application Programming Guide*.)

7.3 USING DATABASIC

DataBasic is a separate product, closely related to V2, that provides a development environment for creating and testing programs using the BASIC programming language. DataBasic can be used on a V2 client machine to develop stored procedures and user-defined functions. The DataBasic development environment provides convenient graphic tools for moving a stored procedure or user-defined function from a client machine to a server machine and installing it in the proper directory. DataBasic allows you to write user-defined functions and stored procedures in BASIC, and automatically generates a "wrapper" program for each function or stored procedure that enables the V2 server to invoke it using C calling conventions.

Here are some reasons why you might choose to use DataBasic as your development environment for creating a stored procedure:

- DataBasic provides a convenient language-oriented debugging environment that enables you to test your stored procedure on the client machine before installing it on the server.

- BASIC is a relatively "safe" language in which to write a stored procedure, since it has no pointers and provides no direct access to system memory.

- DataBasic simplifies the process of installing a stored procedure on a server machine, automatically copying the procedure to the proper directory and updating the DB2CLI.PROCEDURES catalog table.

- Since DataBasic does not use a precompiler, you do not need to manage two copies of your source program, one before precompilation and one after.

- DataBasic provides a level of integration between SQL and BASIC that is not available in other host languages. For example:

  - In a DataBasic program, you do not need an SQL Declare Section. Any BASIC variable of an appropriate type can be used in any SQL statement.

  - With DataBasic, there is a one-to-one correspondence between the parameters passed by the client program in a CALL statement and the parameters received by the stored procedure. In other words, there is no need for the stored procedure to "unpack" its parameters from an SQLDA structure.

  - In a DataBasic stored procedure, there is no need to declare a local SQLCA structure and to copy its content into the parameter SQLCA before returning. The SQLCA structure passed to the stored procedure as a parameter serves double duty as a local SQLCA and is automatically returned to the client program on completion of the stored procedure.

(More information about DataBasic can be found in the manuals *DataBasic Language Reference* and *Databasic Developer's Guide*. See Appendix F for IBM publication numbers.)

7.3.1 Example of a DataBasic Stored Procedure

Let us illustrate the use of DataBasic by rewriting the SERVER1 stored procedure introduced in Section 7.1.1. This stored procedure accepts lists of account numbers and balance changes and applies these changes to a table of accounts on the central database server of a bank. An equivalent stored procedure named SERVER2, written in BASIC, is shown below.

The first thing we notice about SERVER2 is that its parameter list corresponds closely to the actual parameters of the CALL statement by which it is invoked. Rather than being packed into an SQLDA structure, each host variable is passed to the stored procedure as a separate parameter. The individual parameters are followed by an array of null indicators and by an SQLCA structure for return codes.

The SERVER1 stored procedure received a list of account updates in the form of a Blob containing an array of binary numbers. Since BASIC lacks pointers, we find it easier to pass the same information to SERVER2 in the form of a character string in which each number is represented in ASCII and terminated by a comma. For example, the following character string might be used to represent updates to three accounts with account numbers 1, 2, and 3:

```
1,550,2,-75,3,225,
```

The SERVER2 stored procedure uses the BASIC functions Instr, Mid$, and CLng to extract the individual account updates from the character string and apply them to the database using an SQL UPDATE statement. It then commits the transaction if all the updates were successful, or rolls it back if any update failed. The number of successful updates is sent back to the client program in the n_updates parameter to indicate the success or failure of the transaction.

Example Program SERVER2: A Stored Procedure Written in DataBasic

```
'
' Define a type for a CLOB of length 8000 bytes
'
Type SQLCLOB8K
  length As Long        '
  data As String * 8000
End Type
```

```
Sub SERVER2A( _
            n_updates As Long,          _
            update_list As SQLCLOB8K,  _
            null_array() As Integer,    _
            sqlca As sqlca_type        _
          )

    '
    ' No need for an SQL Declare Section.  Any Basic variable can be
    ' used in an SQL statement.  Also no need to declare a local SQLCA.
    '

    Dim acctno As Long          ' account number to be updated
    Dim netchange As Long       ' net change in this account's balance
    Dim counter As Long         ' how many accts updated so far
    Dim p As Integer            ' current position inside BLOB
    Dim start As Integer        ' starting position inside BLOB

    '
    ' The n_updates parameter indicates the number of accounts to be
    ' updated.  The update_list parameter is a Blob containing a list of
    ' (account number, net change) pairs.  All the numbers in this list
    ' are represented in ASCII and followed by commas.  For each account,
    ' we need to extract its account number and net change from the Blob,
    ' and apply the change to the database using an SQL UPDATE statement.

    start = 1
    For counter = 1 To n_updates
       ' Get the account number
       p = InStr(start, update_list.data, ",")
       acctno = CLng(Mid$(update_list.data, start, p - start))
       start = p + 1
       ' Get the net change
       p = InStr(start, update_list.data, ",")
       netchange = CLng(Mid$(update_list.data, start, p - start))
       start = p + 1

       EXEC SQL UPDATE bank.accounts
               SET balance = balance + :netchange
               WHERE acctno = :acctno
       END EXEC

       If (sqlca.sqlcode <> 0) Then Exit For
    Next
```

```
'
' If all updates were successful, commit work;
' otherwise roll back.
'
If (counter = n_updates + 1) Then
   EXEC SQL COMMIT END EXEC
Else
   EXEC SQL ROLLBACK END EXEC
End If


'
' Copy the number of successful updates into the n_updates parameter
' so the client program can diagnose problems.  Set the null indicator
' for the update_list parameter to -128, indicating no need to return
' data in this parameter.
'

n_updates = counter - 1
null_array(0) = 0
null_array(1) = -128

End Sub
```

7.3.2 Example of a Client Program

Stored procedures written using DataBasic can be invoked by client programs written in BASIC and other host languages. As an illustration of a BASIC client program, let us rewrite the CLIENT1A program introduced in Section 7.2.1. The resulting program, named CLIENT2, is shown below. This program illustrates the MsgBox function, which can be used to display messages to the user during execution of a client program.

Example Program CLIENT2: A Client Program Written in DataBasic

```
'
' Define a type for a CLOB of length 8000 bytes
'
Type SQLCLOB8K
  length As Long
  data As String * 8000
End Type
```

```
Sub main()
    '
    '   No need for an SQL Declare Section.  Any Basic variable can be
    '   used in an SQL statement.  Also no need to declare a local SQLCA.
    '
    Dim n_updates_req As Long            ' no. of updates requested
    Dim n_updates As Long                ' no. of successful updates
    Dim update_list As SQLCLOB8K         ' list of update pairs
    Dim dbname As String * 9             ' name of database
    Dim indicator1 As Integer            ' null indicator
    Dim indicator2 As Integer            ' null indicator
    Dim msg1 As String                   ' used for error messages


    '
    ' Collect a series of account updates.
    ' To exercise the stored procedure, we will make up 5 updates.
    ' Each update consists of a pair of integers: (acct. no., net change)
    ' Represent each number in ASCII, followed by a comma.
    '
    n_updates = 5
    n_updates_req = 5
    update_list.length = 40       ' 10 integers, 4 bytes each
    update_list.data = "1,150,"   _' first update
                    & "2,-75,"    _' second update
                    & "3,-100,"   _' third update
                    & "4,90,"      ' fourth update
                    & "5,-20,"    _' fifth update


    '
    ' Connect to the database.
    '
    dbname = "BANKDB" & Chr$(0)              ' add a null terminator
    EXEC SQL CONNECT TO :dbname END EXEC
    If (sqlca.sqlcode <> 0) Then
        msg1 = "Error in connecting to database. " _
             & " SQLCODE = " & sqlca.sqlcode _
             & " SQLSTATE = " & sqlca.sqlstate
        MsgBox msg1
    End If
```

```
'
' Call the stored procedure, passing the number of updates and the
' string containing the changes.  These variables are passed directly
' to the stored procedure, not packed into an SQLDA.  Each parameter
' of the stored procedure has its own null indicator variable.
'
indicator1 = 0
indicator2 = 0

EXEC SQL CALL SERVER2A(:n_updates :indicator1,
                       :update_list :indicator2) END EXEC

If (sqlca.sqlcode = 0) Then
   '
   ' The number of successful updates is returned in n_updates.
   ' Compare this to the number we requested.
   '
   If (n_updates = n_updates_req) Then
      msg1 = "Stored procedure was successful. " _
           & "Number of accounts updated = " & n_updates
   Else
      msg1 = "Error encountered after updating " & n_updates _
           & " accounts.  All updates have been rolled back."
   End If
Else
   msg1 = "Unexpected error in stored procedure. " _
        & " SQLCODE = " & sqlca.sqlcode _
        & " SQLSTATE = " & sqlca.sqlstate
End If
MsgBox msg1


'
' Terminate the database connection.
'
EXEC SQL CONNECT RESET END EXEC

End
End Sub        ' end of client program
```

Tasks and Tools

T here's a lot more to database management than simply running queries and application programs. Databases need to be created, loaded with data, and configured for optimum performance on your hardware and for your mix of applications. Your valuable data needs to be protected against loss by periodic backups. You may want to exercise some control over how your data is distributed on the physical devices attached to your machine. You may also want to monitor various internal database events, such as deadlocks, that may have an effect on the performance of your system.

Statistics need to be collected, so the optimizer will be able to make intelligent choices based on accurate estimates of the cost of various operations. You may wish to control the amount of time spent by the optimizer in choosing an access plan for each SQL statement. In fact, you may wish to find out exactly what access plan the optimizer has chosen for a given statement and how this plan would change if a different set of indexes were available or if the statistics of the tables involved were different.

This chapter is devoted to the various tasks that are involved in the operation of a database system and to the tools provided by V2 for accomplishing these tasks. Many of these tasks are normally performed by database or system administrators and require special authorities. However, some of the tasks described in this chapter, such as rebinding an application program to take advantage of the latest access paths, can be performed by application developers or even by end users.

This chapter summarizes the contents of three IBM manuals: the *DB2 Administration Guide*, the *DB2 Command Reference*, and the *DB2 Database System Monitor Guide and Reference*. These manuals have a combined length of more than 1,200 pages, so for obvious reasons it has been necessary to omit some details. In general, this chapter contains an overall description of V2 administration facilities and provides some examples of the use of each facility, but it does not provide a detailed syntax for the commands involved or an exhaustive list of all the available options. After reading the overview of the various facilities described in this chapter, refer to the IBM manuals listed above for more detailed information and syntax (see Appendix F for IBM publication numbers).

The previous chapters of this book have dealt primarily with SQL *statements*. Most of the facilities in this chapter, however, are controlled by *commands*. The distinction between an SQL statement and a command is

somewhat subtle. Both SQL statements and commands can be executed interactively in a CLP session, simply by typing them on the command line. In
general, SQL statements operate on specific contents of the database, whereas
commands operate on the global state of the database or the system. Also, in
general, SQL statements are recognized by host language precompilers (when
prefixed by EXEC SQL), whereas commands cannot be used in this way. This
book follows the usage in the IBM product documentation regarding the distinction between SQL statements and commands.

Many of the administrative tasks described in this chapter can be accomplished in three different ways: by a command, by a function call from an
application program, or by means of a graphic user interface called the Database Director. I will discuss the command interface first, because you are
already familiar with the environment in which commands are used, the CLP.
Section 8.8 describes how the Database Director provides an easy-to-use
graphic interface that can be used in place of many commands, greatly simplifying the tasks of database and system administrators. I will not describe the
function-call interfaces that enable each command to be invoked from an
application program; these are documented in the *DB2 API Reference*.

8.1 CREATING DATABASES AND MANAGING SPACE

A *database* is a named collection of data containing various kinds of objects
such as tables, indexes, views, and packages. A database is the scope for certain
kinds of authorities, such as DBAUTH. It is also the unit to which an application program or CLP session can connect and within which SQL statements
are executed. Each database contains a set of catalog tables that describes the
content of the database. One of the first tasks in administering a V2 system is
to create one or more databases. In order to understand the process of database creation, we first need to learn something about how V2 manages its
physical storage.

8.1.1 Tablespaces

The physical space within a database is organized into a collection of
tablespaces. Each tablespace, in turn, consists of a collection of *containers*, each
of which is either a directory in your machine's file system, a physical file, or a
device such as a hard disk.

Each table is assigned to one specific tablespace, which contains the primary data for that table—however, a table may optionally keep its indexes in
a second tablespace and its large objects in a third tablespace. The system

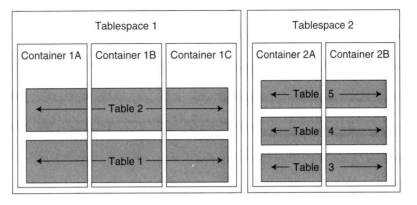

Figure 8-1: Organization of Physical Space into Tablespaces and Containers

attempts to spread the data for each table uniformly across the containers of its tablespace. Figure 8-1 illustrates a database containing two tablespaces, of three and two containers respectively. Tablespace 1 contains two tables and Tablespace 2 contains three tables.

The unit of space allocation within a container is called an *extent*. As a table grows, it occupies new extents in all of the containers in its tablespace. For example, in Figure 8-1, Table 1 occupies extents in containers 1A, 1B, and 1C. The default size of an extent is 16 pages in OS/2 and 32 pages in UNIX environments (a page is 4K bytes). A different default extent size can be defined for your database by a database configuration parameter called DFT_EXTENTSIZE, and you can override the default for a specific tablespace when you create it. If you plan to store many small tables in a tablespace, you may wish to choose a small extent size, since each table will be stored in its own extent.

By assigning tables to tablespaces and mapping tablespaces onto physical devices and directories, you can do a lot to optimize the performance of your database. For example, you can spread your data across multiple disk devices to take advantage of parallel input and output. You can use your fastest storage devices for your most frequently used tables and indexes and store less frequently used data on slower, less expensive devices. Since each tablespace can be independently backed up and restored, you can also cluster closely related tables together in a tablespace so they can be backed up as a unit. (Additional guidelines for assigning tables to tablespaces and mapping tablespaces onto physical storage devices can be found in the *DB2 Administration Guide*.)

V2 provides two different kinds of tablespaces, which are referred to by the terms *System Managed Space* (SMS) and *Database Managed Space* (DMS). An

SMS tablespace uses the facilities of your operating system to manage physical space, whereas in a DMS tablespace, the physical space is managed directly by V2. SMS tablespaces (the default) are easy to create and manage, and are well suited for many small and moderate-sized databases. DMS tablespaces provide an additional degree of control that can be helpful in large databases and high-performance applications, but they also require more sophistication on the part of the database administrator. A single database can contain both SMS and DMS tablespaces. Some of the differences between the two types of tablespaces are summarized in Table 8-1.

Each tablespace is described by a row in the catalog table named TABLESPACES.

The SQL statements for creating, altering, and dropping tablespaces are listed below. In order to use any of these statements, you must have SYSADM or SYSCTRL authority.

CREATE TABLESPACE

In order to create an SMS tablespace, you need to specify the name of the tablespace and the path names of all its containers. Remember that each container in an SMS tablespace is a directory. If a relative path name is given, it is

TABLE 8-1: Properties of Tablespaces

System Managed Space (SMS)	Database Managed Space (DMS)
Each container is a directory in the filespace of your operating system. The space in this directory is not preallocated but grows as data is added to the tablespace. Data is stored in the form of files in the directory. (More files are added as the quantity of data grows.)	A container may be either a fixed-size, pre-allocated file, or a physical device such as a disk (AIX only). In either case, all the storage for the container must be allocated when the container is created. If a container is a device, it must occupy the entire device.
Containers cannot be added to a tablespace after it is created.	Containers can be added to an existing tablespace, using the ALTER TABLESPACE statement.
A container can be shared among multiple tablespaces.	A container cannot be shared among multiple tablespaces.
All the data for a given table, including its indexes and large objects, must be stored in a single tablespace.	The primary data for a table can be stored in one tablespace, its indexes in a second tablespace, and its large objects (LOBs) in a third tablespace. This technique can improve the clustering of the table in physical storage.

interpreted with respect to the local database directory of the database containing the tablespace (see Figure 8-2). If the last level of the path name does not exist, a directory with the given name is created.

In the following example, we create an SMS tablespace containing three containers, implemented by directories on three different disks in an OS/2 or Windows NT file system. We then create a table in the new tablespace, causing the data in the table to be distributed among the three disks. Of course, before executing the CREATE TABLESPACE statement, our application or CLP session must be connected to the database in which the tablespace is to be created.

```
CREATE TABLESPACE sms1 MANAGED BY SYSTEM
    USING ('d:\sms1', 'e:\sms1', 'f:\sms1');
CREATE TABLE accounts.receivable
    (custno  Char(6),
     amount  Money,
     dueDate Date,
     PRIMARY KEY(custno, dueDate))
    IN sms1;
```

When creating a DMS tablespace, it is necessary to specify not only the names of the files or devices that implement the containers, but also their sizes. The size of each file or device is specified as a number of 4K-byte pages, and the specified amount of space is allocated when the tablespace is created. In the following example, we create a DMS tablespace consisting of two containers, each implemented by a file of 10,000 pages.

```
CREATE TABLESPACE dms2 MANAGED BY DATABASE
    USING (FILE 'd:\dms2\dms2.dat' 10000,
           FILE 'e:\dms2\dms2.dat' 10000);
```

V2 recognizes two specialized kinds of tablespaces, called *temporary* and *long* tablespaces. A temporary tablespace provides space for the system to use for temporary results, such as a table that is materialized for sorting during the processing of a query. Every database must have at least one temporary tablespace, and additional temporary tablespaces can be added for improved performance. Either an SMS or a DMS tablespace can be designated as a temporary tablespace at the time of its creation by specifying CREATE TEMPORARY TABLESPACE.

A *long* tablespace is a tablespace that is dedicated to the storage of large objects. When a table is created, the CREATE TABLE statement can specify whether the table will store its large objects mixed with its other data in a regular tablespace or use a separate long tablespace for this purpose. Separating

the large objects from the rest of the data can improve the clustering properties of the table and reduce the number of I/O operations needed to scan the
table. A long tablespace must be a DMS tablespace and is designated at creation time by specifying CREATE LONG TABLESPACE. In the following OS/2
example, we allocate a 50,000-page file to serve as a long tablespace and create
a table that uses the long tablespace to store large objects.

```
CREATE LONG TABLESPACE longspace MANAGED BY DATABASE
    USING (FILE 'f:\longspace\space1.dat' 50000);
CREATE TABLE bridges
    (name      Varchar(32),
     latitude  Double,
     longitude Double,
     photo     Blob(1M))
    IN dms2 LONG IN longspace;
```

A CREATE TABLESPACE statement has the following optional parameters:

- EXTENTSIZE specifies the unit of space allocation inside the containers of the
  tablespace, in pages.

- PREFETCHSIZE specifies the number of pages to be fetched from the
  tablespace in advance of being referenced, in an attempt to anticipate page
  references and reduce waiting for I/O. Prefetching of pages is done automatically when the system is scanning a whole table, or whenever it detects a regular pattern of pages being fetched from disk into main memory.

- OVERHEAD is an estimate of the average latency time (in milliseconds) to
  begin a new I/O operation in the tablespace, and is provided as information
  for the SQL optimizer.

- TRANSFERRATE is an estimate of the time required (in milliseconds) to read
  one 4K-byte page in the tablespace, and is provided as information for the
  SQL optimizer.

These optional parameters are discussed further in the *DB2 SQL Reference*
and the *DB2 Administration Guide*. Each of them has a default value that is
suitable for many applications.

ALTER TABLESPACE

After a tablespace has been created, the only alterations that can be made to it
are as follows:

- The optional performance parameters (PREFETCHSIZE, OVERHEAD, and
  TRANSFERRATE) can be changed, as in the following example:

```
ALTER TABLESPACE userspace1
    PREFETCHSIZE 64;
```

- New containers can be added to a DMS tablespace, as in the following example:

```
ALTER TABLESPACE longspace
    ADD (FILE 'f:\longspace\space2.dat' 50000);
```

When a new container is added to a tablespace, a background process automatically moves some existing data into the new container so that the data in the tablespace will be balanced across all its containers.

DROP TABLESPACE

Dropping a tablespace destroys all the objects (such as tables and indexes) that are completely contained in the tablespace. However, if a table spans multiple tablespaces (for example, it has data in one tablespace and indexes or large objects in another), none of the tablespaces containing parts of the table can be dropped until after the table has been dropped.

The following is an example of a statement that drops a tablespace:

```
DROP TABLESPACE dms2;
```

8.1.2 Creating and Destroying Databases

Now that we understand something about tablespaces, we are ready to discuss the process of creating a database. But first we need to discuss some terminology that, unfortunately, can be confusing. When talking about databases, the terms *catalog* and *directory* are used with more than one meaning. Here is what you need to remember about these terms:

1. As we have seen, each database contains a set of tables called *catalog tables,* which are automatically maintained by the system and which describe the contents of the database.

2. Each instance of V2, installed either as a client or as a server, has a *system database directory,* which lists all the databases that are accessible from that instance. When a database is created, it is automatically entered into the system database directory of the server on which it resides. Additional databases, possibly residing on other servers, can be added to a system database directory by the CATALOG DATABASE command. (Note that the CATALOG DATABASE command has nothing to do with catalog tables.) The content of the system database directory for a given instance of V2 can be displayed by the command LIST DATABASE DIRECTORY.

3. Each database is created in a particular directory in the file system on a server machine. The path name of this directory can be specified (or defaulted) at the time the database is created. This directory is called the *local database directory* of the database. Note that a system database directory is associated with a V2 instance, but a local database directory is associated with a database.

Multiple databases can be created with the same local database directory. The actual content of each database resides in a collection of subdirectories below its local database directory. All the databases having a given path name for their local database directory can be listed by the command LIST DATABASE DIRECTORY ON <path name>.

CREATE DATABASE

A database is created by a CREATE DATABASE command, which requires SYSADM or SYSCTRL authority. A CREATE DATABASE command can be either simple or complex, since it has many options but defaults are provided for almost all of them. Here are two examples:

- This example, the simplest one possible, creates a database named MYDATA, with its location and all its properties chosen by default:

  ```
  CREATE DATABASE mydata;
  ```

- This slightly more complex example creates a database in a specified local database directory and specifies that the database will be used for storing data using a Japanese character set (hence, it will be a double-byte database). A list of supported codesets and territories can be found in an appendix of the *DB2 Planning Guide* for your platform.

  ```
  CREATE DATABASE japan1
     ON '/db/japan1'
     USING CODESET IBM-932 TERRITORY Ja_JP;
  ```

  A CREATE DATABASE statement does all of the following:

- It creates the physical directories to hold the database, under the specified local database directory. If no local database directory is specified, the default is taken from the database manager configuration parameter named DFTDBPATH.

- It creates files to hold the database recovery log and handle other necessary bookkeeping details.

- It creates a set of tablespaces. The characteristics of these tablespaces can be specified explicitly in the CREATE TABLESPACE command or can be defaulted. By default, a new database is created with three SMS tablespaces, named SYSCATSPACE (for catalog tables), USERSPACE1 (for user data), and

TEMPSPACE1 (for temporary storage). Additional tablespaces can be created later. Each database is required to have at least one temporary tablespace.

- In the SYSCATSPACE tablespace, it creates all the system catalog tables and their views and populates them to describe themselves. A new set of catalog tables and views for an empty database occupies about 1.6 megabytes of disk space.
- It sets the values of the database configuration parameters for the new database. Some of these configuration parameters (such as CODESET and TERRITORY) can be specified on the CREATE DATABASE command, while others receive default values. Database configuration parameters are discussed further in Section 8.3.4.
- It binds a set of utility programs to the new database, creating packages for them so that they can be used in the new database.
- It makes an entry for the new database in the system database directory for the V2 instance that created the database. (Later, the new database can be added to the system database directories on other client nodes.)
- It grants DBAUTH authority on the new database to the user who created the database, and it grants CONNECTAUTH, CREATETABAUTH, and BINDAUTH authorities to PUBLIC. This enables any user to connect to the new database, create tables in it, and bind application programs in it. If necessary, the holder of DBAUTH can later revoke these privileges from PUBLIC and replace them with more specific privileges granted to individual users.

DROP DATABASE

Dropping a database is very simple if you hold SYSADM or SYSCTRL authority. Here's an example of how it's done:

```
DROP DATABASE mydata;
```

A database cannot be dropped while any users or applications are connected to it. A database administrator can forcefully disconnect users from a database by using the FORCE command, described in Section 8.3.2.

8.1.3 Where's the Data?

Figure 8-2 shows an example of how a V2 database might be implemented by a collection of physical files in the filespace of the server. The path name of the local database directory is specified at database creation time. Under this directory is found another directory with the name of the V2 instance, and below that is found one directory for each of the databases that share this local database directory. Each database is made up of tablespaces, which in

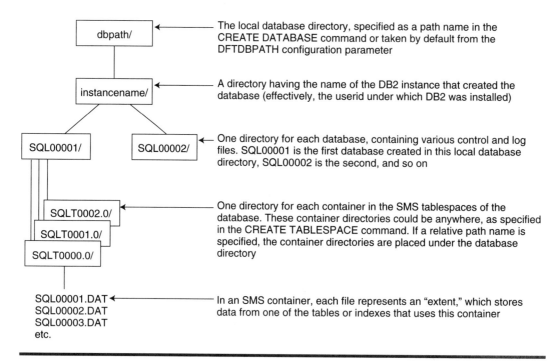

The local database directory, specified as a path name in the CREATE DATABASE command or taken by default from the DFTDBPATH configuration parameter

A directory having the name of the DB2 instance that created the database (effectively, the userid under which DB2 was installed)

One directory for each database, containing various control and log files. SQL00001 is the first database created in this local database directory, SQL00002 is the second, and so on

One directory for each container in the SMS tablespaces of the database. These container directories could be anywhere, as specified in the CREATE TABLESPACE command. If a relative path name is specified, the container directories are placed under the database directory

In an SMS container, each file represents an "extent," which stores data from one of the tables or indexes that uses this container

Figure 8-2: Physical Database Organization Using SMS Tablespaces

turn are made up of containers. Tablespaces are not represented explicitly in Figure 8-2, since they do not map directly onto directories or files. For SMS tablespaces, each container is a directory. The location of the container directories is specified at tablespace creation time, and relative path names are interpreted with respect to the database directory. In an SMS container, the extents in which data is stored are individual files.

TIP: It is very important not to tamper with any of the files shown in Figure 8-2, since this might destroy the database. The database administrator should use the security facilities of the operating system to prevent users from tampering with database files.

8.2 USING YOUR DATABASE

This section describes commands that users and application developers will find helpful in everyday usage of V2 databases.

8.2.1 Operating System–Level Commands

Most of the commands discussed in this chapter are intended to be executed from a CLP session (and most of them also have call interfaces so that they can be invoked from an application program). However, V2 also supports a small number of commands that are intended to be invoked directly from the command line of your operating system (or from a shell script). These commands are very important, because they provide the means to start up your database system and enter a mode where other commands can be used.

The operating system–level commands supported by V2 are listed below. If you have multiple instances of V2 installed on your machine, these commands are directed to the instance named in your DB2INSTANCE environment variable or your most recent ATTACH command, as described in Section 8.3.1.

Most of the commands listed below can be invoked either by typing on your operating system command line, or, if you are using a graphic user interface, by double-clicking on one of the icons in the "DB2" group. For those commands that can be invoked by an icon, the name of the icon is included in the command description.

db2start

Starts the database system. This command requires SYSADM, SYSCTRL, or SYSMAINT authority and must be executed on the server machine. It takes no parameters. The database system must be started before any applications or CLP sessions can connect to a database or any programs can be precompiled. Example:

```
db2start
```

Icon: "Start DB2."

db2stop

Stops the database system. This command requires SYSADM, SYSCTRL, or SYS-MAINT authority and must be executed on the server machine. It takes no parameters. The database system cannot be stopped as long as any application or CLP session remains connected to a database. A system administrator can forcibly disconnect applications from the system by using the FORCE command, which is discussed in Section 8.3.2. Example:

```
db2stop
```

Icon: "Stop DB2."

db2

Starts the CLP. (Usage of the CLP is discussed in Section 2.6.) The following example starts a CLP session with a semicolon delimiter at the end of each SQL statement:

```
db2 -t
```

Icon: "Command Line Processor."

db2dd

Starts the Database Director, a graphic interface for examining the structure of a database and performing database administration tasks. The command takes no parameters. The Database Director is discussed in Section 8.8. Example:

```
db2dd
```

Icon: "Database Director."

db2eva

Invokes the Event Analyzer, a graphic interface for analyzing and displaying data collected by V2 Event Monitors. Event Monitors, as described in Section 8.7.2, can be created to monitor various events, such as database connections, deadlocks, and transaction commits and rollbacks. An Event Monitor collects data on the designated event and saves it in a file. The following example command invokes the Event Analyzer to display the data collected by an Event Monitor named transmon in the database named parts:

```
db2eva -db parts -evm transmon
```

Icon: "Event Analyzer."

db2jobs

Displays a list of all the backup, recover, rollforward, and restart jobs that are currently in progress on this instance of V2, and presents a graphic user interface for controlling these jobs and viewing their output. This command is useful to monitor the progress of jobs that were launched by the Database Director. Example:

```
db2jobs
```

Icon: "Recovery Jobs."

db2rbind

Rebinds all the packages in a database. This might be useful after a reorganization of the database, in which statistics are updated and new indexes are created. Alternatively, the individual packages in the database can be rebound, either explicitly by REBIND commands, or implicitly on their next use. The command in the following example rebinds all the packages in the company database and directs any error messages to a file named rebind.log:

```
db2rbind company -l rebind.log   (AIX syntax)
db2rbind company /l=rebind.log   (OS/2 and Windows syntax)
```

db2sampl

Creates a sample database, named SAMPLE, for experimentation. The sample database consists of 11 tables that describe the employees, departments, and projects of a small company. (The tables in the sample database are described in Appendix E of the *DB2 SQL Reference*.) The command takes an optional parameter that specifies the location (path) where the database is to be created; if no path is specified, the location of the database is determined by the DFTDBPATH configuration parameter. Example:

```
db2sampl
```

Icon: "First Steps."

db2help

Displays a list of all the online documentation available for V2. By double-clicking on the name of one of the online manuals, you can browse the manual and search its content for specific words and phrases. Example:

```
db2help
```

Online manuals can also be accessed from a CLP session by means of the HELP command, described in Section 2.6.4.

Icon: "DB2 Information."

Others

The following operating system–level commands are of interest mainly to system administrators. The detailed syntax of these commands is given in the *DB2 Command Reference*.

db2migdr

Migrates a local database directory from V1 format to V2 format. This makes the database in this local directory accessible for migration to V2.

db2cidmg

Invokes a facility for migrating databases to V2 from V1 or from other database systems in the DB2 family. The database to be migrated may be local or remote.

db2drdat

Invokes a facility for capturing a trace of the messages exchanged between client and server machines using the Distributed Relational Database Architecture (DRDA) protocol. Used mainly for problem determination.

8.2.2 Finding Your Way Around

The commands in this section are useful in a CLP session, after you have connected to a database, to explore the content of the database, examine your own authorities, and obtain general helpful information.

HELP

The HELP command enables you to view the online documentation for the V2 system. If you specify a character string after the word HELP, the system will look for that string in the online *DB2 SQL Reference* or *DB2 Command Reference* and will open a window showing the relevant page of the manual. In this window you can scroll through the manual, do content searches, and follow hypertext links. If you do not provide a character string to search for or if the string you provide is not found, the HELP command opens a window on the table of contents of the *DB2 SQL Reference*. Example:

```
HELP CREATE TRIGGER;
```

LIST TABLES

This command lists all the tables in the database that were created by the current user. If the command is followed by the words FOR ALL, all the tables in the database are listed, regardless of their creator. Examples:

```
LIST TABLES;
LIST TABLES FOR ALL;
```

LIST TABLESPACES

This command lists all the tablespaces in the database to which you are connected. If the command is followed by the words SHOW DETAIL, you get additional details such as the number of containers and extent size in each tablespace. Examples:

```
LIST TABLESPACES;
LIST TABLESPACES SHOW DETAIL;
```

LIST TABLESPACE CONTAINERS

This command lists all the containers in a specific tablespace, which you must identify by its tablespace ID, an integer that you can obtain from the LIST TABLESPACES command. The following command lists the containers for the tablespace whose ID is 2:

```
LIST TABLESPACE CONTAINERS FOR 2;
```

LIST PACKAGES

This command lists all the packages in the database that were bound by the current user. If the command is followed by the words FOR ALL, all the packages in the database are listed, regardless of who bound them. Examples:

```
LIST PACKAGES;
LIST PACKAGES FOR ALL;
```

GET AUTHORIZATIONS

This command displays the instance-level and database-level authorities you hold in the database to which you are currently connected. Example:

```
GET AUTHORIZATIONS;
```

GET CONNECTION STATE

This command displays the name of the database to which you are currently connected, if any. Example:

```
GET CONNECTION STATE;
```

GET INSTANCE

This command displays the name of the instance (that is, the name of the V2 installation) that you are currently using. More than one instance of V2 can exist on the same machine, and you can switch from one instance to another by using the ATTACH command. Example:

```
GET INSTANCE;
```

8.2.3 CLP-Related Commands

A CLP session is begun by the db2 command, discussed in Section 2.6. This section describes several commands that are useful for controlling the behavior of your CLP session.

UPDATE COMMAND OPTIONS

The CLP has a set of command options that specify various aspects of its operation, such as the SQL termination character and the destination file for error messages. (A list of all the CLP command options is given in Section 2.6.2.) These options can be specified when the CLP is invoked, and during a CLP session they can be changed by the command UPDATE COMMAND OPTIONS. The following example turns off the autocommit option, which automatically performs a commit after each SQL statement:

```
UPDATE COMMAND OPTIONS USING c OFF;
```

LIST COMMAND OPTIONS

Lists the CLP command options that are currently in effect. Example:

```
LIST COMMAND OPTIONS;
```

ECHO

The ECHO command simply echoes its content to the output stream. This can be useful for generating labels in an output file. For example, if the CLP is running test cases from an input file and saving the results in an output file, the ECHO command can be used to label the test cases. Example:

```
ECHO Test Case 15;
```

SET CLIENT

This command can be used to change certain characteristics of your CLP session, such as the type of database connections that it uses. (Database connections are discussed in Section 2.9.2.) The SET CLIENT command can be used only when your session is not connected to a database. The command in the following example directs the CLP to use Type 2 connections with a two-phase commit protocol:

```
SET CLIENT CONNECT 2 SYNCPOINT TWOPHASE;
```

QUERY CLIENT

This command displays the client options—such as connection type, commit protocol, and SQL language rules—that are currently in effect. Example:

```
QUERY CLIENT;
```

CHANGE ISOLATION LEVEL

This command changes the level of isolation between your transactions and the transactions of other concurrent users. Choosing a high isolation level can protect you from interference by other users, as described in Section 2.9.1, but it can also affect system performance and limit concurrent access to data.

The supported isolation levels, from highest to lowest, are as follows:

1. *Repeatable Read* (*RR*). Repeated reads of the same data are guaranteed consistent within a transaction.

2. *Read Stability* (*RS*). When performing a repeated read of a table, old rows will be unchanged but new rows may appear.

3. *Cursor Stability* (*CS*). Guarantees that a row of data will not change while your cursor is positioned on it. This is the default isolation level.

4. *Uncommitted Read* (*UR*). Allows you to read updates that have not been committed by other users and that are therefore subject to being rolled back.

The CHANGE ISOLATION LEVEL command can be executed only when you are not connected to a database. Example:

```
CHANGE ISOLATION TO RR;
```

TERMINATE

This command terminates your database connection, if any, and ends your CLP session. If a transaction is in progress, it is committed. Example:

```
TERMINATE;
```

QUIT

This command ends your CLP session but does not terminate your database connection. Example:

```
QUIT;
```

After executing a QUIT command, you can execute some operating system commands and then start a new CLP session by using a db2 command. In your new CLP session, you will still be connected to the same database as you were before the QUIT command.

By default, the CLP executes each SQL statement as a separate transaction, performing a COMMIT after each statement. If you turn off the autocommit option, however, a transaction can span several SQL statements. If such a transaction is in progress when you QUIT, it remains in progress and is neither committed nor rolled back. In your next CLP session (again, with autocommit turned off), you can continue the same transaction.

TIP: As a general rule, it is better to use TERMINATE rather than QUIT to end a CLP session. Leaving a transaction in progress between CLP sessions is a bad idea, because the transaction may be holding locks that will limit access to data by other users. The database connection left active after a QUIT command can also interfere with stopping the database server or changing database configuration parameters.

8.2.4 Package-Related Commands

A *package* is the encapsulated form of an application program, containing the access plans that were selected by the V2 optimizer for the SQL statements in the program. The process of preparing a program for execution by creating a package for it is illustrated by Figure 1-6 and discussed in Section 1.2.4 and Section 2.7.15. The commands that are used for the binding and rebinding of packages are summarized below.

PREP

The PREP command (which can also be spelled PRECOMPILE) is used to precompile an application program and to generate a package and/or a bind file. During the precompilation process, the SQL statements in the application program are replaced by calls to the run-time database system. The program is then ready for compilation using a host language compiler.

In order to precompile a program, you must be connected to a database. You must possess either BINDADD authority on the database (if the program is being precompiled for the first time) or the BIND privilege on the specific package (if it already exists). In addition, you must hold the privileges necessary to execute all the SQL statements contained in the program, and you must hold these privileges as an individual user—privileges granted to groups or to PUBLIC are not sufficient.

If a package is generated during precompilation, it contains an optimized form of each SQL statement in your program, ready to be executed at run time. The package is stored in the database.

If a bind file is generated during precompilation, it contains the SQL statements from your application program, but they have not yet been optimized and converted to executable form. The BIND command can then be used to generate a package from the bind file and to store the package in the database. Unless you specify otherwise, the bind file has the same name as your source program, with an extension of .BND, and is created in the same directory as your source program.

The PREP command has a great many options, which are documented in the *DB2 Command Reference*. I will summarize a few of the more useful options here:

- The BINDFILE option causes the precompiler to create a bind file and to forego creation of a package unless the PACKAGE option is also specified.

- The BLOCKING option controls whether the result sets of queries are returned from the server machine to the client machine one row at a time or in blocks of several rows. Returning blocks of rows improves performance by reducing the number of messages exchanged between server and client, but it leads to problems when cursors are used for positioned updates and deletes (as in DELETE FROM table1 WHERE CURRENT OF cursor1). By default, the system performs blocking of rows for any cursor that is never used for a positioned update or delete. But if your program prepares and executes some dynamic SQL statements, the system cannot be sure that you will not prepare and execute a positioned update or delete on some cursor. If you wish to make a promise that your program will not dynamically prepare and execute any positioned updates or deletes, you can do so by specifying BLOCKING ALL; this promise allows the system to perform blocking of rows in some cases when it would not otherwise do so.

- The COLLECTION option specifies the name of the database schema in which the resulting package will be created. The default schema name is the userid under which the PREP command is executed.

- The CONNECT option specifies whether the program will use Type 1 connections (connecting to only one database in each transaction) or Type 2 connections (connecting to multiple databases in the same transaction). (Type 1 and Type 2 connections are discussed in Section 2.9.2.)

- The DATETIME option specifies the preferred format for dates and times that are generated by the package (such as the value of the CURRENT DATE and CURRENT TIME special registers). The format is specified by a three-letter code such as USA (American standard), EUR (European standard), or JIS (Japanese standard).

- The EXPLSNAP option specifies that "Explain snapshot" information is to be gathered for each SQL statement in the program. This information can be used later with the *Visual Explain* feature of the Database Director to examine the access plan chosen by the optimizer for each statement. The Visual Explain feature is discussed in Section 8.8.1.

- The FUNCPATH option specifies a list of schemas that are to be searched, in order, when resolving function names and datatype names in static SQL statements in the program. The default function path consists of the schemas SYSIBM and SYSFUN, followed by the userid under which the program is being precompiled.

- The ISOLATION option specifies the level of isolation required by the program, in the form of a two-letter code (RR = Repeatable Read, RS = Read Stability, CS = Cursor Stability, UR = Uncommitted Read). (Isolation levels are discussed in Section 2.9.1.)

- The MESSAGES option allows you to specify a filename in which precompiler messages are to be saved (otherwise, these messages are directed to the standard output stream).

- The QUERYOPT option allows you to control the class of optimization techniques to be applied in choosing access plans for SQL statements in the program. Valid values for QUERYOPT are 0, 1, 3, 5, 7, and 9. In general, higher values cause the optimizer to use more time and memory in choosing optimal access plans, potentially resulting in better plans and improved run-time performance. The extreme values 0 and 9 should be used with caution, since they may result in suboptimal plans or long optimization times, respectively. Class 1 is similar to the level of optimization provided by the V1 system. Class 5 is the default level of optimization for V2 and is a good compromise for most applications. Optimization classes are discussed further in Section 8.6.1.

 TIP: Don't confuse the QUERYOPT option with the OPTLEVEL option, which has nothing to do with the optimization of SQL statements and which you probably don't want to use.

- The SYNCPOINT option is used with Type 2 connections to specify how commits and rollbacks are handled for transactions that connect to more than one database. Valid values for this option are ONEPHASE, TWOPHASE, and NONE. The default is ONEPHASE. (The SYNCPOINT option is discussed in Section 2.9.2.)

- The WCHARTYPE option controls the format in which Graphic, Vargraphic, Long Vargraphic, and Dbclob data is exchanged with host variables. WCHARTYPE NOCONVERT (the default) specifies that data is exchanged using two bytes per character, just as it is stored in the database. WCHARTYPE CONVERT specifies that data is exchanged using the `wchar_t` type that is defined by your C compiler and is used with the C "wide character" function library.

The following examples illustrate the use of the PREP command and some of its options:

- The simplest form of a PREP command simply names the program to be pre-compiled:

    ```
    PREP prog1.sqc;
    ```

- This command precompiles a C program named `prog2`, using Repeatable Read isolation and producing both a package and a bind file. The name of the resulting package will be `business.prog2`.

    ```
    PREP prog2.sqc BINDFILE PACKAGE
        COLLECTION business ISOLATION RR;
    ```

- This command precompiles a C++ program named `prog3`, specifying a European format for dates and a function path that includes the SCIENCE and MATH schemas. The user, Jones, includes his own userid in the function path, remembering that the keyword USER is not effective in the FUNCPATH option. Precompiler messages are directed to a file named `prog3.msg` in the current directory.

    ```
    PREP prog3.sqC DATETIME EUR MESSAGES prog3.msg
        FUNCPATH sysibm, sysfun, science, math, jones;
    ```

- This command precompiles a C program named `prog4`. Because the user is very concerned about performance, she specifies the maximum level of optimization and blocking of all cursors. She also specifies EXPLSNAP YES, so she will be able to examine the access plan of each SQL statement using the Visual Explain facility.

    ```
    PREP prog4.sqc QUERYOPT 9 BLOCKING ALL EXPLSNAP YES;
    ```

- This command precompiles a C program named `prog5`. Because the program contains transactions that update multiple databases, the user specifies Type 2 connections and a two-phase commit protocol.

    ```
    PREP prog5.sqc CONNECT 2 SYNCPOINT TWOPHASE;
    ```

BIND

The BIND command generates a package from a bind file created by a PREP command that was executed earlier. I will speak of the BIND command as though it operates on an application program, although it is really operating on the bind file that was generated from a program by extracting its SQL statements. (The role of the BIND command in application program development is illustrated in Figure 1-6.)

When you invoke a BIND command, you must be connected to a database. You must possess either BINDADD authority on the database (if the program is being bound for the first time) or the BIND privilege on the specific package (if it already exists). In addition, you must hold the privileges necessary to execute all the SQL statements contained in the program, and you must hold these privileges as an individual user—privileges granted to groups or to PUBLIC are not sufficient.

A BIND command causes all the names of tables, views, functions, and other objects in the program to be resolved to real objects in the database, possibly with different results than in a previous binding (for example, a function name may be bound to a different function instance). A BIND command also causes a new access plan to be chosen for each SQL statement in the program.

You can use a BIND command to change some of the options associated with a program such as its isolation level and optimization level. The BIND command supports many of the same options as the PREP command, including the BLOCKING, COLLECTION, DATETIME, EXPLSNAP, FUNCPATH, ISOLATION, MESSAGES, and QUERYOPT options described above. The CONNECT, SYNCPOINT, and WCHARTYPE options are not supported by the BIND command; if you want to change these options, you must use the PREP command. Additional BIND options are documented in the *DB2 Command Reference*.

The following examples illustrate use of the BIND command:

- This is the simplest form of the BIND command, merely invoking name resolution and access-path selection to make sure the program named prog1 has a package that reflects the latest conditions in the database:

  ```
  BIND prog1.bnd;
  ```

- This command rebinds the program named prog2, changing its isolation level to RS and its optimization level to 3 and specifying a new function resolution path:

  ```
  BIND prog2.bnd ISOLATION RS QUERYOPT 3
     FUNCPATH sysibm, sysfun, finance, jones;
  ```

REBIND

REBIND is a very simple command that renews the name resolution and access-path selection for an existing package in the database. Each package in the database records the original text of all its SQL statements and all the options that were in effect when it was bound. These SQL statements and bind options are used by the REBIND command to regenerate the package without making any reference to the source program or bind file. A REBIND command is generally more efficient than a BIND or PREP command and should be used when rebinding an existing package without changing the program or its bind options.

As noted in Section 2.7.16, you might choose to rebind an existing package in order to take advantage of the latest indexes or statistics, to use a newly installed function, or to rescue the package from an invalid or inoperative state.

The only operand of the REBIND command is the name of the package to be rebound. If no schema name is specified for the package, a schema name equal to the current userid is implied. The REBIND command is illustrated by the following examples:

```
REBIND prog1;
REBIND business.prog2;
```

8.2.5 Invoking Stored Procedures

Stored procedures are normally invoked by application programs, using the SQL CALL statement. However, the CALL statement is not a dynamic SQL statement and is not accepted by the CLP. A separate INVOKE statement, described below, is provided for invoking a stored procedure from a CLP session. (Stored procedures are described in Chapter 7.)

INVOKE STORED PROCEDURE

This command can be used to invoke a stored procedure from a CLP session. However, if the stored procedure has input parameters or returns a result, it should be invoked from an application program using the SQL CALL statement.

Example:

```
INVOKE proc1;
```

8.3 ADMINISTERING YOUR DATABASE SYSTEM

The commands in this section are intended primarily for use by database administrators rather than by end users. Many of these commands are used "behind the scenes" to keep the database system and its databases configured for optimum performance and to make sure that all the client and server nodes in the network know how to communicate with each other. Other commands are useful in daily tasks, such as forcing users off the system in preparation for a shutdown. All the commands in this section can be executed from a CLP session.

8.3.1 Selecting an Instance

Multiple instances of the V2 database manager may be installed on the same server machine (but if you are running under OS/2 or Windows NT, all the V2 instances must be the same release and modification level). Each V2 instance is given a name at the time it is installed. For example, one V2 instance might be used for testing and another for production, or one V2 instance might be configured for high-volume transactions while another is configured for decision support. Each V2 instance can manage multiple databases, but a database cannot be shared by different V2 instances.

Most SQL statements and many system commands can be executed only if you are connected to a database. Some commands, however, are called *instance-level commands* because they can be executed when no database connection exists. For example, you can execute a CREATE DATABASE command when you are not connected to any existing database. However, the instance-level commands need to be directed to a particular instance of V2 so that they will be executed in the proper context. For example, a CREATE DATABASE command needs to be directed to the V2 instance that is intended to manage the new database.

You can direct your instance-level commands to any V2 instance that is listed in the node directory on your machine. You specify the V2 instance that you wish to use by means of the ATTACH command. You can also specify a default V2 instance by setting the value of the environment variable named DB2INSTANCE. If you execute an instance-level command before any ATTACH command has been executed, your command will be directed to the instance named in the DB2INSTANCE environment variable. The following are examples of how you might define the instance named db2 as your default V2 instance:

- If you are running under a UNIX-based system and using the K-shell, place the following command in your .profile file:

  ```
  export DB2INSTANCE=db2
  ```
- If you are running under OS/2 or Windows NT, place the following command in your CONFIG.SYS file:

  ```
  set DB2INSTANCE=db2
  ```

ATTACH

An ATTACH command specifies the V2 instance to which future instance-level commands will be directed. If no instance name is specified, the ATTACH command returns the name of the instance to which you are currently attached.

Here are some examples of ATTACH commands:

- Attach to the V2 instance named SERVER3, directing all future instance-level commands to this instance. SERVER3 may be installed on the local machine or on a remote server machine that is listed in the local machine's node directory.

```
ATTACH TO server3;
```

- Display the name of the V2 instance to which you are currently attached:

```
ATTACH;
```

DETACH

A DETACH command ends your attachment to a particular V2 instance. If you execute an instance-level command after a DETACH command, it will be directed to the default V2 instance named in your DB2INSTANCE environment variable. A DETACH command requires no authorization and takes no parameters. Here's an example:

```
DETACH;
```

8.3.2 Daily Operations

The commands in this section are used by database administrators for everyday tasks in operating a database system.

DB2START

This command starts the database server. It requires SYSADM, SYSCTRL, or SYSMAINT authority. The database server must be started before any applications or CLP sessions can connect to a database or any programs can be precompiled. Once started, the database server will continue to run until it is explicitly stopped by a DB2STOP command.

The DB2START command takes no parameters. It has an alternate spelling of START DATABASE MANAGER. If more than one database server is installed on (or accessible from) your machine, the server to be started is specified by the most recent ATTACH command.

Examples:

```
DB2START;
START DATABASE MANAGER;
```

TIP: DB2START is both a CLP command and an operating system–level command. If used at the operating system prompt of an AIX or UNIX-based system, it must be typed in lowercase letters.

DB2STOP

This command stops the database server. It requires SYSADM, SYSCTRL, or SYSMAINT authority. The database system cannot be stopped as long as any application or CLP session remains connected to a database. A system administrator can forcibly disconnect applications from the system by using the FORCE command.

The DB2STOP command takes no parameters. It has an alternate spelling of STOP DATABASE MANAGER. If more than one database server is installed on (or accessible from) your machine, the server to be stopped is specified by the most recent ATTACH command.

Examples:

```
DB2STOP;
STOP DATABASE MANAGER;
```

 TIP: DB2STOP is both a CLP command and an operating system–level command. If issued from a CLP session, it stops the database server but does not terminate the CLP session. If issued at the operating system prompt of an AIX or UNIX-based system, it must be typed in lowercase letters.

LIST APPLICATIONS

This command lists all the applications that are connected to a particular database or to all the databases managed by the V2 server to which you are currently attached. The command requires SYSADM, SYSCTRL, or SYSMAINT authority. For each application, the command lists the name of the application, the database to which it is connected, its authorization userid, and its agent ID. The agent ID identifies the process that was created on the server machine to handle requests from the given client. This agent ID may be used in a FORCE command to forcibly disconnect the application from the database.

Here are some examples:

- List all the applications that are connected to the FINANCE database.

  ```
  LIST APPLICATIONS FOR DATABASE finance;
  ```

- List all the applications that are connected to any database managed by the current V2 instance.

  ```
  LIST APPLICATIONS;
  ```

- List all the applications that are connected to any database managed by the current V2 instance and include details such as the state (running or waiting) of each application.

  ```
  LIST APPLICATIONS SHOW DETAIL;
  ```

  An example of output from a LIST APPLICATIONS command is shown below. This sample output describes a CLP session running with authid CHAMBERL and connected to a database named SAMPLE. The agent ID 20332 could be used in a FORCE command to forcibly disconnect this session.

```
Auth Id   Application Name   Agent Id   Application Id                  DB Name
--------  ----------------   --------   ----------------------------   --------
CHAMBERL  db2bp               20332      *LOCAL.chamberl.950626211753   SAMPLE
```

FORCE

This command forcibly disconnects one or more applications from a database. It requires SYSADM or SYSCTRL authority. The FORCE command might be used to disconnect all applications from a database that is about to be shut down.

The applications to be disconnected are specified by their agent IDs, which can be obtained from a LIST APPLICATIONS command. Alternatively, the FORCE command could forcibly disconnect all applications from all databases managed by the V2 instance to which you are currently attached.

Here are some examples:

- Forcibly disconnect the applications with agent IDs 20332 and 20419.

  ```
  FORCE APPLICATION (20332, 20419);
  ```

- Forcibly disconnect all applications connected to databases managed by the current server.

  ```
  FORCE APPLICATION ALL;
  ```

8.3.3 Cataloging Nodes and Databases

As noted in Chapter 1, a client-server database environment can include many machines. A given client machine in the network may be able to connect to several databases managed by V2 instances on several different server machines. Each machine maintains a "map" of the servers and databases that it knows about, in the form of two directories: a *node directory* and a *system database directory*.

The node directory lists all the V2 servers that are known to a given machine. It assigns a local name, called a *node name*, to each server and records the name of the machine on which the server is installed, the instance name of the server on its home machine, and the protocol used to communicate with the server.

The system database directory lists all the databases that are known to a given machine. Some of these databases may be local and some may be remote. The directory assigns a local name, called an *alias*, to each database, and it records the node on which the database resides and the name by which it is known on its home node.

The commands that are used to manage the content of the node directory and the system database directory for a given machine are listed below. These commands have many options, and are explained more fully in the *DB2 Command Reference*.

CATALOG NODE

The CATALOG NODE command is used to enter a new node into a machine's node directory. This command has various options, depending on the protocol used to communicate with the node that is being entered into the node directory (the protocols supported include APPC, IPX/SPX, NetBios, and TCP/IP). There is even a version of the command that can be used to give a new node name to a V2 server installed on the local machine.

The command in the following example might be used on a client machine, to enter a V2 server with an instance name of DB2TEST, running on a remote node with a TCP/IP address of 129.33.70.30, into the node directory with a local name of SPORTS:

```
CATALOG TCPIP NODE sports
    REMOTE 129.33.70.30 SERVER db2test;
```

After SPORTS has been defined as a V2 instance by the command above, applications on the client machine can direct instance-level commands to SPORTS as follows:

```
ATTACH TO sports;
```

CATALOG DATABASE

When a database is created, it is automatically added to the system database directory for the machine on which it resides. Other machines can add the database to their system database directories by using the CATALOG DATABASE command, which records the node where the database resides and assigns it a local alias. Commands that refer to a database must do so by using the alias defined for the database on the machine where the command is executed. The alias by which a database is known on a client machine may or may not be the same as its database name on its home server machine.

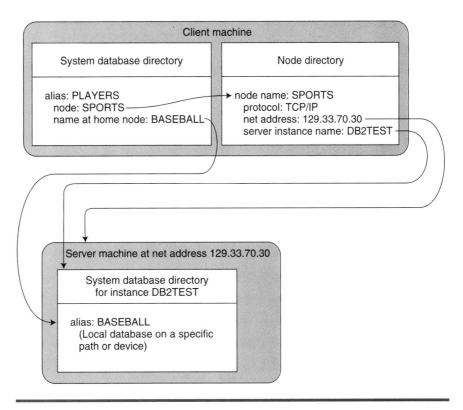

Figure 8-3: Example of System Database Directory and Node Directory

The command in the following example might be used to enter a database named BASEBALL, which is resident on a server node named SPORTS, into the system database directory on a client machine, and to give this database the local alias of PLAYERS. Before this command can be executed, the SPORTS node must be entered into the node directory, so that the client machine knows how to communicate with the V2 server at this node.

```
CATALOG DATABASE baseball AS players AT NODE sports;
```

After execution of the example CATALOG NODE and CATALOG DATABASE commands shown above, the system database directory and node directory at the client machine might contain entries as shown in Figure 8-3.

A user or application at the client machine might execute the SQL statement CONNECT TO PLAYERS. The client's system database directory indicates that the alias PLAYERS refers to a database on the SPORTS node, known at its home node as BASEBALL. The client's node directory indicates that the SPORTS node is a V2 server named DB2TEST, running on a machine that can be reached by the TCP/IP protocol at network address 129.33.70.30. The client machine uses the information in its two directories to send a message to the server machine requesting a connection to the BASEBALL database. The system database directory on the server machine has an entry indicating that BASEBALL is a local database and specifying its location on the server machine.

UNCATALOG

The UNCATALOG command is used to remove an entry from a node directory or system database directory. The following examples might be used to remove the entries that were created in the previous examples:

```
UNCATALOG DATABASE players;
UNCATALOG NODE sports;
```

LIST NODE DIRECTORY

The LIST NODE DIRECTORY command is used to list the content of the node directory on your machine. It takes no operands. Here's an example:

```
LIST NODE DIRECTORY;
```

The output of this example command might be as follows:

```
Node Directory
Number of entries in the directory = 1

Node 1 entry:
  Node name                    = SPORTS
  Comment                      =
  Protocol                     = TCPIP
  Hostname                     = 129.33.70.30
  Service name                 = db2test
```

LIST DATABASE DIRECTORY

The LIST DATABASE DIRECTORY command is used to list the content of the system database directory on your machine. It can also be used with a path name to list the content of a local database directory for a particular database. Remember that a system database directory lists all the databases that can be reached from your machine, while a local database directory contains details about one or more local databases that are stored on a particular path or device. Here are some examples:

- The following command lists the contents of the system database directory:

  ```
  LIST DATABASE DIRECTORY;
  ```

  The output of this command might be as follows. This sample output includes entries for a local database named SAMPLE and a remote database named PLAYERS.

  ```
  System Database Directory
  Number of entries in the directory = 2

  Database 1 entry:
    Database alias                 = SAMPLE
    Database name                  = SAMPLE
    Local database directory       = /home/chamberl
    Database release level         = 6.00
    Comment                        =
    Directory entry type           = Indirect

  Database 2 entry:
    Database alias                 = PLAYERS
    Database name                  = BASEBALL
    Node name                      = SPORTS
    Database release level         = 6.00
    Comment                        =
    Directory entry type           = Remote
  ```

- This command lists the contents of the local database directory on the path /home/chamberl:

  ```
  LIST DATABASE DIRECTORY ON /home/chamberl;
  ```

  The output of this command might be as follows:

  ```
  Local Database Directory on /home/chamberl
  Number of entries in the directory = 1

  Database 1 entry:
    Database alias                 = SAMPLE
    Database name                  = SAMPLE
    Database directory             = SQL00001
    Database release level         = 6.00
    Comment                        =
    Directory entry type           = Home
  ```

8.3.4 Configuring the System and Its Databases

A database management system is like a complex machine with many adjustments. All the adjustments have default settings that are appropriate for typical patterns of use. However, database administrators have the option of changing some of these adjustments in order to configure their systems for a particular hardware environment or mix of applications.

The adjustments that are provided by V2 fall into two general categories: *database manager configuration parameters* and *database configuration parameters*. Each V2 instance has a set of database manager configuration parameters, which apply to the instance as a whole and are independent of any particular database. In addition, each database has its own set of database configuration parameters that apply only to that database.

When a V2 instance is installed, its database manager configuration parameters are set to default values. Some of these parameters deal with resource allocations, such as the amount of memory to be used for buffering messages between client and server. Other parameters record policy decisions such as the names of the groups that hold SYSADM, SYSCTRL, and SYSMAINT authority. Other parameters record how to find things, such as the default directory in which this server will create databases. Some of the parameters must be set to nondefault values in order to enable certain features of the system; for example, distributed transactions require the parameter named TM_DATABASE to be set to the name of the database to be used to coordinate the two-phase commit protocol.

When a database is created, some of its database configuration parameters can be specified by the CREATE DATABASE command, and the remainder are set to default values. Database configuration parameters serve a variety of purposes. Some deal with resource allocations, such as the amount of memory to be used for sorting or for processing SQL statements. Some record policy decisions such as the character set to be used for storing data in this database (which determines whether double-byte datatypes can be used). Some control performance trade-offs, such as the frequency of checking for deadlock or the level of detail required in database statistics. Some control the logging and recovery modes for this database; for example, either the LOGRETAIN or the USEREXIT parameter must be set to ON if the database is to be enabled for forward recovery.

Configuration parameters can be viewed and changed in three ways:

1. By CLP commands, which are described in this section.

2. By using the Database Director, a graphic interface for database administrators, described in Section 8.8.

3. By application programs, using a set of call interfaces described in the *DB2 API Reference*.

Lists of configuration parameters are shown below, in the sample outputs from the GET DATABASE CONFIGURATION and GET DATABASE MANAGER CONFIGURATION commands. Several of these parameters are discussed in other sections of this book—for example, the TM_DATABASE parameter is discussed in Section 2.9.2, and the LOGRETAIN and USEREXIT parameters are discussed in Section 8.4.1. For a detailed discussion of the meaning and use of all the configuration parameters, see the *DB2 Administration Guide*.

UPDATE DATABASE MANAGER CONFIGURATION

This command assigns values to one or more database manager configuration parameters. For example, the following command might be used to assign values to the SYSCTRL_GROUP and SYSMAINT_GROUP parameters:

```
UPDATE DATABASE MANAGER CONFIGURATION USING
    SYSCTRL_GROUP helpers
    SYSMAINT_GROUP workers;
```

TIP: If you are setting more than one parameter with a single command, do not use commas between the parameter settings.

TIP: Configuration parameters that affect the database server do not become effective until the server is restarted. This can be done by the DB2STOP and DB2START commands. Configuration parameters that affect the client do not become effective until the client is restarted. If you are changing configuration parameters from a CLP session, this can be done by using the TERMINATE command (not the QUIT command) and then starting a new CLP session. To make sure that all your changes are effective, it is wise to restart both the client and server after changing configuration parameters.

RESET DATABASE MANAGER CONFIGURATION

This command resets all the database manager configuration parameters to their default values. It takes no parameters. As in the case of UPDATE DATABASE MANAGER CONFIGURATION, the new (default) parameters do not become effective until the server and/or the client has been restarted. Here's an example:

```
RESET DATABASE MANAGER CONFIGURATION;
```

GET DATABASE MANAGER CONFIGURATION

This command displays the current values of all the database manager configuration parameters. If the database manager instance that you wish to investigate is remote, you must first attach to that instance, using the ATTACH command. The following command displays the database manager configuration parameters of the V2 instance to which you are currently attached:

GET DATABASE MANAGER CONFIGURATION;

Shown below is an example of output from a GET DATABASE MANAGER CONFIGURATION command. The parameters listed vary depending on platform (for example, OS/2 or AIX) and depending on whether your DB2 instance is a single-user system or a server. (A discussion of the meaning and use of each parameter can be found in the *DB2 Administration Guide*.)

```
    Database Manager Configuration

  Node type = Database Server with local clients

Database manager configuration release level              = 0x0600

CPU speed (millisec/instruction)          (CPUSPEED) = 4.000000e-05
Max number of concurrently active databases     (NUMDB) = 8
Transaction processor monitor name      (TP_MON_NAME) =

Diagnostic error capture level            (DIAGLEVEL) = 3
Diagnostic data directory path             (DIAGPATH) =

Default database monitor switches
   Buffer pool                     (DFT_MON_BUFPOOL) = OFF
   Lock                               (DFT_MON_LOCK) = OFF
   Sort                               (DFT_MON_SORT) = OFF
   Statement                          (DFT_MON_STMT) = OFF
   Table                             (DFT_MON_TABLE) = OFF
   Unit of work                        (DFT_MON_UOW) = OFF

Database monitor SQL statement size (bytes) (SQLSTMTSZ) = 256

SYSADM group name                        (SYSADM_GROUP) = STAFF
SYSCTRL group name                      (SYSCTRL_GROUP) =
SYSMAINT group name                    (SYSMAINT_GROUP) =

Database manager authentication        (AUTHENTICATION) = SERVER

Default database path                       (DFTDBPATH) = /home/chamberl

Database monitor heap size (4KB)         (MON_HEAP_SZ) = 48
UDF shared memory set size (4KB)          (UDF_MEM_SZ) = 256
```

```
Backup buffer default size (4KB)           (BACKBUFSZ) = 1024
Restore buffer default size (4KB)          (RESTBUFSZ) = 1024

Sort heap threshold (4KB)                  (SHEAPTHRES) = 4096

Directory cache support                    (DIR_CACHE) = YES

Application support layer heap size (4KB)   (ASLHEAPSZ) = 15
Max requester I/O block size (bytes)         (RQRIOBLK) = 32767
Query heap size (4KB)                    (QUERY_HEAP_SZ) = 1000
DRDA services heap size (4KB)             (DRDA_HEAP_SZ) = 128

Priority of agents                          (AGENTPRI) = SYSTEM
Max number of existing agents             (MAXAGENTS) = 200
Max number of concurrent agents          (MAXCAGENTS) = MAXAGENTS
Maximum number of idle agents         (MAX_IDLEAGENTS) = 3

Index re-creation time                      (INDEXREC) = RESTART

Transaction manager database name         (TM_DATABASE) =
Transaction resync interval (sec)      (RESYNC_INTERVAL) = 180

Default accounting string               (DFT_ACCOUNT_STR) =

Directory services type                     (DIR_TYPE) = NONE
Directory path name                   (DIR_PATH_NAME) = /.:/subsys/database/
Directory object name                   (DIR_OBJ_NAME) =
Routing information object name        (ROUTE_OBJ_NAME) =
Default client comm. protocols         (DFT_CLIENT_COMM) =
```

UPDATE DATABASE CONFIGURATION

This command assigns values to one or more database configuration parameters. You do not need to be connected to the database whose parameters are being updated. For example, the following command might be used to assign new values to the NUM_FREQVALUES and NUM_QUANTILES parameters for the SAMPLE database:

```
UPDATE DATABASE CONFIGURATION FOR sample USING
    NUM_FREQVALUES 5
    NUM_QUANTILES 10;
```

TIP: If you are setting more than one parameter with a single command, do not use commas between the parameter settings.

TIP: Database configuration parameters do not become effective until all applications have disconnected from the database. If you are updating database configuration parameters from a CLP session, you can use the DISCONNECT statement to end your database connection (but the new parameters will not become effective until all other applications and CLP sessions have disconnected also).

RESET DATABASE CONFIGURATION

This command resets all the database configuration parameters for a particular database to their default values. The command must include the name of the database, which may be local or remote. The new (default) parameters do not become effective until all applications have disconnected from the database. The following example restores all database configuration parameters to their default values for the SAMPLE database:

```
RESET DATABASE CONFIGURATION FOR sample;
```

GET DATABASE CONFIGURATION

This command displays the current values of all the database configuration parameters for a particular database. You do not need to be connected to a database in order to display its configuration. For example, the following command displays the configuration parameters of the SAMPLE database:

```
GET DATABASE CONFIGURATION FOR sample;
```

Shown below is an example of output from a GET DATABASE CONFIGURATION command. The parameters listed vary depending on the platform (for example, OS/2 or AIX) on which the database resides. Those parameters that do not have a short name in parentheses are not settable by users. (A discussion of the meaning and use of each parameter can be found in the *DB2 Administration Guide*.)

```
Database Configuration for Database sample

Database configuration release level                    = 0x0600
Database release level                                  = 0x0600

Database territory                                      = En_US
Database code page                                      = 850
Database codeset                                        = IBM-850
Database country code                                   = 1
```

```
Directory object name                    (DIR_OBJ_NAME) =

Backup pending                                         = NO
Database is consistent                                 = YES
Roll forward pending                                   = NO

Log retain for recovery status                         = NO
User exit for logging status                           = NO

Number of frequent values retained  (NUM_FREQVALUES) = 10
Number of quantiles retained        (NUM_QUANTILES) = 20

Database heap (4KB)                        (DBHEAP) = 1200
Catalog cache size (4KB)          (CATALOGCACHE_SZ) = 64
Log buffer size (4KB)                    (LOGBUFSZ) = 8
Utilities heap size (4KB)            (UTIL_HEAP_SZ) = 5000
Buffer pool size (4KB)                   (BUFFPAGE) = 1000
Max storage for lock lists (4KB)         (LOCKLIST) = 100

Sort list heap (4KB)                     (SORTHEAP) = 256
SQL statement heap (4KB)                 (STMTHEAP) = 2048
Default application heap (4KB)          (APPLHEAPSZ) = 128
Package cache size (4KB)                (PCKCACHESZ) = 36
Statistics heap size (4KB)           (STAT_HEAP_SZ) = 4384

Interval for checking deadlock (ms)     (DLCHKTIME) = 10000
Percent. of lock lists per application   (MAXLOCKS) = 10
Lock timeout (sec)                     (LOCKTIMEOUT) = -1

Changed pages threshold             (CHNGPGS_THRESH) = 60
Number of asynchronous page cleaners (NUM_IOCLEANERS) = 1
Number of I/O servers                (NUM_IOSERVERS) = 3
Index sort flag                         (INDEXSORT) = YES
Sequential detect flag                  (SEQDETECT) = YES
Default prefetch size (4KB)          (DFT_PREFETCH_SZ) = 32

Default number of containers                         = 1
Default tablespace extentsize (4KB)   (DFT_EXTENT_SZ) = 32

Max number of active applications         (MAXAPPLS) = 40
Average number of active applications    (AVG_APPLS) = 1
Max DB files open per application         (MAXFILOP) = 64
```

```
Log file size (4KB)                           (LOGFILSIZ) = 1000
Number of primary log files                  (LOGPRIMARY) = 3
Number of secondary log files                (LOGSECOND) = 2
Changed path to log files                    (NEWLOGPATH) =
Path to log files = /home/chamberl/chamberl/SQL00002/SQLOGDIR/
Next active log file                                      =
First active log file                                    =

Group commit count                            (MINCOMMIT) = 1
Percent log file reclaimed before soft chckpt (SOFTMAX) = 100
Log retain for recovery enabled              (LOGRETAIN) = OFF
User exit for logging enabled                 (USEREXIT) = OFF

Auto restart enabled                        (AUTORESTART) = ON
Index re-creation time                        (INDEXREC) = SYSTEM (RESTART)
Default number of loadrec sessions        (DFT_LOADREC_SES) = 1
Recovery history retention (days)         (REC_HIS_RETENTN) = 366
```

8.3.5 Migrating Databases

After installing V2, you may have some V1 databases that you would like to migrate to the new system to take advantage of V2 features. V2 provides a migration utility for this purpose, which can be invoked by the MIGRATE DATABASE command. Before you attempt to migrate an old database, you should take a backup of the database so you can recover it if migration fails. You must also make sure that the database to be migrated does not use any schema names that are reserved in V2, such as SYSCAT, SYSSTAT, or SYSFUN. The database to be migrated must be entered in your system database directory (use the CATALOG DATABASE command for this purpose).

MIGRATE DATABASE

In order to use the MIGRATE DATABASE command, you must have SYSADM authority. The command in the following example migrates a database named FINANCE from V1 to V2:

```
MIGRATE DATABASE finance;
```

TIP: After a database is migrated from V1 to V2, all its packages are marked invalid. You can rebind these packages one at a time or use the db2rbind utility to rebind all the packages at once.

8.4 MANAGING DATABASE RECOVERY

One of the most important tasks of a database management system is to protect against loss of data in the event of a hardware or software failure or a power interruption. V2 provides several facilities that can be used by a database administrator to protect databases and to recover from failures. These facilities can be invoked in three ways:

1. By commands in a CLP session. The commands for database recovery are described in this section.

2. By call interfaces from application programs. For details, see the *DB2 API Reference*.

3. By means of the Database Director's graphic interface. The Database Director is discussed in Section 8.8.

One of the basic tools used for protecting against failures is the *backup*. A backup is a copy of a whole database or of some part of a database (one or more tablespaces). If the backup is made on some removable medium such as a tape or diskette, or if it is made on a different physical device from the one that stores the database, it can serve as a protection against failure of the database storage device. At any time, a backup can be used to restore the database to its state at the time the backup was taken. A wise database administrator will have a plan for backing up critical data on a regular basis.

Another important tool for protecting data is the database *log*. A log is a set of files that record all the changes that are made to a database, including information about how the changes are organized into transactions and whether each transaction ended with a commit or a rollback (for a discussion of transactions, see Section 2.9.1). When each transaction is committed, all the log entries pertaining to that transaction are written onto disk so that they will survive a power failure and provide an independent record of the changes made by that transaction. The log is very important in restoring the database to a consistent state after a power or software failure. The system uses the log to ensure that all changes made to the database by committed transactions remain in effect—even if the updated page was in volatile memory at the time of the failure—and that all changes made to the database by transactions that were not committed before the time of the failure are rolled back. The log is also used when it is necessary to reapply the database changes made by a series of committed transactions, as in the case of forward recovery (described below).

The system log is maintained as a set of files in a directory whose path name is specified by the database configuration parameter named LOGPATH. The number of log files is controlled by the LOGPRIMARY configuration parameter, and the size of the log files is controlled by the LOGFILSIZE config-uration parameter. To take advantage of I/O concurrency and to provide pro-tection against media failure, it is wise to keep the log on a different physical device from the database itself.

8.4.1 Types of Recovery

V2 supports the following three types of recovery:

1. *Crash recovery.* Crash recovery is used immediately after a failure to restore the database to a transaction-consistent state in which updates are effective only if they were applied by committed transactions. Crash recovery is invoked by the RESTART command.

2. *Restore recovery.* This form of recovery is used to restore the content of a data-base from a backup that was taken at a previous time. Restore recovery involves the use of the BACKUP and RESTORE commands. It can be used by itself or in conjunction with forward recovery.

3. *Forward recovery.* After a database has been restored from a backup, forward recovery can be used to reapply changes that were made by transactions that committed after the backup was made. In this way, the database can be restored to a transaction-consistent state corresponding to any desired time between the time of the backup and the present. Forward recovery is invoked by the ROLLFORWARD command.

Crash recovery and restore recovery are always available on any database. Forward recovery, however, is available for a given database only if the data-base has been specifically enabled for this form of recovery. The decision of whether to enable forward recovery is an important one. The consequences of this decision are summarized in Table 8-2.

As a database administrator, you can enable forward recovery for your data-base by setting either the LOGRETAIN or the USEREXIT database configura-tion parameter to the value YES. Either of these configuration parameters causes the database log to be configured in such a way that it retains the entries needed for rollback recovery.

If both LOGRETAIN and USEREXIT configuration parameters are set to NO (which is the default), the database log is treated as circular. That is, when the log reaches its maximum size, it wraps around and begins to reuse its own space, deleting its oldest entries. In this case, forward recovery is not enabled, because there is no guarantee that all the entries needed for forward recovery can be found in the log.

If LOGRETAIN is set to YES, the log keeps growing by generating new files and retaining them indefinitely. In this case, you must provide some way to remove old log files to an archive to prevent filling up your disk with log files.

TABLE 8-2: Consequences of Enabling Forward Recovery for a Database

If Forward Recovery Is *Not* Enabled	If Forward Recovery Is Enabled
After a failure, you can recover the database to its last transaction-consistent point before the failure.	Same. Recovery to a transaction-consistent point is always supported.
You can restore the database to its state at the time of any available backup, but you cannot reapply transactions that occurred after the backup.	You can restore the database to its state at the time of any available backup, and in addition you can reapply subsequent committed transactions up to some desired time or up to the present.
You can back up the database only at a time when no applications are connected to the database (this is called an *offline backup*).	You can back up the database while applications are connected to the database and transactions are in progress (this is called an *online backup*). Offline backups are also supported.
Each backup must contain the current state of an entire database.	A backup may contain the current state of a database or of one or more tablespaces. Thus tablespaces within a database can be independently backed up and restored. This gives you the flexibility to back up your more active tablespaces with greater frequency than your less active ones or to omit from your backup certain tablespaces containing large objects that can be reconstructed from another source.

If USEREXIT is set to YES, the log keeps growing by generating and retaining new files, but as each log file becomes full, a user-supplied program (called a *user exit*) is called, which can examine the log directory and move old log files to an archive if necessary. This is a way of automating the process of moving log files to an archive. (For more information about user exits, see Appendix H of the *DB2 Administration Guide*.)

When either the LOGRETAIN or USEREXIT configuration parameter is changed from NO to YES, the database is placed into a *Backup Pending* state in which it cannot be used until a full database backup has been taken.

 TIP: If you use CLP commands to change database configuration parameters such as LOGRETAIN or USEREXIT, you must terminate your CLP session before the new parameter values will become effective. Use the TERMINATE command (not the QUIT command, which leaves a background process connected to the database).

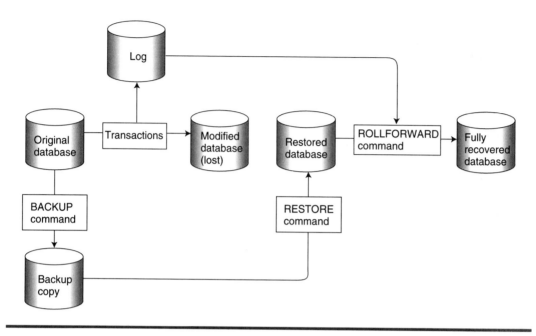

Figure 8-4: Database Backup and Recovery

The commands for controlling database backup and recovery are described below and illustrated in Figure 8-4.

RESTART

RESTART is the first command that should be issued against a database after a failure such as a power outage or a software crash that leaves transactions in progress. It establishes a database connection and uses the database log to restore the database to a transaction-consistent state. All database changes made by transactions that committed before the failure are made effective. All database changes made by transactions that rolled back before the failure, or by transactions that were in progress at the time of the failure, are rolled back.

The following is an example of a RESTART command:

```
RESTART DATABASE finance;
```

You can configure your database to automatically invoke a RESTART command when needed by setting the AUTORESTART database configuration parameter to ON. In this case, the RESTART command will be invoked automatically when the first application attempts to connect to your database after a failure.

If the database that is being restarted is a participant in some *distributed transactions* (transactions that connect to and modify multiple databases, possibly on different servers), it is possible that the status of a distributed transaction may be "in doubt" because a commit request was processed on some but not all servers. If in-doubt transactions are discovered by a RESTART command, you will receive a warning message. You can examine the in-doubt transactions and decide what to do about them by using the LIST INDOUBT TRANSACTIONS command (for details, see the *DB2 Administration Guide*).

BACKUP

The BACKUP command makes a copy of a database, in whole or in part, to a specified device (often a tape) or directory on the server machine. Subject to the constraints in Table 8-2, the backup may be taken either online or offline and may apply either to the whole database or to a set of named tablespaces. In order to use the BACKUP command, you must have SYSADM, SYSCTRL, or SYSMAINT authority.

When using the BACKUP command, you can specify the following information:

- The name of the database to be backed up
- The names of the tablespaces to be backed up (default is the whole database)
- Whether the backup is offline or online (default is offline)
- The name of the device or directory in which the backup files are to be created
- Optionally, a userid and password against which to authorize the backup
- Optionally, some parameters for tuning the input/output process (such as the number and size of the buffers to be used)

A backup command generates one or more backup files in the named device or directory. The generated files have names whose structure is shown in Figure 8-5.

Here are some examples of BACKUP commands:

- This command creates a full database backup of the FINANCE database to a named directory on the server (specified in UNIX format):

```
BACKUP DATABASE finance TO /u/backups/finance;
```

- This command performs an online backup of a named tablespace in the FINANCE database. Applications can continue updating the database while the backup is being taken.

```
BACKUP DATABASE finance
    TABLESPACE userspace1 ONLINE
    TO /u/backups/finance;
```

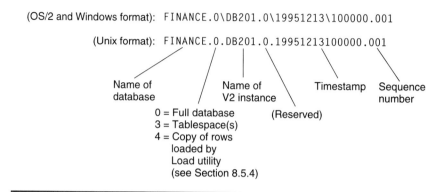

Figure 8-5: Structure of a Backup Filename

 TIP: If you add some containers to a tablespace, it is wise to perform a backup before continuing to use the database. This practice will help you to avoid some complexities that arise if you need to restore a tablespace to which containers have been added since the last backup was made. These complexities are discussed in the *DB2 Administration Guide*.

RESTORE

The RESTORE command restores the content of a database, using the content that was saved in a backup. It does not ordinarily restore the database configuration parameters, but can do so if these parameters have become lost or corrupted. RESTORE can also be used to create a new database and load it with the content saved in a whole-database backup. In order to use the RESTORE command, you must have SYSADM, SYSCTRL, or SYSMAINT authority.

The backup used in a RESTORE command may include the content of either the whole database or a set of tablespaces. Restoring a whole database must be done offline, but restoring tablespaces can be done online, while applications are connected to the database. A RESTORE of a set of tablespaces must be immediately followed by a ROLLFORWARD to the end of the log, which reapplies all changes made to the recovered tablespaces.

When using a RESTORE command, you can specify the following information:

- The name of the database from which the backup was made
- The name of the device or directory on the server machine that contains the backup
- The date and time of the backup you want to use, if there is more than one backup in the directory

- If the RESTORE is directed to a target database that is different from the one that was backed up, the name and location of the target database. If the target database does not exist, it will be created. In this way, multiple independent copies of a database can be made.

- In the case of a tablespace backup, whether the RESTORE is to be done online or offline (default is offline)

- Optionally, a userid and password against which to authorize the RESTORE command

- Optionally, some parameters for tuning the input/output process (such as the number and size of the buffers to be used)

By default, if forward recovery is enabled for your database, the RESTORE command will leave the database (or the tablespaces that were restored) in a state called *rollforward pending*. A database or tablespace in the rollforward pending state cannot be used until a ROLLFORWARD command has been applied to it, to reapply changes made by committed transactions. The rollforward pending state is mandatory if the RESTORE was done from an online backup or from a tablespace-level backup. However, if the RESTORE was done from a whole-database offline backup, the phrase WITHOUT ROLLING FORWARD can be added to the RESTORE command, causing the database to avoid the rollforward pending state and to be usable immediately after the RESTORE is completed.

Here are some examples of RESTORE commands:

- The following command restores the FINANCE database from a backup contained in a specified directory. If forward recovery is not enabled for the FINANCE database, the database will be restored to its state at the time of the backup and will be immediately usable. If forward recovery is enabled, the database will be left in the rollforward pending state and will not be usable until a ROLLFORWARD command has been executed on it.

    ```
    RESTORE DATABASE finance FROM /u/backups/finance;
    ```

- The following command restores the FINANCE database and explicitly specifies that rollforward will not be done and that the database should be immediately usable:

    ```
    RESTORE DATABASE finance FROM /u/backups/finance
        WITHOUT ROLLING FORWARD;
    ```

- The following command restores certain tablespaces in the FINANCE database from a backup contained in a specified directory and taken at a specified date and time. The RESTORE is performed online, while applications continue to use the database. The affected tablespaces are left in a rollforward pending state and will not be usable until a ROLLFORWARD command has been executed to reapply all changes made by committed transactions.

```
RESTORE DATABASE finance
   TABLESPACE ONLINE
   FROM /u/backups/finance TAKEN AT 19950522164034;
```

ROLLFORWARD

The ROLLFORWARD command is invoked after a RESTORE command to perform forward recovery on the database or on some of its tablespaces. It uses the log to reapply database changes made by transactions that committed after the time of the backup. In order to use the ROLLFORWARD command, you must have SYSADM, SYSCTRL, or SYSMAINT authority and the database must be enabled for forward recovery.

A ROLLFORWARD command applies either to the whole database or to one or more tablespaces, whichever is in the rollforward pending state. Ordinarily, this state results from a RESTORE command (but under certain circumstances, a tablespace can be placed into the rollforward pending state by an I/O error). The database or tablespaces that are in the rollforward pending state cannot be used until a ROLLFORWARD has been successfully completed.

If the whole database is being rolled forward, the process must occur offline (with no applications connected to the database), and the database can be rolled forward to any desired point in time between the backup time and the present. If individual tablespaces are being rolled forward, the process can occur either online or offline, but it must roll forward the tablespaces all the way to the present time, reapplying the changes of all committed transactions, to ensure that the recovered tablespaces are consistent with the rest of the database.

When using a ROLLFORWARD command, you can specify the following information:

- The name of the database to be rolled forward

- The date and time to which you want the database to be rolled foward (applies to whole-database recovery only). Only changes made by transactions that committed before the specified time will be reapplied.

- Whether the rollforward process is to take place online or offline (online rollforward applies to tablespaces only)

- Optionally, a directory to search for archived logs, in addition to the regular log directory that is specified by the LOGPATH configuration parameter

- Optionally, a userid and password against which to authorize the ROLLFORWARD command

Here are some examples of ROLLFORWARD commands:

- This command rolls forward the FINANCE database up to the current time. It might be used after restoring the database from a backup, to reapply all transactions that were committed after the backup was taken. The phrase AND STOP is needed to take the database out of the rollforward pending state and make it available for use.

  ```
  ROLLFORWARD DATABASE finance
      TO END OF LOGS AND STOP;
  ```

- This command rolls forward the FINANCE database, reapplying all transactions that were committed before a designated date and time:

  ```
  ROLLFORWARD DATABASE finance
      TO 1995-12-25-10.30.59 AND STOP;
  ```

- This command rolls forward only certain tablespaces within the FINANCE database. The command is issued after a tablespace-level recovery, and it applies only to the tablespaces that were recovered. The command specifies that the forward recovery is to be conducted online and is to proceed all the way to the present time (end of logs).

  ```
  ROLLFORWARD DATABASE finance
      TO END OF LOGS AND STOP
      TABLESPACE ONLINE;
  ```

TIP: Remember that if the database contains some columns of LOB datatypes that were created with the NOT LOGGED option, updates to these columns are not recorded in the log, and forward recovery does not apply to these columns. If, during forward recovery, an update to an unlogged column is encountered, the value of that column will be set to binary zeros.

8.4.2 The Recovery History File

V2 automatically maintains a *recovery history file* for each database, containing a record of all backup, restore, and load operations performed on that database. The record of each operation is retained in the recovery history file for a retention period that by default is 366 days but can be controlled by a database configuration parameter called REC_HIS_RETENTN. The recovery history file provides the database administrator with information about what backups are available for a given database. If the recovery history file for a database becomes lost or corrupted, it can be restored from a backup using a special option of the RESTORE command. The commands that operate on the recovery history file are as follows.

LIST HISTORY

This command displays the content of the recovery history file for a particular database. The simplest form of the command, shown in the following example, displays the entire file:

```
LIST HISTORY ALL FOR DATABASE finance;
```

You can also add clauses to the command to filter its content, selecting only those backup and recovery events that occurred after a certain date and time, or only those events that involved a particular tablespace. Here are some examples of commands with filters:

```
LIST HISTORY SINCE 1995 FOR DATABASE finance;
LIST HISTORY CONTAINING userspace1 FOR DATABASE finance;
```

UPDATE HISTORY

Occasionally you may move some of your backup files from one place to another. Since the recovery history file serves as your record of what backups are available, it is prudent to keep it up-to-date with the current location of each backup. You can do this by means of a command that updates the recovery history file, using a timestamp and sequence number to identify a backup, and specifying the path of its new location. The following example records a new location for a backup created on December 13, 1994, at 10:30 a.m. The phrase DEVICE TYPE D indicates the type of the device that holds the backup (in this case, a disk).

```
UPDATE HISTORY FOR 19941213103000001
    WITH LOCATION /backups/1994 DEVICE TYPE D;
```

PRUNE HISTORY

This command can be used to remove all entries from the recovery history file for events that occurred before a given date and time. The date and time can be specified in the form of a full or partial timestamp. The command in the following example deletes all records of backup and recovery events that occurred on or before December 31, 1993:

```
PRUNE HISTORY 19931231;
```

8.5 MOVING DATA IN BULK

When a database is first created, it is often desirable to load it with data from some external source. Also, during operation of a database, a need sometimes arises to move a large bulk of data into or out of the database, exchanging it with some external source such as a set of files or another database. Of course, it would be possible to write a special-purpose application program to accomplish each of these data transfers, using SQL INSERT and/or SELECT statements embedded in some host programming language. V2 has saved you the trouble of writing many such specialized programs, by providing a set of general-purpose utilities for moving data into and out of databases. These utilities can be summarized as follows:

1. *Export.* This utility extracts data from a database and saves it in a file, using one of several file formats. The data to be extracted is specified by an SQL query.

2. *Import.* This utility is the inverse of Export. It inserts data into a database table from an external file, using the same file formats supported by the Export utility. The Import utility inserts rows into the database table one at a time, using SQL INSERT statements. During the import, the table remains accessible to other applications. All constraints and triggers remain in effect during the import and are activated in the usual way as rows are inserted.

3. *Load.* This utility is a higher-performance alternative to Import. Rather than inserting rows into a table one at a time, the Load utility constructs page images containing many rows and inserts them into the database a page at a time. Indexes are constructed in a separate step after the bulk loading of data. During operation of the Load utility, the tablespace(s) that contain the table being loaded are not accessible to other applications. Also, during the loading of a table, constraints and triggers attached to that table are temporarily suspended. After the table is loaded, its constraints can be reactivated and applied to check the newly loaded data by means of a SET CONSTRAINTS statement, described in Section 8.5.5.

TIP: Check constraints and foreign key constraints are enforced for loaded data at the end of the load process. However, there is no way to find and execute the set of triggers that would have been activated by the loaded data. Therefore, business rules that are implemented by triggers are not guaranteed to be enforced after a load. This is one of the advantages of implementing business rules by constraints rather than by triggers.

8.5.1 File Formats

Four standard file formats are available for use with the Export, Import, and Load utilities. These file formats can be summarized as follows:

1. *Delimited ASCII* (type DEL) files consist of streams of data values, ordered by row and by column within each row. Values are separated by column delimiters (by default, a comma), and rows are separated by row delimiters (by default, a newline character in UNIX and a carriage return/linefeed sequence in OS/2). Character-string values are enclosed in string delimiters (by default, a double quote). Null values are denoted by missing data (column delimiters separated by spaces or by nothing). When you export, import, or load a delimited ASCII file, you can override the default delimiters with your own delimiter characters. A delimited ASCII file contains data values, but it does not contain structural information such as table names and column names.

   The following example shows how four rows of data might be represented in a delimited ASCII file and illustrates the default formats for dates and times in delimited ASCII:

```
"Screwdriver", 5.10, 28, "Acme Tools", 19950115, "09.34.05"
"Hammer", 18.00, 8, "Tools Unlimited", 19950401, "09.34.05"
"Wrench", 24.50, 10, "Bob's House of Tools", 19941230, "21.34.05"
"Wrench, Adjustable", 32.29, 15, "Tools Unlimited", 19950215, "21.34.05"
```

2. *Nondelimited ASCII* (type ASC) files are similar to delimited ASCII files, except that the columns of data within each row are found in fixed positions and therefore do not need to be marked by delimiters. When using a nondelimited ASCII file, the Export, Import, and Load utilities must specify the exact format of the file (that is, the character positions assigned to each column of data).

   The following example shows how the four rows described above might be represented in a nondelimited ASCII file and illustrates the default formats for dates and times in nondelimited ASCII:

```
Screwdriver          5.10 28 Acme Tools              1995-01-15 09.34.05
Hammer              18.00  8 Tools Unlimited         1995-04-01 09.34.05
Wrench              24.50 10 Bob's House of Tools    1994-12-30 21.34.05
Wrench, Adjustable  32.29 15 Tools Unlimited         1995-02-15 21.34.05
```

 TIP: Note that the default representations of dates are different in delimited and nondelimited ASCII files.

3. *Integrated Exchange Format* (type IXF) files are the preferred format for transferring data between databases managed by V2, on the same platform or on

TABLE 8-3: Summary of Filetypes Supported by Export, Import, and Load

	Delimited ASCII (DEL)	Nondelimited ASCII (ASC)	Integrated Exchange Format (IXF)	Worksheet File (WSF)
Export	YES	NO	YES	YES
Import	YES	YES	YES	YES
Load	YES	YES	YES	NO

different platforms.[1] For example, an IXF file can be used to move data between a database running under OS/2 and a database running under AIX, automatically compensating for the different numeric formats used on these two platforms.

An IXF file is a binary file that contains not only data but a description of a table, including its column names, datatypes, and indexes. When a table is exported in IXF format, it can be recreated in another database, complete with its indexes. However, an IXF file does not contain information about primary or foreign keys, constraints, or triggers.

4. *Worksheet* (type WSF) files are intended for interchange of data between V2 and certain versions of the Lotus 1-2-3 and Symphony products. WSF files can contain both column names and data. (More details about WSF files are included in the *DB2 Administration Guide*.)

Table 8-3 summarizes the filetypes that are supported by each of the three utilities for bulk movement of data.

8.5.2 Exporting Data

The Export utility extracts data from the database and saves it in a file using the DEL, IXF, or WSF format. The data to be exported need not come from a single table but can be computed by any SQL query, perhaps containing a join or UNION of multiple tables and/or views. In order to use the Export utility, you must hold SYSADM or DBADM authority, or CONTROL or SELECT privilege on each of the tables or views from which data is being exported.

When exporting data into a DEL file, you can specify characters to be used for row, column, and string delimiters and for decimal points and plus signs.

---

1. V2 uses the personal computer (PC) version of the Integrated Exchange Format, which is not identical to the IXF format used on mainframes.

When exporting data into an IXF file, you can specify column names for the exported data. You can also specify a file in which messages will be saved that are generated during the export process; if no message file is specified, the messages are displayed on standard out.

EXPORT

The Export utility is invoked by the EXPORT command, which is illustrated by the following examples:

- This example exports the entire table named SHOP.TOOLS into a delimited ASCII file named TOOLS.DEL, in the current directory. The phrase OF DEL indicates the type of the file. Messages generated during the export are saved in a file named EXPORT.MSG in the current directory.

```
EXPORT TO tools.del OF DEL
   MESSAGES export.msg
   SELECT * FROM shop.tools;
```

- This example exports certain rows and columns of the SHOP.TOOLS table, specified by an SQL query, into an IXF file named TOOLS.IXF. The line beginning with METHOD N specifies new column names for the exported data.

```
EXPORT TO tools.ixf OF IXF
   METHOD N(toolname, price, acquired)
   MESSAGES export.msg
      SELECT name, price, adate
      FROM shop.tools
      WHERE adate >= '1995-01-01';
```

8.5.3 Importing Data

The Import utility inserts data into a database from a file using one of the four supported file formats. The data from the file is processed one row at a time, using SQL INSERT statements. Any constraints and triggers associated with the target table remain in effect during the import process. If insertion of a row fails (for example, because the row violates a constraint), the Import utility generates a message indicating the row number of the failing row, then proceeds to insert the remaining rows. At the conclusion of the import process, a message is generated summarizing the number of rows that were successfully inserted and the number of rows that failed. The Import utility then commits the transaction.

The Import utility must be invoked in one of the following modes:

INSERT: The target table must exist; new rows are inserted into the target table without affecting the existing content of the table.

INSERT_UPDATE: The target table must exist and have a primary key. New rows that match the primary key of an existing row cause that existing row to be updated. New rows that do not match a primary key of an existing row are inserted into the table.

REPLACE: The target table must exist. Its existing contents are deleted and replaced with the imported data.

CREATE: (IXF files only.) The target table must not exist. The target table (and its indexes, if any) are created from the table description contained in the IXF file. The data in the IXF file is then inserted into the new table.

REPLACE_CREATE: (IXF files only.) If the target table exists, its contents are deleted and replaced with the imported data, leaving the table definition unchanged. If the target table does not exist, it is created (including indexes) from the table description contained in the IXF file, and the data in the file is then inserted into the new table.

In order to use the Import utility, you must have authorities or privileges that are sufficient for what you are trying to do. To insert new rows into an existing table, you need INSERT privilege on that table. To replace the content of a table, you need CONTROL privilege on that table. To create a new table, you need CREATETAB privilege on the database. Of course, SYSADM or DBADM authority is sufficient to perform any of these operations.

When importing data from a delimited ASCII (DEL) file, you can specify characters to be used for row, column, and string delimiters and for decimal points and plus signs.

IMPORT

The Import utility is invoked by the IMPORT command, which is illustrated by the following examples:

- In this example, the content of a delimited ASCII file is inserted into the existing table SHOP.TOOLS2.

```
IMPORT FROM tools.del OF DEL
    MESSAGES import.msg
    INSERT INTO shop.tools2;
```

- In this example, the content of a nondelimited ASCII file is used to replace the content of the existing table named SHOP.TOOLS3. When importing data from an ASC file, the user must specify the exact character positions in the file where each column of data is found. This is done by the line beginning with the phrase METHOD L.

```
IMPORT FROM tools.asc OF ASC
    METHOD L(1 20, 21 26, 29 30, 33 51, 54 63, 66 73)
    MESSAGES import.msg
    REPLACE INTO shop.tools3;
```

- In this example, the content of an IXF file is being used to create a new table named SHOP.TOOLS4. The IXF file contains a definition of the column names of the new table and specifies the indexes to be created on the new table.

```
IMPORT FROM tools.ixf OF IXF
    MESSAGES import.msg
    CREATE INTO shop.tools4;
```

- When data is being imported into a column whose datatype is one of the LOB datatypes (Blob, Clob, or Dbclob), the file being imported may contain either the actual LOB values or the names of files containing the LOB values. The latter case is indicated by the LOBSINFILE option of the IMPORT command, as shown in the following example. This example also illustrates INSERT_UPDATE mode, in which data from the import file is used to update the values of existing rows that have a matching primary key.

```
IMPORT FROM pictures.ixf OF IXF
    MODIFIED BY LOBSINFILE
    MESSAGES import.msg
    INSERT_UPDATE INTO employees;
```

- The following command specifies that the Import utility should skip the first 300 rows in the import file and begin importing data starting with row 301. During the import process, a transaction will be committed after every 50 rows. This command illustrates how the importing of a large file might be restarted after a failure and how regular commit points can be used to protect against subsequent failures.

```
IMPORT FROM bigfile.ixf OF IXF
    COMMITCOUNT 50 RESTARTCOUNT 300
    MESSAGES import.msg
    INSERT INTO bigtable;
```

TIP: An easy way to create a new table with the same column names and datatypes as an existing table is to export the existing table into an IXF file with a WHERE clause that causes zero rows to be exported, then to invoke IMPORT on the IXF file with the CREATE option to create the new table. For example, the following combination of commands creates a new empty table named SHOP.NEWTOOLS and having the same column names and datatypes as the existing table named SHOP.TOOLS:

```
EXPORT TO toolsddl.ixf OF IXF
    SELECT *
    FROM shop.tools
    WHERE 1 < 0;
IMPORT FROM toolsddl.ixf OF IXF
    CREATE INTO shop.newtools;
```

8.5.4 Loading Data

The Load utility, like the Import utility, can load data into a table from a file; it can also load data from a pipe or from a device such as a tape. The main difference between Load and Import is that Load provides significantly higher performance for loading large quantities of data. This performance is accomplished by inserting data into the database one page at a time instead of one row at a time. In order to insert pages into the database, the Load utility must obtain exclusive access to the tablespace(s) being loaded; this processing is called *quiescing* the tablespaces. The Load utility also deactivates triggers and constraints for the table being loaded, for the duration of the load. In order to use the Load utility, you must hold SYSADM or DBADM authority.

The process of loading a table involves the following steps:

1. If the table does not exist, you must create it before invoking the Load utility. You may also create indexes before loading a table. The Load utility will collect index keys during the load process and will use these keys to construct the actual indexes after the data has been loaded. This is the most efficient way to create an index on a large table that is being newly loaded with data.

2. If the table to be loaded has any constraints, including check constraints, foreign key constraints, unique indexes, or a primary key, you must create an *exception table* to be used during the load process. The exception table will be used to contain rows that are discovered to violate one of the constraints on the table. Since all constraints are suspended during the actual loading of data, some extra processing is required after the table is loaded to find rows that violate constraints and move them into the exception table. This extra processing is described in more detail below.

The exception table can have any name you like, but it must have columns that exactly match (in name and datatype) the columns of the table being loaded. In addition, two more columns are recommended for the last two column positions of the exception table. The first of these "extra" columns should have datatype Timestamp and will be used to indicate the time when the violation was discovered. The second "extra" column should have datatype Clob(32K) and will be used to indicate the name(s) of the constraint(s) that were violated by the exceptional row. If an exception table already exists for the table to be loaded (perhaps from a previous load), it would be wise to make sure the exception table is empty before the load begins.

TIP: If a column in the table to be loaded is declared NOT NULL, the corresponding column in the exception table must be declared NOT NULL also.

3. If your database is configured for forward recovery, you must decide whether you want the Load utility to make an extra copy of all the data that is loaded. Forward recovery means that if a failure occurs and the database is restored from an earlier backup, the system is prepared to reapply any committed changes that took place after the time of the backup. In order to reapply the load process, the system needs an extra copy of the loaded data. You can ask the Load utility to create this extra copy by invoking it with the option COPY YES and specifying the name of the file or device where the copy is to be created. If you specify COPY NO or allow the COPY option to default, no copy of the loaded rows will be created. In this case, if your database is configured for forward recovery, the Load utility will leave the tablespace containing the loaded table in a state called *Backup Pending*, in which the data is not accessible until a backup has been made. More details about forward recovery, backups, and the Backup Pending state can be found in Section 8.4.

4. You must also decide whether you want the Load utility to collect statistics on the table being loaded, and/or on its indexes, and save these statistics in the system catalog tables. These statistics measure things like the distribution of values in the columns of the table, and they are useful to the optimizer in choosing access plans for queries against the table. You can use the Load utility to collect statistics only if you are loading the table from scratch, replacing any existing content. This is called *Replace Mode*, and is distinguished from *Insert Mode* in which the new rows are added to the table without affecting existing rows.

To suppress the collection of statistics during loading, invoke the Load utility with the option STATISTICS NO. The default, which collects a limited set of statistics but not the most complete set, is called STATISTICS YES. The maximum set of statistics on the loaded table and all its indexes can be obtained by the option STATISTICS YES WITH DISTRIBUTION AND DETAILED INDEXES ALL. (Other intermediate options are described in the *DB2 Command Reference*.)

5. You must make sure that enough temporary disk space is available for use by the Load utility for storing index keys for all the indexes to be created. By default, the Load utility creates these temporary files in the sqllib/tmp directory for the current V2 instance, but you can specify a different directory if you prefer.

6. To invoke the Load utility, use the LOAD command. Several examples of this command are given below. The Load process consists of the following phases:

- The *load phase*. During this phase, data is loaded into the table, but indexes are not updated, triggers are suppressed, and constraints are not checked.
- The *build phase*. During this phase, any indexes defined on the table are constructed or updated, based on index keys collected in temporary files during the load phase.

- The *delete phase*. During this phase, any rows that are found to violate primary key or unique index constraints are deleted from the loaded table and moved to the exception table. Only primary key and unique index constraints are checked during this phase; foreign key and check constraints are still not checked.

7. If the loaded table has any foreign key or check constraints, the Load utility leaves it in a special state called *Check Pending*. This means that constraints have not been checked for some of the data in the table. If the loaded table is a parent table in any referential integrity relationships, and if the load was done in Replace Mode, the child tables in these relationships are left in Check Pending state also.

A table in Check Pending state cannot be accessed by SQL statements until some action has been taken to remove it from this special state. The usual way to remove a table from Check Pending state is by using the SET CONSTRAINTS statement, which checks the constraints and moves any rows that violate the constraints into the exception table (note that exception tables may be required not only for the loaded table but for its "children" in referential integrity relationships). The Check Pending state and the SET CONSTRAINTS statement are described further in Section 8.5.5.

8. If you did not choose the COPY YES option when you invoked the LOAD command, and your database is configured for forward recovery, the Load utility will leave the tablespace(s) containing the loaded table in Backup Pending state. This means that data stored in these tablespaces will not be accessible until you have made a backup copy of them, using the BACKUP command described in Section 8.4.1.

9. If you specified STATISTICS NO when you invoked the Load utility, the loading of data into your table has probably significantly altered its statistical properties. After you load the table, it would be a good time to invoke the RUNSTATS command, described in Section 8.6.2, to collect accurate statistics on the loaded table and its indexes. The optimizer needs accurate statistical information to generate the best possible access plans for queries against your table.

TIP: When a table is loaded, its rows are placed into physical storage in the order in which they are read from the load file. It is a good practice to select an index that is expected to be used frequently and to load the rows of the table in the order of their key values in this index. The index you selected will then have the *clustering property*, which means that scanning the table using this index will result in the minimum number of I/O operations. Having an index with the clustering property can improve the performance of queries against a table. If you are unable to load the rows of a table in key-value order, you can create a clustering index later by reorganizing the table, using the REORG command described in Section 8.6.3.

LOAD

The Load utility is invoked by the LOAD command, which is illustrated by the examples below. Like IMPORT, LOAD can be invoked either in INSERT mode, which loads new rows into a table and leaves the existing rows unchanged, or in REPLACE mode, which deletes the existing content of the table and replaces it with the newly loaded data. Also like IMPORT, LOAD allows you to specify the characters to be used for row, column, and string delimiters when loading data from a delimited ASCII (DEL) file.

- In this example, the Load utility is being used to insert the content of an IXF file into an existing table named SHOP.TOOLS. Messages generated during loading are saved in the file named LOAD.MSG, and rows that violate primary key or unique index constraints are diverted into an exception file named SHOP.BADTOOLS.

```
LOAD FROM tools.ixf OF IXF
MESSAGES load.msg
INSERT INTO shop.tools
FOR EXCEPTION shop.badtools;
```

TIP: After loading a table, if you attempt to use the table and receive the message "Tablespace access is not allowed" (SQLCODE −290, SQLSTATE 55039), it is probably because your database is configured for forward recovery and you neglected to specify COPY YES on your LOAD command. Your tablespace will not be accessible until you invoke a BACKUP command to back up the tablespace or the whole database.

- In this example, the Load utility is being used to replace the content of a table and to gather a complete set of statistics on the table and all its indexes. This example also makes an extra copy of all the newly loaded rows, for use in forward recovery. The copy file is placed in a directory specified by the LOAD command, and its name is determined by the convention for naming backup files (described in Figure 8-5).

```
LOAD FROM tools.ixf OF IXF
MESSAGES load.msg
REPLACE INTO shop.tools
STATISTICS YES WITH DISTRIBUTION AND DETAILED INDEXES ALL
COPY YES TO /u/backups;
```

TIP: Remember that the STATISTICS option is valid only in REPLACE mode and that the COPY option is valid only if your database is configured for forward recovery.

- In this example, the Load utility is loading a table that includes a column of datatype Clob(10K). Rather than containing actual Clob values, the load file contains the names of the files that in turn contain the Clob values. The LOAD command uses the LOBSINFILE option and specifies the directory in which the Clob files can be found.

```
LOAD FROM students.del OF DEL
LOBS FROM /u/students/resumes MODIFIED BY LOBSINFILE
MESSAGES load.msg
INSERT INTO college.students;
```

The LOAD command has many options, which are described in detail in the *DB2 Command Reference*. Here are a few examples of optional clauses that might be used in a LOAD command:

- RESTART

  Restarts a load process that was previously interrupted, based on status information saved in the message file generated by the load process.

- SAVECOUNT n

  Causes the Load utility to commit a transaction after each n rows have been loaded.

- RESTARTCOUNT n

  Causes the Load utility to skip the first n records in the load file. A LOAD command can also specify RESTARTCOUNT B (start at the build phase to construct indexes) or RESTARTCOUNT D (start at the delete phase, to find records that violate unique indexes).

- ROWCOUNT n

  Causes only the first n records in the file to be loaded.

- WARNINGCOUNT n

  Causes the Load utility to stop after n warnings have been encountered.

The Load utility also provides a LOAD QUERY command, to monitor the status of a load in progress. (See the *DB2 Command Reference* for details.)

8.5.5 Check Pending State

The enforcement of check constraints and foreign key constraints is important to the integrity of the database, but it also carries a cost that must be paid whenever data is modified. For this reason, the Load utility suspends the checking of these kinds of constraints during the bulk loading of data. Whenever it loads data into a table that has check or foreign key constraints, the Load utility leaves that table in a special state called *Check Pending*, to indicate that it contains data against which some constraints have not been checked.

When a table is in Check Pending state, normal access to the table by SELECT, INSERT, UPDATE, and DELETE statements is not allowed. You are also not allowed to create an index on a table while it is in Check Pending state or to process such a table using the EXPORT, IMPORT, REORG, or REORGCHK commands.

When a table is in Check Pending state, you can check its constraints and restore it to a normal state by using a command called SET CONSTRAINTS. When you do this, you need to specify what you want to happen if some rows are found in the table that violate one or more constraints. The best way to do this is by providing an *exception table* into which the offending rows will be moved. The exception table used by the SET CONSTRAINTS command has the same structure as the exception table used by the Load utility to hold rows that violate primary key and unique index constraints. In fact, you may choose to use the same exception table both for a LOAD command and for the SET CONSTRAINTS command that follows it, thus collecting in a single place the rows that violate all kinds of constraints.

As noted in Section 8.5.4, an exception table can have any name you like, but it must have columns that exactly match (in name and datatype, including the NOT NULL property) the columns of the table whose constraints are being checked. In addition, two more columns are recommended for the last two column positions of the exception table. The first of these "extra" columns should have datatype Timestamp; it is used to indicate the time when the violation was discovered. The second "extra" column should have datatype Clob(32K); it is used to indicate the name(s) of the constraint(s) that were violated by the exceptional row. If you invoke the SET CONSTRAINTS command without providing an exception table, the command will stop when it finds the first row that violates a constraint, and the table will be left in Check Pending state.

You can find out whether a given table is in Check Pending state by looking at the STATUS column of the catalog table named TABLES. For a given table, a STATUS value of "N" indicates that the table is in normal state, and a STATUS value of "C" indicates that the table is in Check Pending state. A third status value, "X," applies only to views and indicates that the view is in an inoperative state. The following query might be used to find out whether the table named SHOP.TOOLS is in Check Pending state:

```
SELECT status
FROM syscat.tables
WHERE tabschema = 'SHOP'
AND tabname = 'TOOLS';
```

SET CONSTRAINTS

The use of the SET CONSTRAINTS statement is illustrated by the examples below. In order to use SET CONSTRAINTS, you must hold SYSADM or DBADM authority, or CONTROL privilege on the table(s) to which the statement applies. In addition, if your SET CONSTRAINTS statement inserts rows into an exception table, you must hold the necessary privilege to insert data into this table. The SET CONSTRAINTS statement acquires and holds an exclusive lock on a table while its constraints are being checked.

- This example removes the SHOP.TOOLS table from Check Pending state, checks its contents against the existing check constraints and foreign key constraints, and turns on the enforcement of these constraints for future updates to the table. Since no exception table is specified, the table remains in Check Pending state if any rows are found that violate a constraint.

  ```
  SET CONSTRAINTS FOR shop.tools IMMEDIATE CHECKED;
  ```

- This example checks all the check constraints and foreign key constraints for the tables named SHOP.TOOLS and SHOP.PROJECTS and moves all the rows that are found to violate constraints out of these tables and into their respective exception tables. The SHOP.TOOLS and SHOP.PROJECTS tables are removed from Check Pending state and made available for normal processing, and enforcement of their constraints is resumed for future updates.

  ```
  SET CONSTRAINTS FOR shop.tools, shop.projects
      IMMEDIATE CHECKED
      FOR EXCEPTION IN shop.tools USE shop.badtools,
                   IN shop.projects USE shop.badprojects;
  ```

- This example places the table named SHOP.TOOLS into Check Pending state.

  ```
  SET CONSTRAINTS FOR shop.tools OFF;
  ```

TIP: You might choose to place a table into Check Pending state just before you execute an ALTER TABLE statement to add a new constraint to the table. If an ALTER TABLE statement is used to add a new constraint to a table that is in normal state and contains some rows that violate the new constraint, the ALTER TABLE statement will fail. But if such a table is put into Check Pending state, the ALTER TABLE statement will succeed. A SET CONSTRAINTS statement can then be used to turn on constraint checking, check the new constraint, and move any rows that violate the new constraint into an exception table.

- The SET CONSTRAINTS statement allows you to force a table to be taken out of Check Pending state without having its constraints checked. This is a dangerous thing to do, and presumably you will do it only if you have some independent means of ensuring that the table contains no data that violates constraints. (For example, you might have a program that examines a load file and checks it for violations before the table is loaded.) The command in the following example takes the SHOP.PROJECTS table out of Check Pending state without checking its constraints. After executing this command, the table will be available for normal access and its constraints will be enforced for future updates; however, the system cannot guarantee that all the rows of the table satisfy the existing constraints.

```
SET CONSTRAINTS FOR shop.projects ALL IMMEDIATE UNCHECKED;
```

When you force a table to be taken out of Check Pending state without checking its constraints, you are effectively assuming responsibility for whether its constraints are satisfied. For each table, the system records where the responsibility lies for guaranteeing that all constraints are satisfied. This information is recorded separately for foreign key constraints and for check constraints, in the CONST_CHECKED column of the TABLES catalog table. The first character of this column applies to foreign key constraints, and the second character applies to check constraints. The following encoding is used:

- "Y" means that constraints are enforced and guaranteed by the system.
- "N" means that the table is in Check Pending state and that constraints are not being checked.
- "U" means that the user has taken the table out of Check Pending state by a SET CONSTRAINTS statement with the UNCHECKED option. In this case, the system enforces constraints for new updates to the table, but the ultimate responsibility for ensuring that no rows of the table violate any constraints lies with the user. The table will remain in this state until it is put back into the Check Pending state.

The following query displays the Check Pending status of all the tables in the SHOP schema, including information about whether responsibility for guaranteeing constraints lies with the system or with the user:

```
SELECT tabname, status,
       substr(const_checked, 1, 1) AS fk_checked,
       substr(const_checked, 2, 1) AS cc_checked
FROM syscat.tables
WHERE tabschema = 'SHOP';
```

8.6 TUNING FOR PERFORMANCE

Since SQL is a nonprocedural language, a given SQL statement can often be executed in many different ways. For example, suppose that an SQL query joins two tables named SUPPLIERS and PARTS by matching values in their PARTNO columns. This query might be executed by scanning the SUPPLIERS table and for each row finding the matching rows in PARTS; or by scanning the PARTS table and for each row finding the matching rows in SUPPLIERS; or by sorting both tables into PARTNO order, then computing the join by merging the ordered tables. Each possible algorithm for execution of an SQL statement is called an *access plan*. The choice of an access plan is very important, because the execution time of an SQL statement can vary by more than an order of magnitude, depending on which access plan is selected.

V2 contains an optimizer that automatically chooses an efficient access plan for each SQL statement. The optimizer is said to be *cost-based,* because it works by generating a list of access plans, comparing their costs based on built-in cost formulas, and selecting the plan with the least cost. The access plans that are available for a given SQL statement, and their relative costs, depend on the tables that are accessed by the statement, the indexes that are maintained on these tables, and the statistical properties of the data in the tables. For example, if an SQL query contains a predicate on a column that has an index, and statistics show this column to be very selective, it probably makes sense to apply this predicate early in the access plan.

Compared to the optimizer components of most other relational database systems, the V2 optimizer offers several significant advancements, including the following:

1. It applies *query rewrite algorithms* that can often change a query into a more efficient form. For example, subqueries are often transformed into joins that can be executed more efficiently. Predicates can sometimes be moved to new places in a query where they restrict the size of the result set more quickly, and additional predicates can sometimes be deduced from the predicates provided by the user.

2. It applies *merging algorithms* that can merge an SQL statement together with the view definitions, constraints, and triggers that are referenced or invoked by the statement. The result of this merging process is a single SQL statement that can be analyzed to find the global optimum access plan, rather than optimizing each view, constraint, and trigger separately.

3. Its cost formulas take into account a large collection of statistical information about the database, including distributions of data values within individual columns of tables. The optimizer also considers the physical characteristics of your machine and its storage media. Thus, the access plan selected for a given query might depend on whether your machine is limited by its CPU resources or by its I/O resources.

4. It can use either of two methods for determining the order in which several tables will be joined: *dynamic programming*, which is guaranteed to find the optimal join order, or *greedy join enumeration*, which devotes less time and memory space to the optimization process. Users are given control over the choice of join enumeration methods and other aspects of the optimizer performance.

In order to realize the full benefit of the sophisticated V2 optimizer, users and database administrators have certain responsibilities. Since the optimizer's cost formulas depend on statistical information about the database, it is important that this statistical information be complete and accurate. The physical organization of data in storage also has an important effect on query-processing efficiency. For example, all the employees in a given department can be retrieved more efficiently if the employee table is organized in such a way that employees in the same department are clustered together on a small set of physical pages. This section discusses the tools provided by V2 that allow users to control the optimization process, collect and maintain statistical information, and control the physical organization of data in tables.

8.6.1 Controlling the Optimizer

The V2 optimizer allows the user to control the trade-off between quality of access plan and resources devoted to the optimization process by selecting one of the following *optimization classes*:

Class 0: Minimum optimization

Class 1: Optimization techniques roughly comparable to those of the V1 optimizer.

Class 3: Optimization techniques roughly comparable to those used by DB2 for MVS

Class 5: The default optimization class, using most of the techniques of the V2 optimizer. This class includes the optimization techniques that are felt to be most cost-effective for a typical mix of simple and complex SQL statements and employs heuristic rules to limit the amount of time spent on optimizing dynamic SQL statements.

Class 7: Similar to Class 5, but without the heuristic limits on dynamic optimization time

Class 9: Full use of all the techniques of the V2 optimizer to produce the best possible access plan without regard to the resources used in the optimization process

In general, higher optimization classes cause more time and memory to be used during optimization, potentially resulting in better performance when the SQL statement is executed. For example, dynamic programming is used only at Class 3 and above, and the full set of query rewrite rules is used only at Class 5 and above. Class 0 is recommended only for very simple statements operating on small tables in a dynamic query environment in which it is desired to keep optimization costs to a minimum. Class 9, on the other hand, is recommended only for use on specific "problem queries" that take a very long time to execute. Class 9 should be used in conjunction with Visual Explain (discussed in Section 8.8.1), which enables you to examine the details of the access plan selected by the optimizer. For most applications, the default Class 5 provides a good compromise between optimization cost and query performance.

If the optimizer finds that your system does not have enough memory to complete the optimization of a given SQL statement at a given optimization class, it will automatically fall back to a lower optimization class.

For static SQL statements used in an application program, the optimization class is controlled by the QUERYOPT parameter that was specified on the PREP or BIND command by which the program was bound. The following examples illustrate use of the QUERYOPT parameter on PREP and BIND commands:

```
PREP prog1.sqc QUERYOPT 1;
BIND prog1.bnd QUERYOPT 3;
```

For dynamic SQL statements, the optimization class is controlled by the content of the CURRENT QUERY OPTIMIZATION special register. If this special register has not been set, dynamic SQL statements are optimized using Class 5, the default optimization class. The following example illustrates the use of an SQL statement to set the value of the special register:

```
SET CURRENT QUERY OPTIMIZATION = 3;
```

8.6.2 Statistics

One of the areas in which V2 optimization technology is advanced compared to that of other systems is in the completeness of its statistical information. Listed below are the catalog tables that contain statistical information used by the V2 optimizer. (For more information about catalog tables, see Appendix D.)

- TABLES: This catalog table contains information about each table in the database, including the number of rows in the table, the number of physical pages occupied by the table, and the number of overflow records associated with the table. An overflow record is created when one of the rows of the table is updated in such a way that it no longer fits on its original page.

- COLUMNS: This catalog table contains information about the data values stored in columns of tables. For each column on which information is gathered, COLUMNS records the number of different data values in the column, the second highest and second lowest values, and the average length of data values in the column. The second highest and second lowest values are recorded rather than the highest and lowest values, because the latter values are likely to be "outlying" values that do not reflect the distribution of values in the column.

  Using the information in COLUMNS, the optimizer can make a crude estimate of the selectivity of a predicate on a given column. Better estimates can be made if more detailed information is gathered on the distribution of values in the column—and this is the purpose of the COLDIST catalog table.

- COLDIST: This catalog table contains information about the distribution of data values in individual columns. This information is of two basic kinds: *frequent values* and *quantiles*.

  For each column on which frequent-value information is gathered, COLDIST records the values that occur most frequently in the column and the number of times each of these values occurs. The number of frequent values recorded for each column is controlled by the NUM_FREQVALUES database configuration parameter, which defaults to 10.

  For each column on which quantile information is gathered, COLDIST records a series of values that represent the distribution of data values in the column. For example, if five quantile values are collected, they represent the data values that equal or exceed 20%, 40%, 60%, 80%, and 100% of the data values in the column. The number of quantile values collected for each column is controlled by the NUM_QUANTILES database configuration parameter, which defaults to 20.

  Column-distribution information is particularly important for those columns in which the data values are *skewed*, or nonuniformly distributed. For example, consider a company in which the lowest salary is $10,000 and the highest salary is $90,000. In the absence of column-distribution statistics, the optimizer assumes that salaries are distributed uniformly between these two extremes. But it may happen that most salaries in the company are concentrated in the range between $30,000 and $50,000. In that case, the predicate SALARY BETWEEN 70000 AND 80000 is much more selective than the predicate SALARY BETWEEN 30000 AND 40000. The selectivity of a predicate is very important to the optimizer, because it is an estimate of how useful the predicate is in narrowing the search space of a query. Column-distribution information enables the optimizer to make more accurate estimates of the selectivity of predicates on columns with skewed data distributions.

- INDEXES: This catalog table contains information about each index in the database. An index is a treelike data structure associated with a specific set of columns in a specific table, called the *key columns* of the index. An index defined on multiple key columns can be used as if it were an index on any leading subset of its key columns—for example, an index defined on the COLOR, WEIGHT, and COST columns of the PARTS table can be used to find parts with a given color, a given color and weight, or a given color, weight, and cost.

  Indexes are important to the V2 optimizer, because they provide two very useful properties: the *associative retrieval property* and the *ordering property*. The associative retrieval property means that an index can be used to quickly find rows that have a given key value. This property is useful for evaluating predicates on the key columns. The ordering property means that the index can be used to retrieve all the rows of a table in order of their key values. This property is useful for implementing ORDER BY and GROUP BY clauses and for certain kinds of join algorithms. An *index scan*, which retrieves all the rows of a table in order of the key values of a certain index, is one of the basic access methods used by the V2 optimizer.

  The INDEXES catalog table can be used to record statistical information about an index in two levels of detail. The *basic index statistics* include the number of different values of the index key, considering both the full key and its initial column; the number of physical pages occupied by the index (used in estimating the cost of an index scan); and a measure of how well the index is *clustered*. The clustering measure indicates how well the actual rows of the table are clustered together on physical pages according to the key values of the index and is used to predict the number of data pages that would be fetched during an index scan of a given table. The *detailed index statistics* provide a finer estimate of the number of page fetches required for an index scan, as a function of the size of the buffer in which pages are held during the scan.

- FUNCTIONS: This catalog table contains information about the cost of executing a user-defined function. Both the CPU cost and the I/O cost of the function can be recorded. Since the system has no way to measure or estimate these costs, they can only be supplied by a user who records them directly in the catalog table. If no information is available about the cost of executing a function, the system assumes a default cost.

- TABLESPACES: This catalog table contains information about the performance of the physical storage media used in the database. Each tablespace may be stored on a device with different characteristics. For each tablespace, TABLESPACES records the time required to begin an I/O operation and the rate at which the device is capable of transferring data into main memory. These performance parameters are recorded at the time the tablespace is created (by a CREATE TABLESPACE statement) and can later be modified by an ALTER TABLESPACE statement.

RUNSTATS

Since the optimizer bases its choice of an access plan on the statistical information in the catalog tables, it is very important that this information be current and accurate. V2 provides a command called RUNSTATS, which automatically computes the latest statistics for a table and stores them in the catalog tables. The RUNSTATS command should be invoked to update the statistics for a table whenever the table undergoes a significant change. For example, RUNSTATS should be invoked for a table after the table has been loaded or reorganized; after a significant number of its rows have been inserted, updated, or deleted; or after a new column or index has been added to the table.

In order to invoke the RUNSTATS command, a user must hold SYSADM, SYSCTRL, SYSMAINT, or DBADM authority or the CONTROL privilege on the table for which statistics are being updated.

A user of RUNSTATS can specify the level of detailed statistical information to be gathered about a given table by including or omitting certain phrases in the RUNSTATS command. The phrase WITH DISTRIBUTION indicates that information about distributions of values in the columns of the table is to be gathered and stored in the COLDIST catalog table. The phrase AND INDEXES ALL indicates that statistics are to be gathered about all the indexes associated with a table, as well as about the table itself. The word DETAILED just before INDEXES indicates that the index statistics should include an estimate of the cost of an index scan as a function of buffer size.

The following examples illustrate use of the RUNSTATS command:

- This command collects the basic statistics on the PARTS table in the COMPANY schema but does not collect any information about indexes:

```
RUNSTATS ON TABLE company.parts;
```

TIP: Oddly, the RUNSTATS command does not accept an unqualified table name. Unlike table names used in other places, a table name used in a RUNSTATS command must always be qualified by a schema name.

- This command collects statistics on the COMPANY.PARTS table, including information about the distribution of values in all the columns of the table. The number of frequent values and quantiles recorded for each column are controlled by the NUM_FREQVALUES and NUM_QUANTILES database configuration parameters. The column-distribution statistics are recorded in the COLDIST catalog table.

```
RUNSTATS ON TABLE company.parts WITH DISTRIBUTION;
```

- This command collects statistics on the COMPANY.PARTS table and all its indexes, including only the basic statistics for each index:

```
RUNSTATS ON TABLE company.parts AND INDEXES ALL;
```

TIP: It is a good idea to invoke the RUNSTATS command after creating an index, since statistics on the new index are not collected as part of the CREATE INDEX process.

- This command collects the maximum set of statistics for a table and all its indexes, including column-value distributions and detailed index statistics:

```
RUNSTATS ON TABLE company.parts
WITH DISTRIBUTION AND DETAILED INDEXES ALL;
```

TIP: After updating the statistics for a table and its indexes, you may wish to rebind your application programs that operate on the table to make sure that they are using the best access plan in light of the new statistics.

Updating Your Own Statistics

The recommended way to provide statistical information for use by the V2 optimizer is by using the RUNSTATS command. However, occasionally you may wish to manually update the statistical information in the catalog tables with some values of your own choosing. For example, you may be investigating what access plans would be selected under various hypothetical circumstances.

In order to discuss how to modify statistics in the catalog tables, we must first discuss in greater depth the structure of the catalog tables themselves. The system maintains a set of base catalog tables in the SYSIBM schema. However, users ordinarily access catalog tables by means of *catalog views*. The following two sets of catalog views have been defined:

1. In the SYSCAT schema, a read-only view is provided for each catalog table. Users are advised to use the SYSCAT views rather than the underlying base catalog tables, because the SYSCAT views provide more consistent names. Throughout this book, when we use the term *catalog table* somewhat loosely, we are really referring to the catalog views in the SYSCAT schema.

2. In the SYSSTAT schema, updatable views are provided for certain catalog tables, namely TABLES, COLUMNS, COLDIST, INDEXES, and FUNCTIONS. Each catalog view in SYSSTAT contains only the primary key columns and the statistical columns that users are allowed to update. Furthermore, the SYSSTAT views are defined in such a way that each user can see only those entries that he or she is authorized to update. You may update the statistical information for a table or index if you hold CONTROL privilege for that table or index or if

you hold DBADM authority for the database. You may update the statistical information for a user-defined function if your userid matches the schema name of the function or if you hold DBADM authority.

The two sets of system catalog views are described in detail in Appendix D and illustrated in Figure D-1. To update statistical information in the system catalog tables, you can apply SQL UPDATE statements to the SYSSTAT catalog views. Any updates applied to these views immediately affect the base catalog tables and the SYSCAT views. Of course, changes to statistical information will not affect the access plan chosen for an application program until that program is rebound.

The SYSSTAT catalog views behave just like any updatable table, subject to the following special rules:

- You can modify catalog data only by means of UPDATE statements, not INSERT or DELETE statements.

- For most statistical columns, setting the column to the value −1 indicates that no statistical information is available. In this case, the optimizer will use a default value for the missing statistic.

- If the values that you use to update the catalog statistics are not reasonable, your update will be rejected. For example, you can update the cardinality of a table only to a positive number or to −1, which indicates that no statistics are available. If you attempt to set the cardinality of a table to −25 in SYSSTAT.TABLES, you will receive a message indicating that this value is inconsistent with the definition of the view.

The following examples illustrate manual updating of statistical information in the SYSTATS catalog views:

- This example modifies the statistics for the table named COMPANY.PARTS, to make it appear that the table has 10,000 rows and occupies 250 pages of physical space:

```
UPDATE sysstat.tables
SET card = 10000, npages = 250, fpages = 250
WHERE tabschema = 'COMPANY' AND tabname = 'PARTS';
```

- This example modifies the statistics for the column named QONORDER in the COMPANY.PARTS table, asserting that this column contains 50 distinct values, with the second lowest value being 0 and the second highest value being 500.

```
UPDATE sysstat.columns
SET colcard = 50, low2key = '0', high2key = '500'
WHERE tabschema = 'COMPANY'
AND tabname = 'PARTS'
AND colname = 'QONORDER';
```

TIP: Some of the columns in the SYSSTAT catalog views, such as LOW2KEY and HIGH2KEY, contain values that are copied from columns of real database tables. For example, LOW2KEY and HIGH2KEY record the second lowest and second highest values for each column of data. Since the columns whose values are being recorded may be of any datatype, the LOW2KEY and HIGH2KEY columns contain a character-string representation of the values. A numeric value is represented by a character string containing the literal that would be used to represent that value in an SQL statement, such as '-29' or '3.25E-8'. When updating columns in the SYSSTAT views that represent column values, you must remember to represent each value in character-string form regardless of its datatype.

- This example modifies the statistics for the index named IPARTS1, asserting that the number of distinct key values in the index is 300.

```
UPDATE sysstat.indexes
SET firstkeycard = 300, fullkeycard = 300
WHERE indschema = 'COMPANY'
AND indname = 'IPARTS1';
```

TIP: When updating the key cardinality columns for an index in SYSSTAT.INDEXES, remember to update both FIRSTKEYCARD (the number of distinct values in the first key column) and FULLKEYCARD (the number of distinct key values when all columns are considered). If the index is defined on a single column, FIRSTKEYCARD is equal to FULLKEYCARD. If the index is defined on multiple columns, FIRSTKEYCARD is less than or equal to FULLKEYCARD.

- This example modifies the statistics for a user-defined function in SYSSTAT.FUNCTIONS, asserting that the cost of executing the function is 50,000 machine instructions per invocation. Note that since the RUNSTATS command does not collect information about functions, the only way to provide information about the cost of a function is by directly updating SYSSTAT.FUNCTIONS.

```
UPDATE sysstat.functions
SET insts_per_invoc = 5E4
WHERE funcschema = 'COMPANY'
AND specificname = 'PAYMENT001';
```

TIP: It is wise to identify a function by its specific name, which is always unique within a schema, rather than by its function name, which may not be unique.

Dumping Statistics: db2look

A tool named db2look is provided with V2 for collecting statistical information from catalog tables and saving it in readable form in a file. The information collected can be saved in various formats, including plain text, LaTex, and PostScript. `db2look` is not an internal part of the V2 system but is an application program that runs on top of V2. The following examples illustrate the use of `db2look`:

- This example dumps all statistical information pertaining to tables and indexes in the TRUMP schema in the FINANCE database into a file named `finance.stats` in plain text format:

  ```
  db2look -d finance -u trump -p -o finance.stats
  ```

- This example dumps the same set of statistics from the FINANCE database into a file named `finance.model`. However, this time the statistics are saved in the form of SQL UPDATE statements that could be applied to a second database to make it appear to have the same statistical properties as the FINANCE database. This is called running the `db2look` tool in *mimic mode.* In mimic mode, `db2look` collects statistics on functions and tablespaces as well as on tables and indexes. Of course, in order to apply the saved statistics to a second database, the second database must contain the same tables, indexes, functions, and tablespaces as the FINANCE database.

  ```
  db2look -d finance -u trump -m -o finance.model
  ```

For more information about `db2look`, you can invoke its help text by typing the following on your operating system command line:

```
db2look -h
```

8.6.3 Reorganizing Tables

The units of physical storage that are transferred from disk to main memory during processing of an SQL statement are called *pages.* Each page consists of 4K bytes of data. All the rows of data in the database are assigned to physical pages, usually many rows to a page. The ideal organization for a database table is for its rows to be laid out on pages, ordered by their key values in some frequently used index. An index whose key corresponds to the physical ordering of rows in storage is said to have the clustering property. This is an important property to the optimizer, because a clustering index provides a way to scan over all the rows of a table while fetching the minimum number of pages from disk. When scanning by a clustering index, each page fetched will carry with it many rows with key values in the desired sequence.

Ideally, the rows of a table will nearly fill the pages on which they are stored, leaving a small amount of free space on each page for expansion. If there is too much free space on each page, the number of page fetches required to scan the table will be unnecessarily large. On the other hand, if there is not enough free space on each page, a row that is updated to have a longer value in some column may no longer fit on the page. When that happens, the row is moved to a new page and its position on the original page is filled by an *overflow record* that points to the new location of the row.

When a table is newly loaded, its physical organization can be nearly ideal, provided that the rows are loaded in the order defined by their key values in a clustering index. However, over a period of time, modifications to a table tend to cause its organization to depart from the ideal. If many rows are inserted into the table, they will degrade the clustering property of its clustering index. If many rows are deleted, there may be too much free space on the pages where rows are stored. If many rows are updated, the clustering property will be degraded and some of the rows may be replaced by overflow records. The net result of all these changes is that the number of page fetches required to scan the table is increased.

A table can be restored to its ideal physical organization by means of a command called REORG. Another command called REORGCHK can be used to analyze the physical organization of a table, to determine if it needs to be reorganized. After a table has been reorganized, its rows are packed on pages with the proper amount of free space, overflow records are eliminated, and (if specified in the REORG command) one of the indexes on the table has the clustering property.

REORG

In order to use the REORG command, you must hold SYSADM, SYSCTRL, SYS-MAINT, or DBADM authority or the CONTROL privilege on the table to be reorganized. The only required parameter of the REORG command is the name of the table to be reorganized. An optional parameter is the name of the index that is desired to have the clustering property. If an index name is specified, the rows of the table will be rearranged in physical storage according to their key-value order in the named index. A temporary table is created during the reorganization process, and the REORG command can optionally specify the tablespace in which this temporary table is to be created (by default, it is created in the same tablespace as the original table).

The following example reorganizes the table named COMPANY.PARTS so that the index COMPANY.IPARTS2 has the clustering property:

```
REORG TABLE company.parts INDEX company.iparts2;
```

In a REORG command, both the table name and the name of the clustering index must be qualified by a schema name.

TIP: After reorganizing a table, you should use the RUNSTATS command to collect a new set of statistics on the table and its indexes, then you should rebind any application programs that operate on the table to take advantage of its new organization.

REORGCHK

The REORGCHK command analyzes the physical organization of a table or set of tables and generates a report that can help you to decide which tables are in need of reorganization. In order to use the REORGCHK command, you must hold SYSADM or DBADM authority or CONTROL privilege on the tables to be checked.

A side effect of the REORGCHK command is to update the statistical information in the system catalog tables for each table that is checked (unless you specify by the phrase CURRENT STATISTICS that you want to continue using the current set of statistics).

The following examples illustrate use of the REORGCHK command:

- This example generates a report on the physical organization of the table named COMPANY.PARTS:

```
REORGCHK ON TABLE company.parts;
```

TIP: In a REORGCHK command, the table name must be qualified by a schema name.

- If you invoke REORGCHK without any operands, it generates a report on the physical organization of all the tables that you are permitted to reorganize. Example:

```
REORGCHK;
```

For each table analyzed by REORGCHK, the generated report contains a line describing the table and a line describing each of its indexes.

For each table, three formulas are computed: F1, F2, and F3. Each of these formulas has a specified range of values for a table that is properly organized. F1 measures the number of overflow records in the table, F2 measures the amount of free space on the pages where the table is stored, and F3 measures the number of empty pages that would be fetched in a scan of the table. For each table, REORGCHK provides a three-character summary of the results of computing formulas F1, F2, and F3. For each formula, a hyphen indicates that the value is in the desired range and an asterisk indicates that the value is outside the desired range. For example, a summary of "-**" for a given table would indicate that formula F1 is in the desired range but formulas F2 and F3 are not. A table with one or more asterisks in its summary report is a candidate to be reorganized.

For each index in the REORGCHK report, three formulas are also computed: F4, F5, and F6. F4 measures the clustering property of the index, F5 measures the amount of free space on index pages, and F6 measures whether the index has the appropriate number of levels. As in the case of tables, each index receives a three-character summary in the report, indicating by hyphens and asterisks which of the three formulas are within the desired range. For example, a summary of "*-*" for a given index would indicate that the index lacks the clustering property (measured by F4) and that formula F5 is in the desired range but formula F6 is not. If many indexes defined on a given table have asterisks in their summary reports, that table may be a candidate for reorganization. Remember, however, that in general only one index for a given table can have the clustering property.

Figure 8-6 shows the report generated by running REORGCHK on the sample database created by the db2sampl command. The only indication in this report that reorganization might be needed is an asterisk corresponding to the F2 formula for the EMP_ACT table.

8.6.4 Explaining a Plan

Whenever a static SQL statement is bound or a dynamic SQL statement is prepared for execution, the V2 optimizer analyzes the statement and creates a plan for executing the statement. This plan may involve scanning one or more tables in the database, accessing a table through an index, or joining data from two tables using an algorithm such as a merge join or a nested loop join. In general, the plan for executing a statement can be represented in the form of a graph that shows how data flows from a source (one or more tables or indexes) to a destination (the result set of the SQL statement).

V2 provides a powerful facility called *Explain* that allows you to examine the plans that are created by the optimizer for executing your SQL statements. When you turn on the Explain facility, detailed information about access plans is captured and stored in a set of database tables called the *Explain tables*. You can then examine the Explain tables directly using SQL, or you can display the plans in graphic form using a feature of the Database Director called *Visual Explain*, which is described in Section 8.8.1. By using Explain to examine access plans, you can gain insight into the performance of your SQL statements, and you can learn which indexes are actually being used by the system. This information can be valuable in tuning the performance of your system by dropping unnecessary indexes and creating new indexes to support frequently executed statements.

The Explain facility applies only to those types of SQL statements that have optimized plans: SELECT, INSERT, DELETE, UPDATE, and VALUES. Other SQL statements, such as CREATE and DROP, are executed in straightforward ways and do not require the services of the optimizer.

Before you can use Explain, you need to create the Explain tables that are used to capture the details of access plans. You can do this by connecting to the desired database and executing the CREATE TABLE statements in the file sqllib/misc/EXPLAIN.DDL. For example, you might create the Explain tables in a database named MYDB by executing the following commands from the directory sqllib/misc:

```
Table statistics:

F1: 100*OVERFLOW/CARD < 5
F2: 100*TSIZE / ((FPAGES-1) * 4020) > 70
F3: 100*NPAGES/FPAGES > 80
```

CREATOR	NAME	CARD	OV	NP	FP	TSIZE	F1	F2	F3	REORG
CHAMBERL	DEPARTMENT	9	0	1	1	630	0	-	100	---
CHAMBERL	EMP_ACT	75	0	2	2	2700	0	67	100	-*-
CHAMBERL	EMP_PHOTO	12	0	1	1	84	0	-	100	---
CHAMBERL	EMP_RESUME	8	0	1	1	56	0	-	100	---
CHAMBERL	EMPLOYEE	32	0	2	2	2944	0	73	100	---
CHAMBERL	ORG	8	0	1	1	424	0	-	100	---
CHAMBERL	PROJECT	20	0	1	1	1380	0	-	100	---
CHAMBERL	STAFF	35	0	1	1	1505	0	-	100	---

```
Index statistics:

F4: CLUSTERRATIO or normalized CLUSTERFACTOR > 80
F5: 100*(KEYS*(ISIZE+10)+(CARD-KEYS)*4) / (NLEAF*4096) > 50
F6: 90*(4000/(ISIZE+10)**(NLEVELS-2))*4096/ (KEYS*(ISIZE+10)+(CARD-KEYS)*4)<100
```

CREATOR	NAME	CARD	LEAF	LVLS	ISIZE	KEYS	F4	F5	F6	REORG
Table: CHAMBERL.EMP_PHOTO										
SYSIBM	SQL950625163000290	12	1	1	20	12	100	-	-	---
Table: CHAMBERL.EMP_RESUME										
SYSIBM	SQL950625163008800	8	1	1	20	8	100	-	-	---

Figure 8-6: Example of a Report Generated by the REORGCHK Command

```
db2 connect to mydb
db2 -tf EXPLAIN.DDL
```

By default, the schema name of the Explain tables is the same as your userid. (Thus, each user of the system gets a separate set of Explain tables.) For each statement optimized while the Explain facility is turned on, the Explain tables contain information about when and how the statement was optimized, the text of the statement, and the access plan selected by the optimizer. This information is stored in tables with the following names and contents (for a more detailed description of the Explain tables, see Appendix J of the *DB2 SQL Reference*):

EXPLAIN_INSTANCE: Each row represents a package in which one or more statements have been explained.

EXPLAIN_STATEMENT: Each row represents an SQL statement that has been explained. In this table, you can see the original text of the SQL statement and how this text was modified by merging constraints, triggers, and view definitions into the SQL statement. The columns of this table, which identify the package, statement number, and time of optimization, can be used as keys to access the other Explain tables to retrieve detailed information about the access plan for a given statement.

EXPLAIN_OBJECT: Each row represents one of the sources of data used by a plan, such as a permanent or temporary table or an index.

EXPLAIN_OPERATOR: Each row represents an operation, such as "Union" or "Merge Join," that was selected by the optimizer as part of a plan. In general, each operator has one or more input data flows and an output data flow.

EXPLAIN_ARGUMENT: The rows of this table contain detailed information about the individual operators in a plan, such as the columns to be used for sorting, and whether duplicate values are to be eliminated.

EXPLAIN_STREAM: Each row represents a flow of data between one operator and another or between an object and an operator.

EXPLAIN_PREDICATE: The rows in this table indicate how the predicates of the SQL statement are implemented by the operators in the plan.

As noted above, there are two ways in which you can use the Explain facility to collect and display information about plans:

1. You can use the Explain facility to collect detailed plan information in the Explain tables, which you can then examine using SQL queries. This method is called *Tabular Explain*. Since Tabular Explain allows you to use the power of SQL to examine collections of plans, it is a good method to use when you need global information, such as finding all the plans that use a particular index.

2. You can use the Explain facility to collect plan information in a form called a *snapshot*, which is stored in a Blob column in the EXPLAIN_STATEMENT table. The snapshot information is in an internal format that can be displayed in graphic form using the Visual Explain feature of the Database Director, described in Section 8.8.1. This method is the easiest way to visualize and understand the details of an individual plan.

V2 provides you with independent control over Tabular Explain and Visual Explain, so that you can choose to capture either or both of these kinds of plan information. The controls are provided in the form of bind options named EXPLAIN and EXPLSNAP, and special registers named CURRENT EXPLAIN MODE and CURRENT EXPLAIN SNAPSHOT. The bind options, which can be used on PREP and BIND commands, control the capturing of Explain information during the binding of an application program. The special registers control the capturing of Explain information during processing of dynamic SQL statements. The possible values for the Explain-related bind options and special registers are shown in Table 8-4.[2]

In addition to the bind options and special registers described in Table 8-4, you can obtain Explain information for one specific SQL statement by using a special statement called EXPLAIN. The EXPLAIN statement can be "wrapped around" an explainable (SELECT, INSERT, DELETE, UPDATE, or VALUES) statement, causing the explainable statement to be optimized but not executed and capturing information about the plan chosen by the optimizer. The syntax for the EXPLAIN statement is as follows:

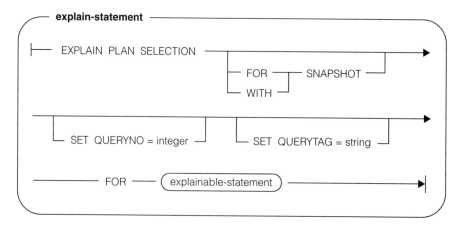

The phrase FOR SNAPSHOT causes snapshot information to be gathered for the statement, and the phrase WITH SNAPSHOT causes gathering of both snapshot and Tabular Explain information. If neither of these phrases is specified, the system gathers only Tabular Explain information. The phrases SET QUERYNO and SET QUERYTAG can be used to provide a label that makes the statement easy to identify in the EXPLAIN_STATEMENTS table. After executing the EXPLAIN statement, you can examine the information you have gathered by executing SQL queries against the Explain tables or, if a snapshot was taken, by using the Visual Explain facility of the Database Director. As an

---

2. The EXPLAIN bind option, the CURRENT EXPLAIN MODE special register, and the EXPLAIN SQL statement are supported beginning with DB2 Version 2.1.1.

TABLE 8-4: Options for Controlling the Explain Facility

	Tabular Explain	Visual Explain
PREP and BIND options	EXPLAIN option. Values: NO: Do not capture Tabular Explain data for SQL statements in this program (this is the default). YES: Capture Tabular Explain data for static SQL statements in this program. ALL: Capture Tabular Explain data for both static and dynamic SQL statements in this program, regardless of the value of CURRENT EXPLAIN MODE.	EXPLSNAP option. Values: NO: Do not capture snapshot data for SQL statements in this program (this is the default). YES: Capture snapshot data for static SQL statements in this program. ALL: Capture snapshot data for both static and dynamic SQL statements in this program, regardless of the value of CURRENT EXPLAIN SNAPSHOT.
Special register	CURRENT EXPLAIN MODE. Values: NO: Do not capture Tabular Explain data for dynamic SQL statements (this is the default). YES: Capture Tabular Explain data for dynamic SQL statements and execute them. EXPLAIN: Capture Tabular Explain data for dynamic SQL statements but do not execute them.	CURRENT EXPLAIN SNAPSHOT. Values: NO: Do not capture snapshot data for dynamic SQL statements (this is the default). YES: Capture snapshot data for dynamic SQL statements and execute them. EXPLAIN: Capture snapshot data for dynamic SQL statements but do not execute them.

example, the following EXPLAIN statement might be used to gather a snapshot of the access plan for a join query on the EMP and DEPT tables introduced in Chapter 3. The snapshot can then be displayed in graphic form by using Visual Explain.

```
EXPLAIN PLAN SELECTION FOR SNAPSHOT
SET QUERYTAG = 'Job Join'
FOR
   SELECT e.name, e.salary, d.location
   FROM emp e, dept d
   WHERE e.deptno = d.deptno
   AND e.job = 'Anthropologist';
```

Since all SQL statements executed via an interactive user interface such as the CLP are considered to be dynamic SQL statements, it is very convenient to use the CLP to gather Explain information for a single statement or for a set of statements. To do this, simply set the value of CURRENT EXPLAIN MODE or CURRENT EXPLAIN SNAPSHOT to YES and execute the SQL statements on which you wish to gather information. As an example of this method, the following statements might be executed via the CLP to gather the same snapshot information obtained by the EXPLAIN statement above:

```
SET CURRENT EXPLAIN SNAPSHOT YES;
SELECT e.name, e.salary, d.location
  FROM emp e, dept d
  WHERE e.deptno = d.deptno
  AND e.job = 'Anthropologist';
SET CURRENT EXPLAIN SNAPSHOT NO;
```

 TIP: Don't forget to set the value of the Explain-related special registers back to NO after collecting the Explain information you need. Otherwise, the system will keep on collecting Explain information about all the dynamic SQL statements you execute, and this information will occupy a significant amount of space in your database.

 TIP: If a dynamic SQL statement fails and is rolled back (for example, a dynamic UPDATE statement violates a check constraint), Explain information will not be collected for that statement, regardless of the setting of the special registers. This is because the gathering of the Explain information is considered part of the statement and is rolled back along with the statement.

8.7 MONITORING THE DATABASE

V2 provides a powerful tool called the *Database Monitor* for use by system and database administrators. Using the Database Monitor, an administrator can acquire comprehensive information about the state of the database system and can collect information about events that occur over a period of time. This information can be useful for tuning performance and diagnosing problems. We have space here for only an overview of the Database Monitor features; a complete description of how to use the Database Monitor can be found in *DB2 Database System Monitor Guide and Reference*.

The Database Monitor really consists of two separate types of monitors with different but related purposes: a *Snapshot Monitor* and a set of *Event Monitors*. Both of these types of monitors can be invoked and controlled via CLP commands, calls from an application program, or a graphic user interface. The purpose of the Snapshot Monitor is to deliver to the user a snapshot of the current state of the database system and the databases under its control. The purpose of the Event Monitors is to keep records on various events that take place over a period of time, directing these event records into a file or a pipe for later analysis.

8.7.1 The Snapshot Monitor

V2 has a large number of predefined *elements* that it knows how to monitor. Some of these elements are counters, such as the number of times a deadlock has occurred. Others represent the current value of something, such as the number of applications that are connected to a database. Others represent a timestamp when something occurred, such as the time when the last transaction was completed. Still others represent the highest recorded value of something, such as the maximum size of the database heap. The Snapshot Monitor allows an administrator to control which of these elements are monitored and to obtain a "snapshot" containing the current values of all the monitored elements at any given time.

In order to use the Snapshot Monitor, you are required to have SYSADM, SYSMAINT, or SYSCTRL authority.

The elements that are controlled by the Snapshot Monitor are classified into the following six groups, which can be independently turned on and off by means of *monitor switches*:

SORT: Information about sorting done by the system, such as number of sorts completed, time spent sorting, and amount of memory allocated for sorting.

LOCK: Information about locks, such as number of locks held, number of deadlocks detected, and time spent waiting for locks.

TABLE: Information about tables, such as the number of rows read and written in each table.

BUFFERPOOL: Information about the internal buffers used by V2 for accessing the database, including the number of input and output operations and the time spent on these operations.

UOW: Information about transactions (units of work), such as the start and stop time of the last transaction and whether it ended with a commit or rollback.

STATEMENT: Information about SQL statements, such as the type of the last statement executed and the amount of CPU time it consumed.

Multiple CLP sessions and/or application programs can use the Snapshot Monitor at the same time; in this case, each session or program gets its own set of monitor switches, which it can control independently.

The Snapshot Monitor can be controlled by CLP commands, by function calls from application programs, or by using the Database Director graphic user interface (described in Section 8.8). The CLP commands used to control the Snapshot Monitor are listed below. (The full syntax of these commands can be found in the *DB2 Command Reference* and the *DB2 Database System Monitor Guide and Reference*.)

UPDATE MONITOR SWITCHES

This command is used to selectively turn on and off the gathering of information about each of the six element groups listed above. Each group has a "switch" that can be independently turned ON or OFF. When a group is turned OFF, all the counters in that group are reset. The following example command might be used to turn on the gathering of information about tables and statements, and to turn off the gathering of information about transactions:

```
UPDATE MONITOR SWITCHES USING TABLE ON STATEMENT ON UOW OFF;
```

Of course, each monitor switch that is turned on causes a slight degradation in performance due to the overhead of collecting data.

GET MONITOR SWITCHES

The GET MONITOR SWITCHES command displays the monitor switch setting (ON or OFF) for each of the six element groups. Information about a particular element is collected by the database monitor only if its group is switched ON. Here's an example of this command:

```
GET MONITOR SWITCHES;
```

RESET MONITOR

This command is used to reset all monitor counters to zero, across all six element groups. The switch settings (ON or OFF) for the six groups are not affected. If you want to reset the counters for only one group, you can do so by switching it OFF and ON. You can reset the counters for all databases, or for a particular database as in the following example:

```
RESET MONITOR FOR DATABASE parts;
```

GET SNAPSHOT

This command displays a "snapshot" containing the current state of the elements being monitored by the Snapshot Monitor. When you ask for a snapshot, you can specify the scope of the information you want, choosing one of the following scopes:

- Information about the state of the database manager itself
- Information about the state of a particular database or all databases that have an active connection
- Information about the state of a particular application or all applications that are currently connected to a database
- Within a particular database, information about tables, locks, tablespaces, or connected applications

The amount of information displayed by the GET SNAPSHOT command depends on the scope you choose. If the selected scope contains some elements whose monitor switch is not turned on, the notation "Not Collected" will be displayed for these elements.

The following are some examples of GET SNAPSHOT commands:

```
GET SNAPSHOT FOR DATABASE MANAGER;
GET SNAPSHOT FOR ALL DATABASES;
GET SNAPSHOT FOR ALL APPLICATIONS;
GET SNAPSHOT FOR LOCKS ON mydata;
GET SNAPSHOT FOR TABLES ON mydata;
GET SNAPSHOT FOR ALL ON mydata;
```

8.7.2 Event Monitors

Users can create multiple Event Monitors to monitor different types of events and can activate and deactivate each Event Monitor independently. Event Monitors differ from the Snapshot Monitor in the following ways:

1. Each Event Monitor is "customized" to monitor a particular set of events that are of interest to the user who created it.

2. Rather than delivering a "snapshot" of the state of the database system at a particular point in time, an Event Monitor delivers a stream of reports on events as they occur. The stream of information generated by an Event Monitor can be directed to a file or to a pipe.

3. An Event Monitor is created in a particular database and monitors events only in that database (unlike the Snapshot Monitor, which can monitor events across databases).

In order to create and use an Event Monitor, you are required to have SYSADM or DBADM authority on the database that contains the Event Monitor.

The commands that are used to create and control Event Monitors are described below.

CREATE EVENT MONITOR

This command creates an Event Monitor, gives it a name, and specifies the types of events to be monitored and the target to which the resulting data is to be directed. Event Monitors have one-part names (not modified by a schema name), and therefore each Event Monitor name must be unique in the database. An Event Monitor can monitor multiple types of events, including any of the following:

- Detection of a deadlock
- Completion of the execution of an SQL statement
- Completion of a transaction (by a COMMIT or ROLLBACK)
- Completion of a database connection (when an application disconnects from the database)

An Event Monitor that is monitoring SQL statements, transactions, or database connections can specify a *filter* that restricts the events to be monitored to those generated by a particular application and/or a particular authid. The filter is specified by a restricted form of a WHERE clause, such as `WHERE APPL_NAME='PAYROLL'` or `WHERE AUTH_ID='MCNAMARA'`.

At any given time, an Event Monitor is either *active* or *inactive*. When first created, the Event Monitor is inactive. The CREATE EVENT MONITOR command can specify that the Event Monitor is to be activated automatically each time the database is started. Event Monitors can also be activated or deactivated manually by the SET EVENT MONITOR STATE command (described below).

Each time an event occurs that conforms to one of the types being monitored by an active Event Monitor and satisfies its filter, the Event Monitor generates an event record and writes it to the target. Each type of event has an event record with a specific format (documented in the *DB2 Database System Monitor Guide and Reference*), and declarations for these event records can be found in `sqllib/include/sqlmon.h`.

The target to which the event records are written may be either a set of files or a named pipe. If the target is a set of files, the CREATE EVENT MONITOR command names the directory in which the event files are to be generated. The Event Monitor will generate event files in this directory with the names `00000000.EVT`, `00000001.EVT`, `00000002.EVT`, and so on. The CREATE EVENT MONITOR command can specify the maximum number of files to be generated and the maximum size of each file. The Event Monitor creates the first file and writes event records into it until it reaches the maximum size, then creates the second file and fills it, and so on. When the directory contains the maximum number of event files and they are all full, the Event Monitor turns itself off. (However, if some other process removes event files as fast as the Event Monitor creates them, the Event Monitor can run indefinitely.) If no limit is specified for the number or size of the event files, the Event Monitor will create an unlimited number of files of maximum size 200 pages (on OS/2) or 1,000 pages (on AIX). One page holds 4K bytes of data.

All the Event Monitors that exist at a given time, both active and inactive, are described in two catalog tables named EVENTS and EVENTMONITORS. Each Event Monitor is described by one row in EVENTMONITORS and by one row in EVENTS for each different type of event that it monitors.

The following are examples of CREATE EVENT MONITOR commands:

- Create an Event Monitor for connection and transaction events that generates a series of event files of default size in a given directory, and specify that it is activated automatically whenever the database is started.

```
CREATE EVENT MONITOR monitor1
    FOR CONNECTIONS, TRANSACTIONS
    WRITE TO FILE '/dbevents/monitor1' AUTOSTART;
```

- Create an Event Monitor that generates an event record for each deadlock event and sends it to a named pipe.

```
CREATE EVENT MONITOR monitor2
    FOR DEADLOCKS
    WRITE TO PIPE '/dbevents/pipe2';
```

- Create an Event Monitor that monitors the execution of SQL statements under the authid "JOHNSON." The monitor should generate a single event file of maximum length 1,000 pages (four megabytes). When this limit is reached, the monitor will automatically turn itself off.

```
CREATE EVENT MONITOR monitor3
    FOR STATEMENTS WHERE AUTHID = 'JOHNSON'
    WRITE TO FILE '/dbevents/monitor3'
    MAXFILES 1 MAXFILESIZE 1000;
```

The monitor in this example will not begin generating event records until it is activated by a SET EVENT MONITOR STATE command (described below). When the monitor is activated, the directory in which the event file is to be generated must be enabled for writing by general users.

When an Event Monitor is no longer needed, it can be dropped by a DROP statement (described in Section 2.8.6), as in the following example:

```
DROP EVENT MONITOR monitor2;
```

SET EVENT MONITOR STATE

This command activates an Event Monitor (by setting its state to 1) or deactivates it (by setting its state to 0). An Event Monitor generates event records only while it is active. All the counters associated with an Event Monitor are reset to 0 each time the Event Monitor is activated. The following are examples of SET EVENT MONITOR STATE commands:

```
SET EVENT MONITOR monitor3 STATE = 1;
SET EVENT MONITOR monitor3 STATE = 0;
```

Analyzing Events

There are two ways to display and analyze the event data collected by an Event Monitor. The easiest way is by means of a graphic interface called the *Event Analyzer*, which can be invoked by the db2eva command or by double-clicking on the "Event Analyzer" icon in your operating system display. The db2eva command allows you to identify the events you wish to analyze, either by naming the database and the Event Monitor or by giving the path name of the file in which event data has been collected, as in the following examples:

```
db2eva -db parts -evm monitor1
db2eva -path /dbevents/monitor1
```

The Event Analyzer creates a window in which you can examine the event data collected by the selected Event Monitor, using various display options. (A more complete description of the Event Analyzer can be found in *DB2 Administrator's Toolkit: Getting Started*.)

The other way to analyze Event Monitor data is to write your own application program to process the event records that are collected in a file or pipe. (The formats of these records are documented in the *DB2 Database System Monitor Guide and Reference*.)

8.8 THE DATABASE DIRECTOR

The Database Director is a graphic interface for database administrators. Most administrative tasks such as configuring, backing up, and restoring databases can be performed in three ways: by CLP commands, by calls from an application program, or by the Database Director. The Database Director is provided with both the single-user and server versions of V2 and is also a part of the Software Developer's Kit (SDK) that runs on client machines. The Database Director can be invoked by typing db2dd at your operating system command prompt, or by double-clicking on the "Database Director" icon in your operating system's desktop user interface.

The Database Director displays a hierarchy of objects, as shown in Figure 8-8. The display includes all the instances of V2 that are installed on your machine, all the databases that are managed by these instances, and the contents of these databases down to the level of individual tables and packages. The Database Director allows you to choose how much detail you wish to see at each level of the hierarchy. Alongside each object that has lower-level details, the Database Director displays one of the icons shown in Figure 8-7. By clicking on these icons, you can expand or conceal the details below each object on the display.

Some of the entries in the Database Director display represent a general class of object (such as Database or Tablespace), while other entries represent specific objects such as specific databases or tablespaces. The Database Director display in Figure 8-8 shows one instance of V2, named CHAMBERL, managing three databases, named FVTDB, NISTTEST, and SB. The SB database is expanded in the display to show that it contains three tablespaces and packages in three schemas. By clicking on the icons in this display, a database administrator can examine the details of the various objects that they represent.

Associated with each entry in the Database Director display is a set of actions. For general entries such as "Databases," the actions include general actions such as creating a new database. For entries that represent specific objects such as the FVTDB database, the actions include tasks that can be applied to that specific object, such as backing up or dropping the database. To see the list of actions that can be applied to a given entry in the Database Director hierarchy, select the entry by clicking on it, then pull down the "Selected" menu at the top of the display. This menu will include all the actions that apply to the selected entry. If you invoke one of the actions on the menu, you may be prompted for additional details of the desired action. (For example, if you invoke the "Recover" action for a particular database, you will be asked for details such as which backup to use.) Of course, to invoke any action using the Database Director, you must hold the appropriate authorities or privileges.

Figure 8-9 shows all the levels of the Database Director display and the actions that apply to each level. The details of these actions are described in the other sections of this chapter, under the commands that can be used to invoke them.

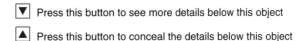

▼ Press this button to see more details below this object

▲ Press this button to conceal the details below this object

Figure 8-7: Icons for Controlling Level of Detail in Database Director Display

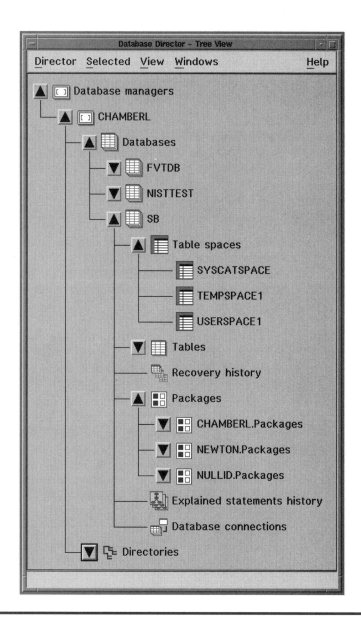

Figure 8-8: Example of a Database Director Display

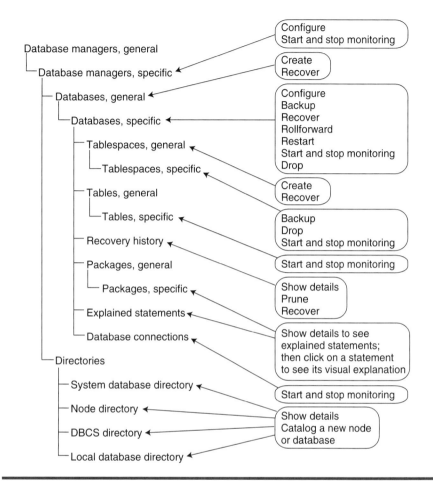

Figure 8-9: Objects and Actions in the Database Director Display

8.8.1 Visual Explain

As described in Section 8.6.4, the Explain facility of V2 allows you to capture detailed information about the access plan selected by the optimizer for any given SQL statement. One of the ways of displaying this information is by using the Visual Explain facility of the Database Director. In order to use this facility, you must capture an *Explain snapshot* for the statement you wish to investigate, using one of the methods discussed in Section 8.6.4.

To invoke Visual Explain on any SQL statement for which an Explain snapshot exists, select a specific database on the Database Director display. The Explain snapshots in this database can be found either under the "Explained statements history" entry or under the entries for specific packages that were bound with an Explain option. Select one of these entries on the Database Director display and invoke the "Show Details" action (on the "Selected" menu) to see a list of the Explain snapshots contained within the selected entry. Each snapshot in the list is identified by the date and time when it was created and the text of its SQL statement. You can click on one of the snapshots in the list and invoke the "Show Access Plan" function (on the "Statement" menu) to see a graphic display of the access plan selected for the given statement. The access plan looks like a graph that represents the flow of data during execution of the plan. Each node in the graph represents some operation, such as an index scan or a merge join. By double-clicking on the nodes of the graph, you can get more information about the operations that they represent and their predicted cost (in arbitrary units called *timerons*). You can also invoke the "Show SQL Text" and "Show Optimized SQL Text" functions (on the "Statement" menu) to display the SQL statement for the snapshot, both as it was originally written and as it was modified during generation of the plan. (The V2 compiler might have modified the statement by adding constraints and triggers or by rewriting it in a more efficient form.) Other menu options allow you to examine the table statistics, optimizer settings, and configuration parameters that were in effect at the time the plan was generated.

Figure 8-10 is an example of a query plan displayed by the Visual Explain facility. It shows, in graphic form, the plan chosen by the optimizer for executing the recursive query in Section 3.8.1 that finds the total number of rivets in a wing. We can see from the figure that this is a recursive query, because the plan graph contains a loop.

TIP: Remember that each Explain snapshot is a large object that occupies space in your database. When you no longer need a given snapshot, select its entry in the "Explained statements history" on the Database Director display and invoke the "Delete" function from the pull-down menu.

8.8.2 Controlling the Snapshot Monitor from the Database Director

Associated with several types of objects in the Database Director display in Figure 8-9 are the actions "Start Monitoring" and "Stop Monitoring." These actions provide a convenient graphic interface to control the Snapshot Monitor in order to collect and display information about the selected object.[3] When you invoke the "Start Monitoring" action, a window appears in which you can specify the kinds of data you wish to be collected and how you wish this data to be displayed. You can, for example, specify that snapshots of one

---

3. Control of Snapshot Monitors from the Database Director display is supported beginning with DB2 Version 2.1.1.

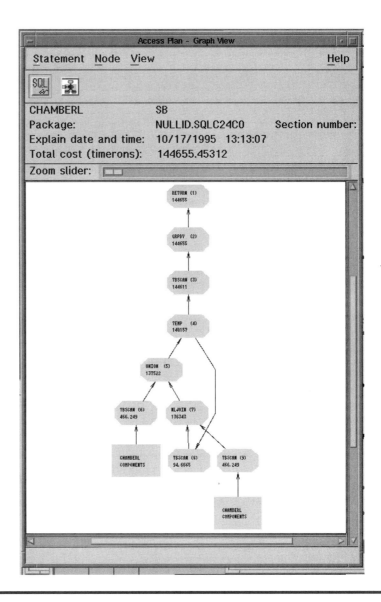

Figure 8-10: A Query Plan Displayed by Visual Explain

or more measured variables are to be collected periodically and displayed in the form of a graph. You can also request an "alert" when some measured variable exceeds a high or low threshold that you specify. The "alert" can consist of logging the event in the database or launching a program that you provide. The kinds of information that can be collected by the Snapshot Monitor are discussed in Section 8.7.1.

Special Registers

S pecial registers contain values, maintained by the system, that describe and control the environment in which an SQL statement is executed. V2 maintains the following special registers:

CURRENT DATE (Datatype: Date)

This register contains the date on which the current statement is being executed. The date information is obtained from the operating system and cannot be manually set.

CURRENT EXPLAIN MODE (Datatype: Char(8))[1]

This register controls the gathering of Tabular Explain data, which can be used to examine the access plans chosen by the optimizer for dynamic SQL statements. (The Explain facility is discussed in Section 8.6.4.) The special register can be given a value by a statement such as the following:

```
SET CURRENT EXPLAIN MODE = YES;
```

The valid values for CURRENT EXPLAIN MODE are as follows:

NO: Do not capture Tabular Explain data for dynamic SQL statements (this is the default).

YES: Capture Tabular Explain data for dynamic SQL statements and execute them.

EXPLAIN: Capture Tabular Explain data for dynamic SQL statements but do not execute them.

CURRENT EXPLAIN SNAPSHOT (Datatype: Char(8))

This register controls the gathering of "snapshot" data, which can be used by the Visual Explain feature of the Database Director to create a graphic display of the access plan for a dynamic SQL statement. (The Explain facility is discussed in Section 8.6.4, and Visual Explain is discussed in Section 8.8.1.) The special register can be given a value by a statement such as the following:

```
SET CURRENT EXPLAIN SNAPSHOT = YES;
```

---

1. The CURRENT EXPLAIN MODE special register is supported beginning with DB2 Version 2.1.1.

The valid values for CURRENT EXPLAIN SNAPSHOT are as follows:

NO: Do not capture snapshot data for dynamic SQL statements (this is the default).

YES: Capture snapshot data for dynamic SQL statements and execute them.

EXPLAIN: Capture snapshot data for dynamic SQL statements but do not execute them.

CURRENT FUNCTION PATH (Datatype: Varchar(254))

This register contains the list of schemas that will be searched to resolve the names of functions and datatypes used in dynamic SQL statements. The schema names are enclosed in double quotes and separated by commas. The value of the register can be set by the SET CURRENT FUNCTION PATH statement (described in Section 4.3.1). The default value is SYSIBM, followed by SYSFUN, followed by the current value of the USER special register.

CURRENT QUERY OPTIMIZATION (Datatype: Integer)

This register specifies the class of optimization techniques to be used in preparing dynamic SQL statements for execution. The special register can be given a value by a statement such as the following:

```
SET CURRENT QUERY OPTIMIZATION = 5;
```

The valid values for CURRENT QUERY OPTIMIZATION are the integers 0, 1, 3, 5, 7, and 9. (The meanings of these values are described in Section 8.6.1.) In general, higher values cause the optimizer to use more time and memory in choosing optimal access plans, potentially resulting in better plans and improved run-time performance. The extreme values 0 and 9 should be used with caution, since they may result in suboptimal plans or long optimization times, respectively. Level 5 is the default level of optimization for V2 and is a good compromise for most applications.

CURRENT SERVER (Datatype: Varchar(18))

This register contains the name of the database to which your application is currently connected. Database connections are controlled by the CONNECT statement (described in Section 2.9.2).

CURRENT TIME (Datatype: Time)

This register contains the time of day at which the current SQL statement is being executed. Multiple references to CURRENT TIME within the same SQL statement will all return the same value. The value of this register is obtained from the operating system and cannot be manually set.

CURRENT TIMESTAMP (Datatype: Timestamp)

This register contains a microsecond-level measure of the date and time at which execution of the current SQL statement began. Multiple references to CURRENT TIMESTAMP within the same SQL statement will all return the same value. The value of this register is obtained from the operating system and cannot be manually set.

CURRENT TIMEZONE (Datatype: Decimal(6,0))

This register contains the difference between Coordinated Universal Time (formerly known as Greenwich Mean Time) and the local time at your server, expressed as a six-digit decimal number representing hours (two digits), minutes (two digits), and seconds (two digits). For example, in California in the winter, the value of CURRENT TIMEZONE is –080000. The value of this register is obtained from the operating system and cannot be manually set.

USER (Datatype: Char(8))

This register contains the userid of the user who is connected to the database and executing the current application. This is the userid that is used for authorization checking of dynamic SQL statements, including statements executed using the CLP. Authorization checking of static SQL statements, on the other hand, is performed against the userid who bound the application, which is not in general the same as the content of the USER register. The value of USER is obtained from the operating system and cannot be manually set.

B Functions

S QL recognizes two types of functions: *scalar functions* and *column functions*. Scalar functions take one or more values as arguments and return a single result. Column functions take one column of values as an argument and return a single result. This appendix describes all the built-in functions of V2. All the built-in column functions, and some of the built-in scalar functions, are in the SYSIBM schema. The remainder of the built-in scalar functions are in the SYSFUN schema. Both of these schemas are on the default function path, so all the built-in functions can be invoked by simple one-part names.

Operators such as + and || are an important special case of scalar functions. An infix operator such as x + y is treated as a call to the scalar function "+"(x,y), and a prefix operator such as -x is treated as a call to the scalar function "-"(x). This appendix describes the built-in operators of V2 as well as the built-in functions.

Each function is identified by its *signature*, which is the combination of its name and the datatypes of its parameters. The signatures of all the built-in functions are listed below, along with their return datatypes. In many cases, a family of functions will have the same name but different signatures. A function call is valid if the actual argument datatypes of the call match the formal parameter datatypes of the function or can be promoted to the formal parameter datatypes by moving to the right in one of the promotion hierarchies shown in Figure B-1.

In the function signatures that follow, it is often necessary to refer to a collection of related datatypes. The following symbols are used:

<any numeric datatype> includes Smallint, Integer, Decimal, and Double

<any string datatype> includes Char, Varchar, Long Varchar, and Clob

<any DBCS datatype> includes Graphic, Vargraphic, Long Vargraphic, and Dbclob

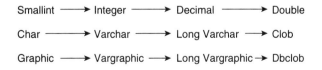

Figure B-1: Promotion Hierarchies for Function Parameters

<any built-in datatype> includes all datatypes except user-defined datatypes

<any short datatype> includes all datatypes except Long Varchar, Long Vargraphic, Blob, Clob, and Dbclob

<any datetime datatype> includes Time, Date, and Timestamp

<date string> means a Char or Varchar of length at least eight characters, containing a string representation of a date in one of the following formats: "1999-12-31" or "12/31/1999" or "31.12.1999"

<time string> means a Char or Varchar of length at least four characters, containing a string representation of a time in one of the following formats: "23:59" or "23:59:00" or "23.59" or "23.59.00" or "11:59 PM" or "11 PM"

<timestamp string> means a Char or Varchar of length 19 or 26 characters, containing a string representation of a timestamp in one of the following formats: "1999-12-31-23.59.00" or "1999-12-31-23.59.00.000000"

<date duration> means a Decimal(8,0) number representing a number of years, months, and days, expressed in format YYYYMMDD

<time duration> means a Decimal(6,0) number representing a number of hours, minutes, and seconds, expressed in format HHMMSS

<timestamp duration> means a Decimal(20,6) number representing a number of years, months, days, hours, minutes, seconds, and microseconds, expressed in format YYYYMMDDHHMMSS.nnnnnn

<same datatype> means that the return datatype of the function is the same as the datatype of its argument

<datatype of highest precedence> means the return datatype of the function is the same as the argument datatype that is farthest to the right in the promotion hierarchy in Figure B-1

B.1 COLUMN FUNCTIONS

Each of the following functions operates on a collection of values (a *column*) to produce a scalar result. In each of these functions, the keyword DISTINCT may precede the argument to indicate that duplicate values are to be eliminated from the argument column before the function is applied. All column functions are found in the SYSIBM schema.

avg (*<any numeric datatype>*) → *<same datatype>*

Returns the average of the non-null values in the argument column. If the argument column is empty, the result is null. There is one exception to the result datatype rule: if the argument datatype is Smallint, the result datatype is Integer.

count (*<any datatype>*) → Integer

count (*) → Integer

Returns the number of non-null values in the argument column. The special form `count(*)` is used for counting rows of a table, including rows that contain null values.

max (*<any short datatype>*) → *<same datatype>*

Returns the maximum value in the argument column. If the argument column is empty, the result is null.

min (*<any short datatype>*) → *<same datatype>*

Returns the minimum value in the argument column. If the argument column is empty, the result is null.

stdev (*<any numeric datatype>*) → Double[1]

Returns the standard deviation of a column of numbers. If the argument column is empty, the result is null.

sum (*<any numeric datatype>*) → *<same datatype>*

Returns the sum of the non-null values in the argument column. If the argument column is empty, the result is null. Exception to the result datatype rule: if the argument datatype is Smallint, the result datatype is Integer. If the argument datatype is Decimal, the result datatype is Decimal with a precision of 31 digits.

variance (*<any numeric datatype>*) → Double[1]

Returns the variance of a column of numbers. If the argument column is empty, the result is null.

B.2 SCALAR FUNCTIONS

The following functions are called scalar functions because both their arguments and their result are scalar values. Some of these functions are built into the V2 implementation and reside in the SYSIBM schema. Others are external functions that are shipped with the system and reside in the SYSFUN schema. The schema in which each function resides is given in parentheses at the end of its description. The SYSIBM functions can in general be expected to have better performance than the SYSFUN functions. Since the default function

---

1. The `stdev` and `variance` functions are supported beginning with DB2 Version 2.1.1.

path includes both the SYSIBM and SYSFUN schemas, you can make use of any of these functions without including a schema name in your function invocation.

abs (*<any numeric datatype>*) → *<same datatype>*

absval (*<any numeric datatype>*) → *<same datatype>*

Returns the absolute value of the argument. There is one exception to the rule that the result datatype is the same as the argument datatype: If the argument datatype is Decimal, the result datatype will be Double, because a Decimal value must be promoted to Double before it can be passed to (or returned from) an external function. (SYSFUN)

acos (Double) → Double

Returns the arccosine of the argument, as an angle expressed in radians. (SYSFUN)

ascii (*<any string datatype>*) → Integer

Returns the ASCII code of the first character of the argument string. (SYSFUN)

asin (Double) → Double

Returns the arcsine of the argument, as an angle expressed in radians. (SYSFUN)

atan (Double) → Double

Returns the arctangent of the argument, as an angle expressed in radians. (SYSFUN)

atan2 (Double *x*, Double *y*) → Double

Returns the arctangent of the quotient *y* / *x*, as an angle expressed in radians. (SYSFUN)

blob (*<any string datatype>*) → Blob

blob (*<any string datatype>*, Integer *n*) → Blob(*n*)

blob (*<any DBCS datatype>*) → Blob

blob (*<any DBCS datatype>*, Integer *n*) → Blob(*n*)

blob (Blob) → Blob

blob (Blob, Integer *n*) → Blob(*n*)

Converts the first argument to a Blob datatype. The second argument, if specified, becomes the maximum length of the result (causing truncation if necessary). (SYSIBM)

ceil (*<any numeric datatype>*) → *<same datatype>*

ceiling (*<any numeric datatype>*) → *<same datatype>*

Returns the smallest integer greater than or equal to the argument. There is one exception to the rule that the return type is the same type as the argument type: If the argument type is Decimal, the return type is Double. (SYSFUN)

char (Date) → Char(10)

char (Date, Keyword *k*) → Char(10)

char (Time) → Char(8)

char (Time, Keyword *k*) → Char(8)

char (Timestamp) ·→ Char(26)

Returns a character-string representation of the argument. The keyword *k*, if present, governs the format of the string representation. Valid values for the keyword argument (which must not be enclosed in quotes) are ISO, USA, EUR, JIS, and LOCAL. (SYSIBM)

char (*<any string datatype>*) → Char( )

char (*<any string datatype>*, Integer *n*) → Char(*n*)

Converts the first argument to a fixed-length Char datatype. The second argument, if specified, becomes the length of the result (causing truncation or padding with blanks if necessary). (SYSIBM)

char (Smallint) → Char(6)

char (Integer) → Char(12)

char (Decimal) → Char( )

char (Decimal, Varchar) → Char( )

Returns a character-string representation of the first argument. If the first argument is Decimal and the second argument is Varchar, the second argument must be a single character and is used to represent the decimal point in the result string. (SYSIBM)

char (Double) → Char(24)

Returns a character-string representation of a double-precision floating-point value. (SYSFUN)

chr (Integer) → Char(1)

Returns the character whose ASCII code is equal to the argument. (SYSFUN)

clob (*<any string datatype>*) → Clob

clob (*<any string datatype>*, Integer *n*) → Clob(*n*)

Converts the first argument to a Clob datatype. The second argument, if specified, becomes the maximum length of the result (causing truncation if necessary). (SYSIBM)

coalesce (*<one or more arguments of compatible datatypes>*) → *<datatype of highest precedence>*

Returns the value of its first non-null argument, or null if all arguments are null. (See Section 4.6.2 for rules governing compatibility of argument datatypes.) coalesce and value are different names for the same function. (SYSIBM)

concat (*<any string datatype>*, *<any string datatype>*) → *<datatype of highest precedence>*

concat (*<any DBCS datatype>*, *<any DBCS datatype>*) → *<datatype of highest precedence>*

concat (Blob, Blob) → Blob

Returns the concatenation of the two string arguments. Equivalent to concat or || used as an infix operator. If the result cannot be represented in the datatype of highest precedence, a suitable datatype is chosen. For example, if a concatenation of two fixed-length strings results in a string of length greater than 254, the result datatype will be Varchar rather than Char. (SYSIBM)

cos (Double) → Double

Returns the cosine of an angle expressed in radians. (SYSFUN)

cot (Double) → Double

Returns the cotangent of an angle expressed in radians. (SYSFUN)

date (*<date string>*) → Date

Converts the argument from a string representation of a Date to an actual Date. The argument may be in any of the following formats (examples represent the last day of the year 1999): (SYSIBM)
"1999-12-31"
"12/31/1999"
"31.12.1999"
"1999365"

date (*<any numeric datatype>*) → Date

Converts the argument to an integer *n* by truncation. Returns the date that is *n* − 1 days after January 1, 0001. (SYSIBM)

date (Timestamp) → Date

date (*<timestamp string>*) → Date

    Returns the date portion of the argument. (SYSIBM)

day (Date) → Integer

day (*<date string>*) → Integer

day (*<date duration>*) → Integer

day (Timestamp) → Integer

day (*<timestamp string>*) → Integer

day (*<timestamp duration>*) → Integer

    Returns the day portion of the argument. (SYSIBM)

dayname (Date) → Varchar(100)

dayname (*<date string>*) → Varchar(100)

dayname (Timestamp) → Varchar(100)

dayname (*<timestamp string>*) → Varchar(100)

    Returns the day of the week corresponding to the argument date, as a character string (Sunday, Monday, and so on). (SYSFUN)

dayofweek (Date) → Integer

dayofweek (*<date string>*) → Integer

dayofweek (Timestamp) → Integer

dayofweek (*<timestamp string>*) → Integer

    Returns the day of the week corresponding to the argument date, as an integer (Sunday = 1, Monday = 2, and so on). (SYSFUN)

dayofyear (Date) → Integer

dayofyear (*<date string>*) → Integer

dayofyear (Timestamp) → Integer

dayofyear (*<timestamp string>*) → Integer

    Returns the day of the year corresponding to the argument date, as an integer between 1 and 366. (SYSFUN)

days (Date) → Integer

days (*<date string>*) → Integer

days (Timestamp) → Integer

days (*<timestamp string>*) → Integer

    Converts the argument to a date, then returns one more than the number of days between January 1, 0001 and this date. (SYSIBM)

dbclob (*<any DBCS datatype>*) → Dbclob

dbclob (*<any DBCS datatype>*, Integer *n*) → Dbclob(*n*)

Converts the first argument to a Dbclob datatype. The second argument, if specified, becomes the maximum length of the result (causing truncation if necessary). (SYSIBM)

decimal (*<any numeric datatype>*) → Decimal(15, 0)

decimal (*<any numeric datatype>*, Integer *p*) → Decimal(*p*, 0)

decimal (*<any numeric datatype>*, Integer *p*, Integer *s*) → Decimal(*p*, *s*)

Returns a decimal representation of the first argument, with the indicated precision and scale. The function name `dec` may be used as a synonym for `decimal`. (SYSIBM)

decimal (Varchar) → Decimal(15, 0)

decimal (Varchar, Integer *p*) → Decimal(*p*, 0)

decimal (Varchar, Integer *p*, Integer *s*) → Decimal(*p*, *s*)

decimal (Varchar, Integer *p*, Integer *s*, Varchar *d*) → Decimal(*p*, *s*)

The first argument is a character-string representation of a decimal number, which is converted to an actual decimal value with the indicated precision and scale. The fourth parameter, if present, is a single character that indicates how the decimal point is represented in the string input. The function name `dec` may be used as a synonym for `decimal`. (SYSIBM)

degrees (*<any numeric datatype>*) → Double

Converts the argument angle from radians to degrees. (SYSFUN)

difference (Varchar(4), Varchar(4)) → Integer

Returns a measure of the difference between two four-byte sound codes computed by the `soundex` function. (SYSFUN) Example of usage:

```
difference(soundex ('Dog'), soundex ('Cat'))
```

digits (Decimal) → Char( )

Returns a fixed-length character string representing the absolute value of the argument, not including its sign or decimal point. For example, digits(–123.45) is "12345." (SYSIBM)

double (*<any numeric datatype>*) → Double

double_precision (*<any numeric datatype>*) → Double

Converts the argument to a double-precision floating-point number. (SYSIBM)

double (Varchar) → Double

If the argument contains a valid representation of a floating-point value, this value is returned. (SYSFUN)

event_mon_state (Varchar) → Integer

The argument is the name of an Event Monitor (defined by a CREATE EVENT MONITOR statement). The function returns 1 if the named Event Monitor is active, 0 if it is inactive. (SYSIBM)

exp (Double x) → Double

Returns e^x, where x is the argument and e is the base of the natural logarithms. (SYSFUN)

float (*<any numeric datatype>*) → Double

Converts the argument to a double-precision floating-point number. (SYSIBM)

floor (*<any numeric datatype>*) → *<same datatype>*

Returns the largest integer less than or equal to the argument. There is one exception to the rule that the return type is the same type as the argument type. If the argument type is Decimal, the return type is Double. (SYSFUN)

graphic (*<any DBCS datatype>*) → Graphic

graphic (*<any DBCS datatype>*, Integer n) → Graphic(n)

Converts the argument to a fixed-length Graphic datatype, of the indicated length. If no length is specified, the length is derived from that of the argument. (SYSIBM)

hex (*<any built-in datatype>*) → Varchar

Returns a hexadecimal representation of the argument value. Each two bytes of the returned string represent one byte of the internal representation of the argument value. (SYSIBM)

hour (Time) → Integer

hour (*<time string>*) → Integer

hour (*<time duration>*) → Integer

hour (Timestamp) → Integer

hour (*<timestamp string>*) → Integer

hour (*<timestamp duration>*) → Integer

Returns the hour part of the argument. If the argument is a time, timestamp, or string, the result is an integer between 0 and 24. If the argument is a duration, the result is an integer between –99 and 99. (SYSIBM)

insert (Varchar x, Integer m, Integer n, Varchar y) → Varchar(4000)

insert (Clob(1M) x, Integer m, Integer n, Clob(1M) y) → Clob(1M)

insert (Blob(1M) x, Integer m, Integer n, Blob(1M) y) → Blob(1M)

The return string is computed by deleting from string x a substring of n characters beginning with character number m, and replacing the deleted substring by string y. (SYSFUN)

integer (*<any numeric datatype>*) → Integer

integer (Varchar) → Integer

Converts the argument to an integer, by truncation of the decimal part if necessary. If the argument is of datatype Varchar, it must be a character-string representation of an integer, such as "–123." The function name `int` may be used as a synonym for `integer`. (SYSIBM)

julian_day (Date) → Integer

julian_day (*<date string>*) → Integer

julian_day (Timestamp) → Integer

julian_day (*<timestamp string>*) → Integer

Returns the number of days between the beginning of the Julian calendar (January 1, 4713 B.C.) and the argument date. (SYSFUN)

lcase (Varchar) → Varchar(4000)

lcase (Clob(1M)) → Clob(1M)

Returns a copy of the argument string in which all the uppercase characters have been converted to lowercase. (SYSFUN)

left (Varchar *x*, Integer *n*) → Varchar(4000)

left (Clob(1M) *x*, Integer *n*) → Clob(1M)

left (Blob(1M) *x*, Integer *n*) → Blob(1M)

Returns the leftmost *n* characters of string *x*. (SYSFUN)

length (*<any built-in datatype>*) → Integer

Returns the length of the argument, in bytes, unless the argument is a double-byte string datatype, in which case the length is measured in characters. If the argument is a numeric or datetime datatype, returns the length in bytes of its internal representation. (SYSIBM)

ln (Double) → Double

Returns the natural logarithm of the argument. (SYSFUN)

locate (*<any string datatype>* *s1*, *<any string datatype>* *s2*) → Integer

locate (*<any string datatype>* *s1*, *<any string datatype>* *s2*, Integer *n*) → Integer

locate (Blob(1M) *s1*, Blob(1M) *s2*) → Integer

locate (Blob(1M) *s1*, Blob(1M) *s2*, Integer *n*) → Integer

Returns the starting position of the first occurrence of argument *s2* inside argument *s1*. The third argument, if any, indicates the position within *s1* where the search is to begin. If *s2* is not found within *s1*, 0 is returned. If any argument is a Clob, it is limited to a length of one megabyte. See `posstr` for a similar function. (SYSFUN)

log (Double) → Double

Returns the natural logarithm of the argument (same as 1n). (SYSFUN)

log10 (Double) → Double

Returns the base-10 logarithm of the argument. (SYSFUN)

long_varchar (*<any string datatype>*) → Long Varchar

Converts the argument to the Long Varchar datatype, which has a maximum length of 32K characters. (SYSIBM)

long_vargraphic (*<any DBCS string datatype>*) → Long Vargraphic

Converts the argument to the Long Vargraphic datatype, which has a maximum length of 16K double-byte characters. (SYSIBM)

ltrim (Varchar) → Varchar(4000)

ltrim (Clob(1M)) → Clob(1M)

Returns a copy of the argument with leading blanks removed. (SYSFUN)

microsecond (Timestamp) → Integer

microsecond (*<timestamp string>*) → Integer

microsecond (*<timestamp duration>*) → Integer

Returns the microsecond part of the argument. (SYSIBM)

midnight_seconds (Time) → Integer

midnight_seconds (*<time string>*) → Integer

midnight_seconds (Timestamp) → Integer

midnight_seconds (*<timestamp string>*) → Integer

Returns the number of seconds between the argument time and the previous midnight. (SYSFUN)

minute (Time) → Integer

minute (*<time string>*) → Integer

minute (*<time duration>*) → Integer

minute (Timestamp) → Integer

minute (*<timestamp string>*) → Integer

minute (*<timestamp duration>*) → Integer

Returns the minute part of the argument. If the argument is a time, timestamp, or string, the result is an integer between 0 and 59. If the argument is a duration, the result is an integer between –99 and 99. (SYSIBM)

mod (Integer *m*, Integer *n*) → Double

Returns the remainder (modulus) of argument *m* divided by argument *n*. (SYSFUN)

month (Date) → Integer

month (*<date string>*) → Integer

month (*<date duration>*) → Integer

month (Timestamp) → Integer

month (*<timestamp string>*) → Integer

month (*<timestamp duration>*) → Integer

Returns the month part of the argument. If the argument is a date, timestamp, or string, the result is an integer between 1 and 12. If the argument is a duration, the result is an integer between –99 and 99. (SYSIBM)

monthname (Date) → Varchar(100)

monthname (*<date string>*) → Varchar(100)

monthname (Timestamp) → Varchar(100)

monthname (*<timestamp string>*) → Varchar(100)

Returns the name of the month part of the argument, as a mixed-case character string. (SYSFUN)

nullif (*<any datatype>*, *<any compatible datatype>*) → *<datatype of highest precedence>*

Returns null if the arguments are equal; otherwise returns the first argument. (SYSIBM)

posstr (*<any string datatype> s1*, Varchar(4000) *s2*) → Integer

posstr (*<any DBCS datatype> s1*, Vargraphic(2000) *s2*) → Integer

posstr (Blob *s1*, Blob(4000) *s2*) → Integer

Returns the starting position of the first occurrence of argument *s2* inside argument *s1*. If *s2* is not found within *s1*, 0 is returned. See locate for a similar function. (SYSFUN)

power (Integer *x*, Integer *n*) → Integer

power (Double *x*, Double *n*) → Double

Returns the first argument raised to the power of the second argument, x^n. (SYSFUN)

quarter (Date) → Integer

quarter (*<date string>*) → Integer

quarter (Timestamp) → Integer

quarter (*<timestamp string>*) → Integer

Returns an integer between 1 and 4 representing the quarter of the year in which the argument occurs. (SYSFUN)

radians (Double) → Double

Converts the argument angle from degrees to radians. (SYSFUN)

raise_error (Varchar, Varchar) → *<void>*

Causes an error condition to be returned in the SQLCA. The first argument must be exactly 5 characters in length and becomes the SQLSTATE. The second argument is a message of up to 70 characters that is placed in the SQLERRMC field of the SQLCA. The SQLCODE is set to –438. The `raise_error` function returns no value but is considered to be compatible with the context in which it is used (often inside a CASE expression). (For a more complete discussion of `raise_error`, see Section 3.2.3.) (SYSIBM)

rand ( ) → Double

rand (Integer) → Double

Returns a random double-precision floating-point number between 0 and 1. The optional argument is used as a "seed" to begin a new random number sequence. (SYSFUN)

repeat (Varchar *x*, Integer *n*) → Varchar(4000)

repeat (Clob(1M) *x*, Integer *n*) → Clob(1M)

repeat (Blob(1M) *x*, Integer *n*) → Blob(1M)

Returns a string consisting of *n* repetitions of the string *x*. (SYSFUN)

replace (Varchar *x*, Varchar *y*, Varchar *z*) → Varchar(4000)

replace (Clob(1M) *x*, Clob(1M) *y*, Clob(1M) *z*) → Clob(1M)

replace (Blob(1M) *x*, Blob(1M) *y*, Blob(1M) *z*) → Blob(1M)

Returns a copy of the string *x*, with all occurrences of the string *y* replaced by string *z*. (SYSFUN)

right (Varchar *x*, Integer *n*) → Varchar(4000)

right (Clob(1M) *x*, Integer *n*) → Clob(1M)

right (Blob(1M) *x*, Integer *n*) → Blob(1M)

Returns the rightmost *n* characters of string *x*. (SYSFUN)

round (Integer *x*, Integer *n*) → Integer

round (Double *x*, Integer *n*) → Double

Rounds the argument *x* in such a way that its least significant digit is *n* digits to the right of the decimal point (if *n* is negative, the least significant digit is to the left of the decimal point). For example, `round(12349, -2)` is 12350. For a related function, see `truncate`. (SYSFUN)

rtrim (Varchar) → Varchar(4000)

rtrim (Clob(1M)) → Clob(1M)

Returns a copy of the argument with trailing blanks removed. (SYSFUN)

second (Time) → Integer

second (*<time string>*) → Integer

second (*<time duration>*) → Integer

second (Timestamp) → Integer

second (*<timestamp string>*) → Integer

second (*<timestamp duration>*) → Integer

> Returns the seconds part of the argument. If the argument is a time, time-stamp, or string, the result is an integer between 0 and 59. If the argument is a duration, the result is an integer between –99 and 99. (SYSIBM)

sign (*<any numeric datatype>*) → *<same datatype>*

> Returns +1 if the argument is positive, –1 if the argument is negative, 0 if the argument is zero. Exception to return type rule: If argument type is Decimal, return type is Double. (SYSFUN)

sin (Double) → Double

> Returns the sine of an angle expressed in radians. (SYSFUN)

smallint (*<any numeric datatype>*) → Integer

smallint (Varchar) → Integer

> Converts the argument to a small integer, by truncation of the decimal part if necessary. If the argument is of datatype Varchar, it must be a character-string representation of an integer between –32,768 and +32,767. (SYSIBM)

soundex (Varchar) → Char(4)

> Returns a four-character code that represents the sound of the words in the argument. For a related function, see `difference`. (SYSFUN)

space (Integer *n*) → Varchar(4000)

> Returns a string consisting of *n* spaces. (SYSFUN)

sqrt (Double) → Double

> Returns the square root of the argument. (SYSFUN)

substr (*<any string datatype>* s, Integer *m*, Integer *n*) → *<string datatype>*

substr (*<any string datatype>* s, Integer *m*) → *<string datatype>*

substr (*<any DBCS datatype>* s, Integer *m*, Integer *n*) → *<DBCS datatype>*

substr (*<any DBCS datatype>* s, Integer *m*) → *<DBCS datatype>*

substr (Blob *s*, Integer *m*, Integer *n*) → Blob

substr (Blob *s*, Integer *m*) → Blob

> Returns a substring of string *s*, beginning at character *m* and containing *n* characters. If the third argument is omitted, the substring begins at character *m* and contains the remainder of string *s*. The argument *s* is padded with blanks if necessary to make a result string of length *n*. The result string

is the same datatype as string *s*, with certain exceptions: If string *s* is a Varchar or Long Varchar and *n* is a constant less than 255, the result datatype is Char(*n*). Similarly, if string *s* is a Vargraphic or Long Vargraphic and *n* is a constant less than 128, the result datatype is Graphic(*n*). (SYSIBM)

table_name (Varchar *t*, Varchar *s*) → Varchar(18)

table_name (Varchar *t*) → Varchar(18)

This function is used to resolve aliases. If the name *t* (or the qualified name *s.t*) is an alias, it is resolved to a table or view. The unqualified name of the resolved table or view is returned. If *t* (or *s.t*) is not an alias, *t* is returned. (SYSIBM)

table_schema (Varchar *t*, Varchar *s*) → Varchar(8)

table_schema (Varchar *t*) → Varchar(8)

This function is used to resolve aliases. If the name *t* (or the qualified name *s.t*) is an alias, it is resolved to a table or view. The schema name of the resolved table or view is returned. If *t* (or *s.t*) is not an alias, the schema portion of the input name is returned (*s*, or if argument *s* is not present, the current authid). (SYSIBM)

tan (Double) → Double

Returns the tangent of an angle expressed in radians. (SYSFUN)

time (Time) → Time

time (*<time string>*) → Time

time (Timestamp) → Time

time (*<timestamp string>*) → Time

Returns the time portion of the argument. If the argument is a string representation of a Time or a Timestamp, it is converted to an actual Time. (SYSIBM)

timestamp (Timestamp) → Timestamp

timestamp (*<timestamp string>*) → Timestamp

Returns the Timestamp represented by the argument. If the argument is a string representing a Timestamp, it is converted to a real Timestamp. (SYSIBM)

timestamp (Date, Time) → Timestamp

timestamp (Date, *<time string>*) → Timestamp

timestamp (*<date string>*, Time) → Timestamp

timestamp (*<date string>*, *<time string>*) → Timestamp

Returns a Timestamp whose date part is taken from the first argument and whose time part is taken from the second argument. The microsecond part of the Timestamp is set to 0. (SYSIBM)

timestampdiff (Integer u, Char(22) d) → Integer

The first argument, u, indicates a time unit, as follows: 256 = years, 128 = quarters, 64 = months, 32 = weeks, 16 = days, 8 = hours, 4 = minutes, 2 = seconds, 1 = microseconds (symbolic constants for these units can be found in `sqllib/include/sqlcli1.h`). The second argument, d, is the result of subtracting two Timestamps and converting the result to character form. The function returns an integer representing an estimation of the interval d expressed in units u. For example, the number of days between Timestamps `t1` and `t2` can be found by `timestampdiff(16, char(t2-t1))`. (SYSFUN)

timestamp_iso (Date) → Varchar(26)

timestamp_iso (Time) → Varchar(26)

timestamp_iso (Timestamp) → Varchar(26)

timestamp_iso (*<timestamp string>*) → Varchar(26)

Converts the argument to a Timestamp, represented as a character string in the ISO format: `'yyyy-mm-dd hh:mm:ss.nnnnnn'`. If the argument is a Date, inserts zeros into the time fields of the Timestamp. If the argument is a Time, inserts the current date into the date fields of the Timestamp. (SYSFUN)

translate (Char) → Char( )

translate (Varchar) → Varchar( )

Returns a copy of the argument string in which all lowercase characters have been translated to uppercase. For a similar function, see `ucase`. (SYSIBM)

translate (Char s, Varchar t, Varchar f) → Char

translate (Varchar s, Varchar t, Varchar f) → Varchar

translate (Graphic s, Vargraphic t, Vargraphic f) → Graphic

translate (Vargraphic s, Vargraphic t, Vargraphic f) → Vargraphic

translate (Char s, Varchar t, Varchar f, Varchar p) → Char

translate (Varchar s, Varchar t, Varchar f, Varchar p) → Varchar

translate (Graphic s, Vargraphic t, Vargraphic f, Vargraphic p) → Graphic

translate (Vargraphic s, Vargraphic t, Vargraphic f, Vargraphic p) → Vargraphic

Returns a copy of string s, in which some of the characters are translated to different characters. String f (the "from string") specifies the characters to be translated, and string t (the "to string") specifies the characters to which they are to be translated. Any character in s that is also found in f is replaced by the corresponding character in t. If string t is shorter than string f, it is padded to the same length by the "pad character" p, which must be a single character. If no pad character is specified, the pad character is assumed to be a single-byte or double-byte blank. (SYSIBM)

truncate (Integer *x*, Integer *n*) → Integer

truncate (Double *x*, Integer *n*) → Double

Truncates the argument *x* in such a way that its least significant digit is *n* digits to the right of the decimal point (if *n* is negative, the least significant digit is to the left of the decimal point). For example, `truncate(12349, -2)` is 12,340. `truncate` can be abbreviated as `trunc`. For a related function, see `round`. (SYSFUN)

ucase (Varchar) → Varchar(4000)

Returns a copy of the argument string in which all lowercase characters have been converted to uppercase. For a similar function, see `translate`. (SYSFUN)

value (*<one or more arguments of compatible datatypes>*) → *<datatype of highest precedence>*

Returns the value of its first non-null argument, or null if all arguments are null. (See Section 4.6.2 for rules governing the compatibility of argument datatypes.) `value` and `coalesce` are different names for the same function. (SYSIBM)

varchar (*<any string datatype>*) → Varchar( )

varchar (*<any string datatype>*, Integer *n*) → Varchar(*n*)

varchar (*<any datetime datatype>*) → Varchar( )

Returns a copy of the first argument converted to datatype Varchar. The second argument, if present, becomes the maximum length of the result string, causing truncation if necessary. (SYSIBM)

vargraphic (*<any DBCS datatype>*) → Vargraphic( )

vargraphic (*<any DBCS datatype>*, Integer *n*) → Vargraphic(*n*)

vargraphic (Varchar) → Vargraphic( )

Returns a copy of the first argument converted to datatype Vargraphic. The second argument, if present, becomes the maximum length of the result string, causing truncation if necessary. (SYSIBM)

week (Date) → Integer

week (*<date string>*) → Integer

week (Timestamp) → Integer

week (*<timestamp string>*) → Integer

Returns the week of the year in which the argument occurs, expressed as an integer between 1 and 53. (SYSFUN)

year (Date) $\rightarrow$ Integer

year (*<date string>*) $\rightarrow$ Integer

year (*<date duration>*) $\rightarrow$ Integer

year (Timestamp) $\rightarrow$ Integer

year (*<timestamp string>*) $\rightarrow$ Integer

year (*<timestamp duration>*) $\rightarrow$ Integer

Returns the year part of the argument. If the argument is a date, timestamp, or string, the result is an integer between 1 and 9,999. If the argument is a duration, the result is an integer between –9999 and 9999. (SYSIBM)

B.3 OPERATORS

B.3.1 Prefix Operators

The following operators can be used as prefix operators (example: -x). These operators are resolved in the same way as unary functions. All these operators reside in the SYSIBM schema.

Operator	Operand Datatype	Result Datatype	Meaning
+	*<any numeric datatype>*	*<same datatype>*	Unary plus. Returns its operand.
–	*<any numeric datatype>*	*<same datatype>*	Unary minus. Returns the negation of its operand.

B.3.2 Infix Operators

The following operators can be used as infix operators (example: x + y). These operators are resolved in the same way as binary functions. All these operators reside in the SYSIBM schema.

Operator	First Operand Datatype	Second Operand Datatype	Result Datatype
+ (addition)	*\<any numeric datatype>*	*\<any numeric datatype>*	*\<datatype of highest precedence>*
+	Date	*\<date duration>*	Date
+	*\<date duration>*	Date	Date
+	Time	*\<time duration>*	Time
+	*\<time duration>*	Time	Time
+	Timestamp	*\<timestamp duration>*	Timestamp
+	*\<timestamp duration>*	Timestamp	Timestamp
− (subtraction)	*\<any numeric datatype>*	*\<any numeric datatype>*	*\<datatype of highest precedence>*
−	Date	Date	*\<date duration>*
−	Date	*\<date string>*	*\<date duration>*
−	*\<date string>*	Date	*\<date duration>*
−	Date	*\<date duration>*	Date
−	Time	Time	*\<time duration>*
−	Time	*\<time string>*	*\<time duration>*
−	*\<time string>*	Time	*\<time duration>*
−	Time	*\<time duration>*	Time
−	Timestamp	Timestamp	*\<timestamp duration>*
−	Timestamp	*\<timestamp string>*	*\<timestamp duration>*
−	*\<timestamp string>*	Timestamp	*\<timestamp duration>*
−	Timestamp	*\<timestamp duration>*	Timestamp
* (multiplication)	*\<any numeric datatype>*	*\<any numeric datatype>*	*\<datatype of highest precedence>*
/ (division)	*\<any numeric datatype>*	*\<any numeric datatype>*	*\<datatype of highest precedence>*
|| (concatenation)	*\<string datatype>*	*\<string datatype>*	*\<datatype of highest precedence>*, or datatype in which result can be represented
||	*\<DBCS datatype>*	*\<DBCS datatype>*	*\<datatype of highest precedence>*, or datatype in which result can be represented
||	Blob	Blob	Blob

APPENDIX

Typecodes

Typecodes are used in the `sqltype` fields of SQLDA descriptors. When a DESCRIBE statement returns an SQLDA describing the results of a query, it uses typecodes to indicate the datatypes in the result set. Typecodes are also used to indicate datatypes whenever values are being exchanged between the application program and the database system via an SQLDA structure (for example, input values in an EXECUTE USING statement). A typecode identifies not just the datatype of the value as it is stored in the database, but also the host language datatype that is being used for input or output.

Each of the built-in SQL datatypes (Integer, Varchar, and so on) has one or more host language datatypes that can be used for exchange of that SQL datatype between applications and the database. Each of these combinations of an SQL datatype and a host language datatype is identified by a typecode. Only a subset of these typecodes are returned by DESCRIBE statements. For example, typecode 460 will never be returned by DESCRIBE, because it denotes a datatype (null-terminated string) that is not used inside the database (though it is a valid host variable).

Typecodes are summarized in Table C-1. The symbolic names for the typecodes and the structures used in their C-language declarations are declared in `sqllib/include/sql.h`. These declarations may be overlaid on storage that is dynamically allocated for exchanging data with a dynamic SQL statement.

TABLE C-1: SQLDA Typecodes and the Datatypes They Represent

SQL Datatype	C-Language Datatype	Typecode If Not Nullable	Typecode If Nullable
Date	char[11]	SQL_TYP_DATE (384)	SQL_TYP_NDATE (385)
Time	char[9]	SQL_TYP_TIME (388)	SQL_TYP_NTIME (389)
Timestamp	char[27]	SQL_TYP_STAMP (392)	SQL_TYP_NSTAMP (393)
Null-terminated double-byte string	wchar_t[n + 1]	SQL_TYP_CGSTR (400)	SQL_TYP_NCGSTR (401)

TABLE C-1: *(Continued)*

SQL Datatype	C-Language Datatype	Typecode If Not Nullable	Typecode If Nullable
Blob(n)	struct sqllob (defined in sql.h)	SQL_TYP_BLOB (404)	SQL_TYP_NBLOB (405)
Clob(n)	struct sqllob (defined in sql.h)	SQL_TYP_CLOB (408)	SQL_TYP_NCLOB (409)
Dbclob(n)	struct sqldbclob (defined in sql.h)	SQL_TYP_DBCLOB (412)	SQL_TYP_NDBCLOB (413)
Varchar(n)	struct sqlchar (defined in sql.h)	SQL_TYP_VARCHAR (448)	SQL_TYP_NVARCHAR (449)
Char(n)	char[n + 1]	SQL_TYP_CHAR (452)	SQL_TYP_NCHAR (453)
Long Varchar	struct sqlchar (defined in sql.h)	SQL_TYP_LONG (456)	SQL_TYP_NLONG (457)
Null-terminated character string	char[n + 1]	SQL_TYP_CSTR (460)	SQL_TYP_NCSTR (461)
Vargraphic(n)	struct sqlgraphic (defined in sql.h)	SQL_TYP_VARGRAPH (464)	SQL_TYP_NVARGRAPH (465)
Graphic(n)	wchar_t[n + 1]	SQL_TYP_GRAPHIC (468)	SQL_TYP_NGRAPHIC (469)
Long Vargraphic	struct sqlgraphic (defined in sql.h)	SQL_TYP_LONGRAPH (472)	SQL_TYP_NLONGRAPH (473)
Double	double	SQL_TYP_FLOAT (480)	SQL_TYP_NFLOAT (481)
Decimal(p,s)	(no C equivalent)	SQL_TYP_DECIMAL (484)	SQL_TYP_NDECIMAL (485)
Integer	long	SQL_TYP_INTEGER (496)	SQL_TYP_NINTEGER (497)
Smallint	short	SQL_TYP_SMALL (500)	SQL_TYP_NSMALL (501)

TABLE C-1: *(Continued)*

SQL Datatype	C-Language Datatype	Typecode If Not Nullable	Typecode If Nullable
Blob File Reference	struct sqlfile (defined in sql.h)	SQL_TYP_BLOB_FILE (804)	SQL_TYP_NBLOB_FILE (805)
Clob File Reference	struct sqlfile (defined in sql.h)	SQL_TYP_CLOB_FILE (808)	SQL_TYP_NCLOB_FILE (809)
Dbclob File Reference	struct sqlfile (defined in sql.h)	SQL_TYP_DBCLOB_FILE (812)	SQL_TYP_NDBCLOB_FILE (813)
Blob Locator	long	SQL_TYP_BLOB_LOCATOR (960)	SQL_TYP_NBLOB_LOCATOR (961)
Clob Locator	long	SQL_TYP_CLOB_LOCATOR (964)	SQL_TYP_NCLOB_LOCATOR (965)
Dbclob Locator	long	SQL_TYP_DBCLOB_LOCATOR (968)	SQL_TYP_NDBCLOB_LOCATOR (969)

Definitions are given below for the structures referred to in the "C-Language Datatype" column of Table C-1.[1] In each of these definitions, data[n] represents an array of sufficient size to hold the data.

```
struct sqlchar            /*  General-purpose VARCHAR          */
      {
      short               length;
      char                data[n];
      };

struct sqlgraphic         /*  General-purpose VARGRAPHIC       */
      {
      short               length;
      wchar_t             data[n];
      };
```

---

1. In sql.h, the definitions of these structures are written using macros and are somewhat more complex, partly for historical reasons and partly for platform independence. Simplified structure definitions are provided here for ease of explanation. See the sql.h and sqlsystm.h files in the sqllib/include directory for details.

```
struct sqllob             /*  General-purpose LOB            */
     {
     unsigned long        length;
     char                 data[n];
     };

struct sqldbclob          /*  General-purpose DBCLOB         */
     {
     unsigned long        length;
     wchar_t              data[n];
     };

struct sqlfile            /*  File reference structure for LOBs  */
     {
     unsigned long        name_length;
     unsigned long        data_length;
     unsigned long        file_options;
     char                 name[255];
     };
```

Note: When double-byte data (SQL datatype Graphic, Vargraphic, Long Vargraphic, or Dbclob) is passed to or received from a host program in an SQLDA structure, the format of the data is controlled by the precompiler option named WCHARTYPE. If the program is precompiled with the option WCHARTYPE CONVERT, all double-byte strings are exchanged in wide-character (wchar_t) format, which is compatible with the wide-character string library declared in wstring.h. If the program is precompiled with the option WCHARTYPE NOCONVERT (the default), double-byte strings are exchanged in multibyte format (two bytes per character, independent of the definition of wchar_t). The C functions named wcstombs() and mbstowcs() can be used to convert data between wide-character format and multibyte format.

System Catalog Tables

The system catalog tables are maintained automatically by the V2 system. They contain *metadata*—that is, information about the data that is stored in the database. The base catalog tables are stored in the SYSIBM schema. For historical reasons, the names of these base catalog tables and their columns do not follow a consistent convention. For this reason, it is recommended that you interact with the catalog tables through two sets of *catalog views* that have been defined on them, which provide more consistent naming. Both sets of catalog views are documented in this appendix.

One set of catalog views is defined in the SYSCAT schema. Any user may read these views, but the views are not updatable. The term *catalog tables* is used loosely throughout this book to refer to the views in SYSCAT.

A second set of catalog views is defined in the SYSSTAT schema and is sometimes referred to as the *updatable catalog views*. The purpose of these views is to provide a means whereby authorized users can manually update statistics that are used for query optimization. It is not necessary for users to update these statistics manually, since the statistics are generated automatically by the RUNSTATS utility. However, manual update of the SYSTAT views provides a way for users to influence the system optimizer or to perform experiments on hypothetical databases.

Figure D-1 illustrates the relationship between the base catalog tables and the views that are defined on them, using the COLUMNS catalog as an example. Every catalog table in SYSIBM has a corresponding view in SYSCAT, and some catalog tables have a view in SYSSTAT as well. The name of the base catalog table underlying a catalog view is usually (but not always) the same as the name of the view with a "SYS" prefix added.

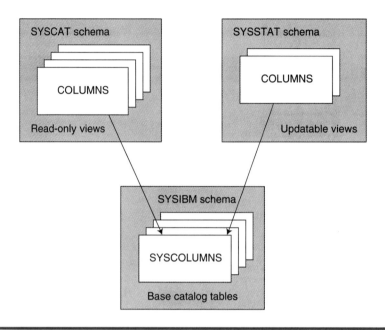

Figure D-1: Views of the System Catalog Tables

D.1 SYSCAT CATALOG VIEWS

All the following views are contained in the SYSCAT schema. None of these views are updatable. The catalog columns do not permit null values, except where noted.

D.1.1 CHECKS

Each row represents a check constraint. Each check constraint applies to a specific table.

Column	Description
CONSTNAME Varchar(18)	Name of the check constraint. Constraint names (including all types of constraints) must be unique within a table. If no name is specified for a constraint when it is created, the system will generate a name automatically.
DEFINER Char(8)	Userid of the definer of the check constraint.

Column	Description
TABSCHEMA Char(8)	Qualified name of the table to which this constraint applies.
TABNAME Varchar(18)	
CREATE_TIME Timestamp	The time at which the constraint was defined. This timestamp is used in resolving functions that are used in this constraint. When the constraint is enforced, no function will be used that was created after the definition of the constraint.
FUNC_PATH Varchar(254)	The function path that was effective at the time the constraint was defined. This function path governs the resolution of functions used by the constraint.
TEXT Clob(32K)	The text of the CHECK clause of the check constraint, exactly as typed by the constraint definer.

D.1.2 COLCHECKS

Each row represents some column that is referenced by a check constraint. This catalog table is useful in finding the check constraints that apply to a given column.

Column	Description
CONSTNAME Varchar(18)	Name of the check constraint. Constraint names (including all types of constraints) must be unique within a table. If no name is specified for a constraint when it is created, the system will generate a name automatically.
TABSCHEMA Char(8)	Qualified name of the table containing the referenced column.
TABNAME Varchar(18)	
COLNAME Varchar(18)	Name of the column that is referenced by the check constraint.

D.1.3 COLDIST

This catalog table contains statistics used by the query optimizer. Each row describes either the nth most frequent value of some column, or the nth quantile (cumulative distribution) value for some column. Statistics are kept for columns of real tables only (not views).

Column	Description
TABSCHEMA Char(8)	Qualified name of the table to which this row applies.
TABNAME Varchar(18)	
COLNAME Varchar(18)	Name of the column to which this row applies.
TYPE Char(1)	Indicates the type of data contained in this row. F = Frequent value Q = Quantile value (for example, if five quantile values are maintained for a given column, 20% of the column values will be less than the first quantile value, 40% of the column values will be less than the second quantile value, and so on)
SEQNO Smallint	If TYPE = F, then n in this column identifies the nth most frequent value. If TYPE = Q, then n in this column identifies the nth quantile value.
COLVALUE Varchar(33) (allows nulls)	The data value, as a character literal, such as $1.23E - 4$. If the length of the literal is greater than 33 characters, it is truncated. A distinct-type value is represented as a value of the underlying base datatype. A null value in COLVALUE indicates that the value being described is null.
VALCOUNT Integer	If TYPE = F, then VALCOUNT is the number of occurrences of COLVALUE in the column. If TYPE = Q, then VALCOUNT is the number of rows whose value is less than or equal to COLVALUE.

D.1.4 COLUMNS

Each row represents a column of a table or view. The columns of the catalog tables and views are listed in COLUMNS, along with the columns of user-defined tables and views.

Column	Description
TABSCHEMA Char(8)	The qualified name of the table or view containing this column.
TABNAME Varchar(18)	
COLNAME Varchar(18)	The name of the column.
COLNO Smallint	The ordinal position of this column among the columns in its table or view (first column = 0).

Column	Description
TYPESCHEMA Char(8)	Qualified name of the datatype of this column.
TYPENAME Varchar(18)	
LENGTH Integer	Maximum length of the data in this column. Zero if the datatype of the column is a distinct type. For double-byte string columns, LENGTH is expressed in characters (multiply by two to get the length in bytes).
SCALE Smallint	Scale if the column datatype is Decimal; zero otherwise.
DEFAULT Varchar(254) (allows nulls)	The default value of the column, expressed as a literal in character-string format. Quotes are used around strings that represent character values, to distinguish them from special registers such as CURRENT DATE. The default value of a distinct type is represented as a casting expression such as SHOESIZE(8). If a column has no default, the value of DEFAULT is the null value. If a column has a default and the default is null, the value of DEFAULT is the unquoted string NULL.
NULLS Char(1)	Y = Column allows null values. N = Column does not allow null values.
CODEPAGE Smallint	Code page used to interpret values in this column. Zero for noncharacter datatypes.
LOGGED Char(1)	Applies only to columns whose datatype is Blob, Clob, Dbclob, or a distinct type based on one of the LOB datatypes (blank otherwise). Y = Column is logged. N = Column is not logged.
COMPACT Char(1)	Applies only to columns whose datatype is Blob, Clob, Dbclob, or a distinct type based on one of the LOB datatypes (blank otherwise). Y = Column is compacted to occupy minimum storage (may adversely affect update performance). N = Column is not compacted.
COLCARD Integer	Number of distinct values in the column (–1 if unknown).
HIGH2KEY Varchar(33)	Second highest data value in the column, represented as a literal in character-string format (zero-length string if unknown).
LOW2KEY Varchar(33)	Second lowest data value in the column, represented as a literal in character-string format (zero-length string if unknown).
AVGCOLLEN Integer	Average length of column values (–1 if unknown or if the datatype of the column is a long or LOB datatype).

Column	Description
KEYSEQ Smallint (allows nulls)	The ordinal position of this column within the primary key of its table, starting with 1 for the first column in the primary key (null if the column is not a part of the primary key).
NQUANTILES Smallint	The number of quantile values recorded in the COLDIST catalog table for this column (–1 if no statistics are available for this column).
NMOSTFREQ Smallint	The number of most frequent values recorded in the COLDIST catalog table for this column (–1 if no statistics are available for this column).
REMARKS Varchar(254) (allows nulls)	Descriptive comment provided by user via COMMENT ON COLUMN statement.

D.1.5 CONSTDEP

Each row represents a dependency of a constraint on some other object. Each constraint applies to a specific table.

Column	Description
CONSTNAME Varchar(18)	Name of the constraint. Constraint names (including all types of constraints) must be unique within a table. If no name is specified for a constraint when it is created, the system will generate a name automatically.
TABSCHEMA Char(8)	Qualified name of the table to which the constraint applies.
TABNAME Varchar(18)	
BTYPE Char(1)	Type of the base object on which the constraint depends. Values: F = Function instance
BSCHEMA Char(8)	Qualified name of the base object on which the constraint depends. In V2, the base object is always a user-defined function. No dependencies are recorded on built-in functions, since these functions cannot be dropped.
BNAME Varchar(18)	

D.1.6 DATATYPES

Each row represents a datatype. Both built-in and user-defined datatypes are represented.

Column	Description
TYPESCHEMA Char(8)	Qualified name of the datatype. For built-in datatypes, the schema name is SYSIBM.
TYPENAME Varchar(18)	
DEFINER Char(8)	Userid under which the datatype was created.
SOURCESCHEMA Char(8) (allows nulls)	Qualified name of the source datatype for distinct types. Null for built-in datatypes.
SOURCENAME Varchar(18) (allows nulls)	
METATYPE Char(1)	S = System (built-in) datatype T = Distinct (user-defined) datatype
TYPEID Smallint	Internal datatype identifier.
SOURCETYPEID Smallint (allows nulls)	Internal datatype identifier of source datatype (null for built-in datatypes).
LENGTH Integer	Maximum length of the datatype. Zero for built-in parameterized datatypes such as Decimal and Varchar.
SCALE Smallint	Scale for distinct types based on the built-in Decimal datatype. Zero for all other datatypes (including Decimal itself).
CODEPAGE Smallint	For string datatypes and distinct types based on string datatypes, the code page used to interpret values of this datatype. Zero for all other datatypes.
CREATE_TIME Timestamp	Creation time of the datatype.
REMARKS Varchar(254) (allows nulls)	Descriptive comment supplied by a user via COMMENT ON DISTINCT TYPE statement.

D.1.7 DBAUTH

Each row represents a set of database-level authorities that have been granted by some grantor to some grantee, which may be an individual user or a group. All privileges granted by a given grantor to a given grantee are recorded in the same row of DBAUTH. All authorities apply to the database that contains the catalog table.

Column	Description
GRANTOR Char(8)	Userid of grantor of authority.
GRANTEE Char(8)	Receiver (holder) of authority. This name may identify an individual user or a group. Groups are defined and managed by the operating system.
GRANTEETYPE Char(1)	U = Grantee is an individual user. G = Grantee is a group.
DBADMAUTH Char(1)	Database Administration authority. Y = held, N = not held
CREATETABAUTH Char(1)	Authority to create tables in the database. Y = held, N = not held
BINDADDAUTH Char(1)	Authority to create (bind) packages in the database. Y = held, N = not held
CONNECTAUTH Char(1)	Authority to connect to the database. Y = held, N = not held
NOFENCEAUTH Char(1)	Authority to create nonfenced external functions in the database. Y = held, N = not held

D.1.8 EVENTMONITORS

Each row represents an Event Monitor. Event Monitors are created by the CREATE EVENT MONITOR statement and controlled by the SET EVENT MONITOR STATE statement. Each Event Monitor monitors a set of events in the database and writes information about them into a given file or pipe.

Column	Description
EVMONNAME Varchar(18)	Name of Event Monitor. Since Event Monitor names are global in a database, they have no schema names.
DEFINER Char(8)	Userid of the user who defined the Event Monitor.

Column	Description
TARGET_TYPE Char(1)	The type of the target to which event data is written. F = File P = Pipe
TARGET Varchar(246)	The name of the target to which event data is written. If the target is a pipe, this column contains the name of the pipe. If the target is a file, this column contains the absolute path name of the directory into which the file will be written. The names of the files to be generated in this directory are 00000001.EVT, 00000002.EVT, and so on.
MAXFILES Integer (allows nulls)	Maximum number of event files that this Event Monitor will generate in the target directory. Null if there is no maximum or if the target type is not FILE.
MAXFILESIZE Integer (allows nulls)	Maximum size (in 4K pages) that each event file can reach before the Event Monitor creates a new file. Null if there is no maximum or if the target type is not FILE.
BUFFERSIZE Integer (allows nulls)	Size (in 4K pages) of the buffer used by the Event Monitor to accumulate event data before writing it into an event file. Null if the target type is not FILE.
IO_MODE Char(1) (allows nulls)	Indicates what happens if an event is detected when the buffer is full. B = Blocked; wait for buffer to be written to disk, then record event. (Prevents loss of data but may adversely affect system performance.) N = Not blocked. (Events may be lost during writing of buffer to disk. Less impact on system performance.) Null if target type is not FILE.
WRITE_MODE Char(1) (allows nulls)	Indicates how this monitor handles existing event data when the monitor is activated. Values: A = Append data to existing file. R = Replace existing file with new file. Null if target type is not FILE.
AUTOSTART Char(1)	Indicates whether the Event Monitor will be activated automatically when the server is started (by a DB2START command). Y = Yes, Event Monitor is activated automatically. N = No, Event Monitor is not activated until a SET EVENT MONITOR STATE command is executed.
REMARKS Varchar(254) (allows nulls)	Reserved for future use by the COMMENT statement to record a descriptive remark about the Event Monitor.

D.1.9 EVENTS

Each row represents an event that is being monitored by some Event Monitor.

Column	Description
EVMONNAME Varchar(18)	Name of Event Monitor that is monitoring this event. An Event Monitor may monitor more than one event. Since Event Monitor names are global in a database, they have no schema names.
TYPE Varchar(18)	The type of event being monitored. The possible values of this column are: DATABASE CONNECTIONS TABLES STATEMENTS TRANSACTIONS DEADLOCKS TABLESPACES
FILTER Clob(32K) (allows nulls)	The full text of the WHERE clause that defines the event that is being monitored, as it was typed in the CREATE EVENT MONITOR statement.

D.1.10 FUNCPARMS

Each row represents either a parameter or the result of a function that has an entry in the FUNCTIONS catalog table.

Column	Description
FUNCSCHEMA Char(8) FUNCNAME Varchar(18)	Qualified name of the function for which this row describes a parameter or result. Several function instances can have the same qualified name, if they have different signatures (this is called *overloading*).
SPECIFICNAME Varchar(18)	Specific name of the function for this row describes a parameter or result. The specific name of a function instance must be unique within its schema.
ROWTYPE Char(1)	Indicates what is described by this row. Values: P = A parameter of the function R = The result of the function, before casting C = The result of the function, after casting (for more details on casting, see the "CAST FROM" clause of the CREATE FUNCTION statement)
ORDINAL Smallint	If ROWTYPE = P, the ordinal position of this parameter among all the parameters of the function; otherwise zero.

Column	Description
TYPESCHEMA Char(8)	Qualified name of the datatype of the parameter or result.
TYPENAME Varchar(18)	
LENGTH Integer	Maximum length of the parameter or result. Zero if the parameter or result is a distinct type or has no well-defined maximum length.
SCALE Smallint	Scale of the parameter or result. Zero if the parameter or result is a distinct type or has no well-defined scale.
CODEPAGE Smallint	Code page used to interpret the parameter or result (zero if it is not a string datatype).
CAST_FUNCID Integer (allows nulls)	Internal Function ID of function used to cast the argument (if this function is sourced on another function) or result (if ROWTYPE = C). Null otherwise.

D.1.11 FUNCTIONS

Contains a row for each user-defined function (including sourced and external functions, scalar and column functions). Also includes system-generated casting and comparison functions, but does not include built-in functions.

Column	Description
FUNCSCHEMA Char(8)	Qualified name of the function. Several function instances can have the same qualified name, if they have different signatures (this is called *overloading*).
FUNCNAME Varchar(18)	
SPECIFICNAME Varchar(18)	Specific name of the function instance (must be unique within its schema).
DEFINER Char(8)	Userid of the user who defined the function.
FUNCID Integer	Function identifier, assigned by the system for internal use.
RETURN_TYPE Smallint	Internal datatype identifier of result datatype of function. Can be joined with TYPEID column in DATATYPES catalog table.
ORIGIN Char(1)	Indicates how the function was created. E = User-defined, external function (written in C) U = User-defined, sourced function (sourced on another function) S = System-generated (for example, cast function of a distinct type)

Column	Description
TYPE Char(1)	S = Scalar function C = Column function
PARM_COUNT Smallint	Number of function parameters. See the FUNCPARMS catalog table for a description of the parameters.
PARM_SIGNATURE Varchar(180) for bit data	Concatenation of up to 90 parameter datatypes, in internal format. Used in function resolution and to guarantee uniqueness. Zero length if function takes no parameters.
CREATE_TIME Timestamp	Timestamp of function creation. Set to zero for V1 functions.
VARIANT Char(1)	Indicates whether two calls to the function with the same parameters will always yield the same result. Used in optimization of queries. Y = Variant (results may differ) N = Invariant (results are consistent) Blank if ORIGIN is not E.
SIDE_EFFECTS Char(1)	Indicates whether the function has side effects (any effect other than returning a result value). Used in optimization of queries. E = Function has side effects (hence number of invocations is important) N = No side effects Blank if ORIGIN is not E.
FENCED Char(1)	Indicates whether the function is allowed to run in the same address as the database or is restricted (fenced) to a separate address space for safety. Y = Fenced N = Not fenced Blank if ORIGIN is not E.
NULLCALL Char(1)	Indicates whether the function should be invoked when one of its arguments is null. Y = Yes, invoke the function with null arguments. N = No, if any argument is null, the function is not invoked and the result is implicitly set to null. Blank if ORIGIN is not E.
CAST_FUNCTION Char(1)	Indicates whether the function is a cast function (meaning that it can be invoked by the notation CAST(type1 AS type2). Y = This is a cast function. N = Not a cast function.
ASSIGN_FUNCTION Char(1)	Indicates whether the function can be invoked implicitly by assigning a value to a target of a different datatype. For example, assigning an Integer to a column of distinct type Hatsize based on Integer will implicitly invoke the function hatsize(Integer). Y = Implicit assignment function N = Not an implicit assignment function

Column	Description
SCRATCHPAD Char(1)	Indicates whether this function has a scratchpad on which it can save information from one invocation to the next. Y = This function has a scratchpad. N = No scratchpad. Blank if ORIGIN is not E.
FINAL_CALL Char(1)	Indicates whether one extra call is made to this function at the end of processing an SQL statement (in addition to the calls for processing each row). Y = Final call is made. N = No final call. Blank if ORIGIN is not E.
LANGUAGE Char(8)	Implementation language of function body (or of the source function's body, if this function is defined on another function). Only C is supported in **V2**. Blank if ORIGIN is not E.
IMPLEMENTATION Varchar(254) (allows nulls)	If ORIGIN = E, contains the path name of the object code module that implements this function. If ORIGIN = U and the source function is built-in, this column contains the name and signature of the source function. Null otherwise.
SOURCE_SCHEMA Char(8) (allows nulls) SOURCE_SPECIFIC Varchar(18) (allows nulls)	If ORIGIN = U and the source function is a user-defined function, contains the specific name of the source function. If ORIGIN = U and the source function is built-in, SOURCE_SCHEMA is "SYSIBM" and SOURCE_SPECIFIC is "N/A for built-in." Null if ORIGIN is not "U."
IOS_PER_INVOC Double	Estimated number of input/output operations per invocation of the function (used in query optimization). –1 if not known.
INSTS_PER_INVOC Double	Estimated number of CPU instructions per invocation of the function (used in query optimization). –1 if not known.
IOS_PER_ARGBYTE Double	Estimated average number of input/output operations per byte of each input parameter (used in query optimization). –1 if not known.
INSTS_PER_ARGBYTE Double	Estimated average number of CPU instructions per byte of each input parameter (used in query optimization). –1 if not known.
PERCENT_ARGBYTES Smallint	Estimated average percent of its input parameter bytes that the function will actually read (used in query optimization). –1 if not known.
INITIAL_IOS Double	Estimated number of "startup" input/output operations performed on the first invocation of the function in an SQL statement (used in query optimization). –1 if not known.

Column	Description
INITIAL_INSTS Double	Estimated number of "startup" CPU instructions executed on the first invocation of the function in an SQL statement (used in query optimization). –1 if not known.
REMARKS Varchar(254) (allows nulls)	Descriptive comment supplied by a user via COMMENT ON FUNC-TION statement.

D.1.12 INDEXAUTH

Each row represents a privilege held on an index.

Column	Description
GRANTOR Char(8)	Userid of the user who granted the privilege (or SYSTEM, if the privilege was granted by the system to the creator of the index).
GRANTEE Char(8)	Receiver (holder) of privilege.
GRANTEETYPE Char(1)	U = Grantee is an individual user. G = Grantee is a group.
INDSCHEMA Char(8)	Qualified name of index on which the privilege is held.
INDNAME Varchar(18)	
CONTROLAUTH Char(1)	Y = Control privilege is held (required to drop the index). N = Control privilege is not held.

D.1.13 INDEXES

Each row represents an index.

Column	Description
INDSCHEMA Char(8)	Qualified name of the index.
INDNAME Varchar(18)	
DEFINER Char(8)	Userid of the user who created the index.

Column	Description
TABSCHEMA Char(8)	Qualified name of the table to which the index applies.
TABNAME Varchar(18)	
COLNAMES Varchar(320)	List of names of the columns to which the index applies. Each column name is preceded by a "+" if the index is ascending on that column, or by a "–" if the index is descending on that column.
UNIQUERULE Char(1)	D = Index allows duplicate key values. U = Key values are required to be unique. P = Index is used to support a primary key (implies unique key values).
COLCOUNT Smallint	The number of columns in the index key.
IID Smallint	Internal identifier of the index.
NLEAF Integer	Number of leaf pages (lowest-level pages) occupied by the index. –1 if not known.
NLEVELS Smallint	Number of levels in the index (used in optimizer cost formulas). –1 if not known.
FIRSTKEYCARD Integer	Number of different values in the first key column of the index. –1 if not known.
FULLKEYCARD Integer	Number of different values in the full index key. –1 if not known.
CLUSTERRATIO Smallint	A measure of how well the ordering of this index corresponds to the physical ordering of rows in storage (used in optimizer cost formulas). –1 if not known.
CLUSTERFACTOR Double	A finer measure of how well the index ordering corresponds to the physical ordering of rows in storage (used in optimizer cost formulas). –1 if not known.
USER_DEFINED Smallint	A 1 indicates that this index was created by a user. An index can be physically destroyed only if USER_DEFINED and SYSTEM_REQUIRED are both 0.
SYSTEM_REQUIRED Smallint	A 1 indicates that this index is being used by the system to enforce a primary key constraint. An index can be physically destroyed only if USER_DEFINED and SYSTEM_REQUIRED are both 0.
CREATE_TIME Timestamp	Time when the index was created.
STATS_TIME Timestamp (allows nulls)	The last time when any change was made to the recorded statistics for this index (for example, by the RUNSTATS utility). Null if no statistics are available for the index.

Column	Description
PAGE_FETCH_PAIRS Varchar(254) for bit data	A list of pairs of integers, represented in character form. Each pair represents the number of pages in a hypothetical buffer and the number of page fetches required to scan the index using that hypothetical buffer. (Zero-length string if no data available.)
REMARKS Varchar(254) (allows nulls)	Descriptive comment supplied by a user via COMMENT ON INDEX statement.

D.1.14 KEYCOLUSE

Lists all columns that participate in a key defined by a primary key or foreign key constraint.

Column	Description
CONSTNAME Varchar(18)	Name of the constraint. Constraint names (including all types of constraints) are unique within a table.
TABSCHEMA Char(8)	Qualified name of the table containing the column.
TABNAME Varchar(18)	
COLNAME Varchar(18)	Name of the column.
COLSEQ Smallint	Ordinal position of the column within the key (first column = 1).

D.1.15 PACKAGEAUTH

Each row represents a set of privileges on a package held by a user or by a group. A package represents the bound form of an application program.

Column	Description
GRANTOR Char(8)	Grantor of the privileges.
GRANTEE Char(8)	Receiver (holder) of the privileges.

Column	Description
GRANTEETYPE Char(1)	U = Grantee is an individual user. G = Grantee is a group.
PKGSCHEMA Char(8)	Qualified name of the package on which the privileges are held.
PKGNAME Char(8)	
CONTROLAUTH Char(1)	Indicates whether the control privilege (needed to drop the package) is held. Y = Privilege is held. N = Privilege is not held.
BINDAUTH Char(1)	Indicates whether the privilege to bind and rebind the package is held. Y = Privilege is held. N = Privilege is not held.
EXECUTEAUTH Char(1)	Indicates whether the privilege to execute the package is held. This privilege is required to successfully run the application program corresponding to this package. Y = Privilege is held. N = Privilege is not held.

D.1.16 PACKAGEDEP

Each row represents a dependency of a package on some object.

Column	Description
PKGSCHEMA Char(8)	Qualified name of the package.
PKGNAME Char(8)	
BINDER Char(8) (allows nulls)	User who bound the package.
BTYPE Char(1)	The type of the object on which the package depends. A = Alias F = Function instance (user-defined functions only) I = Index T = Table V = View

Column	Description
BSCHEMA Char(8) BNAME Varchar(18)	Qualified name of the object on which the package depends. If a function instance on which the package depends is dropped, the package becomes "inoperative" and must be explicitly rebound. If any other kind of object (or privilege) on which the package depends is dropped, the system will automatically attempt to rebind the package on its next use.
TABAUTH Smallint (allows nulls)	If BTYPE is T (table) or V (view), encodes the privileges that are required by this package (may include Select, Insert, Delete, and Update).
PUBLICPRIV Char(1)	Not used in V2. Planned to indicate whether the package is dependent on a public privilege.
TABUSAGE Smallint	If BTYPE is T (table), encodes the operations performed by this package on this table, either directly or indirectly (for example, via a trigger or cascading referential integrity constraint). May also indicate a usage of "Constraint" if the package relies on the existence of a specific constraint on this table.
COLUSAGE Varchar(3000) (allows nulls)	If TABUSAGE indicates Update and/or Constraint usage, records the specific columns that are updated and/or to which the constraint applies. Encoding: one character per column.

D.1.17 PACKAGES

Each row describes a package that was created by binding some application program. The package is stored in the database and contains an optimized plan for executing each SQL statement in the program. This catalog table records some of the options that were specified on the PREP or BIND command that created the package. These options are used when the package is rebound, either implicitly or by an explicit REBIND command.

Column	Description
PKGSCHEMA Char(8) PKGNAME Char(8)	Qualified name of the package.
BOUNDBY Char(8)	Userid of user who bound the package.

Column	Description
VALID Char(1)	Indicates the status of the package. Y = Valid, ready for use. N = Not valid, but will be implicitly rebound on next use. The implicit rebind may restore the package to a valid state. X = Inoperative because some function instance used by the package no longer exists. An inoperative package will not be implicitly rebound; it can be restored to validity only by an explicit BIND or REBIND command.
UNIQUE_ID Char(8)	Time at which the package was originally created. This column serves as a timestamp to check for consistency between the application program and its package.
TOTAL_SECT Smallint	Number of sections in the package. Each section contains an optimized plan for executing one SQL statement.
FORMAT Char(1)	Format used by the package to represent dates and times. Codes: 0 = Derived from country code of database 1 = USA 2 = EUR 3 = ISO 4 = JIS 5 = LOCAL
ISOLATION Char(2) (allows nulls)	Isolation level of this package: RR = Repeatable Read RS = Read Stability CS = Cursor Stability UR = Uncommitted Read
BLOCKING Char(1) (allows nulls)	Cursor-blocking option. Controls whether rows of a query result are transmitted from server to client individually or in "blocks" for efficiency. N = No blocking used. B = Blocking used for fetch-only cursors. In ambiguous cases (no declaration of intent), cursors are assumed to be fetch-only. U = Blocking used for fetch-only cursors. In ambiguous cases (no declaration of intent), cursors are assumed to be updatable.
LANG_LEVEL Char(1) (allows nulls)	0 = SQL statements interpreted in compliance with IBM Systems Application Architecture (SAA) Level 1. Cursors to be used in positioned updates must be declared FOR UPDATE. 1 = SQL statements interpreted in compliance with Multivendor Integration Architecture (MIA) and SQL92 Standard. Cursors to used in positioned updates need not be declared FOR UPDATE.
FUNC_PATH Varchar(254)	The function path used when the package was last bound. The same function path is used on an implicit or explicit rebind of the package.
QUERYOPT Integer	Optimization class under which this package was bound. Values range from 0 to 9, indicating increasing levels of optimization.

Column	Description
EXPLAIN_LEVEL Char(1)	Explain level requested for this package. The Explain facility captures information about access plans in a form that can be displayed visually. (blank) = No Explain requested P = Plan Selection level
EXPLAIN_MODE Char(1)	Is the Tabular Explain facility active for this package? Y = Yes N = No
EXPLAIN_SNAPSHOT Char(1)	Is the Explain snapshot (Visual Explain) facility active for this package? Y = Yes N = No
SQLWARN Char(1)	Y = Positive values for SQLCODE, indicating warning conditions, are returned to the application program. N = Positive values for SQLCODE are suppressed and not returned to the application program.
EXPLICIT_BIND_TIME Timestamp	The time at which this package was last explicitly bound or rebound. When the package is implicitly rebound, no function instance will be selected that was created later than this time.
LAST_BIND_TIME Timestamp	Time at which the plan was last explicitly or implicitly bound or rebound. Used to check validity of EXPLAIN data.
CODEPAGE Smallint	Code page used by application program to interpret character-string data (–1 if not known).
REMARKS Varchar(254) (allows nulls)	Descriptive comment supplied by a user via COMMENT ON PACKAGE statement.

D.1.18 REFERENCES

Each row represents a referential integrity (foreign key) constraint.

Column	Description
CONSTNAME Varchar(18)	Name of the constraint. Constraint names (including all types of constraints) must be unique within a table. If no name is specified for a constraint when it is created, the system will generate a name automatically.
TABSCHEMA Char(8)	Qualified name of child table.
TABNAME Varchar(18)	

Column	Description
DEFINER Char(8)	User who created the constraint.
REFKEYNAME Varchar(18)	Name of the primary key constraint in the parent table.
REFTABSCHEMA Char(8)	Qualified name of parent table.
REFTABNAME Varchar(18)	
COLCOUNT Smallint	Number of columns in the foreign key (in the child table).
DELETERULE Char(1)	Indicates what happens when a row is deleted from the parent table. A = No Action; deletions from the parent table are not allowed if matching rows exist in the child table. C = Cascade; matching rows are deleted from the child table. N = Set Null; foreign key is set to null in matching rows of the child table. R = Restrict; deletions from the parent table are not allowed if matching rows exist in the child table.
UPDATERULE Char(1)	Indicates what happens when a primary key is updated in the parent table. R = Restrict; update not allowed if matching rows exist in child table. A = No Action; update not allowed if matching rows exist in child table.
CREATE_TIME Timestamp	Time at which the referential constraint was defined.
FK_COLNAMES Varchar(320)	List of column names that constitute the foreign key in the child table.
PK_COLNAMES Varchar(320)	List of column names that constitute the primary key in the parent table.

D.1.19 STATEMENTS

Each row contains the text of an SQL statement used to generate one section of a package.

Column	Description
PKGSCHEMA Char(8)	Qualified name of the package.
PKGNAME Char(8)	

Column	Description
STMTNO Smallint	Line number of SQL statement within the source program.
SECTNO Smallint	Section number within the package.
SEQNO Smallint	Sequence number of this row. If the SQL statement occupies more than 3,600 bytes, it is stored in multiple rows, and the SEQNO column is used to number the rows used for a given SQL statement.
TEXT Varchar(3600)	The text of the SQL statement.

D.1.20 TABAUTH

Each row represents a set of privileges on a table or view, granted by a particular grantor to a particular grantee, which may be an individual user or a group. All the privileges granted by a given grantor to a given grantee on a given table or view are combined into a single row of SYSTABAUTH.

Column	Description
GRANTOR Char(8)	Grantor of the privilege.
GRANTEE Char(8)	Receiver (holder) of the privilege.
GRANTEETYPE Char(1)	U = Grantee is an individual user. G = Grantee is a group.
TABSCHEMA Char(8)	Qualified name of the table or view to which the privilege applies.
TABNAME Varchar(18)	
CONTROLAUTH Char(1)	CONTROL privilege; needed to drop the table or view. Implies all other privileges. Y = Privilege is held. N = Not held.
ALTERAUTH Char(1)	ALTER privilege; needed to alter a table or to comment on a table or view. Y = Privilege is held. N = Not held.

Column	Description
DELETEAUTH Char(1)	DELETE privilege; needed to delete rows from a table or view. Y = Privilege is held. N = Not held.
INDEXAUTH Char(1)	INDEX privilege; needed to create an index on a table. Y = Privilege is held. N = Not held.
INSERTAUTH Char(1)	INSERT privilege; needed to insert rows into a table or view. Y = Privilege is held. N = Not held.
SELECTAUTH Char(1)	SELECT privilege; needed to read data from a table or view. Y = Privilege is held. N = Not held.
REFAUTH Char(1)	REFERENCE privilege; needed to create or drop a foreign key constraint that references this table as the parent table. Y = Privilege is held. N = Not held.
UPDATEAUTH Char(1)	UPDATE privilege; needed to update rows of the table or view. Y = Privilege is held. N = Not held.

D.1.21 TABCONST

Each row represents a constraint on a table. Includes check, primary key, and foreign key constraints.

Column	Description
CONSTNAME Varchar(18)	Name of the constraint. Constraint names (including all types of constraints) must be unique within a table. If no name is specified for a constraint when it is created, the system will generate a name automatically.
TABSCHEMA Char(8)	Qualified name of the table to which the constraint applies.
TABNAME Varchar(18)	
DEFINER Char(8)	Userid under which the constraint was defined.

Column	Description
TYPE Char(1)	Type of the constraint. K = Check constraint P = Primary key constraint F = Foreign key (referential integrity) constraint
REMARKS Varchar(254) (allows nulls)	Descriptive comment supplied by a user via COMMENT ON CONSTRAINT statement.

D.1.22 TABLES

Each row represents a table, view, or alias. The system catalog tables and views are represented in TABLES, along with user-defined tables and views.

Column	Description
TABSCHEMA Char(8)	Qualified name of the table, view, or alias.
TABNAME Varchar(18)	
DEFINER Char(8)	Userid of the user who created the table, view, or alias.
TYPE Char(1)	Indicates the type of the object being described. T = Table V = View A = Alias
STATUS Char(1)	Indicates whether the object is in a special status. N = Normal status C = Check Pending status (applies to tables) X = Inoperative status (applies to views)
BASE_TABSCHEMA Char(8) (allows nulls)	If TYPE = A, these columns identify the table, view, or alias that is referenced by this alias; otherwise they are NULL. The object referenced by an alias is not guaranteed to exist.
BASE_TABNAME Varchar(18) (allows nulls)	
CREATE_TIME Timestamp	Time of creation of the table, view, or alias.

Column	Description
STATS_TIME Timestamp (allows nulls)	Last time when any change was made to recorded statistics for this table. Null if no statistics are available.
COLCOUNT Smallint	The number of columns in the table or view.
TABLEID Smallint	Internal table identifier.
TBSPACEID Smallint	Internal identifier of the primary tablespace in which this table is stored. Zero for aliases and views.
CARD Integer	Number of rows in the table. –1 if unknown or if the object being described is not a table.
NPAGES Integer	Number of pages occupied by rows of this table. –1 if unknown or if the object being described is not a table.
FPAGES Integer	Total number of pages in the file used to store this table. –1 if unknown or if the object being described is not a table.
OVERFLOW Integer	The number of overflow records associated with this table. –1 if unknown or if the object being described is not a table.
TBSPACE Varchar(18) (allows nulls)	The name of the primary tablespace in which rows of the table are stored. Null for aliases and views.
INDEX_TBSPACE Varchar(18) (allows nulls)	The name of the tablespace that holds all the indexes created on this table. If this column is null, the indexes are created in the primary tablespace.
LONG_TBSPACE Varchar(18) (allows nulls)	The name of the tablespace that holds all large objects stored in this table (datatypes Long Varchar, Long Vargraphic, Blob, Clob, and Dbclob). If this column is null, the large objects are contained in the primary tablespace.
PARENTS Smallint (allows nulls)	The number of parent tables to which this table is related as a child table in a referential integrity constraint. Zero for aliases and views.
CHILDREN Smallint (allows nulls)	The number of child tables to which this table is related as a parent table in a referential integrity constraint. Zero for aliases and views.
SELFREFS Smallint (allows nulls)	The number of referential integrity constraints in which this table is related to itself as both parent and child. Zero for aliases and views.
KEYCOLUMNS Smallint (allows nulls)	The number of columns in the primary key of this table. Zero for aliases and views.

Column	Description
KEYINDEXID Smallint (allows nulls)	The internal identifier of the index that is used to enforce uniqueness of the primary key for this table. Zero for aliases and views.
KEYUNIQUE Smallint	Number of unique key constraints that are defined on this table. Contains zero since this type of constraint is not yet supported by V2.
CHECKCOUNT Smallint	Number of check constraints that are defined on this table. Zero for aliases and views.
DATACAPTURE Char(1)	Indicates whether updates to this table are captured and propagated to other systems by the Data Propagator product. Y = Table participates in data propagation. N = Does not participate in data propagation.
CONST_CHECKED Char(32)	Indicates the status of the constraints that apply to this table. Byte 1 represents all referential integrity constraints, and byte 2 represents all check constraints. The other bytes are reserved. Status is encoded as follows: Y = Constraints are in normal status, checked and enforced by the system. U = Constraints are not checked by the system and may be violated, but access to the table is allowed. A table can be put into this status by the statement SET CONSTRAINTS FOR <table> IMMEDIATE UNCHECKED. N = Constraints are in Check Pending status (temporarily suspended, usually during loading of data). Constraints are not checked by the system, and normal access to the table is not allowed.
REMARKS Varchar(254) (allows nulls)	Descriptive comment provided by a user via the COMMENT ON TABLE or COMMENT ON ALIAS statement.

D.1.23 TABLESPACES

Each row represents a tablespace.

Column	Description
TBSPACE Varchar(18)	Name of the tablespace. Tablespaces have one-part names (not qualified by a schema name).
DEFINER Char(8)	User who defined the tablespace.
CREATE_TIME Timestamp	Time when the tablespace was created.

Column	Description
TBSPACEID Integer	Internal tablespace identifier.
TBSPACETYPE Char(1)	The type of the tablespace. S = System-managed space D = Database-managed space
DATATYPE Char(1)	The type of data that can be stored in the tablespace. A = All types of data L = Long data only T = Temporary tables only
EXTENTSIZE Integer	The size of the extent used by this tablespace, in 4K pages. This many pages are written to one container in the tablespace before switching to the next container.
PREFETCHSIZE Integer	The number of 4K pages to be read when prefetch is performed in this tablespace.
OVERHEAD Double	The time required to begin an input/output operation, in milliseconds, averaged over the containers in this tablespace. Consists of a combination of controller overhead and disk seek and latency time.
TRANSFERRATE Double	Rate at which data can be read or written in this tablespace. Expressed in terms of milliseconds required to read one 4K page into a buffer, averaged over the containers in this tablespace.
REMARKS Varchar(254) (allows nulls)	Descriptive comment provided by a user via the COMMENT ON TABLESPACE statement.

D.1.24 TRIGDEP

Each row represents a dependency of a trigger on some other object. If an object that a trigger depends on is dropped, the trigger becomes inoperative.

Column	Description
TRIGSCHEMA Char(8)	The qualified name of the trigger.
TRIGNAME Varchar(18)	
BTYPE Char(1)	The type of the object that the trigger depends on. A = Alias F = Function instance T = Table V = View

Column	Description
BSCHEMA Char(8)	The qualified name of the object that the trigger depends on. If the object is a function instance, this is the specific name of the function instance.
BNAME Varchar(18)	

TABAUTH
    Smallint
    (allows nulls)
	If BTYPE = T or V, this column encodes the operations that are performed by this trigger on the table or view. This is a means of recording a dependency of the trigger on the privileges required to perform these operations.

D.1.25 TRIGGERS

Each row represents a trigger.

Column	Description
TRIGSCHEMA Char(8)	The qualified name of the trigger.
TRIGNAME Varchar(18)	
DEFINER Char(8)	Authid under which the trigger was defined.
TABSCHEMA Char(8)	The qualified name of the table to which this trigger applies.
TABNAME Varchar(18)	
TRIGTIME Char(1)	The time when triggered actions are applied to the base table, relative to the event that activated the trigger. B = Trigger applied before event A = Trigger applied after event
TRIGEVENT Char(1)	The event that activates the trigger. I = Insert D = Delete U = Update
GRANULARITY Char(1)	Indicates whether the trigger body is executed only once for the SQL statement that activates the trigger, or once for each row that is modified in the database. R = Row S = Statement
VALID Char(1)	Y = Trigger is valid. X = Trigger is inoperative. The definition of the trigger is retained in the catalog table, but in order to become valid the trigger must be recreated by a CREATE TRIGGER statement.

Column	Description
TEXT Clob(32K)	The full text of the CREATE TRIGGER statement, exactly as typed.
CREATE_TIME Timestamp	The time at which the trigger was created. This timestamp is used in resolving functions used by the trigger. No function will be selected that was created after the trigger was defined.
FUNC_PATH Varchar(254)	Records the function path at the time the trigger was defined. Used in resolving functions used by the trigger.
REMARKS Varchar(254) (allows nulls)	A descriptive comment supplied by a user via the COMMENT ON TRIGGER statement.

D.1.26 VIEWDEP

Each row represents a dependency of a view on some other object.

Column	Description
VIEWSCHEMA Char(8)	The qualified name of the view.
VIEWNAME Varchar(18)	
DEFINER Char(8) (allows nulls)	The user who created the view.
BTYPE Char(1)	The type of object that the view depends on. A = Alias F = User-defined function instance T = Table V = View
BSCHEMA Char(8)	The qualified name of the object that the view depends on.
BNAME Varchar(18)	
TABAUTH Smallint (allows nulls)	If BTYPE is T (table) or V (view), this column indicates which privileges on the underlying table or view are inherited by this view. Revocation of one of these underlying privileges from the definer of the view will cause loss of the same privilege on the view.

D.1.27 VIEWS

Each row represents a view.

Column	Description
VIEWSCHEMA Char(8)	The qualified name of the view.
VIEWNAME Varchar(18)	
DEFINER Char(8)	The user who created the view.
SEQNO Smallint	If the view definition is longer than 3,600 characters, it must be stored in fragments, one fragment per row. This column is a sequence number that permits the fragments to be reassembled into a complete view definition.
VIEWCHECK Char(1)	Indicates the check option that was specified when the view was created. The check option requires rows that are inserted or updated in the view to satisfy the view definition after the insertion or update. N = No check option L = Local check option C = Cascaded check option
READONLY Char(1)	Indicates whether the view is inherently read-only because of its definition. Y = View is read-only. N = Rows of the view can be inserted, deleted, or updated by users with appropriate authorization.
VALID Char(1)	Indicates whether the view is currently in a valid state. Y = View is valid. X = View is inoperative; its definition is retained in the catalog table, but before it can be used it must be recreated by a CREATE VIEW statement.
FUNC_PATH Varchar(254)	The function path of the view creator at the time the view was defined. This path is used for resolving functions used inside the view definition. Function resolution for this view is also influenced by the CREATE_TIME timestamp in the TABLES entry that describes this view.
TEXT Varchar(3600)	The full text of the CREATE VIEW statement, exactly as typed. If the text is longer than 3,600 characters, it is stored in fragments, one per row.

D.2 SYSSTAT UPDATABLE CATALOG VIEWS

All the following catalog views are contained in the SYSSTAT schema. These views are defined in such a way that users see only those rows that they are authorized to update. Users with DBADM authority see all the updatable catalog rows, but other users see only those rows that pertain to objects that they own or for which they have CONTROL privilege.

The SYSSTAT catalog views can be updated by SQL statements, much like other tables. The views support only SQL UPDATE statements, not INSERT or DELETE statements. Furthermore, in each view, only certain columns are updatable. In the following descriptions, only the columns listed below the double line in each catalog are updatable.

Each of the updatable catalog views is defined with certain checks to ensure that the values assigned to its updatable columns are valid statistical values that can be used by the query optimizer. Catalog columns do not permit null values, except as noted.

D.2.1 COLDIST

This view contains statistics gathered about the distribution of data values in the columns of base tables, for use by the query optimizer. Each row describes either the nth most frequent value of some column, or the nth quantile (cumulative distribution) value for some column. Users of this view can see only statistics on those tables for which they hold CONTROL privilege (but users with DBADM authority can see statistics on all tables).

Column	Description
TABSCHEMA Char(8)	Qualified name of the table to which this row applies.
TABNAME Varchar(18)	
COLNAME Varchar(18)	Name of the column to which this row applies.
TYPE Char(1)	Indicates the type of data contained in this row. F = Frequent value Q = Quantile value (for example, if five quantile values are maintained for a given column, 20% of the column values will be less than the first quantile value, 40% of the column values will be less than the second quantile value, and so on)

Column	Description
SEQNO Smallint	If TYPE = F, then *n* in this column identifies the *n*th most frequent value. If TYPE = Q, then *n* in this column identifies the *n*th quantile value.
COLVALUE Varchar(33) (allows nulls)	The data value, as a character literal, such as 1.23E – 4. If the length of the literal is greater than 33 characters, it is truncated. A distinct-type value is represented as a value of the underlying base datatype. A null value in COLVALUE indicates that the value being described is null.
VALCOUNT Integer	If TYPE = F, then VALCOUNT is the number of occurrences of COLVALUE in the column. If TYPE = Q, then VALCOUNT is the number of rows whose value is less than or equal to COLVALUE.

D.2.2 COLUMNS

This view contains information about the values stored in the columns of base tables. Users of this view can see only information on those tables for which they hold CONTROL privilege (but users with DBADM authority can see information on all tables).

Column	Description
TABSCHEMA Char(8)	The qualified name of the table or view containing this column.
TABNAME Varchar(18)	
COLNAME Varchar(18)	The name of the column.
COLCARD Integer	Number of distinct values in the column (–1 if unknown).
HIGH2KEY Varchar(33)	Second highest data value in the column, represented as a literal in character-string format (zero-length string if unknown).
LOW2KEY Varchar(33)	Second lowest data value in the column, represented as a literal in character-string format (zero-length string if unknown).
AVGCOLLEN Integer	Average length of column values (–1 if unknown or if the datatype of the column is a long or LOB datatype).

D.2.3 FUNCTIONS

This view contains information about the cost of executing user-defined functions. This information may be helpful to the optimizer in scheduling the execution of these functions. Information about functions is not provided by the RUNSTATS facility, so the estimates in FUNCTIONS are initialized to –1 (unknown) and remain unknown unless updated by the user. The system supplies default assumptions whenever function costs are unknown. A user of this view sees only information on those function instances whose schema name matches his or her userid (but a user with DBADM authority can see information on all function instances).

Column	Description
FUNCSCHEMA Char(8)	Qualified name of the function.
FUNCNAME Varchar(18)	
SPECIFICNAME Varchar(18)	Specific name of the function instance.
IOS_PER_INVOC Double	Estimated number of input/output operations per invocation of the function. –1 if not known (0 assumed).
INSTS_PER_INVOC Double	Estimated number of CPU instructions per invocation of the function. –1 if not known.
IOS_PER_ARGBYTE Double	Estimated average number of input/output operations per byte of each input parameter. –1 it not known (0 assumed).
INSTS_PER_ARGBYTE Double	Estimated average number of CPU instructions per byte of each input parameter. –1 if not known (0 assumed).
PERCENT_ARGBYTES Smallint	Estimated average percent of its input parameter bytes that the function will actually read. –1 if not known (100 assumed).
INITIAL_IOS Double	Estimated number of "startup" input/output operations performed on the first invocation of the function in an SQL statement. –1 if not known (0 assumed).
INITIAL_INSTS Double	Estimated number of "startup" CPU instructions executed on the first invocation of the function in an SQL statement. –1 if not known (0 assumed).

D.2.4 INDEXES

This view contains statistical information about indexes and their key values. Users of this view can see only information about those indexes for which they hold CONTROL privilege (but users with DBADM authority can see information on all indexes).

Column	Description
INDSCHEMA Char(8)	The qualified name of the index.
INDNAME Varchar(18)	
NLEAF Integer	Number of leaf pages (lowest-level pages) occupied by the index. –1 if not known.
NLEVELS Smallint	Number of levels in the index. –1 if not known.
FIRSTKEYCARD Integer	Number of different values in the first key column of the index. –1 if not known.
FULLKEYCARD Integer	Number of different values in the full index key. –1 if not known.
CLUSTERRATIO Smallint	A measure of how well the ordering of this index corresponds to the physical ordering of rows in storage. –1 if not known. Values may range from 0 to 100.
CLUSTERFACTOR Double	A finer measure of how well the index ordering corresponds to the physical ordering of rows in storage (used in optimizer cost formulas). –1 if not known. Values may range from 0 to 1.
PAGE_FETCH_PAIRS Varchar(254) for bit data	A list of pairs of integers, represented in character form. Each pair represents the number of pages in a hypothetical buffer and the number of page fetches required to scan the index using that hypothetical buffer. (Zero-length string if no data available.)

D.2.5 TABLES

This view contains statistical information about the values stored in base (user) tables. Users of this view can see only information about tables for which they hold CONTROL privilege (but users with DBADM authority can see information on all base tables).

Column	Description
TABSCHEMA Char(8)	The qualified name of the table.
TABNAME Varchar(18)	
CARD Integer	Number of rows in the table (–1 if unknown).
NPAGES Integer	Number of pages occupied by rows of this table (–1 if unknown).
FPAGES Integer	Total number of pages in the file used to store this table (–1 if unknown).
OVERFLOW Integer	The number of overflow records associated with this table (–1 if unknown).

D.3 STORED-PROCEDURE CATALOG TABLE

As discussed in Section 7.1.4, a catalog table named DB2CLI.PROCEDURES is used to list all the stored procedures that are available in a given database, in support of the CLI functions `SQLProcedures()` and `SQLProcedureColumns()`. Unlike the system catalog tables in SYSCAT and SYSSTAT, the PROCEDURES catalog table is not maintained automatically by the system. Instead, it must be created and maintained manually by a database administrator, using the procedures described in Section 7.1.4. The structure of the PROCEDURES catalog table is described below.

D.3.1 PROCEDURES

Each row represents a stored procedure.

Column	Description
PROCSCHEMA Varchar(18)	The qualified name of the stored procedure.
PROCNAME Varchar(18)	
DEFINER Varchar(8)	The user who created the stored procedure.

Column	Description
PKGSCHEMA Varchar(18)	The qualified name of the package that implements the stored procedure.
PKGNAME Varchar(18)	
PROC_LOCATION Varchar(254)	Path name of the executable program that implements the stored procedure.
PARM_STYLE Char(1)	Indicates the convention used to pass parameters to the stored procedure. Always set to the value "D."
LANGUAGE Char(8)	The programming language in which the stored procedure is written. Values: COBOL, C (applies also to C++), REXX, FORTRAN.
STAYRESIDENT Char(1)	Y = Stored procedure is retained in memory after execution. (blank) = Stored procedure is deleted from memory after execution.
RUNOPTS Varchar(254)	Reserved for future use.
PARM_LIST Varchar(3000)	A list of the parameters of the stored procedure. Parameters are assumed to be input parameters unless labelled OUT or INOUT. The following is an example of the syntax used to list the parameters: `x Varchar(20) IN, y Integer OUT, z Decimal(8,2) INOUT`
FENCED Char(1)	Y = Stored procedure is fenced (runs in separate address space). N = Stored procedure is not fenced (runs in same address space as database).
REMARKS Varchar(254) (allows nulls)	A user-supplied description of the stored procedure.
RESULT_SETS Smallint	The number of result sets returned by the stored procedure. Each result set is returned in the form of an open cursor.

APPENDIX

E Syntax for Host Variable Declarations in C and C++

This appendix summarizes the syntax that can be used for declaring host variables inside the SQL Declare Section of a C or C++ application program. In the syntax diagrams, items appearing in italics represent user-supplied names, lengths, and initial values. (Examples of host variable declarations, and an explanation of how they are used, can be found in Section 2.7.)

With each syntax diagram, a table is provided indicating the typecodes that correspond to the declarations in the diagram. Each datatype has two typecodes: an even typecode that indicates non-nullable data and an odd typecode that indicates nullable data. A host variable is considered nullable if it is used together with an indicator variable.

Some of the syntax diagrams in this appendix indicate that host variables can be declared as pointers. If a host variable is declared as a pointer, it must point to an object of a specific size, and it must be dereferenced each time it is used in an SQL statement. For example, the following code fragment declares host variables that are pointers to an integer and to an array of seven characters, respectively, and then uses these variables (properly dereferenced) in an SQL UPDATE statement:

```
EXEC SQL BEGIN DECLARE SECTION;
    long *p1;          /* pointer to long integer      */
    char (*p2)[7];   /* pointer to array of 7 chars */
EXEC SQL END DECLARE SECTION;

long newsalary = 25;
p1 = &newsalary;
p2 = (char(*)[7])"123456";  /* cast string to proper type */

EXEC SQL
    UPDATE emp SET salary = :*p1 WHERE empno = :*p2;
```

E.1 BASIC DATATYPES

Host variables for the basic SQL datatypes are declared in the SQL Declare Section, using pure C/C++ syntax, as shown in the following syntax diagrams.

E.1.1 Numeric Host Variables

Host variables for exchanging numeric data are declared as follows:

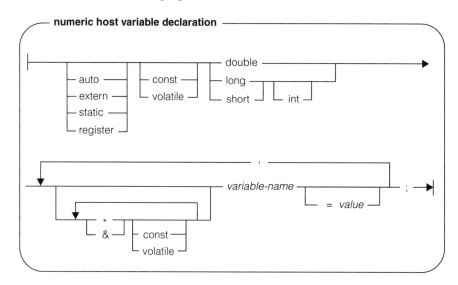

The SQL datatype of a numeric host variable is determined as shown in Table E-1.

TABLE E-1: SQL Datatypes Corresponding to Numeric Host Variables

If the declaration contains . . .	The SQL datatype is considered to be . . .	The SQLTYPE code for this datatype is . . . (not nullable/nullable)
double	Double	480/481
long	Integer	496/497
short	Smallint	500/501

E.1.2 String Host Variables

Host variables for exchanging string data in null-terminated form are declared as follows:

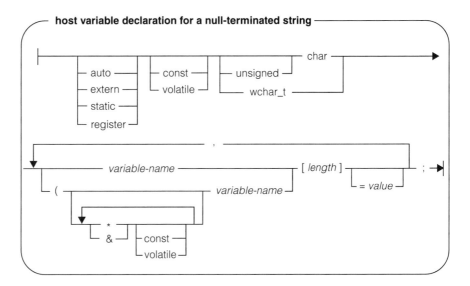

Notes:

- The precompiler permits a string-type variable to be declared without an explicit length, which implies a length of one character. To avoid confusion, we recommend always declaring an explicit length for string-type variables.

- Null-terminated variables should not be used to exchange data with columns declared FOR BIT DATA, since the data stored in these columns may contain binary zeros.

- If a variable is declared to be a pointer, it must point to an object of well-defined length. For example, char (*p)[20] is a pointer to a character string of length 20. Do not use the notation char *p to indicate a pointer to a string of indefinite length.

- Handling of double-byte strings is affected by the WCHARTYPE and LANG-LEVEL precompiler options. See the *DB2 Application Programming Guide* for details.

- To initialize a string variable of type wchar_t, use an L-type C literal such as L"double-byte data".

- The SQL datatype of the host variable is determined as shown in Table E-2.

TABLE E-2: SQL Datatypes Corresponding to Null-Terminated String Host Variables

If the declaration contains . . .	The SQL datatype is considered to be . . .	The SQLTYPE code for this datatype is . . . (not nullable/nullable)
char	Varchar (null-terminated)	460/461
wchar_t	Vargraphic (null-terminated)	400/401

Host variables for exchanging string data in length-prefix form are declared as follows:

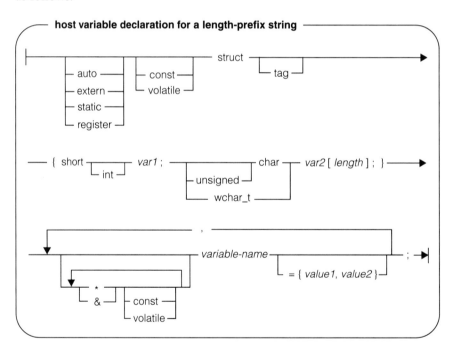

The SQL datatype of a length-prefix host variable is determined as shown in Table E-3.

TABLE E-3: SQL Datatypes Corresponding to Length-Prefix Host Variables

If the declaration contains . . .	The SQL datatype is considered to be . . .	The SQLTYPE code for this datatype is . . . (not nullable/nullable)
`char`, and length is 4,000 or less	Varchar	448/449
`char`, and length is between 4,001 and 32,700	Long Varchar	456/457
`wchar_t`, and length is 2,000 or less	Vargraphic	464/465
`wchar_t`, and length is between 2,001 and 16,350	Long Vargraphic	472/473

E.2 LARGE-OBJECT DATATYPES

V2 has introduced new datatypes called LOBs for representing large objects. Host variables for exchanging data using these new datatypes can be declared in the SQL Declare Section, using new syntax that is translated into C syntax by the SQL precompiler. (The LOB datatypes are discussed in Section 4.1.)

E.2.1 LOB Host Variables

Host variables for exchanging LOB data are declared as follows:

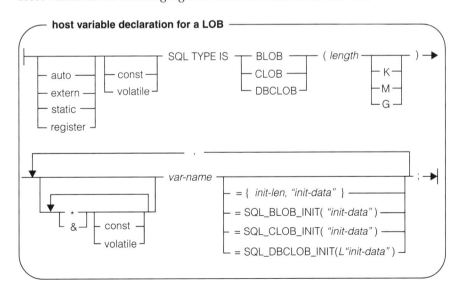

TABLE E-4: SQL Datatypes Corresponding to LOB Host Variables

SQL Datatype	SQLTYPE Code (not nullable/nullable)
Blob	404/405
Clob	408/409
Dbclob	412/413

Notes:

- SQL TYPE IS, BLOB, CLOB, DBCLOB, K, M, and G may be in mixed case.

- The maximum length of an initializing data string is 4,000 bytes.

- To initialize a Dbclob, use an L-type C literal such as L"double-byte data" if your program is precompiled with the option WCHARTYPE CONVERT.

- The syntax in the diagram above can be used to declare host variables of the types listed in Table E-4.

E.2.2 Locators and File References

Host variables for exchanging LOB data by means of locators or file references are declared as follows:

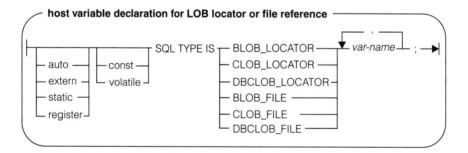

Notes:

- The SQL keywords in the declaration can be in mixed case.

- In a declaration of a LOB locator or file reference, the value of the LOB cannot be initialized. However, the *DB2 Application Programming Guide* describes a variation of the syntax above that permits declaration of a pointer to a locator or file reference, and initialization of the pointer. This syntax has been omitted here for simplicity and clarity.

- The syntax in the diagram above can be used to declare host variables of the types listed in Table E-5.

TABLE E-5: SQL Datatypes Corresponding to Locator and
File-Reference Host Variables

SQL Datatype	SQLTYPE Code (not nullable/nullable)
Blob Locator	960/961
Clob Locator	964/965
Dbclob Locator	968/969
Blob File Reference	804/805
Clob File Reference	808/809
Dbclob File Reference	812/813

APPENDIX

IBM Publications

T he IBM documentation for the V2 product family consists of the publications listed below. If you order one of the CD-ROM versions of the product, all the documentation pertaining to your version will be included on the CD, in PostScript format for printing and also in a format suitable for online viewing. The publications can also be ordered individually, either in hardcopy or on diskette. A publication can be ordered by either of two numbers—its *form number* or its *part number*. Both of these numbers are included for each publication in the tables below (the part number is in parentheses).

F.1 PLATFORM-INDEPENDENT PUBLICATIONS

The publications listed in Table F-1 are shipped with the V2 product and describe aspects of the product family that apply across multiple platforms.

TABLE F-1: Platform-Independent Publications

Form Number (Part Number)	Title and Description
S20H-4580 (59H1088)	*DB2 Administration Guide* Describes how to design, implement, and maintain a database.
S20H-4796 (20H4796)	*DB2 Administrator's Toolkit: Getting Started* Describes facilities provided to support V2 database administrators.
S20H-4984 (59H1089)	*DB2 API (Application Programming Interface) Reference* Describes how to use application programming interfaces to perform database administration functions.
S20H-4643 (59H1090)	*DB2 Application Programming Guide* Describes how to develop and execute application programs containing embedded SQL statements.
S20H-4644 (59H1092)	*DB2 Call Level Interface Guide and Reference* Describes how to develop and execute application programs using the Call Level Interface.

TABLE F-1: *(Continued)*

Form Number (Part Number)	Title and Description
S20H-4645 (59H1093)	*DB2 Command Reference* Describes how to use system commands to perform database administration functions. Also describes how to use the Command Line Processor.
S20H-4871 (20H4871)	*DB2 Database System Monitor Guide and Reference* Describes how to use the database monitor for gathering information about system performance.
S20H-4664 (20H4664)	*DB2 Information and Concepts Guide* Provides a general overview of the V2 product family.
S20H-4808 (59H1100)	*DB2 Messages Reference* Contains explanations for all messages and codes used in V2.
S20H-4779 (20H4779)	*DB2 Problem Determination Guide* Helps in diagnosing errors and problems in V2 applications.
S20H-4665 (59H1101)	*DB2 SQL Reference* Provides a reference manual for the SQL language as used in the V2 product. Also describes system catalog tables.
S20H-4793 (20H4793)	*DDCS User's Guide* Describes concepts and interfaces used in Distributed Database Connection Services (DDCS), which can connect V2 clients to databases managed by other systems.
SC26-4783 (20H4798)	*DRDA Connectivity Guide* Describes how to create a network of distributed relational databases using Distributed Relational Database Architecture (DRDA).

The publications listed in Table F-2 are not shipped with the V2 product, but provide useful background information about the use of V2 and related products.

TABLE F-2: Related Publications

Form Number	Title and Description
SC26-8692	*DataBasic Developer's Guide* Guide to developing stored procedures and external functions in BASIC using the DataBasic product.
SC26-8693	*DataBasic Language Reference* Reference manual for the BASIC language as implemented in the DataBasic product.
SC26-8416	*IBM SQL Reference* Volume 1 describes the SQL language as it is used in all IBM database products. Volume 2 lists the differences among the products and compares IBM SQL with ANSI Standard SQL.

F.2 PLATFORM-SPECIFIC PUBLICATIONS

The publications listed in Table F-3 and Table F-4 describe aspects of the V2 product that apply to specific platforms and have separate versions for the various platforms on which V2 can be installed and used. As before, the form number is listed first, followed by the part number in parentheses.

TABLE F-3: Platform-Specific Publications

Title	AIX Version	OS/2 Version	Windows 95 and NT Version	Windows 3.1 Version
DB2 Installation and Operation Guide	S20H-4757 (59H1096)	S20H-4785 (59H1095)	S33H-0312 (33H0312)	
DB2 Installing and Using Clients	S20H-4666 (59H1098)	S20H-4782 (59H1097)	S33H-0313 (33H0313)	S20H-4789 (59H1099)
DB2 Master Index	S20H-4781 (20H4781)	S20H-4788 (20H4788)		
DB2 Planning Guide	S20H-4758 (20H4758)	S20H-4784 (20H4784)	S33H-0314 (33H0314)	
DB2 Software Developer's Kit: Building Your Applications	S20H-4780 (20H4780)	S20H-4787 (20H4787)	S33H-0310 (33H0310)	S20H-4792 (20H4792)
DDCS Installation and Configuration Guide	S20H-4794 (59H1844)	S20H-4795 (59H1094)	S33H-0311 (33H0311)	

TABLE F-4: Platform-Specific Publications, continued

Title	HP-UX Version	Solaris Version	SINIX Version	Macintosh Version
DB2 Installation and Operation Guide	S34H-0898 (34H0898)	S34H-0893 (34H0893)	S50H-0533 (50H0533)	
DB2 Installing and Using Clients	S34H-0899 (34H0899)	S34H-0894 (34H0894)	S50H-0534 (50H0534)	S50H-0529 (50H0529)
DB2 Planning Guide	S34H-0897 (34H0897)	S34H-0892 (34H0892)	S50H-0532 (50H0532)	
DB2 Software Developer's Kit: Building Your Applications	S34H-0895 (34H0895)	S34H-0890 (34H0890)	S50H-0530 (50H0530)	S50H-0528 (50H0528)
DDCS Installation and Configuration Guide	S34H-0896 (34H0896)	S34H-0891 (34H0891)	S50H-0531 (50H0531)	

Index

Bold page numbers indicate a syntax diagram.

+a CLP option, 86
-a CLP option, 86
access plan, 559, 571–576
access structures, 40–41
activation time of triggers, 342–343
active data features, 323–390
    constraints, 323–342
    defined, 323
    designing databases, 366–384
    STORE program example, 366–384
    triggers, 323, 342–365
acyclic, defined, 211
addWeeks function, 290–292
ADSTAR Distributed Storage Manager (ADSM), 28
after triggers, 355–359
    audit trail, 358–359
    before triggers vs., 350, 351, 354
    constraint interactions, 364–365
    enforcing policies, 355
    linking tables, 355–358
    SQL statements permitted, 354
AIX. *See* operating systems
aliases, 134–136, 388, 524
ALL keyword, 61
ALTER privilege, 167, 340, 347
ALTER TABLESPACE statements, 502–503
ALTER TABLE statements, 133–134, 228–230, 252, 334, 340–342
American National Standards Institute (ANSI), 30–31, 152
AND operators, 54, 59
anomalies due to nulls, 34
ANSI. *See* American National Standards Institute (ANSI)
application developer, 24
application-processing program example, 245–249

application programs. *See* embedding SQL in C and C++ programs; stored procedures
Application Requester protocol, 10
Application Server protocol, 10
arithmetic operators, 52–53, 272
AR protocol, 10
arrows in syntax diagrams, 5
ASC file format, 546, 547
ASC keyword, 142
AS keyword, 73
AS protocol, 10
assignments
    before triggers, 347–349
    datatype families, 321
    distinct types, 257–259
    methods in SQL, 257, 320
    promotion vs., 320
    rules for built-in datatypes, 257–258
    UNION semantics vs., 320
    UPDATE statement SET clause, 78, 257
assignment-statement, **348**
assignment statements, 347–349
atomic compound SQL statements, 112
ATTACH command, 11, 521
audit trail, 358–359
authid, 172
authorities
    catalog tables, 624, 630, 632–633, 638–639
    checking authorization, 172–173
    database-level, 166–167
    defined, 164
    displaying, 511
    granting and revoking, 170–171, 505
    instance-level, 164–166
    V2 enhancements, 176
autocommit feature, 154, 397
AUTOCOMMIT option, 397

automatic revalidation semantics, 387
AUTORESTART parameter, 538

BACKUP command, 539–540
bank program example, 469–473
base tables, 41
base type, 250, 321
BASIC. *See* DataBasic
BCNF. *See* Boyce-Codd Normal Form (BCNF)
before triggers, 350–354
    after triggers vs., 350, 351, 354
    assignment statements, 347–349
    conditioning data, 352
    constraint interactions, 364
    detecting exceptional conditions, 353–354
    SQL statements permitted, 351
BEGIN ATOMIC statements, 345
BETWEEN predicate, 56
Binary Large Object datatype. *See* large objects (LOBs)
BINDADD authority, 167
BIND command
    conservative binding semantics, 283, 385–387
    examples, 518
    FUNCPATH parameter, 261
    ISOLATION parameter, 153–154
    options supported, 518
    overview, 517–518
    privileges required, 173
    rebinding files, 126
BINDFILE option, 17, 123, 515
bind files, 17, 123
binding
    authority, 167
    binding semantics, 385
    conservative binding semantics, 126, 283, 385–387
    defined, 385
    dependencies and, 385
    files, 17, 123

Related titles from Morgan Kaufmann:

Strategic Database Technology: Management for the Year 2000
by Alan R. Simon
This comprehensive guide to emerging database technologies is a thorough investigation of the state-of-the-art in database technology and the latest in research and development efforts. It's an essential source for IS managers, database administrators, systems analysts, and strategic planners.
ISBN 1-55860-264-X; paper; 446 pages; 1995

Joe Celko's SQL for Smarties: Advanced SQL Programming
by Joe Celko
Joe Celko shares his most useful tips and tricks for advanced SQL programming to help the working programmer gain performance and work around system deficiencies. Addressing real problems that people building real applications face, the author provides new and creative ways to solve and avoid these common programming problems.
ISBN 1-55860-323-9; paper; 467 pages; 1995

Understanding the New SQL: A Complete Guide
by Jim Melton and Alan Simon
An effective introduction to SQL and a comprehensive reference describing practical methods of using SQL to solve problems, advanced SQL query expressions, dynamic SQL, transaction models, and database design.
ISBN 1-55860-245-3; paper; 536 pages; 1993